PAXTON CENTER SCHOOL
West Street
Paxton, MA 01612

UCSMP
SCOTTFORESMAN

The University of Chicago School Mathematics Project

Transition Mathematics

Second Edition
Teacher's Edition
Part 2, Chapters 7-13

About the Cover The art on the cover was generated by a computer. The three interlocking rings signify the major themes of this book—algebra, geometry, and applied arithmetic.

Authors

Zalman Usiskin   Cathy Hynes Feldman
Suzanne Davis   Sharon Mallo   Gladys Sanders   David Witonsky
James Flanders   Lydia Polonsky   Susan Porter   Steven S. Viktora

Prentice
Hall

Glenview, Illinois
Needham, Massachusetts
Upper Saddle River, New Jersey

Contents
of Teacher's Edition

T2   **Highlights of *Transition Mathematics, Second Edition***

vi   **Contents of the Student Edition**

4   **Chapter 1**   Decimal Notation

62   **Chapter 2**   Large and Small Numbers

116   **Chapter 3**   Measurement

174   **Chapter 4**   Uses of Variables

236   **Chapter 5**   Patterns Leading to Addition

300   **Chapter 6**   Problem-Solving Strategies

344   **Chapter 7**   Patterns Leading to Subtraction

406   **Chapter 8**   Displays

466   **Chapter 9**   Patterns Leading to Multiplication

528   **Chapter 10**   Multiplication and Other Operations

590   **Chapter 11**   Patterns Leading to Division

640   **Chapter 12**   Real Numbers, Area, and Volume

690   **Chapter 13**   Coordinate Graphs and Equations

T20   **UCSMP Professional Sourcebook**

Section 1   Overview of UCSMP

Section 2   About *Transition Mathematics*

Section 3   General Teaching Suggestions for *Transition Mathematics*

Section 4   Research and Development of *Transition Mathematics*

Section 5   Bibliography

The complete Table of Contents for the Student Edition begins on page *vi*.

Your UCSMP Professional Sourcebook is found at the back of Part 1, starting on page T20.

ISBN: 0-13-058507-6

2 3 4 5 6 7 8 9 10   05 04

CONTENTS

Acknowledgments	*ii*
The University of Chicago School Mathematics Project	*iv*
Table of Contents	*vi*
To the Student	*1*

CHAPTER 1   4

DECIMAL NOTATION

1-1:	Decimals for Whole Numbers	6
1-2:	Decimals for Numbers Between Whole Numbers	10
1-3:	Estimating by Rounding Up or Rounding Down	16
1-4:	Estimating by Rounding to the Nearest	21
1-5:	Knowing Your Calculator	26
1-6:	Decimals for Simple Fractions	31
1-7:	Decimals for Mixed Numbers	37
1-8:	Negative Numbers	41
1-9:	Comparing Numbers	46
1-10:	Equal Fractions	50
	Projects	55
	Summary and Vocabulary	57
	Progress Self-Test	58
	Chapter Review	59

CHAPTER 2   62

LARGE AND SMALL NUMBERS

2-1:	Multiplying by 10, 100, . . .	64
2-2:	Powers	68
2-3:	Scientific Notation for Large Numbers	73
2-4:	Multiplying by $\frac{1}{10}$, $\frac{1}{100}$, . . .	78
2-5:	Percent of a Quantity	84
2-6:	From Decimals to Fractions and Percents	89
2-7:	Circle Graphs	93
2-8:	More Powers of Ten	99
▼	In-class Activity: *Scientific Notation for Small Numbers*	104
2-9:	Scientific Notation for Small Numbers	105
	Projects	109
	Summary and Vocabulary	111
	Progress Self-Test	112
	Chapter Review	113

MEASUREMENT

3-1: Measuring Length   118
3-2: Converting Lengths   125
3-3: Weight and Capacity in the Customary System of Measurement   130
3-4: The Metric System of Measurement   135
3-5: Converting Between Systems   140
3-6: Measuring Angles   145
▼ In-class Activity:
Kinds of Angles   152
3-7: Kinds of Angles   153
3-8: Measuring Area   158
3-9: Measuring Volume   163
Projects   167
Summary and Vocabulary   169
Progress Self-Test   170
Chapter Review   171

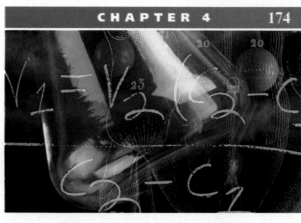

USES OF VARIABLES

4-1: Order of Operations   176
4-2: Describing Patterns with Variables   182
4-3: Translating Words to Algebraic Expressions   187
4-4: Evaluating Algebraic Expressions   193
4-5: Parentheses   197
4-6: Grouping Symbols   203
4-7: Formulas   208
▼ In-class Activity:
Relative Frequency   213
4-8: Probability   214
4-9: Open Sentences   219
4-10: Inequalities   224
Projects   229
Summary and Vocabulary   231
Progress Self-Test   232
Chapter Review   233

CHAPTER 5   236

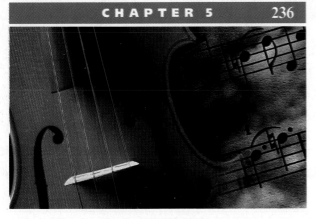

PATTERNS LEADING TO ADDITION

5-1:	Models for Addition	238
5-2:	Zero and Opposites	244
5-3:	Rules for Adding Positive and Negative Numbers	248
▼	In-class Activity: *Combining Turns*	253
5-4:	Combining Turns	254
5-5:	Adding Positive and Negative Fractions	260
5-6:	Adding Probabilities	266
5-7:	The Commutative and Associative Properties	271
5-8:	Solving $x + a = b$	276
▼	In-class Activity: *Polygons*	282
5-9:	Polygons	283
5-10:	Adding Lengths	288
	Projects	293
	Summary and Vocabulary	295
	Progress Self-Test	296
	Chapter Review	297

CHAPTER 6   300

PROBLEM-SOLVING STRATEGIES

6-1:	Being a Good Problem Solver	302
6-2:	Read Carefully	307
6-3:	Draw a Picture	311
6-4:	Trial and Error	315
6-5:	Make a Table	320
6-6:	Use a Spreadsheet	325
6-7:	Special Cases and Simpler Numbers	332
	Projects	338
	Summary and Vocabulary	340
	Progress Self-Test	341
	Chapter Review	342

CHAPTER 7   344

PATTERNS LEADING TO SUBTRACTION

7-1:	Two Models for Subtraction	346
7-2:	The Slide Model for Subtraction	352
7-3:	Solving $x - a = b$	358
7-4:	Solving $a - x = b$	362
7-5:	Counting and Probability with Overlap	367
▼	In-class Activity: *Angles and Lines*	374
7-6:	Angles and Lines	375
7-7:	Angles and Parallel Lines	381
7-8:	Special Quadrilaterals	387
7-9:	The Triangle-Sum Property	393
	Projects	399
	Summary and Vocabulary	401
	Progress Self-Test	402
	Chapter Review	403

CHAPTER 8 406

DISPLAYS

8-1: Graphs and Other Displays 408
8-2: Bar Graphs 415
8-3: Coordinate Graphs 421
8-4: Graphing Lines 428
▼ In-class Activity:
Translations (Slides) 434
8-5: Translations (Slides) 435
8-6: Reflections 440
8-7: Reflection Symmetry 446
8-8: Tessellations 452
Projects 458
Summary and Vocabulary 460
Progress Self-Test 461
Chapter Review 463

CHAPTER 9 466

PATTERNS LEADING TO MULTIPLICATION

9-1: The Area Model for Multiplication 468
9-2: Volumes of Rectangular Solids 476
9-3: Multiplication of Fractions 482
9-4: Multiplying Probabilities 488
9-5: The Rate Factor Model for Multiplication 493
9-6: Multiplication with Negative Numbers and Zero 499
9-7: Size Changes—Expansions 505
9-8: Size Changes—Contractions 511
9-9: Picturing Multiplication with Negative Numbers 516
Projects 521
Summary and Vocabulary 523
Progress Self-Test 524
Chapter Review 525

CHAPTER 10 528

MULTIPLICATION AND OTHER OPERATIONS

10-1: Multiplication as Shortcut Addition 530
10-2: Solving $ax = b$ 535
10-3: Using $ax = b$ 540
10-4: Solving $ax + b = c$ 544
10-5: Solving $ax + b = c$ when a Is Negative 550
10-6: The Distributive Property 555
10-7: The Surface Area of a Box 561
10-8: Dimensions and Units 566
10-9: Areas of Triangles 571
10-10: Areas of Trapezoids 577
Projects 582
Summary and Vocabulary 584
Progress Self-Test 585
Chapter Review 587

CHAPTER 11   590

PATTERNS LEADING TO DIVISION

11-1: Integer Division   592
11-2: The Rate Model for Division   597
11-3: Division of Fractions   601
11-4: Division with Negative Numbers 606
11-5: The Ratio Comparison Model
for Division   611
11-6: Proportions   615
11-7: The Means-Extremes Property   620
▼ In-class Activity:
Proportions in Similar Figures   625
11-8: Proportions in Similar Figures   626
11-9: Proportional Thinking   630
Projects   634
Summary and Vocabulary   636
Progress Self-Test   637
Chapter Review   638

CHAPTER 12   640

REAL NUMBERS, AREA, AND VOLUME

12-1: Converting Decimals to Fractions 642
12-2: Square Roots   646
▼ In-class Activity:
The Pythagorean Theorem   651
12-3: The Pythagorean Theorem   652
▼ In-class Activity:
The Circumference of a Circle   657
12-4: The Circumference of a Circle   658
12-5: The Area of a Circle   664
12-6: Surface Areas of Cylinders and
Prisms   670
12-7: Volumes of Cylinders and Prisms 675
12-8: Spheres   680
Projects   684
Summary and Vocabulary   686
Progress Self-Test   687
Chapter Review   688

CHAPTER 13   690

COORDINATE GRAPHS AND EQUATIONS

13-1: Graphing $y = ax + b$ 692
▼ In-class Activity:
Using an Automatic Grapher   698
13-2: Situations Leading to
$ax + b = cx + d$ 699
13-3: Solving $ax + b = cx + d$ 704
13-4: Fractions and Relative
Frequencies Revisited   709
13-5: Graphs of Formulas   714
13-6: Graphs of Equations with
Symbols for Rounding   719
Projects   725
Summary and Vocabulary   727
Progress Self-Test   728
Chapter Review   729

Selected Answers   732
Glossary   755
Index   764
List of Symbols   773
Photo Acknowledgments   774

Chapter 7 Pacing Chart

Day	Full Course	Minimal Course
1	7-1	7-1
2	7-2	7-2
3	7-3	7-3
4	7-4	7-4
5	Quiz*; 7-5	Quiz*; begin 7-5.
6	7-6	Finish 7-5.
7	7-7	7-6
8	7-8	7-7
9	Quiz*; 7-9	7-8
10	Self-Test	Quiz*; begin 7-9.
11	Review	Finish 7-9.
12	Test*	Self-Test
13		Review
14		Review
15		Test*

*in the Teacher's Resource File

Adapting to Individual Needs

The student text is written for the vast majority of students. The chart at the right suggests two pacing plans to accommodate the needs of your students. Students in the Full Course should complete the entire text by the end of the year. Students in the Minimal Course will spend more time when there are quizzes and more time on the Chapter Review. Therefore, these students may not complete all of the chapters in the text.

Options are also presented to meet the needs of a variety of teaching and learning styles. For each lesson, the Teacher's Edition provides sections entitled: *Video* which describes video segments and related questions that can be used for motivation or extension; *Optional Activities* which suggests activities that employ materials, physical models, technology, and cooperative learning; and *Adapting to Individual Needs* which regularly includes **Challenge** problems, **English Language Development** suggestions, and suggestions for providing **Extra Help.** The Teacher's Edition also frequently includes an **Error Alert,** an **Extension,** and an **Assessment** alternative. The options available in Chapter 7 are summarized in the chart below.

In the Teacher's Edition...

Lesson	Optional Activities	Extra Help	Challenge	English Language Development	Error Alert	Extension	Cooperative Learning	Ongoing Assessment
7-1	●	●	●	●	●	●		Written
7-2	●	●	●	●	●	●	●	Group
7-3	●	●	●	●		●		Written/Oral
7-4	●	●	●	●		●	●	Oral
7-5	●	●	●	●	●	●	●	Written/Oral
7-6	●	●	●	●		●	●	Oral
7-7	●	●	●	●		●	●	Group
7-8	●	●	●	●	●	●	●	Written
7-9	●	●	●	●	●	●	●	Group

In the Additional Resources...

Lesson	In the Teacher's Resource File								
	Lesson Masters, A and B	Teaching Aids*	Activity Kit*	Answer Masters	Technology Sourcebook	Assessment Sourcebook	Visual Aids**	Technology Tools	Video Segments
Opener									
7-1	7-1	67		7-1			67, AM		
7-2	7-2	8, 64, 67	16	7-2			8, 64, 67, AM		
7-3	7-3	67		7-3			67, AM		
7-4	7-4	68, 70		7-4		Quiz	68, 70, AM		Segment 7
7-5	7-5	56, 68, 71		7-5			56, 68, 71, AM		
In-class Activity							AM		
7-6	7-6	68, 72, 73		7-6	Demo 7, Comp 11		68, 72, 73, AM	Geometry	
7-7	7-7	69, 74	17, 18	7-7			69, 74, AM	Geometry	
7-8	7-8	69, 75–77		7-8	Comp 12	Quiz	69, 75–77, AM	Geometry	
7-9	7-9	69, 78–80		7-9	Comp 13		69, 78–80, AM	Geometry	
End of chapter				Review		Tests			

*Teaching Aids, except Warm-ups, are pictured on pages 344C and 344D. The activities in the Activity Kit are pictured on page 344C.

**Visual Aids provide transparencies for all Teaching Aids and all Answer Masters.

Also available is the Study Skills Handbook which includes study-skill tips related to reading, note-taking, and comprehension.

Integrating Strands and Applications

	7-1	7-2	7-3	7-4	7-5	7-6	7-7	7-8	7-9
Mathematical Connections									
Algebra	●	●	●	●	●	●	●		
Geometry	●	●	●	●	●	●	●	●	●
Measurement	●		●	●			●	●	●
Logic and Reasoning	●	●	●	●	●			●	●
Probability					●			●	
Interdisciplinary and Other Connections									
Art						●			
Music		●			●				
Literature	●								
Science	●	●	●	●		●			
Social Studies	●	●	●	●	●	●	●	●	●
Multicultural					●	●		●	
Technology	●	●							●
Career			●						
Consumer	●		●				●		
Sports	●	●		●	●				

Take it to the NET

On the Internet, visit
www.phschool.com
for UCSMP teacher
support, student
self-tests, activities,
and more.

Teaching and Assessing the Chapter Objectives

Chapter 7 Objectives (Organized into the SPUR categories—Skills, Properties, Uses, and Representations)	Lessons	Progress Self-Test Questions	Chapter Review Questions	Chapter Test, Forms A and B	Chapter Test, Forms C	Chapter Test, Forms D
Skills						
A: Subtract any numbers written as decimals or fractions.	7-2	1, 3, 4	1–8	1–5, 16	1	✓
B: Solve sentences of the form $x - a = b$ and $a - x = b$.	7-3, 7-4	10–13	9–18	6–8	2	
C: Find measures of angles in figures with linear pairs, vertical angles, or perpendicular lines.	7-6	16, 17	19–22	14	5	
D: Find measures of angles in figures with parallel lines and transversals.	7-7	18, 23	23–26	12	5	
E: Use the Triangle-Sum Property to find measures of angles.	7-9	21	27–30	13		
F: Find measures of angles and sides in special quadrilaterals without measuring.	7-8	24	31–34	23	4	
Properties						
G: Apply the properties of subtraction.	7-2, 7-3, 7-4	5, 14	35–38	11	2	
H: Know relationships among angles formed by intersecting lines, or by two parallel lines and a transversal.	7-6, 7-7	19, 20	39–45	19	5	
I: Apply the definitions of parallelogram, rectangle, rhombus, and square to determine properties of these figures.	7-8	24, 25	46–49	20–22	4	
J: Explain consequences of the Triangle-Sum Property.	7-9	22	50, 51	24		
Uses						
K: Use the Take-Away Model for Subtraction to form sentences involving subtraction.	7-1, 7-3, 7-4	8	52–55	15	1	
L: Use the Slide Model for Subtraction to form sentences involving subtraction.	7-2, 7-3, 7-4	9	56–58	10	1	
M: Use the Comparison Model for Subtraction to form sentences involving subtraction.	7-1, 7-3, 7-4	6, 7	59–61	9	1	✓
N: Use the Putting-Together with Overlap Model to solve sentences involving subtraction.	7-5	15	62–64	18	3	
Representations						
O: Picture subtraction of positive and negative numbers on a number line.	7-2	2	65, 66	25		
P: Use Venn diagrams to describe or determine overlap.	7-5	15	67, 68	17	3	

In the Assessment Sourcebook

Assessment Sourcebook
Quiz for Lessons 7-1 through 7-4
Quiz for Lessons 7-5 through 7-8
Chapter 7 Test, Forms A–D
Chapter 7 Test, Cumulative Form

 TestWorks
Multiple forms of chapter tests
and quizzes; Challenge items

Activity Kit

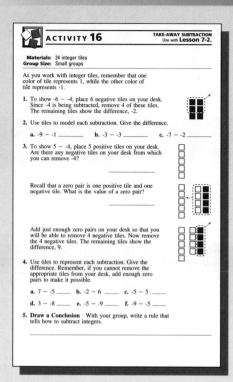

Materials: 24 integer tiles
Group Size: Small groups

As you work with integer tiles, remember that one color of tile represents 1, while the other color of tile represents -1.

1. To show -6 − -4, place 6 negative tiles on your desk. Since -4 is being subtracted, remove 4 of these tiles. The remaining tiles show the difference, -2.

2. Use tiles to model each subtraction. Give the difference.

   a. -9 − -1 _____   **b.** -3 − -3 _____   **c.** -7 − -2 _____

3. To show 5 − -4, place 5 positive tiles on your desk. Are there any negative tiles on your desk from which you can remove -4?

   _____

   Recall that a zero pair is one positive tile and one negative tile. What is the value of a zero pair?

   _____

   Add just enough zero pairs on your desk so that you will be able to remove the 4 negative tiles. Now remove the 4 negative tiles. The remaining tiles show the difference, 9.

4. Use tiles to represent each subtraction. Give the difference. Remember, if you cannot remove the appropriate tiles from your desk, add enough zero pairs to make it possible.

   a. 7 − 1 _____   **b.** -2 − 6 _____   **c.** -5 − 5 _____

   d. 3 − -8 _____   **e.** -5 − -9 _____   **f.** -9 − -5 _____

5. **Draw a Conclusion** With your group, write a rule that tells how to subtract integers.

   _____

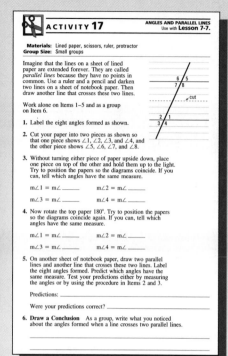

Materials: Lined paper, scissors, ruler, protractor
Group Size: Small groups

Imagine that the lines on a sheet of lined paper are extended forever. They are called *parallel lines* because they have no points in common. Use a ruler and a pencil and darken two lines on a sheet of notebook paper. Then draw another line that crosses these two lines.

Work alone on Items 1–5 and as a group on Item 6.

1. Label the eight angles formed as shown.

2. Cut your paper into two pieces as shown so that one piece shows ∠1, ∠2, ∠3, and ∠4, and the other piece shows ∠5, ∠6, ∠7, and ∠8.

3. Without turning either piece of paper upside down, place one piece on top of the other and hold them up to the light. Try to position the papers so the diagrams coincide. If you can, tell which angles have the same measure.

   m∠1 = m∠ _____   m∠2 = m∠ _____

   m∠3 = m∠ _____   m∠4 = m∠ _____

4. Now rotate the top paper 180°. Try to position the papers so the diagrams coincide again. If you can, tell which angles have the same measure.

   m∠1 = m∠ _____   m∠2 = m∠ _____

   m∠3 = m∠ _____   m∠4 = m∠ _____

5. On another sheet of notebook paper, draw two parallel lines and another line that crosses these two lines. Label the eight angles formed. Predict which angles have the same measure. Test your predictions either by measuring the angles or by using the procedure in Items 2 and 3.

   Predictions: _____

   Were your predictions correct? _____

6. **Draw a Conclusion** As a group, write what you noticed about the angles formed when a line crosses two parallel lines.

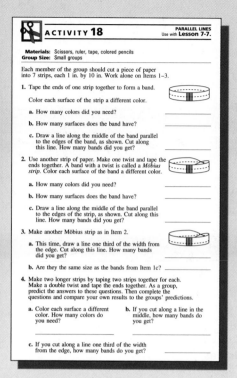

Materials: Scissors, ruler, tape, colored pencils
Group Size: Small groups

Each member of the group should cut a piece of paper into 7 strips, each 1 in. by 10 in. Work alone on Items 1–3.

1. Tape the ends of one strip together to form a band.

   Color each surface of the strip a different color.

   a. How many colors did you need? _____

   b. How many surfaces does the band have? _____

   c. Draw a line along the middle of the band parallel to the edges of the band, as shown. Cut along this line. How many bands did you get?

2. Use another strip of paper. Make one twist and tape the ends together. A band with a twist is called a *Möbius strip.* Color each surface of the band a different color.

   a. How many colors did you need? _____

   b. How many surfaces does the band have? _____

   c. Draw a line along the middle of the band parallel to the edges of the band. Cut along this line. How many bands did you get?

3. Make another Möbius strip as in Item 2.

   a. This time, draw a line one third of the width from the edge. Cut along this line. How many bands did you get?

   b. Are they the same size as the bands from Item 1c?

4. Make two longer strips by taping two strips together for each. Make a double twist and tape the ends together. As a group, predict the answers to these questions. Then complete the questions and compare your own results to the groups' predictions.

   a. Color each surface a different color. How many colors do you need? _____

   b. If you cut along a line in the middle, how many bands do you get? _____

   c. If you cut along a line one third of the width from the edge, how many bands do you get? _____

Teaching Aids

Teaching Aid 8, Number Lines, (shown on page 4D) and **Teaching Aid 64, Checkerboard,** (shown on page 300D) can be used with **Lesson 7-2. Teaching Aid 56, Two-Dice Outcomes,** (shown on page 236D) can be used with **Lesson 7-5.**

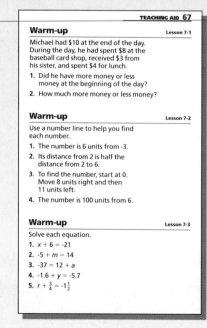

Warm-up Lesson 7-1

Michael had $10 at the end of the day. During the day, he had spent $8 at the baseball card shop, received $3 from his sister, and spent $4 for lunch.

1. Did he have more money or less money at the beginning of the day?

2. How much more money or less money?

Warm-up Lesson 7-2

Use a number line to help you find each number.

1. The number is 6 units from -3.

2. Its distance from 2 is half the distance from 2 to 6.

3. To find the number, start at 0. Move 8 units right and then 11 units left.

4. The number is 100 units from 6.

Warm-up Lesson 7-3

Solve each equation.

1. $x + 6 = -21$

2. $-5 + m = 14$

3. $-37 = 12 + a$

4. $-1.6 + y = -5.7$

5. $r + \frac{3}{4} = -1\frac{1}{2}$

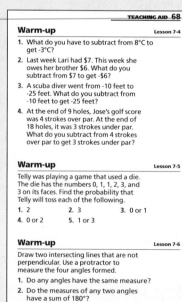

Warm-up Lesson 7-4

1. What do you have to subtract from 8°C to get -3°C?

2. Last week Lari had $7. This week she owes her brother $6. What do you subtract from $7 to get -$6?

3. A scuba diver went from -10 feet to -25 feet. What do you subtract from -10 feet to get -25 feet?

4. At the end of 9 holes, Jose's golf score was 4 strokes over par. At the end of 18 holes, it was 3 strokes under par. What do you subtract from 4 strokes over par to get 3 strokes under par?

Warm-up Lesson 7-5

Telly was playing a game that used a die. The die has the numbers 0, 1, 1, 2, 3, and 3 on its faces. Find the probability that Telly will toss each of the following.

1. 2   2. 3   3. 0 or 1

4. 0 or 2   5. 1 or 3

Warm-up Lesson 7-6

Draw two intersecting lines that are not perpendicular. Use a protractor to measure the four angles formed.

1. Do any angles have the same measure?

2. Do the measures of any two angles have a sum of 180°?

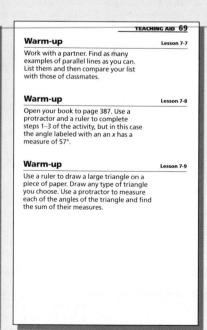

Warm-up Lesson 7-7

Work with a partner. Find as many examples of parallel lines as you can. List them and then compare your list with those of classmates.

Warm-up Lesson 7-8

Open your book to page 387. Use a protractor and a ruler to complete steps 1–3 of the activity, but in this case the angle labeled with an an x has a measure of 57°.

Warm-up Lesson 7-9

Use a ruler to draw a large triangle on a piece of paper. Draw any type of triangle you choose. Use a protractor to measure each of the angles of the triangle and find the sum of their measures.

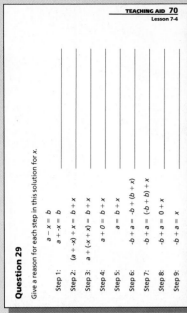

Question 29

Give a reason for each step in this solution for x.

$$a - x = b$$
$$a + -x = b$$

Step 1: $a + -x = b$
Step 2: $(a + -x) + x = b + x$
Step 3: $a + (-x + x) = b + x$
Step 4: $a + 0 = b + x$
Step 5: $a = b + x$
Step 6: $-b + a = -b + (b + x)$
Step 7: $-b + a = (-b + b) + x$
Step 8: $-b + a = 0 + x$
Step 9: $-b + a = x$

Venn Diagrams

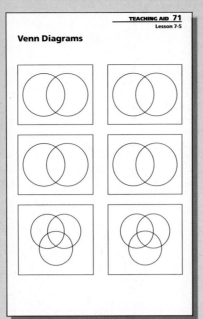

Map of Drexel and Ellis

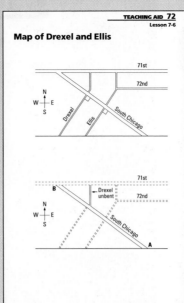

Challenge

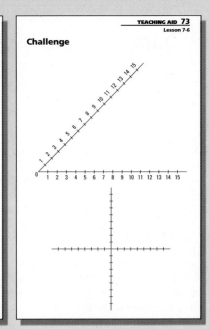

Parallel Lines and Angles

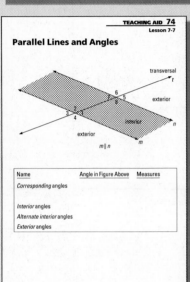

$m \parallel n$

Name	Angle in Figure Above	Measures
Corresponding angles		
Interior angles		
Alternate interior angles		
Exterior angles		

Parallelograms

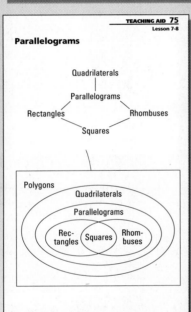

Question 25

25. In the figure below, $ABCD$ and $AEFG$ are parallelograms and $\overline{AB}$ and $\overline{AE}$ are perpendicular. $m\angle ABC = 147°$. $G, A, D,$ and H are on the same line. Find the measure of each indicated angle.

a. $\angle BAG$ b. $\angle GAE$ c. $\angle AGF$ d. $\angle CDH$

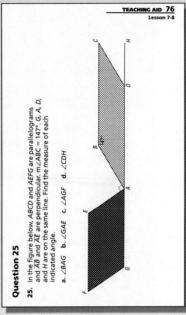

Quadrilaterals

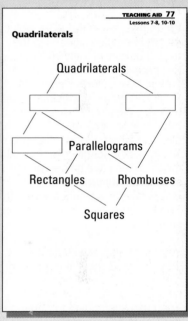

Quadrilaterals

Parallelograms

Rectangles   Rhombuses

Squares

Example 3

Questions 11, 16, 18

11.

16.   18.

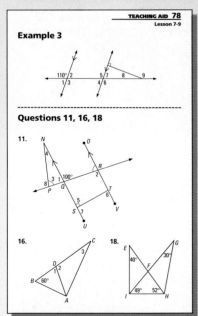

Additional Examples

1. Find the measure of the angle.

   a.   b.

2. Find the measure of $\angle QPR$.

3. Use the information given in the drawing. Explain the steps needed to find $m\angle 1$.

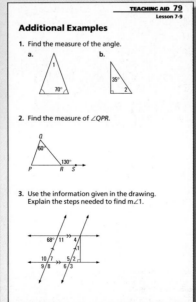

Triangle-Sum Property

Steps 1–2   Step 3

Step 4

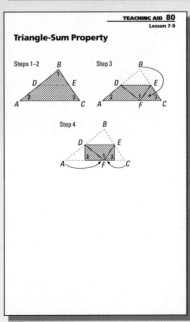

344D

Chapter Opener

Pacing

All the lessons in this chapter are designed to be covered in one day. At the end of the chapter, you should plan to spend 1 day to review the Progress Self-Test, 1–2 days for the Chapter Review, and 1 day for a test. You may wish to spend a day on projects, and possibly a day is needed for quizzes. This chapter should, therefore, take 12–15 days. We strongly advise you not to spend more than 15 days on this chapter; there is ample opportunity to review ideas in later chapters.

Using Pages 344–345

When discussing the table, point out that the negative signs help the reader quickly identify which states lost people in the decade of the 1980s. [Iowa, North Dakota, West Virginia, Wyoming] Decimal notation makes it easy to tell which states have gained large numbers of people. [California, Florida, Georgia, Texas] Ask students why they think these states have gained or lost such large numbers. [Possible responses: movement towards the Sun Belt and away from farms and small towns]

You might also ask students why they think this table is the opener for a chapter on subtraction. [The answer is given below the table.] Then use subtraction to obtain the population of your state in 1980. If the change was negative, tell students that they will learn to subtract a negative number in this chapter. Finally, find the population of some other states in 1980, perhaps those in which a student in the class was born.

7-1   Two Models for Subtraction

7-2   The Slide Model for Subtraction

7-3   Solving $x - a = b$

7-4   Solving $a - x = b$

7-5   Counting and Probability with Overlap

7-6   Angles and Lines

7-7   Angles and Parallel Lines

7-8   Special Quadrilaterals

7-9   The Triangle-Sum Property

344

Chapter 7 Overview

This chapter has three parts. They correspond closely to the three themes of this book: applied arithmetic, pre-algebra, and pre-geometry.

Lessons 7-1 and 7-2 present three models for subtraction—the Take-Away Model, the Slide Model, and the Comparison Model. Students have encountered examples of these models since the early grades. New concepts in this chapter include the names given to the models, the presence of whole numbers, fractions, decimals, and percents, and the use of variables. The Slide Model is used for the relation $x - a = x + -a$ and the subtraction of positive and negative numbers.

Lessons 7-3 and 7-4 introduce sentence solving of the forms $x - a = b$ and $a - x = b$. The rest of the chapter gives applications that involve addition and subtraction.

Lesson 7-5 extends the pattern of the Putting-Together Model of Addition to situations in which there is overlap, thus requiring subtraction of the overlap.

Lessons 7-6 through 7-8 discuss angles and lines. First, we look at linear pairs of angles. If one angle has measure x, the other has measure $180° - x$. This relationship justifies the placement of this content in a chapter on subtraction. If we extend the

PATTERNS LEADING TO SUBTRACTION

Here is a breakdown of the resident population, in 1990, of each state and its gain or loss since 1980, through estimated net migration (moving, births, and deaths).

State	1990 Population	Change Since 1980	State	1990 Population	Change Since 1980
Alabama	4,040,587	146,562	Montana	799,065	12,375
Alaska	550,043	148,192	Nebraska	1,578,385	8,560
Arizona	3,665,228	948,682	Nevada	1,201,833	401,325
Arkansas	2,350,725	64,368	New Hampshire	1,109,252	188,642
California	29,760,021	6,092,257	New Jersey	7,730,188	365,177
Colorado	3,294,394	404,659	New Mexico	1,515,069	211,767
Connecticut	3,287,116	179,552	New York	17,990,455	432,290
Delaware	666,168	71,830	North Carolina	6,628,637	748,542
Florida	12,937,926	3,190,965	North Dakota	638,800	-13,917
Georgia	6,478,216	1,015,234	Ohio	10,847,115	49,512
Hawaii	1,108,229	143,538	Oklahoma	3,145,585	120,098
Idaho	1,006,749	62,622	Oregon	2,842,321	209,165
Illinois	11,430,602	3,193	Pennsylvania	11,881,643	16,923
Indiana	5,544,159	53,945	Rhode Island	1,003,464	56,310
Iowa	2,776,755	-137,053	South Carolina	3,486,703	365,974
Kansas	2,477,574	113,338	South Dakota	696,004	5,236
Kentucky	3,685,296	24,972	Tennessee	4,877,185	286,162
Louisiana	4,219,973	13,857	Texas	16,986,510	2,760,997
Maine	1,227,928	102,885	Utah	1,722,850	261,813
Maryland	4,781,468	564,535	Vermont	562,758	51,302
Massachusetts	6,016,425	279,332	Virginia	6,187,358	840,561
Michigan	9,295,297	33,253	Washington	4,866,692	734,339
Minnesota	4,375,099	299,129	West Virginia	1,793,477	-156,709
Mississippi	2,573,216	52,446	Wisconsin	4,891,769	186,127
Missouri	5,117,073	200,307	Wyoming	453,588	-15,969
Other areas					
D.C.	606,900	-31,532	Guam	133,152	27,173
Puerto Rico	3,522,037	325,517	American		
Virgin Islands	101,809	6,218	Samoa	46,773	14,476

Source: Bureau of the Census, U.S. Dept. of Commerce, 1980 and 1990 Censuses

You can determine the population of your state in 1980 from this table. You must subtract the change since 1980 from the 1990 population for your state. This subtraction may involve positive or negative numbers. It is one of many situations in which subtraction is the operation to use.

In this chapter, you will study many other situations that lead to subtraction. These naturally lead to equations that involve subtraction.

345

Point out that the table exemplifies a common situation in which published information enables a person to determine information not published. Here, by subtracting, students can obtain the 1980 populations of all the states in the United States plus the territories and the District of Columbia.

Photo Connections

The photo collage makes real-world connections to the content of the chapter: patterns leading to subtraction.

Trees in Winter: When temperatures drop to around -40 (deg sign)F, ice crystals form around minute particles of dust or chemical substances that float in the air. When temperatures drop even lower, crystals form directly from water vapor. Depending on the temperature and humidity, the frozen precipitation forms either snow crystals, hail, or sleet.

Globes and People: The growth in world population is represented by this computer-generated graphic. An estimate of human population is determined by a series of equations using both addition and subtraction.

Stones: Garden stones are sold by weight. Subtraction equations model the process used by building supply stores or nurseries to determine the weight of a load of stones.

Girl and Fish: Changes in depth can be modeled by equations using subtraction.

Triangle and Lines: Geometric shapes, such as the triangle, are often incorporated into jewelry, sculpture, and paintings.

Projects

At this time you might want to have students look over the projects on pages 399-400.

lines forming a linear pair, four angles are formed having measures of either x or $180° - x$. If we add a parallel line, eight angles are formed, again with measures of either x or $180° - x$. When another parallel line is added, a parallelogram is formed. This development leads to an investigation of special quadrilaterals. In Lesson 7-9, we develop the formula for the sum of the measures of the angles in a triangle.

Objectives

K Use the Take-Away Model for Subtraction to form sentences involving subtraction.
M Use the Comparison Model for Subtraction to form sentences involving subtraction.

Resources

From the *Teacher's Resource File*
- Lesson Master 7-1A or 7-1B
- Answer Master 7-1
- Teaching Aid 67: Warm-up

Additional Resources
- Visual for Teaching Aid 67

Warm-up

Michael had $10 at the end of the day. During the day, he had spent $8 at the baseball card shop, received $3 from his sister, and spent $4 for lunch.

1. Did he have more money or less money at the beginning of the day? **More money**
2. How much more money or less money? **$9 more**

The cutting edge. *The technician is programming a high-speed saw to ensure that as little lumber as possible is wasted when cuts are made. Even the sawdust is recycled.*

Subtraction as Taking Away

Suppose you walk into a store with $10 and spend $2.56. The amount you have left is found by subtraction: $10 − $2.56 = $7.44. Recall that a model for an operation is a general pattern that includes many of the uses of the operation. This subtraction is an instance of the *Take-Away Model for Subtraction*.

> **Take-Away Model for Subtraction**
> If a quantity y is taken away from an original quantity x with the same units, the quantity left is $x − y$.

Here are other examples of the many different situations that use the take-away model.

Example 1

A piece of wood 32.5 centimeters long is cut from a board of original length 3 meters long. How long is the remaining piece?

Solution

Draw a picture. Units must be consistent, so change 3 meters to centimeters.

Lesson 7-1 Overview

Broad Goals This lesson reviews and algebraically describes the two most important uses of subtraction.

Perspective It is logical to view *taking away* as the counterpart to *putting together*. This is the equivalent of the mathematical relationship of inverse operations, but stated in the language of models for operations.

Although the Take-Away Model itself will be review for students, their prior use of it may have been limited to situations where the numbers are counts. The work in this lesson with length, angle measure, area, and variables is probably new. These applications are not difficult, especially when viewed as extensions of a familiar pattern.

Historically, either of two names has been given to the answer in a subtraction problem—*remainder* or *difference*. Remainder comes from the Take-Away Model; and difference (preferred because remainder has a meaning in division) is from the Comparison Model. More subtraction problems may fit the Comparison Model than any other model.

In this lesson, the comparisons are with positive numbers. In the next lesson, comparisons are made with negative numbers.

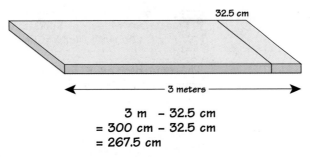

32.5 cm

3 meters

3 m – 32.5 cm
= 300 cm – 32.5 cm
= 267.5 cm

The remaining piece is 267.5 cm long.

Example 1 can be generalized. If the units are the same, a piece C units long cut from a board L units long leaves a piece $L - C$ units long.

Recall from Lesson 5-4, that the angles ABC and CBD drawn below are adjacent angles. The sum of their measures is the measure of angle ABD. If you know m$\angle ABD$ and one of the smaller angles, you can find the other by subtraction. You can think of this as "taking away" one of the smaller angles from the larger.

An old saw. *This saying was probably based upon a comment by noted American author and naturalist, Henry David Thoreau (1817–1862). He said: "They (wood stumps) warmed me twice—once while I was splitting, and again when they were on the fire."*

Example 2

In the drawing below, what is the measure of $\angle ABC$?

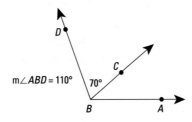

m$\angle ABD = 110°$ 70°

Solution

To find m$\angle ABC$, subtract the measure of $\angle CBD$ from the measure of $\angle ABD$.

$$m\angle ABC = m\angle ABD - m\angle CBD$$
$$= \quad 110° - 70°$$
$$= \quad 40°$$

Subtraction as Comparison

The first number in a subtraction problem is called the **minuend.** The second number is the **subtrahend.** The answer is called the **difference.**

436.2   minuend
−98.5   subtrahend
337.7   difference

The term "difference" comes from a second model of subtraction, the *comparison model.*

Notes on Reading

In class you might discuss the purpose of each example. **Example 1** is a simple application of the Take-Away Model for Subtraction that stresses consistency of units of length. **Example 2** uses the Take-Away Model with angle measures. **Example 3** introduces the Comparison Model for Subtraction and **Example 4** is an instance of the Comparison Model with fractions. **Example 4** also reviews subtraction of fractions.

After discussing **Example 1,** you might have students generalize each example as it was done in **Example 1.**

In comparison subtraction, there is a tendency to worry about which number to put first. This worry is needless since the answer is meaningful regardless of the order. For instance, if you estimate that Mr. Smith weighs 150 pounds and he actually weighs 170 pounds, $150 - 170 = -20$ tells you that your guess was 20 pounds too low, whereas $170 - 150 = 20$ tells that your guess was 20 pounds too high. The important points are to be consistent in a given problem and to be able to make sense of the answer.

Optional Activities

As you are discussing comparison subtraction in **Examples 3 and 4,** you may find that using the number line is useful. For example, if, in the illustration at the right, x is greater than y, $x - y$ is the distance between x and y on the number line. If you do not know which number is greater, then the distance is $|x - y|$, the formula that is often studied in geometry.

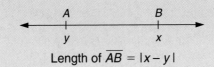

Length of $\overline{AB} = |x - y|$

For **Example 3** and then for **Example 4,** graph the given numbers on a number line. Then ask students for the length of the segment joining the graphs.

Additional Examples

1. **a.** If a sports store has one gross of hockey sticks at the start of a sale and 64 sticks are left after the first day, how many sticks were sold that day?
   80 sticks

   b. A yard is cut off a meterstick. Approximately how long is the remaining piece? **≈ 3.37 in.**

   c. A square vegetable garden is 3 meters on a side. One corner, a square 1.5 meters on a side, will be planted with tomatoes. How many square meters will be left for other vegetables?
   6.75 square meters

2. Use the figure below. ∠XYZ is a right angle. If m∠WYZ = 38°, find m∠WYX. **52°**

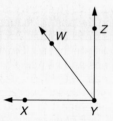

3. In a high school track meet, Marta threw the discus 124 feet 9 inches. The world record (as of 1992) was 252 feet. How much longer is the 1992 world record throw than Marta's throw?
   127 ft 3 in.

4. Theo is making buttermilk pancakes. He put $1\frac{3}{4}$ cups of milk in a bowl with the other ingredients. Then he realized that the recipe calls for $2\frac{1}{2}$ cups of milk. How much more milk should he add?
   $\frac{3}{4}$ **cup**

Comparison Model for Subtraction
$x - y$ is how much more x is than y.

The comparison model for subtraction is commonly used. Here is an example comparing lengths.

Example 3

Penelope is 164 cm tall. Her boyfriend, Ulysses, is 180.5 cm tall. How much taller is Ulysses than Penelope?

Solution

"How much taller" is asking for a comparison, so subtract.
180.5 – 164 = 16.5, so Ulysses is 16.5 cm taller.

The next example compares capacities of $3\frac{2}{3}$ cups and $1\frac{3}{4}$ cups. In it the mixed number $3\frac{2}{3}$ is changed first to $3\frac{8}{12}$ and then to $2\frac{20}{12}$. This can be done because $3\frac{8}{12} = 2 + 1\frac{8}{12} = 2\frac{20}{12}$.

Example 4

A recipe requires $3\frac{2}{3}$ cups of flour. You have $1\frac{3}{4}$ cups. How much more flour do you need?

Solution 1

You need to compare what you have to what you need. So the answer is given by the subtraction $3\frac{2}{3} - 1\frac{3}{4}$. Here is the usual paper-and-pencil algorithm to do this. As with addition, this method requires finding equal fractions with the same denominator.

$$3\frac{2}{3} = 3\frac{8}{12} = 2\frac{20}{12}$$
$$- 1\frac{3}{4} = 1\frac{9}{12} = 1\frac{9}{12}$$
$$\overline{\qquad\qquad\qquad 1\frac{11}{12}}$$

So you need $1\frac{11}{12}$ cups more.

Solution 2

Change both $3\frac{2}{3}$ and $1\frac{3}{4}$ to improper fractions with the same denominator.

$$3\frac{2}{3} = 3\frac{8}{12} = \frac{44}{12}$$
$$- 1\frac{3}{4} = 1\frac{9}{12} = \frac{21}{12}$$
$$\overline{\qquad\qquad\qquad \frac{23}{12} = 1\frac{11}{12}}$$

So you need $1\frac{11}{12}$ cups more.

Adapting to Individual Needs

Extra Help

Materials: 25 red markers and 12 yellow markers

Using Physical Models Help students understand the models for subtraction presented in this lesson by doing the following demonstrations.

a. Put the 25 red markers in a pile. Ask a student to pick up 12 of them, tell how many are left, and explain the action. [13 left; took away 12 red markers]

b. Put the 25 red markers in one pile and the 12 yellow markers in another pile. Ask a student to tell how many more red markers there are than yellow markers. [13 more red markers]

To help students understand how to get the answer, match every yellow marker with a red marker. The remaining pile of 13 red markers shows there are 13 more red markers than yellow markers. In **part b,** note that nothing is taken away as in the Take Away Model; instead the size of the groups are compared.

Solution 3

With a calculator that does fractions, you need only key in $3\frac{2}{3}$, then ⊟, then $1\frac{3}{4}$, then ⊜. The answer $1\frac{11}{12}$ should appear.

QUESTIONS

Covering the Reading

1. **a.** There are 320 passenger seats in one wide-body jet plane. A flight attendant counts 4 vacant seats. How many passengers are on board? **316**
   b. There are S passenger seats in a wide-body jet plane. A flight attendant counts V vacant seats. How many passengers are on board? **$S - V$**

2. **a.** Hungry Hans ate 2 of the dozen rolls his mother prepared for dinner. How many rolls are left for the others at the table? **10**
   b. Hungry Heloise ate A of the dozen rolls her mother prepared for dinner. How many rolls are left for the others at the table? **$12 - A$**

3. Questions 1–2 are instances of what model for subtraction? **the Take-Away Model**

In 4–6, use the picture at the right.

4. Angles ABD and CBD are __?__ angles. **adjacent**

5. If $m\angle ABC = 100°$ and $m\angle DBA = 84°$, what is $m\angle DBC$? **16°**

6. $m\angle ABC - m\angle DBC = m\angle$ __?__. **ABD**

7. Consider the subtraction fact $12 - 8 = 4$. Identify each.
   a. difference **4**   **b.** minuend **12**   **c.** subtrahend **8**

8. State the Comparison Model for Subtraction. **$x - y$ is how much more x is than y.**

9. Jim weighs 150 pounds but wants to get his weight down to 144 pounds. How much does he need to lose? **6 pounds**

10. Nina has $240 saved for a stereo system that costs $395. How much more money does she need? **$155**

11. Lori needs $2\frac{3}{4}$ cups of flour for a cake. She has $2\frac{2}{3}$ cups.
    a. Compare these two quantities by subtraction. **$\frac{1}{12}$ cup difference**
    b. Does Lori have not enough, just enough, or more than enough flour for the cake? **not enough**

12. **a.** To subtract $13\frac{3}{8} - 6\frac{7}{8}$ without using a calculator, how would you rewrite $13\frac{3}{8}$? **$12\frac{11}{8}$**
    b. Do this subtraction. **$6\frac{1}{2}$**

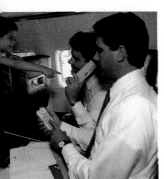

The modern skies. *Many jet planes include high-tech conveniences for the passengers, such as telephones, computers, and fax machines.*

Notes on Questions

Questions 1, 2, and 24 In each of these situations, **part a** is an arithmetic question, and **part b** asks the more general algebraic question. Discuss both answers together.

Questions 5–6 Error Alert Some students may find the angle notation difficult to interpret. Suggest that they sketch the angles, and include the degree measures in the diagram.

Question 12 Point out that this question can be checked by converting the fractions to decimals.

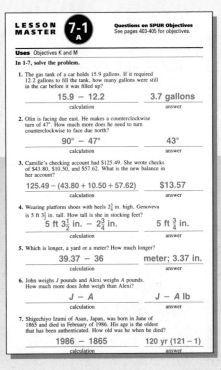

Notes on Questions

Questions 14–16 Error Alert If students have trouble with the distance notation, suggest that they sketch the figure and include the distances. Also note that AD, for example, could have been written as "the length of $\overline{AD}$."

Question 18 Science Connection Marie Sklodowska Curie was born in Warsaw, Poland, in 1867. She studied mathematics, physics, and chemistry in Paris, and became famous as a physicist for her research on radioactivity.

Question 20 This answer could be found by subtracting –17 from 59, a procedure that will be covered in Lesson 7-2.

Questions 22–23 Using simpler numbers in the first question should help students answer the second question.

Question 33 We have found that students are surprised, intrigued, and motivated by this subtraction algorithm. Some students even start using it. Do not dissuade them from using the algorithm; it is very efficient for certain problems, and it is one way subtraction is taught in some parts of the world.

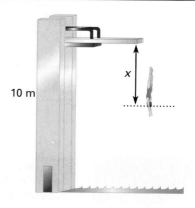

First female Nobel Prize recipient. *Marie Curie received the 1903 Nobel Prize in physics and the 1911 Nobel Prize in chemistry.*

13. The head of a diver is x meters below a diving board that is 10 meters above the water in a pool. How far above the water is the diver's head? **10 – x meters**

In 14–16, use the diagram below of towns A, B, C, and D along a highway.

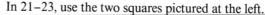

14. Suppose $AD = 10$ km and $AC = 6$ km.
   a. What other distance can be found? **CD**
   b. What is that distance? **4 km**

15. a. The difference $AD - CD$ is the distance between what two towns? **A and C**
   b. $AD - AB - CD = \underline{}$ **BC**

16. Suppose CD is 40% of AD. Also suppose AB is 25% of AD. Then BC is what percent of AD? **35%**

17. Bill's savings account has $510.75 in it. How much will be left after the given withdrawal?
   a. a withdrawal of $40   b. a withdrawal of W dollars
   $470.75   **510.75 – W dollars**

18. The famous scientist Marie Curie was born in 1867 and died in 1934. Using only this information, what was her age when she died? (Watch out. There are two possible answers.) **66 or 67**

19. Use the table on page 345. Determine the 1980 population of each of these places.
   a. New York **17,558,165**
   b. Wyoming **469,557**
   c. the state or area where you live **Answer depends on where you are.**

20. The Roman poet, Livy, was born in 59 B.C. and died in 17 A.D. From this information, what was his age when he died? (Watch out again. There was no year 0. The year 1 A.D. followed 1 B.C.) **74 or 75**

In 21–23, use the two squares pictured at the left.

21. What is the area of the shaded region? $b^2 - a^2$

22. Find the area of the shaded region if $a = 8$ and $b = 10$.
   36 square units

23. Find the area of the shaded region if $a = 4\frac{1}{2}$ and $b = 6.7$.
   24.64 square units

350

350

Adapting to Individual Needs

Challenge
Have students solve the following problem.

Mona leaves at the same time each morning to walk to work. After walking one-fourth of the way, she passes a clock that says 8:00. After walking one-third of the way, she passes another clock that says 8:02. Assuming she walks at a constant rate, what time does she leave home? What time does she arrive at work? [She leaves at 7:54 and arrives at 8:18.]

24. Try simpler numbers if you cannot get the answer right away.
   a. How many integers are between 100 and 1000, not including 100 or 1000? **899**
   b. How many integers are between two integers I and J, not including I or J? $|I - J| - 1$

Review

25. Try positive and negative numbers to see whether it is true that $-(a + b) = -b + -a.$ *(Lesson 6-7)* **See below.**

26. Name one advantage of using a computer spreadsheet.   *(Lesson 6-6)*
   See below.
27. What is the last digit of 7^{1000}?   *(Lesson 6-5)* **1**

28. Solve $-3\frac{1}{2} + x = 4.2$.   *(Lesson 5-8)* **x = 7.7**

29. Give the additive inverse of each number.
   a. 5 **-5**   **b.** -3.4 **3.4**   **c.** 0   *(Lesson 5-2)* **0**

30. *True or false.* $\frac{5}{4} + \frac{5}{4} = \frac{10}{8}$ *(Lesson 5-5)* **False**

31. Evaluate $3p + q^4$ if $p = 4$ and $q = 5$.   *(Lessons 2-2, 4-4)* **637**

32. How many grams are in a pound?   *(Lesson 3-5)* **≈ 454.5 g**

Exploration

33. If the same number is added to both the minuend and the subtrahend, their difference is not changed. For instance, to subtract

$$\begin{array}{r} 4307 \\ -2998 \\ \hline \end{array}$$

you can add 2 to the minuend and subtrahend to get

$$\begin{array}{r} 4309 \\ -3000 \\ \hline \end{array}$$

which is much easier. The answer to both questions is 1309. For each of the subtraction questions below, find a number to add to make the subtraction easier. Then do the subtraction.

a. 136 Add 3. $\begin{array}{r} 139 \\ -100 \\ \hline 39 \end{array}$ $\begin{array}{r} 136 \\ -97 \\ \hline \end{array}$

b. 4905 Add 4. $\begin{array}{r} 4909 \\ -2000 \\ \hline 2909 \end{array}$ $\begin{array}{r} 4905 \\ -1996 \\ \hline \end{array}$

c. 1117 Add 11. $\begin{array}{r} 1128 \\ -1000 \\ \hline 128 \end{array}$ $\begin{array}{r} 1117 \\ -989 \\ \hline \end{array}$

25) Sample: Let $a = 5, b = -2$. Then $-(a + b) = -(5 + -2) = -3$ and $-b + -a = -(-2) + -5 = -3$. Let $a = -9$ and $b = -4$. Then $-(a + b) = -(-13) = 13$ and $-b + -a = 4 + 9 = 13$. It seems true.
26) Sample: Any change in a cell using a formula will result in automatic recalculation.

Practice

For more questions on SPUR Objectives, use **Lesson Master 7-1A** (shown on page 349) or **Lesson Master 7-1B** (shown on pages 350–351).

Assessment

Written Communication Write the numbers $5\frac{1}{2}$, $3\frac{3}{4}$, and $1\frac{3}{4}$ on the board. Ask students to write one problem using these numbers to illustrate the Take-Away Model for Subtraction and one problem that illustrates the Comparison Model for Subtraction. [Problems show understanding of both models. Some students may decide to change each fraction to a decimal and use the decimals in their problems.]

Extension

History Connection Have students research at least four dates in history (two of which are B.C. dates) and then determine how long ago the event occurred or how old the person would be in this year.

Project Update Project 1, *Population Changes*, on page 399, and Project 6, *When x – y is Small*, on page 400, relate to the content of this lesson.

▶ **LESSON MASTER 7-1B** *page 2*

Uses Objective M: Use the Comparison Model for Subtraction to form sentences involving subtraction.

In 8–13, write the calculation and the answer for each question.

8. Kazuo gets $3.50 per week for his allowance. Jason gets $2.25. How much more does Kazuo get than Jason?

$3.5 - 2.25$	$1.25
calculation	answer

9. Which is heavier, a pound or a kilogram? About how much heavier?

$2.2 - 1$	kilogram; ~ 1.2 lb
calculation	answer

10. When Donna was born, she was $20\frac{1}{2}$ inches long. Her twin sister, Lynn, was $19\frac{1}{4}$ inches at birth. How much longer was Donna?

$20\frac{1}{2} - 19\frac{1}{4}$	$1\frac{1}{4}$ inches
calculation	answer

11. If a pork roast weighs $3\frac{1}{4}$ pounds and a beef roast weighs $3\frac{2}{3}$ pounds, how much heavier is the beef roast?

$3\frac{2}{3} - 3\frac{1}{4}$	$\frac{5}{12}$ pound
calculation	answer

12. The seating capacity of the Houston Astrodome is 54,816. The capacity of Three Rivers Stadium in Pittsburgh is 58,727. How many more people can Three Rivers Stadium hold?

$58,727 - 54,816$	3,911 people
calculation	answer

13. L. Frank Baum, the author of *The Wonderful Wizard of Oz*, was born in 1856 and died in 1919, 20 years before the movie, "The Wizard of Oz" was made. What was Baum's age when he died? Give both possible answers.

$1919 - 1856$	62 or 63 years
calculation	answer

14. The library has N novels and B biographies. How many more novels does the library have?

$N - B$ novels
answer

Setting Up Lesson 7-2

Materials If you plan to have students do the *Extension* on page 357, they will need almanacs.

The table on the opening page of this chapter applies the Slide Model for Subtraction and can be used to introduce Lesson 7-2.

Objectives

A Subtract positive and negative numbers written as decimals or fractions.

G Apply the Algebraic Definition of Subtraction.

L Use the Slide Model for Subtraction to form sentences involving subtraction.

O Picture subtraction of positive and negative numbers on a number line.

Resources

From the *Teacher's Resource File*
- Lesson Master 7-2A or 7-2B
- Answer Master 7-2
- Teaching Aids
  - 8 Number Line (Warm-up)
  - 64 Checkerboard
  - 67 Warm-up
- Activity Kit, Activity 16

Additional Resources
- Visuals for Teaching Aids 8, 64, 67
- Almanacs (Extension)

Teaching **7-2**
Lesson

Warm-up

Use a number line to help you find each number. **Teaching Aid 8** contains a number line.

1. The number is 6 units from –3.
   3 or –9
2. Its distance from 2 is half the distance from 2 to 6. **4 or 0**
3. To find the number, start at 0. Move 8 units right and then 11 units left. **–3**
4. The number is 100 units from 6. **106 or –94**

7-2

The Slide Model for Subtraction

Sliding with snowboards. *When temperatures slide down and snow falls, people can slide downhill. These provide images for subtraction.*

Subtraction as Sliding Down

Suppose the temperature is 50° and drops 12°. This situation can be pictured on a number line. Start at 50° and slide 12° to the left.

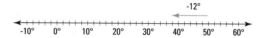

The resulting temperature is 38°.

The answer could also be found by subtracting 50 − 12. This subtraction is not take-away or comparison, but a third model for subtraction called the *slide model.*

❶ | **Slide Model for Subtraction**
If a quantity x is decreased by an amount y, the resulting quantity is $x - y$.

In slide situations, you usually can slide up or down. Results of sliding up are found by addition. Results of sliding down can be found either by adding negative numbers or by subtracting.

	By subtraction	By addition	Answer
A person who weighs 60 kg loses 4 kg. What is the resulting weight?	60 kg − 4 kg	60 kg + -4 kg	56 kg
The temperature is -17° and falls 20°. What is the resulting temperature?	-17° − 20°	-17° + -20°	-37°

Lesson 7-2 Overview

Broad Goals The Algebraic Definition of Subtraction, $a - b = a + -b$, gives an algorithm for subtracting positive and negative numbers. In this lesson, it is introduced through the Slide Model for Subtraction and applied to the calculation of change.

Perspective The Slide Model for Subtraction is related to the Slide Model for Addition. In the latter, positive numbers represent shifts or changes in one direction, and negative numbers represent shifts or changes in the opposite direction. Addition of negative numbers is applied in many situations where, earlier, students would have subtracted. The Slide Model for Subtraction covers many of these situations.

The Slide Model for Subtraction naturally yields situations that use the Algebraic Definition of Subtraction. We call this the *algebraic* definition to distinguish it from definitions students have seen since primary grades. Very often subtraction is also defined as $a - b = c$ if and only if $c + b = a$.

Some teachers have a phrase which informally defines subtraction—subtraction undoes addition. If you like to use this phrase, note that taking away undoes putting together. This idea can be stated as $a + b - b = a$.

These examples show a basic relationship between subtraction and addition. Its formal name is the *Algebraic Definition of Subtraction.* It is also called the *Adding Opposites Property of Subtraction,* or the *Add-Opp Property* for short.

❷ **Algebraic Definition of Subtraction (Add-Opp Property)**
For any numbers x and y,

$$x - y = x + -y.$$

In words, subtracting y is the same as adding the opposite of y.

An Algorithm for Subtraction

The Algebraic Definition of Subtraction allows any subtraction to be converted to an addition. This is helpful because you already know how to add both positive and negative numbers.

Example 1

Simplify -5 − 2.

Solution 1

Use the slide model. Start at -5 and slide down 2.

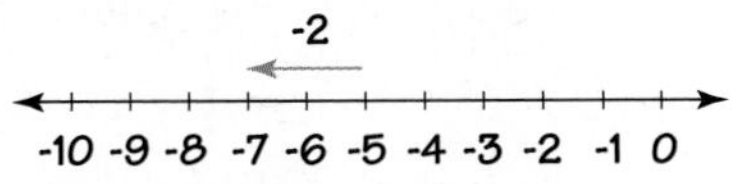

The result is -7. So -5 − 2 = -7.

Solution 2

Use the Algebraic Definition of Subtraction. (Instead of subtracting 2, add -2.)

$$-5 - 2 = -5 + -2 = -7$$

Example 2

Perform each subtraction by converting it to an addition using the Algebraic Definition of Subtraction.

a. 40 − 50.79 **b.** -9 − -11 **c.** $\frac{3}{4} - \frac{7}{8}$ **d.** $x - -y$

Solution

	Given		Convert to Addition		Result
a.	40 − 50.79	=	40 + -50.79	=	-10.79
b.	-9 − -11	=	-9 + 11	=	2
c.	$\frac{3}{4} - \frac{7}{8}$	=	$\frac{3}{4} + -\frac{7}{8} = \frac{6}{8} + -\frac{7}{8}$	=	$-\frac{1}{8}$
d.	x − -y	=	x + y	=	x + y

Notes on Reading

You might want to use the suggestions in *Optional Activities* below to introduce this lesson.

❶ Some situations, such as bank-account transactions, are best represented by the Slide Model for Subtraction. A withdrawal of funds decreases the total amount of money in the bank; a deposit increases the total amount. Weight gain or loss is a similar example. However, temperature-change examples are a pure slide subtraction that should not be construed as take away. Temperatures differ from savings accounts or weights in that their values are scaled values. The 0° temperature does not mean the absence of temperature; it is merely a convenient point on the scale. Therefore, you can decrease a 0° temperature, whereas you cannot take away from an amount of 0 dollars or a weight of 0 kilograms.

❷ When discussing the Algebraic Definition of Subtraction, stress the advantage of addition over subtraction. Addition is commutative and associative; subtraction is neither. As a result, there are no order-of-operation worries with addition. **Example 2** illustrates this point.

Some teachers believe that the "Add-Opp" name helps students understand the rule for subtracting positive and negative numbers. However, we also recognize that some teachers do not like abbreviations and prefer that students give the full name.

Optional Activities

You might want to use *Activity Kit, Activity 16,* as an alternate way to introduce this lesson. In the activity, students use integer tiles to subtract.

After using the activity, you might ask students to explain how the Algebraic Definition of Subtraction allows them to use the two-color counters to subtract. [One possible explanation is to represent each number with counters, then to flip over the counters representing the number to be subtracted, and then to combine as in addition.]

Question 19 of Lesson 7-1 asks students to use the table on page 345 to determine the 1980 populations of various places. Now you can use the data in the table to convince students that the Algebraic Definition of Subtraction works. Subtract the gain for your state from the 1990 population, and you will get the population in 1980. Pick another state for which the gain has the opposite sign, and show that the definition also works for that state.

❸ The three uses of the – sign cause a lot of confusion, so this chart is very important. You may want to read this part of the lesson aloud.

We avoid the use of + signs for positive numbers except when they appear in applications. We also do not use the raised bar to denote negative numbers. Such signs, when applied to variables, are misleading. While it might be clear that $+x$ is the same as x and ^-x is the same as $-x$, the former is not necessarily a positive number, and the latter is not necessarily a negative number. We use parentheses around negative numbers only when taking the opposite of a negative number. Our rule is to use the notation that students will most likely use after this course.

❹ Do not expect students to remember whether the later value or the earlier value comes first in calculating change. If they are confused, recommend that they try simpler numbers.

The application of the Comparison Model for Subtraction to determine change is very important in mathematics. In algebra, it is the reason for the subtractions in the familiar formula for slope.

A major reason for converting subtractions to additions is that addition has the commutative and associative properties. You do not have to worry about order of additions. This is particularly nice if there are more than two numbers involved in the subtraction.

Example 3

Simplify $-5 - {}^-3 + 8 + {}^-2 - 7 - 4$.

Solution

Start with the original expression.	$-5 - {}^-3 + 8 + {}^-2 - 7 - 4$
Convert all subtractions to addition.	$= -5 + 3 + 8 + {}^-2 + {}^-7 + {}^-4$
Rearrange so all negatives are together.	$= -5 + {}^-2 + {}^-7 + {}^-4 + 3 + 8$
Add negatives together and positives together.	$= -18 + 11$
Add the negative total to the positive total.	$= -7$

Uses of the − Sign

You have now learned three uses of the − sign. Each use has a different English word.

❸
where − sign is found	example	in English
between numbers or variables	$2 - 5$	2 *minus* 5
in front of a positive number	-3	*negative* 3
in front of a variable or negative number	$-x$ $-(-4)$	*opposite of* x *opposite of negative* 4

For example, $-3 - {}^-y$ is read "negative three minus the opposite of *y*."

Comparison with Negative Numbers

Special types of the Comparison Model for Subtraction can lead to subtracting negative numbers.

❹ **change = later value − earlier value**

Example 4

The temperature was -3° earlier today. Now it is -17°. By how much has it changed?

Solution

To find the change, start the subtraction with the later value.

$$-17 - {}^-3 = -17 + 3 = -14$$

So the temperature has gone down 14°.

354

Adapting to Individual Needs

Extra Help

At the beginning of this lesson, a temperature change is used as an instance of the Slide Model for Subtraction. In **Example 4**, a temperature change is treated as an instance of the comparison model. Help students see that in the first case, the original temperature and the amount of change are known. The slide model is used to find the resulting temperature. In **Example 4**, the original temperature and the temperature after the change are known. Here, the amount of change, or difference, is found by comparing the temperature before with the temperature after.

354

In questions like that in Example 4, many people get confused. They do not know which number is the later value. This should not cause you to worry, because in comparing numbers, you can subtract in either order. The number $x - y$ is always the opposite of $y - x$. (You are asked to explore this in the Questions.)

For instance, in Example 4 suppose you subtracted -17 from -3.

$$-3 - -17 = -3 + 17 = 14$$

This tells you that the answer to Example 4 is either 14 or -14. Since the temperature went from -3 to -17, it went down. So the correct answer must be the negative one of these, -14.

QUESTIONS

Covering the Reading

1. To picture the subtraction $3 - 4$ on the number line, you can start at __?__ and draw an arrow __?__ units long pointing to the __?__. **3; 4; left**

2. State the Slide Model for Subtraction. **If a quantity a is decreased by an amount b, the result is a quantity $a - b$.**

In 3 and 4, a question is given.
a. Write a subtraction problem that will answer the question.
b. Write an addition problem that will answer the question.
c. Answer the question.

3. The temperature is 74°F and is supposed to drop 20° by this evening. What is the expected temperature this evening?
a) 74 − 20; b) 74 + -20; c) 54°F

4. The temperature is -4°C and is supposed to drop 10° by morning. What is the expected morning temperature?
a) -4 − 10; b) -4 + -10; c) -14°C

5. State the Algebraic Definition of Subtraction (Add-Opp Property)
a. in symbols; b. in words. **a) For any numbers x and y, $x - y = x + -y$.**
b) See below left.

6. $5 - -8 = 5 + $ __?__ . **8**

7. $-x - -y = $ __?__ $+$ __?__ . **-x; y**

In 8–15, simplify.

8. $2 - 5$ **-3**

9. $83 - 100$ **-17**

10. $-8 - 45$ **-53**

11. $-1 - 1$ **-2**

12. $3 - -7$ **10**

13. $0 - -41$ **41**

14. $-\frac{9}{5} - -\frac{6}{5}$ **$-\frac{3}{5}$**

15. $m - -2$ **$m + 2$**

16. Give two reasons why it is useful to be able to convert subtractions to additions.

17. Consider the expression $-43 - -x$.
a. Which of the three dashes (left, center, or right) is read as "minus"?
b. Which dash is read "opposite of"? **a) center; b) right;**
c. Which dash is read "negative"? **c) left**

Too cold to melt. *At -4°C, snow will not change directly to liquid water. However, snow will sublimate or change directly to water vapor.*

5b) Subtracting y is the same as adding the opposite of y.

16) You already know how to add positive and negative numbers; addition has the Commutative and Associative properties.

Adapting to Individual Needs

English Language Development

You might want to spend extra time emphasizing the different uses of the – sign.

(a) As an operation sign: just as + is a symbol for addition, – is a symbol for subtraction. For example, 5 – 3 (5 minus 3) means subtract 3 from 5.

(b) To indicate a negative number: a "–" before a number means it is negative; a "+" or no sign before a number means it

is positive. For example, -3 is negative; 3 is positive.

(c) A "–" in front of a variable means "the opposite of." Students should read $-x$ as the opposite of x. If x is positive, then $-x$ is negative (3 is positive and its opposite, -3, is negative). If x is negative, then $-x$ is positive (-3 is negative and its opposite, -(-3), is positive).

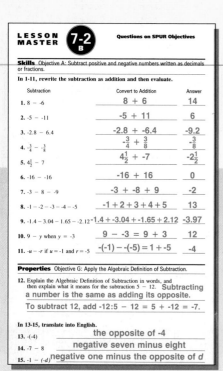

356

---

18. Translate into English: $-A - -4$. **the opposite of A minus negative four**

In 19 and 20, simplify.

19. $-4 - 8 + 6 - 7 + -5 - -3$ **-15**   20. $12 - 24 + -36 - -48 + 60$ **60**

In 21 and 22, calculate the change in temperature from yesterday to today.

21. yesterday, 27°; today, 13° **-14°**   22. yesterday, -9°; today, -8° **1°**

23. Let $x = 46$ and $y = -16$. Give the value of each expression.
    a. $x - y$ **62**   **b.** $y - x$ **-62**   **c.** $(x - y) + (y - x)$ **0**

Applying the Mathematics

24. The formula $p = s - c$ connects profit p, selling price s, and cost c.
    a. Calculate p when $s = \$49.95$ and $c = \$30.27$. **\$19.68**
    b. Calculate p when $s = \$49.95$ and $c = \$56.52$. **-\$6.57**
    c. Your answer to part **b** should be a negative number. What does a negative profit indicate? **a loss**

25. Calculate $a - b + c - d$ when $a = -1$, $b = -2$, $c = -3$, and $d = -4$. **2**

26. Give a key sequence for your calculator that does the subtraction $3 - -4$. **Sample: 3 $\boxed{-}$ 4 $\boxed{+/-}$ $\boxed{=}$**

In 27-29, use trial and error, or test special cases.

27. *Multiple choice.* If $9 = 7 - x$, then $x =$
    (a) 2.   (b) 16.   (c) -2.   (d) -16. **(c)**

28. **a.** For all numbers x, y, and z, is it true that $(x - y) - z = x - (y - z)$? **No**
    b. Does subtraction have the associative property? **No**

29. **a.** In order for subtraction to be commutative, what relationship between any two numbers a and b would have to be true?
    b. Is subtraction commutative? **a) $a - b = b - a$; b) No**

30) 1960–1970: 7,291
    1970–1980: -13,584
    1980–1990: 70,936

30. Here are populations of Portland, Oregon, according to the last four censuses.

1960	372,676
1970	379,967
1980	366,383
1990	437,319

    a. Calculate the change from each census to the next. You should get two positive numbers and one negative number. **See above.**
    b. Add the three numbers you got in part **a**. **64,643**
    c. What does the sum in part **b** mean? **the change in population from 1960 to 1990**

31. Do the addition and subtraction and write your answer as a mixed number:
$$-3\frac{1}{2} + 2\frac{2}{3} - 6\frac{1}{6} \quad \textbf{-7}$$

356

---

32. Daniel weighed $6\frac{15}{16}$ pounds at birth and $21\frac{1}{2}$ pounds on his first birthday. Kiera weighed $7\frac{1}{4}$ pounds at birth and $20\frac{1}{2}$ pounds at one year. How much more weight did Daniel gain in his first year than Kiera gained in hers? *(Lesson 7-1)* $1\frac{5}{16}$ lb

33. A symphony is 43 minutes long. If an orchestra has been playing the symphony for m minutes, how many minutes remain? *(Lesson 7-1)* $43 - m$

Maestro, if you please.
Michael Morgan is shown here conducting the Chicago Youth Symphony Orchestra.

34. Find m∠*HDA* if
m∠*HDR* = 136°
and m∠*ADR* = 54°.
(Lesson 7-1) **82°**

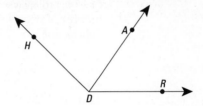

35. In a single elimination tournament a team plays until it is beaten. Eight teams play a single elimination tournament. How many games must be played in this tournament? *(Lesson 6-3)* **7**

36. What property justifies adding the same number to both sides of an equation? *(Lesson 5-8)* **Addition Property of Equality**

37. How many degrees does the minute hand of a watch turn in 1 minute? *(Lesson 5-4)* **6°**

Exploration

38. Use a spreadsheet to evaluate $x - y$ and $y - x$ for at least twenty pairs of values of x and y. Use positives, negatives, fractions, and decimal values for each variable. What relationship do you find between $x - y$ and $y - x$? **The values (x − y) and (y − x) are opposites.**

Lesson 7-2 *The Slide Model for Subtraction* **357**

Practice

For more questions on SPUR Objectives, use **Lesson Master 7-2A** (shown on page 355) or **Lesson Master 7-2B** (shown on pages 356–357).

Assessment

Group Assessment Have students **work in groups** and decide if each of the following sentences is true or false. [Students read the questions correctly and explain their reasoning using the models for subtraction. Some students may choose to use special cases to help them make their decisions.]

1. $a - (b - c) = (a - b) - c$ **False**
2. $x - y = x + -y$ **True**
3. $x - y = y - x$ **False**
4. $-a + b - -c - d + -e = -a + b + c + -d + -e$ **True**
5. $-a + (b + -c) = (-a + b) + -c$ **True**

Extension

Have students use an almanac to find record high and low temperatures for at least five cities. Then have them find the difference between the record high and low for each city.

Project Update Project 1, *Population Changes,* on page 399, relates to the content of this lesson.

▶ **LESSON MASTER 7-2B** *page 2*

Uses Objective L: Use the Slide Model for Subtraction to form sentences involving subtraction.

16. The temperature was 5° this morning. By sunset it was -11°. By how much had it changed?
<u>-11 − 5</u> <u>drop of 16°</u>
calculation answer

17. A submarine was submerged at 111 meters below sea level. After it went down another 80 meters, how far below sea level was the submarine?
<u>-111 − 80</u> <u>191 feet below sea level</u>
calculation answer

18. A river is 2 feet above flood level. By how much would the river have to rise or fall to bring it to 5 feet below flood level?
<u>-5 − 2</u> <u>fall 7 feet</u>
calculation answer

19. Average temperatures for this month were 5° above normal, while average temperatures for the same month last year were 7° below normal. How much higher or lower were this month's average temperatures than those for last year?
<u>5 − (-7)</u> <u>12° higher this year</u>
calculation answer

Representations Objective O: Picture subtraction of positive and negative numbers on a number line.

In 20-23, illustrate the subtraction on the number line and give the result.

20. $3 - 8 =$ <u>-5</u>   -7 -6 -5 -4 -3 -2 -1 0 1 2 3 4 5 6

21. $-2 - 6 =$ <u>-8</u>   -9 -8 -7 -6 -5 -4 -3 -2 -1 0 1 2

22. $-5 - 2 =$ <u>-7</u>   -9 -8 -7 -6 -5 -4 -3 -2 -1 0 1

23. $2 - 6 =$ <u>-4</u>   -6 -5 -4 -3 -2 -1 0 1 2 3 4

Setting up Lesson 7-3

When making the assignment, you may want to mention that Lesson 7-3 is taught through the examples and should be read carefully.

Objectives

B Solve sentences of the form $x - a = b$.

G Apply the properties of addition and subtraction in solving equations.

K Use the Take-Away Model for Subtraction to form sentences involving subtraction.

L Use the Slide Model for Subtraction to form sentences involving subtraction.

M Use the Comparison Model for Subtraction to form sentences involving subtraction.

Resources

From the Teacher's Resource File
- Lesson Master 7-3A and 7-3B
- Answer Master 7-3
- Teaching Aid 67: Warm-up

Additional Resources
- Visual for Teaching Aid 67

Teaching Lesson 7-3

Warm-up

Solve each equation.
1. $x + 6 = -21$ −27
2. $-5 + m = 14$ 19
3. $-37 = 12 + a$ −49
4. $-1.6 + y = -5.7$ −4.1
5. $r + \frac{3}{4} = -1\frac{1}{2}$ $-2\frac{1}{4}$

Notes on Reading

Discuss each example with students as you review the steps for solving an equation.

7-3

Solving $x - a = b$

Hawaiian beef. *The Parker Ranch, located on the island of Hawaii, covers 262,000 acres and is one of the largest ranches in the country. Paniolos (cowboys) are shown here rounding up the herd and collecting strays.*

Consider this problem.

> From a large herd of cattle, cowhands drove away 230 steers. There were 575 steers left in the herd. How large was the original herd?

One way to answer this question is to solve an equation. Let S be the number of steers in the herd. Then, by the Take-Away Model for Subtraction, $S - 230 = 575$.

The equation $S - 230 = 575$ is an equation of the form $x - a = b$, where x is the unknown. To solve this equation, just convert the subtraction to addition using the Algebraic Definition of Subtraction. Then solve the resulting equation as you did in Chapter 5.

Example 1

Solve $S - 230 = 575$ to answer the question at the top of this page.

Solution

Start with the original equation.	$S - 230 = 575$
Convert to addition.	$S + \text{-}230 = 575$
Add 230 to both sides.	$S + \text{-}230 + 230 = 575 + 230$
Simplify.	$S + 0 = 805$
	$S = 805$

The original herd had 805 steers.

Check

If there were 805 steers in the original herd and 230 were driven away, would 575 remain? Yes.

Lesson 7-3 Overview

Broad Goals This lesson discusses the skills and applications associated with solving the equation $x - a = b$.

Perspective This lesson combines ideas from two previous lessons—solving $x + a = b$ (Lesson 5-8) and the Algebraic Definition of Subtraction (Lesson 7-2). Students are asked to change the equation $x - a = b$ which involves subtraction, into $x + \text{-}a = b$ which is a familiar form introduced in Chapter 5, by applying the Algebraic Definition of Subtraction.

The situation in Example 2 leads to another equation of the form $x - a = b$. This time b is negative. Still, the same process used in Example 1 works. Convert the subtraction to addition and solve the resulting equation.

Example 2

A group of divers paused on a natural plateau below the surface of the sea. After descending 20 feet more, they found themselves 53 feet below sea level. What is the elevation of the plateau?

Solution

Let E be the elevation of the plateau (in feet). From the Slide Model for Subtraction, $E - 20 = -53$. Solve this equation.

Original equation	$E - 20 = -53$
Convert to addition.	$E + -20 = -53$
Add 20 to both sides.	$E + -20 + 20 = -53 + 20$
Simplify.	$E + 0 = -33$
	$E = -33$

The plateau is 33 feet below sea level.

The process used in Examples 1 and 2 will work with any equation of the form $x - a = b$. We show this by using the general properties of addition and subtraction on this equation. Since the general properties are true for all numbers, this process will work regardless of the values of a and b.

What is done	What is written	Why it can be done
Original equation	$x - a = b$	
Change to addition.	$x + -a = b$	Algebraic Definition of Subtraction
Add a to each side.	$(x + -a) + a = b + a$	Addition Property of Equality
Regroup.	$x + (-a + a) = b + a$	Associative Property of Addition
Add $-a$ and a.	$x + 0 = b + a$	Property of Opposites
Add 0 and x.	$x = b + a$	Additive Identity Property of Zero

Experienced solvers do not write in all the steps. In Examples 1 and 2, we combined the 3rd and 4th lines. You should begin by writing all (or almost all) of the lines. After a while, you may skip steps. Your teacher may have advice for you to follow.

Scuba diving. *The word* scuba *stands for Self-Contained Underwater Breathing Apparatus. This scuba diver is swimming in an underwater cave in Australia.*

QUESTIONS

Covering the Reading

1. What is the name of the property that enables $x - a$ to be replaced by $x + -a$? **Algebraic Definition of Subtraction (or Add-Opp Property)**

2. What is the only difference between solving an equation of the form $x - a = b$ and solving an equation of the form $x + a = b$? **The equation $x - a = b$ requires an extra step: converting the subtraction to an addition.**

Lesson 7-3 *Solving* $x - a = b$ **359**

❶ You might want to go over this chart in detail. If students have difficulty understanding the steps, use a numerical example as suggested in *Extra Help* on page 360.

To give students more practice writing and solving equations, see *Optional Activities* below.

Additional Examples

1. Solve and check.
   a. $A - 382 = -671$ $A = -289$; $-289 - 382 = -671$
   b. $C - 4.5 = 2.7$ $C = 7.2$; $7.2 - 4.5 = 2.7$

2. Write an equation involving subtraction for the following situation. Solve the equation and answer the question. In Matt Tishun's algebra class, 8 students were excused to attend a special band rehearsal. If 18 students were left in class, what is the regular class size? **Let c stand for class size; $c - 8 = 18$; 26 students**

3. Solve for m: $m - b = kx$. $m = kx + b$

Optional Activities

After discussing the examples, you can use this activity to give students more practice solving equations of the form $x - a = b$.

Ask students to make up situations with questions that can be answered by solving $x - a = b$, and share what they write with each other. Take some of the best situations, and give them to all students in the class for practice.

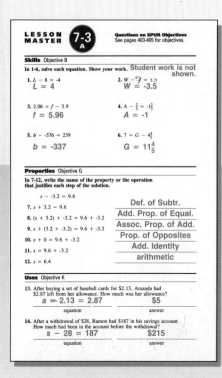

359

Questions 12–13 Some students can undoubtedly do part **c** without answering parts **a** and **b**. The point of these questions is to show that equation solving works, not that equations should be required for easy questions.

Question 14 For some students, it may be helpful to reverse the sides of the equation, writing $s - c = p$. It is important to discuss this question because students will see it again in the next lesson.

Follow-up for Lesson 7-3

Practice

For more questions on SPUR Objectives, use **Lesson Master 7-3A** (shown on page 359) or **Lesson Master 7-3B** (shown on pages 360–361).

Assessment

Written/Oral Communication Have each student write and solve an equation involving subtraction. Then have each student give his or her equation to another student to solve. Then let students compare and discuss their work. [Students can solve equations of the form $x - a = b$ and explain the process.]

360

---

3. Is -42 the solution to $x - 13 = -29$? No

4. Is $y = {}^-1$ the solution to $6 = y - {}^-7$? Yes

In 5–10, an equation is given.
a. Convert the equation to one with only addition in it.
b. Solve.
c. Check.

5. $a - 6 = 9$

5a) $a + {}^-6 = 9$
b) $a = 15$
c) $15 - 6 = 9$

6. $c - 12.5 = 3$

6a) $c + {}^-12.5 = 3$
b) $c = 15.5$
c) $15.5 - 12.5 = 3$

7. $x - 14 = -2$

7a) $x + {}^-14 = -2$
b) $x = 12$
c) $12 - 14 = -2$

8. $73 = y - 28$

8a) $73 = y + {}^-28$
b) $y = 101$
c) $73 = 101 - 28$

9. $B - {}^-5 = 6$

9a) $B + 5 = 6$
b) $B = 1$
c) $1 - {}^-5 = 6$

10. $3.01 = e - 9.2$

10a) $3.01 = e + {}^-9.2$
b) $e = 12.21$
c) $3.01 = 12.21 - 9.2$

11. *Multiple choice.* If $x - a = b$, then $x =$
(a) $a - b.$ (b) $b - a.$ (c) $b + a.$ (d) $b + {}^-a.$ (c)

In 12 and 13, a situation is given.
a. Write an equation involving subtraction describing the situation.
b. Solve the equation.
c. Answer the question.

12. After descending 75 meters, Antoine Clymer is at an elevation of 3,980 meters on the mountain. At what elevation was he before his descent? a) $e - 75 = 3980$; b) $e = 4055$; c) He was at an elevation of 4055 meters before his descent.

13. Greta Lowenz spent $14.39 of her weekly allowance on fancy bows. She has $12.61 left. What is her weekly allowance? a) $A - 14.39 = 12.61$; b) $A = 27$; c) Her weekly allowance is $27.00.

The dancers shown here were among the many performers at the Festival of Philippine Arts and Culture held in Los Angeles, California.

Applying the Mathematics

14. The formula $p = s - c$ relates profit, selling price, and cost. Solve for the selling price s in terms of the profit and the cost. $s = p + c$

15. Scott started with b dollars in his savings account. He withdrew $60. Two days later he withdrew $30, leaving a balance of $237.61. How much was in Scott's account to start with? $327.61

16. A fish starts at a depth of d feet below the surface of a pond. While searching for food it ascends 4 feet, then descends 12 feet. Its final depth is 15 feet below the surface. What was the fish's initial depth? 7 ft below the surface

17. Solve for s: $s - 1\frac{5}{8} = \frac{1}{2}$. $2\frac{1}{8}$

Review

In 18–20, calculate.   *(Lesson 7-2)*

18. $2 - 3 - 10$ -11   19. $-8 - 9$ -17   20. $-\frac{3}{8} - -\frac{2}{3}$ $\frac{7}{24}$

21. The number of Americans of Filipino descent living in the United States in 1980 was 774,652. In 1990, the number of Filipinos in the United States was 1,406,770. What was the change in the Filipino population in the United States from 1980 to 1990? *(Lesson 7-2)* 632,118

360

Adapting to Individual Needs

Extra Help
If students have trouble with the generalizations on page 359, use this instance. Then generalize.

$x - 5 = -12$	
$x + {}^-5 = -12$	Subtracting 5 is the same as adding -5.
$(x + {}^-5) + 5 = -12 + 5$	To get x alone, undo adding -5 by adding 5 to both sides.
$x + ({}^-5 + 5) = -12 + 5$	Regroup so -5 and 5 are together.
$x + 0 = -12 + 5$	The sum of opposites is zero.
$x = -7$	The sum of a number and zero is that number.

This person in Kotzebue, Alaska, is ice fishing—a popular sport in areas where heavy freezing occurs.

22. The highest temperature ever recorded in the United States was 134°F, in Death Valley, California, on July 10, 1913. The lowest temperature ever recorded in the U.S. was -80°F, in Prospect Creek, Alaska, on January 23, 1971.
    a. To the nearest year, how many years separate the two dates?
    b. What is the difference between the temperatures?   *(Lessons 7-1, 7-2)*
    a) 58 years; b) 214°

23. Barry had $312 in his checking account and made out a check for $400. By how much was he overdrawn?   *(Lessons 7-1, 7-2)* $88

24. A person was born in this century in the year B and died in the year D. What are the possible ages of this person at the time of death? (Use special cases if you cannot answer quickly.)   *(Lessons 6-6, 7-1)*
    $D - B$, or $D - B - 1$

25. B is on $\overline{AC}$. If $AC = 1$ meter and $AB = 30$ cm, what is BC?
    (Lessons 3-4, 7-1)   70 cm

26. a. Find x if $-x = -17$. $x = 17$ b. Find x if $-x = 3$.   *(Lesson 5-2)*
    $x = -3$

27. Measure $\angle V$ to the nearest degree.   *(Lesson 3-5)*   10°

In 28–33, rewrite as a decimal.

28. sixty-four millionths   *(Lesson 2-8)*
    .000064

29. 150%   *(Lesson 2-5)*
    1.5

30. 6.34×10^6 *(Lesson 2-3)*
    6,340,000

31. five trillion   *(Lesson 2-1)*
    5,000,000,000,000

32. $\frac{6}{11}$ *(Lesson 1-8)* $.\overline{54}$

33. $\frac{3}{4}$ *(Lesson 1-8)*   .75

34. On personal checks, amounts must be written in English words. Write $4009 as you would need to for a personal check.   *(Lesson 1-1)*
    Four thousand nine dollars

Exploration

35. a. Replace each letter with a digit to make a true subtraction. Different letters stand for different digits. Each letter stands for the same digit wherever it occurs.

    $$\begin{array}{r} \text{TWO} \\ -\text{ONE} \\ \hline \text{ONE} \end{array} \qquad \text{Sample:} \begin{array}{r} 412 \\ -206 \\ \hline 206 \end{array}$$

    b. There is more than one solution. Find as many solutions as you can.
    There are 16 solutions. (ONE, TWO) = (206, 412), (216, 432), (231, 462), (236, 472), (271, 542), (281, 562), (286, 572), (291, 582), (407, 814), (417, 834), (427, 854), (432, 864), (452, 904), (457, 914), (467, 934), (482, 964)

▶ **LESSON MASTER 7-3 B** *page 2*

Uses Objective K: Use the Take-Away Model for Subtraction to form sentences involving subtraction.

15. After withdrawing $16.50 from her bank account, Yoshiko had $71.57 left. How much was in the account before the withdrawal?
    $x - 16.5 = 71.57$ $88.07
    equation   answer

16. After losing 29 points in the game, John had -22 points. How many points did John have before he lost the 29 points?
    $x - 29 = -22$ 7 points
    equation   answer

Uses: Objective L: Use the Slide Model for Subtraction to form sentences involving subtraction.

17. After photographing sea life at 25 meters below the surface of the sea, an oceanographer lowered the camera another 48 meters. At what elevation was the camera's second location?
    $-25 - 48 = e$ 73 feet below sea level
    equation   answer

18. After descending 750 feet, the blimp was 2,200 feet above the stadium. What was its altitude before the descent?
    $b - 750 = 2,200$ 2,950 feet
    equation   answer

Uses Objective M: Use the Comparison Model for Subtraction to form sentences involving subtraction.

19. In the first round of golf, Alfonso scored 3 points under par. In the second round, he scored 4 points over par. How many points higher was Alfonso's second score?
    $4 - -3 = h$ 7 points
    equation   answer

20. Suzi's field-goal average per game 4.8 points lower than the team average. Maria's average was 2.1 points higher than the team average. How many points higher was Maria's average than Suzi's average?
    $2.1 - -4.8 = a$ 6.9 points higher
    equation   answer

Objectives

B Solve sentences of the form $a - x = b$.

G Apply the properties of addition and subtraction in solving equations.

K Use the Take-Away Model for Subtraction to form sentences involving subtraction.

L Use the Slide Model for Subtraction to form sentences involving subtraction.

M Use the Comparison Model for Subtraction to form sentences involving subtraction.

Resources

From the *Teacher's Resource File*
- Lesson Master 7-4A or 7-4B
- Answer Master 7-4
- Assessment Sourcebook: Quiz for Lessons 7-1 through 7-4
- Teaching Aids
  68 Warm-up
  70 Question 29

Additional Resources
- Visuals for Teaching Aids 68, 70

Teaching Lesson 7-4

Warm-up

1. What do you have to subtract from 8°C to get –3°C? **11°C**
2. Last week Lari had $7. This week she owes her brother $6. What do you subtract from $7 to get –$6? **$13**
3. A scuba diver went from –10 feet to –25 feet. What do you subtract from –10 feet to get –25 feet?
   15 feet

Solving $a - x = b$

Georgetown. *Georgetown, a neighborhood in Washington, D.C., has many fine examples of well-preserved, early American architecture. Many of the buildings are 100–200 years old.*

A Situation Leading to $a - x = b$

Here is a portion of the table from the beginning of this chapter.

State	1990 Population	Change Since 1980	State	1990 Population	Change Since 1980
Michigan	9,295,297	33,253	Washington	4,866,692	734,339
Minnesota	4,375,099	299,129	West Virginia	1,793,477	–156,709
Mississippi	2,573,216	52,446	Wisconsin	4,891,769	186,127
Missouri	5,117,073	200,307	Wyoming	453,588	–15,969
Other areas					
D.C.	606,900	–31,532	American		
Puerto Rico	3,522,037	325,517	Samoa	46,773	14,476
Virgin Islands	101,809	6,218	Guam	133,152	27,173

Source: Bureau of the Census, U.S. Dept. of Commerce, 1980 and 1990 Censuses

As you know, from this information you can obtain the 1980 population of each listed state or other area. The general formula comes from the Comparison Model for Subtraction.

$$\text{1990 population} - \text{1980 population} = \text{change}$$

For instance, to find the 1980 population of the District of Columbia (D.C.), let x be the 1980 population. Substitute the known values for the 1990 population and the change.

$$606,900 - x = -31,532$$

❶ The equation to be solved is of the form $a - x = b$. The numbers a and b in this situation have many digits, so we begin by considering a simpler example. Notice that we use almost the same algorithm we used to solve $x - a = b$ in Lesson 7-3. But because the unknown in $a - x = b$ is subtracted, an extra step is needed.

Lesson 7-4 Overview

Broad Goals Solving equations of the form $a - x = b$ is discussed in this lesson along with the idea of equivalent equations and formulas.

Perspective For several reasons, solving $a - x = b$ is more difficult for students than solving $x - a = b$. First, students can either add the opposite of a to both sides, or they can add the variable for which they are solving to both sides. Second, there are more

steps. Third, students usually have had little experience in earlier grades solving corresponding arithmetic problems.

One method for solving $3 - x = 20$ is to add –3 to both sides. This yields $-x = -3 + 20$, and, after simplifying, $-x = 17$. Taking the opposite of both sides results in $x = -17$. Two disadvantages of this method are that it does not generalize easily to formulas, and it does not work easily on inequalities.

There are advantages to solving $3 - x = 20$ by adding x to both sides of the equation. The resulting equation, $3 = 20 + x$, can be solved using methods from Chapter 5 which students already know. This method also helps prepare students to solve equations with variables on both sides which they will encounter in Chapter 12 and to solve inequalities which they will encounter in Algebra.

Example 1

Solve $3 - x = 20$.

Solution 1

Original equation	$3 - x = 20$
Convert to addition.	$3 + {\text-}x = 20$
Add ⁻3 to both sides.	${\text-}3 + 3 + {\text-}x = {\text-}3 + 20$
Simplify.	${\text-}x = 17$
To solve, you need to know x, not $-x$.	
Just take the opposite of both sides.	${\text-}({\text-}x) = {\text-}17$
Simplify.	$x = {\text-}17$

Check

Substitute in the original equation.
Does $3 - {\text-}17 = 20$? Yes.

Solution 2

Another way to solve $3 - x = 20$ is to add x to both sides.

Original equation	$3 - x = 20$
Convert to addition.	$3 + {\text-}x = 20$
Add x to both sides.	$3 + {\text-}x + x = 20 + x$
Simplify.	$3 = 20 + x$

This type of equation you have solved many times before.

Add ⁻20 to both sides.	${\text-}20 + 3 = {\text-}20 + 20 + x$
Simplify.	${\text-}17 = x$

Example 2

Solve the equation $606,900 - x = {\text-}31,532$ to determine the population of the District of Columbia in 1980.

Solution

We use the strategy of Solution 1 from Example 1.

Original equation	$606,900 - x = {\text-}31,532$
Convert to addition.	$606,900 + {\text-}x = {\text-}31,532$
Add ⁻606,900 to each side.	${\text-}606,900 + 606,900 + {\text-}x = {\text-}606,900 + {\text-}31,532$
Simplify.	${\text-}x = {\text-}638,432$
Take the opposite of each side.	${\text-}({\text-}x) = 638,432$
Simplify again.	$x = 638,432$

The population of the District of Columbia in 1980 was 638,432.

What Are Equivalent Equations?

The equations $x = 638,432$ and $606,900 - x = {\text-}31,532$ are **equivalent equations** because they have the same solutions. When you write down the steps to solve an equation, each step should be an equation equivalent to the equations in the previous steps.

Lesson 7-4 *Solving $a - x = b$* **363**

Video

Wide World of Mathematics The segment, *The Census,* presents various population trends and suggests how subtraction may be used to solve problems involving those trends. The segment provides a natural introduction to a lesson on solving equations of the form $a - x = b$. Related questions and an investigation are provided in videodisc stills and in the Video Guide. A related CD-ROM activity is also available.

Videodisc Bar Codes

Search Chapter 34

Play

---

4. At the end of 9 holes, Jose's golf score was 4 strokes over par. At the end of 18 holes, it was 3 strokes under par. What do you subtract from 4 strokes over par to get 3 strokes under par?
7 strokes

Notes on Reading

Two main ideas concerning equivalent equations are presented in this lesson. The first idea is the definition and its relationship to the steps in writing out the work in solving an equation. Each step should be equivalent to the previous step until the simplest equivalent form is reached (the simplest being $x =$ a number). The second idea is the corresponding definition of equivalent formulas.

❶ Make certain that students recognize the difference between the forms $x - a = b$ and $a - x = b$. Since $x + a = b$ and $a + x = b$ are the same, many students fail to appreciate the problem created because there is no commutative property for subtraction.

❷ Two algorithms for solving an equation of the form $a - x = b$ are given in **Example 1.** Students should understand that either is correct. For the reasons outlined in *Lesson 7-4 Overview*, we think the method given in Solution 2 is preferable. However, we present both methods so students and teachers can choose the method that seems to work best for

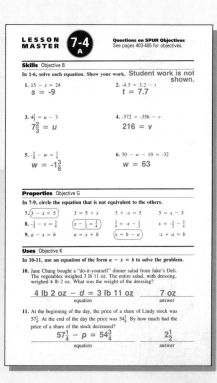

them. Note that in **Question 6** in *Covering the Reading,* students are advised to use the strategy that they like better.

To give students more practice writing and solving equations, see *Optional Activities* on page 363.

Additional Examples

1. Solve $5 - x = 10$.
   Solution 1:
$$5 - x = 10$$
$$5 + \text{-}x = 10$$
$$\text{-}5 + 5 + \text{-}x = \text{-}5 + 10$$
$$\text{-}x = 5$$
$$x = \text{-}5$$
   Solution 2:
$$5 - x = 10$$
$$5 + \text{-}x = 10$$
$$5 + \text{-}x + x = 10 + x$$
$$5 = 10 + x$$
$$\text{-}10 + 5 = \text{-}10 + 10 + x$$
$$\text{-}5 = x$$

2. In 1991, the population of Nicaragua was estimated at 3,751,000. An estimate made in 1984 was 837,000 lower. What was the 1984 estimate?
   2,914,000

3. *Multiple choice.* Which formula is not equivalent to the others? **b**
   a. $x + y = z$
   b. $x = y + z$
   c. $z - y = x$
   d. $z - x = y$

364

Example 3

Multiple choice. Which equation is not equivalent to the others?
(a) $x + 3 = 8$ (b) $2x = 10$ (c) $\text{-}1 = 4 - x$ (d) $x = 5$
(e) $x - 0.4 = 4.96$

Solution

Equations (a), (b), (c), and (d) all have the single solution 5. The solution to equation (e) is 5.36. **Equation (e) is not equivalent to the others.**

Of all equations with solution 5, the simplest is $x = 5$. The idea in solving equations is to find a sentence of the form $x = \underline{\quad}$ that is equivalent to the original equation.

What Are Equivalent Formulas?

Equivalent formulas are like equivalent equations. Here is an example. You have seen the formula $p = s - c$. (Profit on an item equals its selling price minus the cost of obtaining the item.) If the selling price is $49.95 and the cost is $30.27, then the profit is $49.95 - $30.27, or $19.68.

If you solve the formula for s, you will get $s = c + p$. (Selling price equals cost plus profit.) The same three numbers work in the formula $s = c + p$.

$$p = s - c \qquad\qquad s = c + p$$
$$19.68 = 49.95 - 30.27 \qquad 49.95 = 30.27 + 19.68$$

The formulas $p = s - c$ and $s = c + p$ are **equivalent formulas** because the same numbers work in both of them. When you take a formula and solve for a variable in it, you always get an equivalent formula.

QUESTIONS

Covering the Reading

1. Consider the equation $3 - x = 20$. To solve this equation, you can convert the subtraction to an addition. What sentence results?
   $3 + \text{-}x = 20$

2. If $\text{-}x = 30$, then $x = \underline{\;?\;}$. $\text{-}30$

3. If $\text{-}y = \text{-}\frac{1}{2}$, then $y = \underline{\;?\;}$. $\frac{1}{2}$

In 4-6, consider $\text{-}5 = 14 - t$.

4. To solve this equation using the algorithm of Example 1, Solution 1, what should be added to both sides? $\text{-}14$

5. To solve this equation using the algorithm of Example 1, Solution 2, what should be added to both sides? t

6. Solve the equation using the algorithm you like better. $t = 19$

364

Optional Activities

After discussing the examples, you can use this activity to give students more practice solving equations of the form $a - x = b$.

You might have students write equations of the form $a - x = b$ for the situations in *Warm-up* on page 362. Then ask students to make up situations with questions that can be answered by solving equations of the form $a - x = b$. Take some of the best

situations, and give them to all students in the class for practice.

7) x = 302;
300 − 302 = -2

8) y = 119;
61 = 180 − 119

9) z = 90;
-45 = 45 − 90

10) m = 4.3;
4.3 − 3.3 = 1

11) A = -53;
-53 − 57 = -110

12) $B = \frac{-82}{9}$;
$\frac{6}{9} - \frac{-82}{9} = \frac{88}{9}$

In 7–12, solve and check.

7. $300 - x = -2$ **8.** $61 = 180 - y$ **9.** $-45 = 45 - z$

10. $m - 3.3 = 1$ **11.** $A - 57 = -110$ **12.** $\frac{2}{3} - B = \frac{88}{9}$

13. Use the table in this lesson. Solve an equation of the form $a - x = b$ to find the 1980 population of West Virginia. Solve 1,793,477 − x = -156,709 to obtain x = 1,950,186.

14. When are two sentences equivalent? when they have exactly the same solutions

In 15–17, *multiple choice.* Find the sentence that is not equivalent to the others.

15. (a) $x = 5$ (b) $5 - x = 10$ (c) $x = -5$ (a)

16. (a) $y + 1 = 4$ (b) $4 + 1 = y$ (c) $1 + y = 4$ (b)

17. (a) $a + \frac{2}{3} = b$ (b) $a - b = \frac{2}{3}$ (c) $b - a = \frac{2}{3}$ (b)

18. *Multiple choice.* Which formula is not equivalent to the others?
(a) $s = p + c$ (b) $p = s - c$ (c) $p = c - s$ (c)

Applying the Mathematics

19. Solve for c: $p = s - c$. $c = s - p$

In 20–22, the question can lead to an equation of the form $a - x = b$.
a. Give that equation. **b.** Solve the equation. **c.** Answer the question.

20. There were 3500 tickets available for a concert. Only 212 are left. How many tickets have been sold? a) 3500 − s = 212; b) s = 3288; c) 3288 tickets have been sold.

21. The temperature was 14° just 6 hours ago. Now it is 3° below zero. How much has it decreased? a) 14 − d = -3; b) d = 17; c) The temperature has decreased by 17°.

22. The Himalayan mountain climbers pitched camp at 22,500 feet yesterday. Today they pitched camp at 20,250 feet. How far did they come down the mountain? a) 22,500 − d = 20,250; b) d = 2250; c) They came down 2250 feet.

In 23–26, solve. You will have to simplify first.

23. $40 - x + 20 = 180$
x = -120

24. $-6 = -1 - y - 5$
y = 0

25. $13 - 5 \cdot 2 = 9 - K - -7$
K = 13

26. $\frac{6}{5} = \frac{2}{3} - -A$ A = $\frac{8}{15}$

27. *Multiple choice.* Which sentence is equivalent to $A = \ell w$? (Hint: If you do not know the answer quickly, test a special case.)
(a) $A\ell = w$ (b) $Aw = \ell$
(c) $\frac{A}{\ell} = w$ (d) none of these (c)

28. *Multiple choice.* Which of (a) to (c) is not equal to $-b + a$?
(a) $a + -b$ (b) $a - b$
(c) $b + -a$ (d) All equal $-b + a$. (c)

Lesson 7-4 *Solving a − x = b* **365**

Adapting to Individual Needs

English Language Development
You might want to discuss the word *equivalent.* Explain that the statements "The sun is shining" and "It is sunny" are equivalent because they both have the same meaning. A quarter and a dime are equivalent to 7 nickels because both sets of coins have the same value. In mathematics, the equations $x + 6 = 9$, $x + 10 = 13$, and $x = 3$ are equivalent because they all have the same solutions.

Extra Help
If students have trouble recognizing the difference between $x - a = b$ and $a - x = b$, you might discuss the fact that subtraction is not commutative. Have students suggest two different numbers. Demonstrate that for these numbers, $a + b = b + a$, but $a - b \neq b - a$. Ask students if they can find any two different numbers for which $a + b \neq b + a$, or any two different numbers for which $a - b = b - a$.

365

Notes on Questions

Question 29 This question is reproduced on **Teaching Aid 70**. Do not expect high performance on this question. Its purpose is to show students that each step can be justified by a property. The process of justifying steps will help prepare them for future work in algebra and geometry.

Follow-up for Lesson **7-4**

Practice

For more questions on SPUR Objectives, use **Lesson Master 7-4A** (shown on page 363) or **Lesson Master 7-4B** (shown on pages 364–365).

Assessment

Quiz A quiz covering Lessons 7-1 through 7-4 is provided in the *Assessment Sourcebook.*

Oral Communication Have students **work in pairs.** Have each pair write an equation of the form $a - x = b$, solve it, and check the answer. Then have students take turns explaining in their own words how they solved their equation. [Explanations include the reasons for each of the steps and using the terms *negative, minus,* and *the opposite of* correctly.]

Extension

You might extend **Question 38** as follows. Ask students to consider the expression $a - b - c - d - e - f$, with $a = 6, b = 5, c = 4, d = 3, e = 2,$ and $f = 1.$ Have them find all the possible different values of the expression that can be obtained by putting in grouping symbols. [Possible values are the odd integers from –9 to 11.]

366

---

29. Give a reason for each step in this detailed solution of $a - x = b$ for $x.$

Step 1: $\quad a + {-x} = b$	**Algebraic Definition of Subtraction**
Step 2: $(a + {-x}) + x = b + x$	**Addition Property of Equality**
Step 3: $a + ({-x} + x) = b + x$	**Associative Property of Addition**
Step 4: $\quad a + 0 = b + x$	**Property of Opposites**
Step 5: $\quad a = b + x$	**Additive Identity Property of Zero**
Step 6: $-b + a = -b + (b + x)$	**Addition Property of Equality**
Step 7: $-b + a = (-b + b) + x$	**Associative Property of Addition**
Step 8: $-b + a = 0 + x$	**Property of Opposites**
Step 9: $-b + a = x$	**Additive Identity Property of Zero**

Review

30. Solve $x - 11 = -11.$ *(Lesson 7-3)* $x = 0$

31. Solve $8 = y - 40.$ *(Lesson 7-3)* $y = 48$

32. In Montreal, Quebec, the average high temperature in January is -6°C. The average low temperature is -15°C. What is the average difference in the temperatures on a January day in Montreal? *(Lesson 7-2)* 9°C

33. Booker T. Washington was born in 1856 and died in 1915. What was his age when he died? *(Lesson 7-1)* 58 or 59

34. An n-gon has exactly 77 diagonals. What is n? *(Lesson 6-5)* 14

35. Solve for d in terms of c: $c + d = 90.$ *(Lesson 5-8)* $d = 90 - c$

36. 4 kilograms + 25 grams + 43 milligrams equals how many grams? *(Lessons 3-4, 5-1)* 4025.043 g

37. a. Draw two perpendicular lines. See below left.
   b. What kind of angles are formed? *(Lesson 3-7)* right angles

Washington and his sons. *Booker T. Washington was a leader and an educator. In 1881, he founded Tuskegee Normal and Industrial Institute, now called Tuskegee University, and served as its principal until 1915.*

37a) Sample:

Exploration

38. Suppose $a = 5, b = 4, c = 3, d = 2,$ and $e = 1.$ Consider the expression $a - b - c - d - e,$ in which all the dashes are for subtraction. Now put grouping symbols wherever you want. For instance, you could consider $(a - b) - (c - d) - e;$ this gives the values $(5 - 4) - (3 - 2) - 1,$ which simplifies to -1. Or consider $a - [b - (c - d)] - e,$ which is $5 - [4 - (3 - 2)] - 1,$ which simplifies to 1. How many different values of the expression are possible? seven possible values: –5, –3, –1, 1, 3, 5, 7

366

Adapting to Individual Needs

Challenge

For each problem, have students explain the minimum number of times that the coins must be weighed on a balance to determine which coin is lighter.

1. Three silver coins look identical except that one weighs less than the other two. [One time. Weigh 2 coins against each other; if equal, the third coin is lighter; if unequal, choose the lighter of the two coins on the scale.]

2. Of 9 identical-looking gold coins, 8 have the same weight, and one weighs less. [Two times. Weigh 3 coins against 3 coins to find the lighter group—it will be one of the groups of 3 on the scale or the group of 3 that is not on the scale. Then proceed as suggested for the 3 silver coins.]

LESSON

7-5

*Counting
and
Probability
with
Overlap*

Getting a kick out of soccer. *Although soccer has been popular around the world for decades, it did not gain popularity in the U.S. until the 1970s. Now it is one of the fastest growing team sports in the country.*

Last fall at Central Middle School, 43 boys and 54 girls played on a soccer team. Since there is no overlap between boys and girls, it is easy to find how many students played soccer. Use the Putting-Together Model for Addition to get 43 + 54 = 97.

You can draw a picture, called a **Venn diagram,** to illustrate this situation. Separate circles represent quantities with no overlap.

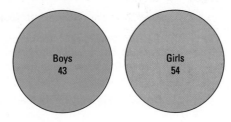

Counting When There Is Overlap

Situations with overlap are more complicated.

Example 1

37 girls from Central Middle School played basketball in the winter. If 9 girls played both soccer and basketball, how many were on at least one of these teams?

Solution

The 54 girls who played soccer overlap with the 37 who played basketball. On the next page, a Venn diagram with intersecting circles for the overlap is drawn to help answer the question.

▶

Lesson 7-5

Objectives

N Use the Putting-Together with Overlap Model to solve sentences involving subtraction.
P Use Venn diagrams to describe or determine overlap.

Resources

From the **Teacher's Resource File**
■ Lesson Master 7-5A or 7-5B
■ Answer Master 7-5
■ Teaching Aids
   56 Two-Dice Outcomes
   68 Warm-up
   71 Venn Diagrams

Additional Resources
■ Visuals for Teaching Aids 56, 68, 71

Teaching 7-5
Lesson

Warm-up

Telly was playing a game that used a die. The die had the numbers 0, 1, 1, 2, 3, and 3 on its faces. Find the probability that Telly will toss each of the following.

1. 2 $\frac{1}{6}$ **2.** 3 $\frac{1}{3}$
3. 0 or 1 $\frac{1}{2}$ **4.** 0 or 2 $\frac{1}{3}$
5. 1 or 3 $\frac{2}{3}$

Notes on Reading

Most people find Venn diagrams very useful in sorting out given information of the type found in this lesson. However, as easy as the ideas are in this lesson, they are tricky. You might wish to read this lesson with your students.

Lesson 7-5 Overview

Broad Goals This lesson generalizes the Putting-Together Model of Addition from Lesson 5-1 and the Probability of Mutually Exclusive Events from Lesson 5-6 to situations where there is overlap. When there is overlap, subtraction of the overlap is involved.

Perspective Suppose there are two sets, A and B. Then there are four distinct

possibilities for an element.
(1) It can be in A but not in B.
(2) It can be in B but not in A.
(3) It can be in both A and B. This is the overlap.
(4) It can be in neither A nor B.

In a Venn diagram that shows A and B intersecting, the number of elements in A is the sum of the number of elements in possibilities (1) and (3). The number of elements in

B is the sum of the number of elements in possibilities (2) and (3). So if we want to find the number of elements in A or B, and we add the number of elements in A to the number of elements in B, possibility (3) has been added twice. Therefore, this number—the overlap—has to be subtracted.

The Putting-Together with Overlap Model holds whether the situation involves combining counts, measures, percents, or probabilities.

Some students might ask why the word Venn is capitalized. Explain that these diagrams are named after John Venn, a 19th-century English logician, who perfected them.

Teaching Aid 71 contains Venn diagrams which you can use when discussing both the reading and the questions.

Sports Connection Dr. James Naismith, the inventor of basketball, originally intended to put up two boxes on either side of the gymnasium. Because he was unable to get two large cartons, he substituted peach baskets instead. These baskets eventually gave the sport its name. Naismith invented basketball in 1892 to serve as an indoor sport that would keep athletes in shape between the fall football season and spring training for baseball and lacrosse.

The origin of the game of soccer can be traced to China (400 B.C.). The Romans played a form of soccer, but the players could not kick the ball. During the 1800s, many schools in England played a game resembling soccer, but each school interpreted the rules of the game differently. In 1848, in Cambridge, England, the first set of rules was drawn up. From that time on soccer began its spread throughout the world. Today soccer is the world's most popular team sport.

❶ As you discuss the Putting-Together with Overlap Model, make sure students understand that z elements are subtracted because z elements have been counted twice. In **Example 1,** z represents the 9 girls that play both soccer and basketball.

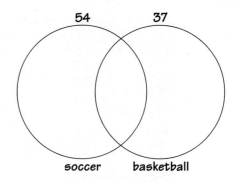

Nine girls belong in the overlap of the circles. Since 54 girls played soccer, $54 - 9 = 45$ girls played only soccer. Likewise, $37 - 9 = 28$ girls played only basketball. So 45 and 28 are in the remaining parts of the circles.

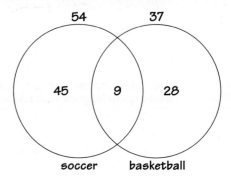

Now there are two ways to answer the question.

1. Add the three numbers: $45 + 9 + 28 = 82$.
2. Add the soccer and basketball totals and subtract the overlap because it has been counted twice: $54 + 37 - 9 = 82$.

So 82 girls played at least one of these sports.

The solution to Example 1 illustrates the combination of putting-together with take-away. The following general principle holds for any counts or other measure.

❶　**Putting-Together with Overlap Model**
If a quantity x is put together with a quantity y, and there is overlap z, the result is the quantity $x + y - z$.

When you know the value of $x + y - z$ and two of the variables in it, you can find the value of the third variable by solving an equation.

② Example 2

The Central Middle School spring concert included both the orchestra and the band. The orchestra has 85 musicians and the band has 75. If 128 students played in the concert, how many played in both the band and the orchestra?

Solution

Think: $x = 85$, $y = 75$, and $x + y - z = 128$, where z is the overlap.

Start with the equation.	$x + y - z = 128$
Substitute.	$85 + 75 - z = 128$
Simplify.	$160 + -z = 128$
Add -160 to both sides.	$160 + -160 + -z = 128 + -160$
Simplify.	$-z = -32$
Take the opposite of both sides.	$z = 32$

32 students played in both the orchestra and the band.

Probability when There Is Overlap

When two events overlap, the probability that one of them occurs can be calculated using this model.

③ Example 3

Use the information given on the preceding page. If there are 175 girls in Central Middle School, what is the probability that a randomly selected girl in the school played soccer or basketball?

Solution 1

From the given information, the probability a girl played soccer is $\frac{54}{175}$; basketball is $\frac{37}{175}$; the probability a girl played both is $\frac{9}{175}$. So the probability a girl played one of the sports can be found using the Putting-Together with Overlap model. It is

$$\frac{54}{175} + \frac{37}{175} - \frac{9}{175} = \frac{82}{175}.$$

The probability a girl played at least one of the sports is $\frac{82}{175}$.

Solution 2

Use the solution to Example 1. 82 girls played at least one of the sports. There are 175 girls in all.

The probability that a girl played soccer or basketball is $\frac{82}{175}$.

All that jazz. Jazz is a style of improvisational music influenced by early African-American spirituals and folk music, and by ragtime music. New Orleans was the home of the first jazz musicians in the early 1900s.

② You might also want to have students make a Venn diagram for this example.

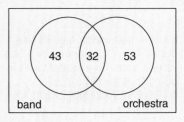

③ Students can use the Venn diagram from **Example 1**, but now they should place the additional number, 93, outside the circles to represent all the girls that are in neither soccer nor basketball. The 93 is found by subtracting 45, 9, and 28 from 175.

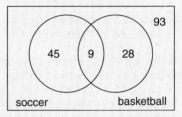

You might ask students to find the probability that a girl played neither soccer nor basketball. $[\frac{93}{175}]$ Note that this is 1 minus the probability that she played at least one sport.

Adapting to Individual Needs

Extra Help Use a Physical Model
To help students understand the Putting-Together with Overlap Model, have students count off beginning with 1. Direct only those students with even numbers to stand and ask how many there are. Then direct only the odd-numbered students to stand, and ask how many there are. Note that no even-numbered student is standing when only the odd-numbered students are standing

and vice versa. Draw a Venn diagram to illustrate this situation. Next illustrate an overlap. Have only the even-numbered students stand, then direct students whose numbers are multiples of 3 to stand. Ask students who are members of both groups to go to the front of the room. Explain that these students represent numbers that are both even and multiples of 3, so they are in the overlap. Draw a Venn diagram illustrating this situation.

369

4 The 36 equally likely outcomes from tossing a pair of dice are reproduced on **Teaching Aid 56.**

Additional Examples

1. Mr. X's math class has 25 students. Ms. Y's science class has 28 students. Five students have both Mr. X and Ms. Y.
   a. Draw a Venn diagram for this situation.

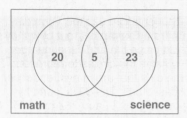

   math   science

   b. How many students are in at least one of these classes?
   48 students

2. In the year 2001, there will be 52 Fridays, and two of them will fall on the 13th of the month. What is the probability that a random day of that year is either a Friday or is the 13th day of a month?
   $\frac{62}{365}$; there are 52 Fridays and 12 days (one for each month) that fall on the 13th, but 2 of these are also Fridays.
   $52 + 12 - 2 = 62$

3. Suppose the students in Mr. X's and Ms. Y's classes (Question 1) are part of the 75 students in a study hall. What is the probability that a randomly selected student from study hall is in Mr. X's class or Ms. Y's class? $\frac{48}{75}$

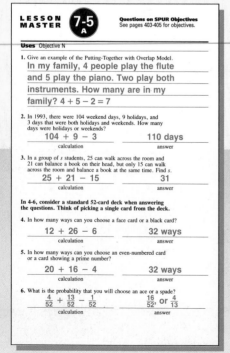

Example 4

If you toss a pair of fair dice once, what is the probability that they will show doubles or a sum greater than seven?

Solution

Examine this diagram; it shows the 36 equally likely outcomes from tossing a pair of dice.

4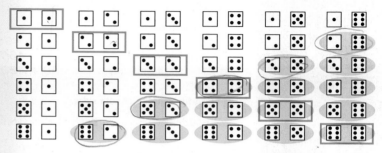

Six outcomes, outlined with rectangles, are doubles.

So the probability of doubles is $\frac{6}{36}$.

Fifteen outcomes, outlined with ellipses, have a sum greater than 7. So the probability that the sum is greater than 7 is $\frac{15}{36}$.

Three outcomes, 4 and 4, 5 and 5, and 6 and 6, have doubles and a sum greater than 7. So the probability of doubles and a sum greater than 7 is $\frac{3}{36}$. This is the probability of the overlap.

So, the probability of doubles or a sum greater than 7 is

$$\frac{6}{36} + \frac{15}{36} - \frac{3}{36} = \frac{18}{36} = \frac{1}{2}.$$

Check

Count the outcomes that are outlined with rectangles or ellipses. There are 18 of them, out of the 36.

QUESTIONS

Covering the Reading

1. Give an example of a situation with overlap. **Sample: 54 girls played soccer, 37 girls played basketball, 9 girls played both.**

In 2 and 3, draw a Venn diagram to illustrate the situation.

2. During 5th period at South Junior High, 23 seventh graders take English, 20 seventh graders take math, and 24 seventh graders are in science.

2)
English 23   Math 20
Science 24

3. Samantha is in 5th-period English with 22 other ninth graders. Her 6th-period math class has 25 students with six students, including Samantha, in both these classes.

3)
17 6 19
English Math

Adapting to Individual Needs

English Language Development
Some students may know the words *over* and *lap,* but will need help understanding *overlap.* Pose this situation and show the overlap: Bill works from 3 until 5, and Sarah works from 4 until 6. They work together (their times overlap) from 4 to 5.

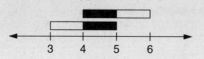

Show the odd numbers from 1 to 20, then show the multiples of 3 from 1 to 20, and then identify the overlap as the multiples of 3 that are also odd numbers.

Odd numbers: 1 3 5 7 **9** 11 13 **15** 17 19
Multiples of 3:   3 6 **9** 12 **15** 18
Overlap: **3 9 15**

The overlap is the intersection of the set of multiples of 3 with the set of odd numbers.

4. In the expression $x + y - z$ for putting-together with overlap, which variable stands for the number in the overlap? **z**

In 5 and 6, refer to the information at the beginning of the lesson.

5. If 65 boys at Central Middle School play basketball and 20 play both soccer and basketball, draw a Venn diagram to represent the soccer and basketball players.

6. If there are 200 boys at Central Middle School, what is the probability a randomly selected boy plays soccer or basketball? $\frac{88}{200}$ or $\frac{11}{25}$

7. Draw a Venn diagram to check the answer to Example 2.

In 8 and 9, consider the situation of Example 4.

8. List the outcomes that overlap. double 4s, double 5s, double 6s

9. Find the probability that a pair of dice will show an even sum or a sum greater than eight. $\frac{24}{36}$ or $\frac{2}{3}$

5)
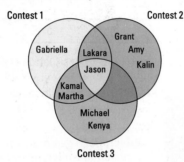
23 | 20 | 45
soccer   basketball

7)
53 | 32 | 43
orchestra   band

Applying the Mathematics

10) The putting-together model is a special case of putting together with overlap when the overlap is 0.

10. Explain how the putting-together model can be considered to be a special case of putting-together with overlap.

11. The Venn diagram below shows the top five scorers at a school for the first 3 math contests of the year.

Contest 1   Contest 2

Grant
Gabriella   Lakara   Amy
Jason   Kalin
Kamal
Martha
Michael
Kenya

Contest 3

a) Gabriella, Lakara, Jason, Kamal, Martha

b) Lakara, Kamal, Martha, Jason

a. List the top 5 scoring students in contest 1.
b. Who finished in the top 5 in at least two contests?
c. Who finished in the top 5 in all three contests? Jason
d. Which two contests had the least overlap? Contest 2 and Contest 3

12. Suppose a school has 600 students. Math teachers gave A's to 20% of the students. English teachers gave A's to 15% of the students. 8% received A's in both math and English.
a. What percent received an A in at least one of the two subjects? 27%
b. How many students received an A in at least one of the two subjects? 162

Lesson 7-5   *Counting and Probability with Overlap*   **371**

Note that students used the idea of overlap when finding common denominators to add fractions. For instance, to add $\frac{4}{15} + \frac{5}{12}$, one considers the sets of multiples of 15 and 12:
   15, 30, 45, 60, 75, . . .
   12, 24, 36, 48, 60, . . .
Any element in the overlap (intersection) can be a common denominator.

4 If you toss a pair of fair dice, what is the probability that you will toss a 4 on the first or second die? $\frac{11}{36}$

Notes on Questions
Question 5 Error Alert If students do not read carefully, they may think that there is not enough information given to determine the number of soccer players. Point out that the directions tell them to refer to the information at the beginning of the lesson. The opening sentence says that 43 boys at Central Middle School play soccer.

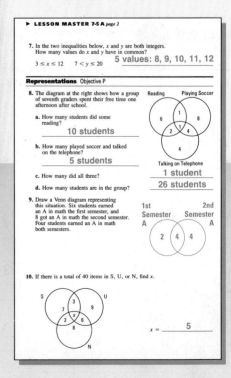

Question 14 This is an example of a Venn diagram with three circles. You may want to put the diagram on the board, and have students determine the number of items in each of these groups.

R   [5 + 6 + 4 + 3 = 18]
S   [2 + 5 + 4 + Y = 11 + Y]
T   [7 + 3 + 4 + Y = 14 + Y]
both R and S   [5 + 4 = 9]
both R and T   [4 + 3 = 7]
both S and T   [4 + Y]
common to R, S, and T   [4]

Question 15c The overlap consists of the numbers that are divisible by both 2 and 3 which are the numbers divisible by 6.

Question 19 The years given for these monarchs are the years of their reigns, not their life spans.

Question 26 A multiple of 36 is used to ensure easier comparison of probabilities.

Follow-up 7-5
for Lesson

Practice

For more questions on SPUR Objectives, use **Lesson Master 7-5A** (shown on pages 370–371) or **Lesson Master 7-5B** (shown on pages 372–373).

LESSON MASTER 7-5 B   Questions on SPUR Objectives

Uses Objective N: Use the Putting-Together with Overlap Model to solve sentences involving subtraction.

1. Write a problem about students with brown hair and students with green eyes so that the situation involves overlap.   **sample: 20 girls have brown hair, 3 have green eyes, and 2 have both. How many students have at least one of these features?**

2. There are 56 students in Concert Choir, 27 in the Girls' Glee Club, and 16 in both. How many students are in at least one singing group?
   56 + 27 − 16   *calculation*   67 students   *answer*

3. There are two shifts at the Right-Tread Tire factory. 114 people work the first shift and 88 work the second shift. If there are 190 factory workers, how many work both shifts?
   190 = 114 + 88 − b   *calculation*   12 workers   *answer*

In 4-7, consider a standard 52-card deck of cards when answering the questions. Think of picking a single card from the deck.

4. In how many ways can you choose a red card or an even-numbered card?
   26 + 20 − 10   *calculation*   36 ways   *answer*

5. In how many ways can you choose a face card or a spade?
   12 + 13 − 3   *calculation*   22 ways   *answer*

6. In how many ways can you choose a numbered card greater than 5 or a card showing a multiple of 4?
   20 + 8 − 4   *calculation*   24 ways   *answer*

7. What is the probability that you will choose a nine or a heart?
   $\frac{4}{52} + \frac{13}{52} - \frac{1}{52}$ *calculation* $\frac{16}{52}$, or $\frac{4}{13}$ *answer*

372

---

13. In the Venn diagram below, if the total number of items in A and B is 37, how many items are in B? **22**

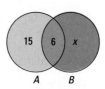

15 6 x

A   B

14. In the Venn diagram below, if a total of 35 items are in R, S, and T, how many are in both S and T? **12**

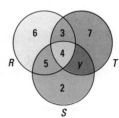

6 3 7
4
R 5 y T
2
S

15. A whole number x such that $1 \le x \le 100$ is chosen at random. Give the probability of each event.
   a. x is divisible by 2. $\frac{1}{2}$ **or 50%**
   b. x is divisible by 3. $\frac{33}{100}$ **or 33%**
   c. x is divisible by 2 or 3. **67%**

The Carson House, built in Eureka, CA, between 1884 and 1886 is an example of Victorian architecture. It was so named because the style was popular during Queen Victoria's reign.

Review

In 16 and 17, a situation is given. **a.** Write an equation involving subtraction to answer the question. **b.** Solve the equation. *(Lessons 7-3, 7-4)*

16. The hot air balloon fell 125 feet from its highest point. The new altitude was 630 ft. How high had it flown? **a) x − 125 = 630; b) 755 ft**

17. In the 1992 Summer Olympics all-around gymnastics competition, a Ukrainian gymnast, Tatiana Gutsu, defeated an American gymnast, Shannon Miller, by twelve hundredths of a point. If Miller's total score was 39.725, what was Gutsu's score? **a) x − 39.725 = 0.12; b) 39.845**

18. Write a simpler equation equivalent to 40 = A + 12. *(Lesson 7-4)* **Sample: A = 28**

19. a. Which of these famous English monarchs had the longest reign?
   King Henry II, who reigned from 1154 to 1189
   King Henry VIII, 1509–1547
   Queen Elizabeth I, 1558–1603
   Queen Victoria, 1837–1901 **Queen Victoria, 64 years**
   b. Queen Elizabeth II ascended to the throne in 1952. In what year could she become the longest reigning English monarch? *(Lessons 7-1, 7-3)* **2016**

Queen Victoria

Adapting to Individual Needs

Challenge
You might wish to describe the ideas of this lesson using the language of set union and intersection. The overlap of two sets A and B is their *intersection* A ∩ B, read "A and B." The number of elements in one or the other of two sets is their *union* A ∪ B, read "A or B." If N(S) stands for the number of elements in a set S, the Putting-Together with Overlap can be described as: N(A ∪ B) = N(A) + N(B) − N(A ∩ B).

The corresponding idea with probabilities is as follows: Let A and B be events from the same set of outcomes (called the *sample space*). Then A ∩ B is the event that both A and B occur. A ∪ B is the event that one of A or B occurs. In general, P(A ∪ B) = P(A) + P(B) − P(A ∩ B). With this symbolism, ask students to describe the Venn diagrams for union (shade both circles) and intersection (shade the common interior) of two sets that overlap.

20. Evaluate $3.\overline{3} + 6\frac{2}{3} - \frac{1}{2} - \frac{5}{6}$. *(Lessons 1-7, 5-5, 7-2)* $\frac{31}{3}$ or $10.\overline{3}$

21. *Multiple choice.* Which of these numbers could be the sum of two consecutive integers? *(Lessons 6-5, 6-7)*
(a) 1992   (b) 1993   (c) 1994   (d) 2000   (b)

22. Use the figure below. If $m\angle BIT = 2°$ and $m\angle GIT = 3°$, what is $m\angle BIG$? *(Lesson 5-4)* **5°**

In 23–24, use the graph below. *(Lessons 2-5, 2-7, 3-6)*

Too Bad for Dad
How men and women think being a father today compares with 20 years ago:

(Numbers add up to 101% due to rounding)

More difficult **81%**

About the same **12%**

Don't know **2%**   Easier **6%**

Source: Brushkin/Goldring Research poll of 1,000 adults for MassMutual Life Insurance Co.

23. Estimate the number of adults who said being a dad today is more difficult. **≈810**

24. a. Without a protractor, estimate the number of degrees in the central angle for "About the same." **Answers will vary.**
    b. Use a protractor to measure the angle in part **a.** You will have to extend the sides of the angle. **≈29°**
    c. What should the number of degrees in the central angle be?
    d. Is the graph accurate? Justify your answer. **c) 43.2°; d) No, viewing the circle at an angle distorts the angle measures.**

25. Which holds more, a half-gallon watering can or a 2-liter watering can? *(Lesson 3-5)* **2-liter watering can**

26) Answers will vary. Samples are given.
a) $\approx \frac{6}{36}$ or $\approx 17\%$
b) $\approx \frac{15}{36}$ or $\approx 42\%$
c) $\approx \left(\frac{6}{36} + \frac{15}{36} - \frac{3}{36} = \frac{18}{36}\right)$ or $\approx 50\%$
d) Answers will vary. Relative frequencies should get closer to the probabilities of the outcomes as the multiple of 36 tosses of the dice increases.

Exploration

26. Toss a pair of dice some multiple of 36 times and record the outcomes.
    a. What is your relative frequency of a double?
    b. What is your relative frequency of a sum greater than 7?
    c. What is your relative frequency of a double or a sum greater than 7?
    d. How do your answers for parts **a, b,** and **c** compare to the probability of each outcome?

Lesson 7-5 *Counting and Probability with Overlap* **373**

Setting up Lesson 7-6
Materials Students will need protractors or **Geometry Templates** for both the In-class Activity and Lesson 7-6. Students using the *Extension* on page 380 will need city maps.

There are many questions in Lesson 7-6. If you are concerned that the assignment will be too long if all questions are assigned, plan to use Questions 8–12, 18–22, 24, and 26 for class discussion, and assign the remainder of the questions for homework.

Assessment
Written/Oral Communication Ask students to draw a Venn diagram showing activities that they are involved in with friends, neighbors, or family members. Then have them explain their diagrams. [Venn diagrams show intersecting (or disjoint) sets depicting two (or more) activities. Explanations show an understanding of overlap.]

Extension
Ask students to draw Venn diagrams to represent the relationships among these collections of three sets.
Sample diagrams are given.
1. animals, vegetables, minerals
2. lions, cats, animals
3. pianists, musicians, violinists
4. insects, mosquitoes, beetles

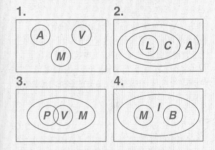

Project Update Project 2, *Probabilities With Playing Cards*, on page 399, relates to the content of this lesson.

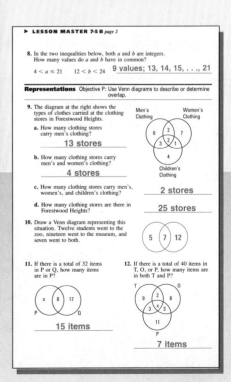

373

Additional Resources
■ Protractors or Geometry Templates

For this activity, students will need protractors or **Geometry Templates**. Be sure all students know how to use a protractor.

As students work, circulate among them to help with any difficulties they might have. In **Step 1** students should find that angles 1 and 2 have measures of 45° and 135°, respectively. If their results are not close to these, help them line up the protractors and read them correctly. Students should understand that the sum of the two measures must be 180° since the two angles form a straight line.

In **Step 3** students should find the measure of angle 3 to be 45°, and the measure of angle 4 to be 135°. Thus, in **Step 4,** they will find that the sum of the measures for each pair is 180°.

Students should record the results of this activity for use with **Question 8** on page 377.

Introducing Lesson 7-6

Angles and Lines

IN-CLASS
ACTIVITY

In the figure below, $\overrightarrow{BA}$ and $\overrightarrow{BC}$ are called **opposite rays** because they have the same endpoint and together they form a line. Angles *DBC* and *DBA* are adjacent angles. Angle *ABC* is called a **straight angle.**

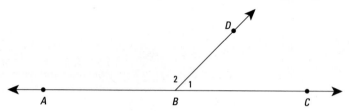

We name the angles 1 and 2 to make reading easier. These angles are called a **linear pair** because they have a common side, $\overrightarrow{BD}$, and their noncommon sides, $\overrightarrow{BA}$ and $\overrightarrow{BC}$, are opposite rays.

1 Measure angles 1 and 2 above and record your results.
  m∠1 = _?_ 45°   m∠2 = _?_ 135°

2 If the ray $\overrightarrow{BE}$ opposite to $\overrightarrow{BD}$ is drawn, angles 3 and 4 are formed. Label ∠*ABE* angle 3 and ∠*CBE* angle 4. Measure angles 3 and 4 and record your results. m∠3 = 45°; m∠4 = 135°

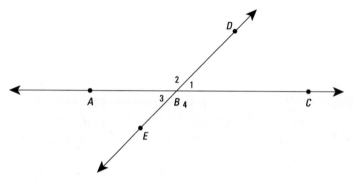

3 Angles 1 and 4 form a linear pair. What is the sum of your measurements of these angles? Angles 2 and 3 form a linear pair. What is the sum of their measures? 180°; 180°

4 *Draw a conclusion.* What is the sum of the measures of the angles in a linear pair? 180°

Optional Activities

Have students **work in groups** and identify things in the real world that form linear pairs. Then have them discuss their examples with the class. Some examples might be a wall and an open door, a building and a flagpole attached to the building, certain positions of two hands of a clock and either a second hand or alarm indicator, and street intersections.

Florida bridge. *Note the variety of angles in the Sunshine State Skyway Bridge, located in Tampa Bay, Florida. This cable-stayed bridge, completed in 1987, spans 1200 feet.*

What Are Vertical Angles?

Angles 1 and 3 on the preceding page are called *vertical angles*. Two angles are **vertical angles** when their sides are opposite rays. Vertical angles always have the same measure, so you should have found that $m\angle 1 = m\angle 3$. Angles 2 and 4 are vertical angles, so you should have found that $m\angle 2 = m\angle 4$.

In general, when two lines intersect, four angles are formed. Two of these have one measure, call it x. The other two each have measure y. The sum of x and y is 180°. That is, $x + y = 180$.

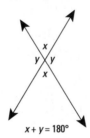

$x + y = 180°$

All of this is related to subtraction. We solve the equation $x + y = 180$ for y.

Original equation	$x + y = 180$
Addition Property of Equality	$-x + x + y = 180 + -x$
Property of Opposites	$0 + y = 180 + -x$
Additive Identity Property of Zero	$y = 180 + -x$
Add-Opp Property of Subtraction	$y = 180 - x$

Lesson 7-6 *Angles and Lines* **375**

Lesson **7-6**

Objectives
C Find measures of angles in figures with linear pairs, vertical angles, or perpendicular lines.
H Know relationships among angles formed by intersecting lines.

Resources
From the *Teacher's Resource File*
- Lesson Master 7-6A or 7-6B
- Answer Master 7-6
- Teaching Aids
  68 Warm-up
  72 Map of Drexel and Ellis Avenues
  73 Challenge
- Technology Sourcebook
  Computer Demonstration 7
  Computer Master 11

Additional Resources
- Visuals for Teaching Aids 68, 72, 73
- Protractors or Geometry Templates
- City maps (Extension)
- Geometry Workshop

Teaching 7-6
Lesson

Warm-up

Diagnostic Draw two intersecting lines that are not perpendicular. Use a protractor to measure the four angles formed.
1. Do any angles have the same measure? **There should be two pairs of angles with equal measures.**

Warm-up continues on page 376.

Lesson 7-6 Overview

Broad Goals The vocabulary of the angles formed by two intersecting lines is introduced and discussed in this lesson.

Perspective Vocabulary is best learned in context, that is, learned through situations in which knowledge of the terms is needed to define and clarify a concept. There is a great deal of vocabulary both in this lesson and in the In-class Activity—opposite rays, linear pair, vertical angles, supplementary

angles, and perpendicular —but all terms are discussed within a frame of reference to give the terms meaning and promote retention.

This lesson applies the ideas of previous lessons. If x is the measure of an angle, then $180 - x$ is its supplement. You might think of "cutting off" (taking away) an angle x from a straight angle of measure 180. The

following two lessons apply the ideas in this lesson to parallel lines and special quadrilaterals.

Do the measures of any two angles have a sum of 180°? There should be four pairs of supplementary angles corresponding to the four linear pairs.

Notes on Reading

Reading Mathematics As students read, they must learn the new terms relating to rays and intersecting lines, and the angles formed by them. Ask students to explain each boldfaced term in their own words, using diagrams if they need to.

❶ You may wish to introduce the term *straight angle* to refer to an angle whose sides are opposite rays. Thus a straight angle is an angle with a measure of 180°. An advantage of having this term is that one can then think of the Angle Addition Property as applying to the two angles in a linear pair. For example, ∠ABC on page 374 is a straight angle; m∠ABD + m∠DBC = m∠ABC.

❷ Call on volunteers to explain how to find the missing measure of one angle in a pair of supplementary angles if the other measure is known, and how to find the three missing measures for angles formed by intersecting lines when the fourth measure is given. Ask different students to illustrate these skills on the board during the discussion.

Emphasize that angles can be supplementary and not form a linear pair. *Extra Help* on page 377 deals with this idea.

❸ One of the nicest applications of angle measure is illustrated here. Students should see that the closer intersecting streets are to being perpendicular, the easier it is for drivers to see the oncoming traffic in both directions.

So if you know *x*, the measure of one angle formed when two lines intersect, the measures of the other three angles are either *x* or 180° − *x*. For instance, if *x* = 110°, then *y* = 180° − *x* = 70°. In the drawing below, one angle measures 110°. The other measures 70°.

❶

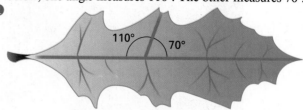

❷ What Are Supplementary Angles?

Two lines intersecting is a common situation. So angles whose measures add to 180° appear often. Such angles are called **supplementary angles.** Supplementary angles do not have to form a linear pair. For instance, any two angles with measures 53° and 127° are supplementary no matter where the angles are located because 53 + 127 = 180.

When two lines intersect to form right angles as in the diagram on the left, all four angles have measure 90°. So any two of the angles are supplementary. Recall that the lines are called perpendicular.

A Situation Leading to Perpendicular Segments

Right angles often occur where streets cross. Here is a sketch of part of a map of Chicago. Drexel and Ellis Avenues go north and south from 71st to 72nd streets. Then they bend so that they intersect South Chicago Avenue at right angles.

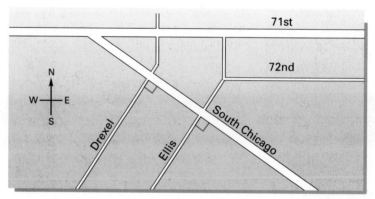

❸ Suppose Drexel did not bend. Then the situation would be as pictured at the top of the next page. A driver going south on Drexel could easily see a car traveling northwest (from *A* to *B*) on South Chicago. But the driver could not easily see a car going southeast (from *B* to *A*) on South Chicago. Because the streets are perpendicular, a driver can see both directions equally well and the intersection is safer.

376

Optional Activities

Activity 1
Materials: Rulers and protractors or **Geometry Templates**

After students have completed the reading, have them attempt to draw pairs of intersecting lines that satisfy each of the following conditions. [2 is impossible; sample responses for 1, 3, and 4 are shown.]
1. Angles of 100°, 80°, 100°, and 80° are formed.

2. Angles of 60°, 40°, 60°, and 40° are formed.
3. Four angles of 90° are formed.
4. Two angles of 32° and two angles of some other measure are formed.

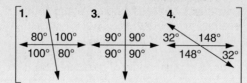

Activity 2 Technology Connection You may wish to use *Technology Sourcebook, Computer Demonstration 7,* to show students how to create and label intersecting lines using the *Geometry Workshop.* Then, you could assign *Technology Sourcebook, Computer Master 11.* Students create and measure angles formed by intersecting lines.

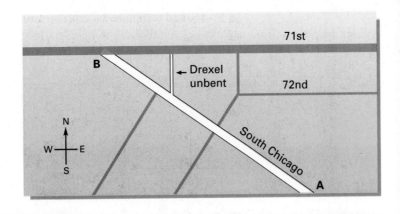

71st

B

← Drexel unbent

72nd

South Chicago

A

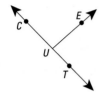

N
W—E
S

QUESTIONS

Covering the Reading

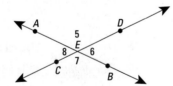

In 1–7, refer to the drawing at the left. *C*, *U*, and *T* are points on the same line.

1. Angle *CUT* is sometimes called a __?__ angle. straight

2. $\overrightarrow{UC}$ and $\overrightarrow{UT}$ are __?__ rays. opposite

3. ∠*CUE* and ∠*EUT* form a __?__. linear pair

4. m∠*CUE* + m∠*EUT* = __?__ degrees. 180

5. If m∠*CUE* = 88°, then m∠*EUT* = __?__. 92°

6. If m∠*CUE* = 90°, then $\overleftrightarrow{CT}$ and $\overleftrightarrow{UE}$ are __?__. perpendicular

7. Angles *CUE* and *EUT* are __?__ angles. supplementary

8. In the In-class Activity on page 374, what did you find for the measures of angles 1, 2, 3, and 4? m∠1 = 45°, m∠2 = 135°, m∠3 = 45°, m∠4 = 135°

In 9–13, $\overleftrightarrow{AB}$ and $\overleftrightarrow{CD}$ intersect at *E*.

A
5
D
E
8
6
7
C
B

9. Name all pairs of vertical angles. Angles 5 and 7, 6 and 8

10. Name all linear pairs. Angles 5 and 6, 7 and 8, 5 and 8, 6 and 7

11. Name all pairs of supplementary angles. Angles 5 and 6, 7 and 8, 5 and 8, 6 and 7

12. If m∠5 = 125°, what are the measures of the other angles? m∠7 = 125°, m∠6 = 55°, m∠8 = 55°

13. Measure angles 5, 6, 7, and 8 (to the nearest degree) with a protractor. m∠5 = m∠7 = 130°, m∠6 = m∠8 = 50°

Lesson 7-6 *Angles and Lines* **377**

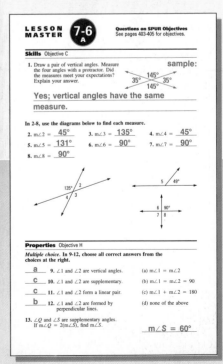

Adapting to Individual Needs

Extra Help
If students have trouble understanding that all linear pairs of angles are supplementary, but pairs of supplementary angles are not necessarily linear pairs, you might use this activity. Draw the following angles on the board.

Ask students which angles are linear pairs? [none] supplementary angles? [2 and 5; 3 and 4] Then ask students to draw (1) a linear pair of angles, and (2) supplementary angles that do not form a linear pair, and (3) explain their answers. [Answers will vary.]

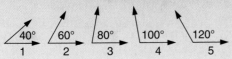

40° 60° 80° 100° 120°
1   2   3   4   5

Questions 18–22 Students can use **Teaching Aid 72** with these questions. Since students' experience with map reading varies greatly, some of them may find these questions difficult.

✎ **Writing Questions 26–27** You might have students share their written explanations with the class.

Questions 29–30 These questions require translating from words to mathematical symbols by interpreting the meaning of *vertical angles* and *supplementary angles*.

In 14–16, find the unknown angle measures without using a protractor.

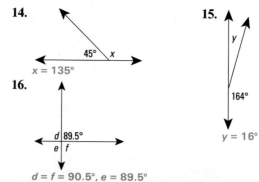

14.
$x = 135°$

15.

16.
$d = f = 90.5°$, $e = 89.5°$

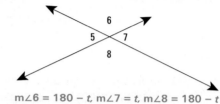
$y = 16°$

17. Two lines intersect below. If $m\angle 5 = t$, find the measures of the other three angles.

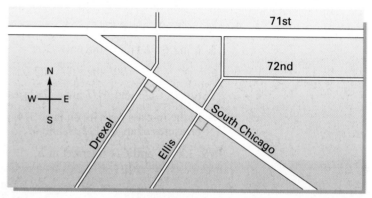

$m\angle 6 = 180 - t$, $m\angle 7 = t$, $m\angle 8 = 180 - t$

In 18–22, use the map below. Assume all the streets are two-way.

18. *True or false.* Drexel and South Chicago intersect at right angles.
True

19. *True or false.* Ellis and 71st intersect at right angles. True

20. How many street intersections are pictured on the map? 6

21. At which intersection is the best visibility of oncoming traffic?
Ellis and 72nd

22. At which intersection is the worst visibility of oncoming traffic?
71st and South Chicago

Adapting to Individual Needs

English Language Development
Because geometry involves so many familiar terms (such as *vertical* and *opposite*) defined in unfamiliar ways, some students may need special attention. You might have them draw or model their concepts of the terms and ideas presented in order to check their understanding.

You might have students write the new terms in this lesson on index cards, along with a drawing or a few words that remind them of the meanings of the terms. They will probably want to include these terms: *opposite rays*, *linear pair*, *vertical angles*, *supplementary angles*, and *perpendicular*.

23) If the ramp is perpendicular to the expressway, the driver has to accelerate into fast-moving traffic while making a 90° turn; if the ramp is nearly parallel, acceleration is much easier.

23. Entrance ramps onto expressways usually form very small angles with the expressway. Perpendicular ramps would allow better visibility. Explain why entrance ramps are not perpendicular to expressways.

In 24 and 25, name all linear pairs shown in the figure.

24.

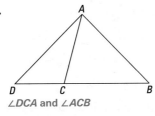

∠DCA and ∠ACB

25.

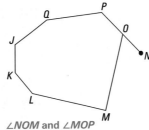

∠NOM and ∠MOP

In 26 and 27, a statement is given.
a. Tell whether the statement is true or false.
b. Explain why you answered part **a** as you did.

26. If one angle of a linear pair is an acute angle, then the other angle is obtuse. **See below left.**

27. If one of two vertical angles is acute, the other is obtuse. **See below left.**

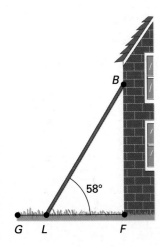

28. A firefighter places a ladder against a building so that m∠*BLF* = 58°, as in the diagram at left. What is m∠*BLG*? **122°**

In 29 and 30, suppose *x* and *y* are measures of two angles. How are *x* and *y* related in the given situation?

29. The angles are vertical angles. *x* = *y*

30. The angles are supplementary. *x* + *y* = 180°

31. An angle has measure 40°. A supplement to this angle has what measure? **140°**

26a) True
b) Since the measures of the angles in a linear pair add to 180°, if one measure is under 90°, the other must be over 90°.

27a) False
b) Vertical angles have the same measure. If one is acute, so is the other.

32. In the figure below, $\overrightarrow{UO}$ and $\overrightarrow{UT}$ are opposite rays. Find the measure of ∠*RUN*. **125°**

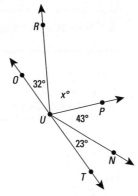

Adapting to Individual Needs

Challenge Art Connection
Have each student do the following:
(1) Draw a 45° angle, and label the vertex 0.
(2) Draw 15 equally spaced marks along each side of the angle and number them 1 through 15. (3) Draw lines connecting all pairs of numbers that have a sum of 16. Or students can use **Teaching Aid 73** and just do step (3). [A sample is shown in the first illustration on the right.] To make the design more interesting, students could draw the

angle on cardboard, and use string or colored yarn to connect the points. As a challenge, have students use the second diagram on the teaching aid to make the design on the right.

▶ **LESSON MASTER 7-6 B** *page 2*

9. ∠*CAT* is a straight angle. Find the measure of ∠*NAP*.

73°

10. Two lines intersect at the right. If m∠1 = *d*, give the other measures.
a. m∠2 = **180° − *d***
b. m∠3 = ***d***
c. m∠4 = **180° − *d***

11. In the figure at the right, m∠*FOG* = 78°. What is the measure of ∠*FOR*?

102°

Properties Objective H: Know relationships among angles formed by intersecting lines.

True or false. In 12-16, tell if the statement is true or false.

12. If ∠1 and ∠2 form a linear pair, then m∠1 + m∠2 = 90°. **false**

13. If one of two vertical angles is obtuse, the other is obtuse. **true**

14. If one of two supplementary angles is acute, the other is acute. **false**

15. Perpendicular lines intersect to form four right angles. **true**

16. Every pair of supplementary angles forms a linear pair. **false**

In 17 and 18, ∠*F* and ∠*G* are supplementary angles.

17. If m∠*F* = 90°, then m∠*G* = **90°**

18. If m∠*F* = 3(m∠*G*) then m∠*F* = **135°**

379

Notes on Questions

Question 39 It is necessary that students know the definition of *complementary angles* to answer the question. Discuss where they might find the meaning of this term.

We have not placed the term *complementary angles* in the lesson because we do not need it for the remainder of this book. However, we feel that students should be expected to learn the term.

Follow-up 7-6
for Lesson

Practice

For more questions on SPUR Objectives, use **Lesson Master 7-6A** (shown on page 377) or **Lesson Master 7-6B** (shown on pages 378–379).

Assessment

Oral Communication Tell students to imagine that a friend is absent from school today. Have them tell how they would explain vertical angles, supplementary angles, and perpendicular segments to the friend over the phone when he or she calls to ask what was done in math class today. [Conversations demonstrate understanding of terms. They include directions for drawing and labeling figures and vocabulary is defined correctly in terms of the figures described.]

Extension

Social Studies Connection Have students **work in groups.** Give each group a city map and have them find safe intersections and intersections that are not safe. Discuss their findings.

Project Update Project 3, *Angles of Chairs,* on page 399, relates to the content of this lesson. Students can begin looking for the chairs they want to use.

33a)

8 5 11

blue jeans sneakers

33. In Casimir Ewell's 5th-period math class, every student wore blue jeans or sneakers. 13 students wore blue jeans. 16 students wore sneakers. 5 students wore both.
    a. Draw a Venn diagram to illustrate this situation.
    b. How many students are in Mr. Ewell's class? *(Lesson 7-5)* 24

In 34–37, solve.

34. $180 - x = 23$ *(Lesson 7-4)* $x = 157$

35. $90 - y = 31$ *(Lesson 7-4)* $y = 59$

36. $17 - (2 - 6) + A = 5 - 2(5 + 6)$ *(Lessons 5-8, 7-2)* $A = -38$

37. $4c = 1200$ *(Lesson 4-9)* $c = 300$

38. Suppose the sign in the cartoon is true. How much would you pay for a down jacket normally selling for $129.95? *(Lesson 2-5)* $2.60

HERMAN®

© 1984 Universal Press Syndicate 8-1

"Salesman of the week gets to go to Hawaii."

39)

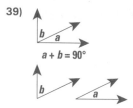

$a + b = 90°$

39. In this lesson you learned about supplementary angles. What are **complementary** angles? Draw at least two examples. two angles whose measures add to 90°; drawings will vary. See samples at the left.

Setting Up Lesson 7-7

Materials Students will need protractors or **Geometry Templates** for the next lesson.

To have students practice listening and visualizing, and to review some vocabulary, you may wish to tell students to keep their books closed, to listen as you read the first paragraph aloud, and then to sketch the figure described. Then have students open their books, reread the paragraph, and compare their sketches with the figure shown.

Angles and Parallel Lines

Train lines. *At a train depot, many lines meet.*

Angles and Intersecting Lines

Two intersecting lines form four angles, as pictured below. Suppose ∠1 has measure x. Then angle 3, vertical to ∠1, has measure x. The other angles have measure $180 - x$.

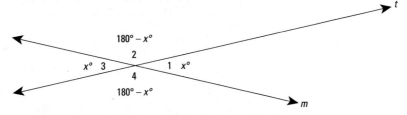

For example, if $x = 25$, then the original angle has measure 25°. The other angles measure either 25° or $180° - 25°$, which is 155°.

Angles Formed by Parallel Lines and a Transversal

Two different lines in a plane are **parallel** if they have no points in common. At the top of the next page, we draw a line n parallel to line m. This can be done easily by aligning line m with one edge of a ruler and drawing line n along the opposite edge. Line n intersects line t to form angles 5, 6, 7, and 8. Because parallel lines go in the same direction, the measures of the four new angles equal the measures of the four angles that were already there.

Lesson 7-7 *Angles and Parallel Lines* **381**

Lesson **7-7**

Objectives

D Find measures of angles in figures with parallel lines and transversals.
H Know relationships among angles formed by intersecting lines, or by two parallel lines and a transversal.

Resources

From the *Teacher's Resource File*
■ Lesson Master 7-7A or 7-7B
■ Answer Master 7-7
■ Activity Kit, Activities 17, 18
■ Teaching Aids
   69 Warm-up
   74 Parallel Lines and Angles

Additional Resources
■ Visuals for Teaching Aids 69, 74
■ Geometry Workshop
■ City maps (Extension)
■ Protractors or Geometry Templates

Teaching **7-7**
Lesson

Warm-up

Work with a partner. Find as many examples of parallel lines as you can. List them and then compare your list with those of classmates. **Samples: opposite sides of the chalkboard, top and bottom edges of a book, lines on notebook paper, railroad tracks, telephone wires**

Lesson 7-7 Overview

Broad Goals This lesson covers the terminology and angle measure relationships associated with two parallel lines cut by a transversal.

Perspective There are several important reasons for Lessons 7-6 through 7-8. First, the angle relationships discussed are an application of the subtraction concepts considered in this chapter. Second, by learning some definitions and notation now, students

become familiar with basic geometric topics and can concentrate on higher-level concepts later on in a formal geometry course. Third, many students enjoy terminology and symbols. For these students, the lessons provide a nice respite from equation solving.

In this lesson, two parallel lines and a transversal are discussed. The situation is thus quite similar to that discussed in Lesson 7-6,

except that there is now a third line which is parallel to one of the two intersecting lines.

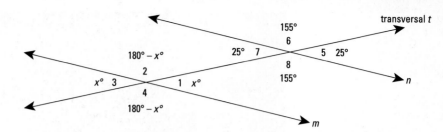

Notes on Reading

See *Activity 2* in *Optional Activities* on page 383 for an alternate way to introduce this lesson.

❶ Spend some time discussing the vocabulary in the chart. Then you might want to use the diagram on **Teaching Aid 74**, or the diagram on this page, to check that students can locate each type of angle in the diagram.

Warn students *not* to learn which angles are corresponding, vertical, and so on, by using the numbers that name them. We vary the relative positions of these numbers to discourage this idea.

Point out that alternate interior, alternate exterior, corresponding, interior, and exterior angles exist whenever two lines are intersected by a transversal. However, the equalities among the angle measures exist only when the two lines are parallel.

Activity 1 in *Optional Activities* below can be used anytime after students have completed the reading.

The line that is not parallel to the others is called a **transversal**. The eight angles have names that tell how they are related to the two parallel lines and the transversal. The interior angles are between the parallel lines. The exterior angles are outside the parallel lines. Alternate interior or alternate exterior angles are on opposite sides of the transversal.

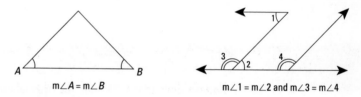

Name	Angles in above figure	Measures
Corresponding angles	1 and 5, 2 and 6, 3 and 7, 4 and 8	equal
Interior angles	1, 2, 7, 8	
Alternate interior angles	2 and 8, 1 and 7	equal
Exterior angles	3, 4, 5, 6	
Alternate exterior angles	3 and 5, 4 and 6	equal

Symbols for Angles

In work with angles, it helps to use special symbols to indicate when angles have the same measure. Use a single arc when two angles have the same measure. For a second pair of equal angles, use a double arc, and so on.

$m\angle A = m\angle B$ $m\angle 1 = m\angle 2$ and $m\angle 3 = m\angle 4$

Symbols for Parallelism

Arrows in the middle of two lines that look parallel mean that they are parallel. If lines *m* and *n* are parallel, you can write *m* // *n*. The symbol // means *is parallel to*. The drawing at the top of this page is repeated at the top of the next page. The symbols for parallel lines and for angles of equal measure are included. Also identified are the interior and exterior angles.

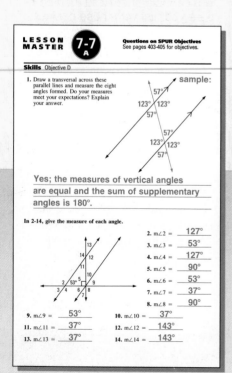

Optional Activities

Activity 1

Materials: Protractors and rulers or **Geometry Templates**

You can use this activity anytime after students have completed the reading. Give them the directions on the right. Then have them generalize their findings. [Alternate interior angles have the same measure and corresponding angles have the same measure. If a transversal is perpendicular to one

of two parallel lines, it is perpendicular to the other.]

1. Draw two parallel lines and a transversal that forms a 50° angle with one of the parallel lines. Find all angle measures. [Four 50° angles and four 130° angles]

2. Draw two parallel lines and a transversal that is perpendicular to one of the parallel lines. Find all angle measures. [All 90° angles]

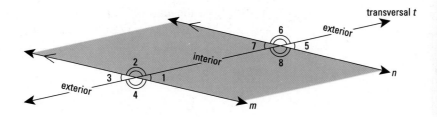

Symbols for Perpendicularity

There are also symbols for perpendicularity. In a drawing, the symbol ⌐ shows that lines or line segments are perpendicular. In writing, ⊥ means *is perpendicular to*.

In drawings, put the ⌐ symbol on only one of the angles at the point of intersection.

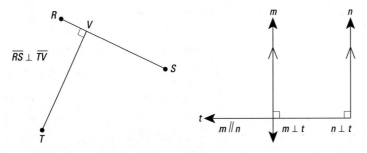

$\overline{RS} \perp \overline{TV}$

$m \| n$ $m \perp t$ $n \perp t$

Notice how these symbols shorten the amount of writing. In the figure above at the right, each parallelism and perpendicularity is indicated twice.

QUESTIONS

Covering the Reading

2) Sample:

1. When are two lines parallel? when they are in the same plane and have no points in common
2. Draw two parallel vertical lines and a transversal.

In 3–8, *m* // *n*. Give the measure of the indicated angle.

3. ∠1 118°   4. ∠2 118°

5. ∠3 62°   6. ∠4 118°

7. ∠5 118°   8. ∠6 62°

9. In the drawing of Questions 3–8, which line is the transversal? p

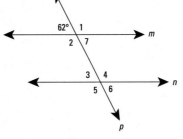

Lesson 7-7 *Angles and Parallel Lines* **383**

383

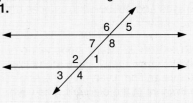
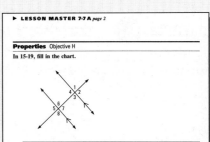

Questions 20–21 Point out that because $\overline{AB}$, $\overline{CE}$, and $\overline{CD}$ are segments and not lengths, choices do not include =, >, or <.

Question 23 Many students do not realize how many angle measures they can find given only one angle measure in the diagram. They can make the one-step deduction to find a missing angle measure, but then they do not realize that *that* measure can be used to find others.

Question 24 This question establishes a pattern that can be used to deduce the sum of the measures of the angles in a triangle. Notice that from the measures of two of the angles, the third angle can be found.

Question 25 Work through this question with students. Review the names for angles and the relationships between angles that can be used to determine all of the measures. Some students may notice that angles 1, 2, 3, and 4 are the angles of a quadrilateral.

In 10–18, use the drawing below. Lines *r* and *s* are parallel.

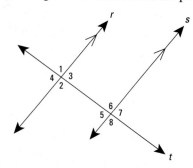

10. Name all pairs of corresponding angles. angles 1 and 6, 4 and 5, 2 and 8, 3 and 7
11. Name the interior angles. angles 2, 3, 5, and 6

12a) They are between the parallel lines and on different sides of the transversal.

12. **a.** Explain why ∠3 and ∠5 are alternate interior angles.
    b. Name the other pair of alternate interior angles. angles 2 and 6
13. Name two pairs of alternate exterior angles. angles 1 and 8, 4 and 7
14. Do the corresponding angles 1 and 6 have the same measure? Yes
15. Do the alternate interior angles 3 and 5 have the same measure? Yes
16. If m∠3 = 84°, give the measure of all other angles. m∠3 = m∠4 = m∠5 = m∠7 = 84°; m∠1 = m∠2 = m∠6 = m∠8 = 96°
17. If m∠5 = *x*, give the measure of all other angles. m∠3 = m∠4 = m∠5 = m∠7 = x; m∠1 = m∠2 = m∠6 = m∠8 = 180 − x
18. If ∠6 is a right angle, which other angles are right angles? all of the angles 1 through 8

In 19–22, use the drawing below. Assume segments that look perpendicular are perpendicular, and segments that look parallel are parallel.

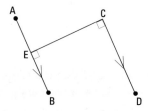

19. Copy the drawing and put in the symbols indicating parallel and perpendicular segments. See drawing above.
20. What symbol completes the statement? $\overline{AB}$ _?_ $\overline{CE}$. ⊥
21. What symbol completes the statement? $\overline{AB}$ _?_ $\overline{CD}$. //
22. Name all right angles. ∠AEC, ∠CEB, ∠ECD

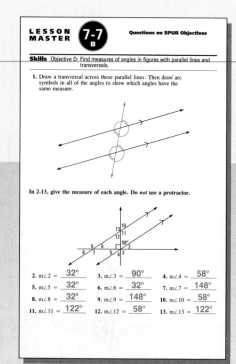
Adapting to Individual Needs

Extra Help
Students who are having trouble remembering the terms presented in the chart on page 382 might benefit from identifying each kind of angle on a separate drawing. For each idea—corresponding angles, interior and alternate interior angles, and exterior and alternate exterior angles—have students draw two parallel lines and a transversal, label the angles 1 through 8, and identify the angles in words (by writing, for

example, "corresponding angles") and then identify the angles by shading areas in different colors.

Students should note that corresponding angles have the same measure and are on the same side of the transversal. Interior angles are between the parallel lines, and exterior angles are outside the parallel lines. Alternate angles have equal measures and are on opposite sides of the transversal.

Applying the Mathematics

23) m∠1 = 90°,
m∠2 = m∠4 = 40°,
m∠3 = 140°

26a) Sample:

27) Sample:

∠1 and ∠2 are a
linear pair.

28) Sample:

Angles 3 and 4 are
vertical angles.

29) Sample:

45°   135°

*Kansas became a state
and adopted its official
seal in 1861. The 34 stars
on the seal indicate
Kansas was the 34th state.
The farmer and cabin
symbolize the anticipated
prosperity through
agriculture.*

In 23 and 24, find the measure of each numbered angle.

23.

24.

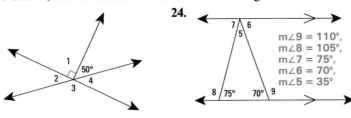

m∠9 = 110°,
m∠8 = 105°,
m∠7 = 75°,
m∠6 = 70°,
m∠5 = 35°

25. Find the sum of the measures of angles 1, 2, 3, and 4 in the drawing below. **360°**

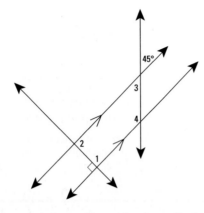

26. Line *m* is parallel to line *n*. Line *m* is perpendicular to line *t*.
  a. Make a drawing of this situation.
  b. Describe how *n* and *t* are related. *n ⊥ t*

Review

In 27–29, draw an accurate example and identify on your drawing.

27. a linear pair   See above left.   **28.** vertical angles   See above left.

29. supplementary angles that are not a linear pair   *(Lesson 7-6)*
See above left.
30. Along I-70 in Kansas, it is 179 miles from Salina to Kansas City, 110 miles from Salina to Topeka, and 150 miles from Abilene to Kansas City. How far is it from Abilene to Topeka?   *(Lesson 7-5)*
81 miles

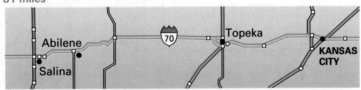

Follow-up 7-7
for Lesson

Practice
For more questions on SPUR Objectives, use **Lesson Master 7-7A** (shown on pages 382–383) or **Lesson Master 7-7B** (shown on pages 384–385).

Assessment
Group Assessment Have students **work in pairs.** Have each student draw two parallel lines cut by a transversal, label the angles, measure one of the angles, and write the measure on the drawing. Then have partners exchange drawings and find the measures of the seven other angles. The partners should check each other's work. [Drawings are accurate and show an understanding of the concepts taught in the lesson.]

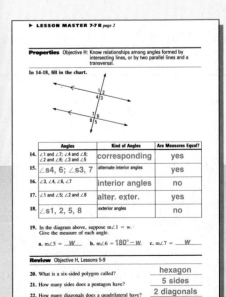

Adapting to Individual Needs

English Language Development
Emphasize that the term *interior* means inside, and the interior angles are between or inside the parallel lines. *Exterior* means outside, and the exterior angles are outside the region bounded by the parallel lines. You might have students continue to write new terms and symbols on index cards, along with a drawing or a few words that remind them of the meanings of the terms. For this lesson they will probably want to

include *parallel lines, transversal, corresponding angles, interior angles, alternate interior angles, exterior angles,* and *alternate exterior angles,* along with the symbols for angle, parallelism, and perpendicularity.

386

Extension

Social Studies Connection You might continue the activity in the *Extension* for Lesson 7-6. Have students **work in groups.** Give each group a city map and tell students to find parallel streets cut by a transversal street. Suggest that they trace the streets and measure the angles formed. Then have them discuss whether or not the streets form safe intersections.

Technology Connection You may wish to have students use the *Geometry Workshop* to draw parallel lines, create transversals, and measure angles.

Project Update Project 3, *Angles of Chairs,* on page 399, relates to the content of this lesson.

---

31. Solve $m - \frac{8}{3} = -3$. *(Lesson 7-3)* $m = -\frac{1}{3}$

32. Subtract $2\frac{6}{7}$ from $5\frac{2}{3}$. *(Lesson 7-1)* $2\frac{17}{21}$

33a) 16 square units
b) Samples: area surrounding a house; area of path around a garden

33. **a.** What is the area of the shaded region between the rectangles below?
    b. Describe at least two real situations where one might have to solve a problem similar to part **a.** *(Lesson 7-1)*

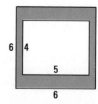

34. Solve for c: $a + b + c = 180$. *(Lesson 5-8)* $c = 180 - a - b$

35. A savings account contains C dollars. How much is in the account after the indicated transactions?
    a. $100 is withdrawn, and $30.45 is deposited. $C - 69.55$ dollars
    b. W dollars are withdrawn (from the original C dollars), and D dollars are deposited. *(Lesson 5-3)* $C - W + D$ dollars

36. Three instances of a pattern are given. Describe the pattern using two variables. *(Lesson 4-2)*
    $$\frac{73 \cdot 5}{5} = 73 \qquad \frac{8/7 \cdot 6}{6} = \frac{8}{7} \qquad \frac{-4.02 \cdot 43}{43} = -4.02 \qquad \frac{a \cdot b}{b} = a$$

Exploration

37) Samples: windows, streets, parking lot stripes, guitar strings, and bridges

37. The photograph below pictures balusters (the parallel vertical supports) and a banister (the transversal) on stairs. Give two other places where it is common to find parallel lines and transversals.

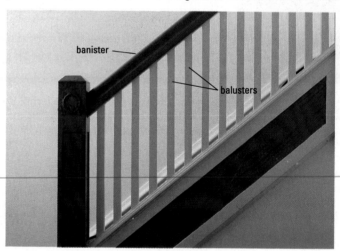

Adapting to Individual Needs

Challenge
Have students solve the following puzzle: Two lines are cut by a transversal. Of the eight angles formed, four have measure 25° and four have measure 155°. However, none of the lines are parallel. Is this possible? If so, draw an example. If not, tell why not. [Yes, it is possible as shown in the diagram on the right.]

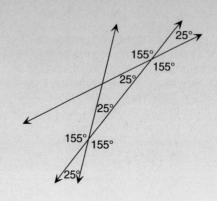

Setting Up Lesson 7-8

Materials Students will need protractors or **Geometry Templates** for Lesson 7-8.

A field of quadrilaterals. *The rectangular panels shown above are part of the AIDS Quilt, a hand-sewn tribute to the tens of thousands of AIDS victims. The quilt was displayed in Washington, D.C., to raise funds for AIDS-related services.*

Here is a drawing of two parallel lines m and n and a transversal t. The pattern of angle measures for vertical angles and linear pairs is shown. Other patterns become clear as more parallel lines are added.

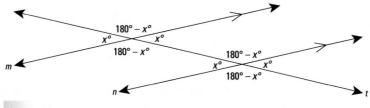

Activity

Step 1

Draw two parallel lines and a transversal as shown above.

Step 2

Choose and label any one angle as $x°$. Label its vertical angle $x°$, and the remaining two angles of the linear pairs $180° - x°$. Label the remaining four angles, using either alternate interior or corresponding angles.

Step 3

Draw another line parallel to the transversal. Label the newly formed angles appropriately. How many angles are now labeled?

Step 4

Trace the interior quadrilateral formed by the lines. Label the four vertices *T, E, A,* and *M* in consecutive order.

Step 5

Measure each angle of *TEAM* to the nearest degree and record your results. Measure the length of each side to the nearest millimeter and record your results.

Lesson 7-8 *Special Quadrilaterals* **387**

Objectives

F Find measures of angles and sides in special quadrilaterals without measuring.

I Apply the definitions of parallelogram, rectangle, rhombus, and square to determine properties of these figures.

Resources

From the *Teacher's Resource File*

- Lesson Master 7-8A or 7-8B
- Answer Master 7-8
- Assessment Sourcebook: Quiz for Lessons 7-5 through 7-8
- Teaching Aids
  69 Warm-up
  75 Parallelograms
  76 Question 25
  77 Quadrilaterals
- Technology Sourcebook, Computer Master 12

Additional Resources

- Visuals for Teaching Aids 69, 75–77
- Geometry Workshop
- Protractors and rulers, or Geometry Templates

Teaching 7-8
Lesson

Warm-up

Open your book to page 387. Use a protractor and a ruler to complete steps 1–3 of the activity, but in this case the angle labeled with an *x* has a measure of 57°. **Check students' drawings. All angles will have a measure of either 57° or 123°.**

Lesson 7-8 Overview

Broad Goals This lesson should make students aware of the relationships among special quadrilaterals. That is, parallelograms include rectangles, rhombuses, and squares; rectangles and rhombuses include squares.

Perspective At this level, we do not *deduce* the properties of figures. Rather, we are content that students can *recognize* the properties. Later, in their study of geometry,

students who know the properties will find it far easier to see the relationships among the figures.

Although students have encountered rectangles and squares before this year, they may have been led to believe that a square is not a rectangle. Thus, in this lesson you may have to "unteach" things students have learned before. Similarly, students may have learned that a rectangle is not a parallelogram.

The term *rhombus* is likely to be new to many students. Stress that a rhombus is also a special kind of parallelogram and that a square is a special type of rhombus. The popular name for a rhombus that is not a square is *diamond*. An alternate plural for rhombus is *rhombi*.

Notes on Reading

Students should record the results of the *Activity* for use with **Questions 3–5** on page 389.

To help students understand relationships among special quadrilaterals, you may wish to use the first visual organizer on **Teaching Aid 75,** which is given below.

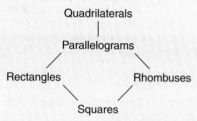

Explain that in this diagram, if all instances of a particular figure (such as a rhombus) have a certain property (such as all sides have equal length), then all instances of figures connected to and below that figure have that property. Point out that the reverse is not always true. A square has the properties of a rhombus, but a rhombus does not always have the properties of a square (a rhombus does not necessarily have all right angles).

You might ask your students which shape below is closest to the shape of a baseball diamond? [a] The fact that a baseball diamond is a square surprises many people.

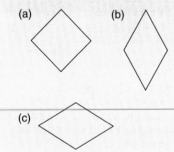

What Is a Parallelogram?

Quadrilateral *TEAM* that you traced in step 4 of the Activity is a *parallelogram*. A **parallelogram** is a quadrilateral with two pairs of parallel sides. Our parallelogram *TEAM* is shown below. In parallelogram *TEAM*, $\overline{TE}$ and $\overline{MA}$ are called **opposite sides.** $\overline{TM}$ and $\overline{EA}$ are also opposite sides. Angles *A* and *T* are **opposite angles.** Angles *E* and *M* are also opposite angles.

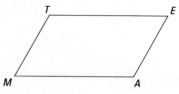

Figures appear smaller than actual size in Teacher's Edition.

Properties of Parallelograms

From the parallel lines, we know that m∠*A* = m∠*T* and m∠*E* = m∠*M*. So opposite angles have the same measure. Also, opposite sides have the same length. So *TE* = *MA* and *TM* = *EA*. This is true in any parallelogram.

> **Properties of Parallelograms**
> In a parallelogram, opposite sides have the same length; opposite angles have the same measure.

For example, *ABCD* is a parallelogram with side and angle measures indicated. The angle measures have been rounded to the nearest degree. The side lengths are to the nearest millimeter.

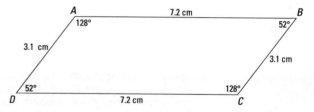

Special Types of Parallelograms

Many common figures are parallelograms. Among these are the rectangle, rhombus, and square. A **rectangle** is a parallelogram with a right angle. All angles of a rectangle have the same measure—they are all right angles. A **rhombus,** or **diamond,** is a parallelogram with all sides the same length. A **square** is a rectangle with the same length and width. Therefore, you can also think of a square as a special type of rhombus. The diagram at the top of the next page summarizes these relationships.

Optional Activities

Activity 1 After students complete the reading, you might have them try to draw each of the following figures. Note that some figures are impossible to draw.
1. A rectangle that is not a square [any rectangle with adjacent sides of different lengths]
2. A square that is not a rectangle [impossible]
3. A parallelogram with a right angle [any rectangle]

4. A parallelogram with only one right angle [impossible]
5. A rectangle that is a rhombus [any square]
6. A quadrilateral that is not a parallelogram [any 4-sided polygon in which at least one pair of opposite sides are not parallel]
7. A parallelogram with four sides of different lengths [impossible]
8. A parallelogram that is not a rectangle [any parallelogram with no right angles]

Activity 2 Technology Connection You may wish to assign *Technology Sourcebook, Computer Master 12.* Students use the *Geometry Workshop* to connect midpoints of sides of quadrilaterals to create new quadrilaterals.

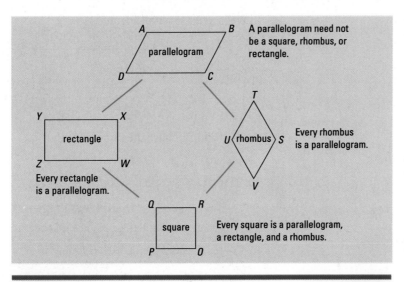

A parallelogram need not be a square, rhombus, or rectangle.

Every rhombus is a parallelogram.

Every rectangle is a parallelogram.

Every square is a parallelogram, a rectangle, and a rhombus.

As you are discussing the lesson, you might ask students to identify everyday items shaped like quadrilaterals. There are many rectangles in any classroom: walls, windows, ceiling or floor tiles, chalkboard sections, and paper. Some of these rectangles may also be squares. Non-rectangular rhombuses and parallelograms may be more difficult to find.

QUESTIONS

Covering the Reading

1. If two paraliel lines intersect one other line, how many angles are then formed? **8**

2. Suppose two parallel lines intersect two other parallel lines.
   a. How many angles are formed? **16**
   b. If one of the angles has measure x, then all angles have either measure __?__ or __?__. **x, $180 - x$**
   c. If one of the angles has measure 30°, then all angles have either measure __?__ or __?__. **30°, 150°**

In Questions 3–5, refer to parallelogram *TEAM* that you traced in step 4 of the Activity in this lesson.

3, 4) Answers are given for diagram on page 388.

3. To the nearest degree, what is the measure of each angle in *TEAM*?
   $m\angle T = m\angle A \approx 120°$, $m\angle E = m\angle M \approx 60°$
4. To the nearest millimeter, what is the measure of each side of *TEAM*?
   $TE = MA \approx 3.8$ cm, $TM = EA \approx 2.2$ cm
5. Does *TEAM* appear to be a rectangle, rhombus, or square? **none of these**

In 6 and 7, refer to quadrilateral *ABCD*.

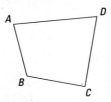

6. N... ...osite sides.   7. Name a pair of opposite angles.
   ...**$\overline{BC}$**   **$\angle A$ and $\angle C$, or $\angle B$ and $\angle D$**

Lesson 7-8   *Special Quadrilaterals*   **389**

Explain this? Class grade

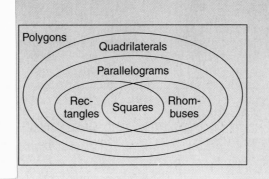

Polygons
Quadrilaterals
Parallelograms
Rectangles   Squares   Rhombuses

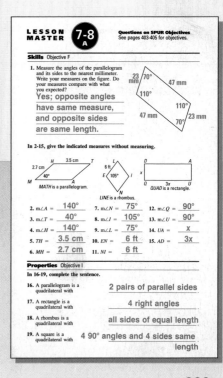

389

Question 11 Note that in this problem more information is given than is needed.

Questions 13–16 These questions clarify the classification of quadrilaterals and can form the basis for a discussion of the relationships among these figures.

Question 13 Error Alert Some students might not identify Figure D as a rectangle. Point out that all squares are rectangles and that tilting a figure does not change the type of figure it is.

Question 14 Remind students that all squares are rhombuses, but not all rhombuses are squares.

Question 21 A Venn diagram can be useful when finding this answer.

Questions 22–23 Students will find the strategy of *drawing a picture* helpful. Notice that the strategy *determining whether there is too little information* also applies to **Question 23.**

Building blocks to a child's development. *Toys often are designed to help children develop their coordination or to increase their awareness of geometric shapes.*

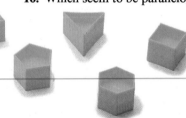

In 8–11, refer to parallelogram *MNPQ*.

8. ∠*N* and _?_ have the same measure. ∠*Q*

9. $\overline{PQ}$ and _?_ have the same length. $\overline{MN}$

10. If m∠*Q* = 70°, then m∠*M* = _?_. 110°

11. If *PQ* = 5 and *PN* = 2.8, then *MN* = _?_. 5

12. What must a parallelogram have in order to be a rhombus? **All sides must be of equal length.**

In 13–16, consider the figures *A* through *H*.

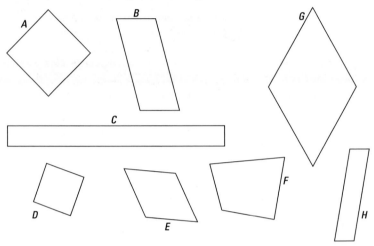

13. Which seem to be rectangles? **A, C, D**

14. Which seem to be rhombuses? **A, D, E, G**

15. Which seem to be squares? **A, D**

16. Which seem to be parallelograms? **A, B, C, D, E, G, H**

Adapting to Individual Needs

English Language Development
To help students learn the names of these special quadrilaterals, have them draw the figures on index cards, and write the English name and the name in their native language. Then suggest that they put the cards with others cards they have made for geometric concepts in this chapter. Have them review the cards periodically with a friend.

In 17–20, consider quadrilaterals, parallelograms, rhombuses, rectangles, and squares.

17. Which have all four sides equal in length? **rhombuses and squares**

18. Which have all four angles equal in measure? **rectangles and squares**

19. Which have both pairs of opposite angles equal in measure?
parallelograms, rhombuses, rectangles, and squares

20. Which have both pairs of opposite sides equal in length?
parallelograms, rhombuses, rectangles, and squares

21. In a collection of 50 parallelograms, 35 are rectangles and 26 are rhombuses. Every figure is a rectangle or rhombus or both. How many squares are in the collection? **11**

In 22 and 23, give the perimeter of each figure.

22. a rhombus with one side having length 10 **40**

23. a parallelogram with one side having length 10 **not enough information**

24a) Sample:

24. One angle of a rhombus has measure 35°.
   a. Draw such a rhombus.
   b. What are the measures of its other angles?
   $m\angle B = m\angle D = 145°$, $m\angle C = 35°$

25. In the figure below, *ABCD* and *AEFG* are parallelograms and $\overline{AB}$ and $\overline{AE}$ are perpendicular. m∠*ABC* = 147°. *G, A, D,* and *H* are on the same line. Find the measure of each indicated angle.
   a. ∠*BAG* **147°**   b. ∠*GAE* **57°**   c. ∠*AGF* **123°**   d. ∠*CDH* **33°**

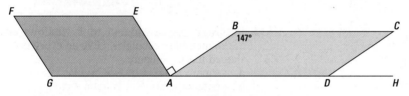

26. If *x* + *y* = 180, then *y* = __?__.   *(Lesson 7-6)*   **180 − x**

In 27–31, use the figure at the left.   *(Lesson 7-6)*

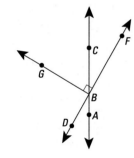

27. Angles *CBG* and __?__ form a linear pair.   **GBA**

28. Angles *ABD* and __?__ are vertical angles.   **CBF**

29. Suppose m∠*FBC* = 30°.   a) ∠DBA, ∠CBD, ∠FBA, ∠GBC, ∠GBA, ∠GBD,
   a. What other angle measures can be found?   ∠ GBF;   b) m∠DBA = 30°,
   b. Find them.   m∠CBD = m∠FBA = 150°, m∠GBC = 60°, m∠ABG = 120°,
   m∠GBD = m∠GBF = 90°

30. Suppose m∠*GBA* = 126°.   ∠GBD, ∠DBA, ∠GBF, ∠FBC, ∠FBA, ∠DBC,
   a. What other angle measures can be found?   ∠GBC
   b. Find them.   m∠GBD = 90°, m∠DBA = 36°, m∠GBF = 90°,
   m∠FBC = 36°, m∠FBA = m∠DBC = 144°, m∠GBC = 54°

31. $\overline{BG}$ __?__ $\overline{DF}$ ⊥

Lesson 7-8   *Special Quadrilaterals*   **391**

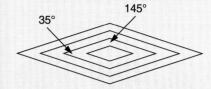
▶ **LESSON MASTER 7-8 B** *page 2*

In 12-19, give the indicated measures without measuring.

12. m∠*E* = __90°__
13. m∠*C* = __90°__
14. *ER* = __a__
15. *EC* = __b__

RECT is a rectangle.

16. m∠*S* = __90°__
17. m∠*Q* = __90°__
18. *QU* = __n__
19. *AU* = __n__

SQUA is a square.

Properties Objective I: Apply the definitions of parallelogram, rectangle, rhombus, and square to determine properties of these figures.

In 20-24, give the most specific name for each description.

20. a parallelogram with all sides the same length   **rhombus**
21. a quadrilateral with two pair of parallel sides   **parallelogram**
22. a rhombus with a right angle   **square**
23. a parallelogram with a right angle   **rectangle**
24. a rectangle with equal length and width   **square**

True or false. In 25-30, tell whether each statement is true or false.

25. In every rhombus, opposite angles have the same measure.   **true**
26. Every rectangle is also a square.   **false**
27. Every square is also a rhombus.   **true**
28. In every parallelogram, all sides have the same length.   **false**
29. A parallelogram could have a right angle.   **true**
30. Every rhombus is also a parallelogram.   **true**

Adapting to Individual Needs

Challenge
Have students solve the following problem. Draw a square. Then draw two straight lines through the square to separate it into four quadrilaterals that are not parallelograms, but have the same size and shape. [Any pair of perpendicular lines through the center but not perpendicular to the sides will satisfy the conditions. A sample answer is given at the right.]

Question 33 Multicultural Connection Milwaukee was originally known as Mahn-a-waukee Seepe (Gathering Place by the River) to the various Indian tribes who first lived there. Students might investigate the origins of the names of their towns.

Follow-up 7-8
for Lesson

Practice

For more questions on SPUR Objectives, use **Lesson Master 7-8A** (shown on page 389) or **Lesson Master 7-8B** (shown on pages 390–391).

Assessment

Quiz A quiz covering Lessons 7-5 through 7-8 is provided in the *Assessment Sourcebook.*

Written Communication Have each student write a paragraph telling what he or she has learned about parallelograms. [Paragraphs contain definitions and diagrams that show understanding of the relationships among parallelograms and special types of parallelograms.]

Extension

There are three other quadrilaterals often discussed in geometry. *Kites* are quadrilaterals with two pairs of distinct adjacent sides that are equal in length. *Trapezoids* are quadrilaterals with at least one pair of parallel sides. (We introduce trapezoids in Chapter 10.) *Isosceles trapezoids* are trapezoids in which base angles are congruent. Have students use the visual organizer on **Teaching Aid 77** to correctly insert the words *trapezoids*, *kites*, and *isosceles trapezoids* onto the diagram.

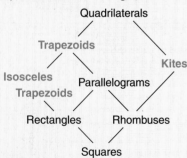

Project Update Project 5, *Automatic Drawing Programs*, on page 400, relates to the content of this lesson.

392

---

32. If you toss a pair of dice once, what is the probability of getting either doubles or a sum of seven? *(Lesson 7-5)* $\frac{12}{36}$ or $\frac{1}{3}$

33. Here are census figures for Milwaukee, Wisconsin.

1950	637,392
1960	741,324
1970	717,372
1980	636,212
1990	628,088

Mitchell Conservatory, Milwaukee, Wisconsin

33a) from 1950 to 1960: 103,932
from 1960 to 1970: -23,952
from 1970 to 1980: -81,160
from 1980 to 1990: -8,124

a. Calculate the change in population from each census to the next. You should get one positive and three negative numbers.
b. Add the four changes you find in part **a.** -9,304
c. What does the sum in part **b** mean? *(Lessons 7-2, 7-4)* From 1950 to 1990, the population of Milwaukee decreased by 9,304 people.

Exploration

34. Rectangles are easy to find. Most windows, chalkboards, and doors are shaped like rectangles. Give an everyday example of something shaped like each figure.
a. a square Sample: crossword puzzle
b. a parallelogram that is not a rectangle Sample: side of a pink eraser
c. a rhombus that is not a square Sample: colored window pane

---

Setting Up Lesson 7-9
Materials Students will need protractors or **Geometry Templates** for Lesson 7-9.

Kayo has been studying triangles. Read this cartoon to see what he considers awesome.

Activity

Draw a triangle on a large sheet of paper. Repeat what Kayo's grandfather did. Do you get the same results?

Lesson **7-9**

Objectives
E Use the Triangle-Sum Property to find measures of angles.
J Explain the consequences of the Triangle-Sum Property.

Resources
From the *Teacher's Resource File*
- Lesson Master 7-9A or 7-9B
- Answer Master 7-9
- Teaching Aids
  69 Warm-up
  78 Example 3, Questions 11, 16, and 18
  79 Additional Examples
  80 Triangle-Sum Property
- Technology Sourcebook, Computer Master 13

Additional Resources
- Visuals for Teaching Aids 69, 78–80
- Geometry Workshop
- Protractors and rulers, or Geometry Templates

Teaching **7-9**
Lesson

Warm-up
Use a ruler to draw a large triangle on a piece of paper. Draw any type of triangle you choose. Use a protractor to measure each of the angles of the triangle and find the sum of their measures. The sum of the angle measures should be near 180°.

Lesson 7-9 Overview

Broad Goals The Triangle-Sum Property, which states that the sum of the measures of the angles of a triangle is 180°, is developed through an activity and used to solve problems.

Perspective In this lesson, the Triangle-Sum Property is developed through a cutting and paper-folding activity.

After the statement of the property, three applications are given with each showing how the measure of angles can be obtained, proceeding from a direct application in Example 1, to a 2-step application in Example 2, to a multi-step application in Example 3.

Students should record the results of the *Activity* for use with **Question 1** on page 396.

Example 1 Some students will do one problem like **Example 1**, see the pattern, and not necessarily solve equations to do similar problems. They will just add the measures of the two given angles, and subtract the sum from 180°. There is nothing wrong with this strategy. It yields the same solution that is found by solving equations.

Example 2 This is a two-step problem in which students find *y* first and then *x*. In the study of geometry later on, students may learn the theorem that the measure of an exterior angle of a triangle equals the sum of the measures of the remote interior angles. This changes the problem to a one-step problem.

Example 3 Go through this example in detail with students. Some students are intrigued by the ability to find the measures of angles located so far away from a given angle. You can use **Teaching Aid 78** to demonstrate how much easier the problem becomes if the information can be written on the drawing itself as each of the facts is determined. This provides a good concrete example of deductive reasoning.

The famous property of triangles illustrated by the cartoon and the activity is the *Triangle-Sum Property*.

Triangle-Sum Property
In any triangle, the sum of the measures of the angles is 180°.

Finding the Measure of the Third Angle of a Triangle

Example 1

Suppose two angles of a triangle have measures 57° and 85°. What is the measure of the third angle?

Solution
First draw a picture. Then let x be the measure of the third angle.

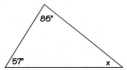

Use the Triangle-Sum Property.
$$57° + 85° + x = 180°$$
$$142° + x = 180°$$

You know how to solve this equation.
$$-142 + 142 + x = -142 + 180$$
$$x = 38$$
So the third angle has measure 38°.

Check
Add the measures. Does 38 + 57 + 85 = 180? Yes.

You have now studied many different ways to find measures of angles. Examples 2 and 3 use some of these ways.

Optional Activities

Materials: **Teaching Aid 80**, rulers, scissors

Instead of having students "tear off" the angles of a triangle and arrange them to form a straight angle, you might want to use this activity. Diagrams to accompany the steps are shown at the right and on **Teaching Aid 80**.

1. Draw a large triangle, and label the vertices *A*, *B*, and *C*. Cut out triangle *ABC*.
2. Fold *A* onto *B* to locate *D*, the midpoint of $\overline{AB}$. Fold *C* onto *B* to locate *E*, the midpoint of $\overline{BC}$. Draw $\overline{DE}$.
3. Fold the top of the triangle down along $\overline{DE}$. *B* should just touch the base $\overline{AC}$ at *F*.
4. Fold the triangle again so that *A* and *C* meet *B* at *F*. Angles 1, 2, and 3 form a straight angle, so the sum of their measures is 180°. Therefore, the sum of the measures of the angles of triangle *ABC* equals 180°.

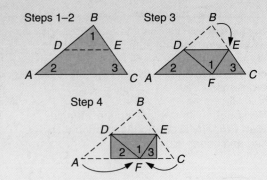

Finding the Measure of an Angle Exterior to a Triangle

Example 2

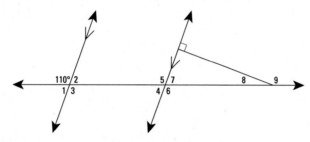

Find the measure of angle *DAC* in the drawing at the left.

Solution

Let *x* be the measure of ∠*DAC*. Let *y* be the measure of ∠*BAC*.
Use the Triangle-Sum Property to find *y*.

$$60° + 70° + y = 180°$$

Simplify. $\qquad\qquad 130° + y = 180°$

Solve for *y*. $\quad -130° + 130° + y = -130° + 180°$

$$y = 50°$$

Now use the fact that angles *DAC* and *BAC* form a linear pair.

$$x + y = 180°$$

Substitute for *y*. $\qquad x + 50° = 180°$

Solve for *x*. $\qquad\qquad x = 130$

So m∠*DAC* = 130°.

Finding the Measures of Angles Given Triangles and Parallel Lines

Example 3

Use the information given in the drawing. Explain the steps needed to find m∠9.

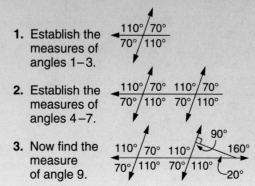

Solution

The drawing is complicated. Examine it carefully. You may wish to make an identical drawing and write in angle measures as they are found.

The arrows indicate that two of the lines are parallel. Angle 5 and the 110° angle are corresponding angles. So m∠5 = 110°. ∠7 forms a linear pair with ∠5, so they are supplementary. Thus m∠7 = 70°. The triangle has a 90° angle created by the perpendicular lines. But it also has ∠7, a 70° angle. The Triangle-Sum Property says that the measures of the three angles add to 180°. This forces m∠8 to be 20°. Finally, ∠9 and ∠8 form a linear pair, so m∠9 = 160°.

Adapting to Individual Needs

Extra Help

Some of the drawings in this lesson can be overwhelming to some students. To help these students, draw the confusing figures on the overhead and work on them section by section, covering up the parts not being used. For example, you might use the following sequence for **Example 3.**

1. Establish the measures of angles 1–3.

2. Establish the measures of angles 4–7.

3. Now find the measure of angle 9.

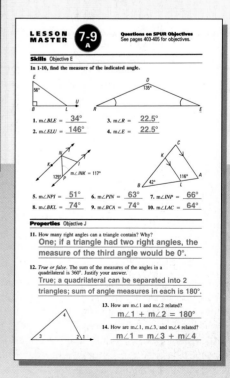

Additional Examples

These examples are shown on
Teaching Aid 79.

1. Find the measure of the angle.

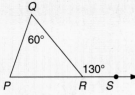

a.

b.

m∠1 = 40°   m∠2 = 55°

2. Find the measure of ∠QPR.

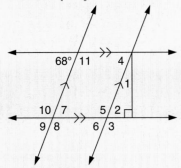

m∠QPR = 70°

3. Use the information given in the
drawing. Explain the steps needed
to find m∠1. **Sample: There are
two sets of parallel lines. Angle
4 and the 68° angle correspond;
m∠4 = 68°. Angles 2 and 4 are
alternate interior angles;
m∠2 = 68°. By the Triangle-
Sum Property m∠1 = 22°.**

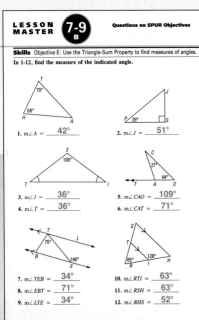

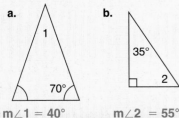
396

Covering the Reading

1. In the Activity, did you get the same results as Kayo's grandfather?
   Results should be about the same.
2. *Multiple choice.* Which is true?
   (a) In some but not all triangles, the sum of the measures of the angles is 180°.
   (b) In all triangles, the sum of the measures of the angles is 180°.
   (c) The sum of the measures of the angles of a triangle can be any number from 180° to 360°. (b)

3. What is the Triangle-Sum Property? In any triangle, the sum of the measures of the angles is 180°.
4. Why did the corners of the triangles in the cartoon fit together to make a straight line? because the angle measures add to 180°

In 5–8, two angles of a triangle have the given measures. Find the measure of the third angle.

5. 30°, 60° **90°** 6. 117°, 62° **1°** 7. 1°, 2° **177°** 8. $x°$, $140° - x°$ **40°**

Applying the Mathematics

9. Find m∠ABC. **74°**

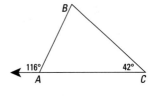

10. Find m∠XYZ. **146°**

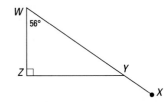

11. Find the measures of angles 1 through 8.

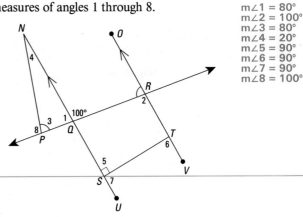

m∠1 = 80°
m∠2 = 100°
m∠3 = 80°
m∠4 = 20°
m∠5 = 90°
m∠6 = 90°
m∠7 = 90°
m∠8 = 100°

396

Adapting to Individual Needs

English Language Development
Most of the terminology in this lesson was
introduced in previous lessons. Students
who are using index cards to help them
learn the terms should continue to use the
cards as needed.

15) If a triangle had two obtuse angles, the sum of their measures would be more than 180°. This contradicts the Triangle-Sum Property.

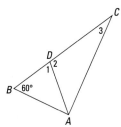

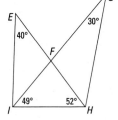

In 12 and 13, *multiple choice.* Use these choices.
(a) complementary
(b) supplementary
(c) neither complementary nor supplementary

12. Which describes angles 5 and 7 of Question 11? (b)

13. Which describes ∠W and ∠ZYW of Question 10? (a)

14. What is the sum of the measures of the four angles of a rectangle? **360°**

15. Explain why a triangle cannot have two obtuse angles. See above left.

16. In the figure at the left, $\overline{BA} \perp \overline{AC}$. Angle BAC is bisected (split into two equal parts) by $\overline{AD}$. m∠B = 60°. Find the measures of angles 1, 2, and 3. **m∠1 = 75°, m∠2 = 105°, m∠3 = 30°**

17. *Multiple choice.* Two angles of a triangle have measures x and y. The third angle must have what measure?
(a) $180 - x + y$ (b) $180 + x + y$
(c) $180 + x - y$ (d) $180 - x - y$ (d)

18. In the figure at the left, $\overline{EH}$ and $\overline{GI}$ intersect at F. Find the measures of as many angles in the figure as you can. **m∠EIH = 88°, m∠EIG = 39°, m∠GHI = 101°, m∠GHE = 49°, m∠IFH = m∠EFG = 79°, m∠IFE = m∠GFH = 101°**

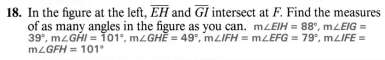

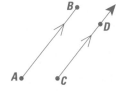

Review

19. a. *True or false.* A square is a special type of rectangle. **True**
    b. *True or false.* A square is a special type of rhombus. *(Lesson 7-8)* **True**

In 20–23, use the drawing below. What is the meaning of each symbol? *(Lesson 7-7)*

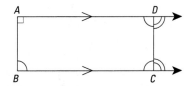

24a) Line segment AB is parallel to ray CD.
b)

20. the arrows on segments $\overline{AD}$ and $\overline{BC}$ **AD and BC are parallel.**

21. the sign that looks like a backward L by angle A **AB and AD are perpendicular.**

22. the single arcs by points B and C **m∠B = m∠BCD**

23. the double arcs by points C and D **The angles have the same measure.**

In 24 and 25, a mathematical sentence is given. **a.** Translate the sentence into an English sentence. **b.** Draw a picture. *(Lesson 7-7)*

24. $\overline{AB} \parallel \overrightarrow{CD}$ **See left.**   **25.** $\overleftrightarrow{EF} \perp \overline{GH}$ **See left.**

25a) Line EF is perpendicular to line segment GH.
b)

26. Solve $-5 = 15.4 - x$. *(Lesson 7-4)* **x = 20.4**

27. Solve $x - 3 = -3$. *(Lesson 7-3)* **x = 0**

Adapting to Individual Needs

Challenge
Have students solve the following problem:

If one side of a triangle measures 6 cm and the other sides have whole-number lengths less than 6 cm, how many different-shaped triangles are possible? [6; triangles with sides 3, 4, 6; 2, 5, 6; 3, 5, 6; 4, 4, 6; 4, 5, 6; and 5, 5, 6] Ask students if they can generalize about the lengths of the other two

sides. [The sum of the two lengths must be greater than 6 and less than 11.]

Notes on Questions
Question 8 Error Alert If students have difficulty, have them find the sum of the two given angles;
$x + (140 - x) = 140$.

Question 11 Tell students that they can find the angle measures in any order they wish, not necessarily the numerical order on the diagram.

Follow-up   **7-9**
for Lesson

Practice
For more questions on SPUR Objectives, use **Lesson Master 7-9A** (shown on page 395) or **Lesson Master 7-9B** (shown on pages 396–397).

Assessment
Group Assessment Have students **work in groups.** Have each group write five questions that require using the Triangle-Sum Property to answer them. [Some groups may decide to make a drawing using parallel lines and triangles and write questions about the drawing, other groups may choose to write true-or-false questions regarding the property, and still other groups may choose problems that require finding the measure of the third angle of a triangle.]

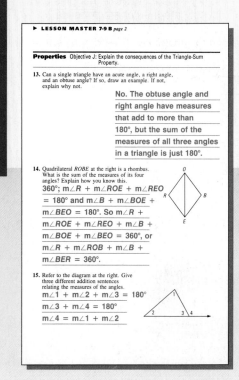

Extension

The activity in the lesson shows one way in which the Triangle-Sum Property is proved. You might want to outline a second proof involving parallel lines. (Students have all the required background except the reason you can draw the parallel line through point *A*—the Parallel Postulate states that through a point not on a line there exists exactly one line parallel to a given line).

Begin with any triangle *ABC* and draw the line parallel to $\overline{BC}$ through *A*.

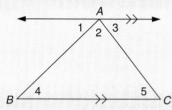

Step 1:
m∠1 + m∠2 + m∠3 = 180°
(Putting together angle measures using the Angle Addition Property)
Step 2:
m∠4 = m∠1 and m∠5 = m∠3
(If two parallel lines are cut by a transversal, then alternate interior angles have the same measure.)
Step 3:
m∠4 + m∠2 + m∠5 = 180°
(Substitution of m∠4 for m∠1, and m∠5 for m∠3 in Step 1.)

Technology Connection You may wish to assign *Technology Sourcebook, Computer Master 13*. Students use the *Geometry Workshop* to construct various types of triangles and investigate their characteristics.

Project Update Project 4, *A Large Triangle*, on page 400, relates to the content of this lesson.

398

---

28. Four people went to a health club. Their weights on February 1 and March 1 are shown below. **a.** How much did each person's weight change? **b.** Who gained the most? **c.** Who lost the most? *(Lesson 7-1)*

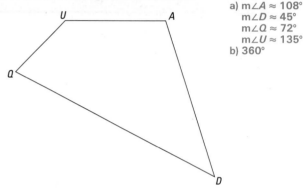

	February 1	**March 1**
Richard	65.3 kg	62.8 kg
Marlene	53.4 kg	54.3 kg
Evelyn	58.6 kg	55.1 kg
Daniel	71.1 kg	72.0 kg

a) Richard: -2.5 kg
Marlene: .9 kg
Evelyn: -3.5 kg
Daniel: .9 kg
b) Marlene and Daniel
c) Evelyn

29. Evaluate $a - b + c - d$ when $a = 0$, $b = -10$, $c = -100$, and $d = -1000$. *(Lesson 7-2)* **910**

30. Evaluate $a - b + c - d$ when $a = -43$, $b = 2$, $c = 5$, and $d = 11$. *(Lesson 7-2)* **-51**

Exploration

31. Here is a quadrilateral that is not a parallelogram. **a.** Measure the four angles. **b.** What is the sum of the measures?

a) m∠A ≈ 108°
m∠D ≈ 45°
m∠Q ≈ 72°
m∠U ≈ 135°
b) 360°

32. *Multiple choice.* What is the sum of the measures of the angles of an *n*-gon?
(a) 180*n*   (b) 180(*n* + 1)   (c) 180(*n* − 2)   (d) 180(*n* + 3) (c)

33. Use computer software that can draw and measure to draw any size or shape of triangle. Then, use the measure tool to measure each of the angles of the triangle and find the sum of the angles. **Answers will vary.**

Measures
∠*BAC*
∠*BCA*
∠*ABC*

A project presents an opportunity for you to extend your knowledge of a topic related to the material of this chapter. You should allow more time for a project than you do for typical homework questions.

1 Population Changes

Obtain census information from the last two censuses for at least 25 towns and communities in your geographic area. Make a table like the one at the beginning of the chapter. Identify the places that are growing the fastest.

2 Probabilities with Playing Cards

Find a standard playing card deck (bridge deck) of 52 cards. Draw an array of the 52 cards similar to that found for dice in Example 4 of Lesson 7-5. Suppose a card is picked at random. Give the probability of each of the following events and explain how you found each answer.

a. The card is an ace.
b. The card is a diamond.
c. The card is the nine of hearts.
d. The card is a nine or a heart.

Make up three other questions of your own and answer them.

3 Angles of Chairs

To measure the angle between a chair leg and the floor, take the smallest of all the angles between the chair leg and lines on the floor drawn through the point of contact with the chair leg. Find ten chairs of different styles and measure the angles between their front legs and the floor. Then measure the angles between their back legs and the floor. Summarize your results.

Chapter 7 Projects

The projects relate to the content of the lessons of this chapter as follows:

Project	Lesson(s)
1	7-1, 7-2
2	7-5
3	7-6, 7-7
4	7-9
5	7-8
6	7-1, 7-3, 7-4

1 Population Changes Students can find census information in almanacs and in *The Statistical Abstract of the United States*. Depending on your geographic area, students may or may not find the data they are looking for in these books. They may need to contact a Government Depository Library; each state has at least one located at the state's capitol. These libraries receive information published by federal agencies. A local library may be able to obtain this information for the students. Students may also get census information by contacting their local town or county office. Once the necessary information has been located, you may want students to offer possible explanations for the population changes that have occurred in their area.

2 Probability with Playing Cards Students with an understanding of probability should have no trouble answering questions a – c. For question d, if students need help getting started, suggest they begin by determining the probability of drawing a nine and then a heart. $[\frac{4}{52}, \frac{13}{52}]$ Explain that these probabilities must be added to predict the final outcome. Ask students to identify any overlap of these two events. [the nine of hearts] Remind students that since this particular outcome has been counted twice, the probability of drawing a single card must be subtracted from the sum of the two probabilities. You may wish to compile the questions the students have written and use them for a class discussion or as an oral assessment.

3 Angles of Chairs Students will need to use protractors to complete this project. Suggest that students make a table for all the information they gather. The table should give a description of the chair as well as the angles of the front and

Possible responses
1. Responses will vary.
2. a. $\frac{4}{52}$ or $\frac{1}{13}$
   b. $\frac{13}{52}$ or $\frac{1}{4}$
   c. $\frac{1}{52}$
   d. $\frac{4}{52} + \frac{13}{52} - \frac{1}{52} = \frac{16}{52}$ or $\frac{4}{13}$
   Responses will vary for students' questions. Samples are given. Give the probability that a card picked at random:
   will be a club or spade, $\frac{26}{52}$ or $\frac{1}{2}$;
   will be a diamond or a queen, $\frac{13}{52} + \frac{4}{52} - \frac{1}{52} = \frac{16}{52}$ or $\frac{4}{13}$;
   will not be a heart, $\frac{39}{52}$ or $\frac{3}{4}$.
3. Responses will vary. In general, most students will find that the angle the front leg of a chair makes with the floor is usually the same as the angle the back leg makes with the floor. These angles may vary between 45° and 90°.

back legs. This will make summarizing their results easier.

4 **A Large Triangle** The key to success in this project is to have students clearly mark and pinpoint the vertices of the triangle. When the vertices are not specific, the measure of the angles may change due to the changing perspective of the viewer. For example, suggest that students pick a specific point on a rooftop, such as the top of a TV antennae, as a vertex.

5 **Automatic Drawing Programs** *The Geometric Supposer* requires that students dictate the lengths of the sides of the quadrilateral. It is compatible with the Apple or IBM computer. *The Geometer's Sketchpad* does not have pre-programmed quadrilaterals for the students to choose from. It is MacIntosh compatible. *GeoExplorer* will automatically construct parallelograms, rectangles, rhombuses, squares, and trapezoids. This program is available through ScottForesman, and is MacIntosh, IBM, and Apple compatible. *Cabri-Geometer* is a French drawing tool that is MacIntosh compatible. There are no pre-programmed quadrilaterals for the students to choose from.

6 **When** *x − y* **Is Small** Here are some general hints that you may wish to give students having difficulty getting started with this project. Tell students that the denominators of the subtrahend and minuend, in lowest terms, are factors of the denominator of the difference and they are not factors of each other.

4 **A Large Triangle**
What is the sum of the measures of the angles in a very large triangle? Pick three points outdoors that are at least 20 meters apart. These points will be the vertices of your triangle. Sight each point from the other two, and, as accurately as you can, measure the angles of the triangle determined by the three points. Add the measures to see what you get. Then repeat this process with another very large triangle.

5 **Automatic Drawing Programs**
There is computer software that will draw geometric figures of various kinds. Among this software are *GeoExplorer, Cabri, The Geometer's Sketchpad,* and *The Geometric Supposer.* Learn how to use this software to draw the various special quadrilaterals of Lesson 7-8. Print out examples of what you have drawn, and explain what you had to do in order to instruct the computer to draw the figures.

6 **When** *x − y* **Is Small**
Suppose $x - y = z$ and z is a small positive fraction, say $z = \frac{1}{100}$. What fractions could x and y be?
a. Find a pair of fractions (in lowest terms) whose denominators are not 100, but whose difference is $\frac{1}{100}$.
b. Then find a pair of fractions (in lowest terms) whose denominators are not 1000, but whose difference is $\frac{1}{1000}$.
c. Then find a pair of fractions (in lowest terms) whose denominators are not 10,000, but whose difference is $\frac{1}{10,000}$.
d. Explain how you could continue this process and get fractions that are closer to each other than any number someone might give.

4. The sum of the angles of a triangle, no matter what the size of the triangle, is always 180°.
5. Responses will vary.
6. Sample responses:
   a. $\frac{1}{4} - \frac{6}{25} = \frac{1}{100}$
   b. $\frac{1}{8} - \frac{31}{250} = \frac{1}{10000}$
   c. $\frac{1}{16} - \frac{39}{625} = \frac{1}{10000}$
   d. The general pattern,
   $\frac{1}{2^n} - (\frac{1}{2^n} - \frac{1}{10^n}) = \frac{1}{10^n}$ where n

represents the number of zeros in the desired difference, can be used to find fractions that are close together. Accept any explanation students can justify from the observations they make.

SUMMARY

Subtraction can arise from take-away, slide, comparison, or overlap situations. In take-away situations, $x - y$ stands for the amount left after y has been taken away from x. In the linear pair below, $m\angle BDA$ can be thought of as the amount left after x is taken from 180°. So $m\angle BDA = 180° - x°$.
Measures of linear pairs add to 180°. The angles are supplementary.

In comparison situations, $x - y$ is how much more x is than y. The word *difference* for the answer comes from this kind of subtraction.

In slide situations, $x - y$ is the result after x has been decreased by y. Earlier this was described as an addition slide situation $x + -y$. Consequently $x - y = x + -y$ always.

Overlap situations arise when two sets have elements in common. This can be pictured by a Venn diagram.

If a quantity x is put together with a quantity y with overlap z, the result is the quantity $x + y - z$.

All of these situations can lead to equations that simplify to $x - a = b$ or $a - x = b$.

Another situation that can lead to equations involving subtraction is the Triangle-Sum Property: In any triangle, the sum of the measures of the angles is 180°.

Two intersecting lines, like $\overleftrightarrow{AB}$ and $\overleftrightarrow{AD}$ below, form two pairs of vertical angles. Adding the line $\overleftrightarrow{DC}$ parallel to $\overleftrightarrow{AB}$ forms eight angles. Adding the line $\overleftrightarrow{BC}$ parallel to $\overleftrightarrow{AD}$ forms the parallelogram $ABCD$. Each of the angles formed has measure $x°$ or $180° - x°$. Special kinds of parallelograms are rectangles, rhombuses, and squares, so these ideas have many uses.

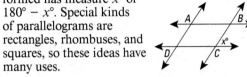

VOCABULARY

You should be able to give a general description and a specific example of each of the following ideas.

Lesson 7-1
Take-Away Model for Subtraction
minuend, subtrahend, difference
Comparison Model for Subtraction

Lesson 7-2
Slide Model for Subtraction
Algebraic Definition (Add-Opp Property) of Subtraction

Lesson 7-4
equivalent equations
equivalent formulas

Lesson 7-5
Venn diagram
Putting-Together with Overlap

Lesson 7-6
straight angle, opposite rays
linear pair, vertical angles
supplementary angles
complementary angles

Lesson 7-7
parallel lines, transversal
corresponding angles, //, ⊥
interior angles, exterior angles
alternate interior angles
alternate exterior angles

Lesson 7-8
parallelogram
opposite angles, opposite sides
rectangle, rhombus, square

Lesson 7-9
Triangle-Sum Property

Chapter 7 *Summary and Vocabulary* **401**

Summary

The Summary gives an overview of the entire chapter and provides an opportunity for students to consider the material as a whole. Thus, the Summary can be used to help students relate and unify the concepts presented in the chapter.

Vocabulary

Terms, symbols, and properties are listed by lesson to provide a checklist of concepts a student must know. Emphasize to students that they should read the vocabulary list carefully before starting the Progress Self-Test. If students do not understand the meaning of a term, they should refer back to the indicated lesson.

Progress Self-Test

For the development of mathematical competence, feedback and correction, along with the opportunity to practice, are necessary. The Progress Self-Test provides the opportunity for feedback and correction; the Chapter Review provides additional opportunities and practice. We cannot overemphasize the importance of these end-of-chapter materials. It is at this point that the material "gels" for many students, allowing them to solidify skills and understanding. In general, student performance should be markedly improved after these pages.

Assign the Progress Self-Test as a one-night assignment. Worked-out *solutions* for all questions are in the Selected Answers section of the student book. Encourage students to take the Progress Self-Test honestly, grade themselves, and then be prepared to discuss the test in class.

Advise students to pay special attention to those Chapter Review questions (pages 403–405) which correspond to questions missed on the Progress Self-Test.

PROGRESS SELF-TEST

Take this test as you would take a test in class. Then check your work with the solutions in the Selected Answers section in the back of the book.

1. Simplify $5 - (-5)$. **10**

2. Picture the subtraction $-6 - 22$ on a number line and give the result. **-28**

   See below for number line.

3. Simplify $\frac{3}{4} - \frac{5}{6}$. **$-\frac{1}{12}$**

4. Evaluate $5 - x + 2 - y$ when $x = 13$ and $y = -11$. **5**

5. Convert all subtractions to additions: $x - y - 5$. **$x + -y + 5$**

6. Valleyview H.S. scored V points against Newtown H.S. Newtown scored N points and lost by L points. How are V, N, and L related? **$V - N = L$, $V = N + L$, or $V - L = N$.**

7. Ray is Z inches tall. Fay is 67 inches tall. How much taller is Ray than Fay? **$Z - 67$ in.**

8. The outer square is 8 meters on a side. The inner square is 4 meters on a side. Find the area of the shaded region. **48 m²**

9. After dropping 7°, the temperature is now -3°.
   a. Solving what equation will tell you what the temperature was before it dropped?
   b. Solve that equation. **a) $t° - 7° = -3°$**
      b) $t = 4°$

In 10–12, solve.

10. $y - 14 = -24$ **$y = -10$**

11. $-50 = 37 - x$ **$x = 87$**

12. $g - 3.2 = -2$ **$g = 1.2$**

13. Solve for a: $c - a = b$. **$c + -b = a$**

14. *Multiple choice.* Which formula is not equivalent to the others?
    (a) $180 = x + y$ (b) $180 - y = x$
    (c) $x - y = 180$ (d) $180 - x = y$ **(c)**

15. Suppose 50 people are drinking coffee on an airplane. If 15 drink it black (with nothing added), 25 add cream, and 20 add sugar, how many drink it with both cream and sugar? **10**

In 16 and 17, use the figure at the right, in which $m\angle ABD = 25°$.

16. $m\angle CBD =$ __?__ **65°**

17. $m\angle ABE =$ __?__ **155° or 205°**

In 18–20, use the figure below. $m \parallel n$

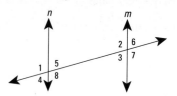

18. If $m\angle 5 = 74°$, then $m\angle 2 =$ __?__ °. **106°**

19. Which angles have measures equal to the measure of angle 6? **$\angle 5$, $\angle 3$, and $\angle 4$**

20. Which angles are supplementary to angle 5? **20) $\angle 7$, $\angle 8$, $\angle 1$, $\angle 2$**

21. Two angles of a triangle have measures 55° and 4°. What is the measure of the third angle? **121°**

22. Why can't a triangle have three right angles?

23. What other angle in the figure below has the same measure as angle E? **$\angle CBE$** 22) See below.

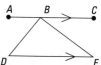

24. In parallelogram $WXYZ$, if $m\angle W = 50°$, what is $m\angle X$? **130°**

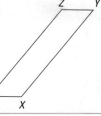

22) The sum of the angle measures would be 270°. By the Triangle Sum Property, the sum must be 180°.

25. Of parallelograms, rectangles, rhombuses, and quadrilaterals, which have all sides equal in length? **rhombuses**

2)
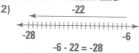
$-6 - 22 = -28$

CHAPTER REVIEW

Questions on SPUR Objectives

SPUR stands for **S**kills, **P**roperties, **U**ses, and **R**epresentations. The Chapter Review questions are grouped according to the SPUR Objectives for this chapter.

SKILLS DEAL WITH THE PROCEDURES USED TO GET ANSWERS.

Objective A: *Subtract any numbers written as decimals or fractions.* *(Lesson 7-2)*

In 1–6, simplify.

1. $-14 - 14$ -28
2. $\frac{1}{2} - \frac{5}{2}$ -2
3. $8.6 - 9.3$ -0.7
4. $-9 - -2$ -7
5. $\frac{2}{3} - (-\frac{4}{5})$ $\frac{22}{15}$ or $1\frac{7}{15}$
6. $11 - (-10)$ 21
7. Evaluate $x - y - z$ when $x = 10.5$, $y = 3.8$, and $z = -7$. 13.7
8. Evaluate $a - (b - c)$ when $a = -2$, $b = -3$, and $c = \frac{1}{4}$. $1\frac{1}{4}$ or 1.25

Objective B: *Solve sentences of the form $x - a = b$ and $a - x = b$.* *(Lessons 7-3, 7-4)*

In 9–16, solve.

9. $x - 64 = 8$ $x = 72$
10. $6 = y - \frac{1}{5}$ $y = 6\frac{1}{5}$ or $y = 6.2$
11. $-4.2 = V - -3$ $V = -7.2$
12. $2 + m - 5 = 4$ $m = 7$
13. $200 - b = 3$ $b = 197$
14. $-28 = 28 - z$ $z = 56$
15. $223 - x = 215$ $x = 8$
16. $\frac{4}{9} - y = \frac{5}{18}$ $y = \frac{1}{6}$
17. Solve for c: $e = c - 45$. $c = e + 45$
18. Solve for y: $180 - y = x$. $y = 180 - x$

Objective C: *Find measures of angles in figures with linear pairs, vertical angles, or perpendicular lines.* *(Lesson 7-6)*

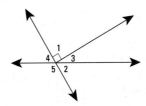

In 19–22, use the figure above to determine the measures.

19. $m\angle 1 = \underline{\ ?\ }$ degrees 90
20. If $m\angle 2 = 60°$, then $m\angle 4 = \underline{\ ?\ }$. 60°
21. If $m\angle 4 = x°$, $m\angle 5 = \underline{\ ?\ }$. $180° - x°$
22. If $m\angle 5 = 125°$, then $m\angle 3 = \underline{\ ?\ }$. 35°

Objective D: *Find measures of angles in figures with parallel lines and transversals.* *(Lesson 7-7)*

In 23–26, use the figure below.

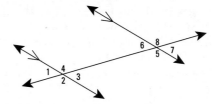

23. Which angles have the same measure as $\angle 6$?
24. If $m\angle 3 = 43°$, then $m\angle 7 = \underline{\ ?\ }$. 43°
25. If $m\angle 2 = y°$, then $m\angle 7 = \underline{\ ?\ }$. $180° - y°$
26. If $m\angle 8 = 135°$, then $m\angle 1 = \underline{\ ?\ }$. 45°
    23) $\angle 7$, $\angle 1$, and $\angle 3$

Chapter 7   *Chapter Review*   **403**

Chapter 7 Review

Resources

From the *Teacher's Resource File*
- Answer Master for Chapter 7 Review
- Assessment Sourcebook: Chapter 7 Test, Forms A–D Chapter 7 Test, Cumulative Form

Additional Resources
- TestWorks

The main objectives for the chapter are organized in the Chapter Review under the four types of understanding this book promotes—Skills, Properties, Uses, and Representations.

Whereas end-of chapter material may be considered optional in some texts, in *UCSMP Transition Mathematics* we have selected these objectives and questions with the expectation that they will be covered. Students should be able to answer these questions with about 85% accuracy after studying the chapter.

You may assign these questions over a single night to help students prepare for a test the next day, or you may assign the questions over a two-day period. If you work the questions over two days, then we recommend assigning the *evens* for homework the first night so that students get feedback in class the next day, then assigning the *odds* the night before the test, because answers are provided to the odd-numbered questions.

It is effective to ask students which questions they still do not understand and use the day or days as a total class discussion of the material which the class finds most difficult.

Objective E: *Use the Triangle-Sum Property to find measures of angles.* *(Lesson 7-9)*

In 27 and 28, use the figure below.

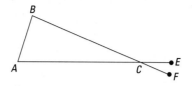

27. If $\overline{AB} \perp \overline{BC}$ and m∠ECF = 40°, find m∠A.
28. If $\overline{AB} \perp \overline{BC}$ and m∠A = 72°, find m∠ECB.
29. Two angles of a triangle measure 118° and 24°. What is the measure of the third angle? 27) 50°;   28) 162°;   29) 38°

30. Two angles of a triangle measure $y°$ and $150° - y°$. What is the measure of the third angle? 30°

Objective F: *Find measures of angles and sides in special quadrilaterals without measuring.* *(Lesson 7-8)*

31. A rhombus has one side of length 2.5 cm. Is this enough to find its perimeter? Yes, 10 cm
32. Each angle of a rectangle has measure ___?___.
33. In parallelogram *ABCD*, if *DC* = 4 and *BC* = 6, find *AB*. 4
34. In parallelogram *ABCD*, if m∠D = 105°, find m∠A. 75°
32) 90°

PROPERTIES DEAL WITH THE PRINCIPLES BEHIND THE MATHEMATICS.

Objective G: *Apply the properties of subtraction.* *(Lessons 7-2, 7-4)*

35. According to the Algebraic Definition of Subtraction, 7 − 3 = 7 + ___?___. -3
36. If 967 − 432 = 535, then 432 − 967 = ___?___.
37. Which sentence is not equivalent to the others? $a + c = b$
$a - c = b$ $a - b = c$ $a + c = b$ $b + c = a$
38. Which sentence is not equivalent to the others? $3 - 8 = x$
$x - 8 = 3$ $3 - 8 = x$ $-x + 3 = -8$ $-8 + x = 3$
36) -535

Objective H: *Know relationships among angles formed by intersecting lines, or by two parallel lines and a transversal.* *(Lessons 7-6, 7-7)*

39. Angles 1 and 2 form a linear pair. If m∠1 = 40°, what is m∠2? 140°
40. Angles 1 and 2 are vertical angles. If m∠1 = 40°, what is m∠2? 40°
41. Angles 1 and 2 are supplementary. If m∠1 = $x°$, what is m∠2? $180° - x°$

In 42–45, use the figure below.

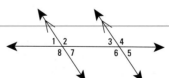

42. Angles 2 and ___?___ are corresponding angles. 4
43. Name the exterior angles. ∠1, ∠8, ∠4, ∠5
44. Angles 3 and ___?___ are alternate interior angles. 7
45. Name four angles supplementary to angle 8. ∠1, ∠7, ∠5, ∠3

Objective I: *Apply the definitions of parallelogram, rectangle, rhombus, and square to determine properties of these figures.* *(Lesson 7-8)*

In 46–49, consider parallelograms, rectangles, rhombuses, and squares.

46. In which of these figures are all sides equal in length? rhombuses and squares
47. In which of these figures are all angles equal in measure? rectangles and squares
48. In which of these figures are both pairs of opposite sides equal in length? all
49. In which of these figures are both pairs of opposite angles equal in measure? all

Objective J: *Explain consequences of the Triangle-Sum Property.* *(Lesson 7-9)*

50. Why can't a triangle have two 100° angles?
51. Can a triangle have three acute angles? Explain your answer.
50) The sum of those two angles would be 200°, which is larger than 180°.
51) Sample: Yes, angles could have measures 40°, 60°, and 80°, which add to 180°.

USES DEAL WITH APPLICATIONS OF MATHEMATICS IN REAL SITUATIONS.

Objective K: *Use the Take-Away Model for Subtraction to form sentences involving subtraction.* (Lessons 7-1, 7-3, 7-4)

52. A one-hour TV program allows $9\frac{1}{2}$ minutes for commercials. How much time is there for the program itself? **50.5 minutes**

53. A 2000 square-foot house was built on a lot of area A square feet. Landscaping used the remaining 3500 square feet. How big was the original lot? **5500 square feet**

54. Anne must keep $100 in a bank account. The account had x dollars in it. Then Anne withdrew y dollars. There was just enough left in the account. How are x, y, and 100 related? **$x - y = 100$**

55. On the line below, $AE = 50$, $BC = 12$, and $CE = 17$. What is AB? **21**

A   B   C D   E

Objective L: *Use the Slide Model for Subtraction to form sentences involving subtraction.* (Lessons 7-2, 7-3, 7-4)

56. O'Hare Airport in Chicago is often 5°F colder than downtown Chicago. Suppose the record low recorded downtown for a day is -13°F. What is the possible low temperature at O'Hare? **-18°F**

57. *Multiple choice.* A person weighs 70 kg and goes on a diet, losing x kg. The resulting weight is y kg. Then $y =$
    (a) $x - 70$.   (b) $70 - x$.
    (c) $x - \text{-}70$.   (d) $\text{-}70 - x$. **(b)**

58. Actor Michael Landon died in 1991 at age 55. When might he have been born? **1936 or 1935**

Objective M: *Use the Comparison Model for Subtraction to form sentences involving subtraction.* (Lessons 7-1, 7-3, 7-4)

59. The number of 16- to 19-year-olds working in 1960 was about 4.1 million. By 1987 the number was about 6.6 million. How many more teens were working in 1987?

60. Yvette believes that her team will win its next game by 12 points. But they lose by 1 point. How far off was Yvette? **13 points too high**

61. An airline fare of F dollars is reduced by R dollars. The lower fare is L dollars. How are F, R, and L related? **$F - R = L$**

59) **2.5 million**

Objective N: *Use the Putting-Together with Overlap Model to solve sentences involving subtraction.* (Lesson 7-5)

62. Of 12 hot dogs, 6 have catsup, 8 have mustard, and 5 have both catsup and mustard. How many hot dogs have neither catsup nor mustard? **3**

63. At International High, 80% of the students speak English. 90% of the students speak a language other than English. What percentage of students speak English and another language? **70%**

64. On a baseball team, 8 people can bat right-handed and 4 people can bat left-handed. Two players are "switch hitters" (can bat either right- or left-handed). How many people are on the team? **10**

REPRESENTATIONS DEAL WITH PICTURES, GRAPHS, OR OBJECTS THAT ILLUSTRATE CONCEPTS.

Objective O: *Picture subtraction of positive and negative numbers on a number line.* (Lesson 7-2)   **65–68) See margin.**

65. Picture the subtraction $\text{-}5 - 3$ on a number line and give the result.

66. Picture the subtraction $8 - 10$ on a number line and give the result.

Objective P: *Use Venn diagrams to describe or determine overlap.* (Lesson 7-5)

In 67 and 68, draw Venn diagrams.

67. 37 people are in the orchestra, 32 are in choir, and 12 are in both.

68. Suppose out of all car owners in a given place, 60% own American-made cars and 50% own foreign cars.

Assessment

Evaluation The *Assessment Sourcebook* provides five forms of the Chapter 7 Test. Forms A and B present parallel versions in a short-answer format. Forms C and D offer performance assessment. The fifth test is Chapter 7 Test, Cumulative Form. About 50% of this test covers Chapter 7, 25% of it covers Chapter 6, and 25% of it covers earlier chapters.

For information on grading, see *General Teaching Suggestions: Grading,* in the *Professional Sourcebook* which begins on page T21 in Volume 1 of this Teacher's Edition.

Additional Answers

65.

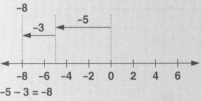

$-5 - 3 = -8$

66.

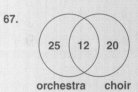

$8 - 10 = -2$

67.

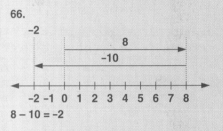

orchestra   choir

68.

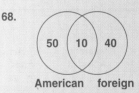

American   foreign

Setting Up Lesson 8-1

Materials Students will need graphs from newspapers or magazines for **Question 26** in Lesson 8-1. They will need an almanac for the *Extension*.

405

Chapter 8 Planner

Adapting to Individual Needs

The student text is written for the vast majority of students. The chart at the right suggests two pacing plans to accommodate the needs of your students. Students in the Full Course should complete the entire text by the end of the year. Students in the Minimal Course will spend more time when there are quizzes and more time on the Chapter Review. Therefore, these students may not complete all of the chapters in the text.

Options are also presented to meet the needs of a variety of teaching and learning styles. For each lesson, the Teacher's Edition provides sections entitled: *Video* which describes video segments and related questions that can be used for motivation or extension; *Optional Activities* which suggests activities that employ materials, physical models, technology, and cooperative learning; and *Adapting to Individual Needs* which regularly includes **Challenge** problems, **English Language Development** suggestions, and suggestions for providing **Extra Help.** The Teacher's Edition also frequently includes an **Error Alert,** an **Extension,** and an **Assessment** alternative. The options available in Chapter 8 are summarized in the chart below.

Chapter 8 Pacing Chart

Day	Full Course	Minimal Course
1	8-1	8-1
2	8-2	8-2
3	8-3	8-3
4	Quiz*; 8-4	Quiz*; begin 8-4.
5	8-5	Finish 8-4.
6	8-6	8-5
7	Quiz*; 8-7	8-6
8	8-8	Quiz*; begin 8-7.
9	Self-Test	Finish 8-7.
10	Review	8-8
11	Test*	Self-Test
12		Review
13		Review
14		Test*

*in the Teacher's Resource File

In the Teacher's Edition...

Lesson	Optional Activities	Extra Help	Challenge	English Language Development	Error Alert	Extension	Cooperative Learning	Ongoing Assessment
8-1	●	●	●	●		●	●	Oral/Written
8-2	●	●	●	●		●	●	Group
8-3	●	●	●	●		●		Oral
8-4	●	●	●	●	●	●	●	Written
8-5	●	●	●	●	●		●	Group
8-6	●	●	●	●		●		Oral
8-7	●	●	●	●	●	●	●	Written
8-8	●	●	●	●		●		Oral

In the Additional Resources...

	In the Teacher's Resource File								
Lesson	Lesson Masters, A and B	Teaching Aids*	Activity Kit*	Answer Masters	Technology Sourcebook	Assessment Sourcebook	Visual Aids**	Technology Tools	Video Segments
8-1	8-1	81, 84		8-1			81, 84, AM		Segment 8
8-2	8-2	81, 85, 86		8-2	Demo 8, Comp 14		81, 85, 86, AM	Graphing/Probability	
8-3	8-3	81, 87		8-3	Comp 15	Quiz	81, 87, AM	Graphing/Probability	
8-4	8-4	82, 87, 88	19	8-4	Comp 16, Calc 10		82, 87, 88, AM	Graphing/Probability	
In-class Activity		86, 89					86, 89, AM	Geometry	
8-5	8-5	82, 87, 90		8-5			82, 87, 90, AM		
8-6	8-6	82, 87, 91, 92		8-6	Comp 17	Quiz	82, 87, 91, 92, AM	Geometry	
8-7	8-7	83, 93, 94	20	8-7	Comp 18		83, 93, 94, AM	Geometry	
8-8	8-8	83, 95	21	8-8			83, 95, AM		
End of chapter		96		Review		Tests			

*Teaching Aids, except Warm-ups, are pictured on pages 406C and 406D. The activities in the Activity Kit are pictured on page 406C.
Teaching Aid 89 which accompanies the In-class Activity is pictured with the lesson notes on page 434.
Teaching Aid 96 which accompanies Project 6 is pictured on page 406D.

**Visual Aids provide transparencies for all Teaching Aids and all Answer Masters.

Also available is the Study Skills Handbook which includes study-skill tips related to reading, note-taking, and comprehension.

Integrating Strands and Applications

	8-1	8-2	8-3	8-4	8-5	8-6	8-7	8-8
Mathematical Connections								
Number Sense	●	●						
Algebra	●		●	●	●	●	●	●
Geometry	●	●	●	●	●	●	●	●
Measurement			●	●	●	●		
Statistics/Data Analysis	●	●	●	●	●	●	●	
Patterns and Functions				●	●	●		
Interdisciplinary and Other Connections								
Art					●	●	●	●
Literature	●							
Science	●	●	●	●	●	●	●	●
Social Studies	●	●	●	●	●	●	●	●
Multicultural		●					●	●
Technology		●	●	●		●	●	
Career					●			
Consumer			●	●				
Sports		●		●				

Take it to the NET

On the Internet, visit **www.phschool.com** for UCSMP teacher support, student self-tests, activities, and more.

Teaching and Assessing the Chapter Objectives

Chapter 8 Objectives (Organized into the SPUR categories—Skills, Properties, Uses, and Representations)	Lessons	Progress Self-Test Questions	Chapter Review Questions	Chapter Test, Forms A and B	Chapter Test, Forms C	Chapter Test, Forms D
Skills						
A: Determine the median, range, and mode of a set of numbers.	8-1	23	1–4	5	1	
B: Draw the reflection image of a figure over a line.	8-6	16	5–8	16	4	
C: Given a figure, identify its symmetry lines.	8-7	13–15	9–12	14	4	✓
D: Make a tessellation using a given figure as a fundamental region.	8-8	17	13, 14	15		✓
Properties						
E: Apply the relationships between figures and their reflection, rotation, and translation images.	8-5, 8-6	21	15–18	7, 20		✓
Uses						
F: Interpret and display information in bar graphs.	8-2	1–5	19–25	2, 3, 6	2	
G: Interpret and display information in coordinate graphs.	8-3	18	26–31	8–10, 13	2	
H: Know reasons for having graphs.	8-1	20	32, 33	1	2	
I: Represent numerical data in a stem-and-leaf display	8-1	22	34, 35	4	1	
Representations						
J: Plot and name points on a coordinate graph.	8-3, 8-4	6–9, 11, 12	36–39	11	3	
K: Graph equations for lines of the form $x + y = k$ or $x - y = k$.	8-4	10	40–43	12	3	
L: Interpret reflections and translations on a coordinate graph.	8-5, 8-6	19	44–47	17–19	5	

Assessment Sourcebook
Quiz for Lessons 8-1 through 8-3
Quiz for Lessons 8-4 through 8-6
Chapter 8 Test, Forms A–D
Chapter 8 Test, Cumulative Form

TestWorks
Multiple forms of chapter tests and quizzes; Challenge items

Activity Kit

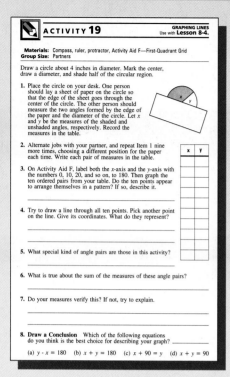
Materials: Compass, ruler, protractor, Activity Aid F—First-Quadrant Grid
Group Size: Partners

Draw a circle about 4 inches in diameter. Mark the center, draw a diameter, and shade half of the circular region.

1. Place the circle on your desk. One person should lay a sheet of paper on the circle so that the edge of the sheet goes through the center of the circle. The other person should measure the two angles formed by the edge of the paper and the diameter of the circle. Let x and y be the measures of the shaded and unshaded angles, respectively. Record the measures in the table.

2. Alternate jobs with your partner, and repeat Item 1 nine more times, choosing a different position for the paper each time. Write each pair of measures in the table.

3. On Activity Aid F, label both the x-axis and the y-axis with the numbers 0, 10, 20, and so on, to 180. Then graph the ten ordered pairs from your table. Do the ten points appear to arrange themselves in a pattern? If so, describe it.

4. Try to draw a line through all ten points. Pick another point on the line. Give its coordinates. What do they represent?

5. What special kind of angle pairs are those in this activity?

6. What is true about the sum of the measures of these angle pairs?

7. Do your measures verify this? If not, try to explain.

8. **Draw a Conclusion** Which of the following equations do you think is the best choice for describing your graph? _____

(a) $y - x = 180$ (b) $x + y = 180$ (c) $x + 90 = y$ (d) $x + y = 90$

x	y

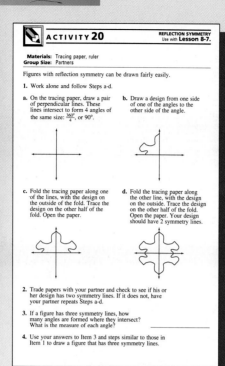
Materials: Tracing paper, ruler
Group Size: Partners

Figures with reflection symmetry can be drawn fairly easily.

1. Work alone and follow Steps a-d.

a. On the tracing paper, draw a pair of perpendicular lines. These lines intersect to form 4 angles of the same size: $\frac{360°}{4}$, or 90°.

b. Draw a design from one side of one of the angles to the other side of the angle.

c. Fold the tracing paper along one of the lines, with the design on the outside of the fold. Trace the design on the other half of the fold. Open the paper.

d. Fold the tracing paper along the other line, with the design on the outside. Trace the design on the other half of the fold. Open the paper. Your design should have 2 symmetry lines.

2. Trade papers with your partner and check to see if his or her design has two symmetry lines. If it does not, have your partner repeats Steps a-d.

3. If a figure has three symmetry lines, how many angles are formed where they intersect? What is the measure of each angle? _____

4. Use your answers to Item 3 and steps similar to those in Item 1 to draw a figure that has three symmetry lines.

Materials: Tracing paper, pin
Group Size: Individuals

1. Carefully trace the outline of one of the white birds in the tessellation above. Leave the tracing in place over the white bird.

2. Can you *slide* your tracing to fit over

a gray bird? _____   a white bird? _____

3. Place the tracing over one of the white birds whose tail contains point A. Push the pin through both sheets of paper at point A.

Can you *rotate* the tracing around point A onto

a gray bird? _____   a white bird? _____

4. Find the label point B, not on the tails, around which a white bird can be rotated onto either another white bird or a gray bird.

5. Find and label point C, around which a white bird can be rotated onto another white bird but *not* onto a gray bird.

Teaching Aids

Warm-up
Lesson 8-1

The following numbers of students were absent from class during the past two weeks.

3, 4, 0, 1, 5, 1, 0, 3, 1, 4

Find the mean, median, and mode of this set of data.

Warm-up
Lesson 8-2

Use the bar graph in Example 1 on page 416.

1. What can you learn from the graph?
2. Who might be interested in this information and why?
3. What are the advantages of having this information in graph form?

Warm-up
Lesson 8-3

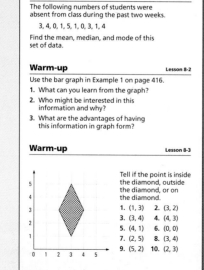

Tell if the point is inside the diamond, outside the diamond, or on the diamond.

1. (1, 3)   2. (3, 2)
3. (3, 4)   4. (4, 3)
5. (4, 1)   6. (0, 0)
7. (2, 5)   8. (3, 4)
9. (5, 2)   10. (2, 3)

Warm-up
Lesson 8-4

Name 5 ordered pairs that satisfy the equation.

1. $x + y = 6$
2. $x - y = 9$
3. $y - x = -2$

Warm-up
Lesson 8-5

1. Graph the triangle with vertices $A = (1, 1)$, $B = (2, 4)$, and $C = (5, 1)$.
2. Add -6 to each x-coordinate and -3 to each y-coordinate. Give the new coordinates.
3. Graph the new triangle.
4. Explain what happened.

Warm-up
Lesson 8-6

Draw any point P. Fold your paper in any way you want, but do not fold it on the point itself. Open the paper and locate the image of P on the other side of the fold line ℓ. Label the image point P'. Give two different ways to locate P'.

Warm-up
Lesson 8-7

Draw the reflection image of the letter A over each line.

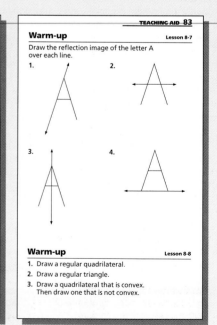

Warm-up
Lesson 8-8

1. Draw a regular quadrilateral.
2. Draw a regular triangle.
3. Draw a quadrilateral that is convex. Then draw one that is not convex.

Additional Examples

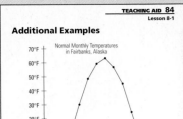

Normal Monthly Temperatures in Fairbanks, Alaska

1. a. What does the graph describe?
   b. What does the horizontal scale represent?
   c. What does the vertical scale represent?
   d. What trend is shown by the graph?
2. The following list gives the ages, at the times of their inaugurations, of all of the presidents of the United States from Theodore Roosevelt to Bill Clinton.
   42, 51, 56, 55, 51, 54, 51, 60, 62, 43, 55, 56, 61, 52, 69, 64, 46
   a. Put this information into a stem-and-leaf display.
   b. Give one feature of this information.
3. Give the range, median, and mode for the data in Example 2.

Additional Examples

1. The following table, from the Urban Institute, gives the number of immigrants who came into the United States by decades. Display the information in a bar graph.

Decade	Number of Immigrants
1910s	5,800,000
1920s	4,100,000
1930s	500,000
1940s	1,000,000
1950s	2,500,000
1960s	3,800,000
1970s	7,000,000
1980s	9,500,000

2. In the book *Dictionary of First Names*, by Alfred J. Kolatch (New York: Perigee Books, 1980), the following numbers of pages are devoted to boys' and girls' names that begin with vowels.

Vowel	A	E	I	O	U
Boys	26	15	4	7	2
Girls	21	10	5	4	2

a. Display this information in a double bar graph.
b. What conclusions can you draw from this information?

Graph Paper

Four-Quadrant Graph Paper

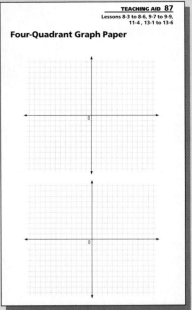

Graphing Equations

Equation: _____

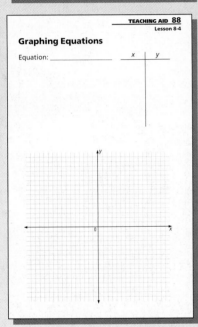

Translation Images

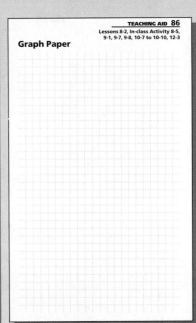

Additional Examples

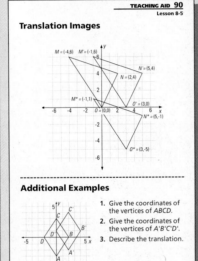

1. Give the coordinates of the vertices of ABCD.
2. Give the coordinates of the vertices of A'B'C'D'.
3. Describe the translation.

Reflection Images

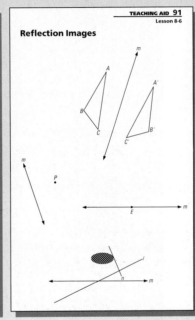

Additional Examples

1.   2.

3.

Questions 9-11

9.   10.

11.

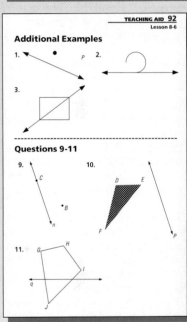

Activity 1

Activity 2

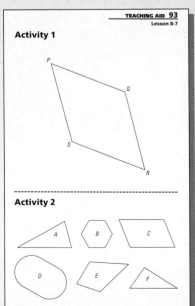

Questions 9-12, 18-19

9.   10.

11.   12.

18.

19.

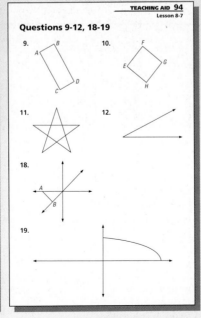

Activity

Questions 10-13

10.   11.

12.   13.

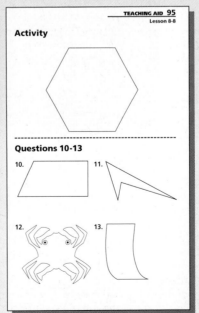

Project 6

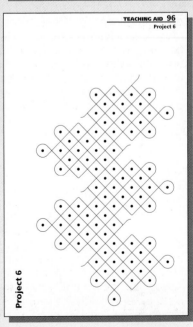

Chapter Opener

Pacing

All lessons in this chapter are designed to be covered in one day. We recommend spending 11–14 days on this chapter, which includes 1 day to review the Progress Self-Test, 1–2 days for the Chapter Review, and 1 day for a test.

Using Pages 406–465

This chapter has two themes. The first theme is the display of numerical information in stem-and-leaf displays (Lesson 8-1), bar graphs (Lesson 8-2), coordinate graphs in general (Lesson 8-3), and graphs of linear equations of the form $x + y = a$ or $x - y = a$ (Lesson 8-4).

The second theme involves transformations. We examine two types of transformations, translations (Lesson 8-5) and reflections (Lesson 8-6). Then reflections are related to reflection symmetry (Lesson 8-7) and translations are associated with tessellations—those repeating patterns that cover the plane (Lesson 8-8).

The topics in this chapter are both important and timely. Some understanding of basic statistical ideas is required for intelligent citizenship and an understanding of what is going on in the world. Stem-and-leaf displays are used by some statisticians to explore data. Bar graphs and coordinate graphs appear in daily newspapers and magazines. In mathematical terms, graphs of solutions to equations are fundamental in understanding relationships and underlie much of advanced mathematics. Transformations play a large part in computer graphics. They also

CHAPTER 8

8-1 Graphs and Other Displays

8-2 Bar Graphs

8-3 Coordinate Graphs

8-4 Graphing Lines

8-5 Translations (Slides)

8-6 Reflections

8-7 Reflection Symmetry

8-8 Tessellations

406

Chapter 8 Overview

A *display* is a presentation of information. The stem-and-leaf displays, bar graphs, and coordinate graphs students will see in the chapter, as well as tables and even prose, are types of displays. The two quotes, one from a famous Russian author and the other from a Chinese author, indicate the universality of the idea of a display. In the projects, we show a completely different type of display from the Tchokwe people of Africa.

To understand displays, students have to be able to "read" them, even if they are pictorial. Also, information can be presented in different types of displays. The bar graph on page 407 displays information that is found (in slightly more detail) in Example 2 of Lesson 8-1.

You may wish to tell students something about the history of the contents of this chapter and, in so doing, give an overview.

The ancient Greeks realized that numbers and operations could be represented geometrically. In the early 1600s, Pierre Fermat and René Descartes worked with coordinate graphs. In the 1790s, William Playfair was the first person to display information in circle graphs, and he was probably the first to use bar graphs. Stem-and-leaf displays were invented by John Tukey in the 1970s.

DISPLAYS

Everything that is visual is a *display* of some sort. Even a written word is a display of a thing, an idea, or a sound. A picture is a display that has been made by someone or something. Every culture has realized the value of pictures.

A picture shows me at a glance what it takes dozens of pages of a book to expound.
　　　　　　　　　—Ivan Turgenev, *Fathers and Sons*

One picture is worth more than a thousand words.
　　　　　　　　　—traditional Chinese proverb

Many people who study the learning of reading believe that the longer a sentence is, the more difficult it is to understand. Here is a display of the lengths of the first 36 sentences in the famous story *Alice's Adventures in Wonderland* by Lewis Carroll. From this information alone, do you think it would be easy or difficult to read this story?

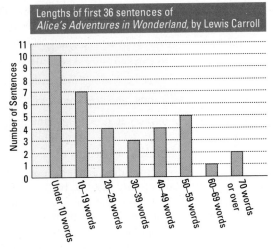

Displays in mathematics usually refer to diagrams, graphs, or tables. In this chapter, you will study stem-and-leaf displays, bar graphs, and coordinate graphs. In Lesson 8-1 you will see a stem-and-leaf display of the same data pictured in this bar graph.

help to explain the symmetry and tessellations which are common in both nature and art, and they themselves are important in geometry, higher algebra, and the study of functions.

Throughout this chapter, we encourage the use of technology that graphs data automatically.

Photo Connections

The photo collage makes real-world connections to the content of the chapter: transformations and ways to display data.

Kimono: Fabric designs often have patterns that are repeated. The Japanese kimono mimics the symmetry and tessellations that can be found in nature.

Forest with Reflection The shore line determines a line of reflection.

Graphs: Graphs can serve as pictures which show general tendencies of data; therefore, they can be used to make predictions.

Flower: In biology, symmetry is the repetition of the parts in a plant or animal in an orderly fashion. A symmetrical flower displays a correspondence of body parts distributed around a central point or axis.

Bees: A honeycomb shows a mass of six-sided compartments called cells, forming a near-perfect tessellation. One square inch (6.5 square centimeters) of a honeycomb has about 25 hexagonal cells.

Projects

At this time you might want to have students look over the projects on pages 458–459.

Transformations were used in the 1700s, but they were not systematized until the 1800s. In 1872, Felix Klein showed that all the geometries known at the time could be described in terms of transformations.

The work of Evariste Galois, about 200 years ago, led to the recognition of the mathematical importance of symmetry. Galois demonstrated that the existence of formulas for solving polynomial equations is related to the existence of certain symmetry groups.

Many cultures have used tilings. A high point was reached during the 1400s with the Moors and other Moslems who used tessellations in tilings. However, the mathematical study of tessellations began only about one hundred years ago.

All kinds of displays have increased in usage recently due to the increased power of computer graphics.

Objectives

A Determine the median, range, and mode of a set of numbers.
H Know reasons for having graphs.
I Represent numerical data in a stem-and-leaf display.

Resources

From the Teacher's Resource File
- Lesson Master 8-1A or 8-1B
- Answer Master 8-1
- Teaching Aids
  81 Warm-up
  84 Additional Examples

Additional Resources
- Visuals for Teaching Aids 81, 84
- A daily newspaper, such as *USA Today*, that contains graphs

Warm-up

Diagnostic The following numbers of students were absent from class during the past two weeks.
  3, 4, 0, 1, 5, 1, 0, 3, 1, 4
Find the mean, median, and mode of this set of data.
Mean 2.2; median 2; mode 1

Graphic illustration. *During his campaign for the U.S. Presidency in 1992, Ross Perot demonstrated how the use of graphs can enhance a presentation.*

Why Use a Graph?

When looking through a newspaper or magazine, you are likely to see graphs of many kinds. People use graphs to display information for many reasons. Here are four.

Graphs can show a great deal of information in a small space.

Graphs are sometimes easier to understand than tables or prose writing.

Graphs can show trends visually.

Graphs can be startling and can be used to sway a reader.

Reading a Graph

When reading a graph, you should follow certain steps to make sure you understand it. First, read the title of the graph and any descriptive text. Then study the scales, if any, to be sure you know what is being measured. Are the numbers in percents, millions, dollars, people, or some other unit? Where does the scale begin? Are the intervals on the scale uniform? All this information can help you decide the purpose of the graph.

Lesson 8-1 Overview

Broad Goals This lesson identifies some important reasons for having graphs and introduces a particular kind of display—the stem-and-leaf display.

Perspective Part of this lesson, which continues through Example 1, is meant to encourage student interest for the entire chapter. Lessons that tell students why they are studying things are as valuable as other kinds of lessons. We feel that if they know

why something is important, they will probably want to learn more about it.

The remainder of the lesson is devoted to stem-and-leaf displays. John Tukey, one of the leading statisticians in the United States over the past few decades, conceptualized the area of statistics known as *exploratory data analysis*. Stem-and leaf-displays are only one of many tools he created to explore data. We introduce stem-and-leaf

displays at this time because they have the advantage of making it easy to determine the median, mode, and range of data.

❶ Example 1

Examine the line graph below.
a. What does this graph describe?
b. What does the horizontal scale represent?
c. What does the vertical scale represent?
d. What trend is shown by the graph?

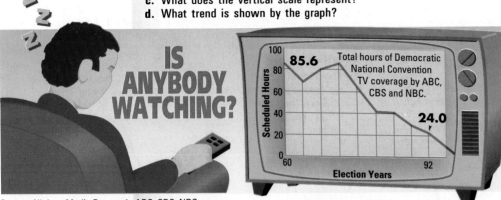

Source: Nielsen Media Research, ABC, CBS, NBC

Solution

a. This graph is about the amount of television coverage of the Democratic National Convention from 1960 to 1992.
b. The horizontal scale represents the years these conventions were held. It is divided into four-year intervals, since presidential elections occur every four years.
c. The vertical scale represents the total number of hours of television coverage by ABC, CBS, and NBC.
d. The amount of coverage has been decreasing.

Notice how the graph of Example 1 visually displays the decrease in television time for the Democratic National Convention. However, the artist has taken liberties with the graph. The graph drops off at the far right, almost to 0. But the graph has no data past 1992. This is a misleading aspect of the graph.

There is another important reason for using graphs and other displays. You can sometimes gain information from a display that would be difficult to see without it. One type of display that is used to explore data for patterns is called a *stem-and-leaf display*.

What Is a Stem-and-Leaf Display?

❷ A **stem-and-leaf display** begins with a set of numbers. First, each number is split between two specific decimal places. For instance, 135 might be split as 1|35 or 13|5. The digits to the left of the vertical line form the **stem**. The digits to the right form the **leaf**. The key to the display is that the stem is written only once, while the leaves are listed every time they appear. For instance, if both 135 and 136 appear and are split as 13|5 and 13|6, then you would write 13|5 6. If you made the split 1|35 and 1|36, then you would write 1|35 36.

Lesson 8-1 *Graphs and Other Displays* **409**

Notes on Reading

There are several terms in this lesson that students are expected to learn: *stem-and-leaf display, range, median, mode,* and *statistic.*

The word *display* used as a noun may be new to students. A display is anything that visually represents something. Students may not have ever realized that written words are visual displays of spoken sounds.

❶ Reading Mathematics Students naturally think that a graph is something to *look at.* They may not realize that a graph can be *read.* To emphasize this, ask these questions. What do the numbers '60 and '92 represent? [1960 and 1992] What does each square between 1960 and 1992 represent? [There are 8 squares and 32 years, so each square represents 4 years.] Estimate the number of hours of Democratic Convention TV time in each of these years. [1964, about 70; 1968, about 80; 1972, about 85; 1976, about 65; 1980, about 42; 1984, about 40; 1988, about 30] What does the broken line going down to the right indicate? [The amount of coverage is decreasing.] What do you think will happen in 1996? [Responses may vary. Some students may think that the declining trend will continue. Others may argue that it is already low and therefore it will go up.]

❷ You will want to go through the discussion of stem-and-leaf displays in detail for some students. Be sure they understand what the numbers mean.

Video

Wide World of Mathematics The segment, *Graphs in the News,* presents different types of animated graphs from recent news reports. The segment provides a basis to launch a discussion on the importance of using graphs and on the type that is most effective in a given situation. Related questions and an investigation are provided in videodisc stills and in the Video Guide. A related CD-ROM activity is also available.

Videodisc Bar Codes

Search Chapter 39

Play

③ Point out that if the regions behind the numerals in the stem-and-leaf display are shaded, a bar graph similar to the one on page 407 would be formed. This connection with the bar graphs, which will be considered in the next lesson, provides another reason for placing stem-and-leaf displays here.

Literature Connection Lewis Carroll's *Alice's Adventures in Wonderland* has been translated into more than 30 languages and into Braille. You might ask if any students have read the book in a language other than English. You might also mention that Carroll wrote many mathematics books under his given name, Charles Lutwidge Dodgson.

(Alice) was looking about for some way of escape, and wondering whether she could get away without being seen, when she noticed a curious appearance in the air; it puzzled her very much at first, but after watching it a minute or two she made it out to be a grin, and she said to herself, "It's the Cheshire Cat; now I shall have somebody to talk to."

. . . from Alice's Adventures in Wonderland, *by Lewis Carroll*

Example 2

The number of words in the first 36 sentences in *Alice's Adventures in Wonderland* (popularly known as *Alice in Wonderland*), by Lewis Carroll, are as follows: 57, 55, 139, 21, 43, 34, 52, 55, 5, 13, 8, 17, 5, 3, 21, 11, 100, 14, 15, 40, 30, 25, 3, 12, 9, 4, 10, 3, 8, 23, 7, 52, 61, 43, 37, 40.
a. Describe this set of numbers with a stem-and-leaf display.
b. What does the display show?

Solution

a. The natural place to split the numbers is between the units place and the tens place. Think of a one-digit number as having a tens digit of 0. Since the largest number is 139, which will be split as 13|9, the largest possible stem is 13. List the possible stems in a vertical column.

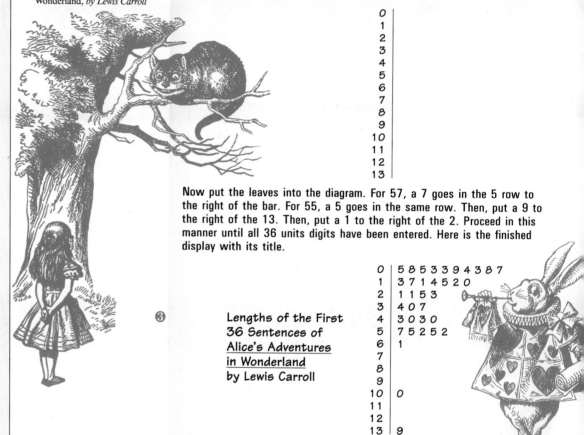

Now put the leaves into the diagram. For 57, a 7 goes in the 5 row to the right of the bar. For 55, a 5 goes in the same row. Then, put a 9 to the right of the 13. Then, put a 1 to the right of the 2. Proceed in this manner until all 36 units digits have been entered. Here is the finished display with its title.

Lengths of the First 36 Sentences of <u>Alice's Adventures in Wonderland</u> by Lewis Carroll

```
0  | 5 8 5 3 3 9 4 3 8 7
1  | 3 7 1 4 5 2 0
2  | 1 1 5 3
3  | 4 0 7
4  | 3 0 3 0
5  | 7 5 2 5 2
6  | 1
7  |
8  |
9  |
10 | 0
11 |
12 |
13 | 9
```

b. The display shows that shorter sentences are more common. There are 10 sentences with fewer than 10 words. However, there are 14 sentences with more than 30 words. The sentence with 139 words is much longer than any other sentence, though there is another with 100 words.

410

Optional Activities

Activity 1 After discussing stem-and-leaf displays in **Example 2**, you might want to use the data at the right, and show students how to make a *back-to-back* stem-and-leaf display. Then have students **work in groups**, research information suitable for a back-to-back stem-and-leaf display, and make the display. Some topics students might research are high and low temperatures, adult and student attendance at events, and grades on two different tests.

Heights (in inches) of the intramural basketball team members:
Boys: 62, 54, 67, 72, 69, 63, 55, 67, 70
Girls: 63, 52, 50, 57, 49, 60, 64, 61

Girls		Boys
9	4	
7 2 0	5	4 5
4 3 1 0	6	2 3 7 7 9
	7	0 2

Stem-and-leaf displays were developed in the 1970s by John Tukey, a professor of statistics at Princeton University. Because of its newness, and because this kind of display is used to explore data, it is not used often to report data. So stem-and-leaf displays are rarely used in newspapers or magazines. But they are helpful in the study of some numerical information.

Why Is a Stem-and-Leaf Display Useful?

Notice that the stem-and-leaf display resembles the bar graph on page 407, turned 90° clockwise. But the stem-and-leaf display shows all the original values. So you can gather more information about the sentence lengths.

For instance, the **mode** of a collection of objects is the object that appears most often. The stem-and-leaf display shows three 3s by the stem 0. No other leaf appears as often in a single stem, so the mode is 3. More of these sentences are 3 words long than any other length.

From the stem-and-leaf display, you can also identify the **range** of the data. This is the difference of the highest and lowest numbers, 139 − 3, or 136. You can also identify the **median,** the middle number if the list were in numerical order. Since there are 36 numbers in all, the middle of the list lies between the 18th and 19th numbers. The 18th number in order is 21; the 19th number is 21. The median sentence length is also 21 words, the mean of the numbers 21 and 21. If there were an odd number of numbers in the list, the median would be the number in the middle and no mean is needed. The range, median, and mode are important *statistics*. A **statistic** is a number that is used to describe a set of numbers.

Example 3

A student scores 89, 72, 99, 93, and 81 on five tests. Give the range, median, and mode of this set of numbers.

Solution

The range is the difference of the largest and smallest numbers.

$$99 - 72 = 27$$

The range is 27.

The median is the middle number if the numbers are in numerical order. So order the numbers: 72, 81, 89, 93, 99. The middle number is 89, the median.

No number appears more often than the others. Therefore, This set of numbers has no mode.

Lesson 8-1 *Graphs and Other Displays* **411**

Additional Examples continue on page 412.

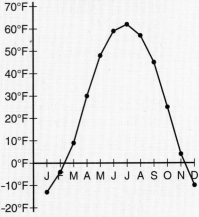
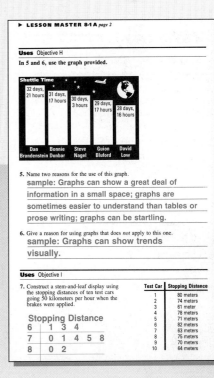

Activity 2 Real-World Graphs
Materials: Graphs from newspapers

After discussing the examples, you might want to give students more practice in reading graphs. Give each **group of students** several graphs. Ask questions about the graphs similar to those asked in **Example 1**.

411

2. The following list gives the ages, at the times of their inaugurations, of all the presidents of the United States from Theodore Roosevelt to Bill Clinton.

42, 51, 56, 55, 51, 54, 51,
60, 62, 43, 55, 56, 61,
52, 69, 64, 46

a. Put this information into a stem-and-leaf display.

```
4   2 3 6
5   1 6 5 1 4 1 5 6 2
6   0 2 1 9 4
```

b. Give one feature of this information. **Sample: Most presidents were in their 50s when they took office.**

3. Give the range, median, and mode for the data in *Additional Example 2*. **range, 27 years; median, 55 years; mode, 51 years**

1) Graphs can show a lot of information in a small space, are sometimes easier to understand than tables or prose writing, can show trends visually, and can be used to sway the reader.

8a)
```
 0 | 6 8 8
 1 | 1 1 4 2
 2 | 4 3 2
 3 | 4 7 0 7
 4 | 5 4 3 5
 5 | 5
 6 | 5
 7 |
 8 | 3 8
 9 |
10 | 8 2
11 | 9
```

QUESTIONS

Covering the Reading

1. Give four reasons for using graphs and other displays.

2. Name at least two steps to follow when reading a graph. **Read the title and descriptive text. Study the scales.**

3. What is a *statistic?* **a number that is used to describe a set of numbers**

In 4–7, use the graph of Example 1.

4. What are the missing values on the horizontal scale? **'64, '68, '72, '76, '80, '84, '88**

5. a. In what year was the most TV coverage of the Democratic National Convention? **1960 or 1972**

b. What was the amount of TV coverage in that year? **≈85 hours**

6. Explain the purpose of the graph. **Sample: to show the decreasing trend of television hours of coverage of a political national convention**

7. Which of the four reasons for graphing do you think apply to this graph? **Graphs can show trends visually.**

8. The next twenty-five sentences of *Alice's Adventures in Wonderland* have the following lengths: 45, 119, 34, 55, 11, 11, 24, 83, 23, 108, 44, 6, 8, 37, 43, 8, 30, 102, 22, 65, 14, 12, 37, 45, 88.

a. Make a stem-and-leaf display of these numbers.

b. What is the range of these numbers? **113**

c. What is the median? **37**

In 9 and 10, a collection of numbers is given.
a. Give the median.
b. Give the range.

9. 10, 9, 9, 10, 10, 7, 9, and 8; the numbers of lessons in the first eight chapters of this book **a) 9; b) 3**

10. 9,400; 6,900; 3,800; 17,300; 11,700; 3,300; 5,400; the areas (in thousands of square miles) of the seven continents **a) 6900; b) 14,000**

In 11–14, give the mode of each collection. (It is possible for a collection to have more than one mode.)

11. the collection of Question 8 **8, 11, 37, 45**

12. the collection of Question 9 **9, 10**

13. 1, 2, 2, 3, 2, 4, 2, 4, 3, 4; the numbers of integer factors of the numbers from one to ten **2**

14. the first 50 decimal places of π (See page 12.) **3 and 9 (bimodal)**

412

Adapting to Individual Needs

Extra Help

Before using **Example 2,** some students may benefit from reading a simple stem-and-leaf display. Give students the data on the right and show them the completed display. First discuss how to read the numbers. Then ask questions about the number of ages represented [7], the youngest and oldest ages [9 and 45 years], the range of the ages [45 − 9 = 36 years] and the middle (median) age [17 years].The ages of members of the Darnel family are 9, 12, 15, 17, 21, 42, and 45.

Stem	Leaf
0	9
1	2 5 7
2	1
3	
4	2 5

15. **a.** Put the information in the graph of Example 1 into a table.
    b. Which do you prefer, the graph or the table, and why?

In 16–18, use the graph below.

16. Give the interval on each scale. **vertical: 1% intervals;**
    horizontal: 4-year intervals
17. Estimate the percent of electoral votes California cast in 1960. **≈6%**

18. Why do you think the graph is on the arm of a strongman flexing his
    bicep? **Sample: The graph shows a clear upward trend, indicating that
    California is politically becoming stronger.**

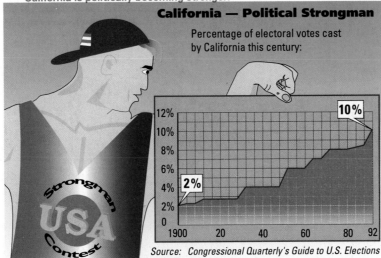

California — Political Strongman

Percentage of electoral votes cast
by California this century:

Source: Congressional Quarterly's Guide to U.S. Elections

Review

19. Given: m∠A = m∠T = 58°. Find m∠H.   *(Lesson 7-9)* **64°**

20. Use the figure below. Lines ℓ and m intersect at P. Find the
    measures of angles 1, 2, 3, 4, and 5.   *(Lesson 7-6)*

    m∠1 = 90°
    m∠2 = 45°
    m∠3 = 45°
    m∠4 = 135°
    m∠5 = 45°

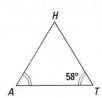

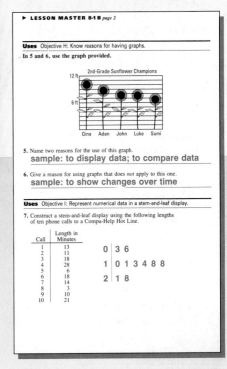

Notes on Questions

Question 22 The key to this question is really determining how many different *hard* additions and subtractions need to be done. Students should realize that **parts d** and **e** are equal, **part d** is the opposite of **part a**, and **part b** is the opposite of **part c**. So the only hard computations needed are those in **parts a** and **c** (or **parts d** and **b**).

Question 25 This question reviews an important skill for the next lesson. In making bar graphs, one picks a unit length and then draws bars relative to that unit.

✎ **Question 26 Writing** As with other questions requiring writing, you may wish to share the best answers with the class.

Follow-up for Lesson **8-1**

Practice
For more questions on SPUR Objectives, use **Lesson Master 8-1A** (shown on pages 410–411) or **Lesson Master 8-1B** (shown on pages 412–413).

Assessment
Oral/Written Assessment Write data on the board that are relevant to students, such as team scores, test scores, absences, or class size. Ask students to tell you all they can about the data. Then have them make a stem-and-leaf display of the data. [Statements will reveal students' abilities to interpret data. Graphs will show their understanding of stem-and-leaf displays.]

Extension
✎ **Writing** In Additional Example 1, students worked with data about Fairbanks, Alaska. Have students **work in groups** and use an almanac or other source to find similar data about another city. Then have them graph the data and write a paragraph about what the graph shows.

Project Update Project 4, *Displays in Newspapers,* Project 6, *Displays of Tchokwe,* and Project 7, *Your Own Data,* all on page 459, relate to the content of this lesson.

---

21. Try at least two special cases with positive and negative numbers to decide whether the pattern is probably true or definitely false for all numbers: $a + -b + -c = -(b + -a + c)$. *(Lesson 6-7)* Samples: $10 + -7 + -1 = -(7 + -10 + 1)$; $-3 + -(-4) + -(-5) = -(-4 + -(-3) + -5)$; probably true.

22. Evaluate each. When possible, use answers to one part to obtain answers to another. *(Lessons 5-3, 5-5, 7-2)*
   a. $6\frac{4}{5} - 3\frac{2}{3}$ $3\frac{2}{15}$
   b. $-6\frac{4}{5} - 3\frac{2}{3}$ $-10\frac{7}{15}$
   c. $6\frac{4}{5} + 3\frac{2}{3}$ $10\frac{7}{15}$
   d. $-6\frac{4}{5} + 3\frac{2}{3}$ $-3\frac{2}{15}$
   e. $-6\frac{4}{5} - -3\frac{2}{3}$ $-3\frac{2}{15}$

23. An age-guesser at a carnival gives a prize if the guess misses your actual age by more than two years. Let G be the guess. If a person is 26 years old, describe the values of G that will give that person a prize. *(Lessons 4-9, 7-2)* $G < 24$ or $G > 28$

24. Steve has h brothers and 4 sisters. There are c children in the family. Give a mathematical sentence relating these numbers. *(Lesson 5-1)* $h + 4 + 1 = c$

25. The segment below represents 1 unit.

(This unit ≈ 51 mm.)

Figures appear smaller than actual size in Teacher's Edition.

1 unit

   a. Draw a segment that represents $\frac{1}{3}$ unit. ≈1.7 cm long
   b. Draw a segment that represents $2\frac{3}{4}$ units. ≈14.0 cm long
   c. Draw a segment that represents 0.6 unit. *(Lesson 3-1)* ≈ 3.1 cm long

Exploration

26. Find a graph in a newspaper or magazine. Copy the graph or cut it out. Explain the purpose of the graph. Answers will vary.

414

Adapting to Individual Needs
Challenge
Have students solve the following problem. For five days, Sergio kept a record of the number of pushups he did each day. Then he compiled these statistics:

Mean: 28   Median: 28
Mode: 24   Range: 10

Find the number of pushups Sergio did each day. [24, 24, 28, 30, 34]

Setting Up Lesson 8-2
Materials Students will need graph paper (**Teaching Aid 86**) for Lesson 8-2. For **Question 30**, on page 420, they will need an almanac or some other source that shows world populations.

Family origins. *This Hispanic family is looking at its family tree. The U.S. Census Bureau has predicted that Hispanics will comprise 14% of the population and be the nation's largest minority group by the year 2010.*

According to the 1990 U.S. census, there were about 22,354,000 people of Hispanic origin living in the U.S. This number includes 13,496,000 people of Mexican ancestry, 2,728,000 of Puerto Rican ancestry, 1,044,000 of Cuban ancestry, and 5,086,000 of other Hispanic origin. The people of "other Hispanic origin" have origins from other Spanish-speaking countries of the Caribbean, Central or South America, or from Spain, or are persons identifying themselves as Spanish, Latino, Hispanic, Spanish-American, and so on.

The preceding paragraph shows numerical information in *prose* writing. **Prose** uses words and numerals but no pictures. Prose allows a person to insert opinions and extra information. It is the usual way you are taught to write.

Making a Bar Graph

Numbers in paragraphs are not always easy to follow. Many people prefer to see numbers displayed. One common display is the *bar graph.* In a **bar graph,** the lengths of bars correspond to the numbers that are represented. For instance, a bar that represents 5,000,000 is twice as long as a bar that represents 2,500,000.

Example 1 shows the steps necessary to display the above data in a bar graph.

Lesson 8-2

Objectives
F Interpret and display information in bar graphs.

Resources
From the *Teacher's Resource File*
- Lesson Master 8-2A or 8-2B
- Answer Master 8-2
- Teaching Aids
  81 Warm-up
  85 Additional Examples
  86 Graph paper
- Technology Sourcebook, Computer Demonstration 8 Computer Master 14

Additional Resources
- Visuals for Teaching Aids 81, 85, 86
- Graphing and Probability Workshop
- Almanac or some other resource for finding world populations (Question 30)

Teaching 8-2
Lesson

Warm-up

Diagnostic Use the bar graph in Example 1 on page 416.
1. What can you learn from the graph? **Sample: the number of people of Hispanic origin living in the United States in 1990**
2. Who might be interested in this information and why? **Sample: schools and businesses**
3. What are the advantages of having this information in graph form? **Sample: it is easier to compare the various numbers.**

Lesson 8-2 Overview

Broad Goals This lesson discusses the rationale, reading, and construction of bar graphs.

Perspective Most students find bar graphs easy to read, but difficult to construct; many of them will make bars whose lengths bear little relation to any uniform scale. You may wish to require that students use rulers or graph paper when making a bar graph.

Students should put enough information in the bar graphs so that readers know what is being graphed. However, allow them some flexibility in their choice of the interval (distance between tick marks) on the scale.

Graphs of all kinds are more commonly used today than in the past because computers can make them automatically from tables and charts. For this reason, it is important that students understand the

principles behind bar graphs and learn how to interpret them. It is also important that they learn how to instruct a computer to draw graphs. Students today will be far more likely, both in later coursework and on a job, to use a computer to do the actual drawing of graphs.

Notes on Reading

Although many spreadsheet programs have the capability of creating bar graphs, we provide this option in the *Graphing and Probability Workshop*.

Note that we use a number line to help students see how to construct uniform scales for the graphs. Explain that although the number line appears three times in **Example 1**, it only has to be drawn once when a graph is actually made. You can Illustrate this idea as you review the questions.

Additional Examples

These examples are given on **Teaching Aid 85.**

1. The following table, from the Urban Institute, gives the number of immigrants who came into the United States by decades. Display the information in a bar graph. **Sample graph is shown below.**

Decade	Number of Immigrants
1910s	5,800,000
1920s	4,100,000
1930s	500,000
1940s	1,000,000
1950s	2,500,000
1960s	3,800,000
1970s	7,000,000
1980s	9,500,000

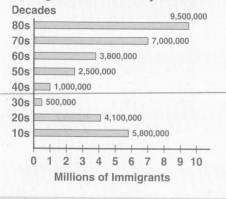

Immigration into U.S. by Decades

Example 1

Display the numerical information on page 415 about persons of Hispanic origin in the United States in a bar graph.

Solution

Step 1: Every bar graph is based on a number line. With a ruler, draw a number line with a *uniform scale*. A **uniform scale** is one on which numbers are equally spaced so that each interval represents the same value. The interval of the scale below was chosen so that all of the numbers will fit on the graph.

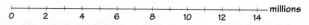

Step 2: Graph each of the numbers.

Step 3: Draw a segment from 0 to each number. Each segment is a *bar* of the bar graph. Then raise each bar above the number line.

Step 4: Identify the bars and write each bar's length by it. Finally, label the entire graph so that someone else will know what you have graphed.

U.S. Population of Hispanic Origin, 1990

- Mexican — 13,496,000
- Puerto Rican — 2,728,000
- Cuban — 1,044,000
- Other — 5,086,000

What Is a Double Bar Graph?

A single bar graph can take up more space than prose. To save space, two related bar graphs can be combined into one. The bars are different colors so that bars of the same color can be easily compared.

Example 2

The information below comes from a survey of the actual and desired ways of spending one's day. The times are averages of the responses of 1,400 adults.

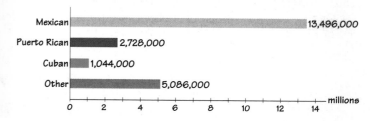

Activity	Real schedule	What people desire
Work/commute	10 hr	8 hr, 18 min
Time with family	1 hr, 54 min	2 hr, 54 min
Physical activity	36 min	1 hr, 6 min

Display this information in a *double bar graph*. ▶

416

Optional Activities

Activity 1 Multicultural Connection
After discussing **Example 1**, you might have students **work in groups**, and make a similar graph for other population groups. Have them select their groups, do their research, and display their findings in bar graphs. Then make a multicultural bulletin board using these graphs along with a copy of the graph for **Example 1**.

Activity 2
Materials: Graphs from newspapers, magazines, science books, or social studies books

✎ **Writing** After students have read the lesson, you might ask them to choose bar graphs from an outside source and write reports about what the graphs show. Students should also give the source of their graphs.

Activity 3 Technology Connection You may wish to use *Technology Sourcebook, Computer Demonstration 8,* to show students how to make a single or double bar graph using the *Graphing and Probability Workshop*. Then, you could assign *Technology Sourcebook, Computer Master 14.*

416

► **Solution**

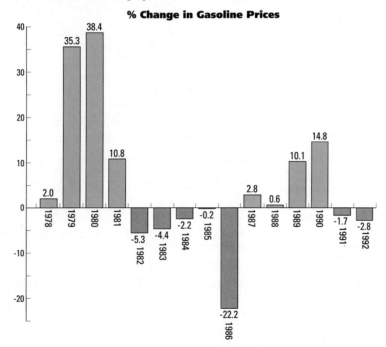

Time spent during the day

■ real
■ desired

Work/commute — 10 hours / 8 hours, 18 minutes

Time with family — 1 hour, 54 minutes / 2 hours, 54 minutes

Physical activity — 36 minutes / 1 hour, 6 minutes

Hours

Each row of the table leads to two bars of the graph. To distinguish the bars, different colors are used.

Creating a Bar Graph from a Spreadsheet

Most spreadsheet programs have the capability of creating bar graphs. To create the bar graph, you first enter data in two rows or two columns. Then you direct the program to convert the information into a graph. For instance, the table below left lists the percent changes in mean gasoline prices from 1978 to 1992. The information for each year is the percent change from the previous year. A negative percent means that the price declined by that percent. The same information is displayed below in a vertical bar graph.

	A	B
1	1978	2.0
2	1979	35.3
3	1980	38.4
4	1981	10.8
5	1982	−5.3
6	1983	−4.4
7	1984	−2.2
8	1985	−0.2
9	1986	−22.2
10	1987	2.8
11	1988	0.6
12	1989	10.1
13	1990	14.8
14	1991	−1.7
15	1992	−2.8

% Change in Gasoline Prices

(vertical bar graph showing values: 1978: 2.0, 1979: 35.3, 1980: 38.4, 1981: 10.8, 1982: −5.3, 1983: −4.4, 1984: −2.2, 1985: −0.2, 1986: −22.2, 1987: 2.8, 1988: 0.6, 1989: 10.1, 1990: 14.8, 1991: −1.7, 1992: −2.8)

Lesson 8-2 *Bar Graphs* **417**

---

2. In the book *Dictionary of First Names*, by Alfred J. Kolatch (New York: Perigee Books, 1980), the following numbers of pages are devoted to boys' and girls' names that begin with vowels.

Vowel	A	E	I	O	U
Boys	26	15	4	7	2
Girls	21	10	5	4	2

a. Display this information in a double bar graph.

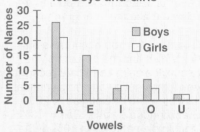

Names Beginning with Vowels for Boys and Girls

■ Boys
□ Girls

b. What conclusions can you draw from this information? **Samples: this book seems to devote fewer pages to girls' names than to boys' names. Those letters which have more names for one sex tend to have more names for the other.**

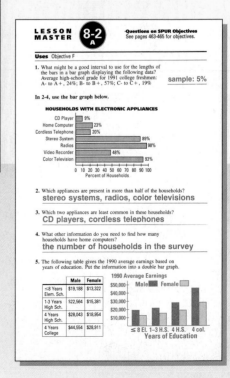

Adapting to Individual Needs

Extra Help

You might want students to establish the interval used in making a uniform scale. Stress that the size of the interval is usually based on the space available. Then discuss with students how they would label an axis in each of these situations.

1. Represent the numbers from 0 to 1000 on a scale using 10 equal intervals. [Label the tick marks 0, 100, 200, 300, and so on.]

2. Represent the years from 1900 to 2000 using 4 equal intervals. [Label the tick marks 1900, 1925, 1950, 1975, and 2000.]

3. Represent the numbers from −15 to 15 using 6 equal intervals. [Label the tick marks −15, −10, −5, 0, 5, 10, and 15.]

Notes on Questions

Making displays is time-consuming. Emphasize the steps given in **Example 1**:
1. Decide on a scale so that all numbers will fit on the graph.
2. Choose an interval for the scale and graph the numbers.
3. Draw a bar for each number.
4. Label each bar.
5. Give the finished graph a descriptive title.

Encourage students to use graph paper or **Teaching Aid 86** and a ruler to make their bar graphs.

Question 18 You might have students also find the percent of the total votes each candidate received. Ask if they notice anything unusual. [Lincoln ≈ 40%, Douglas ≈ 29%, Breckenridge ≈ 18%, Bell ≈ 13%; Lincoln did not receive 50% of the votes.]

Question 19 If we think of a coastline as a fractal, then, in theory, a coastline has no length in our usual way of thinking about it, but only a length based on a particular unit of measure.

418

QUESTIONS

Covering the Reading

In 1–3 refer to Example 1.

1. What is the interval of the scale of the bar graph? **1 million**

2. Are the bars on this graph horizontal or vertical? **horizontal**

3. Identify some information that is in the prose but not in the bar graph. **Sample: a description of what people are identified as of "other Hispanic origin"**

In 4–6, use the bar graph of Example 2.

4. What is the interval of the scale on this graph? **1 hour**

5. **a.** How much time does the average person spend working or commuting? **10 hours**
   b. How much is desired? **8 hours, 18 minutes**

6. Why is this graph called a double bar graph? **It displays two related types of information with two differently colored bars.**

In 7–10, use the bar graph of changes in gasoline prices.

7. What is the interval of the vertical scale? **5%**

8. On this graph, are the bars vertical or horizontal? **vertical**

9. **a.** In which year from 1978 to 1992 did prices increase the most? **1980**
   b. What was the change that year? **38.4%**

10. What does the -5.3 by 1982 mean? **The price of gasoline decreased by an average of 5.3% between 1981 and 1982.**

Applying the Mathematics

In 11–14, a scale on a number line is given.
a. Is the scale uniform?
b. If the scale is uniform, what is its interval? If the scale is not uniform, where is it not uniform?

11a) Yes; b) 2

12a) Yes; b) 3

13a) No; b) The first interval is 1. The other intervals have length 0.05.

14a) No; b) The first two intervals have length 2. The others have length 1.

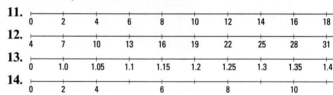

11. 0 2 4 6 8 10 12 14 16 18

12. 4 7 10 13 16 19 22 25 28 31

13. 0 1.0 1.05 1.1 1.15 1.2 1.25 1.3 1.35 1.4

14. 0 2 4 6 8 10

In 15 and 16, suppose a bar graph is to display the numbers 3.39, 3.4, 3.391, and 3.294.

15. Which number will have the longest bar? **3.4**

16. Which two bars will differ the most in length? **3.4 and 3.294**

Adapting to Individual Needs

English Language Development
Some students may have heard the use of the word *uniform* in connection with dress codes, but not in connection with scales. Explain that uniform comes from the Latin *uni-*, meaning one, and *-form,* meaning shape. So a uniform, like a nurse's uniform or a policeman's uniform, means "one shape" for all. Then show students an example of number-line scales in which the intervals are the same length and examples where they are not. Point out that when the intervals are the same, the scale is a *uniform scale.*

In 17 and 18, some information is given. To put the information into a bar graph, what might be a good interval to use for the scale of the graph?

17. annual average unemployment in the United States: 1986, 6.9%; 1987, 6.1%; 1988, 5.4%; 1989, 5.2%; 1990, 5.4%; 1991, 6.6%; 1992, 7.3%

18. popular vote in the Presidential election of 1860: Abraham Lincoln, 1,866,352 votes; Stephen A. Douglas, 1,375,157 votes; John C. Breckinridge, 845,763 votes; John Bell, 589,581 votes

19. Here are the number of miles of coastline of those states bordering on the Gulf of Mexico: Alabama, 53; Florida, 770; Louisiana, 397; Mississippi, 44; Texas, 367.
   a. If you wanted to display this information in a bar graph, what might be a good interval to use?
   b. Draw a bar graph of this information.

20. As of January 1993, the record high and low Fahrenheit temperatures in selected states were: Alaska, 100° and -80°; California, 134° and -45°; and Hawaii, 100° and 12°. Display this information in a double bar graph.

Review

21. Give two reasons for graphs. *(Lesson 8-1)*

22. Which of the states in Question 20 has had the greatest range of temperatures? What is that range? *(Lessons 7-2, 8-1)*

23. a. Solve the equation $105 + 45 + x = 180$.
   b. Write a problem about triangles that can lead to that equation. *(Lessons 5-8, 7-9)*

24. How many degrees are there in the turn with the given magnitude?
   a. half a revolution
   b. one third of a revolution
   c. one fifth of a revolution *(Lesson 3-6)*

In Questions 25 and 26, refer to the circle graph below. It shows the percent of land use of various types in the United States in 1987, excluding Alaska and the District of Columbia.

25. What percent of the land was developed (used for buildings, roads, and so on)? *(Lesson 2-7)*

26. What percent of land was not Federal land? *(Lesson 2-7)*

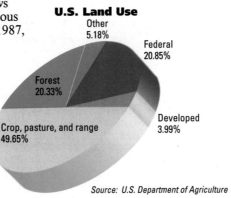

U.S. Land Use
- Other 5.18%
- Federal 20.85%
- Forest 20.33%
- Developed 3.99%
- Crop, pasture, and range 49.65%

Source: U.S. Department of Agriculture

Lesson 8-2 *Bar Graphs* **419**

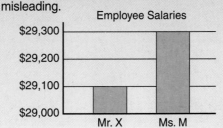
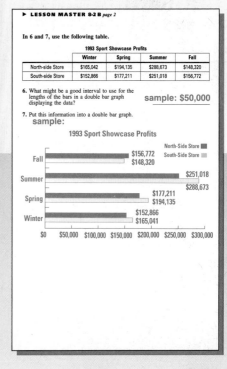

Notes on Questions

Question 30 Students will need an almanac or other source to find the world populations. Note that answers can vary according to the sources used. Also, populations given in a particular source might refer to a metropolitan area rather than to a particular city.

Follow-up 8-2
for Lesson

Practice

For more questions on SPUR Objectives, use **Lesson Master 8-2A** (shown on page 417) or **Lesson Master 8-2B** (shown on pages 418–419).

Assessment

Group Assessment Have students **work in groups.** Have each group decide on a survey question to ask the rest of the class. Then have each group survey the class and make a double-bar graph showing both girls' answers and boys' answers. [Students' graphs will reveal their understanding of bar graphs. Check to see that they have used a uniform scale.]

Extension

Have students **work in groups.** Ask them to use the data in **Example 1** to make a circle graph. Then have them decide which graph does a better job of displaying the data and why. [A circle graph is shown below; students' ideas about which graph is better will vary.]

Project Update Project 4, *Displays in Newspapers*, and Project 7, *Your Own Data*, on page 459, relate to the content of this lesson.

---

27. Use the information from this lesson. The mean price of a gallon of gas was about $1.06 in 1989. What was the mean price in 1990? What was the mean price in 1991? *(Lessons 2-5, 2-6)* **$1.22 in 1990; $1.20 in 1991**

28. Use the information of Question 17. If about 125,000,000 people in the U.S. could work in 1992, how many people were unemployed? *(Lesson 2-5)* **about 9,125,000 people**

29. Round the numbers of Question 18 to the nearest hundred thousand. *(Lesson 1-4)* **1,900,000; 1,400,000; 800,000; 600,000**

Exploration

30. Give the name and approximate population of the largest city in each of the following: Asia, Africa, Europe, North America, Australia, Central or South America. Display this information in a bar graph by hand or by using a spreadsheet program, if one is available. **An almanac may be a good source of information.**

31. Newspapers and magazines use color and imagination to create graphs that will grab the readers' attention. The graph at the right below is far more attractive than the bar graph at the left.

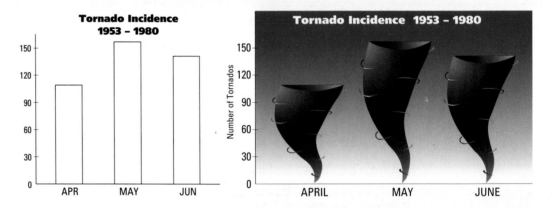

Using the following information, create a bar graph that will attract the readers' attention. Be creative. Use imagination.

**National Basketball Association
1992–1993 Regular Season Scoring Leaders**

Player	Points per game
1. Michael Jordan (Chicago)	32.6
2. Dominique Wilkins (Atlanta)	29.9
3. Karl Malone (Utah)	27.0
4. Hakeem Olajuwon (Houston)	26.1
5. Charles Barkley (Phoenix)	25.6

Source: National Basketball Association
Answers will vary.

420

Setting up Lesson 8-3

Materials Students will need graph paper or **Teaching Aid 87** (Four-Quadrant Graph Paper) for Lesson 8-3.

LESSON 8-3

Coordinate Graphs

Objectives
G Interpret and display information in coordinate graphs.
J Plot and name points on a coordinate graph.

Resources
From the **Teacher's Resource File**
■ Lesson Master 8-3A or 8-3B
■ Answer Master 8-3
■ Assessment Sourcebook: Quiz for Lessons 8-1 through 8-3
■ Teaching Aids
   81 Warm-up
   87 Four-Quadrant Graph Paper
■ Technology Sourcebook, Computer Master 15

Additional Resources
■ Visuals for Teaching Aids 81, 87
■ Graphing and Probability Workshop

Short sleeves in winter? *An elaborate network of enclosed, elevated walkways makes it easy for shoppers and workers to travel in downtown Minneapolis, MN—especially on blustery days or on the cold, snowy days of winter.*

Some patterns involve many *pairs* of numbers. A bar for each pair would take up too much space. *Coordinate graphs* are used instead.

Example 1

Below is a table of temperatures for a cold January morning in Minneapolis. Put this information onto a coordinate graph.

Time of day	Temperature (°F)
1 A.M.	-2
2 A.M.	-2
3 A.M.	-2
4 A.M.	-1
5 A.M.	0
6 A.M.	3
7 A.M.	-1
8 A.M.	0
9 A.M.	3
10 A.M.	7
11 A.M.	11
12 noon	18

Solution

This coordinate graph is based on two number lines. The horizontal number line represents time of day. Its scale goes from 1 to 12 (from 1 A.M. to 12 noon). The vertical number line represents temperature. Its scale goes from -4°F to 18°F. Its interval is chosen as 2° so that all the temperatures will fit on the graph.

▶

Lesson 8-3 Overview

Broad Goals This lesson provides an introduction to the plotting of points on the coordinate plane and the interpretation of sets of points so plotted.

Perspective Making and interpreting coordinate graphs can become quite natural for students, particularly if the graphs are introduced in a familiar context such as the temperature idea used in **Example 1**. In fact,

some science programs introduce coordinate graphs as early as second grade.

Some books distinguish letter names for points from ordered pair names for those points. They use "the point with coordinates (2, 3)" where we use "the point (2, 3)." Instead of writing "$A = (2, 3),$" they will use "*A*: (2, 3)" or "*A*(2, 3)." In this and other UCSMP texts, we view letters and ordered pairs as two different names for the same

thing. We speak of the point (2, 3) and write $A = (2, 3)$. In geometry, we use letters to denote points. In algebra, we use coordinates.

Warm-up

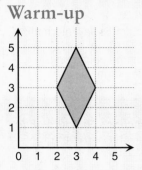

Tell if the point is inside the diamond, outside the diamond, or on the diamond.

1. (1, 3) outside **2.** (3, 2) inside
3. (3, 4) inside **4.** (4, 3) on
5. (4, 1) outside **6.** (0, 0) outside
7. (2, 5) outside **8.** (3, 1) on
9. (5, 2) outside **10.** (2, 3) on

Each row of the table corresponds to one point on the coordinate graph. So the graph contains 12 points.

At 1 A.M. the temperature was -2°. So we go over to 1 on the horizontal line and down to -2. The left point of the graph is the result. The other 11 points are found in the same way.

Time of Day	Temperature (°F)
1 A.M.	-2
2 A.M.	-2
3 A.M.	-2
4 A.M.	-1
5 A.M.	0
6 A.M.	3
7 A.M.	-1
8 A.M.	0
9 A.M.	3
10 A.M.	7
11 A.M.	11
12 noon	18

The coordinate graph has advantages over the table. It pictures the changes in temperature. As the temperature rises, so do the points on the graph. Also, you can insert points between the times on the coordinate graph without making it larger.

Naming Points as Ordered Pairs

When a pair of numbers is being graphed as a point, the numbers are put in parentheses with a comma between them. For instance, the point farthest left on the graph in Example 1 is (1, -2). This means at 1:00 A.M. the temperature was -2°F. The next three points are (2, -2), (3, -2), and (4, -1). The point farthest to the right is (12, 18). It means that at 12:00 noon the temperature was 18°F.

The symbol (a, b) is called an **ordered pair.** *The parentheses are necessary.* The **first coordinate** of the ordered pair is a; the **second coordinate** is b. *Order makes a difference.* In Example 1, the first coordinate is the time of day; the second coordinate is the temperature at that time. At 9 A.M. a temperature of 3°F is graphed as the point (9, 3). This is not the same as a temperature of 9°F at 3:00 A.M., which would be graphed as the point (3, 9).

422

Optional Activities

Activity 1
Materials: A newspaper showing hourly temperatures in your area or a nearby area

After students have studied **Example 1,** they might enjoy making similar graphs for their towns or nearby locations. They should be able to find hourly temperatures in a local newspaper.

Activity 2
Cooperative Learning After discussing the lesson, you might have students **work in groups,** and discuss real-world situations in which using a coordinate grid makes locating things easier. Have each group select one example and explain it to the class. Students might suggest such things as spreadsheets, maps, latitude and longitude, seats in a theater or stadium, and games such as Battleship®.

Activity 3 Technology Connection You
may wish to assign *Technology Sourcebook, Computer Master 15.* Students use the *Graphing And Probability Workshop* to enter coordinates and display graphs.

Example 2

Name points *A, B,* and *C* in the graph below with ordered pairs.

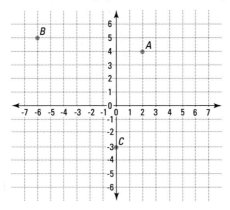

Solution

Find the first coordinate of *A* by looking at the horizontal number line. *A* is above the 2. The second coordinate is found by looking at the vertical number line. *A* is to the right of the 4. So A = (2, 4).
B is above the -6, so the first coordinate of *B* is -6. *B* is to the left of the 5, so the second coordinate of *B* is 5. B = (-6, 5).
C is below the 0 on the horizontal number line. *C* is at the -3 on the vertical number line. So C = (0, -3).

Example 3

Plot the points (-1, -3) and (7, 0) on a coordinate graph.

Solution

To plot (-1, -3), go left to -1 on the horizontal number line. Then go down to -3. That point is *V* on the graph below.

To plot (7, 0), go right to 7 on the horizontal number line. Then stay there! The 0 tells you to go neither up nor down. This is point *T* on the graph.

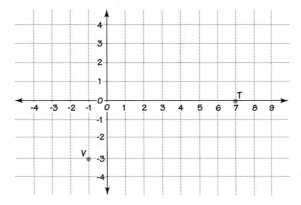

Adapting to Individual Needs

Extra Help

To help students understand how a coordinate graph is developed from two number lines, use a pair of overhead transparencies. The first transparency should show a horizontal number line for integers with vertical lines through the tick marks (grid lines). Highlight the line at 3. Explain that if the number line is labeled *x*, then every point on the line that is highlighted has an *x* coordinate of 3. Then use a transparency that shows a vertical number line labeled *y* and horizontal grid lines. Highlight the horizontal grid line at –2. Establish that every point on the highlighted line has a *y*-coordinate of –2. Superimpose the two transparencies to show that the point at the intersection of the two highlighted lines is (3, –2).

Additional Examples

1. Janet recorded the amount of money she had at the end of each day in a particular week.

   Day 1 $3   Day 5 $4
   Day 2 $1.50   Day 6 $2.50
   Day 3 $ .50   Day 7 $2.50
   Day 4   –$1

   a. Put this information onto a coordinate graph.

   Money at the End of the Day

   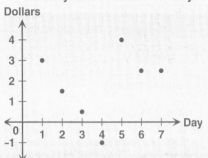

   b. What do you think happened on Days 4 and 5? **Sample: She borrowed money on Day 4 and got her allowance on Day 5.**

2. Give the coordinates of points *A, B, C,* and *D* in the graph below.
   A = (5, 4); *B* = (-1, 2);
   C = (4, -2); *D* = (-1, -5)

   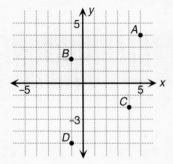

Names for Parts of a Coordinate Graph

When variables stand for coordinates, it is customary to let *x* stand for the first coordinate and *y* stand for the second coordinate. For this reason, the first coordinate of a point is called its **x-coordinate.** The second coordinate is called its **y-coordinate.** For example, the point (-20, 4.5) has *x*-coordinate -20 and *y*-coordinate 4.5. The horizontal number line is called the **x-axis.** The vertical number line is the **y-axis.** The *x*-axis and the *y*-axis intersect at a point called the *origin.* The **origin** has coordinates (0, 0).

The four areas of a graph determined by the axes are called **quadrants** I, II, III, and IV, as shown below.

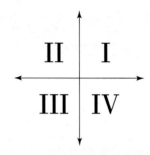

Activity

Graph the following 12 points. Then connect them *in order* by a smooth curve.

(13, 0), (12, 5), (5, 12), (0, 13), (-5, 12), (-12, 5), (-13, 0), (-12, -5), (-5, -12), (0, -13), (5, -12), (12, -5), (13, 0)

QUESTIONS

Covering the Reading

1. Trace the drawing below. Label the *x*-axis, *y*-axis, the origin, and the point (2, 4).

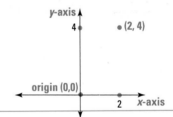

Adapting to Individual Needs

English Language Development
Explain that the word *coordinate* comes from a Latin word meaning "to put in order." In this lesson, the coordinate of a point refers to the ordered pair of numbers that locate the point on a grid. Stress that in an ordered pair, order is important. Show that (2, 3) is not the same as (3, 2) by graphing both points.

In 2–13, use the drawing below. The intervals on the graph are one unit.
What letter names each point?

2. (2, 3) *B*   **3.** (-3, 2) *E*   **4.** (-2, 0) *P*   **5.** (0, 3) *C*

6. (0, -3) *I*   **7.** (-2, -3) *H*   **8.** (0, 0) *R*   **9.** (-3, 0) *F*

10. (3, -2) *K*   **11.** (0, 2) *Q*   **12.** (3, 0) *L*   **13.** (2, -3) *J*

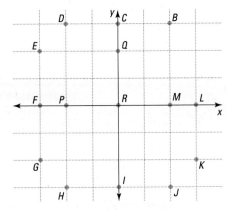

In 14 and 15, draw axes like those shown below. Plot the given points on
your graph.

14. $A = (25, 10)$, $B = (25, 5)$, $C = (25, 0)$, $D = (25, -5)$

15. $F = (-5, -5)$, $G = (-10, -10)$, $H = (-15, -15)$, $I = (15, 15)$

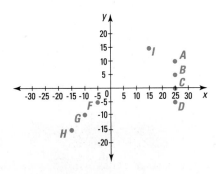

In 16 and 17, refer to Example 1.

16. a. From 3 A.M. to 5 A.M., did the temperature go up or down? up
    b. How is this reflected in the graph? The point for 5 A.M. is higher.

17. Estimate the temperature at 11:30 A.M. 15°

18. The *x*-coordinate of (-3, -1) is __?__. -3

19. The point (0, 3) is on the __?__-axis. *y*

20. The point (0, 0) is called the __?__. origin

---

3. Plot each point. Then tell what
quadrant it is in: $W = (3, 4)$,
$X = (-3, -4)$, $Y = (3, -4)$, and
$Z = (-3, 4)$. See graph below.
W is in the 1st quadrant, *X* is in
the 3rd, *Y* is in the 4th, and *Z* is
in the 2nd.

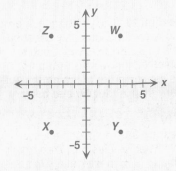

4. Give the coordinates of a point
with each location.
  a. On the *x*-axis any ordered
pair with *y*-coordinate 0
such as (6, 0).
  b. On the *y*-axis any ordered
pair with *x*-coordinate 0
such as (0, 3).
  c. On both axes (0, 0)

Notes on Questions

Questions 14–15 The points in
these questions are *collinear*—they
lie on the same line. Ask students
what is common about the coordinates in each case. [In **Question 14**,
the *x*-coordinate is always 25, or
$x = 25$. In **Question 15**, each
x-coordinate equals the *y*-coordi-
nate, or $x = y$.] These questions pre-
view the idea of equations for lines,
the subject of the next lesson.

Adapting to Individual Needs

Challenge
Have students find as many different
squares as they can with one vertex at
(0, 4) and a second vertex at (4, 0) on a
coordinate grid. Then have them graph the
squares. [The graph is shown at the right.
The possible squares have these vertices:
(0, 0), (4, 0), (4, 4), and (0, 4);
(4, 0), (8, 4), (4, 8), and (0, 4);
(4, 0), (0, 4), (-4, 0), and (0, -4)]

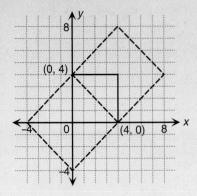

Questions 24–36 These questions should help students make generalizations about the coordinate graph by thinking in terms of quadrants. The three types of questions increase in sophistication.

Question 37 The drawings will be good approximations only because these cities are relatively close to each other. If cities are far apart, then the curvature of the earth causes any map in the plane to be very distorted.

Question 38 You might ask students what conclusions, if any, can be made from these data. [Sample: Atlanta had no very tall buildings before 1961.]

Follow-up for Lesson 8-3

Practice
For more questions on SPUR Objectives, use **Lesson Master 8-3A** (shown on page 425) or **Lesson Master 8-3B** (shown on pages 426–427).

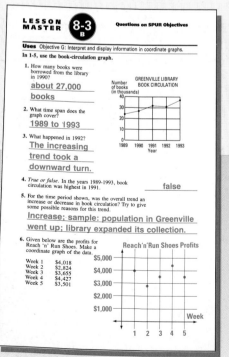

21. The second coordinate of a point is also called its __?__-coordinate. y

22. The x-axis contains the point (-4, __?__). 0

23. When a point is named as an ordered pair, its two coordinates are always placed inside __?__ with a __?__ between them. parentheses, comma

In 24–27, tell in which quadrant the given point lies.

24. (-50, 400) II   25. (78, -78) IV

26. (-.005, -4) III   27. (14, 13) I

28. Show what you found for the Activity in this lesson.

28)

___

Applying the Mathematics

In 29–32, between which two quadrants does the point lie?

29. (0, -4000)   30. (1 millionth, 0) I and IV
    III and IV
31. (-30.43, 0)   32. (0, -989) III and IV
    II and III

In 33–36, in which quadrant is the point (x, y) under the given circumstances?

33. x and y are both negative. III

34. x is positive and y is negative. IV

35. x is negative and y is positive. II

36. x and y are both positive. I

37. Given are the latitudes and longitudes of five European cities. Use these numbers as coordinates in graphing. Use axes like those at the left, but make your drawing bigger. (If correct, your drawing will approximate how these cities are located relative to each other.)

North Latitude

37)
North

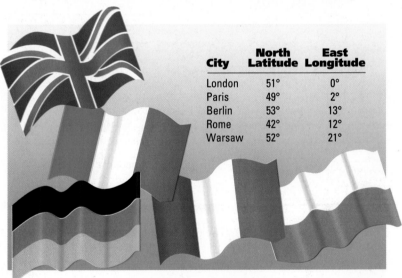

City	North Latitude	East Longitude
London	51°	0°
Paris	49°	2°
Berlin	53°	13°
Rome	42°	12°
Warsaw	52°	21°

426

Review

Standing tall. *The tallest building in Atlanta is the Nations Bank (1988) shown in the forefront.*

38. The 30 tallest buildings in Atlanta, Georgia, as of 1993 were finished in the following years: 1988, 1990, 1973, 1981, 1989, 1980, 1988, 1968, 1985, 1967, 1975, 1991, 1990, 1986, 1986, 1989, 1961, 1975, 1979, 1974, 1987, 1978, 1974, 1975, 1975, 1985, 1987, 1968, 1971, 1972.
  a. Put this information into a stem-and-leaf display. **See below left.**
  b. Put this information into a bar graph in which the bars stand for the numbers of buildings built in the years 1960–69, 1970–79, 1980–89, 1990 or later. **See below left.**
  c. Find the median of the data. **between 1979 and 1980**
  d. Find the range. **30 years**
  e. Which do you prefer, the stem-and-leaf display or the bar graph, and why? *(Lessons 8-1, 8-2)* **Answers will vary.**

39. Draw a picture of two parallel lines and a transversal. Label one pair of alternate interior angles. *(Lesson 7-6)* **See below left.**

40. If one of two vertical angles has measure 20°, what is the measure of the other angle? *(Lesson 7-5)* **20°**

41. Evaluate $y - x$ when $y = -\frac{13}{16}$ and $x = -\frac{17}{32}$. *(Lessons 4-4, 7-2)* $-\frac{9}{32}$

42. If $a + b = 9$, find a when $b = 15$. *(Lesson 5-8)* **-6**

43. Convert this scale from miles to feet. *(Lesson 3-2)*

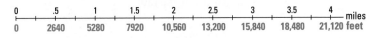

38a)
```
196 | 8718
197 | 35594845512
198 | 819085669757
199 | 010
```

b)
Year in which 30 tallest Buildings in Atlanta, GA, were completed

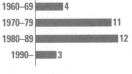

1960–69 4
1970–79 11
1980–89 12
1990– 3

39) Sample:

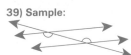

Exploration

44. Most business sections of newspapers contain coordinate graphs. Cut out an example of a coordinate graph from a newspaper or a magazine.
  a. What information is graphed?
  b. Are the scales on the axes uniform?
  c. If so, what are their intervals?
  Answers will vary.

45. Find out the temperature for a recent 12-hour period in your area. Make a graph of this information similar to the graph in Example 1.
  Answers will vary.

Lesson 8-3 *Coordinate Graphs* **427**

Assessment

Quiz A quiz covering Lessons 8-1 through 8-3 is provided in the *Assessment Sourcebook.*

Oral Communication Ask students to explain how the locations of each pair of points are similar and how they are different.
1. (4, 3) and (3, 4)
2. (–3, 2) and (–3, –2).
3. (–4, 6) and (4, 6)
4. (0, –2) and (-2, 0)
[Statements show an understanding of when ordered pairs are on an axis and the difference in locations of positive and negative coordinates.]

Extension

Have students tell what is the same and what is different about the coordinates of the points described below.
1. Points on a line parallel to the *x*-axis [The *y*-coordinate is the same, the *x*-coordinate changes.]
2. Points on a line parallel to the *y*-axis [The *x*-coordinate is the same; the *y*-coordinate changes.]
3. Points on the *x*-axis [The *y*-coordinate is 0; the *x*-coordinate changes.]

Project Update Project 3, *Automatic Graphers*, Project 4, *Displays in Newspapers*, Project 5, *A Display of Temperature*, and Project 7, *Your Own Data*, on pages 458 and 459, relate to the content of this lesson.

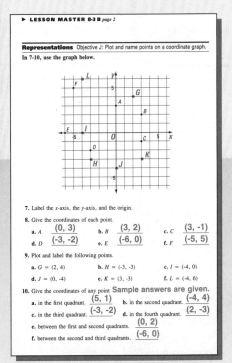

▶ **LESSON MASTER 8-3 B** *page 2*

Representations Objective J: Plot and name points on a coordinate graph.

In 7-10, use the graph below.

7. Label the *x*-axis, the *y*-axis, and the origin.

8. Give the coordinates of each point.
  a. A (0, 3)   **b.** B (3, 2)   **c.** C (3, -1)
  d. D (-3, -2)   **e.** E (-6, 0)   **f.** F (-5, 5)

9. Plot and label the following points.
  a. G = (2, 4)   **b.** H = (-3, -3)   **c.** I = (-4, 0)
  d. J = (0, -4)   **e.** K = (3, -3)   **f.** L = (-4, 6)

10. Give the coordinates of any point **Sample answers are given.**
  a. in the first quadrant. (5, 1)   **b.** in the second quadrant. (-4, 4)
  c. in the third quadrant. (-3, -2)   **d.** in the fourth quadrant. (2, -3)
  e. between the first and second quadrants. (0, 2)
  f. between the second and third quadrants. (-6, 0)

Setting Up Lesson 8-4

Materials Students will need graph paper or **Teaching Aid 87** (Four-Quadrant Graph Paper) for Lesson 8-4.

427

Objectives
J Plot and name points on a coordinate graph.
K Graph equations for lines of the form $x + y = k$ or $x - y = k$.

Resources

From the *Teacher's Resource File*
- Lesson Master 8-4A or 8-4B
- Answer Master 8-4
- Teaching Aids
  82 Warm-up
  87 Four-Quadrant Graph Paper
  88 Graphing Equations
- Activity Kit, Activity 19
- Technology Sourcebook,
  Calculator Master 10
  Computer Master 16

Additional Resources
- Visuals for Teaching Aids 82, 87, 88
- Graphing and Probability Workshop

Teaching
Lesson 8-4

Warm-up
Name 5 ordered pairs that satisfy the equation. **Samples are given.**
1. $x + y = 6$ (0, 6), (6, 0), (−1, 7), (3, 3), (2, 4)
2. $x − y = 9$ (0, -9), (9, 0) (1, −8), (−1, −10), (3, -6)
3. $y − x = −2$ (0, −2), (2, 0), (−1, −3), (1, −1), (3, 1)

LESSON 8-4

Graphing Lines

Lines of support. *A triangular arrangement of cables and support beams is widely used in bridges because of the rigidity and strength of triangles.*

Picturing a Relationship Between Two Variables

In a triangle, the sum of the measures of all three angles is 180°. In a right triangle, one angle has measure 90°. Suppose the other angle measures are x and y. Then x and y must add to 90°. Seven pairs of possible values of x and y are in the table below. These ordered pairs are graphed below the table.

①

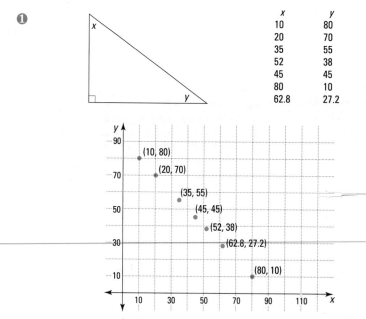

x	y
10	80
20	70
35	55
52	38
45	45
80	10
62.8	27.2

428

Lesson 8-4 Overview

Broad Goals This is a first introduction to the idea of graphing solutions to an equation in two variables. In Chapter 13, the graphing of linear equations is discussed in more detail.

Perspective The phrase "graphing an equation" is short for "graphing all points whose coordinates satisfy the equation." The shorter phrase is universally used in mathematical discourse.

In this lesson, all the lines graphed have equations equivalent to $x + y = k$ or $x − y = k$. If the scales on the axes are the same, then the graphs of these lines are all rotated 45° from the horizontal.

The *x*-coordinate and *y*-coordinate of each point satisfy the equation $x + y = 90$. The seven points lie on a line. This line is the *graph of all the solutions* to $x + y = 90$. The entire line is graphed below. The arrows on the line indicate that the line extends forever in both directions.

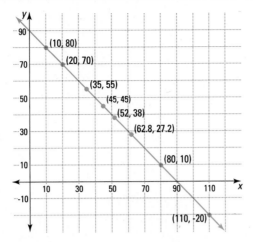

Graphing an Equation

In the equation $x + y = 90$, if you choose a value for one of the variables, you can determine the value of the other. Since there are an infinite number of choices for *x*, there will be an infinite number of solutions, *x* and *y*, to the equation. Some of them, like 110 and -20, involve negative numbers and would not be a solution to the right-triangle question. Only the part of the line in quadrant I contains possible angle measures for the acute angles in a right triangle.

Some graphs of sentences with two variables are beautiful curves. The simplest graphs are lines.

Example 1

Graph all solutions to the equation $x - y = 4$.

Solution

Find some pairs of numbers that work in the equation. You can start with some convenient values of *x*. Then for each *x* value, determine *y*. Keep track of the numbers you find by putting them in a table.

x	y
6	2
4	0
-1	-5

If $x = 6$, then $6 - y = 4$. So $y = 2$.
If $x = 4$, then $4 - y = 4$. So $y = 0$.
If $x = -1$, then $-1 - y = 4$. Solving this equation, $y = -5$.

Now graph the points (*x*, *y*) that you have found. For each equation in this lesson, the graph is a line unless you are told otherwise. You should use at least three points in your table. Two points enable the line to be drawn. The third point is a check.

▶

Lesson 8-4 *Graphing Lines* **429**

Optional Activities

Activity 1 You might want to use *Activity Kit, Activity 19,* as an alternate way to introduce this lesson or as a follow-up to the lesson. In the activity, students measure pairs of supplementary angles, record the measurements in a table, make a graph, and pick a linear equation that describes the graph.

Activity 2 Technology Connection In *Technology Sourcebook, Calculator Master 10*, students use a graphics calculator to graph simple linear equations.

Activity 3 Technology Connection You may wish to assign *Technology Sourcebook, Computer Master 16*. Students collect data regarding expenses for a trip, then use the *Graphing and Probability Workshop* to convert the data from dollars to other currency.

③ If you review **Activity 1** using an automatic grapher connected to an overhead projector, students can see the results rather quickly. Note that many graphers require solving $x - y = a$ for y before beginning. Then you can ask students for various values of a and show the lines quickly. Have students record the results for **Activities 1** and **2** for use in **Questions 5** and **12** on page 431. Remind students to label the x-axis and the y-axis so that it is clear which variable is the first coordinate and which is the second. To save time, give students **Teaching Aid 87.**

Additional Examples

1. Graph all solutions of $x + y = 4$.

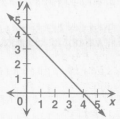

2. Consider the equation $x - y = \frac{1}{2}$.
   a. Find a pair of numbers that satisfies the equation.

   Answers will vary; the x-coordinate should be $\frac{1}{2}$ more than the y-coordinate such as $(3\frac{1}{2}, 3)$.

   b. Find other pairs of numbers that satisfy the equation, and graph the line that contains them.

   Sample points: $(0, -\frac{1}{2})$, $(\frac{1}{2}, 0)$, $(2, 1\frac{1}{2})$, $(-2, -2\frac{1}{2})$

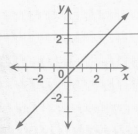

---

③ **Activity 1**

In Example 1, $x - y = 4$ is graphed. This equation is of the form $x - y = a$, with $a = 4$. Graph other lines of the form $x - y = a$. Can you make any conjectures about these lines?

You may have to solve an equation to find a pair of numbers that works in a sentence.

Example 2

Find a pair of numbers that satisfy the equation $y - x = \frac{1}{3}$.

Solution

Pick a value for x, say 6. Substitute 6 for x and solve for y.

When $x = 6$, $y - 6 = \frac{1}{3}$

$$y = 6\frac{1}{3}$$

Thus $(6, 6\frac{1}{3})$ is one point on the graph of $y - x = \frac{1}{3}$.

Substituting other numbers for x and solving for y will give the coordinates of other points that work.

Activity 2

Find three other pairs of numbers that satisfy $y - x = \frac{1}{3}$. Graph the line that contains them.

You are on the right track if your line in Activity 2 is parallel to the line in Example 1.

Adapting to Individual Needs

Extra Help
Be sure students understand that any values of x and y that satisfy an equation will also be the coordinates of a point on the graph of that equation. On the other hand, a pair of values that does *not* satisfy the equation will *not* be coordinates of a point on the graph.

Use $x - y = 5$ as an example. Show how the coordinates (10, 5), (5, 0), and (0, –5)

satisfy the equation. Then graph these points and draw the line. Have students name the coordinates of other points on the line, substitute those values into the equation, and show that they also satisfy the equation. Then have students name points that are not on the line, and show that the coordinates do not satisfy the equation.

QUESTIONS

Covering the Reading

1. Name three pairs of numbers that satisfy $x + y = 90$. **Samples:** (2, 88), (45, 45), (-10, 100)

2. When all pairs of numbers that satisfy $x + y = 90$ are graphed, they lie on a __?__ . **line**

3. Suppose x and y are measures of the two acute angles in a right triangle. How are x and y related? $x + y = 90$

4. Name three pairs of numbers that work in $x - y = 4$. **Samples:** (6, 2), (-1, -5), (0, -4)

5. Describe the common feature of the graphs of lines with equations of the form $x - y = a$. **They are parallel lines.**

In 6–8, an equation and a value of x are given.
a. Find the corresponding value of y.
b. Tell what point these values determine on the line.

6. $x + y = 10; x = 2$
   a) $y = 8$; b) (2, 8)

7. $x - y = 5; x = 3$ a) $y = -2$;
   b) (3, -2)

8. $x = 6 - y; x = 40$ a) $y = -34$; b) (40, -34)

In 9 and 10, graph all solutions to each equation.

9. $x + y = 10$

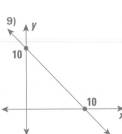
9)

10. $x - y = 6$

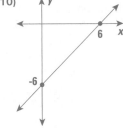
10)

11. *Multiple choice.* The point (2, 3) is not on which line?
    (a) $x - y = -1$
    (b) $-5 = -x - y$
    (c) $x - y = 1$
    (d) $y - x = 1$ (c)

12. Give the coordinates of three points from Activity 2. **Samples:** $(4\frac{2}{3}, 5)$, $(-\frac{1}{3}, 0)$, $(9, 9\frac{1}{3})$

Applying the Mathematics

13. *Multiple choice.* Which graph pictures the solutions to $y - x = 10$? (d)

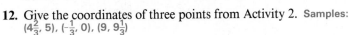

(a)

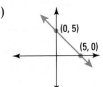
(5, 5)

(b)
(0, 5)
(5, 0)

(c)
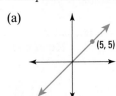
(0, 10)
(10, 0)

(d)
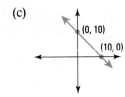
(0, 10)
(-10, 0)

Lesson 8-4 *Graphing Lines* **431**

---

3. Suppose that in Camelot, the evening temperatures (y) are always 10 degrees cooler than the daytime temperatures (x).
   a. Write an equation that relates x and y. [$x - y = 10$]
   b. Graph the solutions to your equation.

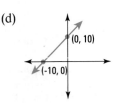

Notes on Questions

We strongly encourage students to use graph paper when making graphs—having the proper materials can cut in half the time required to do a graph. Students can use **Teaching Aids 87 or 88.**

Questions 9 –10 Review these questions carefully with students.

Question 13 Ask students how many points are required to determine a line. [2 points] Algebraically, this means if two points on a line satisfy an equation for a line, all points on the line will satisfy the equation. Substituting points in the equation $y - x = 10$ quickly shows that (d) is correct.

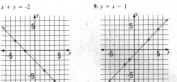

Adapting to Individual Needs

English Language Development

Since there is no new technical vocabulary in this lesson, this might be a good time for students to review the terms from Lesson 8-3. Then you might pair limited-English speaking students with good English-language readers, and let them read the lesson together.

Notes on Questions

Question 17 A table can also be constructed with a spreadsheet. Put 0 in cell A1 and the formula =90−A1 in cell B1. Now you can put other values in column A, and duplicate the formula in the corresponding cells in column B. Or you can use the formula =A1+10 in cell A2, and duplicate that formula down column A. Then duplicate the formula =90−A1 down column B.

Question 18 Error Alert This is a difficult question for many students. Suggest that they try to reproduce the outline on graph paper. Begin with A at (0, 0) and B 12 units up on the y-axis. Ask for the coordinates of B. [B = (0, 12)] Next move to C. Ask which coordinate changes. [The x-coordinate]. Ask for the coordinates of C [C = (8, 12)] and graph the point. Continue in this manner with the other points.

History Connection The first miniature golf course was built in 1916 on the lawn of a North Carolina estate. Now there are around 3,000 miniature golf courses nationwide—half of them built since 1980. Courses compete to attract players with gimmicks like Myrtle Beach, South Carolina's *Hawaiian Rumble*, a 40-foot "volcano" that erupts every 20 minutes.

Question 22 Frank R. Eshman is F. R. Eshman, a freshman.

Question 25 Accept "between 2 and 3" if it is found mentally.

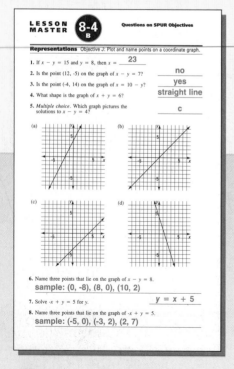

432

14b)

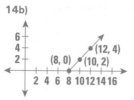

(12, 4)
(8, 0) (10, 2)

15b)

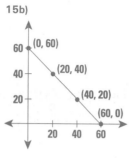

(0, 60)
(20, 40)
(40, 20)
(60, 0)

16c) The graph is a line that passes through the origin and lies in quadrants II and IV at an angle of 45° with either axis.

17a) The first two lines are

X	Y
10	80.

Then the values of X increase by 1 and the values of Y decrease by 1. The last line is

80	10.

b) The first two lines and last line are the same, but now the values of X increase by 10 and the values of Y decrease by 10.

X	Y
10	80
20	70
30	60
40	50
50	40
60	30
70	20
80	10

c) Sample: Change line 20 to
FOR X = 10 TO 100
STEP 5.
Then the first two lines are the same but now the third line is 15 75; the values of X increase by 5 and the values of Y decrease by 5. The last line is 100 -10.

432

In 14 and 15, two variables and a situation are described.
a. Write an equation that relates x and y.
b. Graph all pairs of values of x and y that work in the situation.

14. Margie had x dollars at the beginning of the day. She spent y dollars. She wound up with $8. **a)** $x - y = 8$

15. There are 60 students, x of them in this classroom, y of them next door, none anywhere else. **a)** $x + y = 60$

16. If you need to find many points in a graph, it is a good idea first to solve for one of the variables.
a. Solve $-x - y = 0$ for y. **$y = -x$**
b. Use the solved equation to find three pairs of values of x and y that work in the equation. **Samples: (7, -7), (9, -9), (-3, 3)**
c. Describe the graph of $-x - y = 0$.

17. A table like that on the first page in this lesson can be printed by a computer using the following program.

```
10 PRINT "X", "Y"
20 FOR X = 10 TO 80
30 Y = 90 - X
40 PRINT X, Y
50 NEXT X
60 END
```

a. Type and run this program, and describe the result.
b. Change line 20 as indicated here.

```
20 FOR X = 10 TO 80 STEP 10
```

How does this change what the computer does and what is printed?
c. Change the program so that it prints a different table of coordinates of points on the line. Record the changes you made and describe the table printed.

Review

18. Outlined at the right is a miniature golf hole. All the angles are right angles. Lengths of sides are given. Suppose this outline were graphed with A at (0, 0) and B on the y-axis.
a. Give the coordinates of points B, C, D, E, and F.
b. Give the coordinates of the tee. **(24, 1)**
c. Estimate the coordinates of the hole. *(Lesson 8-3)* **(4, 10)**
a) B = (0, 12); C = (8, 12); D = (8, 2); E = (24, 2); F = (24, 0)

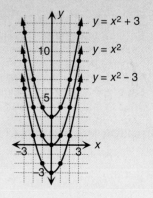

Adapting to Individual Needs

Challenge Technology Connection If graphics calculators are available, you might have students use them with this challenge. Otherwise, students can use **Teaching Aid 88** to make tables and draw the graphs of the equations $y = x^2$, $y = x^2 + 3$, and $y = x^2 - 3$. You might suggest that they choose integer values of x from -3 to 3. Point out that each curve is called a *parabola*. Then have them speculate on where the graph of $y = x^2 + 1$ intersects the y-axis.

[Graphs are shown on the right. The parabolas intersect the y-axis at (0, 0), (0, 3), and (0, -3); $y = x^2 + 1$ will intersect the y-axis at (0, 1)].

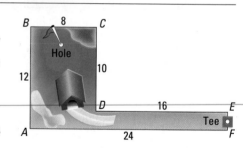
$y = x^2 + 3$
$y = x^2$
$y = x^2 - 3$

19. In which quadrant is the point (-800, 403.28)? *(Lesson 8-3)* II

20. Between which two quadrants is the point (-3, 0)? *(Lesson 8-3)* II and III

21. A point is 5 units directly above (4, -3). What are its coordinates? *(Lesson 8-2)* **(4, 2)**

22. Consider the graph below. *(Lesson 8-2)*

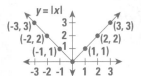

A Day in the Life of Frank R. Eshman

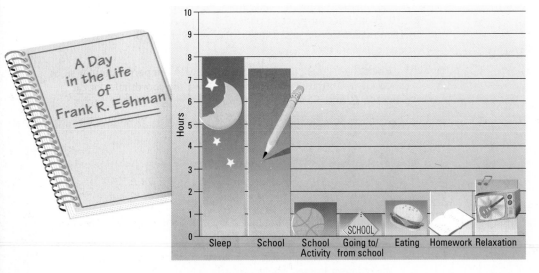

22a) the number of hours the average high school freshman spends in each activity in a day

a. Describe what is being graphed.
b. What is the interval of the scale of the bar graph? **1 hour**
c. Are the bars on this graph horizontal or vertical? **vertical**
d. Frank could spend more time on homework. Where could this time come from? **Sample: relaxation time**
e. Graph a typical day for you, using bars like that in this graph. (Add other bars if you think they are needed.) *(Lesson 8-2)* **Answers will vary.**

23. *Multiple choice.* In this lesson, measures of angles are graphed whose sum is 90°. What are such angles called?
(a) complementary   (b) supplementary
(c) adjacent   (d) vertical   *(Lesson 7-6)* **(a)**

24. An integer is a **palindrome** if it reads the same forward and backward. For example, 252; 12,321; and 18,466,481 are palindromes. How many palindromes are there between 10 and 1000? *(Lesson 6-1)* **99**

25. How many quarts are in a 2-liter bottle of mineral water? *(Lessons 3-4, 3-5)* **2 liters ≈ 2.12 quarts**

26)

$y = |x|$
(-3, 3)   3   (3, 3)
(-2, 2)   2   (2, 2)
(-1, 1)   1   (1, 1)
-3 -2 -1   1 2 3

Exploration

26. Graph $y = |x|$. (Hint: The graph is not a line. Make a table with both positive and negative values for *x*.)

Lesson 8-4 *Graphing Lines* **433**

Setting Up Lesson 8-5

Students who do **Question 22** on page 439 will need a book by M. C. Escher or a book that contains some of his drawings.

You might wish to find out if any students have books about Escher at home; if so, they may bring them in. You might also see if any books containing his drawings are available in your school library. You will also want these books for Lesson 8-8.

Practice

For more questions on SPUR Objectives, use **Lesson Master 8-4A** (shown on page 431) or **Lesson Master 8-4B** (shown on pages 432–433).

Assessment

Written Communication Have students write a paragraph describing how to graph an equation. Then have students exchange their papers and follow their partner's steps to graph the equation. [Check that following the steps given results in the correct graph.]

Extension

Have students **work in groups.** Have them graph each pair of equations given below on the same coordinate grid. Then have them discuss what is similar about the graphs. [The lines are perpendicular.]
1. $x + y = 0$ and $x - y = 0$
2. $x - y = 4$ and $x + y = 4$
3. $x + y = 6$ and $x - y = -2$

Project Update Project 3, *Automatic Graphers*, on page 458, relates to the content of this lesson.

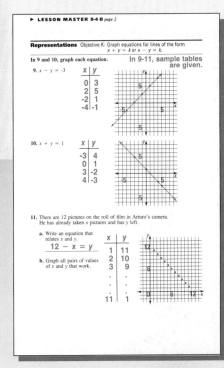

433

In-class Activity

Resources

From the *Teacher's Resource File*
- Teaching Aids
  - 86 Graph Paper
  - 89 Translations

Additional Resources
- Visuals for Teaching Aids 86, 89
- Geometry Workshop

Students can use their own graph paper or **Teaching Aid 86.** Make sure they draw the coordinate axes and the triangle on the same-sized graph paper. Students can use **Teaching Aid 89** to record the coordinates and the changes in the coordinates as they move the triangle. The fourth column in the table can be used if students do *Activity 1* in *Optional Activities* below.

After students find the coordinates of the new positions of A, B, and C, ask them if the x-coordinates increased or decreased. [decreased] Ask if the y-coordinates increased or decreased. [increased] Then repeat the procedure with at least three other moves. Finally have students generalize:
1. A move to the right increases the x-coordinate.
2. A move to the left decreases the x-coordinate.
3. A move up increases the y-coordinate.
4. A move down decreases the y-coordinate.

434

Translations (Slides)

IN-CLASS
ACTIVITY

On graph paper, draw an *x*-axis and a *y*-axis and label each from -10 to 10. From another piece of paper, cut out a right triangle with perpendicular sides 5 and 7 units long. Label the vertices of this triangle A, B, and C.

1 Place the triangle on the graph paper with the perpendicular sides on any grid lines as shown. Write down the coordinates of the vertices A, B, and C. Answers will vary.

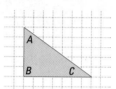

2 Slide the triangle 3 units to the left and 2 units up. Give the new coordinates of A, B, and C. Answers will vary.

3 Compare the coordinates of the new positions of A, B, and C to the old coordinates.

Did the *x*-coordinate of each vertex change? If so, by how much?

Did the *y*-coordinate change? If so, by how much?
x-coordinates are decreased by 3; y-coordinates are increased by 2.

434

Optional Activities

Activity 1 You might have students repeat the activity using other figures, such as various quadrilaterals. After each move, have them compare the new and old coordinates of the vertices, and note what happened. The last column in the table on **Teaching Aid 89** can be used for a fourth coordinate.

Activity 2 Technology Connection You may wish to have students create a polygon and display a slide image of it using *Geometry Workshop.* Have students use the Polygon option to create a shape, then use the Translate option to move it. Ask students to select "coordinate grid" using the Grid option, then compare ordered pairs for the vertices of the image and preimage.

Royal patterns. *The* Omanhene *is the chief of an Ashanti village in Ghana. His robes show the patterns of the type often found in Kente cloth.*

Ashanti people of Ghana translate or slide a design when they paint or stamp patterns on fabric called Kente cloth. If a coordinate grid is placed on the fabric, the slide can be described by looking at the coordinates of points in the design. Any geometric figure can be placed on a coordinate grid. Adding the same number to the coordinates of the points in the figure yields a **translation image** or **slide image** of the original figure.

Horizontal Translations

Begin with triangle *MNO* shown below. Add 3 to each first coordinate. Then graph the new points. The result is a triangle 3 units to the right of *MNO*. We call this △*M′N′O′* (read "triangle *M* prime, *N* prime, *O* prime").

This procedure replaces (0, 0) by (3, 0), (2, 4) by (5, 4) and (-4, 6) by (-1, 6). Each **image** point is 3 units to the right of the **preimage** point.

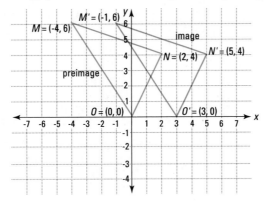

Lesson 8-5 Overview

Broad Goals This lesson introduces the transformation known as a translation and points out its relation to congruent figures in geometry.

Perspective Four types of transformations result in congruent figures. In this book we study three of them—rotations, translations, and reflections. Rotations were mentioned in Chapter 5; translations are presented in this lesson; reflections will be presented in Lesson 8-6. Each of these types of transformations has a name often used with younger students—"turns" for rotations, "slides" for translations, and "flips" for reflections. The fourth type of congruence transformation is the glide reflection or "walk," which students will encounter in UCSMP *Geometry.*

Translations reinforce an important point-plotting concept—the notion that the first coordinate determines the distance right or left, and the second coordinate determines the distance up or down.

Translations also introduce the idea of graphing in geometry. Many students are surprised to see the connection between adding, translations, and congruence. This connection is an extension of the Slide Model for Addition, from the one-dimensional number line to a two-dimensional plane.

Warm-up

Students will need four-quadrant graph paper or **Teaching Aid 87** for this *Warm-up*.

1. Graph the triangle with vertices $A = (1, 1)$, $B = (2, 4)$, and $C = (5, 1)$. **See △ ABC below.**

2. Add -6 to each x-coordinate and -3 to each y-coordinate. Give the new coordinates. $(-5, -2)$, $(-4, 1)$, $(-1, -2)$

3. Graph the new triangle. **See △ A'B'C' below.**

4. Explain what happened. **The new triangle is 6 units to the left and 3 units down from the old triangle.**

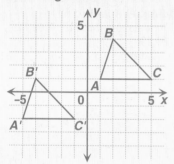

Notes on Reading

Teaching Aid 90 contains the translation images shown on page 436.

You may want to read this lesson aloud with the students. It is important for students to pause as they read to look at the corresponding diagram and figure out just what has been done with the coordinates and the figure. This procedure is particularly true as the concept of translation is developed from a specific case (moving the image 3 units to the right) to a general one (moving the image h units to the right).

Optional Activities

Multicultural Connection The text at the beginning of the lesson mentions that the Ashanti people translate a design when they make Kente cloth. Have interested students research the use of translations in the arts and crafts of various cultures. Suggest that they illustrate their findings and identify the translations. Students might look at the art of Africans, Native Americans, and peoples of Mid- and Far-Eastern countries.

In general, if you add h to each first coordinate, you will get a slide image of the original figure that is h units to the right. (If h is negative, the image will move the opposite of right or left.) This is a two-dimensional version of the Slide Model for Addition that you studied in Chapter 5.

Translations that Are Not Horizontal

What happens if you add a particular number to the *second* coordinate? It's just what you might expect. The preimage slides up or down.

Below, a third triangle is now on the graph. It is the image of △M'N'O' when -5 is added to each second coordinate. We call the image △M*N*O* (triangle M star, N star, O star).

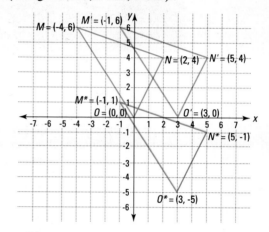

In general, if you add k to the second coordinate of all points in a figure, you will slide the figure k units up. If k is negative, as it is here, then the slide is "negative up," which is down.

Congruent figures are figures with the same size and shape. A translation image is always congruent to its preimage. The three triangles above are congruent.

QUESTIONS

Covering the Reading

In 1–4, what happens to the graph of a figure when the indicated action is taken?

1. 3 is added to the first coordinate of every point on it. **The figure is moved 3 units to the right.**
2. 10 is added to the second coordinate of every point on it. **The figure is moved 10 units up.**
3. -7 is added to the second coordinate of every point on it. **The figure is moved 7 units down.**
4. 6 is subtracted from the first coordinate of every point on it. **The figure is moved 6 units to the left.**
5. Another name for slide is __?__. **translation**

6. When you change coordinates of points of a figure, the original figure is called the __?__ and the resulting figure is called its __?__.
preimage, image

In 7 and 8, graph triangle *ABC* shown below. Then, on the same axes, graph its image under the translation that is described.

7. Add 2 to the first coordinate of each point. **The graph is a triangle with vertices $A' = (3, -5)$, $B' = (7, 2)$, $C' = (-5, 4)$.**
8. Add -3 to the first coordinate and 5 to the second coordinate of each point. **The graph is a triangle with vertices $A' = (-2, 0)$, $B' = (2, 7)$, $C' = (-10, 9)$.**

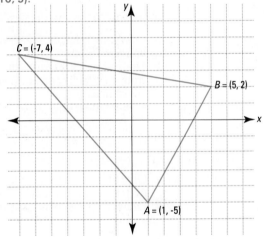

In 9 and 10, tell what happens to the graph of a figure when:

9. k is added to the second coordinate of each point and k is positive. **The graph is moved up k units.**
10. h is added to the first coordinate of each point and h is negative. **The graph is moved h units to the left.**
11. Congruent figures have the same __?__ and __?__. **size, shape**

12. *True or false.* A figure and its slide image are always congruent. **True**

Lesson 8-5 *Translations (Slides)* **437**

Additional Examples
The following additional examples are given on **Teaching Aid 90**.

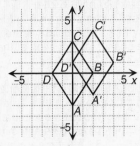

1. Give the coordinates of the vertices of *ABCD*.
$(0, -3), (2, 0), (0, 3), (-2, 0)$
2. Give the coordinates of the vertices of *A'B'C'D'*.
$(2, -2), (4, 1), (2, 4), (0, 1)$
3. Describe the translation.
2 units right, 1 unit up; or add 2 to the *x*-coordinate, add 1 to the *y*-coordinate.

Notes on Questions

Questions 7–8 Students will need a four-quadrant graph (**Teaching Aid 87**).

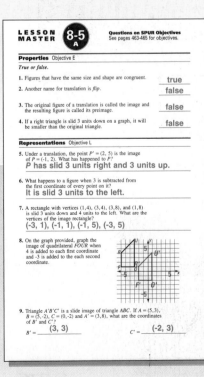

Adapting to Individual Needs

Extra Help

Use Physical Models To help students understand the graph in *Translations that Are Not Horizontal* on page 436, you might use the procedure in the In-class Activity on page 434. Cut out a triangle congruent to △*MNO*. Then, using an overhead projector and **Teaching Aid 87,** show how the triangle is moved horizontally to obtain △*M'N'O'* and then how triangle △*M'N'O'* is moved vertically to obtain △*M*N*O**. Make sure

students see that the triangle has not changed in shape or size; only its position has changed.

You also might use **Teaching Aid 87** and a similar procedure when discussing **Questions 7 and 8** in Covering the Reading.

437

Question 13 This problem is a simplified version of an often-used application of translations. In later courses and in computer work, students may need to translate figures to a more convenient location at the origin.

Question 15 Error Alert Students may have difficulties with this question. Have them look at the *x*-coordinates and then the *y*-coordinates in (0, –4) and (–1, 5). Ask how *x* moved from $x = 0$ to $x = -1$ (1 unit left), and show how *y* moved from $y = -4$ to $y = 5$ (9 units up). Then suggest that students ask themselves the same questions for *A* and *B*. Students may benefit from **working in small groups** and graphing the preimage and the slide image.

Follow-up for Lesson 8-5

Practice

For more questions on SPUR Objectives, use **Lesson Master 8-5A** (shown on page 437) or **Lesson Master 8-5B** (shown on pages 438–439).

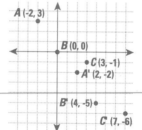

438

13.

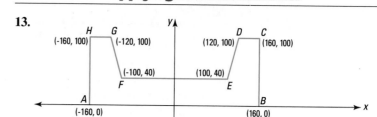

Polygon *ABCDEFGH* outlines a top view of a school building. The architect wishes to send this outline by a computer to a builder. To avoid negative numbers, the architect slides the graph so that the image of point *A* is at the origin.

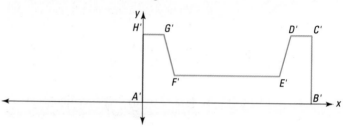

What will be the coordinates of *B'*, *C'*, *D'*, *E'*, *F'*, *G'*, and *H'*?
B' = (320, 0), *C'* = (320, 100), *D'* = (280, 100), *E'* = (260, 40), *F'* = (60, 40), *G'* = (40, 100), *H'* = (0, 100)

14a, b)

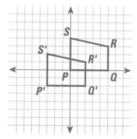

14. a. Draw quadrilateral *PQRS* with *P* = (0, 0), *Q* = (5, 0), *R* = (5, 3), and *S* = (0, 4).
   b. On the same axes, draw the image of *PQRS* when 3 is subtracted from each first coordinate and 2 is subtracted from each second coordinate.
   c. The preimage and image are ? . **congruent**

15. Triangle *A'B'C'* is a slide image of triangle *ABC*. *A* = (0, 0), *B* = (3, 0), *C* = (0, -4), and *C'* = (-1, 5). What are the coordinates of *A'* and *B'*? *A'* = (-1, 9), *B'* = (2, 9)

16. a. Give three instances of the following general pattern: Under a particular transformation, the image of (*x*, *y*) is (*x* + 4, *y* − 5).
   b. Draw the three points and their images.
   a) Samples: image of (-2, 3) is (2, -2); image of (0, 0) is (4, -5); image of (3, -1) is (7, -6).

16b)

A (-2, 3)

B (0, 0)

C (3, -1)

A' (2, -2)

B' (4, -5)

C' (7, -6)

438

Adapting to Individual Needs

English Language Development
Students may be familiar with the word *translation* used in the context of translating from one language to another. Explain that translation can also mean changing from one place or position to another. In the case of a geometric translation, the position of a figure is being changed. Associate the word *slide* with *translation* to help students remember how the position is changed.

Teaching Lesson **8-7**

Warm-up
Draw the reflection image of the letter A over each line.

1.   **2.**

LESSON

8-7

Reflection Symmetry

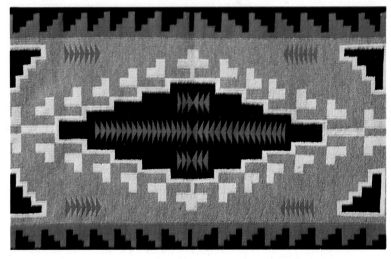

Symmetry in textiles. *This Navajo blanket has two lines of symmetry.*

Nearly a thousand years ago the Diné people, ancestors of today's Navajo in the Southwest United States, learned to weave on looms from the neighboring Pueblo Indians. A Navajo blanket is shown in the photograph above. Notice that if you fold the blanket along a horizontal line through its center, the top and bottom halves match.

What Is Reflection Symmetry?
The same idea occurs with simpler figures. Consider triangle *ABC* shown below. If *ABC* is reflected over line *BD*, the image of *A* is *C*. The image of *C* is *A*. And the image of *B* is *B* itself. The points between these points have images between the points. So the entire triangle coincides with its reflection image. We say that the triangle is **symmetric with respect to line BD.** It has **reflection symmetry.**

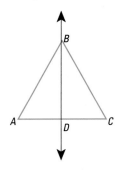

Symmetry lines do not have to be horizontal or vertical.

Lesson 8-7 Overview

Broad Goals It is likely that students have encountered the idea of symmetry before. This lesson connects the ideas of symmetry and reflections.

Perspective Symmetry is an important idea in many areas other than mathematics. Since ancient times, symmetry has been used in art and architecture to create pleasing patterns. Concepts of symmetry are basic for the study of crystals in chemistry,

the study of particle physics, and the study of geometry itself.

The concept of symmetry is familiar to most students. They have either studied it in earlier courses, or noticed it in designs and everyday occurrences. The fundamental idea in this lesson is to relate this very intuitive notion to the more formal language of reflections.

Generally, a figure is symmetric if there is a transformation under which the figure coincides with its image. Symmetries are categorized by the type of transformation; the figures studied in this lesson are called *reflection-symmetric*. Rotation symmetry is covered in the questions. Translation symmetry, though it is not mentioned explicitly, underlies the tessellations of Lesson 8-8.

Review

19a,b,c,d)

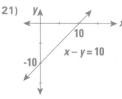

19. Wallpaper designs often involve reflections. Trace the figure below.

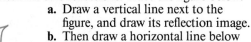

   a. Draw a vertical line next to the figure, and draw its reflection image.
   b. Then draw a horizontal line below the figures, and draw their images.
   c. Repeat steps **a** and **b**. How many figures have been drawn? **16**
   d. Describe how you might extend your design.

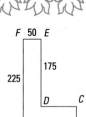

20. The picture of the letter L at the left is to be stored in a computer with point A having coordinates $(0, 0)$ and point B on the x-axis. Give the coordinates of the other points. *(Lesson 8-4)* $B = (150, 0)$; $C = (150, 50)$; $D = (50, 50)$; $E = (50, 225)$; $F = (0, 225)$

21. Graph the line with equation $x - y = 10$. *(Lesson 8-4)*

21)

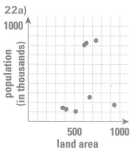

In 22 and 23, use this information about the eight counties in the state of Connecticut.

22a)

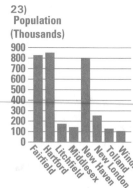

County	Land area (sq mi)	Population (1990 census)
Fairfield	632	828,000
Hartford	739	852,000
Litchfield	921	174,000
Middlesex	373	143,000
New Haven	610	804,000
New London	669	255,000
Tolland	412	129,000
Windham	515	106,000

22. a. Graph the 8 ordered pairs (land area, population).
   b. Is it generally true that the larger counties in area have more people? Explain why or why not. *(Lesson 8-3)* **See below.**

23. Make a bar graph of the populations. *(Lesson 8-2)*

23)

Population (Thousands)

900	
800	
700	
600	
500	
400	
300	
200	
100	
0	

Fairfield, Hartford, Litchfield, Middlesex, New Haven, New London, Tolland, Windham

24. Evaluate $(x - y)^2$ when $x = 6.9$ and $y = 3.4$. *(Lessons 4-4, 4-5)* **12.25**

Exploration

25. Make up some hidden word puzzles like those in Questions 15–18.
Answers will vary.

22b) Sample: Yes, three of the five counties with area over 600 square miles have populations over 800,000. It would seem likely that more people would populate a larger land area provided the land can support urban infrastructure.

Lesson 8-6 *Reflections* **445**

Practice

For more questions on SPUR Objectives, use **Lesson Master 8-6A** (shown on page 443) or **Lesson Master 8-6B** (shown on pages 444 – 445).

Assessment

Quiz A quiz covering Lessons 8-4 through 8-6 is provided in the *Assessment Sourcebook*.

Oral Communication Ask students to explain why translations are sometimes called slides, reflections are sometimes called flips, and rotations are sometimes called turns. Ask them to give examples to support their reasoning. [Statements made and examples given will reveal students' understanding of these transformations.]

Extension

Art Connection Patterns involving translations, reflections, and rotations are found in many quilt designs. Some students might enjoy finding examples of these transformations in actual quilts or in books about quilts. Suggest that they select one design, copy it, and explain the transformations shown. Students might also enjoy making and displaying their own quilt designs.

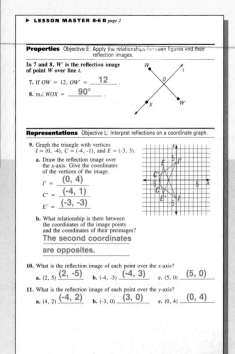

▶ **LESSON MASTER 8-6 B** *page 2*

Properties Objective E: Apply the relationships between figures and their reflection images.

In 7 and 8, W' is the reflection image of point W over line t.

7. If $OW = 12$, $OW' = $ **12** .

8. $m\angle WOX = $ **90°** .

Representations Objective L: Interpret reflections on a coordinate graph.

9. Graph the triangle with vertices $I = (0, -4)$, $C = (-4, -1)$, and $E = (-3, 3)$.
   a. Draw the reflection image over the x-axis. Give the coordinates of the vertices of the image.
   $I' = $ **(0, 4)**
   $C' = $ **(-4, 1)**
   $E' = $ **(-3, -3)**

   b. What relationship is there between the coordinates of the image points and the coordinates of their preimages?
   The second coordinates are opposites.

10. What is the reflection image of each point over the x-axis?
   a. (2, 5) **(2, -5)**   **b.** (-4, -3) **(-4, 3)**   **c.** (5, 0) **(5, 0)**

11. What is the reflection image of each point over the y-axis?
   a. (4, 2) **(-4, 2)**   **b.** (-3, 0) **(3, 0)**   **c.** (0, 4) **(0, 4)**

How to Find a Reflection Image

One way to draw the reflection image of a figure on paper is to fold the paper on the reflecting line. Put the figure on the outside of the fold. Hold the paper up to a light. Then trace the image.

You can also find a reflection image without folding. To do this, you need to find the images of some points. Examine the figure below. If you draw a segment from A to A', the segment is perpendicular to line m. Also, points A and A' are the same distance from line m. The same situation will exist for $\overline{BB'}$ and $\overline{CC'}$. The segments perpendicular to m are drawn below.

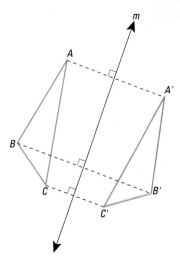

Reflecting a Point Over a Line

❷ One way to locate the reflection image of a point over a line is shown below.

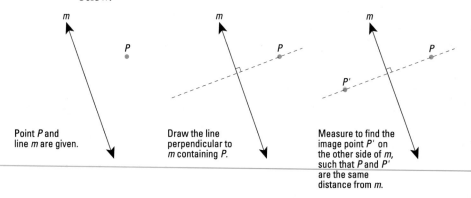

Point P and line m are given.

Draw the line perpendicular to m containing P.

Measure to find the image point P' on the other side of m, such that P and P' are the same distance from m.

The drawings on pages 441–442 are contained on **Teaching Aid 91.**

distance from P to ℓ and locate P' the same distance on the other side of ℓ. Another way is to fold the paper the other way along ℓ and hold it up to a light so that P can be seen and copied on the other side of ℓ.

Notes on Reading

Drawing reflection images can be tricky for students. Let them find images any way they can—with rulers, by folding, or by using a translucent piece of plastic like the Mira. Also, the **Geometry Template** can help them illustrate reflections.

Science Connection Aspartame, an artificial sweetener, is a mirror image of a molecule that occurs naturally in the body. Research chiral isomers (mirror images of molecules) in a chemistry book. Draw and name an example of a molecule and its mirror image.

You might go through the reading with students, even if they have read the material before. Show them how to find reflection images.

❶ When a figure is not symmetric, any reflection image of it will look reversed from the original. This reversal, which does not occur with translations or rotations, can be explained through the concept of *orientation*. Imagine walking around the preimage triangle in the drawing from A to B to C. The triangle will always be on your left. Now imagine walking around the image from A' to B' to C'. The triangle will always be on your right. This difference in directions reflects a change in orientation.

❷ You may wish to introduce the term *perpendicular bisector* to describe the line that is perpendicular to a segment and contains the midpoint of that segment. We do not use this phrase because there are not many opportunities to apply it in this course.

Optional Activities

Activity 1 Using a Physical Model
Materials: A large mirror

You might want to use this activity to introduce the lesson. Have students look in a mirror to observe and report what happens to their reflection image as they: get closer to the mirror, back away from the mirror, turn left, and turn right. Explain that any point on the mirror appears equidistant from the corresponding point on the person

looking into the mirror. Ask whether a mirror switches right and left. [no]

Activity 2 Technology Connection You may wish to assign *Technology Source-book, Computer Master 17*. Students use the *Geometry Workshop* to simulate a miniature golf game. The Reflect option helps students choose the best shot for a hole in one.

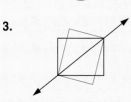
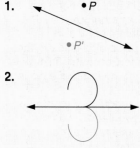
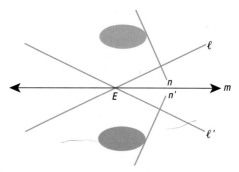

Mirrors can be used in humorous ways.

What Happens to a Point on the Reflecting Line?

❸ If a point is *on* the reflecting line, then it is its own image. We say that it **coincides** with (takes the same position as) its image. In the following figure, the reflecting line *m* is horizontal. The preimage consists of an oval and lines ℓ and *n*. Point *E* on line ℓ coincides with its image.

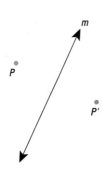

Line ℓ contains *E*, and so does its image, line ℓ'. The angles formed by ℓ and *n* have the same measures as the angles formed by ℓ' and *n'*. In general, notice that figures and their reflection images have the same size and shape. They are congruent even though the reflection image may look reversed.

QUESTIONS

Covering the Reading

In 1–3, point *P'* is the reflection image of point *P* over the reflecting line *m*.

m

P

P'

1. *m* is called the _?_. reflecting line or mirror

2. $\overline{PP'}$ is _?_ to *m*. perpendicular

3. *P* and *P'* are the same _?_ from *m*. distance

4. If a point is on the reflecting line, then it _?_ with its image. coincides

5. *True or false.* A figure to be reflected cannot intersect the reflecting line. False

6. *True or false.* A figure and its reflection image are congruent. True

7. Reflections, rotations, and translations are three types of _?_. transformations

442

In 8 and 9, trace the drawing. Then draw the reflection image of each point over the given line.

8.

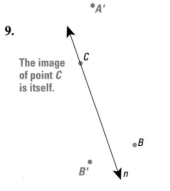

9.

The image of point *C* is itself.

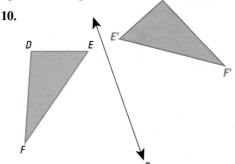

Applying the Mathematics

In 10–11, trace the drawing. Then draw the reflection image of the given figure over the given line.

10.

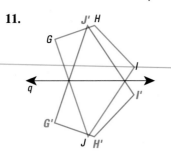

11.

Adapting to Individual Needs

English Language Development
Materials: Mirror

Use a mirror to help students understand the word *reflection*. Have students look into the mirror. Explain that what they see is their reflection. Then put the mirror on line *m* in the drawing on page 440 so that students can see the reflection image of triangle *ABC* in the mirror. Point out that the reflection image looks the same as triangle

A'B'C'. Identify triangle *A'B'C'* as the reflection image.

444

Questions 12–14 These questions link reflections and coordinate graphs with increasing levels of abstraction. **Question 12** specifies a point and reflection line. **Question 13** describes the relation between preimage and image and requires the students to give the reflection line. **Question 14** gives a generalization and requires students to give instances of it. Students can use **Teaching Aid 87** to show these reflections.

Questions 15–18 These questions must be discussed as a prerequisite for **Question 25**.

Question 25 Most students enjoy sharing their original problems. This question also prepares students for **Questions 13–15** in Lesson 8-7.

13a, b)

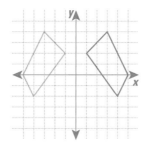

14a) Samples:
Image of (1, 4) is (4, 1);
image of (6, –2) is (–2, 6);
image of (3, 0) is (0, 3);
image of (–4, –8) is (–8, –4).
b) Sample:

12. The point (2, 4) is reflected over the *x*-axis. What are the coordinates of its image? (Hint: Draw a picture.) (2, -4)

13. a. Graph the quadrilateral with vertices (1, 2), (3, 4), (4, -2), and (5, 0).
  b. Change each first coordinate to its opposite and graph the quadrilateral with the new vertices.
  c. Over what line has the preimage been reflected? over the y-axis

14. a. Give four instances of the following general pattern: Under a particular transformation, the image of (*x*, *y*) is (*y*, *x*).
  b. Draw the four points from part **a** and their images.
  c. Describe the transformation. The images are reflection images over the line y = x.

In 15–18, trace the figure. What word results when the figure is reflected over the given line?

15. T O M A T O

16. W H Y

17. ← CHEEK →

18. ← BIKE →

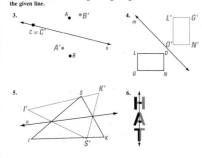

Adapting to Individual Needs

Challenge

Remind students that a palindrome is a number like 1221 that reads the same backwards and forwards. Explain that the word BOB and the group of words MADAM I'M ADAM also form palindromes because they read the same backwards and forwards. Then have students find other words and groups of words that form palindromes. Warn them that it is much easier to find a word palindrome than a group of words that

form a palindrome. [Some examples are MOM, TOOT, NOON, ABLE WAS I ERE I SAW ELBA, and STEP ON NO PETS.]

You might also show students the following sentence. It is not a palindrome, but it has an unusual property. See if they can discover it. [The sentence reads the same way when turned upside down.]
NOW NO SWIMS ON MON

Objectives

B Draw the reflection image of a figure over a line.

E Apply the relationships between figures and their reflection images.

L Interpret reflections on a coordinate graph.

Resources

From the Teacher's Resource File
- Lesson Master 8-6A or 8-6B
- Answer Master 8-6
- Assessment Sourcebook: Quiz on Lessons 8-4 through 8-6
- Teaching Aids
  82 Warm-up
  87 Four-Quadrant Graph Paper
  91 Reflection Images
  92 Additional Examples and Questions 9–11
- Technology Sourcebook, Computer Master 17

Additional Resources
- Visuals for Teaching Aids 82, 87, 91, 92
- Geometry Workshop

Teaching
Lesson **8-6**

Warm-up

Draw any point *P*. Fold your paper in any way you want, but do not fold it on the point itself. Open the paper and locate the image of *P* on the other side of the fold line *ℓ*. Label the image point *P'*. Give two different ways to locate *P'*. **Samples: One way is to draw a line through *P* perpendicular to *ℓ*. Measure the**

Worth reflecting upon. *This extraordinary view is of Mt. Rainier and its reflection in Lake Tipsoo, in the state of Washington.*

Three Kinds of Transformations

Translating is not the only way to get an image of a figure. When you studied turns and their magnitudes in Chapter 5, you rotated points. Rotations, translations, and *reflections* are three ways that geometric figures can be changed or *transformed*. For this reason rotations, translations, and reflections are called **transformations.** You have seen computer-animated graphics. Animations are often done by beginning with a figure then transforming it. (In fact, most of the images in this chapter were drawn by a computer.)

The word "image" suggests a mirror. Mirrors are the idea behind reflections. △ *ABC* and △ *A'B'C'*, its **reflection image over the line (or mirror) *m*,** are shown below.

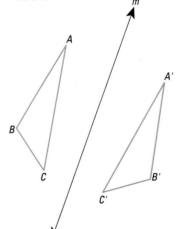

440

Lesson 8-6 Overview

Broad Goals The purpose of this lesson is to introduce the language of reflections and give students practice in making and analyzing reflection images.

Perspective Reflections are fundamental in the study of congruence; for example, the base angles of an isosceles triangle are reflection images of each other. Reflection images also provide the means by which

symmetry can be defined. Symmetry is introduced in the next lesson.

Notice the distinction in mathematics between *reflection* (the transformation) and *reflection image* (the result of applying the transformation). In everyday language, both expressions are called *reflections,* as suggested by the comment, "Look at your reflection in the water."

In the world, reflections are three-dimensional, and the mirror is often vertical. But if the examples used with students are always horizontal or vertical, they would never need to apply the definition of reflection to find images and would not realize the mathematical connections with perpendicularity. Thus the reflecting lines in this lesson are not always horizontal or vertical.

17)

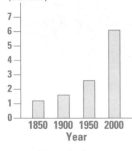

18a)

World Population
(billions)

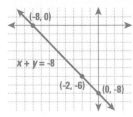

These teens are visiting with a senior citizen in a nursing home.

18b)

World Population
(billions)

Review

17. Graph the line with the equation $x + y = \text{-}8$.   *(Lesson 8-4)*

18. Use the information below.

Year	Estimated World Population
1850	1.2 billion
1900	1.6 billion
1950	2.6 billion
2000	6.1 billion

  a. Display this data with a vertical bar graph.
  b. Graph this data on a coordinate graph. See below left.
  c. What advantage does the coordinate graph have over the vertical bar graph? *(Lessons 8-2, 8-3)* Sample: It is easier to insert additional points.

19. Five people charge the following rates per hour of babysitting: $2.00, $1.50, $2.50, $1.75, $2.00.
  a. Give the median of the charges. $2.00
  b. Give the mode. $2.00
  c. Give the mean (average) charge. $1.95
  d. Give the range of the charges.   *(Lesson 8-1)* $1.00

20. Jasmine scheduled 10 hours to work as a volunteer at the Evans City Nursing Home. She worked $1\frac{1}{2}$ hours on Monday, 2 hours 45 minutes on Tuesday, and 2 hours 15 minutes on Wednesday. Jasmine wants to get her hours in by Friday. How many hours does she need to work Thursday and Friday if she wants to work an equal amount of time on each of those days? *(Lessons 5-5, 7-4)*
$3\frac{1}{2}$ hours ($1\frac{3}{4}$ hours each)

Exploration

21. The square below pictures a floor tile. A corner of the tile is shaded. Sixteen of these tiles are to be arranged to make a 4-by-4 square. Create at least two patterns.   Samples:

22. An artist who used translations is M. C. Escher. Many libraries have books of his work. Find such a book and, from it, trace an example of a figure and its translation image. Answers will vary.

Lesson 8-5   *Translations (Slides)*   **439**

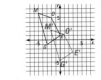

Adapting to Individual Needs

Challenge
Have students graph the triangle with these vertices: $A = (2, 2)$, $B = (4, 6)$, and $C = (6, 2)$. Then have them describe translations that will move △ABC to the following positions.

1. Into Quadrant II [a horizontal slide to the left at least 6 units and a vertical slide up any number of units or down no more than 2 units]

2. Into Quadrant III [a horizontal slide to the left at least 6 units and a vertical slide down at least 6 units]

3. Into Quadrant IV [a horizontal slide to the right any number of units or to the left no more than 2 units and a vertical slide down at least 6 units]

439

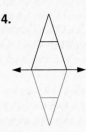

➊ Activity 1

Check that rhombus *PQRS* has two symmetry lines, $\overleftrightarrow{PR}$ and $\overleftrightarrow{QS}$, by tracing *PQRS* and folding it over either of these lines.

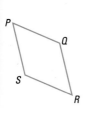 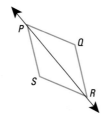 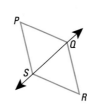

Point out that the figure in 3 coincides with its reflection image.

Notes on Reading

Multicultural Connection Symmetric figures can be seen in the arts and crafts of most Native American cultures. Interested students can investigate examples of symmetry in Native American blankets and rugs, totems, jewelry, pottery, and clothing. Then they might **work in groups** and make a bulletin board display.

Testing for Reflection Symmetry

Many people think that the line *m* shown below at the left is another symmetry line for *PQRS*. But it is not. To test this, reflect *PQRS* over *m*. The image *P′Q′R′S′* is shown below at the right.

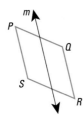 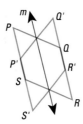

Since *P′Q′R′S′* does not coincide with the original rhombus, *m* is not a symmetry line.

➊ These figures are contained on **Teaching Aid 93**.

Error Alert Some students have difficulty drawing oblique lines of symmetry. Suggest that students trace rhombus *PQRS*, cut out the tracing, and actually fold along the proposed line of symmetry to determine if the line is indeed a line of symmetry.

You also might help students identify oblique lines of symmetry by drawing the same figure with different tilts on an overhead transparency. Project the figure directly onto the board, and trace the projection image with chalk. Then move the projector, and turn the transparency to project the figure in a different location. Ask students to draw the lines of symmetry on each projected figure. Note that the symmetry lines turn as the figure turns.

Some Examples of Figures with Reflection Symmetry

Reflection symmetry is found in many places. Here are some common figures and their lines of symmetry.

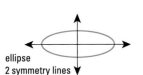
ellipse
2 symmetry lines

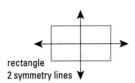
rectangle
2 symmetry lines

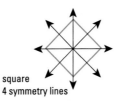
square
4 symmetry lines

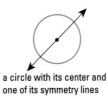
a circle with its center and one of its symmetry lines

Any line through the center of a circle is a line of symmetry. So a circle has infinitely many symmetry lines.

Optional Activities

Activity 1 After students cover the lesson, you might want to use *Activity Kit, Activity 20*, to give students additional opportunities to draw figures with reflection symmetry.

Activity 2 Technology Connection You may wish to assign *Technology Sourcebook, Computer Master 18*. Students use the *Geometry Workshop* to explore lines of symmetry.

Activity 3
Materials: Geometry Template

You can use this activity after students have completed the questions in the text. Have students **work in groups** and find the number of lines of symmetry for each of the 21 figures on the Template. Suggest that they put their information in a table. [Figures 6, 7, 8, 10, 11, 15, 19, 20, have no lines of symmetry; figures 9, 13, 14, 21 have one line of symmetry; figures 1 and 16 have two; figure 4 has three; figure 2 has four; figure 3 has five; figure 5 has six; figure 17 has eight; figures 12, 18 have an infinite number.]

❷ These figures are contained on **Teaching Aid 93.** Note that Activity 2 expands on **Question 8** in *Covering the Reading.*

Additional Examples

1. Draw four reflection-symmetric figures that are different from those in the lesson. Cut and fold to check each drawing.
   Drawings will vary.
2. Draw four figures that will not fold onto themselves.
   Drawings will vary.

❷ **Activity 2**

Trace these figures onto a piece of paper. Draw all the lines of symmetry.

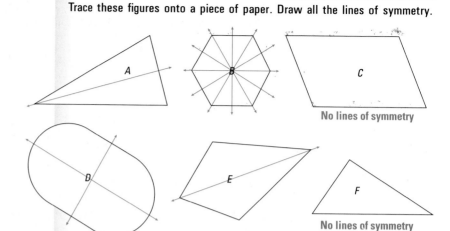

No lines of symmetry

No lines of symmetry

3) Sample:

4) Sample:

5) Sample:

6) Sample:

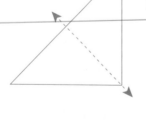

QUESTIONS

Covering the Reading

1. When does a figure have reflection symmetry? when it coincides with its reflection image over some line
2. How many lines of symmetry does a rhombus have? two
3. Draw a figure with no lines of symmetry.
4. Draw a figure that has exactly one symmetry line.
5. Draw a figure that has exactly two lines of symmetry.
6. Draw a figure that has a symmetry line that is neither horizontal nor vertical.
7. How many symmetry lines does a circle have? infinitely many
8. Trace and draw the lines of symmetry for each figure from Activity 2 in this lesson. See above.

Applying the Mathematics

In 9–12, trace the figure, then draw all of its symmetry lines.

9.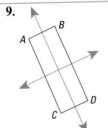

10.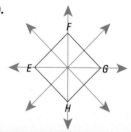

448

Adapting to Individual Needs

Extra Help

If some students have trouble identifying the lines of symmetry in the figures in the lesson, you might have them use **Teaching Aids 93 and 94,** or trace the figures, cut them out, and fold to find the lines of symmetry. Then they can draw the lines of symmetry on the folds.

11.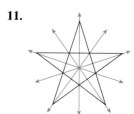

12.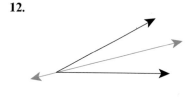

In 13–15, examine these capital letters.

A B C D E F G H I J K L M N O P Q R S T U V W X Y Z

13. Which letters have a horizontal line of symmetry?
B, C, D, E, H, I, O, X

14. Which letters have a vertical line of symmetry?
A, H, I, M, O, T, U, V, W, X, Y

15. Which letters have a symmetry line that is neither horizontal nor vertical? perhaps O

In 16 and 17, a photograph of a living thing is given. In determining the symmetry of natural things like these, it is common to ignore small details.

How many lines of symmetry does the object have?

16. 10

17. 5

Passion flower. *There are about 400 species of the passion flower. Some are grown for their beauty and some, such as the papaya, for their fruit.*

Starfish *The starfish is not a fish but a marine invertebrate. Most are 8 to 12 in. across and live in the ocean. A starfish is capable of growing a new arm if it loses one.*

18)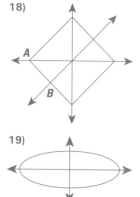

19)

In 18 and 19, part of a symmetric figure is shown. All lines drawn are symmetry lines. Trace what is given, and then draw in the rest of the figure.

18.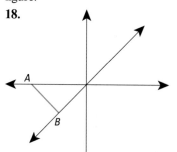

19.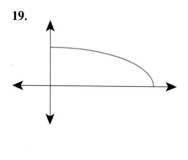

Lesson 8-7 *Reflection Symmetry* **449**

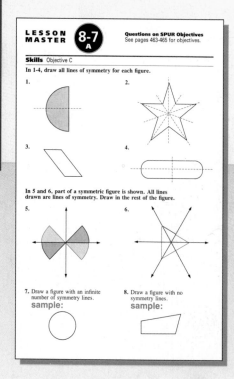

449

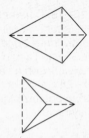
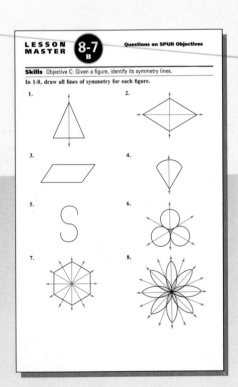
450

---

20) Sample:

21) Sample:

23) This line is a line of symmetry because all points on one side of the line are reflections of points on the other side.

26a)

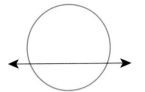

27)

---

20. Draw a hexagon with no lines of symmetry.

21. Draw a hexagon with exactly two lines of symmetry.

In 22 and 23, explain why the given line is or is not a line of symmetry.

22.   **23.**

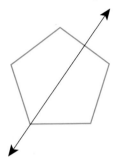

22) This line is not a line of symmetry because it doesn't pass through the center of the circle.

24. Print your full name in capital letters. What percent of the letters in your name have a vertical line as a symmetry line? What percent have a horizontal line as a symmetry line? *Answers will vary.*

Review

25. The point (-3, 8) is reflected over the *x*-axis. What is its image? *(Lesson 8-6)* (-3, -8)

26. a. Graph the quadrilateral with vertices (2, -3), (6, -1), (0, 0), and (-4, -2).
    b. Translate (slide) this quadrilateral up four units and give the vertices of the image quadrilateral. *(Lessons 8-3, 8-5)* Image vertices: (2, 1), (6, 3), (0, 4), (-4, 2)

27. Graph the line with equation $x + y = -4$. *(Lesson 8-4)* Some points on the line are (0, -4), (-4, 0), (-2, -2).

28. The triangle, quadrilateral, pentagon, and decagon pictured in the table on page 284 are **convex polygons.** The other polygons are not convex. Use this information to pick the correct description of convex polygon from this list. A convex polygon is:
(a) a polygon in which two sides are parallel.
(b) a polygon in which there is a right angle.
(c) a polygon in which no diagonals lie outside the polygon.
(d) a polygon with a number of sides that is not a prime number. *(Lesson 5-9)* (c)

450

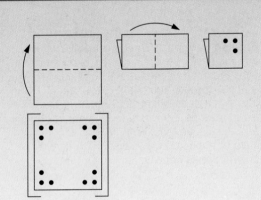
450

Circulation
(millions)

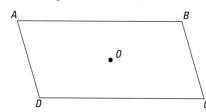

18
16 — 16.3
14 — 14.5
12
10 — 9.7
8.0
8
6
4
2

BHG NG RD TVG

29. Here are average circulations for the last six months of 1992 of four of the best-selling magazines in the United States. Draw a bar graph with this information. *(Lesson 8-2)*

Magazine	Circulation
Better Homes and Gardens	8,002,585
National Geographic	9,708,254
Reader's Digest	16,258,478
TV Guide	14,498,341

30. Find the value of $a + 3(b + 4(c + 5))$ when $a = 1$, $b = 2$, and $c = 3$. *(Lesson 4-5)* **103**

Exploration

31. A figure has **rotation symmetry** if it coincides with an image under a rotation or turn. For instance, all parallelograms have rotation symmetry. Under a 180° rotation (half turn) about point *O, ABCD* coincides with its image.

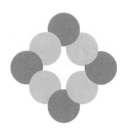

Tell whether the figure below has rotation symmetry. If so, give the magnitude of the smallest rotation under which the figure coincides with its image. **Yes; 90°**

Lesson 8-7 *Reflection Symmetry* **451**

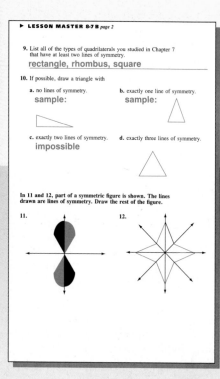

Objectives

D Make a tessellation using a given figure as a fundamental region.

Resources

From the Teacher's Resource File
- Lesson Master 8-8A or 8-8B
- Answer Master 8-8
- Teaching Aids
  83 Warm-up
  95 Activity and Questions 10–13
- Activity Kit, Activity 21

Additional Resources
- Visuals for Teaching Aids 83, 95
- Geometry Template

Teaching Lesson 8-8

Warm-up

Diagnostic

1. Draw a regular quadrilateral. **Students can draw any square.**
2. Draw a regular triangle. **Students can draw any equilateral triangle.**
3. Draw a quadrilateral that is convex. Then draw one that is not convex. **Sample convex quadrilateral shown below on the left; sample quadrilateral that is not convex shown below on the right.**

❶ What Is a Tessellation?

Pictured here are some honeybees in their beehive. Each hexagon behind the bees is a cell in which the bees store honey. Bees are naturally talented at making such cells, so the pattern of hexagons is close to perfect. The pattern of hexagons is an example of a *tessellation*.

A **tessellation** is a filling up of a two-dimensional space by congruent copies of a figure that do not overlap. The figure that is copied is called the **fundamental region** or **fundamental shape** for the tessellation. Tessellations can be formed by combining translation, rotation, and reflection images of the fundamental region.

Shapes that Tessellate

In the beehive the fundamental region is a **regular hexagon**. A **regular polygon** is a convex polygon whose sides all have the same length and angles all have the same measure. A regular polygon with six sides is a regular hexagon.

Only two other regular polygons tessellate. They are the square and the **equilateral triangle**. Pictured here are parts of tessellations using them. A fundamental region is shaded in each drawing.

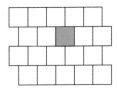

Variations of these regular polygons can also tessellate. There are many different ways to modify the sides of a regular fundamental region so that the resulting figure will tessellate.

452

Lesson 8-8 Overview

Broad Goals The purposes of this lesson are to have fun, to introduce *regular polygons*, to give students practice in putting together geometric shapes, and to review ideas from other parts of the chapter.

Perspective The underlying mathematics of *tessellations* is interesting. This lesson discusses content that, for some teachers and students, is the most memorable of the year.

Any triangle or quadrilateral can be a fundamental region for a tessellation, as illustrated in **Question 11.** Some pentagons do not tessellate, but no one has yet been able to definitively list all pentagons that do tessellate. The only regular polygons that tessellate are equilateral triangles, squares, and regular hexagons. There are *semi-regular tessellations* made up of more than one type of regular polygon. For example, if you try to tessellate regular octagons, you can fit

small squares into the regions not covered by the octagons. This idea is considered in the *Extension*.

Modify a rectangle to create a new tessellation.

Solution

1. Draw and cut any shape out of any side of an index card.

2. Slide the cut-out piece *straight across* to the opposite side. Do not flip it over. Tape it to the opposite side.

3. Pick an uncut side of the rectangle. Draw and cut another shape out of this side, slide it straight across to the opposite side, and tape it to the opposite side.

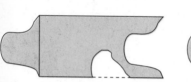

4. On a large sheet of paper, trace around the figure you made.
5. Slide the figure until part of it fits (like a jigsaw puzzle) into part of the tracing you drew. Trace around the figure again.
6. Repeat Step 5 again and again until the page is filled.

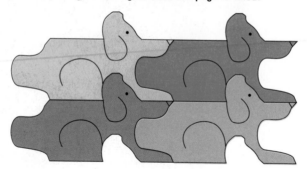

Notes on Reading

❶ Students who have never seen a natural beehive may be surprised to learn that the hive in the picture is made by bees, not by people. The tessellation of hexagons used by bees in making their beehives is extraordinarily accurate.

❷ The **Example** illustrates the easiest way to create a tessellation with a figure that is not a polygon. Go through the solution in some detail. You might also want to go through it using a different modification of the rectangle, or perhaps by modifying a triangle.

Optional Activities

Activity 1 You might want to use *Activity Kit, Activity 21*, after students have completed the lesson. In this activity, students investigate rotations on an Escher-style tessellation.

Activity 2 Every student should, during his or her mathematics (or art) studies, make at least one tessellation using some nonobvious figure as its fundamental region. The Activity on page 454 introduces students to this idea. However, after using the Activity, you might want students to experiment in making their own tessellations. These can be quite attractive if they are carefully and brightly colored.

❸ This hexagon is shown on **Teaching Aid 95**, along with figures students will need for **Questions 10–13.** Students can paste the Teaching Aid onto a piece of cardboard, and cut out the hexagon.

❹ Multicultural Connection If books by Maurits Escher are available, you might show students other designs he created. Many of Escher's tessellations use unusual fundamental regions. However, what is surprising is that even the most complicated tessellations are based on rather simple tessellation designs.

History Connection Tessellation lore contains many interesting facts and puzzles. For example, in 1890 the Russian mathematician Fedorov proved that there are only 17 different symmetry patterns for tessellations in the plane.

Trace the hexagon below onto a piece of cardboard. Modify it to create a new figure that will tessellate. Make a tessellation using the figure as a fundamental region. You may want to illustrate and/or color your design.

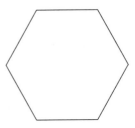

Save your modified figure.

Many other shapes can be fundamental regions for tessellations. The Dutch artist Maurits Escher became famous for the unusual shapes he used in tessellations. Here is part of one of his drawings.

M. C. Escher created this ❹ *periodic design,* Shells and Starfish, *in 1941. He based the design upon tesselations by congruent figures.*

Some shapes do not tessellate. For instance, there can be no tessellation using only congruent regular *pentagons.* (You may want to try, but you will not succeed.)

454

Adapting to Individual Needs

Extra Help Using Physical Models

Materials: Sets of congruent shapes, six each, some of which tessellate and some of which do not.

Before using the example, some students might benefit from actually trying to put congruent figures together—like jigsaw puzzles—to see if they do or do not tessellate. Use sets of congruent triangles, squares, pentagons, hexagons, and circles. For a figure or figures to tessellate, the following conditions must exist: an entire area must be covered, there can be no "holes," and the figures cannot overlap.

QUESTIONS

Covering the Reading

1. What is a tessellation? a filling up of a two-dimensional space by congruent copies of a figure that do not overlap

2. What is the fundamental region for a tessellation? the figure whose copies fill up the space

3. In a beehive, what figure is the fundamental region? a regular hexagon

4. What is a regular polygon? a convex polygon whose sides have the same length and whose angles have the same measure

5. Name three regular polygons that tessellate. equilateral triangles, squares, regular hexagons

6. Can a polygon that is not a regular polygon tessellate? Yes

7. If a figure is not a polygon, can it be a fundamental region for a tessellation? Yes

8. Draw a tessellation with equilateral triangles.

8) Sample:

Applying the Mathematics

9. Use your modified hexagon from the Activity in this lesson to make a tessellation. Answers will vary.

10) Sample:

In 10–13, trace the figure onto cardboard. Make a tessellation with at least 8 copies of the figure as a fundamental region. Figure 12 is from the drawings of Maurits Escher.

11)

10.

11.

12.

13.

12)

13)

Lesson 8-8 *Tessellations* **455**

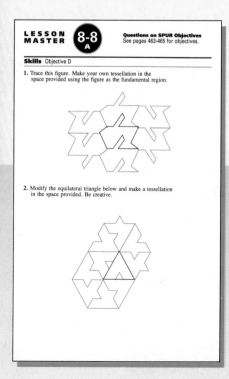

Adapting to Individual Needs

English Language Development
There are several terms you might want to spend some extra time introducing or reviewing: *fundamental region, regular polygon,* and *equilateral triangle.*

When talking about a *fundamental* region, point out that the word fundamental means forming a foundation, or base. In a tessellation, the tessellating figure is the base of the design.

You might contrast *regular* polygons and *nonregular* polygons through illustrations. Emphasize, for example, that any polygon, with 6 sides and 6 angles, is a hexagon. Only when all of the sides and angles are congruent is it a regular hexagon. Point out that *equilateral triangle* is a special name for a regular triangle. Similarly, *square* is a special name for a regular quadrilateral.

455

Question 28 History Connection
The Alhambra was built by Moors.
The Moors lived all around the
Mediterranean and controlled Spain
for hundreds of years. They were
Muslims, and the Muslim religion for-
bids the use of pictures of living
things on the walls of places of wor-
ship. So the Moors' buildings tended
to have intricate abstract designs. In
1492, during the Spanish Inquisition,
the last Moors were driven from
Spain.

Follow-up 8-8
for Lesson

Practice

For more questions on SPUR Objectives, use **Lesson Master 8-8A**
(shown on page 455) or **Lesson
Master 8-8B** (shown on pages
456–457).

14a) A sheet of stamps
is a tessellation;
rectangles tessellate, so
no paper is wasted.
b) Sample: Unusual
stamps are popular with
collectors and can be a
source of income for a
country.

14. Pictured here is a postage stamp from the Polynesian kingdom of
Tonga.
  a. Why are most postage stamps shaped like rectangles?
  b. Why do you think Tonga has stamps shaped like ellipses?

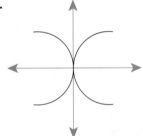

15. How many degrees are in each angle of an equilateral triangle? 60°
(Hint: What is the sum of the measures of the angles?)

16. **a.** Stop signs on highways are in the shape of what regular polygon?
  b. Can this shape be a fundamental shape for a tessellation?
  a) octagon; b) No

17. Another name for *regular quadrilateral* is __?__. square

18. Write a letter to a friend explaining how you modified the hexagon
in the Activity in this lesson. Include a sample tessellation. Answers
will vary.

Review

In 19 and 20, draw all symmetry lines for the given figure. *(Lesson 8-7)*

19. 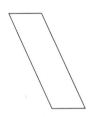   20. no symmetry lines

21. *Multiple choice.* Which is an expression for the measure of one
angle of a regular *n*-gon? *(Lessons 5-9, 6-7, 8-7)*
  (a) $180n(n - 2)$ (b) $\frac{360}{n}$
  (c) $\frac{180(n - 2)}{n}$ (d) $\frac{180}{n}$ (c)

22. A quadrilateral is symmetric with respect to the *y*-axis. Two of the
vertices of the quadrilateral are (4, 8) and (-2, 5). What are the other
two vertices? *(Lessons 8-6, 8-7)* (-4, 8) and (2, 5)

456

Adapting to Individual Needs

Challenge
Have students study regular polygons that
tessellate and regular polygons that do not
tessellate to try to find a property that equilateral triangles, squares, and regular hexagons have that other regular polygons do
not have. [The measure of each angle of
any regular triangle, quadrilateral, and hexagon is a factor of 360; thus the angles can
"fit" together around a point. The angle

measure for a non-tessellating regular polygon is *not* a factor of 360.]

23. Draw the reflection image of triangle *ABC* over line *m*.   *(Lesson 8-6)*

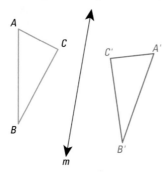

24. Tonya is 5 feet tall. If she grew $1\frac{1}{4}$ inches during the past year, and $\frac{7}{8}$ inch the year before, how tall was she two years ago?
(Lessons 3-2, 7-2) $57\frac{7}{8}$ inches, or 4 feet $9\frac{7}{8}$ inches

25. Solve $a + b + c + d = 360$ for c.   *(Lesson 5-8)* $c = 360 - a - b - d$

26. Write 0.00000 002 in scientific notation.   *(Lesson 2-9)* 2×10^{-8}

Exploration

27. Tiles on floors or ceilings usually form tessellations. Find at least two examples of such tessellations. Sketch the design of each.
Answers will vary.

28. If you visit the Alhambra, you will see many examples of tessellations.
   a. Where is the Alhambra?   **b.** What is it?
   c. Who built it?   **d.** When was it built?
   a) Granada Spain; b) a palace; c) Moorish kings; d) 1248–1354

Shown here is a detail from the Alhambra.

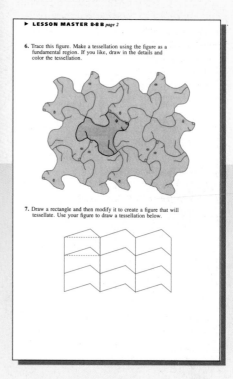

Chapter 8 Projects

Resources

From the Teacher's Resource File
- Teaching Aid 96: Project 6

Additional Resources
- Visual for Teaching Aid 96

Chapter 8 projects relate to the content of the lessons as follows.

Project	Lesson(s)
1	8-8
2	8-7
3	8-3, 8-4
4	8-1, 8-2, 8-3
5	8-3
6	8-1
7	8-1, 8-2, 8-3

1 Tessellations The following sources will provide additional information and instruction on tessellations: *Introduction to Tessellations* by Dale Seymour and Jill Britton; Dale Seymour Publications, 1989. "The Art of Tessellations" by Paul Giganti, Jr. and Mary Jo Cittadino, *Arithmetic Teacher* (1990): 6-14. *"Transformational Geometry and the Artwork of M. C. Escher"* by Sheila Haak, Arithmetic Teacher (1976): 647-652.

2 Symmetry Some students may wish to find symmetry in objects from one specific area, such as architecture or nature. Other students may decide to find symmetry in objects from areas that are of special interest to them such as sports, art, or clothing. Yet other students may find examples of symmetry from a variety of areas. Suggest that students group objects according to the number of lines of symmetry the objects have.

3 Automatic Graphers Sources for automatic graphers include graphing calculators and computer software programs. You may need to explain to students what the terms parameter and scale mean. They can explore how changing the parameters of an equation and the scale will affect their graphs.

458

A project presents an opportunity for you to extend your knowledge of a topic related to the material of this chapter. You should allow more time for a project than you do for typical homework questions.

1 Tessellations
Make a tessellation in which the fundamental region is the shape of an animal or other thing. Design and color your tessellation.

2 Symmetry
Find or take pictures of objects that have different numbers of symmetry lines. For instance, a chandelier may have 10 or 12 symmetry lines; a coin from another country 8 symmetry lines. Find as many different kinds of objects with different symmetries as you can.

458

---

3 Automatic Graphers
Visual displays in mathematics are so helpful that some calculators and computer software have the capability of making coordinate graphs. We call these *automatic graphers,* but no grapher is completely automatic. Learn how to use an automatic grapher. Then use it to graph some of the equations from Lesson 8-4 or other equations of your own choosing. Give an oral or written presentation describing what you have learned.

Responses
1. Responses will vary.
2. Responses will vary.
3. The following information is a sample of what students might include in their projects. Most automatic graphers require the user to input scales for the x- and y-axes. The value of x determines the value of y. If the equation is in slope-intercept form, $y = mx + b$, the parameters of the equation are m and b. As b changes, the line moves up or down. As m changes, the slant of the line changes.

4 Displays in Newspapers

Obtain a large-city Sunday newspaper or a copy of *USA Today*. Cut out every mathematical display in the newspaper. Organize the displays in some fashion, giving the purpose of each display.

5 Display of Temperature

Keep track of the high and low temperatures where you live each day for a week. Display the data in a coordinate graph. Summarize in prose what the temperature has been like for the week.

6 Displays of the Tchokwe

The design below comes from the Tchokwe people of northeast Angola, in the southwestern part of Africa. The Tchokwe draw in the sand and tell stories about what they draw. These drawings almost always begin with setting down a collection of equally spaced points. Then curves are added through and around the points. The drawing below represents a leopard with five cubs. Copy this design and decide where you think the leopard and five cubs are. Make two more designs of this type and write a short story for each.

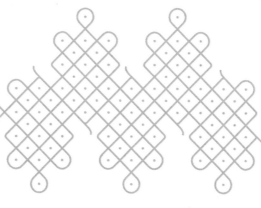

7 Your Own Data

Ask a question that requires collecting some interesting data. Organize the data in several ways, and make at least three different graphs using the data. Report on how you found the data, and summarize what you found.

---

4 Displays in Newspapers Students should look for graphs, sports statistics, stock market information analyses, mortgage rate analyses, and any other comparison charts of topical events. Students may organize displays by type, topic, or range of numbers (magnitude).

5 A Display of Temperature Suggest to students that they draw two separate lines on their graphs, one for the daily low temperatures and one for the daily high temperatures for the week. Students may use different colors for each of the lines and select different scales to display their data. When students have completed their projects, give them an opportunity to compare graphs that display the same data but use different scales.

6 Displays of the Tchokwe You might want to give students **Teaching Aid 96.** Explain to students that each figure is called a *lusona* (plural sonas). Tell students that the simplest lusona is a continuous closed curve with no intersections. You may wish to draw a closed curve on the board and put dots inside and outside the curve. Students should have little difficulty in determining if points lie inside or outside the curve. Suggest to students that their first display be a closed curve and that their story involve inside and outside points. Once students understand simple closed curves, they can move on to a more elaborate display. For more information, students may wish to consult *Ethnomathematics* by Marcia Ascher, published by Brooks/Cole Publishing Company in 1991.

7 Your Own Data Encourage students to avoid survey questions that have simple yes or no answers because the resulting graphs may be simplistic and uninteresting. Students may wish to use a computer software package such as *Transition Mathematics Software* or *StatExplorer* that manipulates data into different graphs.

---

4. Responses will vary.
5. Responses will vary.

6. Designs and stories will vary. Sample response:

7. Responses will vary.

Summary

The Summary gives an overview of the entire chapter and provides an opportunity for students to consider the material as a whole. Thus, the Summary can be used to help students relate and unify the concepts presented in the chapter.

Vocabulary

Terms, symbols, and properties are listed by lesson to provide a checklist of concepts a student must know. Emphasize to students that they should read the vocabulary list carefully before starting the Progress Self-Test. If students do not understand the meaning of a term, they should refer back to the indicated lesson.

SUMMARY

Displays enable a lot of information to be presented in a small space. They can picture trends, are useful for exploring data, and can be used to sway opinions. In this chapter three kinds of displays are discussed: stem-and-leaf displays, bar graphs, and coordinate graphs.

Bar graphs compare quantities by using segments or bars on a specific scale. The scale uses the idea of a number line. By combining two number lines (usually one horizontal, one vertical), pairs of numbers can be pictured on a coordinate graph. Coordinate graphs can show trends and relationships between numbers. Some simple relationships, such as those pairs of numbers (x, y) satisfying equations of the form $x + y = k$ or $x - y = k$, have graphs that are lines.

Relationships between geometric figures can also be displayed. A figure can be put on a coordinate graph. By changing the coordinates of points on the figure, an image of the figure can be drawn. By adding the same numbers to the coordinates, a slide or translation image results.

Any figure can be reflected over a line that acts like a mirror. The image is called a reflection image. If the figure coincides with its image, then it is said to be symmetric with respect to the reflecting line.

Reflections and translations are two types of transformations. So are the rotations you studied in an earlier chapter. Beautiful designs known as tessellations can be created using congruent images of figures under these transformations.

VOCABULARY

You should be able to give a general description and a specific example of each of the following ideas.

Lesson 8-1
stem-and-leaf display, stem, leaf
range
median
statistic
mode

Lesson 8-2
prose
bar graph
uniform scale

Lesson 8-3
coordinate graph
ordered pair
first coordinate
second coordinate
x-coordinate
y-coordinate
x-axis, y-axis
origin
quadrant

Lesson 8-4
graph of the solutions to an equation
palindrome

Lesson 8-5
translation image, slide image
preimage, image
congruent figures

Lesson 8-6
reflection image
reflecting line, mirror
coincide
transformation

Lesson 8-7
reflection symmetry, symmetry with respect to a line
rotation symmetry
convex polygon

Lesson 8-8
tessellation
fundamental region, fundamental shape
regular polygon
regular hexagon
equilateral triangle

PROGRESS SELF-TEST

Take this test as you would take a test in class. You will need graph paper and a ruler or straightedge. Then check your work with the solutions in the Selected Answers section in the back of the book.

In 1–4, use the graph below.

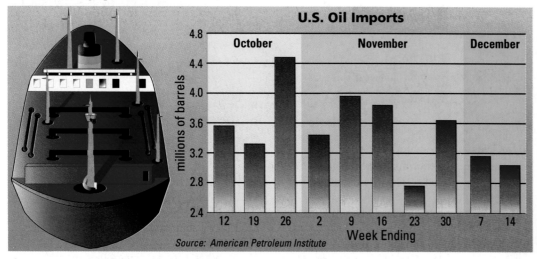

U.S. Oil Imports

Source: American Petroleum Institute

1. In which week of November were the most barrels of oil imported into the U.S.? **Nov. 9**

2. About how many barrels of oil per day were imported into the U.S. during the week of December 14? **≈ 430,000 barrels**

3. What is the interval of the scale on the vertical axis of the graph? **0.4 million barrels**

4. What could be misleading about this graph?

5. A Thanksgiving meal in 1991 cost the typical person about 57¢ for green beans, 81¢ for a beverage, 32¢ for cranberries, 22¢ for sweet potatoes, and $1.18 for turkey. Put this information into a bar graph. **See margin.**

6. Point Q has coordinates (2, 5). What are the coordinates of the point that is ten units directly above Q? **(2, 15)**

7. Graph the line with equation $x - y = 2$. **See graph at the right.**

4) The vertical axis does not begin at 0, so the bars look more different than they actually are.

In 8–10, use the graph below. The interval of each scale is one unit.

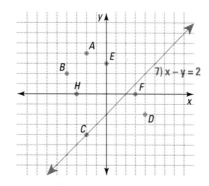

8. **a.** What letter names the point (0, 3)? **E**
   b. What letter names the point (-2, 4)? **A**

9. Which point or points are on the y-axis? **E**

10. Which point or points are on the line $x + y = -2$? **B, since -4 + 2 = -2.**

Progress Self-Test

For the development of mathematical competence, feedback and correction, along with the opportunity to practice, are necessary. The Progress Self-Test provides the opportunity for feedback and correction; the Chapter Review provides additional opportunities and practice. We cannot overemphasize the importance of these end-of-chapter materials. It is at this point that the material "gels" for many students, allowing them to solidify skills and understanding. In general, student performance should be markedly improved after these pages.

Assign the Progress Self-Test as a one-night assignment. Worked-out *solutions* for all questions are in the Selected Answers section of the student book. Encourage students to take the Progress Self-Test honestly, grade themselves, and then be prepared to discuss the test in class.

Advise students to pay special attention to those Chapter Review questions (pages 463–465) which correspond to questions missed on the Progress Self-Test.

Additional Answers
5.

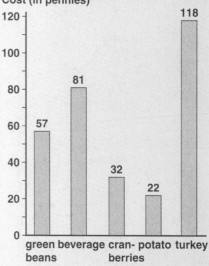

 Cost of a Thanksgiving Meal, 1991
 Cost (in pennies)

Additional Answers

18.

Cost of Mailing Letters 1993

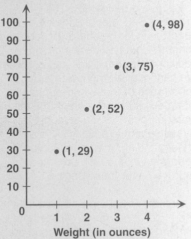

PROGRESS SELF-TEST

In 11 and 12, use the graph of the miniature golf hole below. All angles are right angles. The intervals on the axes are uniform.

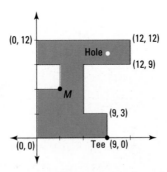

11. Give the coordinates of point *M*. (3, 6)
12. Estimate the coordinates of the hole. (9, 10.5)
13. Draw a quadrilateral with no lines of symmetry. 13–15) See below right.
14. Draw a figure with exactly two lines of symmetry.
15. Draw a square and all its lines of symmetry.
16. Trace triangle *GHI* and line *m* below. Draw the reflection image of triangle *GHI* over line *m*.

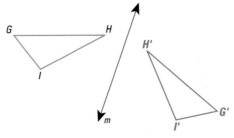

17. Draw part of a tessellation that uses triangle *GHI* as its fundamental region.

18. In 1993, it cost 29¢ to mail a letter weighing 1 oz, 52¢ for a 2-oz letter, 75¢ for a 3-oz letter, and 98¢ for a 4-oz letter. Graph the ordered pairs suggested by this information.
19. In the figure below, *V* is the reflection image of *W* over line ℓ. If m∠*UVW* = 72°, what is m∠*W*? 72°   18) See margin.

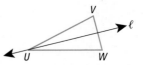

20. Give a reason for having graphs. See below.
21. When are two figures congruent? when they have the same size and shape

In 22–23, use these ages of the first 20 presidents of the United States at the time of inauguration.

57, 61, 57, 57, 57, 58, 57, 61, 54, 68, 51, 49, 64, 50, 48, 65, 52, 56, 46, 54

22. Make a stem-and-leaf display with these numbers. See below.
23. a. What is the median of these numbers? 57
    b. What is the range of these numbers? 22
    c. What is the mode of these numbers? 57

13) Sample: 14) Sample: 15)

20) Sample: Graphs can show a lot of information in a small place. Graphs can picture relationships.

22)
```
4 | 9 8 6
5 | 7 7 7 7 8 7 4 1 0 2 6 4
6 | 1 1 8 4 5
```

CHAPTER REVIEW

Questions on SPUR Objectives

SPUR stands for **S**kills, **P**roperties, **U**ses, and **R**epresentations. The Chapter Review questions are grouped according to the SPUR Objectives for this chapter.

SKILLS DEAL WITH THE PROCEDURES USED TO GET ANSWERS.

Objective A: *Determine the median, range, and mode of a set of numbers.* *(Lesson 8-1)*

In 1–4, give the median, range, and mode of the given numbers.

1. 350, 568, 355, 504, 346, 350, 423, 351, 372 (the heights (in feet) of the 9 tallest buildings in Cincinnati, Ohio) 355; 222; 350

2. 55, 35, 30, 35, 40, 32, 35, 42, 28 (the numbers of stories in the 9 tallest buildings in Miami, Florida) 35; 27; 35

3. 7, 8, 7, 7, 6, 6, 7, 8, 5, 6, 4, 6, 7, 6, 5, 6, 6, 7 (the number of letters in the first names of 20th-century U.S. Presidents) 6; 4; 6

4. 8, 9, 4, 6, 7, 8, 6, 9, 6, 10, 7, 7, 5, 4, 6, 6, 4, 7 (the number of letters in the last names of 20th-century U.S. Presidents) 6.5; 6; 6

Objective B: *Draw the reflection image of a figure over a line.* *(Lesson 8-6)*

In 5–8, trace and use the figures below.

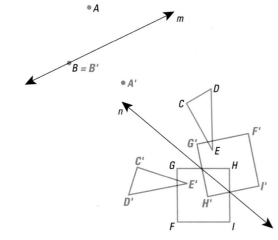

5. Draw the reflection image of point *A* over line *m*.

6. Draw the reflection image of point *B* over line *m*.

7. Draw the reflection image of triangle *CDE* over line *n*.

8. Draw the reflection image of square *FGHI* over line *n*.

5–8) See below left.

Objective C: *Given a figure, identify its symmetry lines.* *(Lesson 8-7)*

In 9–12, draw all symmetry lines for the given figure.

9.

10.
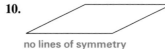

no lines of symmetry

11.
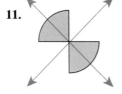

12.
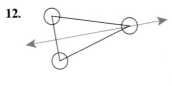

Resources

From the ***Teacher's Resource File***
- Answer Master for Chapter 8 Review
- Assessment Sourcebook: Chapter 8 Test, Forms A–D Chapter 8 Test, Cumulative Form

Additional Resources
- TestWorks

The main objectives for the chapter are organized in the Chapter Review under the four types of understanding this book promotes—Skills, Properties, Uses, and Representations.

Whereas end-of chapter material may be considered optional in some texts, in *UCSMP Transition Mathematics* we have selected these objectives and questions with the expectation that they will be covered. Students should be able to answer these questions with about 85% accuracy after studying the chapter.

You may assign these questions over a single night to help students prepare for a test the next day, or you may assign the questions over a two-day period. If you work the questions over two days, then we recommend assigning the *evens* for homework the first night so that students get feedback in class the next day, then assigning the *odds* the night before the test, because answers are provided to the odd-numbered questions.

It is effective to ask students which questions they still do not understand and use the day or days as a total class discussion of the material which the class finds most difficult.

Evaluation

The *Assessment Sourcebook* provides five forms of the Chapter 8 Test. Forms A and B present parallel versions in a short-answer format. Forms C and D offer performance assessment. The fifth test is Chapter 8 Test, Cumulative Form. About 50% of this test covers Chapter 8, 25% of it covers Chapter 7, and 25% of it covers earlier chapters.

For information on grading, see *General Teaching Suggestions: Grading* in the *Professional Sourcebook* which begins on page T20 in Volume 1 of this Teacher's Edition.

Additional Answers
24a. Sample: 10 calories
  b. Sample:

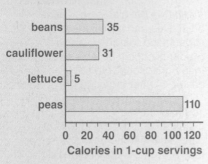
Calories in 1-cup servings

25a. Sample: 1 million
  b. Sample:
     U.S. Population

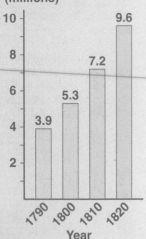

Objective D: *Make a tessellation using a given figure as a fundamental region.* (Lesson 8-8)

13. Make a tessellation using the figure of Question 10 as a fundamental region.
    Sample:

14. Make a tessellation using △ABC below as a fundamental region.

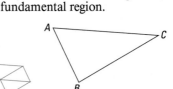

14) Sample:

PROPERTIES DEAL WITH THE PRINCIPLES BEHIND THE MATHEMATICS.

Objective E: *Apply the relationships between figures and their reflection, rotation, and translation images.* (Lessons 8-5, 8-6)

In 15 and 16, use the figure below. *P'* is the reflection image of point *P* over line *t*. Answer with numbers.

15. m∠PQR = __?__. 90°
16. If PQ = 7, then PP' = __?__. 14
17. Triangle ABC is a translation image of triangle DEF. Must the two triangles be congruent? Explain your reasoning.
18. Can one of two congruent figures be the reflection image of the other? Why or why not?

17) Yes, a translation image is always the same size and shape as its preimage.
18) Yes, when one figure is the mirror image of the other over a line of symmetry.

USES DEAL WITH APPLICATIONS OF MATHEMATICS IN REAL SITUATIONS.

Objective F: *Interpret and display information in bar graphs.* (Lesson 8-2)

In 19–23, use the graph below. It shows the average heights of boys and girls for the ages 12–16.

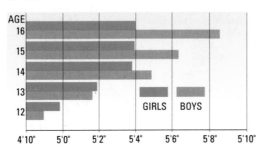

19. What is the interval of the horizontal scale of the graph? 2″
20. At which age do girls and boys differ most in height? 16

21. What is the average height of 12-year-old boys? 4′ 11″
22. Who grows more from age 12 to 13, girls or boys? boys
23) See below.
23. What about this graph could be misleading?
24. The calories in 1-cup servings of some vegetables are: green beans, 35; cauliflower, 31; lettuce, 5; peas, 110.
    a. To display this information in a bar graph, what interval might you use on the scale?
    b. Display in a bar graph. See margin.
25. Use the population of the United States during the first four censuses: 1790, 3.9 million; 1800, 5.3 million; 1810, 7.2 million; 1820, 9.6 million.
    a. To display this information in a bar graph, what interval might you use on the scale?
    b. Display in a bar graph. See margin.

23) The axis does not begin at 0, so the differences between the average heights of boys and girls are magnified.

464

Setting Up Lesson 9-1

Materials Students will need maps of the United States for *Extension* page 475.

We recommend that you assign the Chapter 9 Opener and Lesson 9-1, both reading and some questions, for homework the evening of the test.

Objective G: *Interpret and display information in coordinate graphs.* (*Lesson 8-3*)

In 26–29, use the graph below.

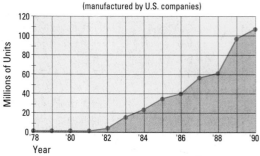

Number of Personal Computers in Use Worldwide
(manufactured by U.S. companies)

26. What major idea is shown in the graph?

27. Name the first year there were more than ten million personal computers in use. **1983**

26) The number of computers in use increased rapidly from 1982 through 1990.

28. In what year were about 30 million personal computers in use? **1985**

29. In what 2-year period did the number of personal computers in use increase the most?

30. Suppose it costs 23¢ a minute for a 1-minute call, 40¢ for a 2-minute call, and 57¢ for a 3-minute call. Graph three ordered pairs suggested by this information.

31. Graph the information of Question 25 on a coordinate graph.

29) 1988–1990; 30, 31) See margin.

Objective H: *Know reasons for having graphs.* (*Lesson 8-1*)

32. Give two reasons why the graph of Questions 19–23 might be useful.

33. Give two reasons why the graph of Questions 26–29 might be useful. **Sample: The graph can show trends and sway the reader.**

32) Sample: The graph is easy to read. The graph saves space.

REPRESENTATIONS DEAL WITH PICTURES, GRAPHS, OR OBJECTS THAT ILLUSTRATE CONCEPTS.

Objective I: *Represent numerical data in a stem-and-leaf display.* (*Lesson 8-1*)

34. Represent the data of Question 2 in a stem-and-leaf display.

35. Here are the latitudes of some of the deepest trenches in the oceans north of the equator: 11°, 10°, 24°, 44°, 31°, 8°, 36°, 7°, 50°, 24°, 14°, 19°, 19°. Represent this information in a stem-and-leaf display.

34, 35) See margin.

Objective J: *Plot and name points on a coordinate graph.* (*Lessons 8-3, 8-4*)

In 36 and 37, use the graph below.

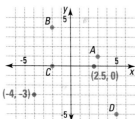

36. Give the coordinates of points *A* and *D*.

37. Give the coordinates of points *B* and *C*.

36) A = (3, 1), D = (5, -5); 37) B = (-2, 4), C = (-2, 0)

38. Graph the point (-4, -3).

39. Graph the point (2.5, 0).

38, 39) See graph below left.

Objective K: *Graph equations for lines of the form $x + y = k$ or $x - y = k$.* (*Lesson 8-4*)

40. Graph the line with equation $x + y = -5$.

41. Graph the line with equation $x - y = 3$.

42. Graph the line with equation $y = x + 2$.

43. Which of the three lines of Questions 40–42 contains the point (-2, -5)? $x - y = 3$

40–42) See margin.

Objective L: *Interpret reflections and translations on a coordinate graph.* (*Lessons 8-5, 8-6*)

44. What are the coordinates of the point 5 units directly above (4, 0)? **(4, 5)**

45. If (2, -3) is reflected over the *y*-axis, what are the coordinates of its image? **(-2, -3)**

46. If (5, 6) is reflected over the *x*-axis, what are the coordinates of its image? **(5, -6)**

47. A triangle with vertices (2, 5), (0, 9), and (3, 7), is slid 2 units down and 7 units to the right. What are the coordinates of the vertices of the image triangle? **(9, 3); (7, 7); (10, 5)**

Chapter 8 *Chapter Review* **465**

34.

35.

40.
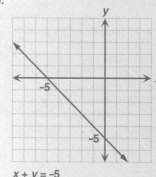

$x + y = -5$

41.
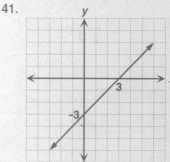

42.
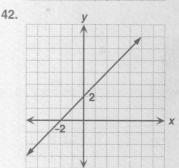

Additional Answers

30.
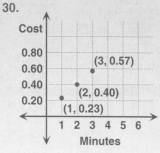

31.
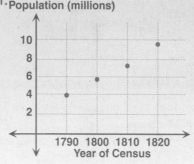

Chapter **9** Planner

Adapting to Individual Needs

The student text is written for the vast majority of students. The chart at the right suggests two pacing plans to accommodate the needs of your students. Students in the Full Course should complete the entire text by the end of the year. Students in the Minimal Course will spend more time when there are quizzes and more time on the Chapter Review. Therefore, these students may not complete all of the chapters in the text.

Options are also presented to meet the needs of a variety of teaching and learning styles. For each lesson, the Teacher's Edition provides sections entitled: *Video* which describes video segments and related questions that can be used for motivation or extension; *Optional Activities* which suggests activities that employ materials, physical models, technology, and cooperative learning; and *Adapting to Individual Needs* which regularly includes **Challenge** problems, **English Language Development** suggestions, and suggestions for providing **Extra Help.** The Teacher's Edition also frequently includes an **Error Alert,** an **Extension,** and an **Assessment** alternative. The options available in Chapter 9 are summarized in the chart below.

Chapter 9 Pacing Chart

Day	Full Course	Minimal Course
1	9-1	9-1
2	9-2	9-2
3	9-3	9-3
4	9-4	9-4
5	Quiz*; 9-5	Quiz*; begin 9-5.
6	9-6	Finish 9-5.
7	9-7	9-6
8	9-8	9-7
9	Quiz*; 9-9	9-8
10	Self-Test	Quiz*; begin 9-9.
11	Review	Finish 9-9.
12	Test*	Self-Test
13	Comprehensive Test*	Review
14		Review
15		Test*
16		Comprehensive Test*

*in the Teacher's Resource File

In the Teacher's Edition...

Lesson	Optional Activities	Extra Help	Challenge	English Language Development	Error Alert	Extension	Cooperative Learning	Ongoing Assessment
9-1	●	●	●	●	●	●		Diagnostic
9-2	●	●	●	●		●	●	Written
9-3	●	●	●	●	●	●	●	Written
9-4	●		●	●			●	Group
9-5	●	●	●	●		●	●	Written
9-6	●	●	●	●		●		Written
9-7	●	●	●	●		●		Written
9-8	●	●	●	●		●		Oral
9-9	●	●	●	●		●		Written

In the Additional Resources...

		In the Teacher's Resource File							
Lesson	Lesson Masters, A and B	Teaching Aids*	Activity Kit*	Answer Masters	Technology Sourcebook	Assessment Sourcebook	Visual Aids**	Technology Tools	Video Segments
9-1	9-1	86, 97, 100–102		9-1			86, 97, 100–102, AM	Geometry	
9-2	9-2	97	22	9-2			97, AM		
9-3	9-3	56, 97, 103		9-3			56, 97, 103, AM		
9-4	9-4	98		9-4		Quiz	98, AM		Segment 9
9-5	9-5	98		9-5			98, AM		Segment 11
9-6	9-6	98	23	9-6			98, AM		
9-7	9-7	86, 87, 99, 104, 105	24	9-7	Demo 9, Comp 19		86, 87, 99, 104, 105, AM	Geometry	
9-8	9-8	86, 87, 99, 105		9-8	Comp 20	Quiz	86, 87, 99, 105, AM	Geometry	
9-9	9-9	87, 99, 105, 106		9-9	Comp 21		87, 99, 105, 106, AM	Geometry	
End of chapter				Review		Tests			

*Teaching Aids, except Warm-ups, are pictured on pages 466C and 466D. The activities in the Activity Kit are pictured on page 466C.

**Visual Aids provide transparencies for all Teaching Aids and all Answer Masters.

Also available is the Study Skills Handbook which includes study-skill tips related to reading, note-taking, and comprehension.

Integrating Strands and Applications

	9-1	9-2	9-3	9-4	9-5	9-6	9-7	9-8	9-9
Mathematical Connections									
Number Sense							●		
Algebra	●	●	●		●	●	●	●	●
Geometry	●	●	●		●	●	●	●	●
Measurement	●	●	●		●	●	●	●	
Logic and Reasoning					●				
Probability				●					
Patterns and Functions	●	●	●	●	●	●	●		●
Interdisciplinary and Other Connections									
Music				●					
Science				●	●	●	●	●	●
Social Studies	●		●		●		●	●	
Multicultural		●			●				●
Technology	●	●	●			·	●	●	●
Career					●		●		
Consumer	●	●		●	●	●		●	
Sports				●	●				

Take it to the NET

On the Internet, visit **www.phschool.com** for UCSMP teacher support, student self-tests, activities, and more.

Teaching and Assessing the Chapter Objectives

Chapter 9 Objectives (Organized into the SPUR categories—Skills, Properties, Uses, and Representations)	Lessons	Progress Self-Test Questions	Chapter Review Questions	Chapter Test, Forms A and B	Chapter Test, Forms C	Chapter Test, Forms D
Skills						
A: Find the area of a rectangle or a right triangle, given its dimensions.	9-1	9, 13	1–4	1, 21		✓
B: Find the volume of a rectangular solid, given its dimensions.	9-2	11	5, 6	19	5	✓
C: Multiply fractions.	9-3	1, 2	7–15	11–13	1	✓
D: Multiply positive and negative numbers.	9-6	3, 4	16–22	14–17	2	
Properties						
E: Identify properties of multiplication.	9-1, 9-2, 9-3, 9-6	6, 7, 25	23–28	2, 3, 7	2	
F: Use properties of multiplication to simplify expressions and check calculations.	9-1, 9-2, 9-3, 9-6	5, 14	29–36	12, 27	2	
Uses						
G: Find areas of right triangles and rectangles and the number of elements in rectangular arrays in applied situations.	9-1	8	37–39	18		✓
H: Find the volume of a rectangular solid in real contexts.	9-2	12	40–43	22	5	✓
I: Calculate probabilities of independent events.	9-4	23, 24	44–47	4, 23	3	
J: Apply the Rate Factor Model for Multiplication.	9-5	10, 18	48–52	5, 20	4	✓
K: Use conversion factors to convert from one unit to another.	9-5	26	53–56	6, 25	4	✓
L: Apply the Size Change Model for Multiplication in real situations.	9-7, 9-8	16, 21, 22	57–60	9		✓
Representations						
M: Picture multiplication using arrays or area.	9-1, 9-3	13, 17	61–64	24	1	
N: Perform expansions or contractions on a coordinate graph.	9-7, 9-8, 9-9	15, 19, 20	65–72	8, 10, 26	6	✓

Assessment Sourcebook
Quiz for Lessons 9-1 through 9-4
Quiz for Lessons 9-5 through 9-8
Chapter 9 Test, Forms A–D
Chapter 9 Test, Cumulative Form
Comprehensive Test, Chapters 1–9

TestWorks
Multiple forms of chapter tests and quizzes; Challenge items

Activity Kit

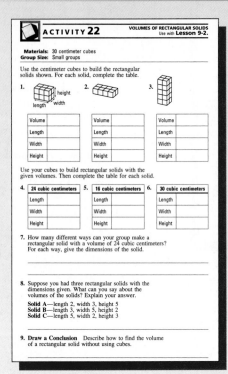

ACTIVITY 22

VOLUMES OF RECTANGULAR SOLIDS
Use with **Lesson 9-2.**

Materials: 30 centimeter cubes
Group Size: Small groups

Use the centimeter cubes to build the rectangular solids shown. For each solid, complete the table.

Volume	
Length	
Width	
Height	

Volume	
Length	
Width	
Height	

Volume	
Length	
Width	
Height	

Use your cubes to build rectangular solids with the given volumes. Then complete the table for each solid.

4. 24 cubic centimeters

Length	
Width	
Height	

5. 16 cubic centimeters

Length	
Width	
Height	

6. 30 cubic centimeters

Length	
Width	
Height	

7. How many different ways can your group make a rectangular solid with a volume of 24 cubic centimeters? For each way, give the dimensions of the solid.

8. Suppose you had three rectangular solids with the dimensions given. What can you say about the volumes of the solids? Explain your answer.
Solid A—length 2, width 3, height 5
Solid B—length 3, width 5, height 2
Solid C—length 5, width 2, height 3

9. Draw a Conclusion Describe how to find the volume of a rectangular solid without using cubes.

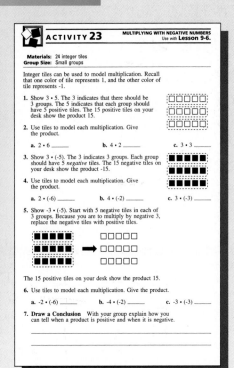

ACTIVITY 23

MULTIPLYING WITH NEGATIVE NUMBERS
Use with **Lesson 9-6.**

Materials: 24 integer tiles
Group Size: Small groups

Integer tiles can be used to model multiplication. Recall that one color of tile represents 1, and the other color of tile represents -1.

1. Show 3 • 5. The 3 indicates that there should be 3 groups. The 5 indicates that each group should have 5 positive tiles. The 15 positive tiles on your desk show the product 15.

2. Use tiles to model each multiplication. Give the product.

a. 2 • 6 _____ **b.** 4 • 2 _____ **c.** 3 • 3 _____

3. Show 3 • (-5). The 3 indicates 3 groups. Each group should have 5 *negative* tiles. The 15 negative tiles on your desk show the product -15.

4. Use tiles to model each multiplication. Give the product.

a. 2 • (-6) _____ **b.** 4 • (-2) _____ **c.** 3 • (-3) _____

5. Show -3 • (-5). Start with 5 negative tiles in each of 3 groups. Because you are to multiply by negative 3, replace the negative tiles with positive tiles.

The 15 positive tiles on your desk show the product 15.

6. Use tiles to model each multiplication. Give the product.

a. -2 • (-6) _____ **b.** -4 • (-2) _____ **c.** -3 • (-3) _____

7. Draw a Conclusion With your group explain how you can tell when a product is positive and when it is negative.

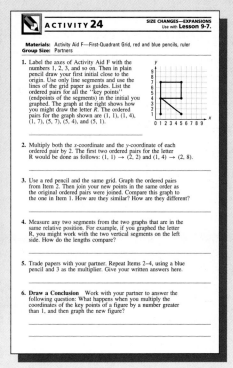

ACTIVITY 24

SIZE CHANGES—EXPANSIONS
Use with **Lesson 9-7.**

Materials: Activity Aid F—First-Quadrant Grid, red and blue pencils, ruler
Group Size: Partners

1. Label the axes of Activity Aid F with the numbers 1, 2, 3, and so on. Then in plain pencil draw your first initial close to the origin. Use only line segments and use the lines of the grid paper as guides. List the ordered pairs for all the "key points" (endpoints of the segments) in the initial you graphed. The graph at the right shows how you might draw the letter *R*. The ordered pairs for the graph shown are (1, 1), (1, 4), (1, 7), (5, 7), (5, 4), and (5, 1).

2. Multiply both the *x*-coordinate and the *y*-coordinate of each ordered pair by 2. The first two ordered pairs for the letter R would be done as follows: (1, 1) → (2, 2) and (1, 4) → (2, 8).

3. Use a red pencil and the same grid. Graph the ordered pairs from Item 2. Then join your new points in the same order as the original ordered pairs were joined. Compare this graph to the one in Item 1. How are they similar? How are they different?

4. Measure any two segments from the two graphs that are in the same relative position. For example, if you graphed the letter R, you might work with the two vertical segments on the left side. How do the lengths compare?

5. Trade papers with your partner. Repeat Items 2–4, using a blue pencil and 3 as the multiplier. Give your written answers here.

6. Draw a Conclusion Work with your partner to answer the following question: What happens when you multiply the coordinates of the key points of a figure by a number greater than 1, and then graph the new figure?

Teaching Aids

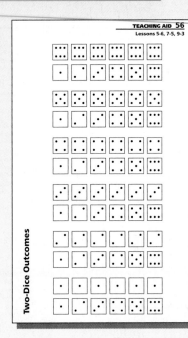

TEACHING AID 56
Lessons 5-6, 7-5, 9-3

Two-Dice Outcomes

TEACHING AID 86
Lessons 8-2, In-class Activity 8-5, 9-1, 9-7, 9-8, 10-7 to 10-10, 12-3

Graph Paper

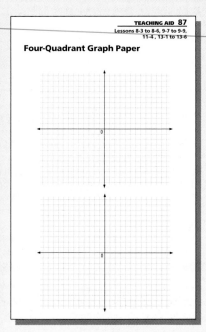

TEACHING AID 87
Lessons 8-3 to 8-6, 9-7 to 9-9, 11-4, 13-1 to 13-6

Four-Quadrant Graph Paper

Warm-up
Lesson 9-1

Explain how you might find the area of each figure. Then, if it is possible, find each area in square units.

1. 2.

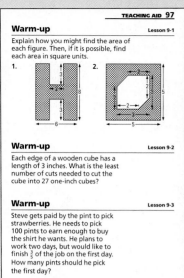

Warm-up
Lesson 9-2

Each edge of a wooden cube has a length of 3 inches. What is the least number of cuts needed to cut the cube into 27 one-inch cubes?

Warm-up
Lesson 9-3

Steve gets paid by the pint to pick strawberries. He needs to pick 100 pints to earn enough to buy the shirt he wants. He plans to work two days, but would like to finish $\frac{3}{5}$ of the job on the first day. How many pints should he pick the first day?

Warm-up
Lesson 9-4

Use the data in Question 22 on page 492. Suppose that the names of the American League stadiums are put into a hat, and one name is picked randomly and then replaced. What is the probability that you will pick a stadium

1. that seats more than 50,000?
2. that was built in the 1970s?
3. built after 1980 or before 1920?
4. with a capacity less than 30,000?
5. with the word *stadium* in its name?

Warm-up
Lesson 9-5

Human hair grows an average of 1.5 to 3.0 millimeters per week. Suppose you had not cut your hair since you were born. Estimate how long your hair would be now if your hair grew at the maximum rate. Write your answer in inches and feet. Remember, 1 inch is exactly equal to 2.5 cm.

Warm-up
Lesson 9-6

Evaluate each expression when $a = 2$ and $b = 7$.

1. $3a + b$
2. $2b + -a$
3. a^4
4. $b^2 + a^3$
5. $(5a)^2$
6. $2.5a + -b$
7. $9b - a$

Warm-up
Lesson 9-7

Graph each point on a coordinate graph.

1. $A = (3, 4)$
2. $B = (0, 6)$
3. $C = (-2, 1)$
4. $D = (3, -4)$
5. $E = (5, 0)$
6. $F = (-6, -6)$
7. $G = (0, 0)$
8. $H = (-1, 3)$

Warm-up
Lesson 9-8

Write each percent as a decimal.

1. 24%
2. 70%
3. 3%
4. 3.2%
5. 2.02%
6. 12.5%
7. 1.63%
8. 80.25%
9. Write the decimals in Questions 1–8 in order from least to greatest.

Warm-up
Lesson 9-9

Name the quadrant or the axis in which each point lies.

1. (-3, 2)
2. (1, 1)
3. (0, -3)
4. (-2.4, 1.6)
5. (-7, -4)
6. (10, 14)
7. (5, -8)
8. (6, 0)

Lesson 9-1

Picturing Multiplication

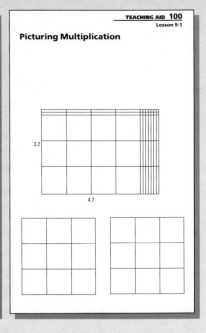

Lesson 9-1

Additional Examples

1. Find the area of the right triangle.
2. Find the area of each triangle. What is the area of the rectangle?

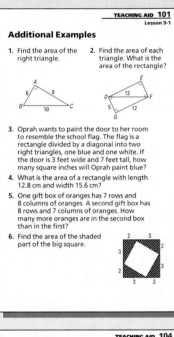

3. Oprah wants to paint the door to her room to resemble the school flag. The flag is a rectangle divided by a diagonal into two right triangles, one blue and one white. If the door is 3 feet wide and 7 feet tall, how many square inches will Oprah paint blue?
4. What is the area of a rectangle with length 12.8 cm and width 15.6 cm?
5. One gift box of oranges has 7 rows and 8 columns of oranges. A second gift box has 8 rows and 7 columns of oranges. How many more oranges are in the second box than in the first?
6. Find the area of the shaded part of the big square.

Lesson 9-1

Questions 18 and 21

18.

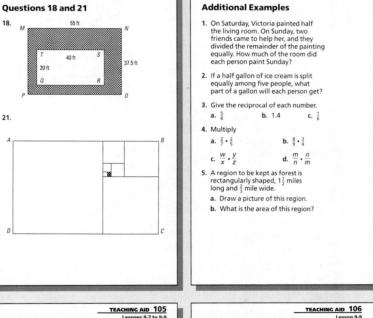

21.

Lesson 9-3

Additional Examples

1. On Saturday, Victoria painted half the living room. On Sunday, two friends came to help her, and they divided the remainder of the painting equally. How much of the room did each person paint Sunday?
2. If a half gallon of ice cream is split equally among five people, what part of a gallon will each person get?
3. Give the reciprocal of each number.
    a. $\frac{5}{8}$
    b. 1.4
    c. $\frac{1}{6}$
4. Multiply
    a. $\frac{2}{7} \cdot \frac{2}{5}$
    b. $\frac{8}{9} \cdot \frac{3}{4}$
    c. $\frac{w}{x} \cdot \frac{y}{z}$
    d. $\frac{m}{n} \cdot \frac{n}{m}$
5. A region to be kept as forest is rectangularly shaped, $1\frac{1}{2}$ miles long and $\frac{2}{3}$ mile wide.
    a. Draw a picture of this region.
    b. What is the area of this region?

Lesson 9-7

Activities 2 and 3

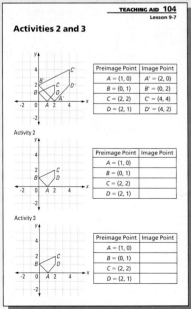

Preimage Point	Image Point
$A = (1, 0)$	$A' = (2, 0)$
$B = (0, 1)$	$B' = (0, 2)$
$C = (2, 2)$	$C' = (4, 4)$
$D = (2, 1)$	$D' = (4, 2)$

Activity 2

Preimage Point	Image Point
$A = (1, 0)$	
$B = (0, 1)$	
$C = (2, 2)$	
$D = (2, 1)$	

Activity 3

Preimage Point	Image Point
$A = (1, 0)$	
$B = (0, 1)$	
$C = (2, 2)$	
$D = (2, 1)$	

Lessons 9-7 to 9-9

Size Changes

Magnitude _____

Preimage Point	Image Point

Magnitude _____

Preimage Point	Image Point

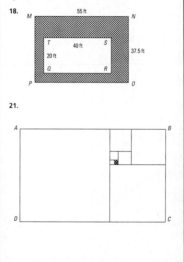

Lesson 9-9

Extension

A.

B.

C.

D.

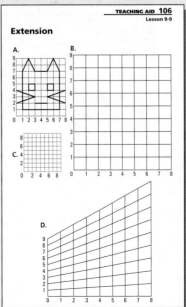
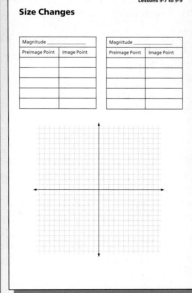

466D

Chapter Opener

Pacing

Every lesson in this chapter is designed to be covered in one day. At the end of the chapter, you should plan to spend 1 day to review the Progress Self-Test, 1–2 days for the Chapter Review, and 1 day for a test. You may wish to spend a day on projects, and possibly a day is needed for quizzes. This chapter should therefore take 12–15 days. We strongly advise you not to spend more than 16 days on this chapter; there is opportunity to review ideas in later chapters.

Using Pages 466–467

Many students have learned to multiply fractions but do not know when they would ever use this simple skill. On this page are five questions leading to the product $\frac{2}{3} \cdot \frac{4}{5}$. They relate to subject matter in this chapter as follows:

1. Area (Lesson 9-1)
2. Independent events (Lesson 9-4)
3. Independent events and area (Lesson 9-4)
4. Rate factor (Lesson 9-5)
5. Size change (Lesson 9-8).

Note that the fraction $\frac{4}{5}$ does not appear in Question 4, but when seconds are converted to minutes for multiplication, 48 seconds becomes $\frac{4}{5}$ minute.

You might ask students to write three questions that lead to the multiplication problem $\frac{1}{3} \cdot \frac{3}{4}$. (In Questions 1, 2, and 5 on this page, students can replace the numbers $\frac{2}{3}$ and $\frac{4}{5}$ to make up these questions.)

CHAPTER 9

9-1 The Area Model for Multiplication

9-2 Volumes of Rectangular Solids

9-3 Multiplication of Fractions

9-4 Multiplying Probabilities

9-5 The Rate Factor Model for Multiplication

9-6 Multiplication with Negative Numbers and Zero

9-7 Size Changes— Expansions

9-8 Size Changes— Contractions

9-9 Picturing Multiplication with Negative Numbers

466

Chapter 9 Overview

Multiplication is a much more diverse operation than addition or subtraction, and in this book two chapters are necessary to cover its applications and its connections with algebra and geometry. Chapter 9 is organized around three major models for multiplication: area (Lessons 9-1 to 9-4), rate factor (Lessons 9-5 and 9-6), and size change (Lessons 9-7 to 9-9). Each of the models for multiplication helps with arithmetic of numbers other than whole numbers. The area model can be used to picture multiplication of fractions. The rate factor model provides situations in which zero and negative numbers are factors. The size change model pictures multiplication by any reals.

Each of the models includes large classes of applications of multiplication. The area model can be extended to volume, and multiplication helps with arithmetic of numbers other than whole numbers. The area model also can picture multiplication of fractions. The rate factor and size change models can provide situations in which zero and negative numbers are factors. The size change model pictures multiplication by any reals: positive, negative, or zero. Each of the models includes large classes of applications of multiplication. The area model can be extended to volume, and can be used to picture probabilities of independent events.

PATTERNS LEADING TO MULTIPLICATION

Multiplication has a wide range of applications. Five quite different situations are described below, each leading to the multiplication $\frac{2}{3}$ times $\frac{4}{5}$. Can you see what the numbers $\frac{2}{3}$ and $\frac{4}{5}$ mean in each situation? Can you answer the questions? In this chapter, you will study several important models for multiplication. They will help you to answer these and other similar questions.

(1) *Area.* A farm is in the shape of a rectangle $\frac{2}{3}$ of a mile long and $\frac{4}{5}$ of a mile wide. What is its area?

(2) *Independent events.* Suppose one of your teachers gives homework 2 out of 3 days and another gives homework 4 of every 5 days on the average. Suppose also that the homework days are random, and the teachers do not discuss with each other when they give assignments. If a day is picked at random, what is the probability that you get homework from both?

(3) *Independent events and area.* About $\frac{2}{3}$ of the surface area of the earth is water. If the probability that an artificial satellite burns up today is $\frac{4}{5}$, what is the probability that it burns up today over water?

(4) *Rate factor.* A bug is traveling at a rate of $\frac{2}{3}$ meter per minute. At this rate, how far will it travel in 48 seconds?

(5) *Size change.* $\frac{4}{5}$ of the students in this class are here today. $\frac{2}{3}$ of those here took the bus to school. What part of the students in the class took the bus to school today?

467

The rate factor model includes the arithmetic equivalents of $d = rt$ and conversion factors. The size change model pictures the "percent of" applications students saw in Chapter 2.

Although repeated addition is the meaning of multiplication with which students are most familiar from earlier courses, repeated addition does not always help in interpreting, using, or understanding the multiplica-

tion of decimals, fractions, or negatives – and many applications of multiplication involve those sorts of numbers. We delay discussion of repeated addition until Chapter 10, when we cover the basic connections between multiplication and the other fundamental operations.

Objectives

A Find the area of a rectangle or a right triangle, given its dimensions.

E Identify the Commutative Property of Multiplication.

F Use properties of multiplication to simplify expressions and check calculations.

G Find areas of right triangles and rectangles, and the number of elements in rectangular arrays in applied situations.

M Picture multiplication using arrays or area.

Resources

From the *Teacher's Resource File*
- Lesson Master 9-1A or 9-1B
- Answer Master 9-1
- Teaching Aids
    86 Graph Paper
    97 Warm-up
    100 Picturing Multiplication
    101 Additional Examples
    102 Questions 18 and 21

Additional Resources
- Visuals for Teaching Aids 86, 97, 100–102
- United States maps (Extension)
- Geometry Workshop

---

*The Area
Model for
Multiplication*

Paper by the square foot. *Allowing for trim, a typical double roll of wallpaper with 55 sq ft will cover a 6-ft section of a wall that is 8 ft high.*

Recall that the area of a plane figure tells you how much space is inside it. The area of any figure is measured in square units. The square shown below is actual size. Its area is 1 square centimeter. It is a *unit square*.

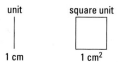

unit

square unit

1 cm

1 cm²

❶ How to Find the Area of a Rectangle

At the left below, the unit squares fit nicely inside the rectangle. So it is easy to find its area. You can count to get 12 square centimeters. However, at the right the unit squares do not fit so nicely. The area cannot be found just by counting. But in both rectangles, the area can be found by multiplying the length of the rectangle by its width.

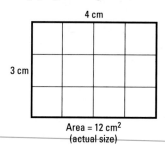

4 cm

3 cm

Area = 12 cm²
(actual size)

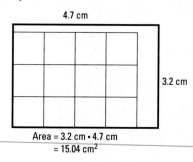

4.7 cm

3.2 cm

Area = 3.2 cm • 4.7 cm
= 15.04 cm²

Lesson 9-1 Overview

Broad Goals The goal of this lesson is to connect multiplication with finding the area of a rectangle and its discrete counterpart, rectangular arrays, and with finding the area of a right triangle.

Perspective Many students already know the formula for the area of a rectangle. What is new is the direct connection made with multiplication; that is, we take advantage of the formula to picture multiplication. Also,

this model helps verify the Commutative Property of Multiplication. The ancient Greeks pictured multiplication with areas of rectangles. Because of that association, the word *square* applies both to the rectangle with equal dimensions and to the multiplication of a number by itself. You may need to point out that the area of a square ($A = s^2$) is a special case of the area of a rectangle ($A = \ell w$); students often think of them as unrelated.

Your students may have been taught that the length of a rectangle always refers to a longer side of the rectangle. This is not the case. When we think of the square as a special type of rectangle, all sides have the same length. The width does not necessarily refer to the shorter side. When a rectangle is upright (as in most bookcases), the width usually refers to the horizontal dimension, the length to the vertical (a bookcase can be wider than it is tall).

These examples are instances of a general pattern. The lengths of the sides of a rectangle are called its **dimensions.** Its area is the product of its dimensions. This pattern is a basic application of multiplication, the *Area Model for Multiplication.*

> **Area Model for Multiplication**
> The area of a rectangle with length ℓ units and width w units is $\ell \cdot w$ (or ℓw) square units.

Arrays

In the picture below, dots have been placed in the unit squares in a 3 × 4 rectangle. The result looks like a box of cans seen from the top. The dots form a **rectangular array** with 3 rows and 4 columns. The numbers 3 and 4 are the *dimensions of the array.* It is called a 3-by-4 array. The total number of dots is 12, the product of the dimensions of the array.

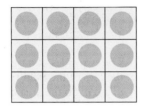

Dimensions and Area

In the physical world, a rectangle with dimensions ℓ and w is called an **ℓ-by-w** or **$\ell \times w$ rectangle.** A room that is 9′3″ × 15′, read "9 feet 3 inches by 15 feet", has area $9\frac{3}{12} \times 15$, or 138.75 square feet. The room has the same area regardless of where it is located. Below are two possible pictures.

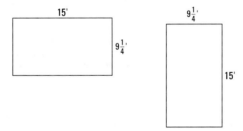

The two rectangles pictured above have the same dimensions. You could say the length and width have been switched. You could also think that one of the rectangles has been rotated 90°. Since the two rectangles have the same area,

$$15 \cdot 9\tfrac{1}{4} = 9\tfrac{1}{4} \cdot 15.$$

Lesson 9-1 *The Area Model for Multiplication* **469**

Warm-up

Explain how you might find the area of each figure. Then, if it is possible, find each area in square units.

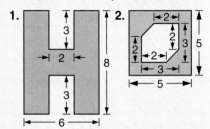

Explanations include dividing the figures into rectangles and triangles. The area of figure 1 is 36 square units. The area of figure 2 is 17 square units.

Notes on Reading

Because the content of Lesson 9-1 is familiar, students should read the lesson on their own.

In class discussion, ask students to identify the important ideas in the lesson. [square units, Area Model for Multiplication, rectangular array, the Commutative Property of Multiplication, the area formula for a right triangle] Note that the lesson goal is to think about the operation and its connection with measurement more than to do a lot of multiplication problems.

❶ You may wish to show how 3.2 · 4.7 = 15.04 with area in more detail than is in the lesson. **Teaching Aid 100** shows the rectangle with this elaboration.

Optional Activities

Activity 1
Materials: **Teaching Aid 86**

Before discussing **Example 2** with students, you might want to have them draw figures made of rectangles, squares, and right triangles, such as the one pictured at the right. Have them draw the figure on graph paper (**Teaching Aid 86**) using the grid lines as units of length. They can calculate the total area of the figure by adding the areas of the triangles and squares. Students can also determine the total area enclosed by each figure by counting the small square units on the graph paper. Then, they can compare the value found by counting with the value found by using formulas.

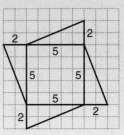

$[A = 4 \cdot \frac{1}{2} \cdot 2 \cdot 5 + 5 \cdot 5 = 45 \text{ sq units}]$

469

You might ask students to represent 1.8×2 and $2.3 \times .9$ with area on the 3-by-3 squares given at the bottom of the teaching aid. [3.6; 2.07]

Error Alert Some students mix up rows and columns in arrays. Point out that the distinction is easy to remember if one thinks of columns as going up and down like architectural columns.

❷ **Error Alert** In reviewing **Example 1**, caution students not to use the length of the hypotenuse in calculating the area of a right triangle. Indeed, you should point out that throughout their study of areas of polygons, whenever they multiply lengths to obtain area, the segments with those lengths will be perpendicular.

To conclude the discussion, you could draw analogies between this introduction of multiplication and those for addition and subtraction. Based on the work with those operations, students can predict some of what is likely to be in the next lessons: multiplication with integers and fractions, properties of multiplication, solving equations with multiplication, and graphing.

The area will be the same regardless of the order of the dimensions: $\ell w = w\ell$. This pictures a fundamental property of multiplication.

> **Commutative Property of Multiplication**
> For any numbers a and b, $ab = ba$.

What Is the Area of a Right Triangle?

It is easy to see that the area of every *right* triangle is half the area of a rectangle.

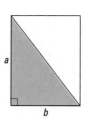 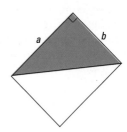 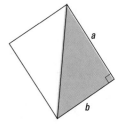

The two sides of a right triangle that are part of the right angle are called the **legs** of the right triangle. The legs in each picture above have lengths a and b. So the area of each rectangle is ab. The area of each right triangle is half of that.

> **Area Formula for a Right Triangle**
> Let A be the area of a right triangle with legs of lengths a and b. Then $A = \frac{1}{2} ab$.

The longest side of a right triangle is called its **hypotenuse.** In each right triangle above, the hypotenuse is a diagonal of the rectangle. You should ignore the hypotenuse when calculating area.

❷ **Example 1**

Find the area of a right triangle with sides of length 3 cm, 4 cm, and 5 cm.

Solution

The hypotenuse is the longest side. It has length 5 cm. So the legs have lengths 3 cm and 4 cm. Thus,

$$A = \frac{1}{2} ab$$
$$= \frac{1}{2} \cdot 3 \text{ cm} \cdot 4 \text{ cm}$$
$$= 6 \text{ cm}^2.$$

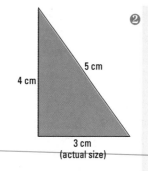

4 cm / 5 cm / 3 cm
(actual size)

Optional Activities

Activity 2 Technology Connection You may wish to have students study area using the *Geometry Workshop.* Have each student divide a rectangle into two triangles, then use the Area option to compare the area of the triangle to the area of the rectangle.

Adapting to Individual Needs

Extra Help
Materials: **Teaching Aid 86**

The following activity should help reinforce students' understanding of the area model for multiplication. Give each student several pieces of graph paper (**Teaching Aid 86**) with unit squares at least 1 cm square. Ask students to draw as many different rectangles as they can with an area of 16 square units. They should find three distinct pairs of

dimensions. [1×16 or 16×1, 2×8 or 8×2, 4×4] Ask students how each dimension is related to 16. [Each is a factor of 16.] Repeat the activity with other areas such as 24, 36, 45, and 60 square units, as needed.

By joining or cutting out right triangles, areas of more complicated figures can be found.

Example 2

A house is to be built on a lot with the following approximate dimensions. What is the area of the lot?

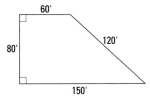

Solution 1

Think of the area as the sum of the areas of a rectangle and a right triangle.

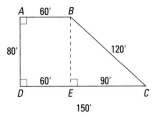

The opposite sides of the rectangle have the same length, so the legs of the right triangle have lengths 80' and 90'.

$$\text{Area of ABCD} = \text{Area of ABED} + \text{Area of } \triangle \text{BCE}$$
$$= 60' \cdot 80' + \frac{1}{2} \cdot 80' \cdot 90'$$
$$= 4800 \text{ sq ft} + 3600 \text{ sq ft}$$
$$= 8400 \text{ sq ft}$$

Solution 2

Think of the area as the difference of the areas of a rectangle and a right triangle.

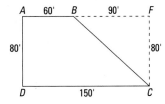

$$\text{Area of ABCD} = \text{Area of AFCD} - \text{Area of } \triangle \text{BFC}$$
$$= 150' \cdot 80' - \frac{1}{2} \cdot 80' \cdot 90'$$
$$= 12,000 \text{ sq ft} - 3600 \text{ sq ft}$$
$$= 8400 \text{ sq ft}$$

Lesson 9-1 The Area Model for Multiplication **471**

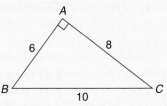
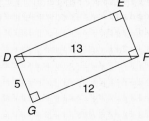
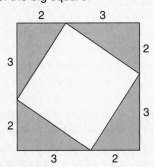
Adapting to Individual Needs

English Language Development
Materials: Counters or other objects

Pair each non-English-proficient student with a student who is proficient in English. Give each pair 24 counters or other objects. Have the English-proficient student make several different arrays and describe each one as follows: The *dimensions* of this *array* are 6 and 4 because there are 6 *columns* and 4 *rows*. Then have the same student make the outline of a rectangle, describe the dimensions as *length* and *width*, and the *area* as the product of length and width. Then the non-English proficient student should do the same activities, using different numbers, describing them in the same way to his or her partner.

471

Notes on Questions

Question 7 Diagnostic The figure is tilted to check understanding of the dimensions of a rectangle. Some students may think length and width should be horizontal and vertical and will try to use the extraneous measure 4.5 in some way.

Remind students to write the word *unit* by any length for which a unit is not given. They also should write *square units* with any area when a measuring unit is not given. Refer students to the *Warm-up* figures to remind them of this notation. The general idea is covered in Lesson 10-8.

2)

The entire rectangle has area 3.2 · 4 cm². Within it is a rectangle with area 3 · 4 cm².

4)
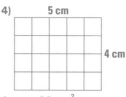

Area = 20 cm²

9a)
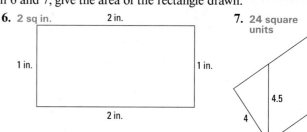

12a)

Covering the Reading

1. What is the area of a rectangle with dimensions 3 cm and 4 cm?
   12 cm²
2. Make an accurate drawing of rectangles to show that the product of 3.2 and 4 is greater than the product of 3 and 4. (Use 1 cm as the unit.)

3. If the length and width of a rectangle are measured in centimeters, the area would probably be measured in what unit? cm²

4. Draw a rectangle that is 4 cm by 5 cm, and give its area.

5. State the Area Model for Multiplication. **The area of a rectangle with length ℓ units and width w units is ℓ · w (or ℓ w) square units.**

In 6 and 7, give the area of the rectangle drawn.

6. 2 sq in.

7. 24 square units

8. Felicia arranged some bottles in the array shown below.

   a. How many rows are in this array? 3
   b. How many columns are in this array? 20
   c. How many bottles did she have in all? 60

9. a. Draw a rectangular array of dots with 7 rows and 5 columns.
   b. How many dots are in the array? 35

10. State the Commutative Property of Multiplication. **For any numbers a and b, ab = ba.**

11. How is the Commutative Property of Multiplication related to area? **Switching dimensions of a rectangle leaves the area unchanged.**

12. a. Draw a right triangle with sides of lengths 9 mm, 40 mm, and 41 mm.
    b. What are the lengths of the legs of this triangle? 9 mm and 40 mm
    c. What is the length of its hypotenuse? 41 mm
    d. What is its area? 180 mm²
    e. What is its perimeter? 90 mm

472

Adapting to Individual Needs

Challenge
Find the area.
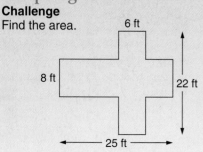

["Sliding" the horizontal part of the figure downward makes it apparent that the figure consists of two rectangles. The total area is 284 square feet.]

13. One wall of E.J.'s bedroom has dimensions as shown below. What is the area of the wall? **71 ft²**

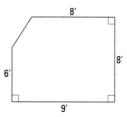

14. Arrange 30 dots in two rectangular arrays with different dimensions. **See left.**
15. Give the dimensions of two noncongruent rectangles each of whose area is 15 square inches. **Samples: 1 in. and 15 in.; 2.5 in. and 6 in.**
16. A rectangular array of dots has *c* columns, *d* dots, and *r* rows. Write an equation relating *c, d,* and *r.* **cr = d**

17. *Multiple choice.* Two stores are shaped like rectangles. Better Bargains is 60 feet wide and 120 feet long. Sales Central is 90 feet wide and 90 feet long. Both stores are all on one floor. Which is true?
    (a) Better Bargains has the greater floor space.
    (b) Sales Central has the greater floor space.
    (c) The two stores have equal floor space.
    (d) Not enough information is given to decide which store has more floor space. **(b)**

14) Sample:

18. Find the area of the shaded region between rectangles *MNOP* and *RSTQ*. **1262.5 ft²**

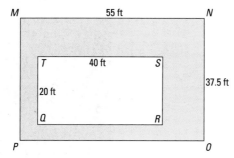

Question 18 This is related to the example in Lesson 4-7, in which the region between squares was shaded. Ask if students can write a formula for the difference of the areas of any two rectangles. If they follow the pattern for squares, they may answer something like $LW - \ell w$ where the capital letters represent the dimensions of the large rectangle and the small letters the dimensions of the small rectangle. This figure is found on **Teaching Aid 102.**

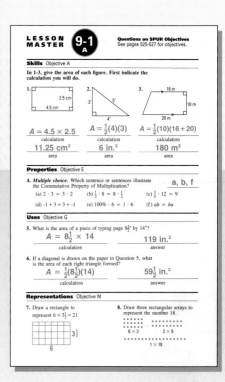

Question 21 The figure is given on **Teaching Aid 102.**

Question 23 History Connection
The Northwest Ordinances of 1784, 1785, and 1787 were enacted by the U.S. Congress to insure the orderly and equitable settlement and political incorporation of the Northwest Territory—the American frontier lying west of Pennsylvania, north of the Ohio River, east of the Mississippi River, and south of the Great Lakes. The Ordinance of 1785 also set aside land for local schools and universities.

Question 26 Here is another chance to talk about the power of powering. An increase of only one hundredth in the dimension of the cube with side 3 increases the volume by over 27 hundredths. The increase is more dramatic when the cubes have dimensions 30.1 and 30.0 mm; the difference is over 270 mm³.

Follow-up
for Lesson **9-1**

Practice

For more questions on SPUR Objectives, use **Lesson Master 9-1A** (shown on page 473) or **Lesson Master 9-1B** (shown on pages 474–475).

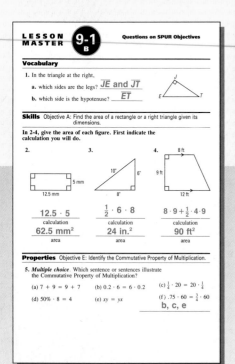

19. A tree is in the middle of a lawn. Around the tree there is a square region where no grass will be seeded. The dimensions of the lawn are shown in the drawing below. How much area will be seeded with grass? **146.5 ft²**

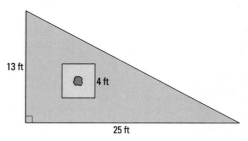

20. *RECT* is a rectangle with length 6 and height h.

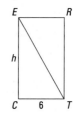

   a. What is the area of triangle *ECT*? **3h**
   b. What is the area of triangle *ERT*? **3h**

21. The design below is made up entirely of squares. The little black square has side of length 1 unit. What is the area of rectangle *ABCD*? **714 square units**

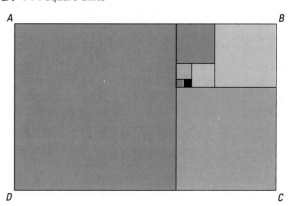

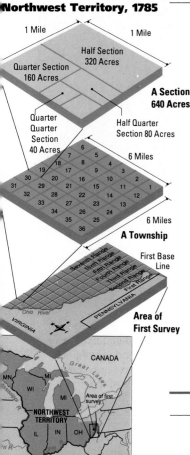

Northwest Territory, 1785

A Section 640 Acres

Half Section 320 Acres

Quarter Section 160 Acres

Half Quarter Section 80 Acres

Quarter Quarter Section 40 Acres

6 Miles

A Township

First Base Line

Seventh Range, Sixth Range, Fifth Range, Fourth Range, Third Range, Second Range, First Range

Ohio River

VIRGINIA

PENNSYLVANIA

Area of First Survey

CANADA

Great Lakes

MN, MI, WI, MI, Area of first survey, NORTHWEST TERRITORY, IL, IN, OH

Map shows present-day boundaries

Prime real estate.
The Northwest Ordinance of 1787 set the terms under which the sections of the Northwest Territory could become states. Eventually the territory became 5 states: Ohio, Indiana, Illinois, Wisconsin, and Michigan.

22a) Sample:

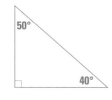

50°

40°

Review

22. **a.** Use a protractor to draw a right triangle with a 40° angle.
    b. What is the measure of the third angle of this triangle?
    (Lessons 3-6, 7-9) a) See below left. b) **50°**

23. The Northwest Ordinance of 1787 divided many areas of the central United States into square-shaped townships 6 miles on a side.
    a. What is the perimeter of such a township? **24 miles**
    b. What is the area? *(Lessons 3-8, 5-10)* **36 square miles**

24. Solve the equation $x + \frac{22}{7} = -\frac{3}{2}$. *(Lesson 5-8)* $x = -\frac{65}{14}$

25. Evaluate $14 - 3(x + 3y)$ when $x = -2$ and $y = 5$. *(Lesson 4-5)*
    -25

26. How much greater is the volume of a cube with edge 3.01 cm than the volume of a cube with edge 3 cm?
    (Lesson 3-9) **0.270901 cm³**

27. One kilogram is approximately equal to how many pounds?
    (Lesson 3-5) **2.2 lb**

28. **a.** Rewrite 48.49 as a simple fraction. *(Lesson 2-6)* **4849/100**
    b. Round 48.49 to the nearest integer. *(Lesson 1-4)* **48**

29. There were about 2,400,000 high school graduates in the United States in 1990. Of these, about 60% went to a 2-year or 4-year college the next year. How many college students is this? *(Lesson 2-5)* **1,440,000**

Exploration

30. **a.** How many entries are needed to complete this multiplication table? **36**

×	3.0	3.2	3.4	3.6	3.8	4.0
7.0	21.0	22.4	23.8	25.2	26.6	28.0
7.2	21.6	23.04	24.48	25.92	27.36	28.8
7.4	22.2	23.68	25.16	26.64	28.12	29.6
7.6	22.8	24.32	25.84	27.36	28.88	30.4
7.8	23.4	24.96	26.52	28.08	29.64	31.2
8.0	24.0	25.6	27.2	28.8	30.4	32.0

b. Fill in the table. See table.
c. Find at least two patterns in the numbers you put into the table.
Possible answers: In any column, the difference between an element and the one just above it is constant. Every number ends in an even digit. Products increase as you go down or to the right.

Lesson 9-1 *The Area Model for Multiplication* **475**

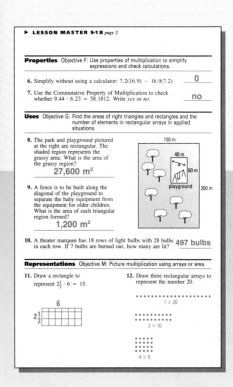

Assessment

Diagnostic As you work through this chapter, try to correct misconceptions students may have about multiplication. To identify some of those misconceptions, give this quiz. In 1–2, answer *true* or *false*.

1. When you multiply two positive numbers, the answer (product) will be larger than either number. **False**

2. When you multiply two positive numbers, the product may be between the two numbers. **True**

In 3–4, answer the questions without using a calculator.

3. What whole number is nearest 7.00034 · 5.99856? **42**

4. What whole number is nearest $\frac{1}{10} \cdot \frac{1}{11}$? **0**

Extension

You might want to have students extend their work with area to estimating areas of several states. Have them use a map of the United States and choose three states that are shaped roughly like a rectangle, right triangle, or a combination of the two. Have students trace the state from the map, draw the geometric shape, and use the map scale to estimate the area.

Project Update Project 1, *Area of Your Residence*, on page 521, relates to the content of this lesson.

Setting Up Lesson 9-2

Question 26 in Lesson 9-1 discusses volume. Use it to refresh students' memories that one multiplies the three dimensions of a cube to get its volume.

Materials The *Notes on Reading* suggest the use of a large box and also a large number of unit cubes for demonstration. The *Extension* requires the use of boxes of various sizes and a tape measure for groups of students to use (one box and one tape measure per group).

Objectives

B Find the volume of a rectangular solid, given its dimensions.

E Identify the Associative Property of Multiplication.

F Use the Associative and Commutative Properties of Multiplication to simplify expressions and check calculations.

H Find the volume of a rectangular solid in real contexts.

Resources

From the *Teacher's Resource File*
- Lesson Master 9-2A or 9-2B
- Answer Master 9-2
- Teaching Aid 97: Warm-up
- Activity Kit, Activity 22

Additional Resources
- Visual for Teaching Aid 97
- Boxes and unit cubes (optional)
- Boxes and tape measures (Extension)

Teaching
Lesson **9-2**

Warm-up

Each edge of a wooden cube has a length of 3 inches. What is the least number of cuts needed to cut the cube into 27 one-inch cubes?

6 cuts

Volumes of Rectangular Solids

Abode sweet adobe. *Many people of Pueblo and Hopi Tribes live in traditional adobe structures. These homes, with their flat roofs, are shaped like rectangular solids.*

❶ How to Describe Boxes

A **box** is a 3-dimensional figure with six **faces** that are all rectangles. A solid box is called a **rectangular solid.** When a box is situated like the one here, we can name the faces *front, back, right, left, top,* and *bottom.* The bottom is sometimes called the **base.** The sides of the faces are called the **edges** of the box. A box has 12 edges. A point at a corner of the box is called a **vertex** of the box. A box has 8 vertices.

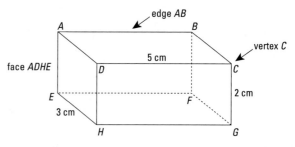

Three edges intersect at each vertex. Their lengths are the **dimensions** of the box. The above box has dimensions 2 cm, 3 cm, and 5 cm. The dimensions are called its **length, width,** and **height.** Sometimes one dimension (either front to back, or top to bottom) is called its **depth.** Notice that the length of every edge of a box equals one of the dimensions. When all the edges have the same length, the box is a cube.

Lesson 9-2 Overview

Broad Goals The goals are to introduce the language of rectangular solids (boxes) and to connect the product of three positive numbers with the volume of a rectangular solid having those numbers as dimensions.

Perspective The volume of a cube was discussed in Chapter 3. The other volumes discussed in this book in Chapter 12 are those of cylinders, prisms, and spheres.

The Associative Property of Multiplication is sometimes written $a(bc) = (ab)c$. In this book, we add the third expression abc, because a key implication of the Associative Property is the removal of all grouping symbols when a collection of numbers is being multiplied. Technically, because of order of operations, $abc = (ab)c$.

Commutativity and associativity, taken together, allow numbers to be multiplied in any order. This is emphasized in both the examples and the questions of this lesson.

How Is the Volume of a Box Found?

Recall that *volume* measures the space inside a 3-dimensional figure, or the space occupied by a solid figure. In Lesson 3-9, you saw that the volume of a cube with edge s was s^3. Now we seek to find the volume of a box whose measurements are known.

Example 1

Find the volume of the box pictured below.

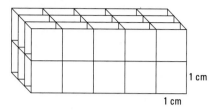

1 cm

1 cm

Solution

Since the dimensions are whole numbers, we can split the box into unit cube compartments. The unit cubes fit evenly into the box. You can count the cubes. There are 15 cubes in each layer. The volume is therefore 30 cubic centimeters, or 30 cm^3.

Notice that in Example 1, the volume is the product of the three dimensions.

$$\text{Volume} = 5 \text{ cm} \cdot 3 \text{ cm} \cdot 2 \text{ cm}$$
$$= 30 \text{ cm}^3$$

The volume of a box or a rectangular solid is always the product of its three dimensions, even when the dimensions are not whole numbers.

> Let V be the volume of a box or a rectangular solid with dimensions a, b, and c.
>
> $$\text{Then } V = abc.$$
> $$\text{Or } V = Bh,$$
>
> where B is the area of the base and h is the height.

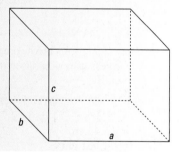

❷ To emphasize the importance of the commutative and associative properties, remind students that problems involving only addition or only multiplication can be done in any order, but that this is not true for subtraction or division. To demonstrate these properties of multiplication, you may want to provide a large number of unit cubes and perform the following demonstration:

1. Arrange the unit cubes into a rectangular solid, and ask for the volume. Note that the volume is the product of the dimensions.
2. Rearrange the cubes, and ask the same question. (The volume will be the same.)

Science Connection You may wish to point out that there are 3-dimensional arrays. Molecules in uniformly solid substances are spaced in such arrays.

Example 2

Find the volume V of a rectangular solid 5.3 cm long, 2.7 cm high, and 3.1 cm deep.

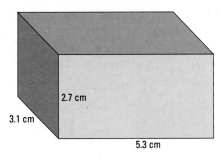

Solution

$V = 5.3 \text{ cm} \cdot 3.1 \text{ cm} \cdot 2.7 \text{ cm} = 44.361 \text{ cm}^3$

Finding the Volume of a Box Using Its Base

Notice in Example 2 that the volume of the box is the area of the base ($5.3 \cdot 3.1$) times its height (2.7). Below, the same box is shown with two different faces as its base. The volume of the figure on the left is the area of the base ($2.7 \cdot 5.3$) times the height (3.1). The volume of the figure on the right is the area of the base ($3.1 \cdot 2.7$) times the height (5.3).

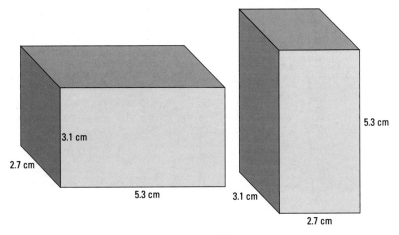

The calculations below confirm that the volume of the box is the same regardless of which base is used. This verifies that multiplication is associative.

$V =\ (a\ \cdot\ b)\ \cdot\ c$
$=\ (5.3 \text{ cm} \cdot 3.1 \text{ cm}) \cdot 2.7 \text{ cm}$
$=\ 16.43 \text{ cm}^2\ \cdot 2.7 \text{ cm}$
$=\ 44.361 \text{ cm}^3$

$V =\ a\ \cdot\ (b\ \cdot\ c)$
$=\ 5.3 \text{ cm} \cdot (3.1 \text{ cm} \cdot 2.7 \text{ cm})$
$=\ 5.3 \text{ cm} \cdot 8.37 \text{ cm}^2$
$=\ 44.361 \text{ cm}^3$

Adapting to Individual Needs

Extra Help

Materials: Identical boxes, 1 per group

Remind students that the base of a rectangular solid is not always the side it is resting on. To emphasize this, have students **work in groups** to find the volume of a box. Each group must decide which face to use as the base and trace around it on paper. Instruct them to find the area of the base, and then to measure the height of the box and multiply it by the area of the base. Stress that height must be measured from the base chosen. Discuss the results in class. Point out how different groups chose different bases and heights for the same box and found the same volume. The activity could be repeated with different boxes.

② Associative Property of Multiplication

For any numbers *a*, *b*, and *c*, $(ab)c = a(bc) = abc$.

Because multiplication is both commutative and associative, numbers can be multiplied in any order without affecting the product. These properties can shorten multiplications.

Example 3

Multiply in your head: $25 \cdot 35 \cdot 4 \cdot 4 \cdot 25$.

Solution

Notice that $4 \cdot 25 = 100$. Multiply these first.

$$\begin{aligned}
\text{Think} \quad 25 \cdot 35 \cdot 4 \cdot 4 \cdot 25 \\
= 35 \cdot (25 \cdot 4) \cdot (4 \cdot 25) \\
= 35 \cdot 100 \cdot 100 \\
= 350{,}000
\end{aligned}$$

QUESTIONS

Covering the Reading

In 1 and 2, refer to the box below. A box of its size and shape was used to pack a laser printer.

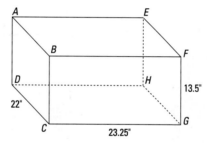

1. **a.** Name its faces. *BFGC, ABCD, AEHD, EFGH, ABFE, DHGC*
   b. Name its edges. $\overline{AB}, \overline{BF}, \overline{FE}, \overline{EA}, \overline{DC}, \overline{CG}, \overline{GH}, \overline{HD}, \overline{BC}, \overline{FG}, \overline{EH}, \overline{AD}$
   c. Name its vertices. *A, B, C, D, E, F, G, H*

2. **a.** What are its dimensions? *23.25″, 22″, and 13.5″*
   b. What is its volume? *6905.25 in³ or 6905 ¼ in³*

In 3 and 4, give the volume of a rectangular solid with the given dimensions.

3. height 6 cm, width 3 cm, and depth 4 cm *72 cm³*

4. height 10 meters, width *w* meters, and depth *d* meters *10wd m³*

Lesson 9-2 *Volumes of Rectangular Solids* **479**

Additional Examples

1. An aquarium is 30 inches long, 15 inches wide, and 15 inches high. How much water can it hold? **6750 in³**

2. **a.** How many square centimeters are in a square meter? **10,000**
   b. How many cubic centimeters are in a cubic meter? **1,000,000**
   c. A paving brick is a rectangular solid, 20 cm long, 8 cm wide, and 6 cm high. How much clay is required to make the 600 bricks needed for a small patio? **576,000 cm³**

3. Multiply mentally:
   a. $2.5 \times 3 \times 10$ **75**
   b. $\frac{1}{2} \times 9 \times 8$ **36**
   c. $2 \times 40 \times 5 \times 6 \times 25$ **60,000**

Notes on Questions

Questions 3–6 Emphasize that the unit used to express volume is the unit of length cubed.

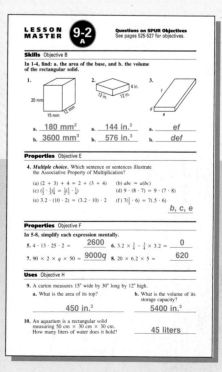

Adapting to Individual Needs

English Language Development
Give each student a box and demonstrate with a large box that all can see. First remind students that a rectangle has 2 *dimensions*, length and width. Then explain that a rectangular solid has 3 dimensions: length, width, and height. Point to each dimension on your box as you speak. Then point to the sides and explain that each side is called a *face*. Have students count the faces on their boxes. [6] Then explain that the segment where two faces meet is called an *edge*. Have students count the edges on their boxes. [12] Then point to a vertex and explain that each corner, or point where 3 or more faces meet, is called a *vertex*. Have students point to each vertex and count. [8] Point to the inside of the box and explain that the amount of space inside, or the *volume*, is the product of the three dimensions.

Question 10 You might wish to show the steps using the properties:

$$5 \cdot 437 \cdot 2$$
$$= 5 \cdot (437 \cdot 2)$$
$$= 5 \cdot (2 \cdot 437)$$
$$= (5 \cdot 2) \cdot 437$$
$$= 10 \cdot 437$$

Obviously no one goes through all of these steps when he or she does the multiplication mentally, but students should be informed of the connection between the mental process and the properties of multiplication.

Question 17 Multicultural Connection Students might be interested in the following information. The Sony Corporation, a major Japanese manufacturer of consumer electronics products, was formed in 1946 to apply the advanced technology developed during World War II to the manufacture of consumer products. In 1957, Sony introduced the world's first pocket-sized, all-transistor radio; in 1960, it produced an 8-inch transistorized television set. Interested students might research the "firsts" of other consumer electronic companies.

Question 21b This approaches an equation of a line from a slightly new perspective. You could start out by demonstrating on a grid that there can be an infinite number of lines through that point. Then ask students to suggest how to find an equation for one of them.

15a)

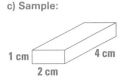

c) Sample:

Play on. *Since a boom box is portable and has excellent sound quality, it is often used in exercise classes.*

In 5–7, give the volume of a rectangular solid in which:

5. the area of the base is 40 square centimeters and the height is 4 centimeters. **160 cm³**

6. the base is 10 inches by 2 feet, and the height is 1.5 inches. **360 in³**

7. the base has area A and the height is h. *Ah* cubic units

8. State the Associative Property of Multiplication. For any numbers a, b, and c, $(ab)c = a(bc) = abc$.

9. Give an instance of the Associative Property of Multiplication. Sample: $(3 \cdot 4) \cdot 0.5 = 3 \cdot (4 \cdot 0.5)$

In 10–12, use the properties of multiplication to do these problems in your head. Do no calculator or pencil-and-paper calculations.

10. $5 \cdot 437 \cdot 2$ **4370**

11. $6 \cdot 7 \cdot 8 \cdot 9 - 9 \cdot 8 \cdot 7 \cdot 6$ **0**

12. 50% of 67 times 2 **67**

Applying the Mathematics

13. The floor of a rectangular-shaped room is 9 feet by 12 feet. The ceiling is 8 feet high. How much space is in the room? **864 cu ft**

14. Give two possible sets of dimensions for a rectangular solid whose volume is 144 cubic units. Samples: 12 units, 12 units, and 1 unit; 12 units, 4 units, and 3 units

15. a. Draw a rectangular solid whose volume is 8 cm³ and which has all dimensions the same length. See above left.
    b. What is this rectangular solid called? cube
    c. Draw a second rectangular solid whose volume is 8 cm³ but whose dimensions are not equal. See above left.

16. Give the volume of this box. **1080 in³**

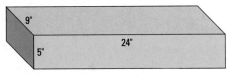

17. *Multiple choice.* A portable cassette player is nearly a rectangular solid with dimensions 12 cm × 9 cm × 4 cm. One "boom box" is also nearly rectangular, with dimensions 18 cm × 55 cm × 19 cm. About how many times as much volume does the boom box occupy as the portable cassette player?
    (a) 4 (b) 6 (c) 12 (d) 24 (e) 40 (e)

Adapting to Individual Needs

Challenge
Have students solve the following problem: The areas of the faces of a box are 40, 80, and 50 square centimeters. Find the volume of the box. [400 cubic centimeters]

18. a. *True or false.* If $x = 7.6092$, then $3(x + 4) = (x + 4) \cdot 3$. True
  b. *True or false.* $\frac{2}{3} \cdot \frac{4}{5} = \frac{4}{5} \cdot \frac{2}{3}$ True
  c. What general principle is exemplified by parts **a** and **b**? *(Lesson 9-1)*
  Commutative Property of Multiplication

19. A computer has a display screen that can show up to 364 rows and 720 columns of dots. How many dots can be on that screen?
(Lesson 9-1) **262,080 dots**

20. Find the area of the rectangle with vertices (2, 4), (5, 4), (5, 10), and (2, 10). *(Lessons 8-3, 9-1)* **18 square units**

21. a. In which quadrant is the point (4, -1)? **fourth (IV)**
  b. Give an equation for a line that goes through (4, -1).
  (Lessons 6-1, 8-3, 8-4) **Sample: y = x − 5**

22. Refer to the triangle at the left.
  a. What is the value of y? $47\frac{1}{2}°$
  b. How many angles are acute? **two**
  c. How many angles are obtuse? *(Lessons 3-7, 7-9)* **one**

23. Solve the equation $83 - x = 110$. *(Lesson 7-4)* **x = -27**

24. To divide a decimal by .001, how many places should you move the decimal point, and in what direction? *(Lessons 2-4, 2-6, 6-7)*
three places to the right

25. If $n = 10$, what is the value of $(3n + 5)(2n - 3)$? *(Lesson 4-5)* **595**

26. 2.6 kilometers is how many meters? *(Lesson 3-4)* **2600 meters**

In 27–29, put one of the signs <, =, or > in the blank. *(Lesson 1-9)*

27. -4 − 4 __?__ -4 + 4 <

28. -7.352 __?__ -7.351 <

29. 2/3 __?__ .66666666 >

30. What digit is in the thousandths place of 54,321.09876? *(Lesson 1-2)*
8

Exploration

31. Choose a room where you live that is shaped like a rectangular solid. Find its dimensions and calculate its volume.

32. Suppose the dimensions of the box given in Question 16 were estimates, the result of rounding the lengths *to the nearest inch*. For instance, the shortest edge might have had a length as small as 4.5 in. or as large as 5.5 in. To the nearest cubic inch, find the smallest and largest volumes the rectangular solid could have.
31) Answers will vary. Sample: If a room has a 9′ by 12′ floor and is 8′ high, its volume is 864 cubic feet.
32) The smallest possible volume is 23.5″ · 8.5″ · 4.5″, or about 899 in³. The largest possible volume is 24.5″ · 9.5″ · 5.5″, or about 1280 in³.

Setting Up Lesson 9-3
Materials The *Extension* for Lesson 9-3 requires students to use stock prices from a newspaper.

Question 29 Students may think that these are equal. Point out that .66666666 is a terminating, not an infinite, decimal.

Follow-up for Lesson 9-2

Practice
For more questions on SPUR Objectives, use **Lesson Master 9-2A** (shown on page 479) or **Lesson Master 9-2B** (shown on pages 480 – 481).

Assessment
Written Communication Ask each student to write three multiplication problems that can be solved mentally by using the commutative and associative properties of multiplication. Have them exchange their problems with another student and find the answers mentally. [Problems model the properties and contain numbers appropriate for mental arithmetic.]

Extension
Materials: Boxes of various sizes, tape measures

Divide students into groups, giving each group a box and a tape measure. Ask each group to determine how many boxes like the one they have would fill the classroom.

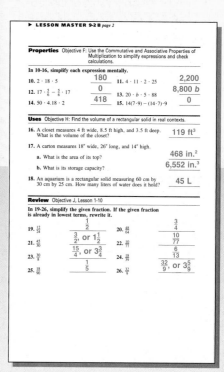

Objectives

C Multiply fractions.
E Identify properties of reciprocals.
F Use properties of multiplication to simplify expressions and check calculations.
M Picture multiplication of fractions using areas of rectangles.

Resources

From the *Teacher's Resource File*
■ Lesson Master 9-3A or 9-3B
■ Answer Master 9-3
■ Teaching Aids
   56 Two-Dice Outcomes
   97 Warm-up
  103 Additional Examples

Additional Resources
■ Visuals for Teaching Aids 56, 97, 103
■ Newspapers (Extension)

Teaching
Lesson **9-3**

Warm-up

Steve gets paid by the pint to pick strawberries. He needs to pick 100 pints to earn enough to buy the shirt he wants. He plans to work two days, but would like to finish $\frac{3}{5}$ of the job on the first day. How many pints should he pick the first day? **60 pints**

Notes on Reading

Emphasize that a full understanding of multiplying fractions involves more than memorizing a rule for computation. Looking at the operation from many viewpoints helps students to

---

Can you cut it? *Think about how you would cut this cake if you wanted a large number of pieces.*

Multiplication of Unit Fractions

A large cake was bought for a class party. First the cake was cut into 20 pieces as shown. These pieces were too large, so each was cut into 2 smaller pieces.

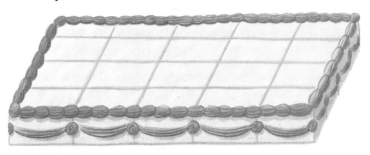

Example 1

At the party, Kris ate one of the smaller pieces. What part of the cake did she eat?

Solution 1

Since each of 20 pieces was cut into 2, there were 40 smaller pieces. If all smaller pieces were the same size, Kris ate $\frac{1}{40}$ of the cake.

Solution 2

The original pieces were each $\frac{1}{20}$ of the cake. Kris ate $\frac{1}{2}$ of $\frac{1}{20}$. To find $\frac{1}{2}$ of $\frac{1}{20}$, multiply the fractions: $\frac{1}{2} \cdot \frac{1}{20} = \frac{1}{40}$. Again, Kris ate $\frac{1}{40}$ of the cake.

482

Lesson 9-3 Overview

Broad Goals The goal of this lesson is to use applications to review the algorithm for multiplication of fractions.

Perspective Most students have learned the rule for multiplying fractions, but they treat it as just another one of the many rules of mathematics. In this lesson, we try to justify that rule, to put the rule on firm ground, and to give students a way to get the answers to problems even if they forget the rule.

This lesson includes each of the four dimensions of the SPUR approach to understanding. It includes the skill of multiplying fractions (in both arithmetic and algebraic contexts); the properties that connect multiplication, division, reciprocals, and fractions; uses and applications to real situations; and the area model representation.

Do not ignore the algebra here. Fractions are dealt with in algebra just as they are in arithmetic.

The fractions $\frac{1}{2}$, $\frac{1}{3}$, $\frac{1}{4}$, and so on, are unit fractions. A unit fraction is a fraction with 1 in its numerator and a positive integer in its denominator. The rule for multiplying two unit fractions is quite simple to state.

Multiplication of Unit Fractions Property
For all nonzero numbers a and b, $\frac{1}{a} \cdot \frac{1}{b} = \frac{1}{ab}$.

Fractions and Division

The ancient Egyptians used unit fractions extensively. In fact, they used no fractions other than unit fractions and the fraction $\frac{2}{3}$. Through some very ingenious methods, they wrote all other fractions as sums of unit fractions.

Today we look at fractions differently. We look at $\frac{2}{3}$ as being 2 times $\frac{1}{3}$, and in general we look at any fraction $\frac{a}{b}$ as being a times $\frac{1}{b}$. Because the fraction $\frac{a}{b}$ is equal to the quotient $a \div b$, this pattern gives a fundamental relationship between multiplication and division. It is sometimes called the *Algebraic Definition of Division*.

Algebraic Definition of Division
For all numbers a and nonzero numbers b, $a \cdot \frac{1}{b} = \frac{a}{b} = a \div b$.

Example 2

The 23 students in Kris's class each ate one piece of the cake. How much of the cake did these students eat altogether?

Solution

They ate 23 times $\frac{1}{40}$ of the cake. $23 \cdot \frac{1}{40} = \frac{23}{40}$.

When 40 of the pieces were eaten, then $40 \cdot \frac{1}{40}$ of the cake was eaten. This is 100% of the cake. Thus $40 \cdot \frac{1}{40} = 100\%$. More simply, $40 \cdot \frac{1}{40} = 1$.

What Are Reciprocals?

Two numbers whose product is 1 are called **reciprocals** or **multiplicative inverses** of each other. Above we explained why $\frac{1}{40}$ and 40 are reciprocals of each other. This is one instance of a general pattern involving reciprocals.

appreciate what is really going on. You may wish to outline the content using the SPUR categories.

Skills: $\frac{1}{2} \cdot \frac{1}{20} = \frac{1}{40}$ (**Example 1**); $23 \cdot \frac{1}{40} = \frac{23}{40}$ (**Example 2**); $40 \cdot \frac{1}{40} = 1$ (page 483); $\frac{2}{3} \cdot \frac{4}{5} = \frac{8}{15}$ (**Example 4**)

Properties: The Multiplication of Fractions Property, the Multiplication of Unit Fractions Property, The Property of Reciprocals, and the Algebraic Definition of Division

Uses: Splitting problems, as in **Examples 1 and 2**

Representations: The volume picture in **Example 1** and the area picture after **Example 4**

Optional Activities

You might want to use this activity after students have read the lesson. Have students **work in groups** to make up three situations that can be answered by multiplying the fractions $\frac{2}{3}$ and $\frac{1}{6}$. (Sample: Six people shared a pizza equally. Mary ate $\frac{2}{3}$ of her share. What part of the pizza did she eat?) Each group can then present its situations to the class for discussion.

❶ To focus on the mathematical rationales for the algorithm for the Multiplication of Fractions Property, you may want to closely examine the picture of the farm which illustrates $\frac{2}{3} \cdot \frac{4}{5}$. Ask students why the denominator of the answer is 15. [There are 15 small rectangles in all.] Then ask why the numerator of the answer is 8 and what the answer $\frac{8}{15}$ means? [8 of the small rectangles represent the farm; $\frac{8}{15}$ of the region is occupied by the farm.]

Error Alert A common mistake students make in multiplying fractions is to ignore the fraction bar and think that the answer is greater than either factor because the numerator and denominator are larger numbers. Use decimals to show students that $\frac{8}{15}$ is less than either $\frac{2}{3}$ or $\frac{4}{5}$.

Additional Examples

These Additional Examples can be found on **Teaching Aid 103.**

1. On Saturday, Victoria painted half the living room. On Sunday, two friends came to help her, and they divided the remainder of the painting equally. How much of the room did each person paint on Sunday? $\frac{1}{6}$

2. If a half gallon of ice cream is split equally among five people, what part of a gallon will each person get? $\frac{1}{10}$

3. Give the reciprocal of each number.
   a. $\frac{5}{8}$ $\frac{8}{5}$
   b. 1.4 $\frac{5}{7}$ or .$\overline{714285}$
   c. $\frac{1}{6}$ 6

   We discourage the use of $\frac{6}{1}$ as the reciprocal of $\frac{1}{6}$. That practice encourages students to wrongly think that $\frac{6}{1}$ is a number different from 6.

484

> **Property of Reciprocals**
> For any nonzero number a, a and $\frac{1}{a}$ are reciprocals.
> That is, $a \cdot \frac{1}{a} = 1$.

Notice that *the reciprocal of a number is 1 divided by that number.* All nonzero numbers have reciprocals, no matter how they are written.

Example 3

Write the reciprocal of 12.5 as a decimal.

Solution

The reciprocal of 12.5 is $\frac{1}{12.5}$. A calculator shows that $1 \div 12.5$ is equal to 0.08. The reciprocal of 12.5 is 0.08.

Check

Does $12.5 \cdot 0.08 = 1$? Yes.

Most scientific calculators have a reciprocal key $\boxed{1/x}$. Enter 12.5 and then press this key. The reciprocal of 12.5 should be displayed.

Multiplication of Any Fractions

The most general pattern involving multiplication of fractions is that the product of the fractions $\frac{a}{b}$ and $\frac{c}{d}$ equals $\frac{ac}{bd}$. That is, the product can be written as a fraction whose numerator is the product of the numerators of the given fractions, and whose denominator is the product of the denominators of the given fractions. The pattern is much easier to state with variables than in words. We call it the *Multiplication of Fractions Property.*

> **Multiplication of Fractions Property**
> For all numbers a and c, and nonzero numbers b and d, $\frac{a}{b} \cdot \frac{c}{d} = \frac{ac}{bd}$.

Example 4

A farm is in the shape of a rectangle $\frac{2}{3}$ of a mile long and $\frac{4}{5}$ of a mile wide. What is its area?

Solution

The area (in square miles) is the product of $\frac{2}{3}$ and $\frac{4}{5}$. Using the Multiplication of Fractions Property, $\frac{2}{3} \cdot \frac{4}{5} = \frac{2 \cdot 4}{3 \cdot 5} = \frac{8}{15}$.

The area is $\frac{8}{15}$ square mile, or about .53 square mile.

Corn country. *The U.S. produces more than $\frac{2}{3}$ of the world's supply of corn. Some surplus corn is converted into non-food uses such as ethanol and biodegradable trash bags.*

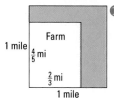

1 mile

Farm

$\frac{4}{5}$ mi

$\frac{2}{3}$ mi

1 mile

Figure 1

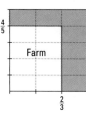

Figure 2

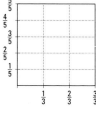

Farm

$\frac{2}{3}$

Figure 3

❶ Picturing Multiplication of Fractions

There is probably no algorithm in arithmetic simpler than the Multiplication of Fractions Property. But why does it work? One way to explain why it works uses the Area Model for Multiplication. Look back at the situation of Example 4.

Think of the farm as being inside a square mile (Figure 1 at the left). Divide that square mile into rectangles that are $\frac{1}{5}$ mile by $\frac{1}{3}$ mile (Figure 2). You can see that 15 of these rectangles fit into the square mile. So the area of each small rectangle is $\frac{1}{15}$ square mile.

The farm, because it is $2 \cdot \frac{1}{3}$ miles wide, and $4 \cdot \frac{1}{5}$ miles long, includes $2 \cdot 4$, or 8 of these rectangles (Figure 3). So the farm has area $8 \cdot \frac{1}{15}$ square mile, or $\frac{8}{15}$ square mile.

QUESTIONS

Covering the Reading

1. Consider the case of Example 1. Suppose each of the 20 pieces had been cut into 3 equal pieces. Then each smaller piece is what part of the original cake? $\frac{1}{60}$

2. What is meant by a *unit fraction*? **a fraction with 1 in its numerator and a positive integer in its denominator**

In 3–8, give the product as a fraction in lowest terms or as a whole number.

3. $\frac{1}{3} \cdot \frac{1}{4}$ $\frac{1}{12}$

4. $\frac{1}{40} \cdot \frac{1}{x}$ $\frac{1}{40x}$

5. $\frac{1}{a} \cdot \frac{1}{b}$ $\frac{1}{ab}$

6. $2 \cdot \frac{1}{3}$ $\frac{2}{3}$

7. $\frac{1}{8} \cdot 16$ 2

8. $\frac{1}{x} \cdot 5$ $\frac{5}{x}$

9. State the Algebraic Definition of Division. **For all numbers a and nonzero b, $a \cdot \frac{1}{b} = \frac{a}{b} = a \div b$.**

In 10–15, simplify.

10. $\frac{6}{5} \cdot \frac{2}{9}$ $\frac{12}{45}$, or $\frac{4}{15}$

11. $\frac{3}{5} \cdot \frac{5}{3}$ 1

12. $\frac{1}{9} \cdot \frac{9}{2}$ $\frac{1}{2}$

13. $(7 \cdot \frac{1}{12}) \cdot (3 \cdot \frac{1}{4})$ $\frac{7}{16}$

14. $12 \cdot \frac{3}{4}$ $\frac{36}{4} = 9$

15. $\frac{a}{b} \cdot \frac{c}{d}$ $\frac{ac}{bd}$

16. A farm is rectangular in shape, $\frac{1}{2}$ mile by $\frac{2}{3}$ mile. Use a drawing to explain why the area of the farm is $\frac{1}{3}$ square mile.

In 17 and 18, give the reciprocal of the number.

17. 10 $\frac{1}{10}$

18. 4.5 $\frac{2}{9}$

19. Write the reciprocal of 40 as a decimal. **0.025**

16)

$\frac{1}{2}$

farm

$\frac{1}{3}$ $\frac{2}{3}$ 1

The farm occupies 2 of 6 equal pieces of the square mile.

4. Multiply:
   a. $\frac{2}{7} \cdot \frac{2}{5}$ $\frac{4}{35}$
   b. $\frac{8}{9} \cdot \frac{3}{4}$ $\frac{2}{3}$
   c. $\frac{w}{x} \cdot \frac{y}{z}$ $\frac{wy}{xz}$
   d. $\frac{m}{n} \cdot \frac{n}{m}$ 1

5. A region to be kept as forest is rectangularly shaped, $1\frac{1}{2}$ miles long and $\frac{2}{3}$ mile wide.
   a. Draw a picture of this region.
   b. What is the area of this region?

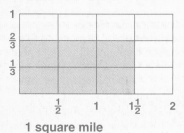

1

$\frac{2}{3}$

$\frac{1}{3}$

$\frac{1}{2}$ 1 $1\frac{1}{2}$ 2

1 square mile

LESSON MASTER 9-3 A

Questions on SPUR Objectives
See pages 525-527 for objectives.

Skills Objective C

In 1-6, write the product as a whole number or as a fraction in lowest terms.

1. $\frac{1}{2} \cdot \frac{1}{5} = $ __$\frac{1}{10}$__
2. $\frac{1}{p} \cdot \frac{1}{q} = $ __$\frac{1}{pq}$__
3. $6 \cdot \frac{1}{3} = $ __2__
4. $\frac{1}{t} \cdot 7 = $ __$\frac{7}{t}$__
5. $\frac{3}{10} \cdot \frac{3}{5} = $ __$\frac{9}{50}$__
6. $\frac{4}{9} \cdot \frac{3}{8} = $ __$\frac{1}{6}$__

Properties Objective E

7. What are reciprocals? Use examples in your explanation.
   Reciprocals are two numbers whose product is 1; 6 and $\frac{1}{6}$ are reciprocals.

In 8-11, give the reciprocal.

8. $\frac{5}{8}$ __$\frac{8}{5}$__
9. 6 __$\frac{1}{6}$__
10. $3\frac{1}{2}$ __$\frac{2}{7}$__
11. $\frac{m}{n}$ __$\frac{n}{m}$__

Properties Objective F

In 12 and 13, simplify.

12. $\frac{q}{r} \cdot \frac{r}{q} = $ __1__
13. $\frac{3}{4} \cdot \frac{5}{6} \cdot \frac{4}{3} = $ __$\frac{5}{6}$__

Representations Objective M

14. What multiplication is pictured below?
    $\frac{2}{5} \times \frac{4}{5} = \frac{8}{25}$

15. Picture $\frac{1}{3} \cdot \frac{3}{4}$ using an area model.
    $\frac{1}{3} \times \frac{3}{4} = \frac{3}{12}$

Adapting to Individual Needs

English Language Development
Materials: Apple or other fruit

Students who are just learning English might benefit from this activity which stresses translating "of" as "times" when dealing with fractions. Display an apple and write "1 apple" on the board. Say "If I had three *of* these, I would have 3 apples." Write $3 \times 1 = 3$ on the board. Then ask students what equation could be written to show $\frac{1}{2}$ *of*

the apple, emphasizing the word *of*. Write $\frac{1}{2} \times 1 = \frac{1}{2}$ on the board. Cut the apple to show $\frac{1}{2}$. Repeat the activity showing $\frac{1}{2}$ of $\frac{1}{2}$ the apple is $\frac{1}{4}$ the apple and write $\frac{1}{2} \times \frac{1}{2} = \frac{1}{4}$ on the board. Have students explain $\frac{1}{2}$ of $\frac{1}{4}$ the apple.

Notes on Questions

Questions 27–28 Students need to see that multiplying any number by a fraction less than 1 gives a product less than the original number. Likewise, multiplication by a fraction greater than 1 gives a product greater than the original number. These questions address these issues.

Question 34 When discussing this question, you might want to use **Teaching Aid 56**.

Question 35 Geography Connection In discussing this question, you might want to share these additional facts. Alaska is the largest state of the United States with an area of 591,004 square miles (1,530,700 square km) and the state with the least number of people per square mile—the estimated population in 1990 was 576,000.

20. Kyle presses 16 .
    a. What will the calculator do? **It displays 0.0625, which is $\frac{1}{16}$.**
    b. How can he check his answer? **key in** 1 ÷ 16 =

21. State the Property of Reciprocals. **For any nonzero number a, a and $1/a$ are reciprocals. That is, $a \cdot 1/a = 1$.**

22. Stephen has to blow up $\frac{1}{4}$ of all balloons needed for a celebration. He has a friend who will equally share Stephen's part of the job.
    a. How much of the total job will the friend do? $\frac{1}{8}$
    b. If the total job pays $100, how much should Stephen's friend receive? **$12.50**

Applying the Mathematics

23. Verify that $\frac{5}{8}$ is the reciprocal of $\frac{8}{5}$ by converting both fractions to decimals and multiplying. **$0.625 \cdot 1.6 = 1$**

24. Write the reciprocal of $1\frac{1}{2}$ as a fraction. $\frac{2}{3}$

25. Explain why 0 has no reciprocal. **Sample: The reciprocal would be $\frac{1}{0}$, but you cannot divide by 0.**

26. Each edge of a cubical box is $\frac{1}{2}$ meter long. What is the volume of the box? $\frac{1}{8}$ cubic meter

27. a. Multiply $\frac{1}{2} \cdot \frac{1}{3} \cdot \frac{1}{4}$. $\frac{1}{24}$
    b. How do you know that the answer to part **a** must be a number less than 1, without doing any multiplication? **Sample: $\frac{1}{2}$ of $\frac{1}{3}$ is less than $\frac{1}{3}$; $\frac{1}{4}$ of that is even smaller.**

28. a. Multiply $\frac{3}{2} \cdot \frac{5}{4} \cdot \frac{7}{6}$. $\frac{35}{16}$, or $2\frac{3}{16}$
    b. How do you know that the answer to part **a** must be a number greater than 1, without doing any multiplication? **All factors are greater than 1.**

29. a. Multiply $3\frac{1}{2} \cdot 2\frac{3}{4}$. Write your answer as a mixed number. $9\frac{5}{8}$
    b. How can you check your answer to part **a**? **Sample: Convert fractions to decimals and multiply.**

Review

30. Give the volume of a box with dimensions 9 cm, 15 cm, and 20 cm. *(Lesson 9-2)* **2700 cm³**

31. Find the area of right triangle *ABC*. *(Lessons 6-2, 9-1)*
    210 square units

486

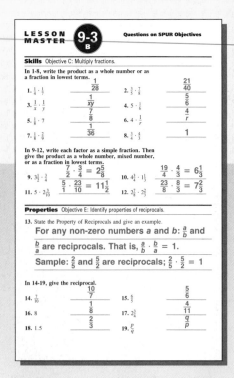

Adapting to Individual Needs

Challenge
Have students solve the following problems.
1. While flying across the country, an airline passenger fell asleep halfway toward her destination. When she awakened, the distance remaining to be traveled was half the distance she had traveled while asleep. What part of the trip was she asleep? $[\frac{1}{3}]$

2. Find three fractions between $\frac{1}{2}$ and 1 whose product is $\frac{1}{2}$. [Sample answer: $\frac{6}{7} \cdot \frac{3}{4} \cdot \frac{7}{9} = \frac{1}{2}$]

In 32 and 33, $\overline{PQ} \parallel \overline{ST}$ and angle measures are as shown on the figure.

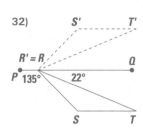

32.

32. Trace the figure and draw the reflection image of $\triangle RST$ over the line containing $\overline{PQ}$. *(Lesson 8-6)*

33. Find the measures of the three angles of triangle RST.
(Lessons 7-6, 7-7, 7-9) $m\angle SRT = 23°$, $m\angle S = 135°$, $m\angle T = 22°$

34) Yes. They cannot happen at the same time. If one die shows a 5, the sum must be greater than 5.

34. Two ordinary dice are tossed.
$A =$ the sum of the numbers showing on the dice is 5.
$B =$ one of the dice shows a 5.
Are A and B mutually exclusive? Why or why not? *(Lesson 5-6)*

35. If it snowed three days last week in Barrow, Alaska, what percent of the week did it not snow? Answer to the nearest percent.
(Lesson 4-8) **57%**

36. a. Order from smallest to largest: $\dfrac{1}{4}$ $\dfrac{4}{7}$ $\dfrac{7}{40}$. $\dfrac{7}{40}, \dfrac{1}{4}, \dfrac{4}{7}$
b. Order from smallest to largest: $-\dfrac{1}{4}$ $-\dfrac{4}{7}$ $-\dfrac{7}{40}$.
(Lessons 1-6, 1-8) $-\dfrac{4}{7}, -\dfrac{1}{4}, -\dfrac{7}{40}$

Way up north. *These children in Barrow, Alaska, are playing on a trampoline made from animal skins. Barrow, on the coast of the Arctic Ocean, is the northernmost community in the United States.*

Exploration

37. Examine this pattern involving unit fractions.
$$\frac{1}{2} = \frac{1}{3} + \frac{1}{6}$$
$$\frac{1}{3} = \frac{1}{4} + \frac{1}{12}$$
$$\frac{1}{4} = \frac{1}{5} + \frac{?}{} \quad \frac{1}{20}$$

a. Fill in the blank and then write the next two equations in the pattern.
b. Use the pattern to write $\frac{1}{2}$ as the sum of ten different unit fractions.
a) $\frac{1}{5} = \frac{1}{6} + \frac{1}{30}; \frac{1}{6} = \frac{1}{7} + \frac{1}{42}$
b) **Sample:** $\frac{1}{2} = \frac{1}{6} + \frac{1}{30} + \frac{1}{20} + \frac{1}{13} + \frac{1}{156} + \frac{1}{10} + \frac{1}{90} + \frac{1}{72} + \frac{1}{56} + \frac{1}{42}$

Setting Up Lesson 9-4

Questions 34 and 35 in this lesson review ideas that are helpful for the Lesson 9-4.

Practice
For more questions on SPUR Objectives, use **Lesson Master 9-3A** (shown on page 485) or **Lesson Master 9-3B** (shown on pages 486–487).

Assessment
Written Communication Draw a 6-by-8 grid on the board. Ask students to copy the grid and show the multiplication of $\frac{1}{3}$ by $\frac{5}{8}$ on the grid. [Students may use colored pencils or different types of shading to represent appropriate fractions. Encourage creativity in these visual displays of fraction multiplication.]

Extension
Have students find the stock market reports in a newspaper. Have them choose a stock and calculate the cost of 50 shares.

Project Update Project 6, *Multiplying Fractions Versus Multiplying Decimals or Percents*, on page 522, relates to the content of this lesson.

▶ **LESSON MASTER 9-3 B** *page 2*

Properties Objective F: Use properties of multiplication to simplify expressions and check calculations.

In 20-23, simplify.

20. $\frac{3}{5} \cdot \frac{1}{3} \cdot \frac{5}{3}$ _____ $\frac{1}{3}$ **21.** $\frac{1}{a} \cdot a \cdot 6$ _____ 6

22. $9 \cdot \frac{1}{8} \cdot \frac{1}{9} \cdot 2$ _____ $\frac{1}{4}$ **23.** $3 \cdot \frac{1}{10} \cdot \frac{10}{3}$ _____ 1

Representations Objective M: Picture multiplication of fractions using areas of rectangles.

In 24-26, tell what multiplication is pictured.

24.   **25.**   **26.**

$\frac{2}{5} \cdot \frac{3}{4}$ $\frac{1}{6} \cdot \frac{5}{6}$ $2 \cdot \frac{1}{3}$

In 27-29, picture the multiplication using the area model.

27. $\frac{1}{2} \cdot \frac{1}{4}$ **28.** $\frac{2}{3} \cdot \frac{4}{5}$ **29.** $3 \cdot \frac{1}{4}$

Review Objective J, Lesson 4-8

30. A spinner in a game is pictured. Assume all positions of the spinner are equally likely. The angles which form the regions have the measures given at the right. Give the probability, as a fraction in lowest terms, of landing on each region.

Region I: 36° $\frac{1}{10}$
Region II: 90° $\frac{1}{4}$
Region III: 60° $\frac{1}{6}$
Region IV: 54° $\frac{3}{20}$
Region V: 120° $\frac{1}{3}$

Objectives

I Calculate the probability of *A* and *B*, when *A* and *B* are independent events.

Resources

From the *Teacher's Resource File*
■ Lesson Master 9-4A or 9-4B
■ Answer Master 9-4
■ Teaching Aid 98: Warm-up
■ Assessment Sourcebook: Quiz for Lessons 9-1 through 9-4

Additional Resources
■ Visual for Teaching Aid 98

Teaching Lesson **9-4**

Warm-up

Use the data in **Question 22** on page 492. Suppose that the names of the American League stadiums are put into a hat, and one name is picked randomly and then replaced. What is the probability that you will pick a stadium

1. that seats more than 50,000? $\frac{4}{7}$
2. that was built in the 1970s? $\frac{1}{7}$
3. built after 1980 or before 1920? $\frac{3}{7}$
4. with a capacity less than 30,000? 0
5. with the word *stadium* in its name? $\frac{1}{2}$

Notes on Reading

Because the ideas in this lesson may be new to students, this is an appropriate lesson for students to read aloud.

Outside of mathematics, the word *independent* means "on one's own," or "without interference from others." This is the idea behind independent events.

❶ In reviewing **Example 1**, note that the events are independent because winning or losing one of the events does not affect winning or losing the other.

A probable favorite? *Field hockey is a fast-paced team sport that became popular with women in the U.S. in the early 1900s. Women's field hockey became an Olympic sport at the 1980 Summer Games.*

In Lesson 5-6, you learned that when events *A* and *B* are mutually exclusive, the probability of the event *A or B* is the sum of the probabilities of *A* and *B*. For instance, in tossing two dice:

$$\begin{array}{ccc} \text{probability of} & = & \text{probability of} & + & \text{probability of} \\ A \text{ or } B & & A & & B \end{array}$$

$$\begin{array}{ccc} \text{probability of a} & = & \text{probability of a} & + & \text{probability of a} \\ \text{sum of 7 or 11} & & \text{sum of 7} & & \text{sum of 11} \end{array}$$

This is possible only because the sums of 7 and 11 cannot occur at the same time.

The Probability of *A and B*

What happens if *A* and *B* *can* occur at the same time? That is, what is the **probability of the event *A and B*** if the probability of *A* and the probability of *B* are known? It may surprise you that the probability can sometimes be found by multiplication. In this lesson, we examine when that can be done and when it cannot. We use the abbreviation *Prob(A)* for the probability of the event *A*.

❶ **Example 1**

Two school teams are competing today. It is thought that the baseball team, with the amazing Kendall Hepitch on the mound, has an 85% chance of winning. The field hockey team, however, is thought to have only a 1 in 4 chance of winning. What is the probability that both teams will win?

▶

Lesson 9-4 Overview

Broad Goals Students should learn that to find the probability of a set of independent events, one can multiply the probabilities of the events.

Perspective If the probability that an event *A* will happen is *x*, and the probability that an event *B* will happen is *y*, and *A* and *B* are independent events, then the probability that both *A* and *B* will occur is *xy*. Because we so often represent probabilities as

fractions, one of the most prevalent uses of multiplication of fractions is in the calculation of probability. That is why this lesson is placed where it is.

The notation *Prob(E)*, introduced here for the probability of the event *E*, is an example of function notation, used in a setting in which it is quite natural. Read *Prob(E)*, or *P(E)*, as "the probability of the event *E*."

Solution

First name the individual events.

Let B = the baseball team wins. From the information, *Prob(B)* = 85%.

Let H = the field hockey team wins. From the information, *Prob(H)* = $\frac{1}{4}$.

B and H is the event that both teams win. The question asks for *Prob(B and H)*.

In this situation, we can assume that if one team wins, it does not affect the other team's result. So $\frac{1}{4}$ of the time the baseball team wins, the field hockey team will also win. This tells us how to find the answer:

$$\text{Prob(B and H)} = 85\% \cdot \frac{1}{4} = 21.25\% \approx 21\%.$$

The probability that both teams will win is about 21%.

When Are Events Independent?

In Example 1, we say that winning the baseball game and winning the field hockey game are *independent events*. The idea of independent events is that the occurrence of one does not depend on the occurrence of the other. In general, two events *A* and *B* are **independent events** when and only when *Prob(A and B) = Prob(A) · Prob(B)*.

❷ **Example 2**

On a TV game show there are three doors. The grand prize for the day is behind one of them. What is the probability that contestants will guess the correct door on the next two shows?

Solution 1

Let A be the event of guessing correctly on the next show. Let B be the event of guessing correctly on the second show. It is realistic to think that the guesses of contestants are random and independent.

Because of randomness, *Prob(A)* = $\frac{1}{3}$ and *Prob(B)* = $\frac{1}{3}$.
Because of independence,

$$\text{Prob(A and B)} = \text{Prob(A)} \cdot \text{Prob(B)} = \frac{1}{3} \cdot \frac{1}{3} = \frac{1}{9}.$$

Solution 2

Name the doors 1, 2, and 3. Then the possible guesses of doors for the two days are (1, 1), (1, 2), (1, 3), (2, 1), (2, 2), (2, 3), (3, 1), (3, 2), and (3, 3). Only one of these nine pairs will be correct, so The probability is $\frac{1}{9}$.

❸ Notice how easy it is to calculate the probability of *A and B* when the events *A* and *B* are independent. The difficulty is deciding whether *A* and *B* are independent. For instance, consider the probability of rain. Storm systems tend to be in an area for more than one day. So rain today increases the probability of rain tomorrow. Rain today and rain tomorrow are not independent events.

Lesson 9-4 *Multiplying Probabilities* **489**

Video

Wide World of Mathematics The segment, *Two-Sport Athlete,* profiles a man who competes professionally in two sports—and shows how he calculates his sports statistics. The segment may be used to launch a lesson on finding the probability of the occurrence of two independent events. Related questions and an investigation are provided in videodisc stills and in the Video Guide. A related CD-ROM activity is also available.

Videodisc Bar Codes

Search Chapter 44

Play

---

❷ In **Example 2**, the TV show that is most famous for having three doors is "Let's Make a Deal," but random events occur on many other shows.

For some events *A* and *B*, the word "and" in *A* and *B* may have as many as three possible interpretations:
(1) Both events occur simultaneously.
(2) Event *A* occurs, then event *B* occurs, but the two are not affected by each other. In many cases, this means "and then, with replacement."
(3) *A* occurs and affects the chances of *B* occurring. In this interpretation, *and* means "and then, without replacement."

The examples of the lesson are all of the form "*A* and then *B*," following interpretation (2). But **Example 1** can also be thought of as being Interpretation (1), and **Questions 11 and 14** are clearly of this type. When events *A* and *B* are independent, these two interpretations all yield the same value for *P(A and B)*. But if *A* and *B* are dependent, then the interpretations can yield different values. The contrast in these two cases is brought out in *Optional Activities* on page 490.

❸ An example of *dependent events* is given between **Examples 2** and **3**. You may wish to explain in more detail why the events might be dependent. Think of a situation in which there is one very small storm that may hit an area. It may come today or tomorrow, and the probability that it will come is $\frac{1}{3}$. But if it comes today, it will leave and then there will be no storm tomorrow. Thus the probability of rain on both days could be 0 despite the probability of rain being $\frac{1}{3}$ on each day.

If the storm is a long storm, then it is more likely that if it hits today it will continue on to tomorrow. There is a high probability it will be stormy on both days. Thus the probability of rain on both days could be as high as $\frac{1}{3}$. In general, if events A and B have probabilities of $\frac{1}{3}$ each, then the probability of A and B can be as high as $\frac{1}{3}$ and as low as 0. If the probability is $\frac{1}{9}$, then the events are independent.

❹ There are two reasons for **Example 3**. One is the important idea of the independence of more than two events. Also, this particular context explains why a high level of accuracy is needed on simple arithmetic computation, and why calculators and computers are used. In this example, we assume that an error in one computation does not affect an error in the others. That is what makes the events independent.

Additional Examples

1. Your favorite singer is giving a concert. She sings your favorite song at 1 out of 2 concerts. She sings your least favorite song at 1 out of 4 concerts. What are your chances of hearing both songs?
$\frac{1}{8}$

Suppose the probability of rain today is $\frac{1}{3}$ and the probability of rain tomorrow is $\frac{1}{3}$. Is the probability of rain both days then $\frac{1}{9}$, as in Example 2? No. The events are not independent and there is no simple way to calculate the probability that they will both happen.

An Example with More than Two Independent Events

Arithmetic errors are usually not independent. If you make an error in one place, you are more likely to make an error someplace else. But for the next example, we assume that errors are independent. Notice that it is possible for three or more events to be independent.

❹ **Example 3**
Suppose you are 98% accurate on basic arithmetic facts. A problem requires 10 basic facts. What is the probability that you will get all 10 facts correct?

Solution
Let E_1 = getting the first fact correct. Then $Prob(E_1) = 98\% = .98$. Similarly, let E_2 = getting the second fact correct, and so on, with E_{10} = getting the tenth fact correct. Then the event of getting all 10 facts correct is (E_1 and E_2 and E_3 and . . . and E_{10}). Assume the facts are independent. Then

$$Prob(E_1 \text{ and } E_2 \text{ and } E_3 \text{ and } \ldots \text{ and } E_{10})$$
$$= Prob(E_1) \cdot Prob(E_2) \cdot Prob(E_3) \cdot \ldots \cdot Prob(E_{10})$$
$$= \underbrace{.98 \cdot .98 \cdot .98 \cdot \ldots \cdot .98}_{10 \text{ factors}}$$
$$= .98^{10}$$
$$\approx .817$$

So there is about an 82% chance of getting all 10 facts correct.

There are many occasions when you might need to get 10 or more basic facts correct to solve a problem. But 82% accuracy in computation is not very high. This is why teachers want you to have even greater accuracy than 98% on basic facts, and why calculators are used today for complicated computations.

QUESTIONS

Covering the Reading

1. Translate into English words: $Prob(A)$. probability of the event A

2. Let Y = you wear a brown coat today.
Let F = your best friend wears a brown coat today.
   a. Describe the event Y *or* F.   **b.** Describe the event Y *and* F.

2a) Either you or your friend wears a brown coat today.
b) Both you and your friend wear brown coats today.

490

Optional Activities

After students have answered **Question 23**, you might want to have them **work in groups** and consider the following problem. Imagine tossing two dice, one green and one red. Let A = getting a sum of 6 on the two dice and let B = getting a 5 on the green die. $P(A) = \frac{5}{36}$ and $P(B) = \frac{1}{6}$. If $P(A$ and $B)$ means these events are to occur at the same time, are A and B independent events? Why? [No; $P(A$ and $B) = \frac{1}{36}$ (of the

36 possible tosses, only the toss of green = 5 and red = 1 satisfies), so $P(A$ and $B) \neq P(A) \cdot P(B)$]. If $P(A$ and $B)$ means that A occurs on one toss and then B occurs on another toss, are A and B independent? Why? [yes; $P(A$ and $B) = P(A) \cdot P(B)$]

3. Give a definition of *independent events*. **A and B are independent events when and only when Prob(A and B) = Prob(A) · Prob(B).**

4. Suppose on a TV game show there are four doors. The grand prize for the day is behind one of them. One contestant each day is able to guess which door has the prize behind it.
   a. What is the probability that a contestant will guess the correct door on a particular day? $\frac{1}{4}$
   b. What is the probability that the contestants will guess the correct door two days in a row? $\frac{1}{16}$
   c. What is the probability that the contestants will guess the correct door three days in a row? $\frac{1}{64}$
   d. Are guessing the correct doors today and tomorrow independent events? **Yes**

5. Let A = it snows today. Let B = it snows tomorrow. Explain why A and B are not independent events. **Snow today can affect the probability of snow tomorrow.**

6. Suppose you are 98% accurate when doing arithmetic computation. If a situation requires 5 independent arithmetic computations, what is the probability that you will get all 5 correct? $(.98)^5 \approx 90.392\%$

7) Answers will vary. Sample: You might need to get 10 basic facts correct to solve a problem and 82% accuracy on 10 basic facts is not very high.

7. Explain why 98% accuracy in basic facts is not very high.

Applying the Mathematics

8. Consider the situation of Example 1.
   a. What is the probability that the baseball team will lose? **15%**
   b. What is the probability that the field hockey team will lose? $\frac{3}{4}$
   c. What is the probability that both teams will lose? **11.25%**

9. Answer Question (2) on page 467. $\frac{8}{15}$ or $\approx 53\%$

10. Suppose a basketball player makes 74% of his free throws. If free throws are independent events, what is the probability that the player makes two free throws in a row? $\approx 55\%$

11) No. Since $P(A) = \frac{9}{10}$ and $P(B) = \frac{17}{24}$, $P(A) \cdot P(B) = \frac{51}{80}$. However, $\frac{3}{4}$ of the right-handed people are right-eyed, so $P(A \text{ and } B) = \frac{3}{4} \cdot \frac{9}{10} = \frac{27}{40}$. This shows that $P(A \text{ and } B) \neq P(A) \cdot P(B)$.

11. About $\frac{9}{10}$ of people are right-handed, and $\frac{1}{10}$ are left-handed. People can also be "right-eyed" or "left-eyed." According to the *Encyclopedia Britannica*, "about three fourths of right-handed and one third of left-handed persons are right-eyed in sighting." Let A = a person is right-handed, and let B = a person is right-eyed. Are A and B independent events? Explain why or why not.

12. One summer camp has 136 applicants for 50 openings. A second camp has 200 applicants for 65 openings. Suppose each camp fills its openings randomly from the applicants. If you were to apply to both camps, what is the probability that both would accept you? $\approx 12\%$

Lesson 9-4 *Multiplying Probabilities* **491**

---

2. Imagine tossing five coins. Let A = the first two coins both show heads. Let B = the last three all show tails.
   a. What is *Prob(A and B)*? $\frac{1}{32}$
   b. Are A and B independent? Why? **Yes, $P(A) = \frac{1}{4}$ and $P(B) = \frac{1}{8}$, $\frac{1}{4} \cdot \frac{1}{8} = \frac{1}{32}$, so $P(A) \cdot P(B) = P(A \text{ and } B)$**

3. Suppose there are 6 different independent systems in a car (ignition, exhaust, and so on). If each system works 99.9% of the time, and the systems are independent, what is the probability that the car will start? **about 99.40%**

Notes on Questions

Question 10 Studies of free-throw shooting tend to indicate that free throws are rather close to independent events. This goes counter to intuition.

Question 11 An answer can be given without calculating. Since right-handed people are more likely to be right-eyed, the events are not independent. Calculation verifies this: $P(A) = \frac{9}{10}$, $P(B) = \frac{17}{24}$, and $P(A \text{ and } B) = \frac{3}{4} \cdot \frac{9}{10} = \frac{27}{40}$, which is not the product of $P(A)$ and $P(B)$.

Question 12 The key word in this question is "randomly." In the real world, camps seldom select applicants randomly, so the events might not be independent.

Adapting to Individual Needs

English Language Development

Some students might have trouble with the term *independent*. Have student A stand next to a desk without touching it. Have student B lean against another desk. Ask students what would happen to each student if you moved the desk away. Point out that student A's position is independent of the position of the desk. Student B's position is not independent of the position of the desk.

Notes on Questions

Question 18 Point out to students that they have a choice of computing with either fractions or decimals. Calculators may be used, but are not necessary.

Practice

For more questions on SPUR Objectives, use **Lesson Master 9-4A** (shown on pages 489–490) or **Lesson Master 9-4B** (shown on pages 491–492).

Assessment

Quiz A quiz covering Lessons 9-1 through 9-4 is provided in the *Assessment Sourcebook.*

Group Assessment Have students **work in groups**. Ask each group to prepare a quiz covering the material in this lesson. Each student in the group should write at least one quiz question. Have each group take another group's quiz and check the other group's answers to their own quiz. [Questions should reflect the content of the lesson. Questions and answers will probably parallel the examples.]

Project Update Project 4, *Streaks,* on page 522, relates to the content of this lesson.

► **LESSON MASTER 9-4 B** *page 2*

8. What is the probability of tossing tails on a fair coin and tossing a number less than 5 on a fair die?

$\frac{1}{2} \cdot \frac{2}{3}$
calculation

$\frac{1}{3}$
answer

9. You have two decks of cards and draw one card from each. What is the probability that both cards are hearts?

$\frac{1}{4} \cdot \frac{1}{4}$
calculation

$\frac{1}{16}$
answer

10. You have two decks of cards and draw one card from each. What is the probability that both cards are kings?

$\frac{1}{13} \cdot \frac{1}{13}$
calculation

$\frac{1}{169}$
answer

11. If you toss a fair coin, what is the probability of tossing 6 heads in a row?

$\left(\frac{1}{2}\right)^6$
calculation

$\frac{1}{64}$
answer

12. In one of your drawers, 3 of 8 T-shirts are black. In another drawer, 4 of 5 pairs of pants are jeans. If you select at random, what is the probability that you will pull out a black T-shirt and a pair of jeans?

$\frac{3}{8} \cdot \frac{4}{5}$
calculation

$\frac{3}{10}$
answer

13. Ty Cobb was the American League batting champion 12 times. His best average was .420. Use this as his probability of getting a hit in a single at bat and assume each is an independent event. If Ty Cobb were to bat four times in a game, what is the probability he would *not* get a hit?

$(.58)^4$
calculation

.113165
answer

14. Are the assumptions in Question 15 necessarily valid? Explain your thinking.
No; sample: Circumstances are not identical for each time at bat. Health, weather, the pitch, and so on, all affect the outcome.

---

14) If you toss a 7, you cannot toss an 11. So Prob(both events) = 0. This is not the product of the individual probabilities.

21) The area is multiplied by 5^2 or 25. Examples: $2 \cdot 3 = 6$, and $5(2) \cdot 5(3) = 25(6) = 150$; $4 \cdot 1 = 4$, and $5(4) \cdot 5(1) = 25(4) = 100$. Sample pattern: If dimensions of a rectangle are multiplied by n, the area is multiplied by n^2.

More than just a stadium.
The SkyDome is home to Toronto's professional football team, the Argonauts, and baseball team, the Blue Jays. The SkyDome covers 8 acres; features a retractable roof that can be closed in a matter of minutes; and includes a hotel and entertainment mall.

22a)
```
3 | 3
4 | 84073
5 | 235780
6 | 4
7 | 4
```

---

13. Suppose you are 98% accurate at arithmetic computation without a calculator and 99% accurate with a calculator. How much larger is the probability of getting 100 independent arithmetic computations correct with the calculator? ≈ **23.3%**

14. Two dice are tossed once. Explain why tossing a sum of 7 and tossing a sum of 11 are not independent events.

Review

In 15–20, calculate. *(Lessons 5-5, 9-3)*

15. $\frac{3}{4} \cdot 4$ **3**

16. $\frac{1}{2} \cdot \frac{3}{4} \cdot \frac{2}{3}$ $\frac{1}{4}$

17. $\frac{1}{2} + \frac{1}{2} \cdot \frac{1}{5}$ $\frac{3}{5}$

18. $2.6 + \frac{7}{25}$ **2.88, or $\frac{72}{25}$**

19. $x \cdot \frac{1}{x}$ **1**

20. $\frac{1}{a} \cdot \frac{1}{b}$ $\frac{1}{ab}$

21. If the dimensions of a rectangle are multiplied by 5, what happens to its area? Give two examples and the general pattern. *(Lessons 4-2, 9-1)*

22. Here are the seating capacities of American League baseball stadiums:

Team	Stadium (year built)	Seating Capacity
Baltimore Orioles	Oriole Park at Camden Yards (1992)	48,000
Boston Red Sox	Fenway Park (1912)	33,925
California Angels	Anaheim Stadium (1966)	64,593
Chicago White Sox	Comiskey Park (1991)	44,321
Cleveland Indians	Cleveland Stadium (1932)	74,483
Detroit Tigers	Tiger Stadium (1912)	52,416
Kansas City Royals	Kauffman Stadium (1973)	40,625
Milwaukee Brewers	Milwaukee County Stadium (1953)	53,192
Minnesota Twins	Hubert H. Humphrey Metrodome (1982)	55,883
New York Yankees	Yankee Stadium (1923)	57,545
Oakland A's	Oakland-Alameda County Coliseum (1968)	47,313
Seattle Mariners	Kingdome (1977)	58,823
Texas Rangers	Arlington Stadium (1965)	43,521
Toronto Blue Jays	SkyDome (1989)	50,516

a. In your head, round the capacities down to the nearest thousand. Then put the rounded values into a stem-and-leaf display. See left.

b. What is the median capacity? *(Lessons 1-3, 8-1)* **51,466**

Exploration

23. a. Give an example different from any in this lesson of two events that are not independent.
b. Give an example different from any in this lesson of two events that are independent.
Sample: a) picking a red card and picking a diamond from a standard deck of 52 cards b) picking a king card and picking a diamond from a standard deck of 52 cards

---

Adapting to Individual Needs

Challenge
Have students solve the following problem: A die is rolled three times in a row. What is the probability that the same number will occur each time? [The probability that a particular number will occur three times in a row is $\frac{1}{6} \times \frac{1}{6} \times \frac{1}{6}$, or $\frac{1}{216}$. Since, there are six possible ways this can happen, the answer is $\frac{6}{216}$, or $\frac{1}{36}$.]

Setting Up Lesson 9-5

Materials Students will need newspapers for the *Notes on Questions* and the *Assessment* in Lesson 9-5.

LESSON

9-5

The Rate Factor Model for Multiplication

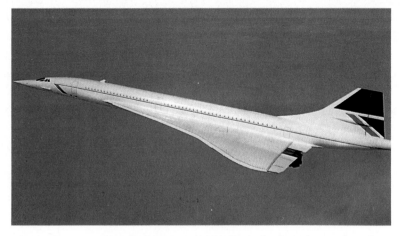

Faster than sound. *The BAC/Aérospatiale Concorde, shown here, is the only supersonic jet used for passenger service. It can cruise at speeds up to Mach 2.2—which is 2.2 times as fast as the speed of sound, or about 1450 mph at 36,000 ft.*

What Is a Rate?

A quantity is a rate when its unit contains the word "per" or "for each" or some synonym. Here are some examples of *rates*.

> 55 *miles per hour* (speed limit)
> 25.3 *students per class* (average class size)
> 107 *centimeters* of snow *per year* (average snowfall in Boston)
> $2\frac{1}{2}$ *pieces for each student* (result of splitting up a pie)

Every rate has a **rate unit.** Above, the rate units are in italics.

When used in an expression, the slash / or horizontal bar—means "per." Notice how the above rate units are written in fraction notation.

Using the slash		**Using the bar**
55 mi/hr	$=$	$55\,\frac{mi}{hr}$
25.3 students/class	$=$	$25.3\,\frac{students}{class}$
107 cm/yr	$=$	$107\,\frac{cm}{yr}$
$2\frac{1}{2}$ pieces/student	$=$	$2\frac{1}{2}\,\frac{pieces}{student}$

Multiplying by a Rate

Suppose a woman gains 2 pounds per month during pregnancy. Her rate of weight gain is then

$$2\,\frac{pounds}{month}.$$

Lesson 9-5

Objectives

J Apply the Rate Factor Model for Multiplication.
K Use conversion factors to convert from one unit to another.

Resources

From the **Teacher's Resource File**
■ Lesson Master 9-5A or 9-5B
■ Answer Master 9-5
■ Teaching Aid 98: Warm-up

Additional Resources
■ Visual for Teaching Aid 98
■ Newspapers (Notes on Question 17 and Assessment)

Teaching Lesson 9-5

Warm-up

Human hair grows an average of 1.5 to 3.0 millimeters per week. Suppose you had not cut your hair since you were born. Estimate how long you hair would be now if your hair grew at the maximum rate. Write your answer in inches and feet. Remember, 1 inch is approximately equal to 2.5 cm. **Answers will vary.**

Lesson 9-5 Overview

Broad Goals Students should see the broad roles of rates and rate units in multiplication.

Perspective The unit in a rate is written with the fraction bar or slash because the *calculation* of rate is a fundamental use of division. For instance, if a person travels 200 miles in 5 hours, the rate is $\frac{200\ miles}{5\ hours} =$ 40 miles/hour $= 40\,\frac{miles}{hour}$. Lesson 11-2

discusses the corresponding Rate Model for Division.

Historically, most teachers of mathematics avoid units and are criticized by science teachers for it. We think their criticisms are justified. It is true that putting units in an equation can be quite confusing. Even scientists who use units to check formulas seldom keep units going through a calculation. But elsewhere, keeping track of units can be

a big help. (The use of units to help set up or answer a problem is called *dimensional analysis*.)

In this lesson it is useful to keep track of units. By keeping track of units, students have one more way to check answers and to figure out which operation is reasonable. Also, work with units in rate factor multiplication reinforces multiplication of fractions.

Suppose she keeps this rate up for 5 months. Multiplication gives the total she gains.

$$5 \text{ months} \cdot 2 \frac{\text{pounds}}{\text{month}} = 10 \text{ pounds}$$

❶ Look at the units in the multiplication above. They work as if they were whole numbers and fractions. The unit "months" at left cancels the unit "month" in the denominator. The unit that remains is pounds. You can see where the 10 comes from.

Here is a similar example of multiplying by a rate.

❷ **Example 1**

A person buys 7 cans of tuna at $1.39 per can. What is the total cost?

Solution

Here is the way it looks with all units included.

$$7 \text{ cans} \cdot 1.39 \frac{\text{dollars}}{\text{can}} = 9.73 \text{ dollars}$$

Here is how it looks using the usual dollar signs and a slash.

$$7 \text{ cans} \cdot \$1.39/\text{can} = \$9.73$$

The Rate Factor Model for Multiplication

The quantity $1.39 \frac{\text{dollars}}{\text{can}}$ in Example 1 is a rate that is multiplied. So it is a **rate factor.** The general idea behind Example 1 is the Rate Factor Model for Multiplication.

Rate Factor Model for Multiplication
The product of (a $unit_1$) and $\left(b \frac{unit_2}{unit_1}\right)$ is (ab $unit_2$), signifying the total amount of $unit_2$ in the situation.

Some multiplications from earlier lessons in this chapter can be thought of as rate factor multiplications.

Example 2

(Array) An auditorium contains 12 rows with 19 seats per row. How many seats are in the auditorium?

Solution

Here $unit_1$ is rows, and $\frac{unit_2}{unit_1}$ is $\frac{\text{seats}}{\text{row}}$. $Unit_2$, the unit of the product, is seats.

$$12 \text{ rows} \cdot 19 \frac{\text{seats}}{\text{row}} = 228 \text{ seats}$$

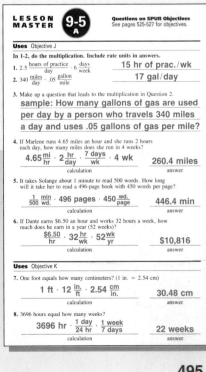

A run for your money. *In recent years, the New York City Marathon has begun with about 26,000 entrants crossing the 4260-ft-long Verrazano-Narrows Bridge. Usually over 95% of the entrants complete the marathon.*

Converting Units Using Rates

A *conversion factor* is a special kind of rate factor. Start with a conversion formula. Here is an example.

$$1 \text{ mile} = 5280 \text{ feet}$$

Since the quantities are equal, dividing one by the other gives the number 1.

$$\frac{1 \text{ mile}}{5280 \text{ feet}} = 1 \quad \text{and} \quad \frac{5280 \text{ feet}}{1 \text{ mile}} = 1$$

You could say there is 1 mile for every 5280 feet or there are 5280 feet for every mile. The quantities $\frac{1 \text{ mile}}{5280 \text{ feet}}$ and $\frac{5280 \text{ feet}}{1 \text{ mile}}$ are conversion factors. A conversion factor is a rate factor that equals the number 1.

Example 3

(Conversion) 40,000 feet equals how many miles?

Solution

Multiply 40,000 feet by the conversion factor with miles in its numerator and feet in its denominator. The mile unit is needed in the product, so feet needs to be in the denominator to cancel.

$$40,000 \text{ feet} \cdot \frac{1 \text{ mile}}{5280 \text{ feet}} = \frac{40,000}{5280} \text{ miles}$$
$$= 7.\overline{57} \text{ miles}$$

Example 4

(Conversion) 26.2 miles, the approximate length of a marathon, is how many feet?

Solution

Use the conversion factor with miles in its denominator.

$$26.2 \text{ miles} \cdot \frac{5280 \text{ feet}}{1 \text{ mile}} = 138,336 \text{ feet}$$

Uta Pippig of Germany, on the left wearing F3, won the women's division of the 1993 New York City Marathon with a time of 2:26:24. Andres Espinosa of Mexico won the men's division with a time of 2:10:04.

Lesson 9-5 *The Rate Factor Model for Multiplication* **495**

Adapting to Individual Needs

Extra Help

Remind students of the importance of reading a problem carefully so that they know what units to use in the answer. If a conversion is involved, knowing the unit to be used in the answer will help in choosing the correct conversion factor for the problem. For example, if a problem asks for the number of inches in 9 feet, have students write the following equation.

$$9 \text{ feet} \times \frac{12 \text{ inches}}{1 \text{ foot}} = \underline{\hspace{2cm}} \text{ inches}$$

Point out that "inches" in the answer means that "feet" will have to cancel, thus it is the unit to be used in the denominator of the conversion factor. Help students see that if $\frac{1 \text{ foot}}{12 \text{ inches}}$ were used in the same equation, no unit would cancel. Also remind students to always check their answers for reasonableness.

④ **Example 5** should be discussed carefully. Given this information, students are often confused about which operation(s) to use to obtain the answer. Getting the units right is a big help in getting the answer.

Additional Examples

1. A piece of notebook paper is about .04 inch thick. A ream of paper contains 500 sheets. How thick is a ream? **500 sheets ·**

$$\frac{.04 \text{ inch}}{\text{sheet}} = 20 \text{ inches}$$

2. A box contains 12 jars in each of 6 rows. Determine how many jars are in the box using rate factor multiplication. $\frac{12 \text{ jars}}{\text{row}} \cdot 6 \text{ rows} =$

72 jars

3. Multiply conversion factors to find how many yards are in 5280 feet.

$$5280 \text{ ft} \cdot \frac{1 \text{ yd}}{3 \text{ ft}} = \frac{5280}{3} = 1760 \text{ yd}$$

4. Multiply conversion factors to determine how many inches are in a mile. $\frac{12 \text{ inches}}{\text{foot}} \cdot \frac{5280 \text{ feet}}{\text{mile}} =$

$$\frac{63,360 \text{ in.}}{\text{mi}}$$

5. A calligrapher charges 5 cents a word to do fancy lettering. If a graduating class has 128 students and each student has a first, a middle, and a last name, how much will the calligrapher charge to write the names on the diplomas? $\frac{0.05}{\text{word}} \cdot \frac{3 \text{ words}}{\text{student}} \cdot$

$$\frac{128 \text{ students}}{\text{class}} = \frac{\$19.20}{\text{class}}$$

Multiplying Two or More Rates

In some situations, two rates are to be multiplied. Again the units are multiplied as you would multiply fractions.

④ **Example 5**

An administrative assistant has 8 letters to type. Each letter is 4 pages long. Each page takes 6 minutes to type. How long will it take to type all the letters?

Solution

Think rates. There are 4 pages per letter. There are 6 minutes per page.

$$8 \text{ letters} \cdot 4 \frac{\text{pages}}{\text{letter}} \cdot 6 \frac{\text{minutes}}{\text{page}}$$

$$= 32 \text{ pages} \cdot 6 \frac{\text{minutes}}{\text{page}}$$

$$= 192 \text{ minutes}$$

QUESTIONS

Covering the Reading

In 1 and 2, a sentence is given.
a. Copy the sentence and underline the rate.
b. Write the rate with its unit in fraction notation using the slash.
c. Write the rate with its unit in fraction notation using the fraction bar.

1. Only 4 tickets per student are available for the basketball game.
   b) 4 tickets/student   c) $4 \frac{\text{tickets}}{\text{student}}$

2. The speed limit there is 45 miles per hour.
   b) 45 miles/hour   c) $45 \frac{\text{miles}}{\text{hour}}$

3. Consider the multiplication $3 \text{ hr} \cdot 50 \frac{\text{km}}{\text{hr}} = 150 \text{ km}$.
   a. Identify the rate factor. $50 \frac{\text{km}}{\text{hr}}$
   b. Identify the unit of the rate factor. $\frac{\text{km}}{\text{hr}}$
   c. Make up a situation that could lead to this multiplication.
      Sample: If you travel for 3 hours at $50 \frac{\text{km}}{\text{hr}}$, how far have you gone?

In 4–7, do the multiplication.

4. $5 \text{ classes} \cdot 25 \frac{\text{students}}{\text{class}} \cdot 30 \frac{\text{questions}}{\text{student}}$ 3750 questions

5. $8.2 \text{ pounds} \cdot \$2.29/\text{pound}$ $18.778

6. $\frac{1.06 \text{ quarts}}{\text{liter}} \cdot 6 \text{ liters}$ 6.36 quarts

7. $2 \frac{\text{games}}{\text{week}} \cdot 8 \frac{\text{weeks}}{\text{season}}$ $16 \frac{\text{games}}{\text{season}}$

8. a. Do this multiplication. $30,000 \text{ ft} \cdot \frac{1 \text{ mile}}{5280 \text{ ft}} \approx 5.68 \text{ miles}$
   b. Make up a question that leads to this multiplication. Sample: Convert 30,000 feet to miles.

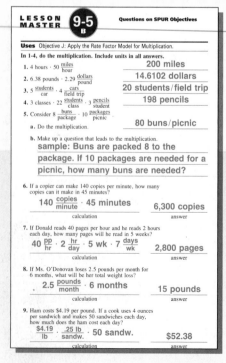

LESSON MASTER 9-5 B Questions on SPUR Objectives

Uses Objective J: Apply the Rate Factor Model for Multiplication.

In 1-4, do the multiplication. Include units in all answers.

1. $4 \text{ hours} \cdot 50 \frac{\text{miles}}{\text{hour}}$ **200 miles**

2. $6.38 \text{ pounds} \cdot 2.29 \frac{\text{dollars}}{\text{pound}}$ **14.6102 dollars**

3. $5 \frac{\text{students}}{\text{car}} \cdot 4 \frac{\text{cars}}{\text{field trip}}$ **20 students/field trip**

4. $3 \text{ classes} \cdot 22 \frac{\text{students}}{\text{class}} \cdot 3 \frac{\text{pencils}}{\text{student}}$ **198 pencils**

5. Consider $8 \frac{\text{buns}}{\text{package}} \cdot 10 \frac{\text{packages}}{\text{picnic}}$

   a. Do the multiplication. **80 buns/picnic**

   b. Make up a question that leads to the multiplication.
   sample: Buns are packed 8 to the package. If 10 packages are needed for a picnic, how many buns are needed?

6. If a copier can make 140 copies per minute, how many copies can it make in 45 minutes?
   $140 \frac{\text{copies}}{\text{minute}} \cdot 45 \text{ minutes}$ **6,300 copies**
   calculation   answer

7. If Donald reads 40 pages per hour and he reads 2 hours each day, how many pages will he read in 5 weeks?
   $40 \frac{\text{pp}}{\text{hr}} \cdot 2 \frac{\text{hr}}{\text{day}} \cdot 5 \text{ wk} \cdot 7 \frac{\text{days}}{\text{wk}}$ **2,800 pages**
   calculation   answer

8. If Ms. O'Donovan loses 2.5 pounds per month for 6 months, what will be her total weight loss?
   $2.5 \frac{\text{pounds}}{\text{month}} \cdot 6 \text{ months}$ **15 pounds**
   calculation   answer

9. Ham costs $4.19 per pound. If a cook uses 4 ounces per sandwich and makes 50 sandwiches each day, how much does the ham cost each day?
   $\frac{\$4.19}{\text{lb}} \cdot \frac{.25 \text{ lb}}{\text{sandw.}} \cdot 50 \text{ sandw.}$ **$52.38**
   calculation   answer

Adapting to Individual Needs

English Language Development
For students who are just learning English, slight changes in wording can be confusing. Help them by making a list of words and phrases commonly used to signify a rate. Include *per*, *for each*, *for every*, *a* or *an* (as in 50 times a minute). Have these students write the list on an index card or in their journals if they are keeping them.

9. If an animal gains 1.5 kg a month for 7 months, how many kg will it have gained in the seven months? 10.5 kg

10. A typist can type 40 words a minute. At this rate, how many words can be typed in 20 minutes? 800 words

11) $\frac{1 \text{ mile}}{5280 \text{ ft}}$ and $\frac{5280 \text{ ft}}{1 \text{ mile}}$

11. Name the two conversion factors for converting between feet and miles.

12. An airplane flying 35,000 feet up is how many miles up?
≈ 6.63 miles

13. A section of a football stadium has 50 rows with 20 seats in each row. How many people can be seated in this section? 1000 people

---

Applying the Mathematics

14a) $\frac{1 \text{ in.}}{2.54 \text{ cm}}$ and $\frac{2.54 \text{ cm}}{1 \text{ in.}}$

14. Recall that 1 inch = 2.54 cm.
  a. What two conversion factors does this formula suggest?
  b. Use one of the factors to convert 10 cm to inches. ≈3.94 in.

15. If a heart beats 70 times a minute, how many times will it beat in a day? 100,800 beats

16. Solve for x: 4 hours · x = 120 miles. 30 miles/hour

17. When the twins went to France in August of 1993, they found that 5.7 francs were worth 1 dollar. In Spain, they found that 1 franc was worth 22.8 pesetas. How many pesetas could they get for $10?
1299.6 pesetas

18. Suppose a particular car has a 14-gallon tank and can get about 25 miles per gallon. What do you get when you multiply these quantities?
350 miles

Review

BINGO!

19. Sarah feels she has a 2 out of 7 chance of getting a B in English and a 4 out of 5 chance of getting an A in mathematics. If these events are independent, what is the probability that both will happen?
(Lesson 9-4) $\frac{8}{35}$

20. Suppose the probability that you win a game of bingo is $\frac{1}{15}$.
  a. What is the probability that you will win the first two games you play? $\frac{1}{225}$
  b. What is the probability that you will win the first three games you play? *(Lesson 9-4)* $\frac{1}{3375}$

21. Three shirts are in a drawer and four skirts are on hangers. In the dark, you pick out a shirt and skirt. What are your chances of choosing the particular shirt and skirt you want? *(Lesson 9-4)* $\frac{1}{12}$

22. Rebecca had $86.48 to spend during her vacation. She spent half of her money the first day and one fourth of what was left on the second day. How much money did she have left after the second day? *(Lesson 9-3)* $32.43

Lesson 9-5 *The Rate Factor Model for Multiplication* **497**

Notes on Questions
✎ **Question 30 Writing** Estimates
may vary depending on the method
used and pages selected as samples. It is important that students justify their answer with a reasonable
process.

Follow-up
for Lesson **9-5**

Practice

For more questions on SPUR Objectives, use **Lesson Master 9-5A**
(shown on page 495) or **Lesson
Master 9-5B** (shown on pages
496–497).

Assessment
Written Communication
Materials: Newspapers
Have students look through newspapers to find examples of rates. Have
them write questions using the rate
that was cited in the paper. [Ques-
tions demonstrate an understanding
of rates and the Rate Factor Model
for Multiplication.]

Extension

You might want to have students
research the most recent census
data and find the population density
for 10 states or 10 major cities. Point
out that density is a rate: number of
people per square mile. Discuss
why it is useful for city, state, or
federal governments to have such
information.

Project Update Project 3, *Effects
of Different Rates,* on page 521,
relates to the content of this lesson.

---

23) $1\frac{1}{4}$ square miles

A downtown haven.
*Central Park, in the
middle of Manhattan, is
the largest of New York
City's parks. It includes
the Mall, where outdoor
concerts are held, and the
Ramble, an enclosed bird
sanctuary.*

30) a) **Count the words
on a few pages.
Take their average
(a rate), and
multiply this
average by the
number of pages.**
b) **Answers will
vary.**

498

---

23. Central Park in New York City is shaped like a rectangle, about $2\frac{1}{2}$ miles long and $\frac{1}{2}$ mile wide. What is its area?   *(Lessons 9-1, 9-3)*

24. *Multiple choice.* $\frac{2}{3} - \left(-\frac{2}{3}\right) =$
(a) $-\frac{4}{3}$ (b) 0   (c) $\frac{4}{9}$ (d) $\frac{4}{3}$ (e) none of these
(Lessons 5-5, 7-2) (d)

25. Seven teams are to play each other in a tournament. Each team will play every other team once. How many games will be played? *(Lesson 6-3)* **21 games**

26. A diving team went 267.8 feet below sea level and then rose 67.9 feet.
a. What addition tells where the team would be? **-267.8 + 67.9**
b. What was their final position? *(Lessons 5-1, 5-3)*
199.9 ft below sea level
In 27–29, give an abbreviation for the unit. *(Lessons 3-3, 3-4)*

27. pound **lb**   **28.** kilogram **kg**   **29.** milliliter **mL**

Exploration

30. Depending on the number of words it contains, a work of prose is often classified as a short story, a novelette, or a novel. A short story is usually less than 10,000 words. To find the number of words in a work of prose, editors rarely count them all, but use rate factors.
a. Describe how you might estimate the number of words in a work of prose.
b. Estimate the number of words in this chapter.

Adapting to Individual Needs
Challenge
Have students solve the following problem: A car is traveling at a rate of 60 miles
per hour. Change this rate to feet per second. [88 feet/second]

A negative rate. *Sometime lakes are "drawn down" or drained in winter to prevent shoreline damage from the freezing water. These park rangers are controlling the rate at which water flows out of Pine Barrens Lake in New Jersey.*

A Situation Involving Multiplication by a Negative Number

Any loss can lead to a negative rate. Suppose a person loses 2 pounds per month on a diet. The rate of change in weight is then

$$-2 \, \frac{\text{pounds}}{\text{month}}.$$

If the person keeps losing weight at this rate for 5 months, multiplying gives the total loss.

$$5 \text{ months} \cdot -2 \, \frac{\text{pounds}}{\text{month}} = -10 \text{ pounds}$$

Ignoring the units, a positive and a negative number are being multiplied. The product is negative.

$$5 \cdot -2 = -10$$

The number of months does not have to be a whole number. The rate does not have to be an integer.

Example 1

On a medically supervised diet lasting $3\frac{1}{2}$ months, a person lost 2.4 kg per month. What was the net change in weight?

Solution

Use the Rate Factor Model for Multiplication. The rate is $-2.4 \, \frac{\text{kg}}{\text{month}}$.

$$-2.4 \, \frac{\text{kg}}{\text{month}} \cdot 3\frac{1}{2} \text{ months}$$

$$= -2.4 \, \frac{\text{kg}}{\text{month}} \cdot 3.5 \text{ months}$$

$$= -8.4 \text{ kg}$$

The net change is a loss of 8.4 kg.

Lesson 9-6 *Multiplication with Negative Numbers and Zero* **499**

Lesson 9-6

Objectives

D Multiply positive and negative numbers.
E Identify the Multiplication Properties of Zero and –1.
F Use the Multiplication Properties of Zero and –1 to simplify expressions and check calculations.

Resources

From the *Teacher's Resource File*
- Lesson Master 9-6A or 9-6B
- Answer Master 9-6
- Teaching Aid 98: Warm-up
- Activity Kit, Activity 23

Additional Resources
- Visual for Teaching Aid 98

Teaching Lesson 9-6

Warm-up

Evaluate each expression when $a = 2$ and $b = 7$.
1. $3a + b$ 13
2. $2b + -a$ 12
3. a^4 16
4. $b^2 + a^3$ 57
5. $(5a)^2$ 100
6. $2.5a + -b$ –2
7. $9b - a$ 61

Lesson 9-6 Overview

Broad Goals The skill of multiplying negative numbers is easy, but students wonder why they need to learn it. The point of this lesson and Lesson 9-9 is to present situations that involve multiplication with negative numbers.

Perspective The rules for multiplication with negative numbers are usually presented as in the simple statements shown at the bottom of page 501. We also encourage the

operator view, stated at the bottom of page 500. It stresses that the sign of the answer is determined by what one factor does to the other.

Although the multiplication properties of zero and -1 are quite easy, students should still consider the examples and questions carefully. The examples and questions discuss consequences of the properties that

are not so obvious and that students may have missed or misunderstood.

Students can do this lesson independently, since the generalizations are clear and straightforward. Students should be able to give the rules in class along with some real-world situations to illustrate them.

❶ **Example 4** provides computation with an even number of negative numbers. Help students see that if an even number of factors have opposite signs, then, by repeatedly applying the Multiplication Property of –1, the answer will have no opposite sign. If an odd number of factors have opposite signs, then the answer (when simplified) will have an opposite sign. Caution students again and again that this works only when multiplication is the only operation used.

Additional Examples

Evaluate.
1. –.001 · 536 –0.536
2. 10 · –$\frac{1}{2}$ –5
3. –28 · 5 –140
4. Tell whether the number is positive or negative.
   a. –1 · –10 · –100 · –1000 · –10,000 negative
   b. –1 · 2 · –3 · 4 · –5 · 6 · –7 positive
   c. $(-3)^5$ negative
   d. x^4 when $x = -11$ positive
   e. –2.5 · –4 positive
   f. –2.5 + –4 negative
5. The temperature has been dropping 3 degrees an hour for the past four hours. Describe the temperature four hours ago. **The temperature was 12° higher.**
6. Find the product:
   a. –$\frac{1}{7}$ · –7 1
   b. –3 · 1$\frac{1}{2}$ · –2.3 · 0 · –50 · $\frac{1}{4}$ · –9 0

Example 1 demonstrates that when a positive number is multiplied by a negative number, the product is negative.

Example 2

What is 5 · –4.8?

Solution

Think of this as a loss of 4.8 kg per month for 5 months. The result is a loss, so the answer is negative. Since 5 · 4.8 = 24,

$$5 \cdot -4.8 = -24.$$

Example 3

What is –7 · 4?

Solution

–7 · 4 = 4 · –7. Think of this as a loss of 7 kg each month for 4 months.

$$-7 \cdot 4 = -28$$

Multiplication with Two Negative Numbers

What happens if both numbers are negative? Again think of a weight-loss situation. Suppose a person loses 2 pounds a month. At this rate, 5 months *ago* the person weighed 10 pounds more. Going back is the negative direction for time. So here is another multiplication for this situation.

$$5 \text{ months ago} \cdot \text{loss of } 2 \frac{\text{pounds}}{\text{month}} = 10 \text{ pounds more}$$
$$-5 \text{ months} \cdot -2 \frac{\text{pounds}}{\text{month}} = 10 \text{ pounds}$$

Ignoring the units: –5 · –2 = 10

In general, the product of two negative numbers is a positive number.

There is another way to think of multiplication with positive and negative numbers.

> When a number is multiplied by a positive number, the sign of the product (positive or negative) is the same as the sign of the number.
>
> When a number is multiplied by a negative number, the sign of the product (positive or negative) is the opposite of the sign of the number.

Optional Activities

Activity 1
You can use *Activity Kit, Activity 23*, to introduce this lesson. In this activity, students use integer tiles to multiply integers.

Activity 2
Before students answer **Question 25,** you might want to present an alternative method of justifying multiplication of positive and negative numbers. Show students the following patterns and ask them to fill in the blanks.

5 · 3 = 15	3 · 4 = 12
5 · 2 = 10	2 · 4 = 8
5 · 1 = 5	1 · 4 = 4
5 · 0 = 0	0 · 4 = 0
5 · –1 = [–5]	–1 · 4 = [–4]
5 · –2 = [–10]	–2 · 4 = [–8]

These patterns provide an additional way of remembering rules for multiplication of positive and negative numbers if one has forgotten them.

❶ **Example 4**

Is -2 · -5 · 3 · -4 · 6 · -2 · -1 · -3 positive or negative?

Solution

Each multiplication by a negative changes the product's sign. Each two changes keeps it positive. Since there are 6 negative numbers, the sign is positive.

Check

Use your calculator to verify that the product is 4320.

Caution: The kind of thinking in the Solution to Example 4 works because the numbers are all multiplied. It does not work for addition or subtraction.

Multiplication by -1

Multiplication by -1 follows the above pattern, but it is even more special.

$$-1 \cdot 53 = -53$$
$$-1 \cdot -4 = 4$$
$$-1 \cdot \frac{2}{3} = -\frac{2}{3}$$

Multiplication by -1 changes a number to its opposite. Here is a description with variables.

> **Multiplication Property of -1**
> For any number x, $-1 \cdot x = -x$.

You have now seen that the product of a positive number and a negative number is negative. You have also seen that the product of two negative numbers is positive. Of course you already know that the product of two positive numbers is positive. These facts can be summarized as follows:

> The product of two numbers with the same sign is positive. The product of two numbers having opposite signs is negative.

Adapting to Individual Needs

Extra Help

If students have trouble remembering the rules for multiplying with negative numbers, illustrate 3 × -3.6 on a number line, making 3 jumps of 3.6 units each to the left from zero, landing at -10.8. Then point out that multiplying -3 × -3.6 would mean the same jumps, but in the opposite direction, which would be to the right, landing at 10.8.

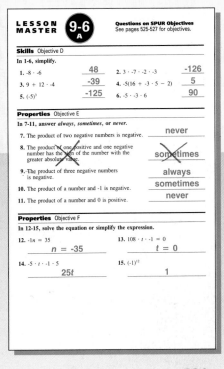

LESSON MASTER 9-6 A

Questions on SPUR Objectives
See pages 525-527 for objectives.

Skills Objective D

In 1-6, simplify.

1. -8 · -6 _____ 48
2. 3 · -7 · -2 · -3 _____ -126
3. 9 + 12 · -4 _____ -39
4. -5(16 + -3 · 5 − 2) _____ 5
5. (-5)³ _____ -125
6. -5 · -3 · 6 _____ 90

Properties Objective E

In 7-11, answer *always, sometimes,* or *never.*

7. The product of two negative numbers is negative. _____ never
8. The product of one positive and one negative number has the sign of the number with the greater absolute value. _____ sometimes
9. The product of three negative numbers is negative. _____ always
10. The product of a number and -1 is negative. _____ sometimes
11. The product of a number and 0 is positive. _____ never

Properties Objective F

In 12-15, solve the equation or simplify the expression.

12. -1n = 35 _____ n = -35
13. 108 · t · -1 = 0 _____ t = 0
14. -5 · t · -1 · 5 _____ 25t
15. (-1)¹² _____ 1

Multiplication by 0

What about multiplying numbers by zero, a number which is neither positive nor negative? Notice what happens when the number 5 is multiplied by positive numbers that get smaller and smaller.

$$5 \cdot 2 = 10$$
$$5 \cdot 0.43 = 2.15$$
$$5 \cdot 0.07 = 0.35$$
$$5 \cdot 0.000148 = 0.00074$$

The smaller the positive number, the closer the product is to zero. You know what happens when 5 is multiplied by 0. The product is 0.

$$5 \cdot 0 = 0$$

There is a similar pattern if you begin with a negative number. Multiply -7 by the same numbers as above.

$$-7 \cdot 2 = -14$$
$$-7 \cdot 0.43 = -3.01$$
$$-7 \cdot 0.07 = -0.49$$
$$-7 \cdot 0.000148 = -0.001036$$

The products are all negative, but again they get closer and closer to zero. You can check the following multiplication on your calculator.

$$-7 \cdot 0 = 0$$

These examples are instances of an important property of zero.

Multiplication Property of Zero
For any number x, $x \cdot 0 = 0$.

QUESTIONS

Covering the Reading

1. What is the negative rate in this sentence? A person loses 3.8 pounds per month for 3 months. -3.8 lb/month

In 2–4, a situation is given.
a. What multiplication problem involving negative numbers is suggested by the situation?
b. What is the product and what does it mean?

2. A person loses 3 pounds a month for 2 months. How much will the person lose in all?

2a) $\frac{-3 \text{ pounds}}{\text{month}} \cdot 2$ months
b) -6 pounds; a total loss of 6 lb

3. A person loses 5 pounds a month. How will the person's weight 4 months from now compare with the weight now?

3a) $\frac{-5 \text{ pounds}}{\text{month}} \cdot 4$ months
b) -20 pounds; 20 lb lighter

4. A person has been losing 6 pounds a month. How does the person's weight 2 months ago compare with the weight now?

4a) $\frac{-6 \text{ pounds}}{\text{month}} \cdot -2$ months
b) 12 pounds; 12 lb heavier

502

Adapting to Individual Needs

English Language Development
Students who are just learning English might confuse a phrase like *5 months ago* with the phrase *5 months from now*. Have each of these students work with a partner who is proficient in English. Ask the English-proficient student do the following: First, say a phrase like *5 months ago* or *5 months from now* and ask the other student to identify that month; then give a date in the past or future (within 12 months of the present) and have the first student identify the correct phrase, *n months ago*, or *n months from now*.

Controlling weight.
Bicycle riding is an excellent way to exercise and maintain good health.

In 5 and 6, fill in the blank with one of these choices.
(a) is always positive (b) is always negative
(c) is sometimes positive, sometimes negative

5. The product of two negative numbers __?__. (a)

6. The product of a positive and a negative number __?__. (b)

In 7–12, simplify.

7. -4 · 8 -32

8. 73 · -45 -3285

9. -6 · -3 18

10. -2 · 5 -10

11. 1.8 · -3.6 -6.48

12. -4.1 · -0.3 1.23

In 13–16, tell whether xy is positive or negative.

13. x is positive and y is positive.
positive

14. x is positive and y is negative.
negative

15. x is negative and y is positive.
negative

16. x is negative and y is negative.
positive

17. State the Multiplication Property of 0. For any number x, $x \cdot 0 = 0$.

In 18–21, simplify.

18. 8 · -1 -8

19. -1 · -1 · -1 -1

20. 0 · -6 0

21. -3 · -2 · -1 · 0 0

22. Multiplication of a number by __?__ results in the opposite of the number. -1

23. Tell whether -5 · -4 · -3 · -2 · -1 · 1 · 2 · 3 · 4 · 5 is positive, negative, or zero. Then explain why. Negative; since there are an odd number of negative factors, and no zero, the product must be negative.

24. Calculate.
   a. 3 + -3 0
   b. 3 − (-3) 6
   c. 3 · -3 -9

Applying the Mathematics

25. Find the value of -5x for the given value of x.
   a. 2 -10   b. 1 -5   c. 0 0   d. -1 5   e. -2 10

26. Evaluate 3 + -7a + 2b when a = -4 and b = -10. 11

27. In Europe, the number zero is sometimes called the *annihilator*. What is the reason for this name? Sample: Multiplication by zero annihilates the number, making it zero.

In 28–31, simplify.

28. -5 · -5 · -5 · -5 625

29. $(-4)^3$ -64

30. $-\frac{1}{2} \cdot \frac{7}{3}$ $-\frac{7}{6}$

31. $\left(\frac{2}{5}\right)\left(-\frac{5}{7}\right)\left(-\frac{7}{2}\right)$ 1

32. *Multiple choice.* Morry is now $2500 in debt. He has been incurring additional debt at the rate of $200/week. Which expression tells how he was doing 5 weeks ago?
   (a) 2500 − 5 · 200   (b) -2500 + -200 · -5
   (c) -2500 + 5 · -200   (d) 2500 + -5 · -200 (b)

Practice

For more questions on SPUR Objectives, use **Lesson Master 9-6A** (shown on page 501) or **Lesson Master 9-6B** (shown on pages 502–503).

Assessment

Written Communication Have students write a general rule explaining how to determine if the product of several positive and negative numbers is positive or negative. [Students should try several examples with various combinations of positive and negative numbers. Students will conclude that examples with an odd number of negative numbers yield a negative solution and examples with an even number of negative numbers yield a positive solution. The number of positive numbers in the example does not effect the sign of the solution.]

Extension

You might want to write the following questions on the board and ask students to explain their answers.
1. Is $(-x)(-y)$ a positive number, a negative number, or zero? **Any of those depending on the value of the variables.**
2. If $x \neq 0$, is x^2 always positive? Is x^3 always positive? **yes; no**
3. Give the sign of x^n when x is a negative number and n is a positive integer. **Positive when n is even; negative when n is odd.**

38a)

Review

In 33 and 34, write the rate using fraction notation and abbreviations.   *(Lesson 9-5)*

33. kilometers per second **km/sec**

34. grams per cubic centimeter $\frac{g}{cm^3}$

35. A computer prints at the rate of 12 pages/min. How long will it take to print 2400 documents with 3 pages per document?   *(Lesson 9-5)* **600 minutes, or 10 hours**

36. Joann runs 5.85 miles each hour. At the same rate, how far will she run in 3 hours?   *(Lesson 9-5)* **17.55 miles**

37. If your probability of spelling a hard word correctly is 90%, what is the probability that you will correctly spell all 10 hard words on a test?   *(Lesson 9-4)* $(.90)^{10} \approx .349 \approx 35\%$

38. **a.** Picture a rectangular park that is $\frac{2}{3}$ mile by $\frac{3}{5}$ mile.
    b. Calculate the area of the park.   *(Lesson 9-3)* $\frac{6}{15}$, or $\frac{2}{5}$ sq mi

39. If the edges of a cube are tripled in length, what happens to its volume?   *(Lessons 9-2, 3-9)* **It is multiplied by 27.**

40. What are supplementary angles?   *(Lesson 7-6)* **two angles whose measures add to 180°**

41. Give an example of a positive number and a negative number whose sum is positive.   *(Lessons 5-1, 5-3)* **Sample: $3 + {}^-2 = 1$**

42. Graph all solutions to $x > 5$ on a number line.   *(Lesson 4-10)*

Exploration

43. Find an example of a rate in a newspaper or magazine. **Answers will vary.**

Setting Up Lesson 9-7

Materials Students will need graph paper for this lesson. **Teaching Aid 86** is graph paper and **Teaching Aid 87** is four-quadrant graph paper.

LESSON
9-7

Size Changes— Expansions

An expanded view. *This projection of a computer image onto the large screen is an example of an expansion. The two images are similar.*

Size Changes of Lengths

The segment below has length L.

$$L \rule{2cm}{0.4pt}$$

Place 2 such segments end to end to form a new segment. The total length of the new segment is $L + L$ or $2L$. Multiplying by 2 lengthens the segment. The new segment has twice the length of the original.

$$L + L \bullet\!\!\rule{2cm}{0.4pt}\!\!\bullet$$
$$2L \rule{2.5cm}{0.4pt}$$

Place another copy. The length is $2L + L$ or $3L$. Multiplying by 3 expands the segment even more.

$$3L \rule{3cm}{0.4pt}$$

Activity 1

Consider the segment above with length L. Draw a segment with length $2.5L$.

These examples show that multiplying by a number can be pictured as changing the size of things. The number is called the **size change factor.** Above, the size change factors are 2, 3, and 2.5.

Lesson 9-7 Overview

Broad Goals This is the first of three lessons covering the arithmetic, algebraic, and geometric applications of multiplication that are included under the broad heading of size changes.

Perspective For many people, the coordinate representations in this and the next two lessons provide an effective way of thinking of multiplication. The idea of changing size is also fundamental in applications of geometry, with or without coordinates. The size change transformation is as basic to the study of similarity as reflections, rotations, and translations are to congruence. Moreover, computers enlarge and contract figures by utilizing multiplications with coordinates analogous to those given here. Graphs of functions can be similarly modified.

Lesson 9-7

Objectives

L Apply the Size Change Model for Multiplication in real situations.
N Perform expansions on a coordinate graph.

Resources

From the *Teacher's Resource File*
■ Lesson Master 9-7A or 9-7B
■ Answer Master 9-7
■ Teaching Aids
   86 Graph Paper
   87 Four-Quadrant Graph Paper
   99 Warm-up
  104 Activities 2 and 3
  105 Size Changes
■ Activity Kit, Activity 24
■ Technology Sourcebook, Computer Demonstration 9 Computer Master 19

Additional Resources
■ Visuals for Teaching Aids 86, 87, 99, 104, 105
■ Inch rulers or Geometry Templates (Question 14)
■ Geometry Workshop

Teaching Lesson 9-7

Warm-up

Graph each point on a coordinate graph. Students can use **Teaching Aid 87.**

1. $A = (3, 4)$ **2.** $B = (0, 6)$
3. $C = (-2, 1)$ **4.** $D = (3, -4)$
5. $E = (5, 0)$ **6.** $F = (-6, -6)$
7. $G = (0, 0)$ **8.** $H = (-1, 3)$

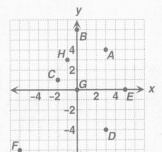

Notes on Reading

Reading Mathematics With three activities, this lesson requires active reading. If the lesson is read in class, then allow time for each of the activities. You can use **Teaching Aid 104** when discussing Activities 2 and 3. **Teaching Aid 105** can be used with any size changes.

Students should record the results of the **Activities** for use with **Questions 2, 6,** and **7** on page 508.

The Size Change Model for Multiplication covers a huge number and variety of multiplication situations, including the familiar "times as many," "part of," and "percent of." The general idea is that there is a quantity multiplied by a scalar (a quantity with no unit). The answer is then a second quantity with the same unit:

$$\begin{pmatrix} \text{size} \\ \text{change} \\ \text{factor} \end{pmatrix} \times \begin{pmatrix} \text{first} \\ \text{quantity} \end{pmatrix} = \begin{pmatrix} \text{second} \\ \text{quantity} \end{pmatrix}$$

When the size change factor is greater than 1, the second quantity is greater than the original, and we say that an *expansion* has taken place. When the absolute value of the size change factor is a number less than 1, a *contraction* has taken place. (Lesson 9-8 deals with contractions.)

When discussing size changes, have students concentrate on the coordinate multiplications, especially the generalizations after **Example 2** and Activity 3. Students can show their work for Activities 2 and 3 on **Teaching Aid 104**. You might ask students to predict what size change factor would yield a smaller rather than a larger image.

Size Changes with Other Quantities

The idea of size change can involve quantities other than lengths.

Example 1

John weighed 6.3 pounds at birth. By the time he was a year old, his weight had tripled. How much did he weigh at age 1?

Solution

"Tripled" means a *size change of magnitude 3,* so multiply John's birth weight by 3. He weighed 3 · 6.3, or 18.9 pounds.

Example 2

Maureen works in a store for $7 an hour. She gets time and a half for overtime. What does she make per hour when she works overtime?

Solution

"Time and a half" means to multiply by $1\frac{1}{2}$ or 1.5. Working overtime, she makes 1.5 · $7.00, or $10.50 per hour.

In each of the above examples, there is a beginning quantity and a size change factor. They are multiplied together to obtain a final quantity. This is the idea behind the Size Change Model for Multiplication.

> **Size Change Model for Multiplication**
> Let *k* be a nonzero number without a unit. Then *ka* is the result of applying a **size change of magnitude *k*** to the quantity *a*.

Picturing Size Changes

A size change can be nicely pictured using coordinates. We begin with a quadrilateral. Then we multiply both coordinates of all its vertices by 2. The image has sides 2 times as long as the preimage. Also, the image sides are parallel to the corresponding preimage sides. The image quadrilateral has the same shape as the preimage.

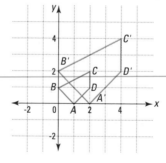

Preimage point	Image point
A = (1, 0)	A' = (2, 0)
B = (0, 1)	B' = (0, 2)
C = (2, 2)	C' = (4, 4)
D = (2, 1)	D' = (4, 2)

Optional Activities

Activity 1 You can use *Activity Kit,* Activity 24, before covering the lesson or you might also choose to use the activity as an alternative to Activity 2 on page 507. In this activity, students observe that multiplying the coordinates of the points of a figure by a number greater than 1 results in an expansion of the figure.

Activity 2 You might want to use the following as an alternative to Activity 1 on page 505. Have students draw a segment of any length on their paper. Call the length *h.* Then instruct them to draw segments of length 2*h,* 3*h,* 4*h,* 1.5*h,* and 2.5*h.* Point out that the coefficients of *h* are size change factors.

Activity 3 Technology Connection You may wish to use *Technology Sourcebook, Computer Demonstration 9,* to show students how to expand shapes using the *Geometry Workshop.* Then, you could assign *Technology Sourcebook, Computer Master 19.* Students use the Size option to create and expand a shape.

This transformation is called a *size change of magnitude 2*. The image of any point (x, y) is (2x, 2y). Because the image figure is bigger, this size change is also called an **expansion** of magnitude 2. The number 2 is the size change factor.

Activity 2

Draw quadrilateral *ABCD* as shown on page 506 on graph paper. Multiply the coordinates of its vertices by 3. Call the image points *A**, *B**, *C**, and *D**. Draw *A*B*C*D**.

❶ The transformation in Activity 2 is a size change of magnitude 3. In general, under a size change of magnitude 3, the image of (x, y) is (3x, 3y).

Two figures that have the same shape are called **similar figures.** Under a size change, the preimage and the image are always similar. In Activity 2, you should find that *A*B*C*D** is bigger than *A'B'C'D'*. But it is still similar to *ABCD*.

Activity 3

On a new graph, multiply the coordinates of *ABCD* by 2.25. Draw the preimage and image. How do they compare?

In Activity 3, you have performed a size change of magnitude 2.25. Under this transformation, the image of (x, y) is (2.25x, 2.25y). Activities 2 and 3 are instances of a two-dimensional size change.

Size Change Model for Multiplication (two-dimensional version)
Under a size change of magnitude *k*, the image of (x, y) is (kx, ky).

---

❷ **Size Changes with Magnitude 1**

If the magnitude of a size change is 1, then the image of (x, y) is (1 · x, 1 · y), or (x, y) itself. That is, each point is its own image. It keeps its identity. That is how you can remember the name of the *Multiplicative Identity Property of One*.

Multiplicative Identity Property of One
For any number *x*, 1 · x = x.

---

❶ Ask students to explain the difference between similar and congruent figures. Several students can draw examples of similar figures and congruent figures. Point out to students that if figures are congruent, then they are also similar.

❷ When the size change factor equals 1, no change takes place. In this case, the transformation is called the *identity transformation*. (It is the same transformation as a rotation of 0°.) For this reason, we include the familiar Multiplication Identity Property of One here.

Adapting to Individual Needs

Extra Help
The following might help students better understand the use of expansions in everyday life. Mention that a photographer uses an enlarger when making prints from negatives. Ask what magnitude of expansion would be needed to make an 8 x 12 picture from a 2 × 3 negative [magnitude 4]. Then tell students to consider a blueprint, or any scale drawing of a building. If the front of a building is 18 inches on the drawing and the building is 30 times the size of the blueprint, how long is the front of the building? [540 inches, or 45 feet]

Additional Examples

1. From 1967 to 1993, the cost of housing was multiplied by about 4.4. If a house cost $20,000 in 1967, what is an estimate for its cost in 1993? **$88,000**

2. After practicing typing for two months last summer, Kyle increased his speed to $2\frac{1}{2}$ times his original speed. If his original typing speed was 18 words a minute, how many words per minute can he type now?
45 words per minute

3. Draw a kite with vertices (3, 0), (0, 2), (–2, 0), and (0, –2) as the preimage. On the same axes, draw the images of this kite under size changes of magnitudes 2, 3, and 4. Students can use **Teaching Aid 87.**

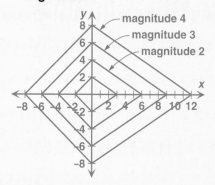

508

Now you see it, now you don't. *Some people take up magic as a hobby and earn money performing at parties.*

6)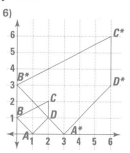

7)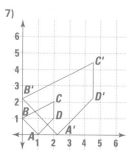

9)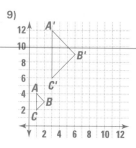

508

QUESTIONS

Covering the Reading

1. Suppose this segment has length x. **(Segment has length 4.5 cm.)**

   Figures appear smaller than actual size in Teacher's Edition.
   a. Copy this segment and then draw a segment of length $2x$. **9 cm**
   b. Draw a segment of length $3x$. **13.5 cm**
   c. Draw a segment of length $3.5x$. **15.75 cm**
   Check student drawings.

2. Show the results of Activity 1. **Length L is 1.2 cm or 0.5 in; 2.5L should be length 3 cm or 1.25 in.**

3. Draw a line segment that is 1.5 times as long as the segment at the right.
   Segment at right is 2.5 cm. Student segment should be 3.75 cm.

4. David saved $25.50. After doing three magic shows, his savings had tripled.
   a. What size change factor is meant by the word *tripled*? **3**
   b. How much money does he have now? **$76.50**

5. Megan earns $2.50 an hour for baby-sitting. After 10 P.M., she gets time and a half.
   a. What does she make per hour after 10 P.M.? **$3.75**
   b. What will Megan earn for baby-sitting from 7 P.M. to 11 P.M.? **$11.25**

6. Show the results of Activity 2. **Image: $A^* = (3, 0)$, $B^* = (0, 3)$, $C^* = (6, 6)$, $D^* = (6, 3)$. See graph at the left.**

7. Show the results of Activity 3. **Image: $A' = (2.25, 0)$, $B' = (0, 2.25)$, $C' = (4.5, 4.5)$, $D' = (4.5, 2.25)$. See graph at the left.**

8. Under a size change, a figure and its image have the same shape. They are called _?_ figures. **similar**

9. A triangle has vertices (1, 4), (2, 3), and (1, 2). Graph the triangle and its image under a size change with magnitude 3. **(Image has vertices (3, 12), (6, 9), and (3, 6).)**

10. Under a size change with magnitude k, the image of (x, y) is _?_. **(kx, ky)**

11. a. Graph the quadrilateral with vertices (1.5, 4), (4, 0), (2, 1), and (1, 2). **See margin.**
    b. Find the image of this quadrilateral under an expansion of magnitude 2. **Image: (3, 8), (8, 0), (4, 2), and (2, 4)**
    c. How do lengths of the sides of the image compare with lengths of the sides of the original quadrilateral? **They are twice as long.**
    d. How do the measures of the angles in the preimage and image compare? **The measures are equal.**

12. State the Multiplicative Identity Property of One. **For any number x, $1 \cdot x = x$.**

Adapting to Individual Needs

English Language Development
Help students relate phrases like *size change of magnitude 2* and *size change of magnitude 3* to common terms like *double* and *triple*. Alternate phrases would be *2 times as great* or *3 times as great*. Be sure students do not incorrectly use *2 times greater* or *3 times greater* in these situations. If they do, point out that *2 times greater* really means the original size *plus* 2 times the size, resulting in a size that is 3 times the original.

13. A microscope lens magnifies 150 times. Some human hair is about 0.1 mm thick.
    a. How thick would the hair appear under this microscope? **15 mm**
    b. What is the size change factor in this situation? **150**

14. The bookcase pictured is $\frac{1}{40}$ of the actual size. This means that the actual bookcase is 40 times as wide, 40 times as high, and 40 times as deep. Will the actual bookcase fit a space 5 feet wide? **No, the actual bookcase is 85 inches wide.**

15. An object is 4 cm long. A picture of the object is 12 cm long. The image of the object is __?__ times actual size. **3**

16. Each word suggests an expansion. What is the magnitude of the expansion?
    a. doubled **2**
    b. quintupled **5**
    c. octupled **8**
    d. quadrupled **4**

Review

In 17–20, perform the indicated operations.   *(Lessons 9-6, 9-3, 5-5)*

17. $-1 \cdot -8 + -11 \cdot -8$ **96**

18. $-\frac{1}{2} \cdot -\frac{2}{3}$ **$\frac{1}{3}$**

19. $\left(\frac{1}{2} + -\frac{1}{6}\right) \cdot (-30)$ **-10**

20. $6 \cdot -\frac{1}{6} + 5 \cdot 0 \cdot -\frac{1}{5}$ **-1**

In 21–26, let $x = 10$ and $y = -1$. Give the value of each expression.
(Lessons 9-6, 4-4)

21. xy **-10**

22. $-x \cdot -y$ **-10**

23. x^y **.1**

24. y^x **1**

25. $x^2 + y^2$ **101**

26. $x^3 + y^3$ **999**

27. About 51% of the babies born in the United States are boys. Suppose a family has two children. Assume the births of babies are independent events. How much more likely is a family to have two boys than two girls?   *(Lesson 9-4)* **2%**

Lesson 9-7 *Size Changes—Expansions* **509**

Notes on Questions

Students can use either **Teaching Aid 86** or **Teaching Aid 87** to show the answers to the questions involving graphs.

Question 14 This question requires students to measure the length of the drawing, and then multiply by 40. Since the final answer needs to be in feet, the measure must be taken in inches and converted to feet (or the five feet converted to inches). Students can use the **Geometry Template** for measuring.

Additional Answers

11 a, b

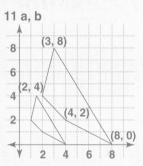

▶ **LESSON MASTER 9-7B** *page 2*

8. Give the image of (p, q) under a size change of magnitude 75. **$(75p, 75q)$**

9. Draw a segment with length $1.5 \cdot AB$.

10. Graph the triangle with vertices (-2, 1), (-1, 4), and (2, 0), and its image under an expansion of magnitude 3.

11. Graph the quadrilateral with vertices (-3, 1), (-2, 4), (3, -1), and (0, -2), and its image under an expansion of magnitude 2.5.

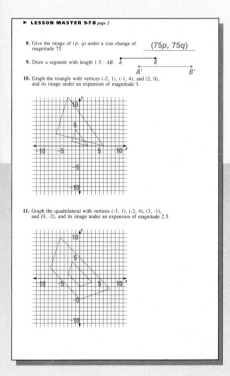

Question 28 Because the distribution is reasonably balanced, the mean and the median are relatively close together.

Question 32 The distance Marlene drives is given in kilometers because Canada uses the metric system. You might point out that if you drive through Canada, you will buy gasoline in liters, not in gallons, and that fuel efficiency is measured in $\frac{kilometers}{liter}$, not $\frac{miles}{gallon}$.

Geography Connection Canada occupies the northern two fifths of North America and covers 3,849,675 square miles (9,970,610 square km). Canada stretches about 2,860 miles (4,600 km) from north to south and nearly 3,340 miles (5,380 km) from east to west. Interested students might find the dimensions of other countries and locate them on a world map.

Question 33 Students need to look in an encyclopedia, science book, or similar reference book.

Follow-up for Lesson 9-7

Practice

For more questions on SPUR Objectives, use **Lesson Master 9-7A** (shown on page 507) or **Lesson Master 9-7B** (shown on pages 508–509).

Assessment

Written Communication Have students graph a quadrilateral with vertices (3, 2), (0, –4), (–2, –1), and (1, 5). Then have each student choose two size changes and graph both images. [Check students' drawings. Be sure images accurately represent size changes they have chosen.]

Extension

Have students use a rectangle to explore the relationship between the size change factor and the changes in perimeter and area. [Perimeters are multiplied by the size change factor itself; area, by the square of the size change factor.]

Project Update Project 2, *Copies of All Sizes*, on page 521, relates to the content of this lesson.

---

28. Here are the films that have generated the highest video rental incomes (as of January, 1993) of all those released in the given year. (Source: *Variety*, January, 1993)

Year Released	Movie Title	Total Video Rentals (in millions of dollars)
1980	The Empire Strikes Back	141.7
1981	Raiders of the Lost Ark	115.6
1982	E.T., the Extra-Terrestrial	228.6
1983	Return of the Jedi	169.2
1984	Ghostbusters	132.7
1985	Back to the Future	105.5
1986	Top Gun	79.4
1987	Three Men and a Baby	81.4
1988	Rainman	86.8
1989	Batman	150.5
1990	Home Alone	140.1
1991	Terminator 2	112.5
1992	Home Alone 2	102.0

A shot from Ghostbusters. Shown here is a scene with the loveable marshmallow man.

a. Give the mean of the total rental amounts. ≈126.6 million dollars
b. Give the median of the total rental amounts. *(Lessons 8-1, 4-6)* 115.6 million dollars

29. Solve $x - 64.2 = -18.9$. *(Lesson 7-3)* 45.3

30. A horse race was $1\frac{1}{8}$ miles long. For the first third of a mile, Lover's Kiss led the race. For the next $\frac{3}{4}$ mile, Kisser's Hug was in the lead. For the rest of the race, Hugger's Love was in front. For how long a distance did Hugger's Love lead the race? *(Lessons 7-1, 5-5)* $\frac{1}{24}$ mile

31. Give an example of a negative number whose absolute value is between 0 and 1. *(Lesson 5-3)* Any number between –1 and 0 is correct.

32. Marlene needs to drive 500 km to visit her grandfather in Canada. Can she do this in a day without speeding? Explain why or why not. *(Lessons 9-5, 3-5)* Yes, she can. Sample: A km is shorter than a mile, so she can drive at a rate of 50 km/hr for 10 hours.

Exploration

33. What is the magnitude of a size change you might find in an electron microscope? Answers will vary. Sample: 20,000

Setting Up Lesson 9-8

Use **Question 31** to review absolute value.

Poly-contractions. *The colorful bird in the contractions is a macaw, the largest member of the parrot family. Macaws may be found from Mexico to Bolivia. Many of the 315 parrot species are endangered because habitats have been destroyed by humans.*

What Are Contractions?

In Lesson 9-7, all of the size change factors were numbers larger than 1. So the products are larger than the original values. In this lesson, we multiply by numbers between 0 and 1. This results in products with smaller values. For instance, if 8 is multiplied by 0.35, the product is 2.8. The number 2.8 is smaller than 8.

This can be pictured. Consider the segments below.

A ——————— 8 cm ——————— B

C —— 2.8 cm —— D

AB = 8 cm. CD = 0.35 · 8 cm = 2.8 cm. CD is shorter.

Think of $\overline{AB}$ as having been reduced in size to 2.8 cm by a shrinking, or a *contraction*. A **contraction** is a size change with a magnitude whose absolute value is between 0 and 1. In the situation above, the *magnitude of the contraction* is 0.35.

Lesson 9-8 *Size Changes—Contractions* **511**

Lesson **9-8**

Objectives
L Apply the Size Change Model for Multiplication in real situations.
N Perform contractions on a coordinate graph.

Resources
From the *Teacher's Resource File*
■ Lesson Master 9-8A or 9-8B
■ Answer Master 9-8
■ Teaching Aids
  86 Graph Paper
  87 Four-Quadrant Graph Paper
  99 Warm-up
  105 Size Changes
■ Assessment Sourcebook: Quiz for Lessons 9-5 through 9-8
■ Technology Sourcebook, Computer Master 20

Additional Resources
■ Visuals for Teaching Aids 86, 87, 99, 105
■ Geometry Workshop
■ Rulers or Geometry Templates

Teaching 9-8
Lesson

Warm-up
Write each percent as a decimal.
1. 24% .24   2. 70% .7
3. 3% .03   4. 3.2% .032
5. 2.02% .0202 6. 12.5% .125
7. 1.63% .0163 8. 80.25% .8025
9. Write the decimals in Questions 1–8 in order from least to greatest. .0163, .0202, .03, .032, .125, .24, .7, .8025

Lesson 9-8 Overview

Broad Goals In this, the second of three lessons on size changes, size changes with magnitudes between 0 and 1 are considered.

Perspective There is continuity with size changes. If the magnitude of a size change is greater than 1, then images are larger than preimages. If the magnitude of a size change is 1, then images and preimages are identical and therefore they are the

same size. If the magnitude of a size change is between 0 and 1, then the image is smaller; hence we call this size change a *contraction*.

If all coordinates are multiplied by 0, then the image of every point is (0, 0). This is sometimes considered a transformation but sometimes not (some authors require transformations to be one-to-one functions); the result is an *annihilation* of the figure.

Although all the size changes in these lessons are centered at the origin, this need not be the case. Under a size change of magnitude k centered at the point (a, b), the image of (x, y) is (k(x − a) + a, k(y − b) + b).

This lesson has content that is similar to that of the previous lesson, and the questions include types of applications seen earlier in the book—such as percents of and fractions of. The purpose here is to think of these as multiplication.

We suggest that you have students do this lesson on their own. Then ask for a brief summary of the reading, and spend the rest of the class discussion on troublesome questions.

❶ **Teaching Aid 105** can be used to illustrate the idea of a contraction on the coordinate plane.

You may wish to point out that if a figure F is the image of a figure G under a contraction, then G is the image of F under an expansion. It provides another application of reciprocals. For instance, in the contraction pictured on page 512, *PENTA* is the image of *P'E'N'T'A'* under an expansion, and the magnitudes of the expansion and contraction, 2 and $\frac{1}{2}$, are reciprocals. The sides of *P'E'N'T'A'* are one half the lengths of sides of *PENTA*, so sides of *PENTA* have twice the lengths of sides of *P'E'N'T'A'*. If you were only given the figures and did not know which figure was the preimage and which the image, you could pick either one as the preimage and the other as the image.

There are no examples of size changes here with magnitudes between –1 and 0. They too are contractions. Examples are found in the next lesson.

Picturing Contractions

Below a two-dimensional contraction is pictured. The preimage is the large pentagon *PENTA*. We have multiplied the coordinates of all its vertices by $\frac{1}{2}$. Since $\frac{1}{2}$ is between 0 and 1, the resulting image $P'E'N'T'A'$ is smaller than the original. Again the preimage and image are similar figures. In this case, sides of the image have $\frac{1}{2}$ the length of sides of the preimage. Corresponding angles on the preimage and image have the same measure.

❶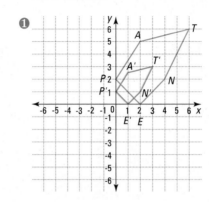

Preimage point	Image point
$P = (0, 2)$	$P' = (0, 1)$
$E = (2, 0)$	$E' = (1, 0)$
$N = (4, 2)$	$N' = (2, 1)$
$T = (6, 6)$	$T' = (3, 3)$
$A = (2, 5)$	$A' = (1, 2.5)$

So the image of (x, y) is $\left(\frac{1}{2}x, \frac{1}{2}y\right)$.

Contractions with Other Quantities

Contractions also occur with quantities that are not lengths.

Example 1

Suppose an airline has a plan in which a spouse can travel for $\frac{2}{3}$ the regular price and a child under 12 can travel for $\frac{1}{2}$ the regular price. Under this plan, what will it cost a married couple and their 11-year-old child to fly if the regular price of a ticket is $150?

Solution
It will cost one adult $150.
It will cost the spouse 2/3 of $150. This can be calculated by multiplying fractions: $\frac{2}{3} \cdot \$150 = \frac{\$300}{3} = \$100$.
It will cost the child $\frac{1}{2}$ of $150. That is $\frac{1}{2} \cdot \$150$, or $75.
The total cost will be $150 + $100 + $75, or $325.

In Example 1, the size change factors are $\frac{2}{3}$ and $\frac{1}{2}$. Size change factors for contractions are often written as fractions or percents. You have seen the type of question in Example 2 before. Now you can think of it as an example of size change multiplication.

Optional Activities

Activity 1
Materials: Transparency of any simple figure, white poster board

Before students read the lesson, you might want to use the following activity. Draw a four-quadrant grid on white poster board and mount it at the front of the room. Put a transparency of a simple figure on the overhead and project it onto the poster board. Have a student trace the figure on the poster board using a colored marker. Then move the projector so it is farther away from the poster board. Have another student trace the image using a different color. Let students compare the positions of vertices and sides of the two tracings on the coordinate grid. If there is no distortion due to the angle of projection, the poster board will show figures and their size change images.

Activity 2 Technology Connection You may wish to assign *Technology Sourcebook, Computer Master 20.* Students use the *Geometry Workshop* to create and contract a shape.

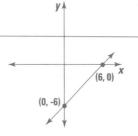

Twins Millie Reiger and Addie Moran were 100 years old on April 8, 1993.

Example 2

In the year 2000, about 1.5% of the people in the United States were 85 or older. If the U.S. population was about 270,000,000, how many people were 85 or older?

Solution

The size change factor is 1.5%, or 0.015.
0.015 · 270,000,000 people = 4,050,000 people.
About 4.05 million people in the United States are over 85.

QUESTIONS

Covering the Reading

1. **a.** By measuring, determine t in the drawing at the right to the nearest millimeter.
   b. Draw a segment with length $0.3t$.
   c. What is the magnitude of the contraction?

   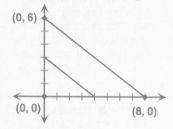

2. What is a *contraction*?

In 3–5, give the image of the point (6, 4) under the contraction with the given magnitude.

3. 0.5   4. 0.75   5. $\frac{1}{4}$

6. **a.** Graph the pentagon with vertices (10, 10), (10, 5), (0, 0), (0, 5), and (5, 10).
   b. Graph its image under a contraction with magnitude 0.8.
   c. How do the lengths of the corresponding sides of the preimage and image compare?
   d. How do the measures of corresponding angles in the preimage and image compare?

7. Repeat Example 1 if the regular cost of a ticket for an adult is $210.

8. About 9.0% of the U.S. population in 1990 were classified as being of Hispanic origin. If the population then was about 248,700,000, about how many people in the U.S. in 1990 were of Hispanic origin?

9. In Question 8, what is the size change factor?

Applying the Mathematics

10. The actual damselfly is similar but half the length of its picture at the left. How long is the actual damselfly?

11. In doing Question 10, some students measure lengths of this insect in centimeters. Others measure in inches. If they measure accurately, will they get equal values for the length of the damselfly?

12. What is the image of (12, 5) under a contraction with magnitude k?

Lesson 9-8   *Size Changes—Contractions*   **513**

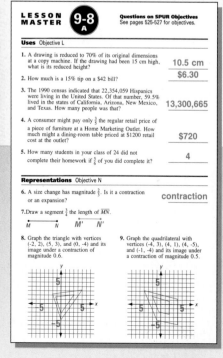
Adapting to Individual Needs

Extra Help

Help students understand why the absolute value of the magnitude of a contraction is between 0 and 1. Point out that a size change with magnitude of 1 produces the original quantity, changes with magnitude greater than 1 would be expansions, and a change of magnitude 0 would eliminate the original quantity. Therefore, multiplying any number by a number between 0 and 1 will give a product greater than 0 but less than the original number.

Question 15 Making reasonable generalizations is one of the skills emphasized throughout this course. By now students should have developed some skill at describing patterns. Drawing a picture may help. A nice aspect of this generalization is the unexpected connection between graphing and reciprocals.

Question 16 History Connection
You might want to share the following information with your students. Memorial Day is a patriotic holiday which honors Americans who died in any war while serving the United States. The people of Waterloo, N.Y., first observed the holiday on May 5, 1866, when they decorated the graves of soldiers killed in the Civil War. Today, people continue to observe the holiday by placing flowers and flags on the graves of military personnel. Community organizations often march in parades and take part in special programs. Interested students can find out how local communities observe Memorial Day, or Decoration Day as it is also known.

Question 31 You may wish to give students the hint to trace the stick figure onto a coordinate graph. Students can use either **Teaching Aid 86** or **Teaching Aid 87**.

15b) If figure *A* is the image of figure *B* under a size change of magnitude *k*, then figure *B* is the image of figure *A* under a size change of magnitude $\frac{1}{k}$.

19b) Being poor and being white are not independent events. A white person has a slightly smaller chance (about 17% less) of being poor.

22)

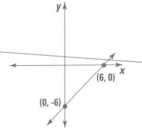

514

13. *Multiple choice.* A car was priced at $7000. The salesperson offers a discount of $350. What size change factor, applied to the original price, gives the discount?
   (a) 0.02   (b) 0.05   (c) 0.20   (d) 0.245   (b)

14. *Multiple choice.* A car was priced at $7000. The salesperson offers a discount of $350. What size change factor, applied to the original price, gives the offered price?
   (a) 0.05   (b) 0.20   (c) 0.80   (d) 0.95   (d)

15. A size change of magnitude $\frac{1}{2}$ was applied to a pentagon in this lesson. Suppose the preimage and image were switched.
   a. A size change of what magnitude would now be pictured? 2
   b. Generalize the idea of this question.

Review

16. Jay asks for $5 an hour to mow a lawn. On holidays, he asks for time and a half. How much will he earn for a three-hour job on Memorial Day? *(Lesson 9-7)* $22.50

17. If the length of a 12.5 cm segment is quintupled, what is its new length? *(Lesson 9-7)* 62.5 cm

18. Give the value of $-4(x - 1)^2$ when x has the indicated value. *(Lessons 9-6, 5-3, 4-5)*
   a. 2 -4   **b.** 1 0   **c.** 0 -4   **d.** -1 -16   **e.** -2 -36

19. According to the Bureau of the Census, in 1990 about 13.5% of people in the United States were classified as "poor." About 80.3% of the population were classified as "White." *(Lesson 9-4)*
   a. If being poor is independent of being white, what percent of the population would you expect to be classified as "poor and white"? ≈ 10.8%
   b. Actually, about 9.0% of the population were classified as "poor and white." Explain why this number is lower than the answer to part **a.**

20. How many boxes 50 cm long, 30 cm wide, and 20 cm high can be packed into a railroad car 3 m wide, 3 m high, and 15 m long? *(Lesson 9-2)* 4500

21. Negative five is added to the second coordinate of every point on the graph of a figure. What happens to the graph of that figure? *(Lesson 8-5)* The graph is translated five units down.

22. Graph the line $x - y = 6$. *(Lesson 8-4)*

23. List three reasons for using graphs. *(Lesson 8-1)* Sample: Graphs can contain a lot of information in a small space, can show trends visually, and can be used to sway a reader.

514

Adapting to Individual Needs

English Language Development
It is often helpful to point out terms that mean the opposite of each other. Before students read this lesson, remind them of Lesson 9-7 where they worked with expansions. Ask how an expansion compared in size with its preimage. [larger] Show them the word *contraction* in the lesson title on page 511 and remind students that a contraction is smaller than its preimage. Use hand motions as you say, "expand means to get larger" and "contract means to get smaller."

In 24–26, use the figure below. *(Lesson 7-7)*

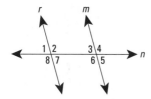

24. Angle 3 and __?__ are corresponding angles. **angle 1**

25. Name the pairs of alternate interior angles. **angles 2 and 6, and angles 3 and 7**

26. If lines r and m are parallel and $m\angle 3 = 70°$, what are the measures of the other angles? **$m\angle 3 = m\angle 5 = m\angle 1 = m\angle 7 = 70°$; $m\angle 4 = m\angle 6 = m\angle 2 = m\angle 8 = 110°$**

27. Joe is saving to buy a present for his father's birthday. He has $5 now and adds $2 a week. *(Lesson 6-5)*
    a. How much will he have in 6 weeks? **$17**
    b. How much will he have in w weeks? **$5 + 2 \cdot w$ dollars**

28. List all the divisors of 48. *(Lesson 6-2)* **1, 2, 3, 4, 6, 8, 12, 16, 24, 48**

29. Helen walked $3\frac{1}{4}$ miles on Monday, $3\frac{1}{8}$ miles on Tuesday, $2\frac{1}{3}$ miles on Wednesday, and x miles on Thursday. She walked a total of $12\frac{2}{3}$ miles. How far did she walk on Thursday? *(Lesson 5-8)* **$3\frac{23}{24}$ miles**

Exploration

30. A map (like a road map or a map of the United States) is a drawing of a contraction of the world. The scale of the map is the size change factor. If $1''$ on the map represents 1 mile on Earth, then the scale is,

$$\frac{1''}{1 \text{ mile}} = \frac{1''}{5280 \text{ feet}} = \frac{1''}{5280 \cdot 12 \text{ in.}} = \frac{1''}{63{,}360''} = \frac{1}{63{,}360}.$$

This is sometimes written as 1:63,360. Find a map and determine its scale. **Answers will vary.**

31. Below is a drawing. Make a drawing that is similar and 2.5 times the size.

Check by connecting the right hand and left foot on the drawing (the preimage) and doing the same on the image. The image connection should be 2.5 times as long as the connection on the preimage.

Lesson 9-8 *Size Changes—Contractions* **515**

Follow-up 9-8 for Lesson

Practice

For more questions on SPUR Objectives, use **Lesson Master 9-8A** (shown on page 513) or **Lesson Master 9-8B** (shown on pages 514–515).

Assessment

Quiz A quiz covering Lessons 9-5 through 9-8 is provided in the *Assessment Sourcebook*.

Oral Communication Ask students to describe situations that suggest contractions. Have students estimate the size change factor for each example. [Some sample answers are prices of sale items, decreases in population, dolls, models of cars, airplanes, or trains, pictures of items in catalogs, and maps. Estimates will vary.]

Extension

Many students enjoy drawing similar figures, either larger or smaller, like the one requested in **Question 31.** This skill is often used in adapting designs for quilts, stenciling, and so on. Students could find such a pattern and perform the size change. Allow them to pick the magnitudes of the size changes they use.

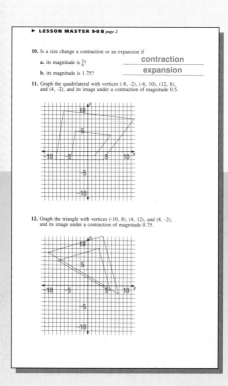

Lesson 9-9

Objectives

N Perform expansions or contractions with negative magnitude on a coordinate graph.

Resources

From the *Teacher's Resource File*
- Lesson Master 9-9A or 9-9B
- Answer Master 9-9
- Teaching Aids
  86 Graph Paper
  87 Four-Quadrant Graph Paper
  99 Warm-up
  105 Size Changes
  106 Extension
- Technology Sourcebook, Computer Master 21

Additional Resources
- Visuals for Teaching Aids 87, 99, 105, 106
- Geometry Workshop

Teaching Lesson 9-9

Warm-up

Name the quadrant or the axis in which each point lies.

1. (–3, 2) II
2. (1, 1) I
3. (0, –3) *y*-axis
4. (–2.4, 1.6) II
5. (–7, –4) III
6. (10, 14) I
7. (5, –8) IV
8. (6, 0) *x*-axis

LESSON 9-9

Picturing Multiplication with Negative Numbers

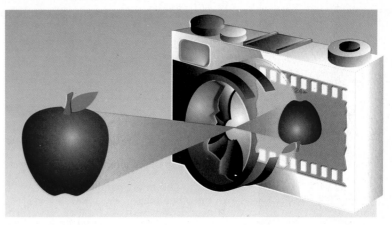

Negatives are negatives. *All cameras use the same basic principle: light is focused by the lenses onto the film to form an image in which up is down, and left is right. This is just like the image formed when multiplying by negative numbers.*

Remember that multiplication can be pictured by expansions or contractions. In Lessons 9-7 and 9-8, the coordinates of preimage points were positive. But coordinates can be any number. So the preimage can be anywhere. Here the preimage is a quadrilateral with a shaded region near one vertex.

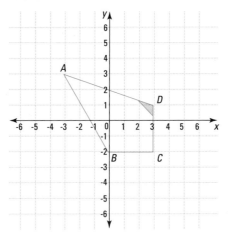

Preimage vertices

$A = (-3, 3)$
$B = (0, -2)$
$C = (3, -2)$
$D = (3, 1)$

An Expansion of Magnitude 2

First we multiply all coordinates by 2. You know what to expect.

1. The image is similar to the preimage.
2. The sides of the image are 2 times as long as the corresponding sides of the preimage.
3. The sides of the image are parallel to corresponding sides of the preimage.

Lesson 9-9 Overview

Broad Goals The second half of the chapter is extended and summarized by examining the picture of multiplication given by size changes with negative magnitudes.

Perspective This lesson opens with a detailed review of material from Lesson 9-7. The new content, size changes of negative magnitude, and a summary of characteristics of a size change of magnitude *k* follows. Because of the logical, gradual progression

of picturing transformations on the coordinate graph, this lesson is not difficult. It serves to convince many students that multiplication by negative numbers is a useful idea.

The lesson provides an opportunity to apply absolute value, because size changes of magnitudes *k* and –*k* have much in common. In both cases, the length is multiplied by the absolute value of the magnitude *k*.

For instance, a size change of magnitude 7 and one of magnitude –7 will both multiply lengths by 7.

The notion that multiplication by a negative number reverses directions is a geometric way of stating that multiplication by a negative number changes the sign of a number, the characterization that was given in Lesson 9-6.

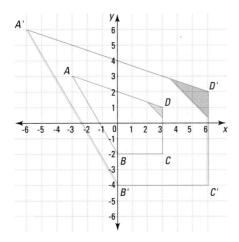

Preimage vertices

$A = (-3, 3)$
$B = (0, -2)$
$C = (3, -2)$
$D = (3, 1)$

Image vertices

$A' = (-6, 6)$
$B' = (0, -4)$
$C' = (6, -4)$
$D' = (6, 2)$

Notice also:

4. The line containing a preimage point and its image also contains (0, 0).

5. Each image point is 2 times as far from (0, 0) as its preimage.

6. The preimage and the image quadrilateral have the same tilt.

An Expansion of Magnitude -2

Now we find the image of the same quadrilateral under an expansion with the negative magnitude, -2. This is done by multiplying all coordinates by -2. We call this image $A''B''C''D''$. (Read this "A double prime, B double prime, and so on.")

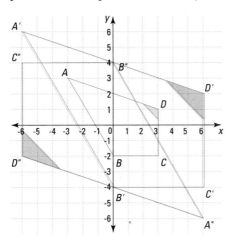

Preimage vertices

$A = (-3, 3)$
$B = (0, -2)$
$C = (3, -2)$
$D = (3, 1)$

Image vertices

$A'' = (6, -6)$
$B'' = (0, 4)$
$C'' = (-6, 4)$
$D'' = (-6, -2)$

Again:

1. The preimage and image are similar.

2. The sides of $A''B''C''D''$ are 2 times as long as the corresponding sides of $ABCD$.

Lesson 9-9 *Picturing Multiplication with Negative Numbers* **517**

Optional Activities

✎ **Activity 1 Writing** After students have completed this lesson, you might want to ask them to do the following writing activity. Ask students to write out how they would explain to a student in an earlier grade why $2 \cdot -3 = -6$ and then why $-2 \cdot -3 = 6$.

Activity 2 Technology Connection You may wish to assign *Technology Sourcebook, Computer Master 21*. Students use the *Geometry Workshop* to create a polygon. The students multiply the coordinates by a negative number and create an image of the polygon. Students compare the preimage to the image.

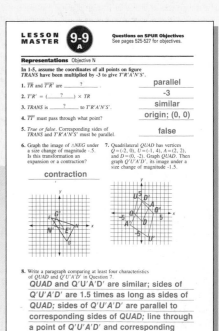

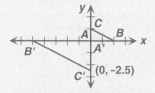
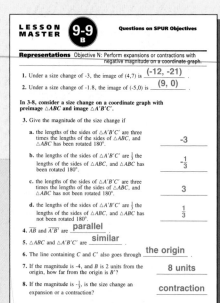

518

---

3. Corresponding preimage and image sides are parallel.
4. The line containing a preimage point and its image contains (0, 0).
5. Each image point is 2 times as far from (0, 0) as its preimage.

But one new thing has happened.

6. The figure has been rotated 180°. It has been turned upside down. What was right is now left. What was up is now down.

> **Multiplication by a negative number reverses directions.**

❶ Multiplying the coordinates of all points on a figure by the number *k* performs the transformation known as a *size change of magnitude k*. The number *k* may be positive or negative. But in all cases:

1. The resulting figure (the image) is similar to its preimage.
2. Lengths of sides of the resulting figure are $|k|$ times lengths of corresponding sides of the preimage.
3. Corresponding sides are parallel.
4. Corresponding preimage and image points lie on a line that goes through the origin.
5. Image points are $|k|$ times as far from the origin as corresponding preimage points.
6. If *k* is negative, the figure is rotated 180°.

The examples have pictured what happens when *k* = 2 and when *k* = -2.

Activity
Draw quadrilateral *ABCD* from the beginning of this lesson. Apply a size change of magnitude $-\frac{1}{2}$ to the quadrilateral. Name the image *A*B*C*D**. Verify the properties numbered 1–6 mentioned above for *ABCD* and *A*B*C*D**.

QUESTIONS

Covering the Reading

1. In a size change of magnitude -2, the image of (4, 5) is (__?__).
   (-8, -10)
2. In a size change of magnitude -5, the image of (-10, 7) is (__?__).
   (50, -35)
3. In any size change, a figure and its image are __?__. similar
4. In a size change of magnitude -3, lengths on the image will be __?__ times the corresponding lengths on the preimage. 3
5. In any size change, a segment and its image are __?__. parallel

518

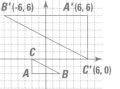

7)

B'(-6, 6)   A'(6, 6)

C

A   B   C'(6, 0)

9a)

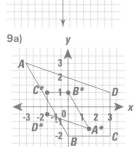

Big blue marble. *This shot of Earth was taken by an astronaut aboard Apollo 16. In the middle of the picture is southern California.*

18)

W

Z   X

Y

6. What is the major difference between a size change of magnitude -3 and one of magnitude 3? **For a size change of magnitude -3, the image is rotated 180°.**

7. Let $A = (-2, -2)$, $B = (2, -2)$, and $C = (-2, 0)$. Graph $\triangle ABC$ and its image under an expansion of magnitude -3.

8. Multiplication by a negative number __?__ directions. **reverses**

9. **a.** Show what you obtained as a result of the Activity of this lesson.
   b. Is the result an expansion, a contraction, or neither? **a contraction**

10. A size change of magnitude -2 is like one of magnitude 2 followed by a rotation of what magnitude? **180°**

Applying the Mathematics

11. Let $P = (3.45, -82)$. Suppose that P' is the image of P under a size change of magnitude -10. *True or false?* $\overleftrightarrow{PP'}$ contains $(0, 0)$. **True**

12. **a.** Are the quadrilaterals $A'B'C'D'$ and $A''B''C''D''$ in this lesson congruent? **Yes**
    b. If so, why? If not, why not? **One is the rotation image of the other.**

13. Recall that the four quadrants of the coordinate plane are numbered from 1 to 4, as shown at the left. Consider a size change with magnitude -2.3. If a preimage is in quadrant 4, in which quadrant is its image? **2**

2	1
3	4

Review

14. Suppose $\frac{4}{5}$ of the students in Mr. Mboya's class are here today, and $\frac{2}{3}$ of them took the bus to school. What fraction of the students in that class took the bus to school today? *(Lesson 9-8)* $\frac{8}{15}$

15. Simplify: $0 \cdot a + 1 \cdot b + -1 \cdot c + -1 \cdot -d$ *(Lesson 9-6)* **b − c + d**

16. Translate each phrase into a numerical expression or equation.
    a. spending $50 a day **-$50/day**
    b. 4 days from now **4 days**
    c. 4 days ago **-4 days**
    d. If you spend $50 a day for 4 days, you will have $200 less than you have now. $\frac{-\$50}{day} \cdot 4 \text{ days} = -\$200$
    e. If you have been spending $50 a day, 4 days ago you had $200 more than you have now. *(Lesson 9-5)* $\frac{-\$50}{day} \cdot -4 \text{ days} = \$200$

17. About 71% of the earth's surface is covered by water. (Some people think we should call our planet Water, not Earth.) If a large meteor were to hit the earth, what are the chances it would hit land on a Sunday? *(Lessons 9-4, 9-3)* **≈4%**

18. Draw part of a tessellation that uses quadrilateral $WXYZ$. *(Lesson 8-8)*

Lesson 9-9 *Picturing Multiplication with Negative Numbers* **519**

Notes on Questions

Students can use either **Teaching Aid 87** or **Teaching Aid 105** to graph their answers.

Question 11 A student may draw a picture to answer this. Ask why it is not necessary to do so. [Some students might observe that the situation is an instance of the sixth characteristic of size changes.]

Question 14 Multicultural Connection Students may think that Mb at the beginning of a name is an error, but it is a common English way of spelling a sound that is common to a number of African and South American languages. Thomas Mboya (1930–1969) was a political leader in Kenya. Mbabane is the capital and largest town in Swaziland, in Southern Africa. The Mbayá are South American Indians who live in Argentina, Paraguay, and Brazil.

(*Notes on Questions continue on page 520.*)

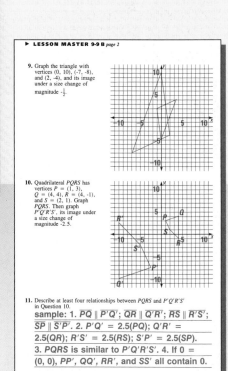

▶ **LESSON MASTER 9-9 B** *page 2*

9. Graph the triangle with vertices (0, 10), (-7, -8), and (2, -4), and its image under a size change of magnitude $-\frac{1}{2}$.

10. Quadrilateral $PQRS$ has vertices $P = (1, 3)$, $Q = (4, 4)$, $R = (4, -1)$, and $S = (2, 1)$. Graph $PQRS$. Then graph $P'Q'R'S'$, its image under a size change of magnitude -2.5.

11. Describe at least four relationships between $PQRS$ and $P'Q'R'S'$ in Question 10.
   sample: 1. $\overline{PQ} \parallel \overline{P'Q'}$; $\overline{QR} \parallel \overline{Q'R'}$; $\overline{RS} \parallel \overline{R'S'}$; $\overline{SP} \parallel \overline{S'P'}$. 2. $P'Q' = 2.5(PQ)$; $Q'R' = 2.5(QR)$; $R'S' = 2.5(RS)$; $S'P' = 2.5(SP)$. 3. $PQRS$ is similar to $P'Q'R'S'$. 4. If $O = (0, 0)$, PP', QQ', RR', and SS' all contain O.

Adapting to Individual Needs

English Language Development
Materials: Grid paper or **Teaching Aid 86**

As you discuss the six characteristics on page 518 review the following terms:

1. *Similar:* From grid paper cut out two similar rectangles that are not the same size. Hold them up and remind students that they have the same shape but not the same size so they are similar.

2. *Corresponding:* Use the rectangles from step 1 and color a short edge of each rectangle with a marker. Hold up the two rectangles with each darkened edge on top. Have a student point to the two darkened edges and then tell the students that these are corresponding sides.

3. *Image* and *Preimage:* Illustrate by using the graphs on pages 516–517. Remind students that *pre* means "before" so the preimage was there first.

519

Notes on Questions

Question 27 Do not expect students to add $3a + 2a$ to get $5a$. This idea is covered in the next chapter.

Question 29b Students should not have to calculate to answer this question, because $\frac{3}{4} = 75\%$.

Follow-up 9-9
for Lesson

Practice
For more questions on SPUR Objectives, use **Lesson Master 9-9A** (shown on page 517) or **Lesson Master 9-9B** (shown on pages 518–519).

Assessment
Written Communication Have students write a summary of Lessons 9-7 through 9-9. Students should be allowed to use their books, but summaries should be in their own words. Ask students to also write about the concepts that they found particularly easy or difficult in these lessons. [The summary should include an explanation of how size change is a model of multiplication. The self evaluation will vary.]

Extension
Give each student a copy of **Teaching Aid 106**. Have them graph the picture of the cat from Grid A onto Grids B, C, and D using the coordinates from Grid A. Ask them how the cat has changed on each grid and why. [Since the squares on Grid B are larger than those on Grid A, the cat is larger. Similarly, the squares on Grid C are smaller, so the cat is smaller. Grid D is a distortion of Grid A, so the figure is distorted.] Students might enjoy drawing the cat or another figure on a distorted grid of their own making.

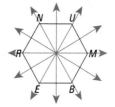

19. Trace hexagon *NUMBER* at the left and then draw all of its lines of symmetry. *(Lesson 8-7)*

20. Trace the figure below. Draw the reflection image of triangle *XYZ* over line *p*. *(Lesson 8-6)*

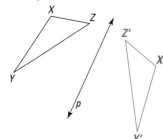

21. List all composite numbers *n* where $15 < n < 25$. *(Lesson 6-2)*
    16, 18, 20, 21, 22, 24

22. Is 41 prime or composite? Explain your answer. *(Lesson 6-2)*
    Prime; 41 is divisible by only 1 and itself.

In 23–25, name the kind of polygon. *(Lesson 5-9)*

23.   24.   25.

hexagon   dodecagon or 12-gon   pentagon

26. Find the value of $-5x + 6$ when $x = -9$. *(Lesson 4-4)* **51**

27. Find the value of $3a + 2a$ when $a = -7$. *(Lesson 4-4)* **-35**

28. Three instances of a pattern are given. Describe the pattern using one variable. *(Lesson 4-2)*

$$-3 \cdot 5 + 4 \cdot 5 = 5$$
$$-3 \cdot 7.8 + 4 \cdot 7.8 = 7.8$$
$$-3 \cdot -1 + 4 \cdot -1 = -1 \qquad -3n + 4n = n$$

29. One thousand two hundred sixty students were asked whether they thought Hardnox High would win its next football game. Seventy-five percent thought it would win.
    a. How many students is this? **945**
    b. Is the answer to part **a** greater than, equal to, or less than $\frac{3}{4}$ of 1260? *(Lesson 2-5)* **equal to**

30. Write 5^{10} as a decimal. *(Lesson 2-2)* **9,765,625**

31. Which is largest: $-\frac{2}{3}$, -0.6, or -0.66? *(Lesson 1-9)* **-0.6**

Exploration

32. Draw a figure on a coordinate grid. Then draw the images, in different colors, of the figure under size changes of magnitudes 3, $\frac{1}{3}$, $-\frac{1}{3}$, and -3. Describe how the four images and the preimage compare.
    Answers will vary.

Adapting to Individual Needs

Challenge
Have students draw a triangle that has vertices in three of the quadrants of a coordinate grid. Then have them perform the following transformations and answer each question.
1. Multiply only the *x*-coordinate of each vertex by –1. Graph the image. How is a triangle affected by multiplying each *x*-coordinate by –1? [The triangle is reflected over the *y*-axis.]

2. Multiply only the *y*-coordinate of each vertex in the preimage by –1. Graph the image. How is a triangle affected by multiplying each *y*-coordinate by –1? [The triangle is reflected over the *x*-axis.]

A project presents an opportunity for you to extend your knowledge of a topic related to the material of this chapter. You should allow more time for a project than you do for typical homework questions.

1 Area of Your Residence

The floor area of an apartment or house is the area enclosed by the outer walls of the residence. Sketch the shape of the place where you live and, through measuring, multiplication, and addition, calculate this area for your residence.

2 Copies of All Sizes

Some copy machines enlarge and/or reduce. Start with an interesting original picture. Make copies of various sizes. Then make copies of copies to obtain still other sizes. Put all the copies together in a display explaining what you have done and giving the magnitudes of the size changes from the original picture.

3 Effects of Different Rates

Suppose you have to type up an essay that is 1000 words long. Then if you can type 25 words per minute, it will take you 40 minutes. Fill in at least fifteen rows of the following table. (One row is already filled in.)

typing speed	time to type
25 $\frac{\text{words}}{\text{min}}$	40 min

Graph the pairs of numbers you find. (For instance, (25, 40) should be on your graph.) Use the graph to describe how an increase in typing speed affects the amount of time it takes to type up the essay.

Possible responses

1. Responses will vary.
2. Responses will vary.
3. Sample responses:

Speed words/minute	Minutes to type 1000 words
10	100
15	67
20	50
25	40
30	33
35	29
40	25
45	22
50	20
55	18
60	17
65	15
70	14
75	13
80	12

Responses continue on page 522.

Chapter 9 Projects

Chapter 9 projects relate to the content of the lessons as follows.

Project	Lesson(s)
1	9-1
2	9-7, 9-8
3	9-5
4	9-4
5	9-8
6	9-3

1 Area of Your Residence Make sure that students understand that in the United States living area is measured in square feet. Students may be interested in knowing that living area in Japan is often measured by the number of *tatami* mats it takes to cover the floor. If a student's home is an irregular shape, have them separate the region into right triangles, rectangles, and squares, find the area of each shape and then add to find the total area. Remind students who live in two-story homes to find the area of each level. Students who live in some apartments will not be able to measure outside walls to find the area of their home. They may be able to obtain a layout of their apartment from the building's owner or manager.

Suggest that students change dimensions measured in feet and inches to a decimal equivalent in feet before computing the area of their home.

2 Copies of All Sizes If students have difficulty selecting a picture to work with, suggest that they use their own school picture, a picture of a famous work of art, or a picture of a sports team's logo.

Many copy machines can reduce a picture from 99% to 64% of its original size. Contractions smaller than 64% will need to be done in more than one step. Similarly, many copy machines can enlarge a picture from 101% to 154% of the original size. Remind students that to find the magnitude of the size change from the original picture, they will have to record the magnitude of each size change and multiply the magnitudes together.

3 Effects of Different Rates Suggest that students select some typing speeds that are less than 25 words per minute. Students may decide to choose the same interval between typing speeds, such

521

as intervals of two or five, while others may choose to vary the intervals between the speeds they choose. Point out to students that in either case, their graph must be labeled to show equal increments.

4 Streaks Alert students that they should record the result of each toss in order, indicating whether it was a head or a tail. To answer parts b, c, and d, students must go to the data, find each head (pair of heads, triple of heads), and count the number of times a head followed. In each case the relative frequency is written as the ratio of the number of times a head follows after a head to the number of heads (pairs of heads, triples of heads).

5 Half-size You One possible way to have students create a paper model is to have each student cut a rectangle out of butcher paper or any other large-sized paper. The length of the rectangle is one half of the height of the student and the width is one half the distance from their right little finger to their left little finger when their hands are hanging at their sides. Students can use this entire rectangle to draw in their features.

6 Multiplying Fractions Versus Multiplying Decimals or Percents Some students may think that it is always easier to use a calculator to multiply decimals and percents than it is to multiply fractions. Have these students explain how they figure out the cost of an item that is on sale for 50% off the original price. Remind students that dividing by two is the same as multiplying by one half.

4 Streaks
Toss a coin at least 250 times, recording heads or tails for every toss. Answer the following questions to help you decide whether or not the results of your tosses are independent.

a. What is the relative frequency of heads for your tosses?

b. After each head, what is the relative frequency that the next toss is heads?

c. After each pair of heads, what is the relative frequency that the third toss is heads?

d. After each three heads in a row, what is the relative frequency that the fourth toss is heads?

e. Judging from what you find in parts **a** through **d,** do you think that tossing heads on one toss affects what happens on the next toss? Explain why or why not.

5 Half-size You
Make a two-dimensional contraction of yourself by measuring the length and width of your legs, toes, arms, hands, fingers, neck, face, nose, mouth, eyes, and so on. Make a paper model of yourself that is half your real size.

6 Multiplying Fractions Versus Multiplying Decimals or Percents
Instead of multiplying 2.5 by 3.75, you could multiply $\frac{5}{2}$ by $\frac{15}{4}$. Instead of taking 20% of some quantity, you could take $\frac{1}{5}$ of that quantity. When is it easier to multiply fractions? When is it easier to multiply with decimals or percents? Write an essay giving examples and your opinions.

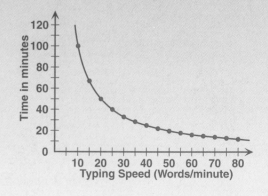

522

Additional responses, page 521

The graph shows that when the typing speed increases from a slow rate to slightly higher rate, the amount of time it takes to type an essay drops quickly. When the typing speed increases from a high rate to a slightly higher rate, the amount of time drops only slightly.

Time in minutes vs. Typing Speed (Words/minute)

SUMMARY

Like addition, multiplication is commutative and associative. There is an identity (the number 1) and every number x but zero has a multiplicative inverse (its reciprocal $\frac{1}{x}$). Multiplying any number by 0 gives a product of 0. Multiplying by -1 changes a number to its opposite.

Given the dimensions, you can multiply to find the area of a rectangle, the area of a right triangle, the number of elements in a rectangular array, and the volume of a rectangular solid. Areas of parts of rectangles and rectangular solids can picture multiplication of fractions: the product of $\frac{a}{b}$ and $\frac{c}{d}$ is $\frac{ac}{bd}$. Multiplication is also used to determine probabilities. If two or more events are independent, the product of their probabilities is the likelihood that they will both occur.

Another important use of multiplication involves rate factors. Examples of rate factors are the quantities 600 miles/hour, $2.50 per bottle, 27.3 students per class, and -3 kg/month. When rate factors are multiplied by other quantities, the units are multiplied like fractions. Rate factors like 5280 feet/mile can be used to convert units and to explain how to multiply with negative numbers.

Size changes can picture multiplication by a positive number or by a negative number. They show direction as well as size. Multiplying by a number greater than 1 can be pictured as an expansion. Multiplying by a number between 0 and 1 can be pictured as a contraction. Multiplying by a negative number rotates the picture 180°. So negative · positive = negative, and negative · negative = positive. In all cases, the figure and its size-change image are similar.

VOCABULARY

You should be able to give a general description and a specific example of each of the following ideas.

Lesson 9-1
Area Model for Multiplication
dimensions
rectangular array
Commutative Property of
    Multiplication
right triangle, legs, hypotenuse
Area Formula for a Right
    Triangle

Lesson 9-2
box, rectangular solid
edge, vertex, face
dimensions, length, width,
    height, depth
volume, base
Associative Property of
    Multiplication

Lesson 9-3
unit fraction
Multiplication of Unit
    Fractions Property
Algebraic Definition of
    Division
multiplicative inverse,
    reciprocal
Property of Reciprocals
Multiplication of Fractions
    Property

Lesson 9-4
independent events
Probability of the event A and B

Lesson 9-5
rate, rate unit, rate factor
Rate Factor Model for
    Multiplication
conversion factor

Lesson 9-6
Multiplication Property of -1
Multiplication Property of
    Zero

Lesson 9-7
size change factor
size change of magnitude k
expansion
similar figures
Size Change Model for
    Multiplication
Multiplicative Identity
    Property of One

Lesson 9-8
contraction

Chapter 9 *Summary and Vocabulary* **523**

4. a.– d. Responses will vary.
   e. Based on students' data, the answer will probably be no, because the relative frequency for heads following one head, two heads, or three heads should remain around .5, indicating that the results of the tosses are independent.
5. Responses will vary.
6. The following is a sample of what students might include in their projects.

It seems easier to multiply fractions when (a) the denominators are small numbers, (b) the fraction is a unit fraction with the denominator a factor of the number being multiplied, or (c) the fraction is a nonterminating decimal. It seems easier to multiply with decimals and percents when (a) the numbers are given as decimals, (b) using a calculator even if it is a fraction calculator, (c) the number

is not an "easy" fraction, or (d) the numbers are very large or small. Examples will vary.

Progress Self-Test

For the development of mathematical competence, feedback and correction, along with the opportunity to practice, are necessary. The Progress Self-Test provides the opportunity for feedback and correction; the Chapter Review provides additional opportunities and practice. We cannot overemphasize the importance of these end-of-chapter materials. It is at this point that the material "gels" for many students, allowing them to solidify skills and understanding. In general, student performance should be markedly improved after these pages.

Assign the Progress Self-Test as a one-night assignment. Worked-out *solutions* for all questions are in the Selected Answers section of the student book. Encourage students to take the Progress Self-Test honestly, grade themselves, and then be prepared to discuss the test in class.

Advise students to pay special attention to those Chapter Review questions (pages 525–527) which correspond to questions missed on the Progress Self-Test.

Additional Answers

18a. $8.50 \frac{\text{dollars}}{\text{hour}} \cdot 37.5 \frac{\text{hours}}{\text{week}} =$

$318.75 \frac{\text{dollars}}{\text{week}}$

b. The person earns $318.75 per week.

19.

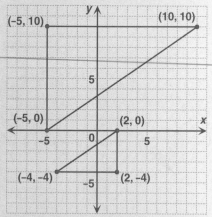

20. Sample: The corresponding angles in the preimage and image are equal. The corresponding sides are not equal.

PROGRESS SELF-TEST

Take this test as you would take a test in class. Then check your work with the solutions in the Selected Answers section in the back of the book.

In 1–5, simplify.

1. $4 \cdot \frac{1}{3} \cdot \frac{5}{4}$ $\frac{5}{3}$

2. $\frac{1}{x} \cdot \frac{7}{16}$ $\frac{7}{16x}$

3. $5 \cdot -9$ -45

4. $-3 \cdot 3 + -2 \cdot -2$ -5

5. $a + 1 \cdot a + b + 0 \cdot b + -21 \cdot c + c$
   $2a + b - 20c$

In 6 and 7, name the general property.

6. $(12 \cdot 43) \cdot 225 = 12 \cdot (43 \cdot 225)$ Associative Prop. of Mult.

7. $m \cdot \frac{1}{m} = 1$ Property of Reciprocals

8. An auditorium has r rows with s seats in each row. Five seats are broken. How many seats are there to sit in? $rs - 5$

9. Give the area of the right triangle pictured here. 58.82 m²

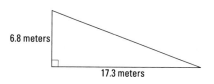

6.8 meters
17.3 meters

10. What multiplication with negative numbers is suggested by the following situation? For four hours, the flood waters receded three centimeters an hour. See below.

11. What is the volume of a rectangular solid with dimensions 3 feet, 4 feet, and 5 feet? 60 ft³

12. Could a jewelry box with a volume of 3375 cm³ fit in a dresser drawer with dimensions 40 cm, 12 cm, and 45 cm? Explain your answer. See below.

13. Give dimensions for two noncongruent rectangles, each with an area of 16. 1 × 16, 3.2 × 5

14. Round the reciprocal of 38 to the nearest thousandth. ≈0.026

15. What is the image of (8, 2) under an expansion of magnitude 4? (32, 8)

16. Alta earns $5.80 per hour. She gets time and a half for overtime. How much does she make per hour of overtime? $8.70

17. a. What multiplication of fractions is pictured below? $\frac{2}{3} \cdot \frac{1}{4}$

b. What is the product? $\frac{1}{6}$

18. A person makes $8.50 an hour and works 37.5 hours a week. a. Multiply the two rates in this situation. b. Explain the meaning of the result. See margin.

In 19 and 20, a triangle has vertices (2, 0), (-4, -4), and (2, -4).

19. Graph this triangle and its image under an expansion of magnitude -2.5.

20. Name one thing that is the same about the preimage and image and one thing that is different. 19, 20) See margin.

21. $\frac{3}{25}$ of Clemente High students are in the band. There are 850 students at Clemente High. How many students are in the band? 102

22. Larry earned a scholarship which will pay for $\frac{2}{3}$ of his $8400 college tuition. How much is his scholarship? $5600

23. You have a one in ten chance of guessing a correct digit. What are your chances of guessing three correct digits in a row? $\frac{1}{1000}$

24. You feel you have a 2 in 3 chance of getting an A on a history test and a 2 in 5 chance of getting an A on your upcoming math test. If these are independent events, what are your chances of getting an A on both tests? $\frac{4}{15}$

25. *Multiple choice.* Which number is the reciprocal of 1.25?
   (a) 0.125 (b) -1.25 (c) 0.8 (d) 0.75 (c)

26. The highest mountain in Africa, Mount Kilimanjaro, is 19,340 ft high. How many miles is this? ≈ 3.66 mi

10) $4 \text{ hr} \cdot -3\frac{\text{cm}}{\text{hr}} = -12 \text{ cm}$ 12) It would probably fit since the volume of the dresser is 21,600 cm³, much larger than the volume of the jewelry box.

CHAPTER REVIEW

Questions on SPUR Objectives

SPUR stands for **S**kills, **P**roperties, **U**ses, and **R**epresentations. The Chapter Review questions are grouped according to the SPUR Objectives for this chapter.

SKILLS DEAL WITH THE PROCEDURES USED TO GET ANSWERS.

Objective A: *Find the area of a rectangle or a right triangle, given its dimensions.* *(Lesson 9-1)*

1. What is the area of a rectangle with length 7 cm and width 3.5 cm? **24.5 cm²**

2. What is the area of a rectangle with length 5 and width w? **5w sq units**

3. What is the area of a right triangle with legs 6 and 9? **27 sq units**

4. What is the area of the right triangle pictured here? **2400 sq units**

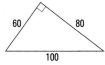

60   80
100

Objective B: *Find the volume of a rectangular solid, given its dimensions.* *(Lesson 9-2)*

5. What is the volume of the rectangular solid pictured below? **1875 cubic units**

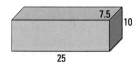

7.5
10
25

6. What is the volume of a rectangular solid with dimensions x, y, and z? **xyz cubic units**

Objective C: *Multiply fractions.* *(Lesson 9-3)*
In 7–15, perform the multiplication and write the answer in lowest terms.

7. $3 \cdot \frac{1}{6}$ $\frac{1}{2}$

8. $\frac{4}{5} \cdot \frac{4}{3}$ $\frac{16}{15}$

9. $100 \cdot \frac{3}{8}$ $\frac{75}{2}$

10. $\frac{2}{5} \cdot \frac{2}{5} \cdot \frac{2}{5}$ $\frac{8}{125}$

11. $10\frac{1}{8} \cdot 10$ $\frac{405}{4}$

12. $2\frac{1}{2} \cdot 3\frac{2}{3}$ $\frac{55}{6}$

13. $\frac{6}{7} \cdot \frac{7}{8} \cdot \frac{8}{9}$ $\frac{2}{3}$

14. $\frac{3}{10} \cdot 3.25$ $\frac{39}{40}$, or 0.975

15. $1\frac{1}{3} \cdot 1\frac{1}{5}$ $\frac{8}{5}$

Objective D: *Multiply positive and negative numbers.* *(Lesson 9-6)*
In 16–21, simplify.

16. $-8 \cdot -2$ **16**

17. $3 + -10 \cdot 9$ **-87**

18. $5 \cdot -5 \cdot 4 \cdot -4$ **400**

19. $6x - 5$ when $x = -1$ **-11**

20. $(-8)^2$ **64**

21. $5 \cdot (-4)^3$ **-320**

22. If $x = -3$ and $y = -16$, what is the value of $5x - 2y$? **17**

23) For any x, $x \cdot 0 = 0$.
24) Associative Property of Multiplication
25) Commutative Property of Multiplication

PROPERTIES DEAL WITH THE PRINCIPLES BEHIND THE MATHEMATICS.

Objective E: *Identify properties of multiplication.* *(Lessons 9-1, 9-2, 9-3, 9-6)*

23. State the Multiplication Property of Zero.

24. What property justifies that $(78 \cdot 4) \cdot 25 = 78 \cdot (4 \cdot 25)$? **See above right.**

25. What property justifies that $a \cdot b = b \cdot a$?

26. A number not equal to zero multiplied by its reciprocal equals what value? **1**

27. *True or false.* The product of any two negative numbers is a negative number. **False**

28. What is the reciprocal of $\frac{2}{3}$? $\frac{3}{2}$

Chapter 9 *Chapter Review* **525**

Chapter 9 Review

Resources
From the *Teacher's Resource File*
■ Answer Master for Chapter 9 Review
■ Assessment Sourcebook: Chapter 9 Test, Forms A-D Chapter 9, Cumulative Form Comprehensive Test, Chapter 1-9

Additional Resources
■ TestWorks

The main objectives for the chapter are organized in the Chapter Review under the four types of understanding this book promotes – Skills, Properties, Uses, and Representations.

Whereas end-of chapter material may be considered optional in some texts, in *UCSMP Transition Mathematics* we have selected these objectives and questions with the expectation that they will be covered. Students should be able to answer these questions with about 85% accuracy after studying the chapter.

You may assign these questions over a single night to help students prepare for a test the next day, or you may assign the questions over a two-day period. If you work the questions over two days, then we recommend assigning the *evens* for homework the first night so that students get feedback in class the next day, then assigning the *odds* the night before the test, because answers are provided to the odd-numbered questions.

It is effective to ask students which questions they still do not understand and use the day or days as a total class discussion of the material which the class finds most difficult.

Assessment

Evaluation The *Assessment Sourcebook* provides six forms of the Chapter 9 Test. Forms A and B present parallel versions in a short-answer format. Forms C and D offer performance assessment. The fifth test is Chapter 9 Test, Cumulative Form. About 50% of this test covers Chapter 9, 25% of it covers Chapter 8, and 25% of it covers earlier chapters. In addition to these tests, Comprehensive Test Chapter 1-9 gives roughly equal attention to all chapters covered thus far.

For information on grading, see *General Teaching Suggestions: Grading* in the *Professional Sourcebook* which begins on page T20 of the Teacher's Edition.

Objective F: *Use properties of multiplication to simplify expressions and check calculations.*
(Lessons 9-1, 9-2, 9-3, 9-6)

In 29–33, simplify without using a calculator.

29. $ab - ba$ 0
30. $\frac{1}{2} \cdot 2 \cdot \frac{1}{3} \cdot 3$ 1
31. $\frac{7}{8} \cdot \frac{8}{7}$ 1
32. $-1 \cdot -1 \cdot -1 \cdot -1 \cdot 7$ 7
33. $\frac{1}{2} \cdot \frac{1}{5} \cdot 5 \cdot x$ $\frac{x}{2}$

34) $6.54 \cdot 2.48 = 16.2192$

34. Use the Commutative Property of Multiplication to check whether $2.48 \cdot 6.54 = 16.2192$.

35. a. Find the product of $\frac{1}{8}$ and $\frac{1}{5}$. $\frac{1}{40}$
    b. Check by converting the fractions to decimals. $0.125 \times 0.2 = 0.025$

36. a. What is the reciprocal of $\frac{9}{10}$? $\frac{10}{9}$
    b. Check your answer by converting the fractions to decimals and finding their product. $.9 \times 1.\overline{1} = 1$

USES DEAL WITH APPLICATIONS OF MATHEMATICS IN REAL SITUATIONS.

Objective G: *Find areas of right triangles and rectangles, and the number of elements in rectangular arrays in applied situations.*
(Lesson 9-1)

37. The flag of the United States has as many stars as states. How many states did the U.S. have when the flag below was in use?   48

38. The smaller rectangle below is the space for a kitchen in a small restaurant. The larger rectangle is the space for the restaurant. The shaded region is space for seating. What is the area available for seating?   900 ft²

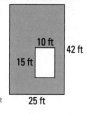

39. An 8″ by 10.5″ rectangular sheet of paper is cut in half along its diagonal. What is the area of each half?   42 in²

Objective H: *Find the volume of a rectangular solid in real contexts.*   *(Lesson 9-2)*

40. A stick of margarine is approximately 11.5 cm long, 3 cm wide, and 3 cm high. What is the volume of the stick?   103.5 cm³

41. A computer was packed in a box 51 cm by 48 cm by 35 cm. What is the volume of this box?   85,680 cm³

42. A plastic container has a base with area 72 square centimeters and height 14 cm. Can it hold a liter of soup? Explain why or why not.   Yes, 1008 cm³ > 1000 cm³ = 1 L

43. A typical yardstick is 3 feet long (of course), $1\frac{1}{8}″$ wide, and $\frac{1}{8}″$ thick. To the nearest cubic inch, what is its volume?   5 in³

Objective I: *Calculate probabilities of independent events.*   *(Lesson 9-4)*

44. In 1993, Mark Price missed only about 5% of the free throws he attempted. Suppose his free throws are independent events. What is the probability that he would miss two free throws in a row at the end of a ball game?   .0025, or $\frac{1}{400}$, or .25%

45. At the 1992 U.S. National Indoor Rifle and Pistol Championships, Air Rifle champion Debra Sinclair hit the bull's eye 595 out of 600 times. Assume her shots are independent events. If you took a picture of two random shots in a row, what is the probability that both shots hit the bull's eye?   ≈ 98.34%

46. Suppose that, for a particular plant, the probability that a seed will not sprout is $\frac{1}{20}$. What is the probability that two seeds will both not sprout?   .0025, or $\frac{1}{400}$

47. Five of seven days are weekdays. Resttown gets hit by a snowstorm about once every 5 years. What are the chances of Resttown being hit by a snowstorm next year on a weekday? $\frac{1}{7}$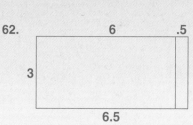

526

Additional Answers, page 527

48b. Sample: If John eats an average of 2 cookies each day, how many cookies does John eat in a year?

49b. Sample: How far can you drive in 5 hours at an average speed of 25 miles per hour?

61.

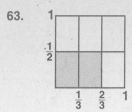

There are 20 dots in this 5 × 4 array.

62.

6   .5

3

6.5

63.

1

$\frac{1}{2}$

$\frac{1}{3}$ $\frac{2}{3}$ 1

Area = $\frac{2}{6}$ or $\frac{1}{3}$ km²

Objective J: *Apply the Rate Factor Model for Multiplication.* *(Lesson 9-5)*

In 48 and 49, a multiplication problem is given. **a.** Do the multiplication. **b.** Make up a question that leads to this multiplication.

48. $2 \frac{\text{cookies}}{\text{day}} \cdot 365 \frac{\text{days}}{\text{year}}$ a) 730 cookies per year
    b) See margin.

49. $5 \text{ hours} \cdot 25 \frac{\text{miles}}{\text{hour}}$ a) 125 miles
    b) See margin.

50. A person makes $10.50 an hour and works 37.5 hours a week. How much does the person earn per year? **$20,475**

51. Fire laws say there is a maximum of 60 people allowed per small conference room. There are 6 small conference rooms. Altogether, how many people can meet in them? **360 people**

52. If Lois has been losing weight at the rate of 2.3 kg per month, how did her weight 4 months ago compare with her weight now? **Four months ago, Lois was 9.2 kg heavier.**

Objective K: *Use conversion factors to convert from one unit to another.* *(Lesson 9-5)*

53. Name the two conversion factors from the conversion equation 1 foot = 30.48 cm.
$$\frac{1 \text{ ft}}{30.48 \text{ cm}}, \quad \frac{30.48 \text{ cm}}{1 \text{ ft}}$$

54. 500 cm equals about how many ft? **≈ 16.4'**

55. 150 hours equals how many days? **$6\frac{1}{4}$ days**

56. Name the two conversion factors from the conversion equation 1 mile = 1760 yards.
$$\frac{1 \text{ mi}}{1760 \text{ yd}}, \quad \frac{1760 \text{ yd}}{1 \text{ mi}}$$

Objective L: *Apply the Size Change Model for Multiplication in real situations.* *(Lessons 9-7, 9-8)*

57. Mrs. Kennedy expects to save $\frac{1}{8}$ of her weekly grocery bill of $150 a week by using coupons from a newspaper. How much money does she expect to save? **$18.75**

58. On the average, the cost of medical care in the U.S. quintupled from 1970 to 1991. If an item cost x dollars in 1970, what did it cost in 1991? **5x dollars**

59. If you make $4.75 an hour, what will you make per hour of overtime, if you are paid time and a half? **$7.13**

60. Mr. Jones tithes. That is, he gives one-tenth of what he makes to charity. If he makes $500 a *week*, how much does he give every *year* to charity? **$2600**

REPRESENTATIONS DEAL WITH PICTURES, GRAPHS, OR OBJECTS THAT ILLUSTRATE CONCEPTS.

Objective M: *Picture multiplication using arrays or area.* *(Lessons 9-1, 9-3)*

61. Show $5 \cdot 4 = 20$ using a rectangular array.

62. Show that $6.5 \cdot 3$ is larger than $6 \cdot 3$ using rectangles with accurate length and width. (Use centimeters as the unit.)

63. Picture a rectangular park $\frac{1}{2}$ km by $\frac{2}{3}$ km and find its area.

64. Explain why $75 \cdot 23 = 23 \cdot 75$ using ideas of area.
61–64) See margin.

Objective N: *Perform expansions or contractions on a coordinate graph.*
(Lessons 9-7, 9-8, 9-9)

65. Graph the triangle with vertices (0, 5), (6, 2), and (4, 4) and its image under an expansion of magnitude 2.5. **See margin.**

66. What is the image of (x, y) under an expansion of magnitude 1000? **(1000x, 1000y)**

67. Is a size change of magnitude $\frac{3}{7}$ an expansion or a contraction? **contraction**

68. Graph the segment with endpoints (4, 9), and (2, 3). Graph its image under a size change of magnitude $\frac{1}{3}$. **See margin.**

69. What is the image of (40, -80) under a size change of magnitude -0.2? **(-8, 16)**

70. Under a size change of magnitude -5, how will a quadrilateral and its image be the same and how will they be different?

71. Let $A = (-4, 5)$, $B = (2, 0)$, and $C = (0, -3)$. Graph $\triangle ABC$ and its image under a size change of magnitude -2. **70, 71) See margin.**

72. A size change of magnitude -12 is like a size change of magnitude 12 followed by a rotation of what magnitude? **180°**

68.
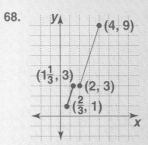

70. Sample: The corresponding angles in the quadrilateral will be equal in both the preimage and image, and the shape is the same. The image will be 5 times bigger and rotated 180°.

71.
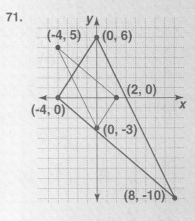

64.
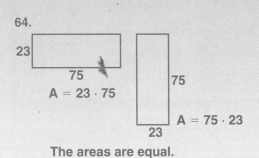
A = 23 · 75
A = 75 · 23
The areas are equal.

65.
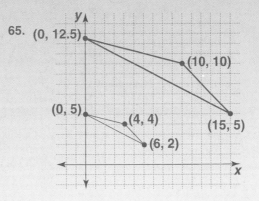

Setting Up Lesson 10-1

We recommend that you assign Lesson 10-1, both reading and some questions, for homework the evening of the test. It gives students work to do after they have completed the test and keeps the class moving.

Chapter **10** Planner

Adapting to Individual Needs

The student text is written for the vast majority of students. The chart at the right suggests two pacing plans to accommodate the needs of your students. Students in the Full Course should complete the entire text by the end of the year. Students in the Minimal Course will spend more time when there are quizzes and more time on the Chapter Review. Therefore, these students may not complete all of the chapters in the text.

Options are also presented to meet the needs of a variety of teaching and learning styles. For each lesson, the Teacher's Edition provides sections entitled: *Video* which describes video segments and related questions that can be used for motivation or extension; *Optional Activities* which suggests activities that employ materials, physical models, technology, and cooperative learning; and *Adapting to Individual Needs* which regularly includes **Challenge** problems, **English Language Development** suggestions, and suggestions for providing **Extra Help.** The Teacher's Edition also frequently includes an **Error Alert,** an **Extension,** and an **Assessment** alternative. The options available in Chapter 10 are summarized in the chart below.

Chapter 10 Pacing Chart

Day	Full Course	Minimal Course
1	10-1	10-1
2	10-2	10-2
3	10-3	10-3
4	10-4	10-4
5	Quiz*; 10-5	Quiz*; begin 10-5.
6	10-6	Finish 10-5.
7	10-7	10-6
8	Quiz*; 10-8	10-7
9	10-9	Quiz*; begin 10-8.
10	10-10	Finish 10-8.
11	Self-Test	10-9
12	Review	10-10
13	Test*	Self-Test
14		Review
15		Review
16		Test*

*in the Teacher's Resource File

In the Teacher's Edition...

Lesson	Optional Activities	Extra Help	Challenge	English Language Development	Error Alert	Extension	Cooperative Learning	Ongoing Assessment
10-1	●		●		●	●		Written
10-2	●	●	●	●		●	●	Group
10-3	●	●	●	●		●	●	Written/Oral
10-4	●	●	●	●	●	●	●	Group
10-5	●	●	●	●	●	●	●	Oral
10-6	●	●	●	●	●	●	●	Oral
10-7	●	●	●	●	●	●	●	Group
10-8	●	●			●	●	●	Written
10-9	●	●	●		●	●		Written
10-10	●	●	●	●		●		Written

In the Additional Resources...

Lesson	Lesson Masters, A and B	Teaching Aids*	Activity Kit*	Answer Masters	Technology Sourcebook	Assessment Sourcebook	Visual Aids**	Technology Tools	Video Segments
					In the Teacher's Resource File				
10-1	10-1	107		10-1			107, AM		
10-2	10-2	107, 110	25	10-2			107, 110, AM		
10-3	10-3	107		10-3			107, AM		
10-4	10-4	108, 110	26	10-4		Quiz	108, 110, AM		
10-5	10-5	108, 111		10-5	Demo 10, Comp 22		108, 111, AM	Spreadsheet	
10-6	10-6	108		10-6			108, AM		
10-7	10-7	86, 109, 112		10-7		Quiz	86, 109, 112, AM		
10-8	10-8	86, 109	27	10-8			86, 109, AM		Segment 10
10-9	10-9	86, 109, 113, 114		10-9	Comp 23		86, 109, 113, 114, AM	Geometry	
10-10	10-10	77, 86, 109, 115, 116		10-10	Comp 24		77, 86, 109, 115, 116, AM	Geometry	
End of chapter				Review		Tests			

*Teaching Aids, except Warm-ups, are pictured on pages 528C and 528D. The activities in the Activity Kit are pictured on page 528C.

**Visual Aids provide transparencies for all Teaching Aids and all Answer Masters.

Also available is the Study Skills Handbook which includes study-skill tips related to reading, note-taking, and comprehension.

Integrating Strands and Applications

	10-1	10-2	10-3	10-4	10-5	10-6	10-7	10-8	10-9	10-10
Mathematical Connections										
Algebra	●	●	●	●	●	●	●	●	●	●
Geometry	●	●	●	●	●	●	●	●	●	●
Measurement	●		●	●		●	●	●	●	●
Probability				●	●					
Patterns and Functions		●	●	●	●					
Interdisciplinary and Other Connections										
Science	●			●		●				
Social Studies		●	●	●	●	●		●	●	●
Multicultural			●		●		●			
Technology	●				●	●		●	●	●
Consumer	●		●	●		●	●			

Take it to the NET

On the Internet, visit **www.phschool.com** for UCSMP teacher support, student self-tests, activities, and more.

Chapter 10 Objectives (Organized into the SPUR categories—Skills, Properties, Uses, and Representations)	Lessons	Progress Self-Test Questions	Chapter Review Questions	In the Assessment Sourcebook		
				Chapter Test, Forms A and B	Chapter Test, Forms	
					C	D
Skills						
A: Solve and check equations of the form $ax = b$.	10-2, 10-5,	10, 13, 14	1–8	5, 11, 12	1	
B: Solve and check equations of the form $ax + b = c$.	10-4, 10-5	15, 16	9–16	13, 14	2	
C: Apply properties of multiplication to simplify expressions.	10-1, 10-6	1–5	17–24	1	4	
D: Find the area of a triangle.	10-9	10, 18, 19	25–28	7–9, 21		
E: Find the area of a trapezoid.	10-10	20	29–32	10, 21	6	
Properties						
F: Recognize and use the Distributive Property, the Repeated Addition Property of Multiplication, and the Multiplication Property of Equality.	10-1, 10-2, 10-6	6, 7	33–36	2–4, 17	3	
Uses						
G: Find unknowns in real situations involving multiplication.	10-3, 10-4, 10-5	17, 21	37–41	15, 19	2	✓
H: Find the surface area of a rectangular solid in real contexts.	10-7	12	42–44	20	5	✓
I: Pick appropriate units in measurement situations.	10-8	8	45–48	6	5	✓
Representations						
J: Represent equations of the form $ax = b$ and $ax + b = c$ with a balance scale diagram.	10-2, 10-4	22	49, 50	16		
K: Represent the Distributive Property by areas of rectangles.	10-6	11	51, 52	18	3	

Assessment Sourcebook

Quiz for Lessons 10-1 through 10-4   Chapter 10 Test, Forms A–D
Quiz for Lessons 10-5 through 10-7   Chapter 10 Test, Cumulative Form

TestWorks
Multiple forms of chapter tests and quizzes; Challenge items

Activity Kit

ACTIVITY 25
SOLVING $ax = b$
Use with **Lesson 10-2.**

Materials: Envelopes, paper clips
Group Size: Partners

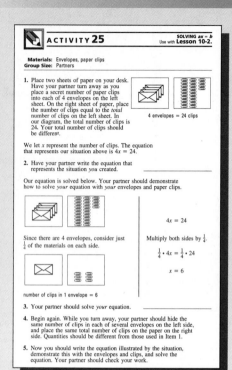

1. Place two sheets of paper on your desk. Have your partner turn away as you place a secret number of paper clips into each of 4 envelopes on the left sheet. On the right sheet of paper, place the number of clips equal to the *total* number of clips on the left sheet. In our diagram, the total number of clips is 24. Your total number of clips should be different.

4 envelopes = 24 clips

We let x represent the number of clips. The equation that represents our situation above is $4x = 24$.

2. Have your partner write the equation that represents the situation *you* created.

Our equation is solved below. Your partner should demonstrate how to solve *your* equation with *your* envelopes and paper clips.

$$4x = 24$$

Since there are 4 envelopes, consider just $\frac{1}{4}$ of the materials on each side.

Multiply both sides by $\frac{1}{4}$.

$$\frac{1}{4} \cdot 4x = \frac{1}{4} \cdot 24$$

$$x = 6$$

number of clips in 1 envelope = 6

3. Your partner should solve *your* equation.

4. Begin again. While you turn away, your partner should hide the same number of clips in each of several envelopes on the left side, and place the same total number of clips on the paper on the right side. Quantities should be different from those used in Item 1.

5. Now you should write the equation illustrated by the situation, demonstrate this with the envelopes and clips, and solve the equation. Your partner should check your work.

ACTIVITY 26
SOLVING $ax + b = c$
Use with **Lesson 10-4.**

Materials: Envelopes, paper clips
Group Size: Partners

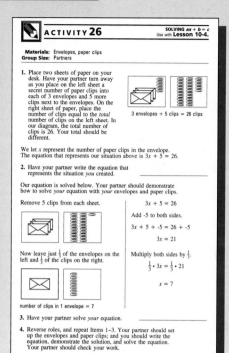

1. Place two sheets of paper on your desk. Have your partner turn away as you place on the left sheet a secret number of paper clips into each of 3 envelopes and 5 more clips next to the envelopes. On the right sheet of paper, place the *total* number of clips equal to the *total* number of clips on the left sheet. In our diagram, the total number of clips is 26. Your total should be different.

3 envelopes + 5 clips = 26 clips

We let x represent the number of paper clips in the envelope. The equation that represents our situation above is $3x + 5 = 26$.

2. Have your partner write the equation that represents the situation *you* created.

Our equation is solved below. Your partner should demonstrate how to solve *your* equation with *your* envelopes and paper clips.

Remove 5 clips from each sheet.

$$3x + 5 = 26$$

Add -5 to both sides.

$$3x + 5 + -5 = 26 + -5$$

$$3x = 21$$

Now leave just $\frac{1}{3}$ of the envelopes on the left and $\frac{1}{3}$ of the clips on the right.

Multiply both sides by $\frac{1}{3}$.

$$\frac{1}{3} \cdot 3x = \frac{1}{3} \cdot 21$$

$$x = 7$$

number of clips in 1 envelope = 7

3. Have your partner solve *your* equation.

4. Reverse roles, and repeat Items 1–3. Your partner should set up the envelopes and paper clips; and you should write the equation, demonstrate the solution, and solve the equation. Your partner should check your work.

ACTIVITY 27
DIMENSIONS AND UNITS
Use with **Lesson 10-8.**

Materials: Centimeter grid paper, centimeter ruler, string, scissors, 8″ × 11″ cardboard, straight pins
Group Size: Partners or small groups

1. Draw a large triangle on centimeter grid paper. Then work alone to estimate the area of the triangle in square centimeters by counting. Then find the average of your group's estimates.

my estimate	average of estimates

2. Now place the grid paper on the cardboard. Run a length of string around the perimeter of the triangle, using pins to hold the string in place. Then cut off the extra string. Remove the string and measure it to give the perimeter of the triangle in centimeters.

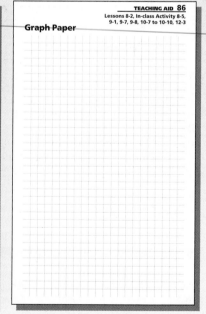

3. Predict whether every figure with the same *perimeter* as that of the triangle also has the same *area* as that of the triangle. Write *yes* or *no*.

4. Use the piece of string to outline another closed figure on the grid paper. It need not be a polygon. Use the full length of the string so the new figure has the same perimeter as that of the triangle. Pin the string in place. Give an estimate of the area of your new figure. Then find the average of your group's estimates.

my estimate	average of estimates

5. Was your prediction in Item 3 correct?

6. Each person should cut another piece of string the same length as the string from Item 2. See who can find a figure with the greatest area. You each get two tries. What was the winning area? Describe the figure.

7. Repeat Item 6, but find the figure with the least area. If you run into difficulty with this challenge, give an explanation. Otherwise, give the winning area, and describe the figure.

Teaching Aids

TEACHING AID 36
Lesson 3-8

Centimeter Grid

TEACHING AID 77
Lessons 7-8, 10-10

Quadrilaterals

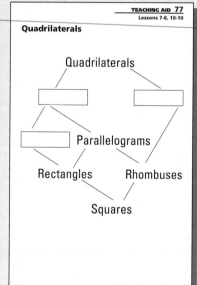

Quadrilaterals

Parallelograms

Rectangles   Rhombuses

Squares

TEACHING AID 86
Lessons 8-2, In-class Activity 8-5, 9-1, 9-7, 9-8, 10-7 to 10-10, 12-3

Graph Paper

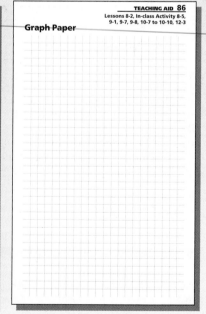

Warm-up
Lesson 10-1

Find the total cost of the groceries excluding tax.

2 gallons of milk at $1.89 per gallon

4 loaves of bread at $1.19 a loaf

3 pounds of apples at $.59 a pound

5 rolls of paper towels at $.69 a roll

Warm-up
Lesson 10-2

Every multiplication fact $a \cdot b = c$ has two related division facts: $b = \frac{c}{a}$ and $a = \frac{c}{b}$. Write the corresponding division facts for each multiplication fact.

1. $9 \cdot 7 = 63$
2. $3.1 \cdot 6 = 18.6$
3. $\frac{1}{2} \cdot 80 = 40$
4. $\frac{2}{3} \cdot \frac{3}{2} = 1$

Warm-up
Lesson 10-3

For each question, write an equation, solve it, and check your work.

1. This week Dakota earned $12.75 baby-sitting. This is one third the amount she earned last week during her spring vacation. How much did she earn during her vacation?

2. What is the total amount of money Dakota earned in the last two weeks?

Warm-up
Lesson 10-4

Choose the correct solution.

1. $\frac{3}{5}x + 7 = 16$
   a. $x = 15$
   b. $x = 27$

2. $\frac{5}{8}n - 4 = 26$
   a. $n = 36$
   b. $n = 25$

3. $-27 = 3y - 12$
   a. $y = 5$
   b. $y = -5$

4. $0.8m + 2.8 = 402.8$
   a. $m = 500$
   b. $m = 5000$

5. $2.5x = 150$
   a. $x = 60$
   b. $x = 37.50$

6. $4t - .4 = 2.8$
   a. $t = 0.2$
   b. $t = 0.5$

Warm-up
Lesson 10-5

Fill in the blanks.

1. The product of two negative numbers is always a _____ number.

2. The product of one positive and one negative number is always a _____ number.

3. The reciprocal of a negative number is a _____ number.

Warm-up
Lesson 10-6

Last week, Lia worked 6 hours, Maria, 10 hours, and Jason, 9 hours. Each earned $4.40 an hour. What is the total amount they earned? Explain how you found your answer.

Warm-up
Lesson 10-7

Find the area of each figure.

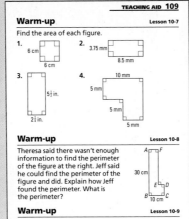

Warm-up
Lesson 10-8

Theresa said there wasn't enough information to find the perimeter of the figure at the right. Jeff said he could find the perimeter of the figure and did. Explain how Jeff found the perimeter. What is the perimeter?

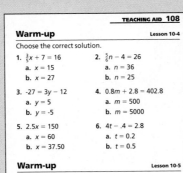

Warm-up
Lesson 10-9

Find each product mentally.

1. $\frac{1}{2} \times 46$
2. $\frac{1}{2} \times 9 \times 6$
3. $\frac{1}{2} \times 7 \times 2$
4. $\frac{1}{2} \times (7 + 21)$
5. 0.5×22
6. $0.5 \times (3.2 + 1.8)$

Warm-up
Lesson 10-10

It costs $100 to sod a lawn that is 30 feet by 15 feet. How much will it cost to sod a lawn that is twice as long and twice as wide?

Balance-Scale Diagrams

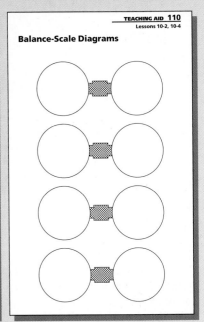

Challenge

How many △s would balance the O on the last set of scales? The other scales are balanced.

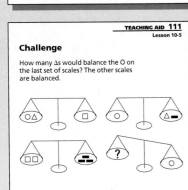

Surface Area of a Box

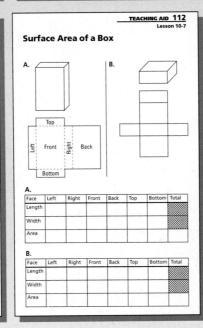

A.

Face	Left	Right	Front	Back	Top	Bottom	Total
Length							
Width							
Area							

B.

Face	Left	Right	Front	Back	Top	Bottom	Total
Length							
Width							
Area							

Area of a Triangle

By drawing an altitude and measuring lengths, find the area of this triangle to the nearest square inch.

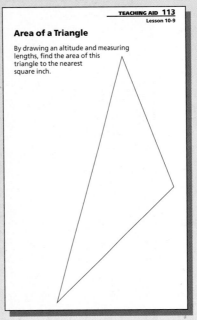

Additional Examples

1. Find the area of this triangle.

2. Find the area of △XYZ.

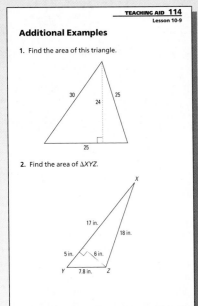

Additional Examples

Find the area of each trapezoid.

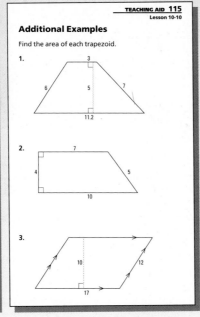

Area of a Trapezoid

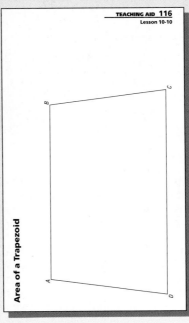

528D

Chapter Opener

CHAPTER 10

Pacing

All lessons in this chapter are designed to be covered in one day. At the end of the chapter, you should plan to spend 1 day to review the Progress Self-Test, 1–2 days for the Chapter Review, and 1 day for a test. You may wish to spend a day on projects, and possibly a day is needed for quizzes. This chapter should therefore take 13–16 days. We strongly advise you not to spend more time than this on this chapter; there are important ideas to cover in later chapters.

Using Pages 528-529

It can be argued that there are three fundamental operations of arithmetic: addition, multiplication, and powering. Subtraction, division, and the taking of roots are respective special cases of these operations. Whereas addition is the most basic of these operations, multiplication is the pivotal operation, in the sense that it provides a shortcut for certain additions, and in turn powering provides a shortcut for certain multiplications.

On this page, multiplication is related to addition, subtraction, and division, and it is pictured by area models.

Discuss how the areas of the rectangles relate to each of the multiplication problems on this page. Try to elicit the following for the operations:

Multiplication and Addition: $8 \cdot 3.5$ is the area of a rectangle with dimensions 8 and 3.5; the rectangle can be split into 8 smaller rectangles with dimensions 3.5 and 1; adding the areas of the smaller rectangles gives the area of the entire rectangle.

10-1 Multiplication as Shortcut Addition

10-2 Solving $ax = b$

10-3 Using $ax = b$

10-4 Solving $ax + b = c$

10-5 Solving $ax + b = c$ When a Is Negative

10-6 The Distributive Property

10-7 The Surface Area of a Box

10-8 Dimensions and Units

10-9 Areas of Triangles

10-10 Areas of Trapezoids

528

Chapter 10 Overview

This chapter contains two parts of roughly equal length. The first half of the chapter deals with the solving of equations involving multiplication, proceeding from $ax = b$ (Lessons 10-2 and 10-3) to $ax + b = c$ (Lessons 10-4 and 10-5). The Distributive Property, which underlies Lesson 10-1, is discussed overtly in Lesson 10-6, and provides a bridge between the two parts of the chapter.

The rest of the chapter deals with area: the surface area of rectangular solids, which requires the area formula for a rectangle (Lesson 10-7), the area of a triangle (Lesson 10-9), and the area of a trapezoid (Lesson 10-10). Lesson 10-8 is a critical lesson, reminding students of the differences between area and perimeter. The Distributive Property enters the second part of the chapter in two ways: as a shortcut for calculating the surface area of rectangular solids,

and as a justification for the area formulas for triangles and trapezoids.

The applications in this chapter are varied. The various models for multiplication studied in Chapter 9 provide settings for the simplest equations. Some of the patterns studied first in Chapters 4 and 5 return here for the linear equations of Lessons 10-4 and 10-5. Area provides many additional applications.

MULTIPLICATION AND OTHER OPERATIONS

Chapter 9 covered uses of multiplication without reference to other operations. But multiplication is related to all the other basic operations of arithmetic. Each of these relationships can be pictured using area.

Multiplication and Addition

Multiplication provides a shortcut for adding many instances of the same number.

$$3.5 + 3.5 + 3.5 + 3.5 + 3.5 + 3.5 + 3.5 + 3.5 = 8 \cdot 3.5$$

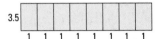

Multiplication and Subtraction

Sometimes subtraction can help with a multiplication. Here is a way to multiply by 99 in your head.

$$62 \cdot 99 = 62 \cdot 100 - 62 \cdot 1$$
$$= 6200 - 62$$
$$= 6138$$

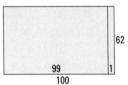

Multiplication and Division

Every multiplication fact gives rise to division facts.

$7 \cdot 9 = 63$ means $\frac{63}{9} = 7$
and $\frac{63}{7} = 9$.

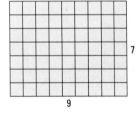

In this chapter, you will study the general algebraic patterns that relate multiplication to addition and subtraction. These relationships have applications to the areas of two-dimensional figures and the surface areas of three-dimensional figures.

529

Multiplication and Subtraction: The area of the left rectangle is 62 · 99. The area of the entire figure is 62 · 100; subtract the area of the right rectangle, 62 · 1, from that, and you get the area of the left rectangle.

Multiplication and Division: The area of the entire figure is 63 square units. Divide 63 by either dimension of the figure, and the result is the other dimension.

Photo Connections

The photo collage makes real-world connections to the content of the chapter: multiplication and other operations.

Balls: An array of objects can be grouped by rows or columns, allowing one to find the total number of objects by multiplying the number of objects in each group by the number of groups.

Boxes: The surface area of a box is the amount of wrapping paper needed to cover it exactly without any overlapping paper.

Sailboat: Sails come in different shapes and sizes, and over the years have been made from flax fibers, cotton, and most recently Dacron. The amount of cloth in a sail can be calculated using the formula for the area of a triangle, $A = \frac{1}{2}bh$.

Iceberg: "This is only the tip of the iceberg." Many students understand the origin of this expression from science class; that is, about one eighth of the mass of an iceberg projects above the water. If the mass of the "tip" of the iceberg were known, students could mulitply to find its entire mass, and they also could determine the portion below water.

Bobsled: A bobsled course that qualifies for an international competition must be at least 1500 meters long. Four-man sleds reach speeds up to 160 kilometers per hour (100 mph). The average rate of speed over a course can be determined by the equation $d = rt$, where d is the length of the course and t is the time of the run.

Objectives
C Apply the Repeated Addition Property of Multiplication to simplify expressions.
F Recognize and use the Repeated Addition Property of Multiplication.

Resources
From the *Teacher's Resource File*
- Lesson Master 10-1A or 10-1B
- Answer Master 10-1
- Teaching Aid 107: Warm-up

Additional Resources
- Visual for Teaching Aid 107

Teaching Lesson 10-1

Warm-up
Find the total cost of the groceries excluding tax.
2 gallons of milk at $1.89 per gallon
4 loaves of bread at $1.19 a loaf
3 pounds of apples at $.59 a pound
5 rolls of paper towels at $.69 a roll
[$13.76]

Notes on Reading
Reading Mathematics Since the reading is straightforward, you may wish to ask only if there are any questions on various parts of the reading. Then to ensure that students understand what they have read, ask if there are any questions on page 530. If not, ask what 5*x* equals, according to the Repeated Addition Property. [*x* + *x* + *x* + *x* + *x* = 5*x*] For **Example 1**, ask: what is the perimeter of a square with side

---

LESSON 10-1

Multiplication as Shortcut Addition

Food for thought. *The FDA now recommends a minimum of five daily servings of fruits and vegetables to maintain good health.*

Shortcut Addition with One Variable

Suppose you buy 5 different items at a grocery store.

The clerk will add the costs to arrive at your total cost.

$$a + b + c + d + e$$

But if you buy 5 items that are the same, the checkout clerk has a choice.

The prices can be added:

$$x + x + x + x + x.$$

Or, the price of the one item can be multiplied by 5. The total cost to you is 5*x*.

Lesson 10-1 Overview

Broad Goals This lesson introduces the Repeated Addition Property of Multiplication in its algebraic form, $nx = x + x + \ldots + x$, where there are *n* addends. Then students apply that property to questions on perimeter and to simplifying expressions.

Perspective Multiplication as repeated addition has limited applicability. In Chapter 9, we saw that any positive real number can represent the length or width of a rectangle,

or can be involved in size changes. Any number, positive or negative, can be a rate factor. In repeated addition, however, one of the factors has to be a whole number. Thus, repeated addition does not help in interpreting, using, or understanding the multiplication of decimals, fractions, or negatives. All of the examples in this lesson involve small whole-number multiples of the variable, the kind of situation for which repeated addition is effective.

Usually repeated addition is conceived of as a way of turning multiplication into addition. In actual applications the reverse is the case: an addition situation with equal addends is turned into a multiplication situation.

At this point, we do not state the Distributive Property because it is far more general than the Repeated Addition Property of Multiplication.

Multiplication can be a shortcut for addition because the addends are equal. This property of multiplication is called the *Repeated Addition Property*.

Repeated Addition Property of Multiplication
If n is a positive integer, then

$$nx = \underbrace{x + x + \ldots + x.}_{n \text{ addends}}$$

Specifically:

$$1x = x$$
$$2x = x + x$$
$$3x = x + x + x$$
$$4x = x + x + x + x$$

and so on.

Example 1

What is the perimeter of a square with side length s?

Solution

The perimeter is the sum of the lengths of the sides: $s + s + s + s$. By repeated addition, The perimeter is $s + s + s + s = 4s$.

Shortcut Addition with Two Variables

Think again about the grocery situation. Suppose you buy amounts of two different items.

What is the total cost? By adding, the total cost is

$$(e + e + e + e + e) + (x + x + x).$$

This, due to the Repeated Addition Property of Multiplication, equals

$$5e + 3x.$$

The clerk can multiply the first cost by 5 and the second cost by 3, and then add them together. No other simplification can be made.

Optional Activities

After students finish the lesson, you might have each student write a grocery list or use an actual one that applies to his or her family. Students can go to a grocery store, find the prices of the items on their lists, and calculate the total cost of the groceries. Have them explain how they used the Repeated Addition Property of Multiplication.

6? [24 units] For **Example 2** ask: what is the perimeter if $\ell = 14$ and $w = 13$? [54 units] Then ask if there are any questions about **Example 3** and the paragraph below it. If not, ask if $3x$ and $3y$ are like terms? [No] Are $3x$ and $3x^2$ like terms? [No]

Additional Examples

1. A regular hexagon has sides of length f. What is its perimeter? $6f$
2. What is the perimeter of a parallelogram with adjacent sides of lengths a and b? $2a + 2b$
3. Simplify: $s + 3s + 5 + t + 2t - 7$. $4s + 3t - 2$
4. A ticket to Saturday night's concert costs $7.50.
   a. If Judi wants to buy 6 tickets, how much money will she need? $45
   b. If Todd wants to buy t tickets, how much money will he need? 7.50t$

531

Question 11 Science Connection
Beekeepers in the United States tend about $4\frac{1}{4}$ million hives and produce about 200 million pounds of honey every year. The 4 million pounds of beeswax produced every year is used in candles, lipsticks, polishes, and other products. Both natural and artificial hives usually have hexagonal compartments, as pictured here.

Question 13 Error Alert Many students get the answer 4. Have these students substitute a number for e and simplify. Remind them to follow order of operations. Also remind students that $e = 1e$ by the Multiplicative Identity Property of One.

Questions 17–18 When discussing these questions, emphasize the phrase "adding the same number to both sides" and remind students that this phrase is called the Addition Property of Equality.

(Notes on Questions continue on page 534.)

This idea can be used to obtain a formula for the perimeter of a rectangle.

Example 2

What is the perimeter of a rectangle with length ℓ and width w?

Solution

$$\text{perimeter} = \ell + w + \ell + w$$

Commutative and Associative Properties of Addition	$= \ell + \ell + w + w$
Repeated Addition Property of Multiplication	$= 2\ell + 2w$

From Examples 1 and 2 come the formulas $p = 4s$ for the perimeter of a square and $p = 2\ell + 2w$ for the perimeter of a rectangle.

Example 3

Simplify $8x + 4y + x + 3 + 2y + 3x + 6$.

Solution 1

Write the multiplications as repeated addition, then rearrange.
$8x + 4y + x + 3 + 2y + 3x + 6$
$= x + x + x + x + x + x + x + x + y + y + y + y + x + 3 + y + y + x + x + x + 6$
$= x + x + x + x + x + x + x + x + x + x + x + x + y + y + y + y + y + y + 3 + 6$
$= 12x + 6y + 9$

Solution 2

Think repeated addition. Group the like terms together.
$8x + 4y + x + 3 + 2y + 3x + 6$
$= (8x + x + 3x) + (4y + 2y) + 3 + 6$
$= 12x + 6y + 9$

As Solution 2 indicates, $8x$, x, and $3x$ are called *like terms* because they are multiples of the same variable. $12x$ and $6y$ are *unlike terms*. Like terms can be combined into a single term. Unlike terms cannot be simplified into a single term.

QUESTIONS

Covering the Reading

1. Suppose you buy 3 shirts at $10.99 each and 2 more shirts at $4.99 each.
   a. Write out the cost as an addition.
   b. Write out the cost using multiplication for the repeated additions.
   a) $10.99 + 10.99 + 10.99 + 4.99 + 4.99$ b) $3(10.99) + 2(4.99)$

In 2–4, simplify.

2. $x + x + x$ $3x$ 3. $\ell + w + \ell + w$ $2\ell + 2w$

4. $25 + 20 + 20 + 25 + 20 + 20 + 25 + 20 + 25$ 200

Adapting to Individual Needs

Extra Help
To help students understand the ideas of *like terms* and *unlike terms*, suggest that they think of the variables as labels. For example, use the expression $8x + 4y + 3x$. Let x represent one loaf of French bread and y represent one stick of butter. Students can then see that there are 11 loaves and 4 sticks. The quantity of bread could not be combined with the quantity of butter.

5. The ℓ and w in Question 3 might represent what real-world
quantities?

6. Give the perimeter of this outline of a pencil. $2a + 2b + c$

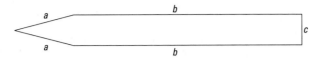

In 7 and 8, change the multiplications to additions.

7. $6y$ $\;$ $y + y + y + y + y + y$

8. $2x + 4z$
$x + x + z + z + z + z$

In 9 and 10, simplify.

9. $m + 1 + n + 2m + 4n + 6m$ $\;$ $9m + 5n + 1$

10. $4 + A + 2A + A + 6 + B$
$4A + B + 10$

Applying the Mathematics

11. Part of a beehive is drawn at the left. Each cell is a regular hexagon.
What is the sum of the lengths of the pictured segments? $28s$

12. Suppose frozen orange juice costs \$1.39 per can in a grocery store.
   a. A shopper buys 6 cans. Name two ways the shopper can figure
   out the total cost.
   b. A shopper buys c cans. What is the total cost? $c(1.39)$
   a) **Multiply 6(1.39), or add 1.39 + 1.39 + 1.39 + 1.39 + 1.39 + 1.39**

In 13 and 14, simplify.

13. $4e - e$ (Hint: Change all operations to additions.) $3e$

14. $11x - 2x + 3x$ $\;$ $12x$

15. a. Write $8 \cdot -\frac{1}{2}$ as repeated addition.
   b. Calculate $8 \cdot -\frac{1}{2}$. -4
   a) $-\frac{1}{2} + -\frac{1}{2} + -\frac{1}{2} + -\frac{1}{2} + -\frac{1}{2} + -\frac{1}{2} + -\frac{1}{2} + -\frac{1}{2}$

16. Give a formula for the perimeter p of an equilateral triangle if one
side has length s. $p = 3s$

Review

17. Solve $5 = 80 + u$. *(Lesson 5-8)* $u = -75$

18. Solve $-3 + x = 1140$. *(Lesson 5-8)* $x = 1143$

19. Which pairs of numbers are reciprocals? *(Lesson 9-3)*
   (a) 100 and 0.01 $\qquad$ (b) 2 and $\frac{1}{2}$
   (c) 2.5 and $\frac{2}{5}$ $\qquad$ (d) $\frac{7}{4}$ and $\frac{4}{7}$
   (e) 3.5 and $\frac{3}{5}$ $\qquad$ (f) 16 and -16
   (g) 1.5 and $0.\overline{6}$ $\qquad$ (h) 3 and .3 $\;$ (a), (b), (c), (d), (g)

Practice
For more questions on SPUR objectives, use **Lesson Master 10-1A**
(shown on page 531) or **Lesson
Master 10-1B** (shown on pages
532–533).

Assessment
Written Communication Have students write a paragraph describing
two different ways to find the perimeter of a square and of a rectangle.
[Paragraphs show understanding
of the Repeated Addition Property
of Multiplication and use diagrams
or examples as part of their
explanations.]

Extension
Have students tell if the following
sentences are *always true*, *sometimes true*, or *never true*.
1. $7x + 1 + 2x = 10x$
   sometimes true
2. $7m + m + 2m = 10m$
   always true
3. $n + n = n^2$ sometimes true
4. $t^2 + t^2 = 2t^2$ always true
5. $2d^3 - d^3 = d^3$ always true

Project Update Project 5, *Multiplication of Numbers in Scientific Notation*, on page 583, relates to the
content of this lesson.

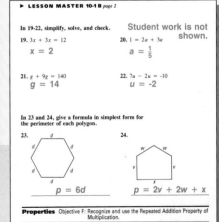

▶ **LESSON MASTER 10-1B** *page 2*

In 19-22, simplify, solve, and check. $\qquad$ **Student work is not
shown.**
19. $3x + 3x = 12$ $\qquad\qquad$ 20. $1 = 2a + 3a$
   $x = 2$ $\qquad\qquad\qquad$ $a = \frac{1}{5}$

21. $g + 9g = 140$ $\qquad\qquad$ 22. $7u - 2u = -10$
   $g = 14$ $\qquad\qquad\qquad$ $u = -2$

In 23 and 24, give a formula in simplest form for
the perimeter of each polygon.
23. $\qquad\qquad\qquad\qquad$ 24.

$p = 6d$ $\qquad\qquad\qquad$ $p = 2v + 2w + x$

Properties Objective F: Recognize and use the Repeated Addition Property of
Multiplication.

25. **a.** Explain how the Repeated Addition Property of
   Multiplication can be used to simplify $2x + 3x$.
   **$2x$ is $(x + x)$ and $3x$ is $(x + x + x)$, so
   $2x + 3x$ is $(x + x) + (x + x + x)$, or $5x$.**

   b. Will your explanation in Part a work for $2x + 3y$?
   Explain your answer.
   **No; $2x + 3y = (x + x) + (y + y + y)$;
   the xs and ys cannot be combined**

533

534

Notes on Questions

Question 23 When discussing this question, you might ask students to compare the two equations. [Both sides of the first equation were multiplied by 3.] Tell students that this question makes use of the Multiplication Property of Equality which they will use in Lesson 10-2.

Question 24 This review helps to prepare students for Lesson 10-7.

Question 25 It is important for students to realize that area does not depend upon the way a figure is tilted.

Question 28 Ask students to explain why no calculation is needed to answer the question.

Question 29 The property is $\frac{1}{\frac{1}{n}} = n$

and corresponds to the Opposite of the Opposite Property of Addition: $-(-n) = n$. In words, the reciprocal of the reciprocal of a number is the original number; you could call it the Reciprocal of a Reciprocal (Rec-Rec) Property.

✎ **Question 30c Writing** Some calculators allow the constant key to be used with a variety of operations. Be sure that students document their explorations in writing. You might ask volunteers to read their answers to the class.

20) Associative Property of Addition
21) Associative Property of Multiplication
22) Algebraic Definition of Subtraction
23) Multiplication Property of Equality

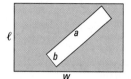

29b) The calculator has taken the reciprocal of the reciprocal of 5.
c) 0.2 is displayed.
d) If you press the reciprocal key an even number of times, you will get the original number. If you press the key an odd number of times, you will get its reciprocal.

30a) 5 is repeatedly added to the number displayed.
b) 5 is repeatedly added to the number displayed, which began at 8 (not 5 as in part a).

534

In 20–23, name the general property. *(Lessons 3-2, 5-7, 7-2, 9-2)*

20. $a + (b + c) = (a + b) + c$ **21.** $\frac{1}{5}(5w) = \left(\frac{1}{5} \cdot 5\right)w$

22. $35 + {-}78 = 35 - 78$ **23.** Since 1 in. = 2.54 cm, 3 in. = 3 · 2.54 cm.

24. A box has dimensions 2′, 3′, and 4′. Consider the largest face of the box. *(Lessons 5-10, 9-1)*
   a. What are its dimensions? **3′ by 4′**
   b. What is the area of this face? **12 ft²**
   c. What is the perimeter of this face? **14 ft**

25. A rectangle with dimensions a and b is tilted inside a rectangle with dimensions ℓ and w.
   a. Is this enough information to give a formula for the area of the shaded region? **Yes**
   b. If so, what is the formula? If not, why not? *(Lessons 7-1, 9-1)*
   $\ell w - ab$

26. Find the measures of the numbered angles, given that $m \parallel n$. *(Lesson 7-7)* **m∠1 = m∠3 = m∠4 = 145°; m∠2 = 35°**

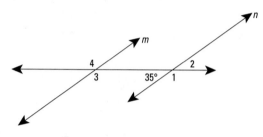

27. What is the expected temperature? *(Lesson 7-2)*
   a. The temperature is 7°F and is expected to drop 8°. **−1°F**
   b. The temperature is w°F and is expected to drop z°. **$w - z$ degrees**

28. *True or false.* $1.005 \cdot 2.34567893456 > 2.34567893456$ *(Lesson 4-10)*
   True

Exploration

29. Enter 5 on your calculator. Press the reciprocal key [1/n] twice.
   a. What number is displayed? **5**
   b. What has happened?
   c. What will happen if you press the reciprocal key 75 times?
   d. Make a generalization.

30. Some calculators have a constant key, often named [K].
   a. If your calculator has such a key, press 5 [+] [K] [=] [=] [=] . . . What happens as you continue to press [=]?
   b. Press 5 [+] [K] 8 [=] [=] [=] . . . What happens now?
   c. Explore what happens in parts **a** and **b** if the [+] key is replaced by keys for other operations. **Sample: If [−] is used, the constant will be subtracted each time [=] is pressed.**

Adapting to Individual Needs

Challenge
Have students solve the following problem:

A cardboard box is circled with 4 pieces of masking tape as shown. If there is one inch of overlapping tape on each piece, how much tape is used? [$(8z + 4x + 4y + 4)$ in.]

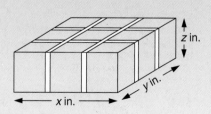

Laws of equality. *This statue of the* Scales of Justice, *which is atop New York City Hall, symbolizes the belief that justice should be applied equally to all. In this lesson, you will also see scales used to show equality.*

Picturing the Solving of $ax = b$

Here is an equation you should be able to solve in your head. (Think of a solution before reading on.)

$$3w = 6$$

This equation can be represented with a balance scale.

Three boxes with unknown weight w per box are on the left side of the scale. They balance the 6 one-kilogram weights on the right side. This situation pictures $3w = 6$.

Since the weight is shared equally among the three boxes, one box weighs 2 kilograms.

Lesson 10-2

Objectives
A Solve and check equations of the form $ax = b$.
F Recognize and use the Multiplication Property of Equality.
J Represent equations of the form $ax = b$ with a balance scale diagram.

Resources
From the **Teacher's Resource File**
■ Lesson Master 10-2A or 10-2B
■ Answer Master 10-2
■ Teaching Aids
107 Warm-up
110 Balance Scale Diagrams
■ Activity Kit, Activity 25

Additional Resources
■ Visuals for Teaching Aids 107, 110

Teaching 10-2
Lesson

Warm-up
Every multiplication fact $a \cdot b = c$ has two related division facts: $b = \frac{c}{a}$ and $a = \frac{c}{b}$. Write the corresponding division facts for each multiplication fact.

1. $9 \cdot 7 = 63$ $9 = \frac{63}{7}$; $7 = \frac{63}{9}$
2. $3.1 \cdot 6 = 18.6$
   $6 = \frac{18.6}{3.1}$; $3.1 = \frac{18.6}{6}$
3. $\frac{1}{2} \cdot 80 = 40$ $\frac{1}{2} = \frac{40}{80}$; $80 = \frac{40}{\frac{1}{2}}$
4. $\frac{2}{3} \cdot \frac{3}{2} = 1$ $\frac{2}{3} = \frac{1}{\frac{3}{2}}$; $\frac{3}{2} = \frac{1}{\frac{2}{3}}$

Lesson 10-2 Overview

Broad Goals This lesson applies the Multiplication Property of Equality to solve equations of the form $ax = b$.

Perspective This lesson has three SPUR dimensions: the skill of solving equations of the form $ax = b$; the use of the Multiplication Property of Equality; and the representation of the equation and the property with a balance scale. Uses for equations of the form $ax = b$ are delayed until Lesson 10-3

in order to provide a day for students to concentrate on the skill of solving equations in this form.

Each idea in this lesson is related to ideas students have encountered earlier in this book. The balance scale was used with addition. The Multiplication Property of Equality was in Chapter 3. The development of a method for solving more complicated equations of the form $ax = b$ parallels the

solving of equations of the form $x + a = b$ in Lesson 5-8. Students may have balked at the use of the Addition Property of Equality to solve an equation they could do in their heads, but one reason for using that property was to make this lesson easier.

Do not worry if students cannot solve equations of the form $ax = b$ in a single day. There is a lot of time throughout this chapter for them to gain that skill.

Reading Mathematics Since this lesson contains some technical reading, you might wish to have students read and discuss it in class. There are many connections to make, and the examples are important. Reading aloud and discussing important points as you go along may work well here. **Teaching Aid 110** contains balance scale diagrams which can be used as you discuss the lesson and questions.

After students have read the lesson, discuss the similarity between the Multiplication Property of Equality and the Addition Property of Equality from Lesson 5-8. Since students know how to use the latter, they already have an idea about how to apply this new property.

Each of the examples illustrates a use of the Multiplication Property of Equality. **Example 1** is a straightforward application with an explanation of each step. **Example 2** illustrates an equation that is difficult to solve mentally. **Example 3** is the first percent problem in the book that is not a "percent of" question, and it is quite difficult to solve without an equation.

As always, the writing font shows the steps you might expect students to show on their papers. Even after students become proficient, it is effective to require the original equation, a line showing what each side is multiplied by, and a line showing the solution. Also, stress the importance of checking answers.

Optional Activities

You might want to use *Activity 25* in the *Activity Kit* to introduce this lesson. In this activity, students represent equations of the form $ax = b$ and demonstrate how to solve the equation using concrete materials.

Sharing equally gives the same result as multiplying both sides of the equation $3w = 6$ by $\frac{1}{3}$. Example 1 shows the same steps without the balance scale.

Example 1

Solve $3w = 6$.

Solution

$$3w = 6$$
$$\frac{1}{3} \cdot 3w = \frac{1}{3} \cdot 6 \qquad \text{Multiply both sides by } \frac{1}{3}.$$
$$w = 2 \qquad \text{Arithmetic}$$

Check

Substitute 2 for w in the original equation. Does $3 \cdot 2 = 6$? Yes.

Notice why both sides of $3w = 6$ are multiplied by $\frac{1}{3}$. The product of 3 and $\frac{1}{3}$ is 1. So, $\frac{1}{3} \cdot 3w = \left(\frac{1}{3} \cdot 3\right)w = 1w = w$. Thus, multiplying both sides of the equation in Example 1 by $\frac{1}{3}$ leads to an equivalent equation of the form $x = \underline{\quad}$. This solves the equation.

Solving $ax = b$ Using the Multiplication Property of Equality

In general, multiplying both sides of an equation by any nonzero number will not affect its solutions. This situation is an instance of the *Multiplication Property of Equality* which you studied in Lesson 3-2.

Multiplication Property of Equality
If $x = y$, then $ax = ay$.

The Multiplication Property of Equality can be used to solve any equation of the form $ax = b$, if $a \neq 0$. To solve for x, just multiply both sides by $\frac{1}{a}$, the reciprocal of a. This method is particularly effective in solving equations which don't have obvious solutions.

Example 2

Solve $\frac{3}{5}m = \frac{1}{4}$ and check the solution.

Solution

First write the equation, leaving room for work below it.

$$\frac{3}{5}m = \frac{1}{4}$$

This is an equation of the form $ax = b$. Here $a = \frac{3}{5}$, $x = m$, and $b = \frac{1}{4}$. We want to multiply both sides by a number that will leave m by itself on the left side. That number is $\frac{5}{3}$, the reciprocal of $\frac{3}{5}$.

▶

$$\frac{5}{3} \cdot \left(\frac{3}{5} \cdot m\right) = \frac{5}{3} \cdot \frac{1}{4}$$

Because all numbers on the left-hand side are multiplied, the Associative Property of Multiplication lets us drop the parentheses.

$$\frac{5}{3} \cdot \frac{3}{5} \cdot m = \frac{5}{3} \cdot \frac{1}{4}$$

The hard part is done. Now you just simplify.

$$1 \cdot m = \frac{5}{3} \cdot \frac{1}{4}$$

Using $1 \cdot m = m$, and multiplying the fractions on the right side,

$$m = \frac{5}{12}.$$

Check

Substitute $\frac{5}{12}$ for m in the original equation.

Does $\frac{3}{5} \cdot \frac{5}{12} = \frac{1}{4}$?

The product of the fractions on the left side is $\frac{1}{4}$ in lowest terms. **Yes, it does.** So $\frac{5}{12}$ is the solution.

The next example may seem hard, but it can be solved using an equation.

Example 3

Six percent of a number is 30. What is the number?

Solution

First translate into an equation. Let the number be n.

Six percent   of   a number   is   30.
  ↓   ↓   ↓   ↓   ↓
 .06   ·   n   =   30

Here we solve using the Multiplication Property of Equality. Multiply both sides by the reciprocal of .06.

$$\frac{1}{.06} \cdot .06n = \frac{1}{.06} \cdot 30$$

Now simplify.

$$n = \frac{30}{.06}$$
$$n = 500$$

Check

6% of 500 = .06 × 500 = 30

To use the Multiplication Property of Equality, you need to know how to find reciprocals, how to multiply fractions, and how to find equal fractions. Now you can see why these ideas were discussed in previous chapters! But you still might wonder when these equations are solved outside of mathematics classes. That is the subject of the next lesson.

Lesson 10-2 *Solving ax = b*   **537**

Additional Examples

In 1–2, solve and check.
1. $240 = 1.5k$
   $k = 160; 240 = (1.5)(160)$
2. $\frac{1}{3}m = \frac{5}{8}$ $m = \frac{15}{8}; \frac{1}{3} \cdot \frac{15}{8} = \frac{5}{8}$
3. Fifteen percent of a number is 12. What is the number? 80

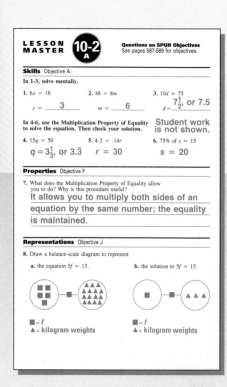

Adapting to Individual Needs

Extra Help
Help students see the parallel between solving addition equations of the form $x + a = b$ and solving multiplication equations of the form $ax = b$. Ask students how they would solve an addition equation of the form $x + a = b$. Help them recall that they would add the opposite of a, or *additive inverse* of a, to both sides of the equation. Point out that in solving any equation, the goal is to get the variable alone on one side. Since the sum of additive inverses is zero and $x + 0 = x$, that goal is accomplished. Remind students that another name for *reciprocal* is *multiplicative inverse*. Since the product of multiplicative inverses is 1 and $1 \cdot x = x$, the goal is accomplished when both sides of $ax = b$ are multiplied by $\frac{1}{a}$.

Notes on Questions

Questions 11–14 Point out that each of these problems uses the same form of equation to solve it. Each is a size-change multiplication in which the size-change factor and the result are known. What is not known is the original number.

Question 15 Students need to see unknowns on the right side of an equation, and realize that there is no difference between solving $b = ax$ and solving $ax = b$.

Question 18 Although students do not have to master the names for every property in this question, they should realize that steps follow one another and that there is a good reason for each step.

Questions 23–24 History Connection Andrew Jackson was the first to use the donkey as a political symbol. By the 1880s, the use of the donkey in political cartoons had caught the public's attention, and the donkey was established as the symbol for the Democratic Party. Political cartoons played a similar role in establishing the elephant as a symbol for the Republican party. In 1874, *Harper's Weekly* carried a cartoon which showed an elephant representing the Republican vote. The idea caught on, and the elephant soon came to stand for the Republican party.

1a) Sample:
■ = w
● = kilogram weights

Covering the Reading

1. **a.** Draw a balance scale diagram representing the equation $4w = 12$.
   b. Solve the equation. $w = 3$

2. **a.** To solve $3x = 0.12$ using the Multiplication Property of Equality, by what number would both sides be multiplied? $\frac{1}{3}$
   b. Solve $3x = 0.12$ using the Multiplication Property of Equality. $1/3 \cdot 3x = 1/3 \cdot 0.12; x = 0.04$

3. **a.** To solve $5y = 80$ using the Multiplication Property of Equality, by what number should you multiply both sides? $\frac{1}{5}$
   b. Solve $5y = 80$. $y = 16$

4. If $x = y$, then $6x = \underline{\ ?\ }$. $6y$

5. Question 4 is an instance of what property?
   Multiplication Property of Equality

6. Delilah said the solution to $\frac{2}{3}x = 5$ is $\frac{15}{2}$. Is she correct? Yes

7. **a.** To solve $\frac{6}{25} \cdot A = \frac{2}{9}$, it is most convenient to multiply both sides by what number? $\frac{25}{6}$
   b. Solve this equation. $A = \frac{25}{27}$

In 8–10, solve and check.

8. $\frac{2}{3}x = 8$ $x = 12;$
   $\frac{2}{3} \cdot 12 = 8$

9. $\frac{t}{9} = 40$ $t = 360;$
   $\frac{360}{9} = 40$

10. $\frac{4}{7}y = \frac{1}{8}$ $y = \frac{7}{32}$
    $\frac{4}{7} \cdot \frac{7}{32} = \frac{1}{8}$

11. Seven times a number is 413. What is the number? 59

12. Seven percent of a number is 84. What is the number? 1200

13. 40% of what number is 25? 62.5

Applying the Mathematics

14. Ten-thirds of a number is 30. What is the number? 9

In 15–17, solve and check.

15. $16.56 = 7.2y$
    $y = 2.3; 16.56 = 7.2 \cdot 2.3$

16. $\frac{2}{3}k = 62\%$ $k = 93\%;$
    $(2/3) \cdot 93\% = 62\%$

17. $x + x + x = 5.736$
    $x = 1.912$
    $1.912 + 1.912 + 1.912 = 5.736$

18. Give the property telling why each step follows from the previous one.
    $$\frac{7}{4} \cdot A = \frac{1}{5}$$

    Step 1 $\frac{4}{7} \cdot \left(\frac{7}{4} \cdot A\right) = \frac{4}{7} \cdot \frac{1}{5}$ Multiplication Property of Equality

    Step 2 $\left(\frac{4}{7} \cdot \frac{7}{4}\right) \cdot A = \frac{4}{7} \cdot \frac{1}{5}$ Associative Property of Multiplication

    Step 3 $1 \cdot A = \frac{4}{7} \cdot \frac{1}{5}$ Property of Reciprocals

    Step 4 $A = \frac{4}{35}$ Multiplication of fractions, Multiplication Identity Property of 1

19. If $\frac{4}{3}$ of a number is 1200, what is $\frac{3}{4}$ of that number? 675

538

Adapting to Individual Needs

English Language Development

This is a good time for students to review all the terms that they have defined on index cards. Cards should include definitions and examples of *reciprocal*, *percent*, and the *Associative Property of Multiplication*, which are used in this lesson. Then have students add the Multiplication Property of Equality to their sets of cards.

LESSON MASTER 10-2 B   Questions on SPUR Objectives

Skills Objective A: Solve and check equations of the form $ax = b$.

In 1–6, solve mentally.

1. $9x = 18$ $x = \underline{2}$
2. $35 = 7g$ $g = \underline{5}$
3. $10y = 85$ $y = \underline{8.5}$
4. $\frac{1}{2}d = 12$ $d = \underline{24}$
5. $\frac{c}{5} = 3$ $r = \underline{15}$
6. $11 = 50\%$ of c $c = \underline{22}$

In 7–15, use the Multiplication Property of Equality to solve the equation. Then check your solution.   Student work is not shown.

7. $7u = 154$ $u = 22$
8. $22a = 77$ $a = \frac{7}{2}$, or 3.5
9. $\frac{4}{5}y = 84$ $y = 105$

10. $\frac{1}{2}d = \frac{9}{4}$ $d = \frac{9}{2}$, or $4\frac{1}{2}$
11. $412 = \frac{v}{8}$ $v = 3296$
12. $1.9m = 475$ $m = 250$

13. $3.64 = .52q$ $q = 7$
14. $\frac{7}{12} = \frac{11}{6}j$ $j = \frac{7}{22}$
15. 85% of $p = 272$ $p = 320$

538

In 20 and 21, simplify. *(Lesson 10-1)*

20. $7 + 2x + 5x + 3$ **21.** $y + z + 2z$

22. Draw a figure that has exactly 3 symmetry lines. *(Lesson 8-7)*

In 23 and 24, consider the following information about the U.S. Senate.

Years	Democrats	Republicans
1983–85	46	54
1985–87	47	53
1987–89	54	46
1989–91	57	43
1991–93	57	43
1993–95	58	42
1995–97	47	53
1997–99	45	55
1999–2001	46	54

Changing Congressional faces. *In 1948, Margaret Chase Smith became the first woman elected to a full six-year Senate term. When the 106th Congress convened in January 1999, there were 9 female senators and 58 female representatives.*

23. What is the mean number of Democrats in the U.S. Senate from 1983–95? *(Lesson 4-6)*

24. The ordered pairs (Democrats, Republicans) for these nine two-year periods all lie on a line. What is an equation for that line? *(Lesson 8-4)*

25. Since there was no year that we number 0, how many years were between the given years?
  a. 2 A.D. and 2 B.C.   **b.** 4 A.D. and 4 B.C.
  c. 10 A.D. and 10 B.C.   **d.** n A.D. and n B.C. *(Lesson 7-2)*

26. **a.** To solve $\frac{31}{6} + m = -\frac{5}{8}$, what number can be added to both sides?
  b. Solve $\frac{31}{6} + m = -\frac{5}{8}$. *(Lesson 5-8)*

27. Use a protractor to measure $\angle ABC$ to the nearest degree. *(Lesson 3-6)*

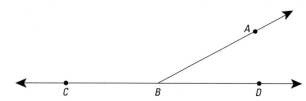

28. Write one millionth in the requested form.
  a. as a decimal   **b.** as a power of 10 *(Lessons 1-2, 2-8)*

Exploration

29. 144 seats can be arranged in a rectangular array with 12 rows and 12 columns. How many other rectangular arrays are possible?

Adapting to Individual Needs

Challenge
Have students solve the following problem:

On an outdoor running track, there are 12 equally spaced poles around the track. A runner starts at the first pole and reaches the eighth pole in 36 seconds. If the runner keeps running at the same rate, how long will it take the runner to reach the twelfth pole? [$56\frac{4}{7}$ sec]

Practice

For more questions on SPUR Objectives, use **Lesson Master 10-2A** (shown on page 537) or **Lesson Master 10-2B** (shown on pages 538–539).

Assessment

Group Assessment Have students **work in pairs** to solve the following equations and to represent the procedures for finding both solutions on **Teaching Aid 110.**
1. $4x = 64$ $x = 16$
2. $75 = 5n$ $15 = n$
[Students use the Multiplication Property of Equality to solve both equations and picture the procedures on balance scales.]

Extension

Have students study the nine equations below and then group together all those equations that have the same solution.

1. $\frac{m}{3} = 8$ **2.** $3m = 8$

3. $8 = \frac{1}{3}m$ **4.** $8 = 3m$

5. $m - 3 = 8$ **6.** $m = 2\frac{2}{3}$

7. $8 = -3 + m$ **8.** $11 = m$

9. $m = 24$

1, 3, and 9; 2, 4, and 6; 5, 7, and 8.

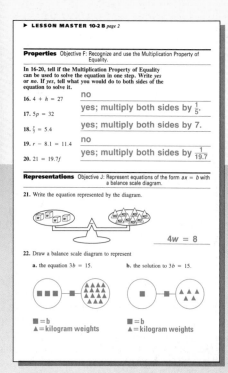

▶ **LESSON MASTER 10-2 B** *page 2*

Properties Objective F: Recognize and use the Multiplication Property of Equality.

In 16-20, tell if the Multiplication Property of Equality can be used to solve the equation in one step. Write *yes* or *no*. If *yes*, tell what you would do to both sides of the equation to solve it.

16. $4 + h = 27$ no

17. $5p = 32$ yes; multiply both sides by $\frac{1}{5}$.

18. $\frac{x}{7} = 5.4$ yes; multiply both sides by 7.

19. $r - 8.1 = 11.4$ no

20. $21 = 19.7f$ yes; multiply both sides by $\frac{1}{19.7}$

Representations Objective J: Represent equations of the form $ax = b$ with a balance scale diagram.

21. Write the equation represented by the diagram.

$4w = 8$

22. Draw a balance scale diagram to represent
  a. the equation $3b = 15$.   **b.** the solution to $3b = 15$.

■ = b   ■ = b
▲ = kilogram weights   ▲ = kilogram weights

539

G Find unknowns in real situations involving multiplication.

Resources
From the *Teacher's Resource File*
- Lesson Master 10-3A or 10-3B
- Answer Master 10-3
- Teaching Aid 107: Warm-up

Additional Resources
- Visual for Teaching Aid 107

Teaching
Lesson 10-3

Warm-up
Diagnostic For each question, write an equation, solve it, and check your work.
1. This week Dakota earned $12.75 baby-sitting. This is one third the amount she earned last week during her spring vacation. How much did she earn during her vacation? $\frac{1}{3}s = 12.75$; $s = 38.25$; she earned $38.25; $\frac{1}{3}(38.25) = 12.75$
2. What is the total amount of money Dakota earned in the last two weeks? $t = 12.75 + 38.25$; $t = 51$; she earned $51; $51 = 12.75 + 38.25$

Notes on Reading
Reading Mathematics Since this lesson, like Lesson 10-2, has quite a bit of reading, you might wish to have students read it aloud in class.

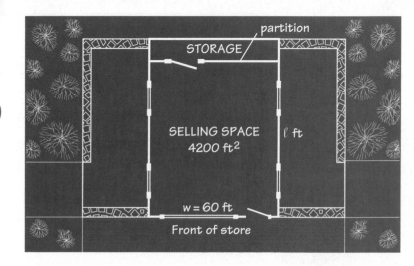

You have learned a variety of applications of multiplication:

> areas of rectangles
> arrays
> rate factors
> expansions (times as many)
> contractions (part of)
> percents of

Any of these applications can lead to an equation of the form $ax = b$. Here is an example involving areas of rectangles.

An Example Involving Area

Example 1

Claus's Clothes occupies a rectangular floor space. The store is 60 feet wide as shown in the diagram above. The store must be split into selling space and storage space by a partition. Mrs. Claus wants 4200 square feet for selling space. Where should the partition be located?

Solution

The selling space is a rectangle. One dimension of the rectangle is known to be 60 feet. The area is to be 4200 square feet. Now apply the formula for the area of a rectangle.

$$A = \ell\, w$$

Substitute 4200 for A and 60 for w in the formula.

$$4200 = \ell \cdot 60$$

▶

Lesson 10-3 Overview

Broad Goals This lesson considers questions that can be answered by solving equations of the form $ax = b$.

Perspective The list of applications that introduces the lesson reminds students of the different uses of multiplication that have been covered: area, arrays, volume, repeated addition, size change, and percents of. **Example 1** may be solved without writing an equation, but **Examples 2 and 3** are

more difficult. Again the purpose is to convince students of the need for the general algorithm for solving even an equation as simple in form as $ax = b$.

▶ Solve this equation in your head or by using the Multiplication Property of Equality.

$$\ell = \frac{4200}{60} \text{ feet}$$
$$\ell = 70 \text{ feet}$$

The partition should be 70 ft from the front of the store.

Check

You should always check answers with the original question. If the depth (length) of the selling space is 70 feet, will there be 4200 square feet of selling space? Yes, because $60 \cdot 70 = 4200$.

An Example Involving Size Changes

The next example involves a size change. Before you begin, read the question carefully. Without solving, you should know whether the answer will be greater than 12.60 or less than 12.60.

Example 2

A worker receives time and a half for overtime. If a worker gets $12.60 an hour for overtime, what is the worker's normal hourly wage?

Solution

Recall that time and a half means the worker's normal wage is multiplied by $1\frac{1}{2}$ to calculate the overtime wage. Let W be the normal hourly wage.

Then $1\frac{1}{2} \cdot W = \$12.60$.

Now the job is to solve this equation. First change the fraction to a decimal.

$$1.5 \cdot W = 12.60$$
$$W = \frac{12.60}{1.5}$$
$$W = \$8.40$$

The worker's normal hourly wage is $8.40.

Check

Ask: If a worker makes $8.40 an hour, will that worker get $12.60 for overtime? Yes; half of $8.40 is $4.20, and $4.20 plus $8.40 is $12.60.

Job requirements.
To compete for permanent future jobs, young people will need good communication, interpersonal, and analytic skills.

❶ General Advice

In answering these kinds of questions, many people find it useful to think of the following steps.

(1) Read carefully. Determine what is to be found and what is given.

(2) Let a variable equal the unknown quantity.

(3) Write an equation.

(4) Solve the equation.

(5) Check your answer back in the original question.

Lesson 10-3 *Using ax = b* **541**

Optional Activities

Writing You might want to give students the following activity after discussing **Question 8.** Have students bring in models of objects such as planes, trains, cars, and furniture. Then have students **work in small groups** to write problems about these models. They may need almanacs and other resources that give life-size measures.

3. Suppose the sales tax in a community is 8%. If the Buy Cycle bicycle store sent the state $2,000 in sales taxes for March, what were the total sales of the store in that month?
$.08s = 2000$; $s = \$25,000$;
$.08(25000) = 2000$

Notes on Questions

Questions 6–9 Each of these questions has been designed so that it is difficult to answer without solving an equation. Setting up the equation is not difficult, so students can devote attention to solving the equation.

Question 8 It is fine if students multiply 188 mm by 12 to obtain the solution, but point out they would get the same product if they solved $\frac{1}{12}w = 188$ using the Multiplication Property of Equality.

Question 10 Social Studies Connection Kennedy narrowly won the election, defeating Nixon by a margin of only 118,550 votes. A major factor in the campaign was a then-unique series of four televised debates between the two men. The debates reached an estimated 85,000,000 to 120,000,000 American viewers. Interested students can monitor television for one week to see how politicians utilize the media to gain support for their programs and further their goals.

542

An Example Involving Percents

Here is a size-change example using percents.

Example 3

In a small-town election, it was reported that Phineas Foghorn got about 38% of the votes. It was also reported that he received 405 votes. How many people voted?

Solution

Let v be the number of people who voted. Given that 38% of v equals 405, translate this into an equation.

$$.38v = 405$$
$$\frac{.38v}{.38} = \frac{405}{.38} \qquad \text{Multiply both sides by } \frac{1}{.38}$$
$$v \approx 1065.8$$

There were approximately 1066 voters.

Check

Suppose 1066 people voted and Phineas received 405 votes. Is this 38%?

$$\frac{405}{1066} = 0.37992 \ldots$$

When rounded, this number equals 38%. So the answer checks.

QUESTIONS

Covering the Reading

2) Sample: The original problem is the question that is asked, not the equation, which may have been set up incorrectly.

1. What is the first step you should do in solving a problem like those in this lesson? Read carefully. Determine what is to be found and what is given.

2. You solve a problem using an equation. Why should you first check the equation's solution in the original problem, not in the equation?

3. In Example 1, suppose the width of Claus's Clothes was increased to 80 feet. Where should the partition now be located? 52.5 ft from the front of the store

4. Stacey gets paid time and a half for each hour she baby-sits after midnight. She made $3.60 per hour after midnight on New Year's Eve. How much did she make for each hour before midnight? $2.40

5. In an election, it was reported that Belinda Bellows received 1,912 votes, 54% of the total. How many votes were cast? ≈ 3541

Applying the Mathematics

In 6–9, write an equation, solve it, and check your work.

6. A pair of in-line skates is on sale at 70% of the original price. The sale price is $189.95. What was the original price? $271.36

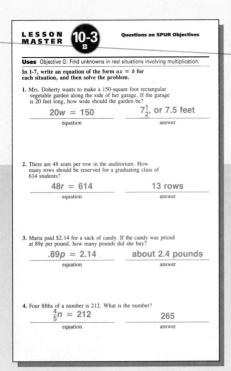

542

Adapting to Individual Needs

Extra Help

For students who have trouble writing an equation after reading a word problem, suggest an intermediate step. This step involves condensing the facts into a short sentence that can then be translated into a mathematical equation. Have students identify which facts of the problem are known and which are unknown. Then they can try writing one simple sentence using these facts. For **Example 2**, they might write: One

and one half times the normal wage is $12.60.

$$1\frac{1}{2} \quad \cdot \quad w \quad = \quad \$12.60$$

For **Example 3**, the sentence could be: 38% of the voters is 405 people.

$$.38 \quad \cdot \quad v \quad = \quad 405$$

7. At an average speed of 550 mph, how long will it take an airplane to fly from Los Angeles to Manila, a distance of 7300 miles? **≈ 13.27 hours**

8. Doll house models are often $\frac{1}{12}$ actual size. If a doll house window is 188 mm wide, how wide is the real window? **2256 mm, or 2.256 m**

9. A Macintosh Classic screen has 175,104 pixels in a rectangular array. There are 512 columns in this array. How many rows are there? **342 rows**

10. From 1932 until 1992, the largest percent of people eligible to vote who actually voted in a presidential election was 62.8%. This occurred in the 1960 election between John Kennedy and Richard Nixon. About 68,839,000 votes were cast. How many people were old enough to vote then but didn't? **≈ 40,777,000**

11. In the Chinese game of mah-jongg, the player "going mah-jongg" (or winning) receives the value w of the winning score from two of the other players and double the winning score from the player designated East. If East wins, the other three players give that person double the winning score. Let T be the total value received by the winner.
    a. Write an equation relating w and T if East does not win. **T = 4w**
    b. If the winning score in part **a** is 900, find T. **T = 3600**
    c. If East wins, write an equation relating w and T. **T = 6w**
    d. If the winning score in part **c** is 900, find T. **T = 5400**

Going mah-jongg. Shown is one example of a winning mah-jongg hand of tiles. In Chinese, mah-jongg means "sparrow." Therefore, a sparrow or mythical "bird of 100 intelligences" appears on the 1s tiles.

Review

In 12–14, solve. *(Lessons 10-1, 10-2)*

12. $14n = 4$ $n = \frac{2}{7}$ $= 0.285714 \approx 0.286$
13. $a + a + a + a = 30$ $a = 7.5$
14. $2170 = 2\frac{1}{3}x$ $x = 930$
15. Simplify $1 - 5 - 4$. *(Lessons 4-1, 7-2)* **-8**

16. As of January 1993, the world record for the 5000-meter run was 12 minutes, 58.39 seconds for men (set by Said Aouita of Morocco in 1987) and 14 minutes 37.33 seconds for women (set by Ingrid Kristiansen of Norway in 1986). Who ran faster, and by how much? *(Lesson 7-1)* **Aouita, by 1 minute 38.94 seconds**

17. Make a tessellation using copies of quadrilateral *ABCD*. *(Lesson 8-8)*

A
D
B
C

17)

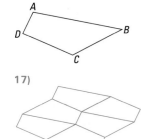

In 18–20, evaluate if $x = 3.2$ and $y = 7.8$. *(Lesson 4-4)*

18. $100x + 200$ **520** 19. $100x + 200x$ **960** 20. $100x + 200y$ **1880**

21. 2 cm is how many meters? *(Lesson 3-4)* **0.02 m**

Exploration

22. Suppose the area of a rectangularly shaped farm is 240 acres, or $\frac{3}{8}$ of a square mile. What might be the dimensions of the farm, in feet?
Sample: 3200 ft by 3267 ft

Lesson 10-3 *Using ax = b* **543**

Practice
For more questions on SPUR Objectives, use **Lesson Master 10-3A** (shown on page 541) or **Lesson Master 10-3B** (shown on pages 542–543).

Assessment
Written/Oral Communication
Write the equation $0.25t = 15$ on the board. Ask each student to write an application question for which the equation would provide a solution, solve it, and check the answer. [Problems show understanding of questions that use equations of the form $ax = b$ to solve them.]

Extension
Give students the following problem.

A coat that had been reduced by $33\frac{1}{3}$% is on sale now for half of that reduced price. If the current price tag on the coat reads $90, what was the original price? **$270**

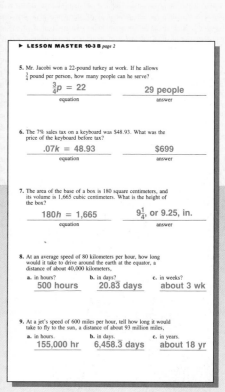

Objectives

B Solve and check equations of the form $ax + b = c$.

G Find unknowns in real situations leading to equations of the form $ax + b = c$.

J Represent equations of the form $ax + b = c$ with a balance scale diagram.

Resources

From the Teacher's Resource File

■ Lesson Master 10-4A or 10-4B
■ Answer Master 10-4
■ Assessment Sourcebook: Quiz for Lessons 10-1 through 10-4
■ Teaching Aids
  108 Warm-up
  110 Balance Scale Diagrams
■ Activity Kit, Activity 26

Additional Resources

■ Visuals for Teaching Aids 108, 110

LESSON

10-4

Solving $ax + b = c$

Algebra in action. *Suppose each kitten weighs the same. If the cat weighs 9 pounds, and the cat and kittens together weigh 19 pounds, then the equation $4w + 9 = 19$ could be used to find the weight of each kitten.*

❶ **Picturing the Solving of $ax + b = c$**

Here is a balance-scale picture of the equation $3w + 5 = 14$. On the scale, three boxes of equal unknown weight and 5 one-kilogram weights balance with 14 one-kilogram weights.

You can find the weight w of one box in two steps. Each step keeps the scale balanced.

Step 1 Remove 5 one-kilogram weights from each side.

Lesson 10-4 Overview

Broad Goals This lesson introduces an algorithm for solving equations of the form $ax + b = c$, and offers several applications.

Perspective Usually the skill of solving equations in the form $ax + b = c$ cannot be mastered in a single day. Students will continue to work on the skill in Lesson 10-5 and in later chapters (and in *UCSMP Algebra*). The idea of the lesson is to get students off to a good start. Concentrate on students

using the required steps and understanding how the properties are applied.

The basic strategy in all sentence solving is to convert equations into simpler ones which can be more easily solved. When solving equations, the object of writing down the steps is to eventually arrive at a sentence whose solution is obvious. You may wish to review the idea of *equivalent sentences*. The goal in solving $ax + b = c$ for x

is to end up with an equivalent sentence of the form $x = k$. This type of equation is frequently referred to as a two-step equation, since two major operations are necessary to get to the form $x = k$.

Some students immediately see the general pattern in solving $ax + b = c$. They subtract b from c and divide by a. We see nothing wrong with this procedure; it's the mark of an excellent pattern finder.

Step 2 Distribute the remaining weight equally among the boxes.

Therefore, one box weighs 3 kilograms. Example 1 shows the same steps without the balance scale.

❷ Example 1

Solve $3w + 5 = 14$.

Solution

$3w + 5 + -5 = 14 + -5$	Addition Property of Equality (Add −5 to each side.)
$3w = 9$	Simplify.
$\frac{1}{3} \cdot 3w = \frac{1}{3} \cdot 9$	Multiplication Property of Equality (Multiply both sides by $\frac{1}{3}$.)
$w = 3$	Simplify.

Check

Substitute 3 for w in the original equation.

Does $3w + 5 = 14$?
$3 \cdot 3 + 5 = 14$?
$9 + 5 = 14$?
$14 = 14$? Yes.

Solving $ax + b = c$ Using Properties

In the equation $3w + 5 = 14$, the unknown w is multiplied by a number. Then a second number is added. We call this an **equation of the form $ax + b = c$**. In this case, $a = 3$, $b = 5$, $c = 14$, and $x = w$. All equations in this form can be solved for x with two major steps. First add $-b$ to both sides. This step gets the term with the variable alone on one side. Then multiply both sides by $\frac{1}{a}$.

Example 2 illustrates this strategy. The original sentence may look complicated, but it can be simplified to a sentence of the form $ax + b = c$.

Optional Activities

You might want to use *Activity 26* in the *Activity Kit* to introduce the lesson. In this activity, students use paper clips and envelopes to represent and solve equations of the form $ax + b = c$.

Warm-up
Choose the correct solution.
1. $\frac{3}{5}x + 7 = 16$ a
   a. $x = 15$ **b.** $x = 27$
2. $\frac{5}{6}n - 4 = 26$ a
   a. $n = 36$ **b.** $n = 25$
3. $-27 = 3y - 12$ b
   a. $y = 5$ **b.** $y = -5$
4. $0.8m + 2.8 = 402.8$ a
   a. $m = 500$ **b.** $m = 5000$
5. $2.5x = 150$ a
   a. $x = 60$ **b.** $x = 37.50$
6. $6.4t - .4 = 2.8$ b
   a. $t = 0.2$ **b.** $t = 0.5$

Notes on Reading

❶ When discussing this section, you may want to use **Teaching Aid 110** which contains balance scale diagrams.

❷ Be certain that students focus on the two-step nature of the process in **Example 1**. Ask what needs to be done to get w by itself on one side of the equation [add −5 and multiply by $\frac{1}{3}$] and which operation should be done first [add −5 to both sides]. **Example 2** requires a simplification to get to the form $ax + b = c$, and **Example 3** illustrates using $ax + b = c$ in a real situation. The origin of the expression $1.20 + .30n$ may be clearer to students if they think of n as the number of times the meter clicks.

In 1–2, solve and check.
1. $-20 = 15 + 7v$ $-5 = v$ Check:
   $15 + 7(-5) = 15 + -35 = -20$
2. $10 + 8w - 4 = 14$ $w = 1$ Check:
   $10 + 8(1) - 4 = 10 + 8 - 4 = 14$
3. A taxicab in a certain town
   charges $0.75 plus 10¢ for each
   quarter mile.
   a. How much will a trip of 5.5
      miles cost? $2.95
   b. How far can you travel for
      $5.05? 10.75 miles

Fair fares. *Wilhelm Bruhn invented the taximeter in 1891, enabling commercial drivers to determine accurately a fee for each ride. The modernization of taxicabs (which were named after the taximeter) paralleled that of the automobile.*

Example 2

Solve $10 + 6h - 14 = 32$.

Solution

First simplify the left-hand side. You may not need to write all the steps that are shown here.

$10 + 6h - 14 = 32$	
$10 + 6h + -14 = 32$	Algebraic Definition of Subtraction
$10 + -14 + 6h = 32$	Associative and Commutative Properties of Addition
$-4 + 6h = 32$	Arithmetic

This is an equation like the one solved in Example 1. Add 4 to both sides.

$4 + -4 + 6h = 4 + 32$	Addition Property of Equality
$6h = 36$	Arithmetic

You can solve this equation in your head. Otherwise, either multiply both sides by $\frac{1}{6}$ or divide both sides by 6.

$$h = 6$$

Check

Substitute: Does $10 + 6 \cdot 6 - 14 = 32$?
$10 + 36 - 14 = 32$?
$46 - 14 = 32$? Yes.

Here is a typical problem that leads to an equation of the form $ax + b = c$.

Example 3

In a recent year, taxicabs in New York City began each trip by setting the meter at $1.50. The meter added 25¢ for each $\frac{1}{5}$ mile traveled. If a trip cost $17.75, how far did the cab travel?

Solution

Let n be the number of $\frac{1}{5}$ miles traveled. Then
$$\text{total cost} = 1.50 + .25n$$
$$17.75 = 1.50 + .25n$$

Subtract 1.50 from each side.
$$16.25 = .25n$$

Multiply each side by $\frac{1}{.25}$. This is the same as dividing by .25.

$$65 = n$$

The taxi traveled $65 \cdot \frac{1}{5}$ miles, or 13 miles altogether.

Adapting to Individual Needs

Extra Help

When solving two-step equations, it might help some students to think of the term that contains the variable as a single quantity. Write $5x + -3 = 67$ on a transparency before turning on the overhead projector (or write it on the board before students enter the room). Cover up the term $5x$ with a card. Show the equation to the students and ask what it says. [Some number plus negative 3 equals 67.] Ask what can be done to solve it

[Add 3 to both sides] and proceed to write the following steps:

■ + -3	=	67
■ + -3 + 3	=	67 + 3
■ + 0	=	70
■	=	70

Then take off the card, have students describe the resulting equation, and ask how to solve it. [Five times some number equals 70; multiply both sides by $\frac{1}{5}$.] Show

the following steps:
$$5x = 70$$
$$\tfrac{1}{5} \cdot 5x = \tfrac{1}{5} \cdot 70$$
$$x = 14$$

Have students check that $5(14) + -3 = 67$ is a true statement.

If you cannot write an equation right away, a good strategy is to make a table. For Example 3, you might make a table like this one.

$\frac{1}{5}$ miles traveled	Cost
0	1.50
1	1.50 + .25
2	1.50 + .25 · 2
3	1.50 + .25 · 3
·	·
·	·
·	·

Continue writing until you see the pattern.

n	1.50 + .25n

Then, since the cost was $17.75, the equation to be solved is
$17.75 = 1.50 + .25n$.

1)
■ = w
● = kilogram weights

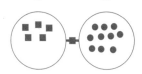

QUESTIONS

Covering the Reading

1. Illustrate how to solve the equation $5w + 2 = 12$ using a balance scale.

In 2–5, the equation is of the form $ax + b = c$. Identify a, b, and c.

2. $3x + 8 = 12$ $a = 3, b = 8, c = 12$ 3. $17 = 11 + \frac{1}{2}x$ $a = \frac{1}{2}, b = 11, c = 17$

4. $-4 + 2y = 9$ $a = 2, b = -4, c = 9$ 5. $2x - 8 = 12$ $a = 2, b = -8, c = 12$

6. a. To solve the equation $4x + 25 = 85$, first add __?__ to both sides. -25
   b. Solve $4x + 25 = 85$. Show your work. $x = 15$

7. a. What should be the first step in solving $3 + 4x + 5 = 6$? add 3 and 5
   b. Solve this equation. Show your work. $x = -\frac{1}{2}$

In 8–11, solve the equations of Questions 2–5. 8) $x = \frac{4}{3}$; 9) $x = 12$; 10) $y = 13/2$; 11) $x = 10$

In 12–17, solve and check. Show your work. See check at the left.

12) $2(17) + 7 = 34 + 7 = 41$
13) $300 + 120(10) = 300 + 1200 = 1500$
14) $8(\frac{1}{4}) - 2 = 0$
15) $17 + 60(\frac{4}{3}) + 3 = 17 + 80 + 3 = 100$
16) $\frac{5}{8}(104) + 20 = 65 + 20 = 85$
17) $-20 + 4(2) = -20 + 8 = -12$

12. $2y + 7 = 41$ $y = 17$ 13. $300 + 120t = 1500$ $t = 10$

14. $8y - 2 = 0$ $y = \frac{1}{4}$ 15. $17 + 60m + 3 = 100$ $m = \frac{4}{3}$

16. $\frac{5}{8}x + 20 = 85$ $x = 104$ 17. $-20 + 4x = -12$ $x = 2$

18. Use the situation in Example 3.
    a. How much would it cost to take a cab 2 miles? $4.00
    b. How far did the cab travel if a trip cost $9.50? 6.4 miles

19. To take a cab in a certain city, it costs 75¢ plus 15¢ for every $\frac{1}{5}$ mile traveled. If a cab fare is $10.05, how long was the trip? 12.4 miles

Lesson 10-4 *Solving* $ax + b = c$ **547**

Adapting to Individual Needs

English Language Development
Use copies of **Teaching Aid 110** to illustrate the steps used in solving these equations.

$$3m + 4 = 7$$
$$18 = 5y + 8$$
$$2x + 1 = 15$$

Do not give the equations or steps on the diagrams. Then work individually with each student and listen as he or she explains the pictures and writes the steps.

547

Question 21 Part a is intended to give a hint for the equation needed to solve **part b.** If students still cannot determine an equation, suggest that they use the problem-solving strategies of making a table and looking for a pattern.

Geography Connection Brazil, whose population in 1992 was around 150,000,000, covers an area of 3,286,487 square miles. Brazil covers nearly half of the total land area of South America. Interested students can find the cost for air fare to Brazil.

Question 22 Error Alert Many students do not realize that they should substitute 68 for *F* in the formula. If they substitute 68 for *C*, they will obtain 154.4 for an answer. Inform students that the *F* in the formula is a variable and should be replaced by a number that is the temperature measured in degrees Fahrenheit. The *F* in 60°F tells the scale used to measure the temperature and it is not a variable.

Question 23 This kind of detail is not intended as a model for student solutions.

Relaxing in Rio. *The city Rio de Janeiro lies along part of Brazil's 7400 km (over 4500 mi) of coastline. One of the main attractions of Rio is its beautiful white-sand beaches, such as the famous Copacabana Beach shown here.*

Applying the Mathematics

20. French fries have about 11 calories apiece. So, if you eat F French fries, you take in about $11F$ calories. A plain 4-oz hamburger with a bun has about 500 calories.
    a. Together, how many calories do the hamburger and F French fries have?
    b. How many calories are in a plain 4-oz hamburger on a bun and 20 French fries?
    c. How many French fries can you eat with a plain 4-oz hamburger on a bun for 800 total calories?

21. Paolo estimates that a trip to Brazil to see relatives will cost $1500 for air fare and $90 a day for living expenses.
    a. What will it cost to stay n days?
    b. How long can Paolo stay for $2500?

22. Use the formula $F = \frac{9}{5}C + 32$ to find the Celsius equivalent of 68°F.

23. Meticulous Matilda likes to put in every step in solving equations. Here is her solution to $5m + 7 = 17$. Give a reason for each step.
    a. $(5m + 7) + {-7} = 17 + {-7}$
    b. $5m + (7 + {-7}) = 17 + {-7}$
    c. $5m + 0 = 17 + {-7}$
    d. $5m = 10$
    e. $\frac{1}{5} \cdot (5m) = \frac{1}{5} \cdot 10$
    f. $\left(\frac{1}{5} \cdot 5\right)m = \frac{1}{5} \cdot 10$
    g. $1 \cdot m = 2$
    h. $m = 2$

24. Solve $2x + 3 + 4x + 5 = 6$.

25. a. To solve $mx + n = p$ for x, what could you add to both sides?
    b. Solve this equation.

Review

26. If the area of a rectangular plot of land is $\frac{3}{8}$ sq mi and one dimension of the plot is $\frac{1}{2}$ mi, what is the other dimension? *(Lesson 10-3)*

27. If $11x = 1331$, what is x? *(Lesson 10-2)*

28. a. Give the perimeter of this polygon in simplified form. *(Lesson 10-1)*

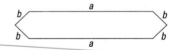

    b. What kind of polygon is this figure? *(Lesson 5-9)*

548

Adapting to Individual Needs

Challenge

Have students solve the following problem:

The weight of object B is $\frac{3}{4}$ the weight of object A. If A is placed on one side of a balance scale, it is balanced by object B and a $\frac{3}{4}$-pound weight. How much does object A weigh? [3 pounds]

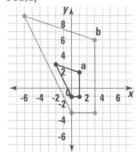

30a,b)

29. A size change has magnitude $\frac{5}{6}$. Is it a contraction or an expansion?
(Lessons 9-7, 9-8) contraction

30. a. Graph the quadrilateral with vertices (1, 2), (-2, 3), (0, -1), and
(1, -1). *(Lesson 8-3)*
b. Graph the image of this quadrilateral under a size change of
magnitude 3. *(Lesson 9-7)*

31. One hat contains 4 slips of paper labeled 0 and 6 slips of paper
labeled 1. A second hat contains 26 slips, each labeled with a
different letter of the alphabet. You draw a 1 from the first hat and
an *R* from the second hat. A person is allowed one guess. What are
the chances that the person will guess what you drew? *(Lesson 9-4)*
3/130

32. Trace the figure below and draw its lines of symmetry. *(Lesson 8-7)*

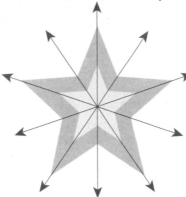

33. On January 1 about 2500 deer were in the White Forest. During the
year, *D* deer died, *B* were born, and *S* were relocated. At the end of
the year about 2300 deer were in the forest. Give an equation
relating all of these numbers and variables. *(Lessons 5-1, 7-1)*
Sample: 2500 − *D* + *B* − *S* = 2300

Exploration

34. a. Find rates for taxi rides near where you live.
b. How far can you travel for $10.00?
Answers will vary.

Follow-up
for Lesson 10-4

Practice
For more questions on SPUR Objectives, use **Lesson Master 10-4A**
(shown on page 547) or **Lesson
Master 10-4B** (shown on pages
548–549).

Assessment
Quiz A quiz covering Lessons 10-1
through 10-4 is provided in the
Assessment Sourcebook.

Group Assessment Have every
student **work with a partner.** Ask
each student to draw balance scales,
or use **Teaching Aid 110,** to illustrate an equation of the form $ax + b$
$= c$ and the steps used to arrive at
the solution. Tell them not to write
the equation or steps on the drawing.
Have partners exchange papers and
write the equation and steps. [Alge-
braic steps match the balance drawings, showing understanding of both
the concrete and symbolic methods
of solving equations.]

Extension
Project Update Project 3, *How
Often Is a Solution to an Equation
an Integer?*, on page 582, relates to
the content of this lesson.

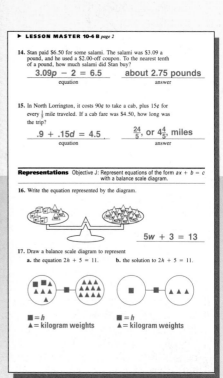

Objectives

A Solve and check equations of the form $ax = b$.

B Solve and check equations of the form $ax + b = c$ when a is negative.

G Find unknowns in real situations leading to equations of the form $ax + b = c$ when a is negative.

Resources

From the *Teacher's Resource File*
■ Lesson Master 10-5A or 10-5B
■ Answer Master 10-5
■ Teaching Aid
   108 Warm-up
   111 Challenge
■ Technology Sourcebook,
   Computer Demonstration 10
   Computer Master 22

Additional Resources
■ Visuals for Teaching Aids 108, 111

Teaching Lesson 10-5

Warm-up

Fill in the blanks.

1. The product of two negative numbers is always a <u>positive</u> number.

2. The product of one positive and one negative number is always a <u>negative</u> number.

3. The reciprocal of a negative number is a <u>negative</u> number.

Food distribution. *Shown here are volunteers from a relief organization as they distribute food to the needy. Food pantries in large cities may give out 1000 lb of food per day. See Question 22.*

Solving $ax = b$ When a Is Negative

The equation $-4x = 3$ is an equation of the form $ax = b$, with $a = -4$ and $b = 3$. This equation can be solved using the Multiplication Property of Equality. But first you must be able to find the reciprocals of negative numbers.

The reciprocal of n is $\frac{1}{n}$, because $n \cdot \frac{1}{n} = 1$. The reciprocal of $-n$ is $-\frac{1}{n}$, because $-n \cdot -\frac{1}{n} = 1$.

For example, the reciprocal of -4 is $-\frac{1}{4}$, or -0.25. The reciprocal of $-\frac{2}{3}$ is $-\frac{3}{2}$, or -1.5.

Activity

a. Enter -5 into a calculator. Press the reciprocal key to see what the calculator shows. $-.2$

b. Repeat part **a** for $-\frac{2}{7}$. -3.5

Example 1

Solve $-4x = 30$.

Solution

Work as you did before, with equations of the form $ax = b$. Multiply both sides by the reciprocal of -4. Because of the Multiplication Property of Equality, this does not change the solution.

$$-\frac{1}{4} \cdot -4x = -\frac{1}{4} \cdot 30$$

▶

Lesson 10-5 Overview

Broad Goals This lesson considers the solution of the same type of equation covered in Lessons 10-2 and 10-4, except that the coefficient of the unknown is now allowed to be negative. You may wish to consider this material as being wholly algebra—not pre-algebra—and mastery of the skill is not expected.

Perspective We find that for many students, this is an intriguing lesson. They

have a technique for solving equations of the forms $ax = b$ or $ax + b = c$ and they are curious to see it work on equations with negative numbers. Emphasize that no new ideas are needed to answer the questions in this lesson.

▶ Because $-\frac{1}{4} \cdot -4 = 1$, the left-hand side simplifies to $1 \cdot x$, which equals x. The numbers on the right-hand side can be multiplied as usual.

$$x = -\frac{30}{4}$$
$$= -7.5$$

Check

Substitute -7.5 for x in the original equation.

$$\text{Does } -4 \cdot -7.5 = 30?$$

Yes, so the solution checks.

When solving equations with negative numbers, you should first decide whether the solution is positive or negative. Is it obvious in Example 1 that x is negative? In Example 2, you should realize before solving that m is positive.

Example 2

Solve $-4.5m = -27$.

Solution

$$-4.5m = -27$$

Multiply both sides by $-\frac{1}{4.5}$, the reciprocal of -4.5.

$$-\frac{1}{4.5} \cdot -4.5m = -\frac{1}{4.5} \cdot -27$$

All that is left is to simplify both sides.

$$1 \cdot m = -\frac{-27}{4.5}$$
$$m = 6$$

Check

Does $-4.5 \cdot 6 = -27$? Yes, it does.

Solving $ax + b = c$ When a Is Negative

In the next example, there is a starting amount from which a certain amount is subtracted at a constant rate. The question leads to a sentence of the form $ax + b = c$ where a is negative.

Example 3

Water in a swimming pool is currently 2.8 meters deep. After opening a valve, the depth of the water will decrease 2 centimeters, or .02 meter, per minute. In how many minutes will the water be 1.5 meters deep?

Solution

Let t be the time (in minutes) the valve is open. The height (in meters) of the water after t minutes is

$$2.8 - .02t.$$

▶

Lesson 10-5 *Solving $ax + b = c$ When a Is Negative* **551**

Notes on Reading

Before students look at the solution to **Example 1**, ask them how they can tell that the solution must be negative. [The product of a positive and a negative number could not be 30, and obviously $x \neq 0$.] Similarly, ask them how they can tell that the solution to **Example 2** must be positive. [The product of two negatives could not be -27.]

One of the difficulties in **Example 3** is that one fact is given in meters and the other in centimeters. Point out that 2 centimeters is changed to .02 meters so that both sides represent meters. Explain that the problem could have been solved in centimeters, in which case the equation to solve would be $280 - 2m = 150$.

Additional Examples

In 1–2, solve and check.
1. $-6q = 5$ $q = -\frac{5}{6}$; $-6 \cdot -\frac{5}{6} = 5$
2. $15 = -2.5s$
   $s = -6$; $-2.5 \cdot -6 = 15$
3. Write an equation whose solution answers the question. Then answer the question.

   A clock is currently 3 seconds behind time and is losing .04 second a day. How long will it be before the clock is a minute behind?
   $-3 - .04d = -60$; 1425 days
4. Solve and check: $25 - \frac{1}{2}y = 30$.
   $y = -10$; $25 - \frac{1}{2}(-10) = 25 + 5$
   $= 30$

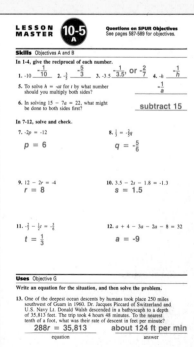

Question 13 Some students might multiply both sides by $\frac{1}{2}$ or $\frac{-1}{2}$ as their first step. This is fine provided they can use the distributive property (Lesson 10-6) correctly. Other students might add $2v$ to both sides first. This is fine, too, but doing either of these steps first will add an extra step. It is important that students see that there are several possibilities for first steps. However, using the methods in this lesson, students would add -8 first so as to isolate the variable on the left side. Allow for diversity if students can solve the equation correctly.

▶ So we need to solve

$$2.8 - .02t = 1.5.$$

First convert the subtraction to addition using the Algebraic Definition of Subtraction.

$$2.8 + -.02t = 1.5$$

Add -2.8 to both sides.

$$-.02t = -2.8 + 1.5$$
$$-.02t = -1.3$$

Now solve the equation as you did Example 2. Multiply both sides by the reciprocal of $-.02$.

$$-\frac{1}{.02} \cdot -.02t = -\frac{1}{.02} \cdot -1.3$$
$$t = \frac{1.3}{.02}$$
$$t = 65$$

In 65 minutes the water will be 1.5 meters deep.

QUESTIONS

Covering the Reading

In 1–6, write the reciprocal of each number.

1. -8 $-\frac{1}{8}$, or -0.125
2. $-\frac{1}{3}$ -3
3. $\frac{9}{5}$ $\frac{5}{9}$, or $0.\overline{5}$
4. -1.2 $-0.8\overline{3}$, or $-\frac{5}{6}$
5. $-x$ $-\frac{1}{x}$
6. $-\frac{1}{x}$ $-x$

7. What results did you get for the Activity in this lesson? part a: -0.2; part b: -3.5
8. To solve $-ax = b$, by what number should you multiply both sides? $-\frac{1}{a}$

In 9–12, solve and check.

9. $-4x = 8$ $x = -2$; $-4(-2) = 8$
10. $-4.5y = -81$ $y = 18$; $-4.5(18) = -81$
11. $1.2 = -1.2B$ $B = -1$; $-1.2(-1) = 1.2$
12. $-\frac{2}{15} = -\frac{5}{3}t$ $t = \frac{2}{25}$; $-\frac{5}{3}\left(\frac{2}{25}\right) = -\frac{2}{15}$
13. a. To solve the equation $8 - 2v = -50$, first ___?___ to both sides. add -8
    b. Solve $8 - 2v = -50$. $v = 29$

In 14 and 15, solve and check.

14. $100 = 160 - 20h$ $h = 3$; $160 - 20(3) = 160 - 60 = 100$
15. $-2c + 5 = 17$ $c = -6$; $-2(-6) + 5 = 12 + 5 = 17$
16. What property enables both sides of an equation to be multiplied by the same number without the solutions being affected? Multiplication Property of Equality
17. Consider the situation of Example 3.
    a. Where does the number $-.02$ come from?
    b. In how many minutes will the water be 1 meter deep? 90 minutes
    c. In how many minutes will the pool be empty? 140 minutes
    a) The water is decreasing at a rate of 2 cm per minute. Converting to meters, 2 cm = 0.02 m.

552

Adapting to Individual Needs

English Language Development
Have students work together taking turns explaining to each other how to solve equations in the form $ax + b = c$ when a is negative.

552

In 18–21, solve and check.

18. $-\frac{2}{3}m + \frac{1}{3} = 11$ $m = -16$

18) Check:
$-\frac{2}{3}(-16) + \frac{1}{3} =$
$\frac{32}{3} + \frac{1}{3} = \frac{33}{3} = 11$

19. $6 - 30n - 18 = 69$ $n = -\frac{27}{10}$, or -2.7

19) Check:
$6 - 30(-2.7) - 18 =$
$6 + 81 - 18 = 87 - 18$
$= 69$

20. $-4 = -4 - 4a$ $a = 0$;
$-4 - 4(0) = -4 - 0 = -4$

21. $2b + 2 + 3b + 3 - 4b - 4 = 5$
$b = 4$

21) Check:
$2(4) + 2 + 3(4) + 3 -$
$4(4) - 4 = 8 + 2 +$
$12 + 3 - 16 - 4 = 25 -$
$20 = 5$

22. A relief agency began the year with 20 tons of food. Suppose 0.3 ton of food was used each day.
   a. After d days, how much food was left? $20 - 0.3d$ tons
   b. After how many days are only 1.5 tons of food left? $61\frac{2}{3}$ days

23. Suppose the original length of a pencil is $7\frac{1}{2}$ inches. Marna thinks she can use the pencil until it is 3 inches long. If she uses $\frac{1}{5}$ inch a day, how many days will it last? $22\frac{1}{2}$ days

24. Is the solution to $5.83146 = -24.987t$ positive or negative?   negative

25. Suppose $xy = z$ and both x and z are negative. What can be said about y? y is positive.

26. Find the integer between -1111 and 1111 that is the solution to the equation $-11x - 111 = -11111$.   1000

27. Solve $9u - 47 = 214$.   *(Lesson 10-4)* $u = 29$

28. a. At Elm Grove High School, 600 students are on at least one of the school teams. This is 30% of all students. How many students are at Elm Grove High?   2000
   b. At Maple Middle School, 30% of the 600 students are enrolled in a computer class. How many students is this?   *(Lessons 2-5, 10-3)*   180

29. Under a size change of magnitude -4, how will a quadrilateral and its image be the same, and how will they be different?   *(Lesson 9-9)*   See below.

30. Solve $0x = 7$.   *(Lesson 9-6)*   There is no solution since any number multiplied by 0 is 0.

31. Suppose a person makes $9.25 an hour and works 28 hours a week. How much does this person earn per year?   *(Lesson 9-5)* $13,468

29) They will have the same shape, but the length of the sides of the image will be 4 times the lengths of the corresponding sides of the preimage, and the image will be rotated 180° from the position of the preimage.

Question 22 Multicultural Connection The largest relief agency in the world is the International Movement of the Red Cross and Red Crescent, with branches in 135 countries. In countries with mostly Christian populations, the branch is called the Red Cross. In Muslim countries the branch is called the Red Crescent. The organization is committed to preventing misery in time of war or peace and to serving all peoples regardless of race, nationality, or religion. In the United States, the American Red Cross has more than 10 million volunteers.

Question 26 This equation can be solved using the methods of this lesson, or in the following way: First solve $y - 111 = -11,111$; then solve $-11x = y$.

Question 28 Error Alert Some students might get the same answer for these two different percent problems because the problems use the same numbers. Point out that **part b** is of the type found in Chapter 2 and **part a** is of the type found in this chapter.

Adapting to Individual Needs

Challenge
Write the following problem on the board, or give students **Teaching Aid 111.**

How many △s would balance the ○ on the last set of scales? The other scales are balanced.[5 △s]

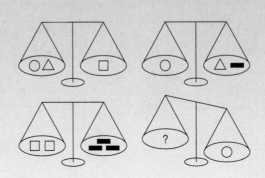

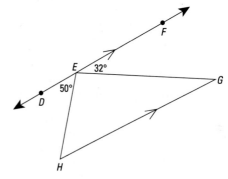

Practice

For more questions on SPUR Objectives, use **Lesson Master 10-5A** (shown on page 551) or **Lesson Master 10-5B** (shown on pages 552–553).

Assessment

Oral Communication Have students **work in groups**. Write the following equations on the board, assigning a different one for each group.

1. $4 - 7m = -52$ $m = 8$
2. $-5n + 17 = 18$ $n = -\frac{1}{5}$
3. $-0.2w + 13.8 = -0.2$ $w = 70$
4. $24.5 = -2.5 - 3z$ $z = -9$
5. $8 = -\frac{2}{3}x + 16$ $x = 12$
6. $-15 = 15 - \frac{1}{2}y$ $y = 60$

Have students work together to solve their assigned equations. Then have each group explain to the class how they solved the equation. [Explanations show understanding of the reasons for each step and include use of the word *reciprocal*. Students should include a check as part of their work.]

Extension

Give students formulas such as $F = \frac{9}{5}C + 32$, $d = rt$, and $P = 2\ell + 2w$, and ask them to solve for one of the other variables. $[C = \frac{5}{9}(F - 32);$

$\frac{d}{t} = r, \frac{d}{r} = t, w = \frac{P - 2\ell}{2},$

$\ell = \frac{P - 2w}{2}]$

32)

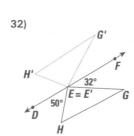

32. Trace the drawing and draw the reflection image of $\triangle EGH$ over $\overleftrightarrow{DF}$. *(Lesson 8-6)*

33. Find the measures of all angles of $\triangle EGH$. *(Lessons 7-7, 7-9)*
$m\angle HEG = 98°$, $m\angle H = 50°$, $m\angle G = 32°$

34. Find $m\angle DBC$ in terms of x. *(Lesson 7-6)* $180° - x$

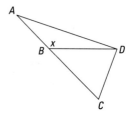

35. The probability that a sum S will appear when two ordinary dice are thrown is $(6 - |S - 7|)/36$. (S will always be an integer from 2 to 12.) Use this formula to calculate the probability that a sum of 3 will appear. *(Lessons 4-6, 5-3)* $\frac{1}{18}$

Exploration

36b) x will be positive when $b < c$ and $a > 0$, or when $b > c$ and $a < 0$.

c) x will be negative when $b > c$ and $a > 0$, or when $b < c$ and $a < 0$.

d) $x = 0$ when $b = c$ and $a \neq 0$.

36. a. Solve for x: $ax + b = c$. (Assume $a \neq 0$.) $x = \frac{c - b}{a}$
   b. Without solving, how can you predict when the solution will be positive?
   c. Without solving, how can you predict when the solution will be negative?
   d. Without solving, how can you predict when the solution will be zero?

Mathematics in art. *The Dutch painter Piet Mondrian specialized in abstract forms using the simple harmonies of straight lines, right angles, and the primary colors. How could the Distributive Property be used to relate the areas of some of the rectangles in his painting above?*

Suppose you need to find the total area of these rectangles.

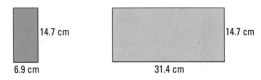

One obvious way is to find $6.9 \cdot 14.7$ and $31.4 \cdot 14.7$. Then add the two products.

❶ **Activity 1**

Do these calculations to find the total area. 563.01 cm²

Another way to find the area involves a simpler addition and only one multiplication. Join the rectangles.

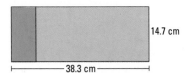

One dimension is still 14.7 cm. The other dimension is 6.9 cm + 31.4 cm, or 38.3 cm. Multiplying the two dimensions, 14.7 cm and 38.3 cm, gives the area.

Lesson 10-6 *The Distributive Property* **555**

Lesson 10-6

Objectives
C Apply the Distributive Property to simplify expressions.
F Recognize and use the Distributive Property.
K Represent the Distributive Property by areas of rectangles.

Resources
From the *Teacher's Resource File*
■ Lesson Master 10-6A or 10-6B
■ Answer Master 10-6
■ Teaching Aid 108: Warm-up

Additional Resources
■ Visual for Teaching Aid 108

Teaching 10-6
Lesson

Warm-up
Diagnostic Last week, Lia worked 6 hours, Maria, 10 hours, and Jason, 9 hours. Each earned $4.40 an hour. What is the total amount they earned? Explain how you found your answer. $110; (6 × $4.40) + (10 × $4.40) + (9 × $4.40) or (6 + 10 + 9) × $4.40; equality of methods is due to the Distributive Property)

Notes on Reading
❶ Just as the Distributive Property of Multiplication over Addition combines multiplication and addition, the rectangle display of this property combines area, a model for multiplication, and putting together lengths, a model for addition.

Lesson 10-6 Overview

Broad Goals This lesson formally introduces the two forms $ax + bx = (a + b)x$ and $x(a + b) = ax + bx$ of the Distributive Property of Multiplication over Addition, and the corresponding forms for the Distributive Property of Multiplication over Subtraction.

Perspective All forms of the Distributive Property derive from either one of the basic properties $ax + bx = (a + b)x$ and $x(a + b) = xa + xb$. In the first, one begins

with an addition and converts it to a multiplication. In the second, one begins with a multiplication and converts it to an addition.

There are additional differences between these two forms: the multiplier appears on a different side and there are different common names given to the forms. Converting $ax + bx$ to $(a + b)x$ is called *adding like terms*. Converting $x(a + b)$ to $xa + xb$ is *multiplying the binomial by the monomial*

factor. Although the only mathematical difference between these forms is the Commutative Property of Multiplication, the differences in appearance cause students to consider these as two entirely different properties. The two forms of the Distributive Property of Multiplication over Subtraction are easy once the addition forms are known.

Because many students find the Distributive Property difficult, discuss the reading and the examples in detail. The Area Model provides a good visual interpretation of distributivity, and the examples indicate the utility of the Distributive Property in mental arithmetic.

As you review each example, have students make up similar situations. You might want to have students **work in groups** of four, with each student making up an example and then answering the examples of the other three students.

❷ The Distributive Property of Multiplication over Subtraction follows naturally because of the inverse relationship between addition and subtraction. You may prefer to have students convert the subtractions to addition and not consider this as a separate property.

❸ The rectangle display of the Distributive Property of Multiplication over Subtraction combines the Area Model for Multiplication and the Take-Away Model for Subtraction.

Activity 2

Find 38.3 × 14.7. Compare your answer to what you found in Activity 1.
563.01; It is equal to the area found in Activity 1.

Distributing Multiplication over Addition

The above activities indicate that

$$6.9 \cdot 14.7 + 31.4 \cdot 14.7 = (6.9 + 31.4) \cdot 14.7.$$

Since multiplication is commutative and associative, the 14.7 could be at the left of each multiplication. Thus the rectangles also picture

$$14.7 \cdot 6.9 + 14.7 \cdot 31.4 = 14.7(6.9 + 31.4).$$

The general patterns are known as the *Distributive Property of Multiplication over Addition.*

> **The Distributive Property of Multiplication over Addition**
> For any numbers *a*, *b*, and *x*,
>
> $$ax + bx = (a + b)x$$
> $$\text{and } x(a + b) = xa + xb.$$

The Distributive Property gets its name because it says that multiplications "distributed" over several quantities can be combined into one multiplication. In Example 1 below, the 4 is distributed over 1.75 and 0.29 as a common factor. The two multiplications can be written as one.

Example 1

April bought 4 greeting cards at $1.75 each and 4 stamps at $0.29 each. What was the total cost?

Solution

By the Distributive Property, $a \cdot x + b \cdot x = (a + b)x$.

$$\$1.75 \cdot 4 + \$0.29 \cdot 4 = (\$1.75 + \$0.29)4$$
$$= (\$2.04) \cdot 4$$
$$= \$8.16$$

The total cost was $8.16.

Using the Distributive Property to Calculate in Your Head

In Example 2, the distributive property is used to multiply 18 and 10.50. It enables you to do the calculation in your head.

Optional Activities

Activity 1 You might want to use this activity after discussing **Examples 1–4.** Read each multiplication aloud and ask students to compute mentally. When a correct answer has been given for each exercise, ask volunteers to explain how the Distributive Property can be used in each computation.

1. 8 · 999 [7992; 8 · (1000 − 1) = (8 · 1000) − (8 · 1)]

2. 16 · 1003 [16,048; 16 · (1000 + 3) = (16 · 1000) + (16 · 3)]

3. 5 · 88 [440; 5 · (80 + 8) = (5 · 80) + (5 · 8)]

4. 9 · 65 [585; 9 · (60 + 5) = (9 · 60) + (9 · 5)]

5. 15 · 12 [180; 15 · (10 + 2) = (15 · 10) + (15 · 2)]

Example 2

A store owner bought 18 blouses for $10.50 each. Mentally calculate the total cost to the store owner.

Solution

Think of 10.50 as 10 and 0.50. Here are the mental steps.

$$18 \cdot 10.50 = 18(10 + 0.50)$$
$$= 18 \cdot 10 + 18 \cdot 0.50$$
$$= 180 + 9$$
$$= 189$$

The total cost to the store owner was $189.

Distributing Multiplication over Subtraction

There is also a Distributive Property of Multiplication over Subtraction. You may have already used it in doing mental arithmetic.

> **The Distributive Property of Multiplication over Subtraction**
> For any numbers *a*, *b*, and *x*,
> $$ax - bx = (a - b)x.$$
> $$\text{and } x(a - b) = xa - xb.$$

Example 3

What will 7 pairs of socks at $3.98 a pair cost? Do this in your head.

Solution

Think of 3.98 as 4 − 0.02. $7 \cdot 3.98 = 7(4 - 0.02)$
Apply the Distributive Property of $= 7 \cdot 4 - 7 \cdot 0.02$
Multiplication over Subtraction.
These multiplications can be done mentally. $= 28 - 0.14$
You are taking 14¢ from 28 dollars. $= 27.86$

Seven pairs of socks will cost $27.86.

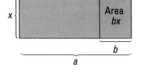

At the left is an area picture of the Distributive Property of Multiplication over Subtraction. What is the area of the blue rectangle?

Answer 1: The dimensions of the blue rectangle are *x* and *a* − *b*. So its area is $(a - b)x$.

Answer 2: The area of the whole figure is *ax*. The area of the orange rectangle is *bx*. So the area of the blue rectangle is $ax - bx$.

Since the answers must be equal, $(a - b)x = ax - bx$.

Additional Examples

1. Find the total cost of 5 gifts at $4.25 each and 5 cards at $1.25 each. $5 \cdot 4.25 + 5 \cdot 1.25 = 5 \cdot (4.25 + 1.25)$; $27.50

2. The cost of a book is $6.02, including tax. Mentally calculate the total cost of 12 of these books. $12 \cdot 6.02 = 12 \cdot 6 + 12 \cdot .02$; $72.24

3. Find the product $8 \cdot 5.96$ in your head. $8 \cdot 5.96 = 8(6 - .04) = 8 \cdot 6 - 8 \cdot 0.04$; 47.68

4. Multiply.
   a. $-5(3p - 4)$ $-15p + 20$
   b. $\frac{1}{2}(12 + 6f - 9g)$
   $6 + 3f - 4.5g$

5. Simplify and check.
   a. $5a + 2.4a$ $7.4a$; let $a = 3$;
   $5 \cdot 3 + 2.4 \cdot 3 = 15 + 7.2 = 22.2 = 7.4 \cdot 3$
   b. $5a - 2.4a$ $2.6a$; let $a = 4$:
   $5 \cdot 4 - 2.4 \cdot 4 = 20 - 9.6 = 10.4 = 2.6 \cdot 4$
   c. $6b - 4b + 8 - 2$ $2b + 6$;
   let $b = 2$: $6 \cdot 2 - 4 \cdot 2 + 8 - 2 = 12 - 8 + 8 - 2 = 10$, and
   $2 \cdot 2 + 6 = 4 + 6 = 10$

6. Use diagrams of rectangles to illustrate $ax + bx = (a + b)x$. Begin with two rectangles.

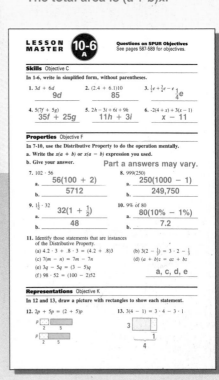

   Sum of areas is $ax + bx$. Put the rectangles together.

   The total area is $(a + b)x$.

Optional Activities

Activity 2 You may want to show students an alternative method to solve equations of the form $ax + b = c$. Give students the following equation and the steps that can be used to solve it.

$$18 - 3x = 12$$
$$\tfrac{1}{3}(18 - 3x) = \tfrac{1}{3} \cdot 12$$
$$6 - x = 4$$
$$-x = -2$$
$$x = 2$$

Discuss the reasons for multiplying by one third. Ask students what properties are used in the second step. [Distributive Property and Multiplication Property of Equality] Solve several more equations, and then have students **work in groups** to solve the following equations using the Distributive Property.

1. $15 - 5x = 75$ $[x = -12]$
2. $2.8 = 3.6 - .2m$ $[m = 4]$
3. $\tfrac{3}{4}y - 6 = \tfrac{1}{8}$ $[y = 8\tfrac{1}{6}]$

LESSON MASTER 10-6 A

Questions on SPUR Objectives
See pages 587-589 for objectives.

Skills Objective C
In 1-6, write in simplified form, without parentheses.

1. $3d + 6d$ 9d
2. $(2.4 + 6.1)10$ 85
3. $\frac{1}{2}e + \frac{3}{4}e - e$ $\frac{1}{4}e$
4. $5(7f + 5g)$ $35f + 25g$
5. $2h - 3i + 6i + 9h$ $11h + 3i$
6. $-2(4 + x) + 3(x - 1)$ $x - 11$

Properties Objective F
In 7-10, use the Distributive Property to do the operation mentally.
a. Write the $x(a + b)$ or $x(a - b)$ expression you used.
b. Give your answer.   Part a answers may vary.

7. $102 \cdot 56$ a. $56(100 + 2)$ b. 5712
8. $999(250)$ a. $250(1000 - 1)$ b. $249,750$
9. $1\frac{1}{2} \cdot 32$ a. $32(1 + \frac{1}{2})$ b. 48
10. 9% of 80 a. $80(10\% - 1\%)$ b. 7.2

11. Identify those statements that are instances of the Distributive Property.
   (a) $4.2 \cdot 3 + .8 \cdot 3 = (4.2 + .8)3$
   (b) $3(2 - \frac{1}{3}) = 3 \cdot 2 - \frac{1}{3}$
   (c) $7(m - n) = 7m - 7n$
   (d) $(a + b)z = az + bz$
   (e) $3q - 5q = (3 - 5)q$
   (f) $98 \cdot 52 = (100 - 2)52$
   a, c, d, e

Representations Objective K
In 12 and 13, draw a picture with rectangles to show each statement.
12. $2p + 5p = (2 + 5)p$
13. $3(4 - 1) = 3 \cdot 4 - 3 \cdot 1$

Notes on Questions

Question 3 Ask students for their explanations before finding out which person they think did it correctly. The explanation carries more weight when students disagree.

Question 8 Bravo to a student who writes $8(x + y)$. You could say that this student has seen that 8 is a like term! Point out that in algebra this change from an addition situation to a multiplication is called *factoring*.

Questions 10–13 Checking these products is conceptually important in that students can see how the Distributive Property works. The checks also provide a review of order of operations.

Question 27 Do not let students be intimidated by the size of the second factor. Suggest that they write out the problem for multiplication first, 732 times $(1,000,000,000,000,000 - 1)$, and then evaluate.

Distributing Multiplication over Addition and Subtraction

The distributive properties over addition and subtraction can be combined.

Example 4

Multiply $3(5x + y - 8)$.

Solution

Use the distributive properties.
$$3(5x + y - 8) = 3 \cdot (5x) + 3 \cdot y - 3 \cdot 8$$
$$= 15x + 3y - 24$$

Check

Substitute a different number for each variable. We use $x = 2$ and $y = 4$. The values for the given expression and the answer should be the same.

Given expression: $3(5x + y - 8) = 3(5 \cdot 2 + 4 - 8) =$
$$3(10 + 4 - 8) = 3(6) = 18$$
Answer: $15x + 3y - 24 = 15 \cdot 2 + 3 \cdot 4 - 24 =$
$$30 + 12 - 24 = 18$$

Since the values are equal, the answer checks.

---

2) The total area of the rectangles is $3x + 5x$. Put them together and the area is $(3 + 5)x$.

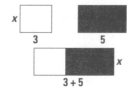

10) Sample: use $x = 2$,
$50(2 + 4) = 50 \cdot 6 = 300$, $50(2) + 200 = 100 + 200 = 300$

11) Sample: use $n = 2$,
$2(6 + 7(2)) = 2(6 + 14) = 2(20) = 40$, $12 + 14(2) = 12 + 28 = 40$

12) Sample: use $a = 4$, $b = 2$, $c = 3$, $4(2 + 2(3)) = 4(2 + 6) = 32$, $4(2) + 2(4)(3) = 8 + 24 = 32$

13) Sample: use $t = 2$, $u = 3$, $5(100 + 2 + 3) = 5(105) = 525$, $500 + 5(2) + 5(3) = 500 + 10 + 15 = 525$

15) Sample:

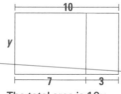

The total area is $10y$. Subtract $3y$ and the remaining part has area $7y$.

558

QUESTIONS

Covering the Reading

1. a. What is the total area of these rectangles? **70 w**

b. How can you check your answer to part **a**? Sample: Put the rectangles together to form one large rectangle and find the area.

2. Draw a picture with rectangles to show that $3x + 5x = (3 + 5)x$. See above left.

3. Fred believes that $6m - m = 5m$. Nell believes that $6m - m = 6$. Who is correct and how can you tell? Fred; $6m - m = 6 \cdot m - 1 \cdot m = (6 - 1)m = 5m$. You can check by substitution.

In 4–9, combine like terms.

4. $10 \cdot 3.95 + 6 \cdot 3.95$ **63.2**   **5.** $4x + 6x$ **10x**

6. $4y + 6y + 8$ **10y + 8**   **7.** $2.4v + 3.5v + v$ **6.9v**

8. $8x + 8y$ **8x + 8y**   **9.** $11A + 11B$ **11A + 11B**

In 10–13, multiply and check. See check at the left.

10. $50(x + 4)$ **50x + 200**   **11.** $2(6 + 7n)$ **12 + 14n**

12. $a(b + 2c)$ **ab + 2ac**   **13.** $5(100 + t + u)$ **500 + 5t + 5u**

14. Give an instance of the Distributive Property of Multiplication over Subtraction. Sample: $15x - 3x = (15 - 3)x = 12x$

15. Draw a picture with rectangles to show that $10y - 3y = 7y$.

Adapting to Individual Needs

Extra Help
If students have trouble seeing how one form is derived from the other when using the Distributive Property, write the following numerical example on the board.

$$3(5 + 6) = 3 \cdot 5 + 3 \cdot 6$$

Ask students to compute both sides using the standard order of operations to see that the results are the same. Have a volunteer write the steps on the board as follows:

$$3(5 + 6) = 3 \cdot 5 + 3 \cdot 6$$
$$3 \cdot 11 = 15 + 18$$
$$33 = 33$$

In 16 and 17, show how you can apply the Distributive Property of Multiplication over Subtraction to find the total cost in your head.

16. You buy three sweaters at $29.95 each. $3(30 - 0.05) = 90 - 0.15 = 89.85$

17. You purchase 8 tapes at $8.99 each. $8(9 - 0.01) = 72 - 0.08 = 71.92$

In 18–21, use the Distributive Property to rewrite the expression.

18. $5x - 2x$ $(5 - 2)x = 3x$

19. $12 \cdot \$3.75 - 2 \cdot \$3.75$
$10 \cdot \$3.75 = \$37.50$

20. $a(b - c)$ $ab - ac$

21. $4(a - 5b + 3c)$ $4a - 20b + 12c$

Applying the Mathematics

22. Use a calculator to verify that

$$3.29(853 + 268) = 3.29 \cdot 853 + 3.29 \cdot 268.$$

As you evaluate each side, write down the key sequence you use and the final display. left: 3.29 ⊗ ⓘ 853 ⊕ 268 ⓘ ⊜ ③688.09;
right: 3.29 ⊗ 853 ⊕ 3.29 ⊗ 268 ⊜ ③688.09

23. A hamburger costs x cents. Dave bought 3 hamburgers. Sue bought 2. How much did they spend altogether? $3x + 2x$, or $5x$ cents

24. Suppose an acre of land will yield B bushels of wheat. The McAllisters planted 400 acres. Mr. Padilla planted 120 acres. Mrs. Smith planted 240 acres. How many bushels of wheat can the three expect to harvest altogether? $760B$ bushels

In 25 and 26, apply the Distributive Properties.

25. $a(a + a^2)$ $a^2 + a^3$

26. $3x(3y - 3z)$ $9xy - 9xz$

27. Multiply 732 by 999,999,999,999,999. $732 \cdot 10^{15} - 732 \cdot 1 =$
27) $732(1,000,000,000,000,000 - 1) =$
$732,000,000,000,000,000 - 732 = 731,999,999,999,999,268$

28. Phil, Gil, and Will each bought a CD player costing t dollars, an amplifier costing a dollars, and speakers costing s dollars. How much did they spend altogether? $3(t + a + s)$ or $3t + 3a + 3s$ dollars

In 29 and 30, apply the Distributive Properties. Then simplify if possible.

29. $-2(3 + x) + 5(0.4x)$ -6

30. $\frac{1}{3}(3m + n) + \frac{1}{3}(3m - n)$ $2m$

Review

In 31–33, solve. *(Lessons 10-2, 10-5)*

31. $14x = 42$ $x = 3$

32. $5y - 3 = 20$
$y = \frac{23}{5}$ or 4.6

33. $6 - 4y = 20$ $y = -\frac{7}{2}$
or -3.5

34. A swimming pool has a depth of $2\frac{1}{2}$ ft now. It is being filled at a rate of $\frac{1}{20}$ ft per minute.
  a. What will its depth be in m minutes? *(Lesson 6-5)* $\left(\frac{5}{2} + \frac{1}{20}m\right)$ ft
  b. When will it be 9 feet deep? *(Lesson 10-4)*
  130 minutes

Lesson 10-6 *The Distributive Property* **559**

Combining the work.
Combines (com'bines) are machines used to cut and thresh wheat. Teams of people with combines travel from Texas to Canada to harvest the wheat as it ripens.

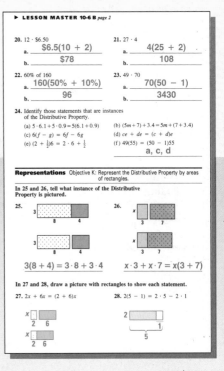

▶ **LESSON MASTER 10-6 B** *page 2*

20. $12 \cdot \$6.50$
  a. $\$6.5(10 + 2)$
  b. $\$78$

21. $27 \cdot 4$
  a. $4(25 + 2)$
  b. 108

22. 60% of 160
  a. $160(50\% + 10\%)$
  b. 96

23. $49 \cdot 70$
  a. $70(50 - 1)$
  b. 3430

24. Identify those statements that are instances of the Distributive Property.
  (a) $5 \cdot 6.1 + 5 \cdot 0.9 = 5(6.1 + 0.9)$ (b) $(5m + 7) + 3.4 = 5m + (7 + 3.4)$
  (c) $6(f - g) = 6f - 6g$ (d) $ce + de = (c + d)e$
  (e) $(2 + \frac{1}{2})6 = 2 \cdot 6 + \frac{1}{2}$ (f) $49(55) = (50 - 1)55$
  a, c, d

Representations Objective K: Represent the Distributive Property by areas of rectangles.

In 25 and 26, tell what instance of the Distributive Property is pictured.

25.   **26.**

$3(8 + 4) = 3 \cdot 8 + 3 \cdot 4$ $x \cdot 3 + x \cdot 7 = x(3 + 7)$

In 27 and 28, draw a picture with rectangles to show each statement.

27. $2x + 6x = (2 + 6)x$ **28.** $2(5 - 1) = 2 \cdot 5 - 2 \cdot 1$

Adapting to Individual Needs

English Language Development
Have students add the Distributive Property to the terms they have defined on index cards. If some need help understanding the word *distributive*, demonstrate by holding two books and say, "These books are for . . ." and name two students. Then say, "I will distribute the books to these two students" and give each one a book.

Challenge
Each of the following expressions can easily be evaluated mentally. Have students discover a method and make up similar problems.

1. $(1993 + 1993) \cdot 50$
  $[1993 \cdot 2 \cdot 50 = 1993 \cdot 100 = 199,300]$

2. $(387 + 387 + 387 + 387) \cdot 25$
  $[387 \cdot 4 \cdot 25 = 387 \cdot 100 = 38,700]$

Notes on Questions

Question 38 This question anticipates the use of the Distributive Property to multiply binomials, an important property that students encounter in the study of algebra: $(a + b)(c + d) = (a + b)c + (a + b)d = ac + bc + ad + bd$.

Follow-up 10-6
for Lesson

Practice
For more questions on SPUR Objectives, use **Lesson Master 10-6A** (shown on page 556) or **Lesson Master 10-6B** (shown on pages 558–559).

Assessment
Oral Communication Ask students to explain how they could use the Distributive Property to mentally find the amount of money they should leave as a tip for restaurant service. Remind them that approximately 15% of a restaurant bill is often left as a tip. Explain that the amount of the bill should be rounded up to the nearest dollar. [Explanation reveals understanding of the Distributive Property by showing that multiplying by 15% is the same as multiplying by 10% and then by 5% and adding the two amounts together.]

Extension
Have students evaluate each expression when $a = 24$, $b = 4$, $c = 2$.
1. $a \div (b + c)$ 4
2. $(a \div b) + (a \div c)$ 18
3. $a + (b \cdot c)$ 32
4. $(a + b) \cdot (a + c)$ 728
Ask students to compare their answers for 1 and 2, and for 3 and 4, before answering questions 5 and 6.
5. Is division distributive over addition? Explain. **No; there are numbers for which $a \div (b + c) \neq (a \div b) + (a \div c)$.**
6. Is addition distributive over multiplication? **No; there are numbers for which $a + b \cdot c \neq (a + b) \cdot (a + c)$.**

Project Update Project 6, *Different Methods of Multiplication*, on page 583, relates to the content of this lesson.

---

35. **a.** What is the reciprocal of $\frac{6}{7}$? *(Lesson 9-3)* $\frac{7}{6}$
    b. Solve $\frac{6}{7}x = 84$. *(Lesson 10-2)* $x = 98$

36. Consider triangle *ABC*.

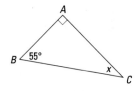

    a. What is the value of x? 35°
    b. How many angles of $\triangle ABC$ are acute? two
    c. How many angles of $\triangle ABC$ are obtuse? *(Lessons 3-7, 7-9)* none

---

Exploration

37. Here is a worked-out multiplication of 372×681.

    37) This process uses the fact that
    $372 \cdot 681 = (2 + 70 + 300) \cdot 681 =$
    $2 \cdot 681 + 70 \cdot 681 + 300 \cdot 681 =$
    $1362 + 47670 + 204300 =$
    253332.

    $$\begin{array}{r} 681 \\ \times\ 372 \\ \hline 1362 \\ 4767 \\ 2043 \\ \hline 253332 \end{array}$$

    Explain how this process is an application of the Distributive Property of Multiplication over Addition.

38. One way to express the area of the entire figure is $(a + b)(c + d)$. What is another expression for the area? Sample: $ac + ad + bc + bd$

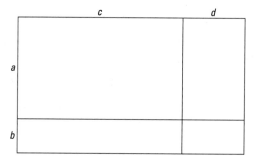

Setting Up Lesson 10-7
Materials Students will need gift boxes of various sizes and rulers for the *Assessment* in Lesson 10-7.

Lesson **10-7**

Objectives

H Find the surface area of a rectangular solid in real contexts.

Resources

From the **Teacher's Resource File**
■ Lesson Master 10-7A or 10-7B
■ Answer Master 10-7
■ Assessment Sourcebook: Quiz for Lessons 10-5 through 10-7
■ Teaching Aids
  86 Graph Paper
  109 Warm-up
  112 Surface Area of a Box

Additional Resources
■ Visuals for Teaching Aids 86, 109, 112
■ Gift boxes of various sizes, inch rulers or Geometry Templates (Assessment)

From the grape vine. *These claymation raisins are used by the California Raisin Advisory Board to promote consumption of raisins. California, the only state producing raisins commercially, is the world's leading raisin-grape producer.*

Each face of the raisin box at the right is a rectangle. (In a perspective drawing, you view some faces at an angle. So some of the faces may not seem to be rectangles.)

The surface of this raisin box can be constructed by cutting a pattern out of a flat piece of cardboard. The pattern is called a **net** for the 3-dimensional surface. The construction is pictured below. The dashed segments show where folds are made. The folds become the edges of the box. (For a real box, some overlap is needed. But the same idea is used.)

the net   after one fold

A rectangular solid consists of a box and all points inside it. The **surface area** of a rectangular solid is the sum of the areas of its faces. The raisin box has six faces: top, bottom, right, left, front, and back. The surface area tells you how much cardboard is needed to make the box.

Lesson 10-7 *The Surface Area of a Box* **561**

Warm-up

Find the area of each figure.

1. 6 cm
6 cm
36 cm²

2. 3.75 mm
8.5 mm
31.875 mm²

3. $5\frac{1}{2}$ in.
$2\frac{1}{4}$ in.
$12\frac{3}{8}$ sq. in.

4. 10 mm
5 mm
5 mm
5 mm
75 mm²

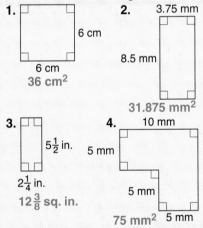

Lesson 10-7 Overview

Broad Goals The lesson discusses how to calculate the total surface area of a rectangular solid (box).

Perspective Lesson 9-2 discussed the volume of a rectangular solid as the three-dimensional analog of the Area Model for Multiplication. We did not introduce surface area earlier because its computation is more involved than either area or volume. Students are more likely to understand the

difference between surface area and volume and to successfully complete the multistep calculation when these ideas are separated as they are here.

Students will particularly be more likely to see the difference if actual boxes are unfolded for demonstration purposes. In teaching this lesson and the next, differentiate between the two as often as possible: surface area is wrapping; volume is filling.

Flatten an actual box. (In advance, you may wish to cut off the overlapping parts of the top and bottom.) Once the box is flattened, there is no volume, and the idea of surface area is clear.

❶ To help students calculate surface area, encourage them to make a chart like the one on this page. In doing so, students will need to name the faces of the solid, something they may never have done before. You can use **Teaching Aid 112** when discussing this lesson.

We use a raisin box in the lesson because it is small and because one for each student can be purchased at low cost. For demonstration, however, a cereal box works better.

You may wish to do this lesson more algebraically. If the dimensions of the box are *L*, *W*, and *H*, then the areas of the six faces are *LW, LH, WH, LW, LH,* and *WH*. The sum is, by repeated addition, 2*LW* + 2*LH* + 2*WH*, or using the Distributive Property, 2*(LW + LH + WH)*.

Have students record the results of the *Activity* on page 562 for use with **Question 4** on page 563.

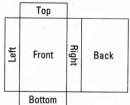

❶ **Activity**

Find the surface area of a miniature raisin box

Step 1 Take the raisins out and eat them (if allowed), or put them away.

Step 2 Flatten the box by cutting along edges.

Step 3 Copy and complete the chart below. Use your ruler to measure edges to the nearest millimeter.

Face	Length (mm)	Width (mm)	Area (mm²)
Left			
Right			
Front			
Back			
Top			
Bottom			

Step 4 Adding the six areas gives the total surface area. Do this.

Example

Find the surface area of a rectangular solid 10 in. high, 4 in. wide, and 3 in. deep.

Solution

First, draw a picture. You may want to separate the faces as shown here.

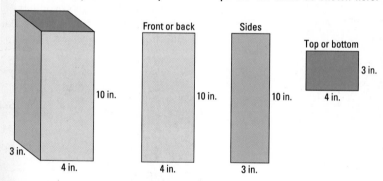

Now just add the areas of the faces. The surface area is

$$10 \cdot 4 + 10 \cdot 4 + 10 \cdot 3 + 10 \cdot 3 + 3 \cdot 4 + 3 \cdot 4$$
$$= 40 + 40 + 30 + 30 + 12 + 12$$
$$= 164 \text{ square inches}$$

The surface area is 164 square inches.

Optional Activities

After students have read the lesson, you might want to have them **work in groups** to solve this problem.

A gallon of paint usually covers about 1000 square feet. A room 10 ft long, 12 ft wide, and 10 ft high is being painted. Ignoring doors and windows, will a half gallon of paint be enough? (Note: It is not necessary to paint the floor.) [560 sq ft; a half gallon is not enough.]

6a)

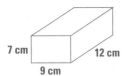

7 cm   12 cm
9 cm

b)

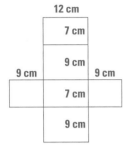

12 cm
7 cm
9 cm   9 cm   9 cm
7 cm
9 cm

7a)

3"
3"   3"

b) Sample:

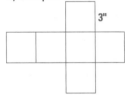

3"

QUESTIONS

Covering the Reading

1. A raisin box and all points inside it is an example of a figure called a __?__. **rectangular solid**

2. What is the surface area of a solid? **the sum of the areas of its faces**

3. How many faces does a rectangular solid have? **6**

4. Give the surface area, to the nearest square millimeter, that you found for the miniature raisin box in the Activity.
Answers will vary.

5. What is a net for a 3-dimensional figure? **a 2-dimensional pattern which can be folded into that figure**

In 6 and 7, dimensions for a box are given.
a. Make a sketch of the box.
b. Draw a net for the box.
c. Find the surface area of the box.

6. dimensions 9 cm, 12 cm, and 7 cm a,b) See left.   c) 510 cm²

7. dimensions 3", 3", and 3" a,b) See left.   c) 54 square inches

Applying the Mathematics

8. A box is pictured.

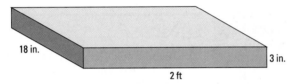

18 in.
3 in.
2 ft

a. Find its surface area in square inches. **1116 square inches**
b. Find its volume in cubic inches. **1296 cubic inches**

9. A rectangular solid has length ℓ, width w, and height h.
a. What is its volume? **ℓwh**
b. What is its surface area? **$2\,\ell w + 2\,\ell h + 2\,hw$**

10. A shirt to be given as a gift is put into a box. The dimensions of the box are 14", 9", and 2.5". What is the least amount of wrapping paper needed to wrap the gift? (You are allowed to use a lot of tape.) **367 sq inches**

11. Refer to the Example in this lesson. Suppose that the surface of the box is made from a rectangular sheet of cardboard.
a. What are the smallest dimensions the cardboard could have?
b. How much material will be wasted?
a) **16 in. by 14 in.** b) **60 sq in.**

12. Use a sheet of notebook paper, a ruler, tape, and scissors to construct a box. You may use any dimensions you wish.
Boxes will vary.

Lesson 10-7   *The Surface Area of a Box*   **563**

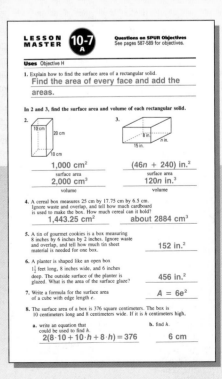

Question 14 Note that this question does not require any folding. It is most easily done in its given unfolded state.

Question 16 Multicultural Connection Years ago, a day for honoring mothers was observed in England. Slavic and other people also observed similar days. In 1907 Anna Jarvis began a campaign for a nationwide observance of Mother's Day in the United States. She chose the second Sunday in May as Mother's Day, and she also began the custom of wearing a carnation. In 1915 President Woodrow Wilson authorized Mother's Day as an annual national observance.

Question 28 This is an appropriate problem to be done **in groups**. Few students will come up with all the patterns. The joint effort will usually encourage students to attack this problem more vigorously. You may have to explain why two different

looking nets, for example, [net]

and [net], are the same net.

They are reflection images of each other and so are congruent.

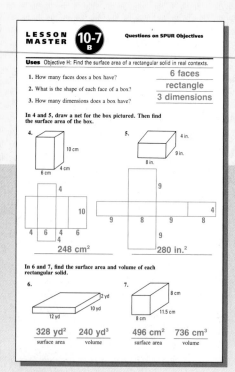

13. Patricia Tern wanted to make a rectangular box out of cardboard. She drew the following net. It is not correct. Draw a corrected net by moving one rectangle. **Move one of the top rectangles to the bottom.**

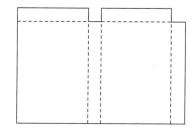

14. A net for a cube is shown below. All sides of the squares have length 5. What is the surface area of the cube? **150 square units**

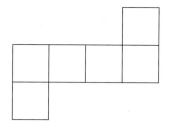

15. The bottom of a box has dimensions 24 cm and 20 cm. The box is 10 cm high and has no top. What is the surface area of the box? **1360 cm²**

Review

16. Bill bought a dozen roses for Mother's Day at $2.50 each and a dozen carnations at $.50 each. Explain how the total amount he spent can be calculated with one multiplication. *(Lesson 10-6)*
Apply the Distributive Property to get 12(2.50 + .50), and simplify.

In 17–19, simplify. *(Lessons 10-1, 10-6)*

17. $3x + 8x$ **11x**

18. $2y + y - 5y$ **-2y**

19. $8m + 2n - 20m - n$ **-12m + n**

20. Mel weighs 180 lb. If he goes on a diet and loses 2 lb every thirty days, how long will it take him to reach 150 lb? *(Lesson 10-5)* **450 days**

21. Solve $3x - x = 1$. *(Lesson 10-5)* $x = \frac{1}{2}$

22. Solve for y: $x - y = 34$. *(Lesson 7-4)* $y = x - 34$

23. Simplify $\frac{1}{6} - \frac{3}{18} - \frac{2}{3} + \frac{5}{9}$. *(Lesson 7-2)* $-\frac{1}{9}$

24. What is the perimeter of a rectangle with length 40 and width 60? *(Lesson 5-10)* **200 units**

25. What property guarantees that $x + 45$ equals $45 + x$? *(Lesson 5-7)*
Commutative Property of Addition

Adapting to Individual Needs

English Language Development
The use of the term *face* in this lesson could be confusing for some students. Demonstrate by touching each side of a box and saying, "This is a *face*." Then explain that *surface* means all of the faces combined. Refer to diagrams and the chart on page 562 to reinforce this fact.

26. Let *n* be a number. Translate into mathematics.
  a. 2 less than a number *n* − 2
  b. 2 is less than a number. 2 < *n*
  c. 2 less a number *(Lesson 4-3)* 2 − *n*

27. What is the volume of the cube illustrated in Question 14?
  (Lesson 3-9) **125 cubic units**

Exploration

28. In Question 14 a net was given for a cube. Here is a different net. (Nets are different if they are not congruent.)

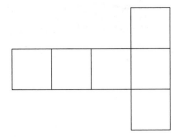

Draw all possible different nets for a cube.

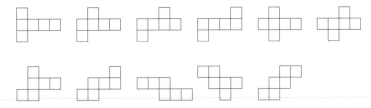

Adapting to Individual Needs

Challenge
Have students solve the following problems:
1. Centimeter cubes are arranged on a wooden tabletop to make the rectangular solid at the right. How many cubes have no visible faces? [640 cubes]
2. Suppose the solid is built on a glass table. How many cubes have no visible faces? [512 cubes]

6 cm
10 cm
18 cm

Follow-up 10-7
for Lesson

Practice
For more questions on SPUR objectives, use **Lesson Master 10-7A** (shown on page 563) or **Lesson Master 10-7B** (shown on pages 564–565).

Assessment
Quiz A quiz covering Lessons 10-5 through 10-7 is provided in the *Assessment Sourcebook.*

Group Assessment
Materials: gift boxes of various sizes, rulers or Geometry Templates

Have students **work in groups**. Give each group a gift box. Tell students that a craft project requires that the box be covered with felt on all sides except the bottom, and there should be no overlap. Their job is to find the amount of felt needed. [Correct answers show understanding of surface area of a box.]

Extension
Ask students to write an expression for the surface area of a cube with side *s*. **6*s*²**

Project Update Project 4, *Surface Areas and Volumes of Boxes,* on page 583, relates to the content of this lesson.

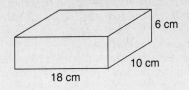

► **LESSON MASTER 10-7 B** *page 2*

8. A rectangular solid is 5 in. wide, 6 in. long, and *h* in. high. What is its surface area? **(22*h* + 60) in.²**

9. The length of the edge of a cube is *e* units.
  a. What is the surface area of the cube? **6*e*² square units**
  b. What is the volume of the cube? **e³ cubic units**

10. A cracker tin is a box measuring 12 cm by 12 cm by 24 cm. Ignore waste and overlap and tell how much tin sheet material is needed for one box. **1,440 cm²**

11. A redwood planter is shaped like an open box 30 inches long, 8 inches wide and 8 inches deep. Mrs. Sato is staining the outside surface. What is the area of the surface she is staining? **848 in.²**

12. A box of sugar cubes measures 5 cm by 13 cm by 20 cm.
  a. Ignore waste and overlap and tell how much cardboard is needed to make the box. **850 cm²**
  b. How many 1-cm cubes of sugar can the box hold? **1300 cubes**

13. The surface area of a box is 232 square inches. The box is 4 inches wide and 8 inches long. If it is *h* inches high.
  a. write an equation that could be used to find *h*. **24*h* + 64 = 232**
  b. find *h*. **7 in.**

14. The volume of a box is 540 cubic centimeters. The box is 9 centimeters long and 12 centimeters high.
  a. How wide is the box? **5 cm**
  b. What is the surface area of the box? **426 cm²**

15. What is the length of an edge of a cube whose surface area and volume have the same numerical value? (Hint: Refer to Question 9.) **6**

Objectives
I   Pick appropriate units in measurement situations.

Resources
From the *Teacher's Resource File*
- Lesson Master 10-8A or 10-8B
- Answer Master 10-8
- Teaching Aids
  86 Graph Paper
  109 Warm-up
- Activity Kit, Activity 27

Additional Resources
- Visuals for Teaching Aids 86, 109

Teaching Lesson **10-8**

Warm-up
Theresa said there wasn't enough information to find the perimeter of the figure below. Jeff said he could find the perimeter of the figure and did. Explain how Jeff found the perimeter. What is the perimeter? *FE* + *DC* = 30 cm, *AF* + *ED* = 10 cm; 30 cm + 10 cm + 30 cm + 10 cm = 80 cm

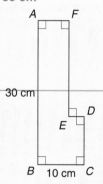

Fishing room galore. *With an area of 8320 km² (about 3200 mi²), Lake Titicaca is the second largest lake in South America. It is also the world's highest navigable lake for large vessels, located 3810 m (about 12,500 ft) above sea level.*

Measuring the Size of a One-Dimensional Figure
The size of a line segment is given by its length.

Measuring the Size of Two-Dimensional Figures
Rectangles and other polygons are two-dimensional. There are two common ways of measuring these figures. Perimeter measures the boundary. Area measures the space inside the figure.

Perimeter and area are quite different. The perimeter of the rectangle pictured below is 6 ft + 100 ft + 6 ft + 100 ft, or 212 *feet*. That's how far you have to go to walk around the rectangle. Perimeter is measured in units of length. The area of the rectangle pictured below is 100 ft · 6 ft or 600 *square feet*. That's how much space it occupies. Area is measured in square units.

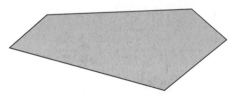

100 ft

6 ft

566

Lesson 10-8 Overview

Broad Goals This lesson focuses entirely on appropriate units of measure for length, area, and volume; no new skill is introduced.

Perspective It is an enigma to many high-school geometry teachers why students confuse area with perimeter and surface area with volume. One reason for the confusion is that students may never have had real-world meanings for perimeter and area

(such as coastline and fishing room), and they may never have used units. Consequently, all they have for intuition is that these ideas measure the size of the figure. By focusing directly on the units of measure themselves, we hope to correct misconceptions early and avoid mistakes later. Students should realize that two figures with the same volume can have quite different surface areas, and two figures with the

same surface area can have quite different volumes.

Since a figure with a given perimeter can have many different areas, it is natural to ask how large that area can be. Of all quadrilaterals, a square has the most area for a given perimeter. More generally, of all figures with the same perimeter, the circle has the most area. Equivalently, of all

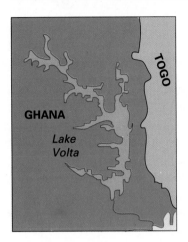
6 cm
3 cm

The perimeter of the rectangle at the left is 6 cm + 3 cm + 6 cm + 3 cm, or 18 cm. Its area is 6 cm · 3 cm, or 18 cm². Perimeter and area can never actually be equal because the units are different. In a situation like this one, the perimeter and area are called *numerically equal*.

❶ In lakes, perimeter measures shoreline. Area measures fishing room. Below are maps of Lake Volta in the African country of Ghana, and Lake Titicaca, which lies in the South American countries of Peru and Bolivia. Lake Volta has only a little more fishing room despite having much more shoreline. It has a small area for its perimeter.

Measuring the Size of Three-Dimensional Figures

There are three different common ways to measure the size of a three-dimensional figure. Consider the shoe box below. We can measure the total length of its edges. Like perimeter, this is one-dimensional. We can measure its surface area, which is two-dimensional. Or we can measure its volume, which is three-dimensional.

The shoebox has edges of lengths 14 inches, 5 inches, and 7 inches. There are four edges of each length. (Some are hidden from view.) The total length of all edges is 4 · 5″ + 4 · 7″ + 4 · 14″, or 104 *inches*.

5 in.
7 in.
14 in.

The surface area of this shoe box is found by adding the areas of the six rectangular faces. You should check that it is 406 *square inches*.

The volume of this box measures the space occupied by the box. It is 5 in. · 7 in. · 14 in., or 490 *cubic inches*.

Lesson 10-8 *Dimensions and Units* 567

figures with the same area, the circle has the least perimeter. The three-dimensional analogues are: Of all boxes with the same surface area, the cube has the most volume. More generally, of all figures with the same surface area, the sphere has the most volume. Equivalently, of all figures with the same volume, the sphere has the least surface area. Thus, for a given amount of soap enclosing some air, to get minimum surface tension, the soap should form a sphere around the area. (This is why soap bubbles are spheres.) These ideas are discussed in *UCSMP Geometry*.

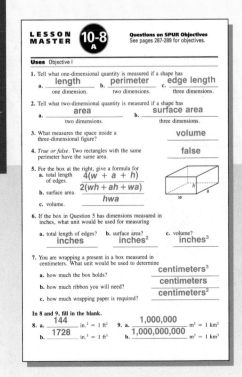

LESSON MASTER 10-8 A

Questions on SPUR Objectives
See pages 287-289 for objectives.

Uses Objective I

1. Tell what one-dimensional quantity is measured if a shape has
   a. **length** one dimension.
   b. **perimeter** two dimensions.
   c. **edge length** three dimensions.

2. Tell what two-dimensional quantity is measured if a shape has
   a. **area** two dimensions.
   b. **surface area** three dimensions.

3. What measures the space inside a three-dimensional figure? **volume**

4. *True or false.* Two rectangles with the same perimeter have the same area. **false**

5. For the box at the right, give a formula for
   a. total length of edges. **4(w + a + h)**
   b. surface area. **2(wh + ah + wa)**
   c. volume. **hwa**

6. If the box in Question 5 has dimensions measured in inches, what unit would be used for measuring
   a. total length of edges? **inches**
   b. surface area? **inches²**
   c. volume? **inches³**

7. You are wrapping a present in a box measured in centimeters. What unit would be used to determine
   a. how much the box holds? **centimeters³**
   b. how much ribbon you will need? **centimeters**
   c. how much wrapping paper is required? **centimeters²**

In 8 and 9, fill in the blank.
8. a. **144** in.² = 1 ft²
   b. **1728** in.³ = 1 ft³
9. a. **1,000,000** m² = 1 km²
   b. **1,000,000,000** m³ = 1 km³

This is a good time to demonstrate that the units, if handled carefully, take care of themselves. In finding perimeter of a rectangle 3 cm by 5 cm, one adds the lengths: 3 cm + 5 cm + 3 cm + 5 cm = 16 cm. But the area of the same rectangle is 3 cm × 5 cm = 3 × cm × 5 × cm = 3 × 5 × cm × cm = 15 cm². Using the same method with volume yields cubic units. In science courses, units are regularly handled in this way.

Additional Examples

1. Two boxes have the same volume, 320 cm³. Box A measures 10 cm x 8 cm x 4 cm and Box B measures 8 cm x 5 cm x 8 cm. Which one requires more cardboard? **Box A**

2. Rectangle *ABCD* is 10 cm long and 2 cm wide. Find the dimensions of another rectangle which has the same area as *ABCD*, but its perimeter is less than the perimeter of *ABCD*. **Sample: a rectangle with dimensions of 4 cm and 5 cm**

Surface area and volume have different units. They measure different things, as the example below shows.

Example

The spaghetti box and tea bag box each have a volume of 750 cubic centimeters. Which box requires more cardboard?

Solution

The surface area of the spaghetti box is the sum of the areas of its faces.

front + back + top + bottom + right + left =
$30 \cdot 5 + 30 \cdot 5 + 30 \cdot 5 + 30 \cdot 5 + 5 \cdot 5 + 5 \cdot 5 = 650 \text{ cm}^2$.

The surface area of the box of tea bags is
$10 \cdot 10 + 10 \cdot 10 + 10 \cdot 7.5 + 10 \cdot 7.5 + 10 \cdot 7.5 + 10 \cdot 7.5$, or
500 cm^2.

So the spaghetti box requires more cardboard.

QUESTIONS

Covering the Reading

In 1–4, suppose that length is measured in centimeters. In what unit would you expect each to be measured?

1. perimeter cm

2. volume cm^3

3. area cm^2

4. surface area cm^2

5. __?__ measures the space inside a 2-dimensional figure. Area

6. __?__ measures the space inside a 3-dimensional figure. Volume

7. __?__ measures the distance around a 2-dimensional figure. **Perimeter**

8. __?__ measures the surface of a 3-dimensional figure. Surface area

9. In this lesson, the area of Lake Titicaca is measured in square kilometers.
   a. In what unit would you expect its shoreline to be measured? km
   b. In what unit would you expect its fishing room to be measured? km^2

10. Draw a lake that has a large perimeter but very little area.

11. Suppose a side of a square has length 4.
    a. *True or false.* The perimeter and area of the square are equal. **False**
    b. Explain your answer. **They are only numerically equal; 4 units is not the same as 4 square units.**

12. Find the area of each face of the shoe box in this lesson. 35 in^2; 98 in^2; 70 in^2

10) Sample:

Video

Wide World of Mathematics The segment, *Chunnel,* describes the construction of the transportation tunnels connecting England and France beneath the English Channel. A variety of statistics related to the tunnel are given, providing a foundation for a discussion of dimensions and units. Related questions and an investigation are provided in videodisc stills and in the Video Guide. A related CD-ROM activity is also available.

Videodisc Bar Codes

Search Chapter 49

Play

13. Give an example of two rectangular solids with the same volume but with different surface areas. **Sample: 24 by 2 by 1; 6 by 4 by 2**

14. A small box has dimensions 11 mm, 12 mm, and 13 mm.
    a. Find the total length of its edges. **144 mm**
    b. Find its surface area. **862 mm²**
    c. Find its volume. **1716 mm³**

Applying the Mathematics

15. A box has dimensions ℓ, w, and h. What is the total length of its edges? **4ℓ + 4w + 4h**

16. A rectangle has a perimeter of more than 100 inches. But its area is less than 1 square inch.
    a. Is this possible? **Yes**
    b. If so, give the dimensions of such a rectangle. If not, tell why it is not possible. **Sample: 200 in. by 0.001 in.**

In 17–19, tell whether the idea concerns surface area or volume.

17. the amount of wrapping paper needed for a gift **surface area**

18. how many paper clips a small box can hold **volume**

19. the weight of a rock **volume**

20. 640 acres = 1 square mile. A farm is measured in acres.
    Multiple choice. What is being measured about this farm?
    (a) its land area   (b) its perimeter   (c) its volume **(a)**

21. Recall that a liter is a metric unit equal to 1000 cm³.
    Multiple choice. What does a liter measure?
    (a) length   (b) area   (c) volume **(c)**

Review

22. This program calculates and prints the surface area and volume of a box. Two lines are incomplete.

```
10 PRINT "SIDES OF BOX"
15 INPUT A, B, C
20 PRINT "VOLUME", "SURFACE AREA"
30 VOL = ____
40 SA = ____
50 PRINT VOL,SA
60 END
```

22b)
SIDES OF BOX
2, 3, 4
VOLUME SURFACE AREA
24   52

c) Sample:
SIDES OF BOX
10, 15, 7.5
VOLUME SURFACE AREA
1125   675

a. Complete lines 30 and 40 to make this program give correct values for *VOL* and *SA*. **A * B * C; 2 * A * B + 2 * A * C + 2 * B * C**
b. What will the computer print if $A = 2$, $B = 3$, and $C = 4$?
c. Run the completed program with values of your own choosing to test it. *(Lessons 9-2, 10-7)*

Lesson 10-8   *Dimensions and Units*   **569**

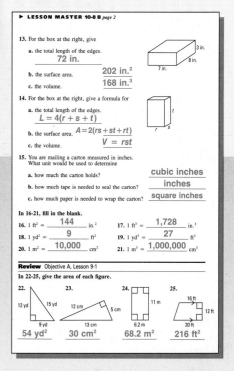

▶ **LESSON MASTER 10-8 B** *page 2*

13. For the box at the right, give
    a. the total length of the edges. **72 in.**
    b. the surface area. **202 in.²**
    c. the volume. **168 in.³**

14. For the box at the right, give a formula for
    a. the total length of the edges. **L = 4(r + s + t)**
    b. the surface area. **A = 2(rs + st + rt)**
    c. the volume. **V = rst**

15. You are mailing a carton measured in inches. What unit would be used to determine
    a. how much the carton holds? **cubic inches**
    b. how much tape is needed to seal the carton? **inches**
    c. how much paper is needed to wrap the carton? **square inches**

In 16-21, fill in the blank.
16. 1 ft² = **144** in.²   17. 1 ft³ = **1,728** in.³
18. 1 yd² = **9** ft²   19. 1 yd³ = **27** ft³
20. 1 m² = **10,000** cm²   21. 1 m³ = **1,000,000** cm³

Review Objective A, Lesson 9-1
In 22-25, give the area of each figure.
22. **54 yd²**   23. **30 cm²**   24. **68.2 m²**   25. **216 ft²**

569

Practice

For more questions on SPUR Objectives, use **Lesson Master 10-8A** (shown on page 567) or **Lesson Master 10-8B** (shown on pages 568–569).

Assessment

Written Communication Present the following situations and have students write their answers.

1. Suppose you are wrapping a present. Tell whether you need to measure length, surface area, or volume, and whether you would use cm, cm², or cm³ to determine:
   a. how much the box holds.
      volume, cm³
   b. how much wrapping paper to use. **surface area, cm²**
   c. how much ribbon to use.
      length, cm

2. Choose a book that you have with you. Then measure it and determine the dimensions of the smallest possible box the book would fit into. Find the volume and surface area of the box. [Answers show understanding of the distinctions between length, area, and volume and the units used for each.]

Extension

Ask students to find the perimeter of a square with area 25 square units. [20 units.] Then have students **work in groups** to find a polygon with perimeter 20 and area less than 25 square units. Then ask groups to draw a polygon with area 25 square units whose perimeter is greater than 20 units. You might want to suggest that students work on graph paper or **Teaching Aid 86**.
Samples

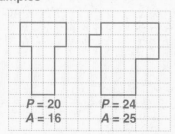
P = 20   P = 24
A = 16   A = 25

Project Update Project 1, *Units for Land Area,* on page 582, relates to the content of this lesson.

---

27)
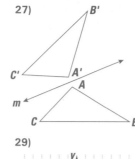

29)
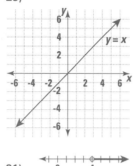
y = x

31)

0   4

Shades of the 50s. *The first movie requiring 3-D glasses was produced in 1952 by Arch Obeler.*

---

23. *Multiple choice.* Which expression is equal to $\frac{2}{3}x - x$?
    (Lesson 10-6)
    (a) $\frac{2}{3}$ (b) $-\frac{1}{3}$ (c) $-\frac{1}{3}x$ (d) none of these **(c)**

24. Simplify $100x - 5y + 8x - 23 + 9y - 1 + x + 80y$.   *(Lesson 10-6)*
    $109x + 84y - 24$

25. Solve $3c + 5c + 12 = 240$.   *(Lessons 10-4, 10-6)* **c = 28.5**

26. Find the area of the triangle with vertices $(4, -8)$, $(-3, -8)$, and $(-3, 11)$.   *(Lessons 8-3, 9-1)* **66.5 square units**

27. Trace the drawing. Then reflect triangle *ABC* over the line *m*. *(Lesson 8-6)* **See left.**

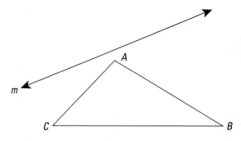
m
A
c   B

28. The point $(8, -4)$ is translated 10 units down. What is its image? *(Lesson 8-5)* **$(8, -14)$**

29. Graph the line with equation $y = x$.   *(Lesson 8-4)* **See left.**

30. In this figure, $\angle 2$ is a right angle and $m\angle 1 = 140°$. What is $m\angle 3$? *(Lessons 7-6, 7-7)* **130°**

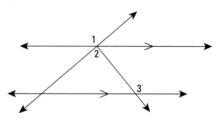

31. Graph all solutions to the inequality $x > 4$.   *(Lesson 4-10)*
    See left.

32. a. Rewrite 3 trillion in scientific notation. **3×10^{12}**
    b. Rewrite 3 trillionths in scientific notation.   *(Lessons 2-3, 2-8)*
       3×10^{-12}

33. Rewrite each number as a percent. a. $\frac{1}{3}$ b. $\frac{2}{3}$ c. $\frac{4}{5}$ *(Lessons 1-6, 2-4)*
    a) 33.$\overline{3}$%; b) 66.$\overline{6}$%; c) 80%

Exploration

34. The "D" in 3-D movies is short for "dimensional."
    a. Are these movies actually three dimensional? **No**
    b. When you watch a 3-D movie in a theater, you must wear special glasses. How do these glasses work? **Sample: Each lens of the glasses is a different color and blacks out part of the picture. Each eye sees a slightly different image, so the brain thinks the viewer is seeing 3-D.**

Adapting to Individual Needs

Extra Help
Materials: Graph paper or **Teaching Aid 86**, string, tape, scissors, ruler or **Geometry Template**

Have students draw a large rectangle on graph paper. Then have them lay a piece of string along the border of the rectangle, fastening it at each corner. Next, have students cut the string at the last corner, straighten it, and measure its length. Point out that this is the perimeter of the rectangle and it is measured in units of length. Then have students find the number of squares inside the rectangle. Say that this is the area and it is measured in square units. Then have students imagine that the rectangle is the base of a box that is 5 units tall. Tell students that the number of cubes needed to fill the box is the volume of the rectangular solid, which is measured in cubic units.

LESSON

10-9

Areas of Triangles

© The Walt Disney Company

Triangular support. *Buckminster Fuller invented the geodesic dome. Geodesic spheres, like this one at EPCOT Center, consist of lightweight triangular faces.*

Finding the Area of a Triangle from the Area of a Related Rectangle

You saw in Lesson 9-1 that the area of any right triangle is half the area of a rectangle. The area of rectangle *DFEG* below is *bh*. So the area of triangle *DEG* is $\frac{1}{2}bh$.

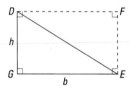

Every triangle has half the area of a related rectangle.

❶   Activity 1

Trace two copies of triangle *ABC* onto a sheet of paper. Trace rectangle *ABDE* onto another sheet of paper.

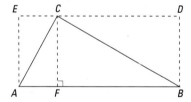

Cut out both triangles. Then cut one of the triangles at $\overline{CF}$. Show that the three triangles you now have fill the entire rectangle.

Lesson 10-9 *Areas of Triangles*   **571**

Objectives
D Find the area of a triangle.

Resources
From the **Teacher's Resource File**
■ Lesson Master 10-9A or 10-9B
■ Answer Master 10-9
■ Teaching Aids
    86 Graph Paper
    109 Warm-up
    113 Area of a Triangle
    114 Additional Examples
■ Technology Sourcebook, Computer Master 23

Additional Resources
■ Visuals for Teaching Aids 86, 109, 113, 114
■ Geometry Workshop

Teaching 10-9
Lesson 10-9

Warm-up
Mental Mathematics Find each product mentally.
1. $\frac{1}{2} \times 46$ **23**
2. $\frac{1}{2} \times 9 \times 6$ **27**
3. $\frac{1}{2} \times 7 \times 2$ **7**
4. $\frac{1}{2} \times (7 + 21)$ **14**
5. 0.5×22 **11**
6. $0.5 \times (3.2 + 1.8)$ **2.5**

Notes on Reading
❶ Activity 1 is important, as it shows physically that the area of a triangle is half the area of a related rectangle.

Lesson 10-9 Overview

Broad Goals In Lesson 9-1, students found the area of any right triangle using the area formula $A = \frac{1}{2}bh$. This lesson extends the use of the formula to any triangle.

Perspective It is not obvious to all people that the area of a triangle should be determined just by the length of a side and the altitude to that side. The formula $A = \frac{1}{2}bh$

given in this lesson is derived by considering the triangle as half a rectangle with dimensions *b* and *h*.

A second possible derivation is to use the Distributive Property and the area formula for right triangles. This method would generalize **Examples 1 and 2**.

Some students have trouble finding the area of a triangle that does not have a horizontal base. They want the altitude to be vertical. If students have trouble understanding **Example 1** or Activity 2 for this reason, suggest that they turn the page until the base is horizontal. Then the altitude is vertical.

❷ Encourage students to begin their work by stating an appropriate formula, as shown in the solution to **Example 1**. If students are in the habit of writing the formula first and then making substitutions, they will not be confused by problems that require solving for the height or the base, rather than the area.

❸ As an extra activity, or as an alternative for Activity 2, you might want to use **Teaching Aid 113**. The activity is the same, but the triangle is larger and obtuse. The area of the triangle on the teaching aid is approximately 10 square inches. Ask for volunteers to tell which altitude and base they used, and to explain how they calculated the area of the triangle. You might want to have students draw the two altitudes they didn't use.

Have students record the results of *Activity 2* on page 573 for use with **Question 7** on page 574. If students used **Teaching Aid 113** as an alternative to *Activity 2,* accept those results as the answer for **Question 7.**

The Activity verifies that the area of △*ABC* is $\frac{1}{2}$ the area of rectangle *ABDE.* One dimension of the rectangle is *AB.* The other dimension equals *CF.* $\overline{CF}$ is the segment from point *C* perpendicular to the opposite side $\overline{AB}$. It is called the **height,** or **altitude,** of △*ABC.*

A height (or altitude) of a triangle does not have to be the length of a vertical line segment. Every triangle has three altitudes, one from each vertex perpendicular to the opposite side. The side to which the altitude is drawn is called the **base** for that altitude. Below are three copies of △*PQR.* The three altitudes are drawn with a blue line. Also drawn are three rectangles. The area of the triangle is always one-half the area of the rectangle. That is, the area of a triangle is half the product of a side (the base) and the altitude drawn to that side.

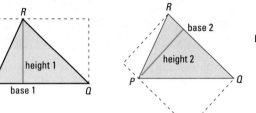

> **Area Formula for Any Triangle**
> Let *b* be the length of a side of a triangle with area *A.* Let *h* be the length of the altitude drawn to that side. Then
> $$A = \tfrac{1}{2}\,bh.$$

Using an Area Formula to Find the Area of a Triangle

❷ **Example 1**

$\overline{VY}$ is perpendicular to $\overline{XZ}$. Find the area of △*XYZ.*

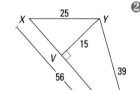

Solution

$\overline{VY}$ is the only altitude shown. Its base is $\overline{XZ}$. So use $\overline{XZ}$ as the base in the formula.

$$
\begin{aligned}
\text{Area of } \triangle XYZ &= \tfrac{1}{2} \cdot bh \\
&= \tfrac{1}{2} \cdot XZ \cdot VY \\
&= \tfrac{1}{2} \cdot 56 \cdot 15 \\
&= 420
\end{aligned}
$$

The area of △XYZ is 420 square units.

Adapting to Individual Needs
Extra Help
Materials: Graph paper or **Teaching Aid 86**

Some students might have trouble with the fact that the altitude of a triangle is not one of its sides, except in the case of a right triangle. Have students draw any rectangle *ABCD* on graph paper. Then have students mark point *E* on side $\overline{AB}$, two units from *A;* and point *F* on side $\overline{DC}$, two units from *D.*

Then draw $\overline{DE}$ and $\overline{CE}$. The figure might look like this:

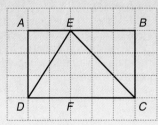

Remind students that Activity 1 on page 571 verifies that the area of △*DEC* equals half the area of rectangle *ABCD.* The area of the rectangle is *AD · DC.* So the area of △*DEC* equals $\frac{1}{2} \cdot AD \cdot DC.$ Point out that *AD* = *EF.* So the area of △*DEC* is $\frac{1}{2} \cdot EF \cdot DC.$ This should help them see that using one side of the triangle as the base, and multiplying it by the altitude to that base, will give the area.

Example 2

Find the area of △ABC.

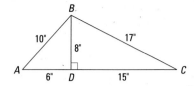

Solution 1

Separate △ABC into the two right triangles ABD and BDC.

Area of △ABD = $\frac{1}{2}$ · 6 · 8 square inches

Area of △BDC = $\frac{1}{2}$ · 8 · 15 square inches

Add the areas to get the area of △ABC.

Area of △ABC = $\frac{1}{2}$ · 6 · 8 + $\frac{1}{2}$ · 8 · 15

$\qquad = \quad$ 24 $\quad + \quad$ 60

$\qquad$ = 84 square inches

Solution 2

Use the formula for the area of a triangle. Since $\overline{BD} \perp \overline{AC}$, BD is the height for the base $\overline{AC}$.

Area = $\frac{1}{2}$ bh = $\frac{1}{2}$ · (6 + 15) · 8 = $\frac{1}{2}$ · 21 · 8 = 84 square inches

Measuring to Find the Area of a Triangle

In Example 2, more information was given than was needed. The 10″ and 17″ lengths were not used. In the next Activity, no lengths are given. But by measuring, you can estimate the area.

❸ **Activity 2**

Trace this triangle. By drawing an altitude and measuring lengths, estimate the area of this triangle to the nearest square inch.

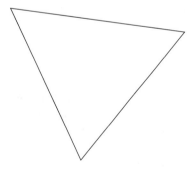

If your estimate is about 2 square inches, you probably did Activity 2 correctly.

Lesson 10-9 *Areas of Triangles* **573**

Additional Examples

Teaching Aid 114 contains both of these examples.

1. Find the area of this triangle

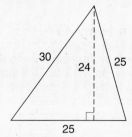

300 square units

2. Find the area of △XYZ

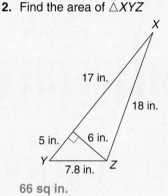

66 sq in.

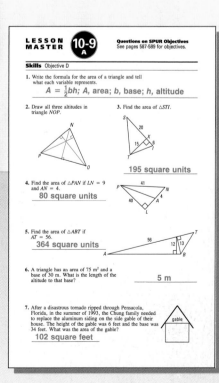

Optional Activities

Activity 1
Materials: Graph paper or **Teaching Aid 86**

You might want to use this activity after students have done Activity 1 on page 571. Have students draw several different rectangles on graph paper and find the area of each. Then show students how to draw a triangle inside each rectangle where one side of the rectangle becomes the base of the triangle, and the third vertex of the triangle lies on the opposite side of the rectangle, but not at a vertex (as shown in *Extra Help* on page 572). Have students count squares to estimate the area of each triangle. Ask them to compare the area of each triangle to the area of the rectangle. [The area of the triangle is one half the area of the rectangle.]

573

Notes on Questions

For most classes, review **Questions 1–7** in order to ensure that the basic ideas of the lesson are clear to students.

Question 9 Error Alert Some students will not know what to do because they are being asked to find an altitude, not an area. Tell them to write the formula first and then make substitutions. They will need to solve an equation of the form $ax = b$.

Question 10 History Connection The fourth-dynasty (c.2575–2465 B.C.) Pyramids of Giza were erected on a rocky plateau on the west bank of the Nile River near al-Jizah, Egypt. The three pyramids are included among the Seven Wonders of the Ancient World. The largest and oldest of the three is called the Great Pyramid. It was built by Khufu, the second king of the 4th dynasty. According to the Greek historian Herodotus, 100,000 men labored 20 years to build the Great Pyramid. Approximately 2,300,000 blocks of stone were used in this structure, each weighing an average of 2.5 tons.

Question 11 The altitude to base $\overline{RE}$ is outside the triangle. Ask students what kind of triangle has two of its altitudes outside the triangle. [an obtuse triangle.]

(Notes on Questions continue on page 576.)

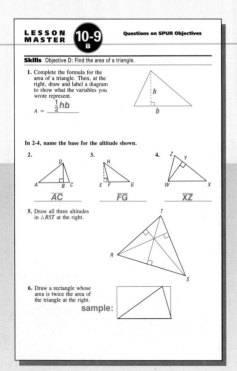

Covering the Reading

1. Find the area of $\triangle DEF$.   **468 sq units**

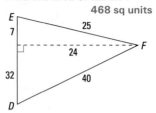

2. Find the area of $\triangle ABC$.   **84 sq units**

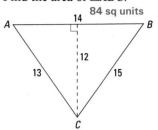

3. Trace $\triangle XYZ$.

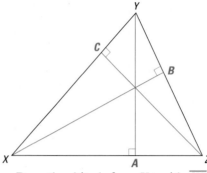

a. Draw the altitude from Y to side $\overline{XZ}$.
b. Draw the altitude from X to side $\overline{YZ}$.
c. Draw the altitude from Z to side $\overline{XY}$.

4. Give another name for each.
   a. altitude   height
   b. the side of a triangle to which the altitude is perpendicular base
5. Draw a rectangle whose area is twice the area of this triangle.

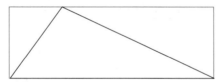

6) Let b be the length of a side of a triangle with area A, and let h be the length of the altitude drawn to that side. Then $A = \frac{1}{2} bh$.

6. Give a formula for the area of a triangle.

7. In Activity 2, what are the dimensions of the side you measured and of the altitude to that side? The sides have approximate lengths 2.24", 2.05", and 2.05". The altitudes to these sides have approximate lengths 1.72", 1.86", and 1.86".

Optional Activities

Activity 2 Technology Connection You may wish to assign *Technology Sourcebook, Computer Master 23*. Students use *Geometry Workshop* to display a triangle. Then students explore the relationships between altitude, base length, and area.

Applying the Mathematics

8. Each square in the grid below is 1 unit on a side. Find the area of △*MNP*. Explain the method you used. **21 sq units; by counting squares, base *MN* = 6, height = 7.**

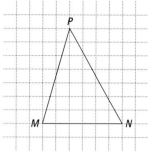

9. The triangle below has a base with length 40 cm and an area of 300 cm². What is the length of the altitude to that base? **15 cm**

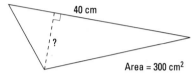

Area = 300 cm²

10. Below is a photograph of three of the great pyramids of Giza in Egypt. Each face of the largest pyramid is a triangle whose base is about 230 meters long. The height of each face is about 92 meters. What is the area of a face? **10,580 square meters**

The pyramids of ancient Egypt, built as royal tombs, are the largest stone structures in the world.

11. Find the area of △*EAR* below. **132 square units**

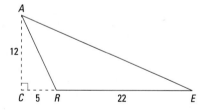

Lesson 10-9 *Areas of Triangles* **575**

Adapting to Individual Needs

Challenge
Any triangle can be divided into four congruent triangles by a simple process. Have students discover how to do this by actually cutting out a large triangle and then cutting it into four congruent triangles. [Locate the midpoints of all three sides of the triangle and connect the midpoints. The four triangles formed are congruent. See △*ABC* at the right.]

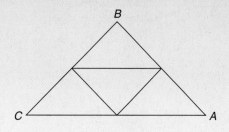

Follow-up 10-9
for Lesson

Practice
For more questions on SPUR Objectives, use **Lesson Master 10-9A** (shown on page 573 or **Lesson Master 10-9B** (shown on pages 574–575).

Assessment
Written Communication Have students draw three triangles. The first triangle should have an altitude that is one of the sides of the triangle, the second triangle should have an altitude inside the triangle, and the third triangle should have an altitude outside the triangle. Have students measure the altitude and base of each triangle and find its area. [Drawings and answers show understanding of the meaning of *altitude* and *base* of a triangle and of finding the area of a triangle.]

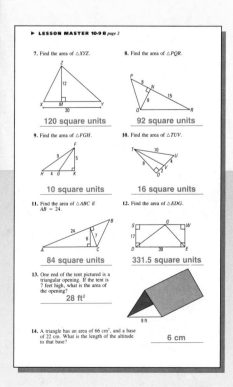

▶ **LESSON MASTER 10-9 B** *page 2*

7. Find the area of △*XYZ*. **120 square units**

8. Find the area of △*PQR*. **92 square units**

9. Find the area of △*FGH*. **10 square units**

10. Find the area of △*TUV*. **16 square units**

11. Find the area of △*ABC* if *AB* = 24. **84 square units**

12. Find the area of △*EDG*. **331.5 square units**

13. One end of the tent pictured is a triangular opening. If the tent is 7 feet high, what is the area of the opening? **28 ft²**

14. A triangle has an area of 66 cm², and a base of 22 cm. What is the length of the altitude to that base? **6 cm**

Extension

Activity Give students the following activity.
1. Draw a large triangle *ABC*.
2. Draw the three altitudes for △*ABC*.
3. Measure the altitudes and the sides of △*ABC*.
4. Calculate the area of △*ABC* using side
   a. $\overline{AB}$. **b.** $\overline{BC}$. **c.** $\overline{AC}$.
5. Repeat steps 1–4 using a different kind of triangle.
6. What does this activity show? [Sample answer: Each of the areas calculated in step 4 are about the same. To find the area of a triangle, you can use any side as the base and you must use the altitude drawn to that base.]

Notes on Questions

Question 15 The Distributive Property should be used to avoid more than one multiplication by 5.671.

12. A box has dimensions 30 cm, 26 cm, and 12 cm. *(Lessons 3-9, 10-7)*
    a. What is the area of the largest face of the box? 780 cm²
    b. What is the total surface area of the box? 2904 cm²
    c. What is the volume of the box? 9360 cm³

13. Multiply $a(a + 2)$. *(Lesson 10-6)* $a^2 + 2a$

14. Solve $1.7x - 0.4 = 3.0$. *(Lesson 10-4)* $x = 2$

15. Evaluate $3x + 14x + 2x + x$ when $x = 5.671$. *(Lesson 10-1)* 113.42

16. What is the value of $-4m$ when $m = -4$? *(Lessons 4-4, 9-6)* 16

17. How many two-digit numbers satisfy both of the following conditions?
    (1) The first digit is 1, 3, 5, or 7.
    (2) The second digit is 2, 4, or 6. *(Lessons 6-1, 9-4)* 12 numbers

In 18–22, refer to these polygons. *(Lesson 7-8)*

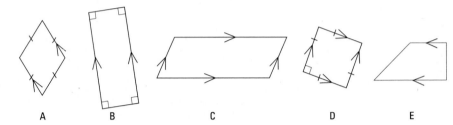

A   B   C   D   E

18. The polygons are all __?__. trapezoids

19. Which of the polygons are parallelograms? A, B, C, D

20. Which of the polygons are rectangles? B, D

21. Which of the polygons are rhombuses? A, D

22. Which of the polygons are squares? D

23. Add: $\frac{2}{5} + \frac{1}{3} + \frac{1}{4}$. *(Lesson 5-5)* $\frac{59}{60}$

24. What simple fraction in lowest terms equals $\frac{0.46}{9.2}$? *(Lesson 1-10)* $\frac{1}{20}$

25. Translate into English: 345.29. *(Lesson 1-2)* three hundred forty-five and twenty-nine hundredths

26. Identify an object where you live that has the shape of a triangle. (For example, you might use part of a roof or a side of a piece of furniture.) Draw a copy of the object, give or estimate the lengths of its sides and at least one altitude, and find its area.
    Answers will vary.

576

Setting Up Lesson 10-10

Questions 18–22 on this page review the various kinds of quadrilaterals. Point out that all of figures A to E are trapezoids, so the formula that students will see in Lesson 10-10 applies to all of these figures.

Trapezoids in architecture. *The design of this hotel in Cancun, Mexico, illustrates the use of trapezoidal shapes in depicting a thunderbird. In North American Indian mythology, thunderbirds are powerful spirits.*

Pentagon *ABCDE* is split into three triangles.

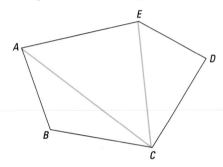

To find the area of *ABCDE,* you could add the areas of the triangles. This is one reason you learned how to find the area of a triangle. *Any polygon can be split into triangles.*

Finding the Area of a Trapezoid by Splitting It into Triangles

When a figure is split into two or more triangles that have the same altitude, their areas can be added using the Distributive Property. A simple formula can be the result. This can always be done if the figure is a *trapezoid.* A **trapezoid** is a quadrilateral that has at least one pair of parallel sides.

Lesson 10-10 Overview

Broad Goals This lesson has two goals: to point out that the area of any polygon can be found by splitting it into triangles, a process called *triangulating the polygon*; and to use triangulation and the Distributive Property to derive the formula $A = \frac{1}{2} h(b_1 + b_2)$ for the area of any trapezoid.

Perspective The definition given here of trapezoid—a quadrilateral with *at least* one pair of parallel sides—differs from that given in some books. Some people prefer to restrict trapezoids to those figures which have *exactly* one pair of parallel sides. We see no reason for such a restriction. The area formula for trapezoids works for parallelograms, and it is efficient to have trapezoids include parallelograms in the way that parallelograms include rectangles and rhombuses, and each of these includes squares. Our definition is found in many

other books and is one of the two definitions given in the James and James *Mathematics Dictionary.*

In *UCSMP Geometry,* students will learn the hierarchy relating the various types of quadrilaterals shown on **Teaching Aid 77**.

Lesson 10-10

Objectives
E Find the area of a trapezoid.

Resources
From the *Teacher's Resource File*
- Lesson Master 10-10A or 10-10B
- Answer Master 10-10
- Teaching Aids
  77 Quadrilaterals
  86 Graph Paper
  109 Warm-up
  115 Additional Examples
  116 Area of a Trapezoid
- Technology Sourcebook, Computer Master 24

Additional Resources
- Visuals for Teaching Aids 77, 86, 109, 115, 116
- Geometry Workshop

Teaching 10-10
Lesson

Warm-up
It costs $100 to sod a lawn that is 30 feet by 15 feet. How much will it cost to sod a lawn that is twice as long and twice as wide? $400

Notes on Reading
Because memorizing the formula for the area of a trapezoid is not recommended, students can focus on learning to divide a trapezoid into two triangles whose areas they can easily find. This process can be used for any polygon. Help students follow the use of the Distributive Property in deriving the formula.

The formula for the area of a trapezoid is one of the more complicated area formulas a student will encounter. The difficulty is caused by the subscripts and the parentheses in it, two features of many formulas with which students are unfamiliar. It is given here because it is standard content, because it exemplifies the Distributive Property, and because it provides good practice of many concepts. At this level, you should not expect students to memorize it.

❶ Some people like to reorder the formula as $A = h \cdot \frac{1}{2}(b_1 + b_2)$ and then restate it as follows: the area of a trapezoid is the product of its height and the mean (or average) length of its bases. The drawing below explains why; the area of the trapezoid (thick lines) equals the area of the rectangle (dotted lines). The dimensions of the rectangle are the trapezoid's height and the average of the lengths of its bases.

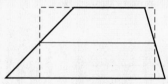

❷ Stress that the definition of *trapezoid* includes any quadrilateral with at least one pair of parallel sides; however, the quadrilateral may have two pairs of parallel sides. One way to develop an appreciation of the implications is to show that the formula $A = \frac{1}{2}h(b_1 + b_2)$ becomes $A = hb$ if the figure is a parallelogram ($b_1 = b_2$); it becomes $A = \ell w$ if the figure is a rectangle ($h = \ell$, $b_1 = b_2 = w$); and it becomes $A = s^2$ if the figure is a square ($h = s$, and $b_1 = b_2 = s$).

Find the area of trapezoid *TRAP*.

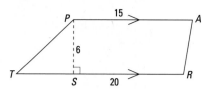

Solution

Draw the diagonal $\overline{PR}$. This splits the trapezoid into two triangles, *PAR* and *PRT*. Each triangle has altitude 6.

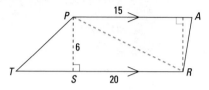

$$\text{Area of trapezoid } TRAP = \text{Area of } \triangle PAR + \text{Area of } \triangle PRT$$
$$= \frac{1}{2} \cdot 6 \cdot 15 + \frac{1}{2} \cdot 6 \cdot 20$$
$$= 3 \cdot 15 + 3 \cdot 20$$
$$= 45 + 60$$
$$= 105$$

The area of TRAP is 105 square units.

❶ **A Formula for the Area of a Trapezoid**

The parallel sides of a trapezoid are called its **bases.** The distance between the bases is the **height,** or **altitude,** of the trapezoid. The example shows that you need only the lengths of the bases and the height to find the area of a trapezoid.

To find a general formula, replace the specific lengths with variables. Let the bases have lengths b_1 and b_2. b_1 means the "first base," b_2 means the "second base." Let the height be h.

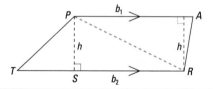

$$\text{Area of trapezoid } TRAP = \text{Area of } \triangle PAR + \text{Area } \triangle PRT$$
$$= \frac{1}{2} \cdot h \cdot b_1 + \frac{1}{2} \cdot h \cdot b_2$$

Now use the Distributive Property. The following formula is the result.

578

Optional Activities

Activity 1

Materials: Geometry Templates

After students complete the lesson, you might have them trace each trapezoid given on the Geometry Template. Then have them measure and estimate the area of each figure. Remind students that squares, rectangles, rhombuses, and parallelograms are trapezoids because they have a pair of parallel sides.

Activity 2 Technology Connection You may wish to assign *Technology Sourcebook, Computer Master 24.* Students use the *Geometry Workshop* to create a trapezoid. Then students draw a diagonal to divide the trapezoid into two figures. Finally, students compare the sum of the areas of the two triangles to the area of the trapezoid.

Area Formula for a Trapezoid
Let A be the area of a trapezoid with bases b_1 and b_2 and height h.
Then $A = \frac{1}{2} \cdot h(b_1 + b_2)$.

You can check that this formula gives the answer found in the Example.
There $h = 6$, $b_1 = 15$, and $b_2 = 20$.

$$A = \tfrac{1}{2}h(b_1 + b_2)$$
$$= \tfrac{1}{2} \cdot 6(15 + 20)$$
$$= 105$$

Some people prefer the formula in words.

> The area of a trapezoid is one half the product of its height and the sum of the lengths of its bases.

For What Figures Does This Formula Work?

Trapezoids come in many different sizes and shapes. Here are some trapezoids with bases drawn in blue. Heights of the trapezoids below are dashed. In the trapezoid at the far right, one base has to be extended to meet the height.

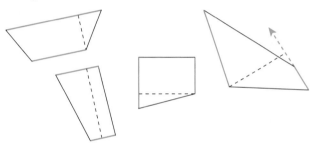

❷ Rectangles, squares, rhombuses, and parallelograms have parallel sides, so they are all trapezoids. Therefore, whatever is true for all trapezoids is true for all rectangles, squares, rhombuses, and parallelograms. The area formula for a trapezoid works for all these figures.

However, there is no general formula that works for the area of all polygons.

Lesson 10-10 *Areas of Trapezoids* **579**

Adapting to Individual Needs

Extra Help
Materials: Graph paper or **Teaching Aid 86**

Some students may need help identifying the bases and the height of a trapezoid. Draw trapezoid *ABCD* so that $\overline{AB} \parallel \overline{CD}$. Have students draw it on grid paper. Help students see that the distance between sides $\overline{AB}$ and $\overline{DC}$ is constant. Therefore,

they are parallel and can be considered bases of the trapezoid. The distance between the bases is the height. On the other hand, the distance between sides $\overline{AD}$ and $\overline{BC}$ varies, depending on where the measurement is taken, so sides $\overline{AD}$ and $\overline{BC}$ are not parallel and cannot be considered bases of the trapezoid.

Additional Examples

Teaching Aid 115 contains all of these additional examples. Have students find the area of each trapezoid.

1.

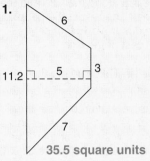

35.5 square units

2.

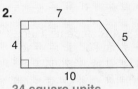

34 square units

3.

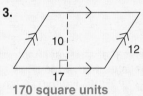

170 square units

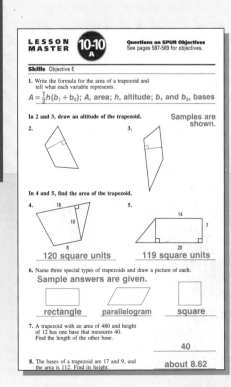

579

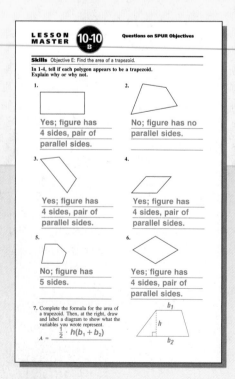

580

QUESTIONS

Covering the Reading

1. Why is the area formula for a triangle so important?

1) Sample: Any polygon can be split up into triangles. By adding the areas of the triangles, you can get the area of the polygon.

2. How can you tell if a figure is a trapezoid? **If it has at least one pair of parallel sides, it is a trapezoid.**

In 3–7, *true or false.*

3. All quadrilaterals are trapezoids. **False**

4. All squares are trapezoids. **True**

5. All trapezoids are rectangles. **False**

6. The formula for the area of a trapezoid can be used to find the area of a parallelogram. **True**

7. There is a formula for the area of any polygon. **False**

8. Use the trapezoid at the left.
   a. Give the lengths of its bases. **20, 17**
   b. Give its height. **22**
   c. Give its area. **407 sq units**

9. a. Draw a trapezoid with bases of length 4 cm and 5 cm and height of 2 cm.
   b. Find the area of this trapezoid. **9 cm²**

10. A trapezoid has bases b_1 and b_2 and height h. What is its area?

10) $\frac{1}{2} h(b_1 + b_2)$

11. In words, state the formula for the area of a trapezoid. **The area of a trapezoid is one-half the product of its height and the sum of its bases.**

9a) (not to scale)

Applying the Mathematics

12. Find the area of the parallelogram drawn below. **320 sq units**

13. The shape of Egypt roughly approximates a trapezoid. The north border of Egypt is about 900 km long, the south border is about 1100 km long, and the height is about 1100 km. What is the approximate area of Egypt? **about 1,100,000 km²**

580

14) Sample:

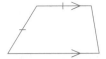

16) figure, polygon, quadrilateral, trapezoid, parallelogram, rectangle, square

17a) One example of an altitude is the dashed segment between the parallel sides. See drawing.

b) $AB \approx 21$ mm, $DC \approx 39$ mm, $AE \approx 25$ mm; Area ≈ 750 mm^2

14. Draw a trapezoid with exactly two sides of equal length.

15. A trapezoid has an area of 60 square meters. Its height is 10 meters. One of the bases is 5 meters long. What is the length of the other base? **7 m**

16. Order these seven terms from most general to most specific.
polygon   square   trapezoid   figure
rectangle   quadrilateral   parallelogram

17. a. Trace trapezoid *ABCD* and draw an altitude.
b. Measure the bases and the altitude to the nearest millimeter. Use these measurements to estimate the area of *ABCD*.

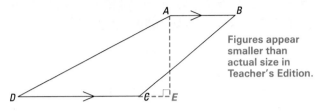

Figures appear smaller than actual size in Teacher's Edition.

Review

18. Two-thirds of a piece of cloth was used. The starting amount was *A*. How much is left?   *(Lesson 10-6)* $\frac{1}{3}A$ or $\frac{A}{3}$

19. a. Solve $8x - 10 = 70$. $x = 10$
b. Solve $-8y - 10 = 70$. $y = -10$
c. Solve $-8(z + 3) - 10 = 70$.   *(Lessons 10-4, 10-5, 10-6)* $z = -13$

20. Use the figure shown at the left. Find the area of $\triangle ABC$ in two different ways.   *(Lesson 9-1)* 1) $\frac{1}{2} \cdot 80 \cdot 60 = 2400$ sq units; 2) $\frac{1}{2} \cdot 100 \cdot 48 = 2400$ sq units

21. Find the area of a right triangle with sides of lengths 12 ft, 16 ft, and 20 ft.   *(Lesson 9-1)* **96 sq ft**

22. *True or false.*   If the diagonal of a rectangle is drawn, the perimeter of each right triangle is one-half the perimeter of the rectangle. *(Lesson 5-10)* **False**

23. To the nearest integer, what is the sum of $2\frac{1}{3}$, $3\frac{1}{4}$, and $4\frac{1}{5}$? *(Lesson 5-5)* **10**

Exploration

24a) Sample: a quadrilateral with no sides parallel

24b) Sample:

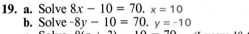

24. Words often have many meanings. Sometimes those meanings do not agree with each other. One of the meanings of trapezoid is "trapezium."
a. Look in a dictionary to find another meaning of "trapezium."
b. Draw a trapezium.

Lesson 10-10   *Areas of Trapezoids*   **581**

Adapting to Individual Needs

Challenge
Have students draw and cut out a trapezoid that has one pair of parallel sides, tape it along any one of its sides to a pencil (or a piece of string), turn the pencil 360°, and then describe the three-dimensional figure that would be formed by turning the trapezoid. Have students repeat the activity by taping different sides of the trapezoid. Some students might want to repeat the activity with different trapezoids. [Answers will vary.]

Practice

For more questions on SPUR Objectives, use **Lesson Master 10-10A** (shown on page 579) or **Lesson Master 10-10B** (shown on pages 580–581).

Assessment

Written Communication Draw a large trapezoid on a sheet of paper, or use **Teaching Aid 116.** Give no dimensions of the trapezoid but have students estimate its area in square inches. Ask students to write a paragraph explaining how they found the area of the trapezoid. [Answer and explanation will reveal understanding of finding area of a trapezoid by triangulating or by drawing an altitude and measuring.]

Extension

If your students did the *Extension* for Lesson 7-8 (page 392), review the definitions of isosceles trapezoid and kite and their placement in the diagram on **Teaching Aid 77.** If you did not assign the extension, you might have students complete the teaching aid at this time.

Project Update Project 2, *Areas of Special Types of Trapezoids* on page 582, relates to the content of this lesson.

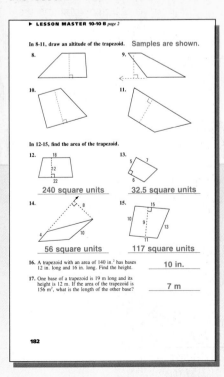

581

Chapter 10 Projects

Chapter 10 projects relate to the content of the lessons as follows.

Project	Lesson(s)
1	10-8
2	10-10
3	10-4
4	10-7
5	10-1
6	10-6

1 Units for Land Area Information about units of area can be found in most almanacs or encyclopedias. The metric unit *are* and the U. S. unit *square rod* may not be familiar to students. Have students find how these units are related to other units in their measurement systems. An are is equal to 100 square meters and a square rod is equal to 30.25 square yards.

2 Areas of Special Types of Trapezoids The area formulas for parallelograms, rectangles, and squares can be found in Chapter 4. Once students have found that the area of each figure can be found using either formula, you may wish to discuss with them how the formula for each specific figure is derived from the formula for a trapezoid.

3 How Often Is a Solution to an Equation an Integer? There are 6^3 or 216 possible different equations that can be formed by tossing three dice to find the value of *a*, *b*, and *c* in the equation $ax + b = c$. Eighty-five of these solutions are positive, eighty-four are integers, and twenty-six are positive integers. Remind students when they are determining relative frequencies of each event that zero is an integer, but not a positive integer.

PROJECTS 10 CHAPTER TEN

A project presents an opportunity for you to extend your knowledge of a topic related to the material of this chapter. You should allow more time for a project than you do for typical homework questions.

1 Units for Land Area
In the metric system, land is often measured using a unit called the *hectare*. In the U.S. system, a commonly used unit of land area is the *acre*. Write an essay telling how these units are related to other units within their system, and determine how hectare and acre are related to each other.

2 Areas of Special Types of Trapezoids
Parallelograms, squares, rectangles, and rhombuses are all special types of trapezoids. Each of these types of figures has its own area formula. Find a formula for the area of each type. Then find the area of a specific example of each type, using the formula you have found and then using the formula for the area of a trapezoid given in Lesson 10-10.

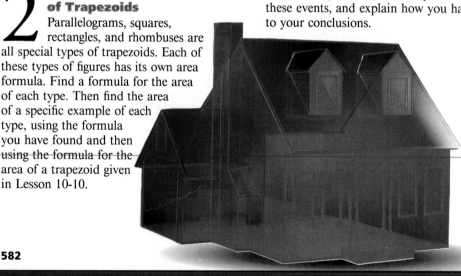

3 How Often Is a Solution to an Equation an Integer?
Even if the numbers you deal with are small positive integers, solutions to many equations are not integers. To verify this, try this experiment. Find three six-sided dice and call them *a*, *b*, and *c*. Toss the dice and substitute the numbers into the equation $ax + b = c$. For instance, if the die *a* shows 2, *b* shows 5, and *c* shows 1, then the equation will be $2x + 5 = 1$. Write down 50 equations using this procedure. Determine the relative frequencies of the following events:
a. The solution is positive.
b. The solution is an integer.
c. The solution is a positive integer. Write down what you think are the probabilities of these events, and explain how you have come to your conclusions.

582

Possible responses
1. The following information is a sample of what students might include in their projects. One hectare is equal to 10,000 square meters and 100 ares. One square kilometer is equal to 100 hectares or 1,000,000 square meters. One acre is equal to 160 square rods, 4,840 square yards, or 43,560 square feet. One square mile is equal to 640 acres. One acre is equal to 0.405 hectare and one hectare is approximately equal to 2.469 acres.
2. Area formulas:
parallelogram: $A = b \times h$
square: $A = s^2$
rectangle: $A = l \times w$
rhombus: $A = b \times h$
Areas of specific figures will vary. The area of each figure will be the same whether the trapezoid formula or the specific formula for that shape is used.

4 Surface Areas and Volumes of Boxes

Students should decide what unit of measurement they are going to use before starting the project. Have students label each box in some way and suggest that they make a table showing the volume and surface area of each box. If students have more than one box with the same surface area, have students compare the volumes and the shapes of these boxes.

5 Multiplication of Numbers in Scientific Notation

Have students use special cases to develop rules for multiplying numbers in scientific notation. Suggest that they use whole number values for *a* and *b*, find products mentally, and come up with a rule. Then have them pick some nonintegers for *a* and *b* and use a calculator to test if the rule they came up with applies to these numbers as well. If a computer spreadsheet is available, suggest that interested students use this tool to generate their samples. Remind students that the exponents can have negative as well as positive values.

6 Different Methods of Multiplication

Both Napier's bones and the Russian Peasant algorithm are used solely for multiplication. The abacus, however, is used for adding, subtracting, and dividing, as well. If students have difficulty finding information about multiplying on an abacus, they can use the book *The Abacus* by Jesse Dilson, St. Martin's Press, New York.

John Napier was a Scottish mathematician who made a calculating device that used rods carved from bones. This method is sometimes called lattice multiplication. Students may find it helpful to use large grid paper to show how to multiply using this method.

The advantage of the Russian Peasant algorithm is that it requires only the abilities to add, multiply by two, and divide by two.

4 Surface Areas and Volumes of Boxes

Find at least six boxes of various sizes and calculate their surface areas and volumes. Explain why a box that has greater volume might not have greater surface area.

6 Different Methods of Multiplication

A variety of ways of multiplying two whole numbers have been developed over the centuries. Find out about one of the following methods of multiplication:
(a) using an abacus,
(b) Napier's bones (shown below),
(c) the Russian Peasant algorithm.
Show how to multiply 364×27 using the method you have chosen.

5 Multiplication of Numbers in Scientific Notation

Suppose two numbers are given in scientific notation: $a \cdot 10^m$ and $b \cdot 10^n$. What is the product of those numbers in scientific notation? By experimenting with your calculator or by hand, come up with rules for multiplying numbers in this form.

3. a.– c. Relative frequencies will vary. The probability of each event is:
   a. 85/216
   b. 7/18
   c. 13/108.
4. Responses will vary. In general, students will find that cube-shaped boxes have the greatest volume for a given surface area. Therefore, a cube-shaped box may have a greater volume than a box shaped like a rectangular prism that has a greater surface area.
5. $(a \cdot 10^m) \cdot (b \cdot 10^n) = ab \cdot 10^{m+n}$

(Responses continue on page 584.)

Summary

The Summary gives an overview of the entire chapter and provides an opportunity for students to consider the material as a whole. Thus, the Summary can be used to help students relate and unify the concepts presented in the chapter.

Vocabulary

Terms, symbols, and properties are listed by lesson to provide a checklist of concepts a student must know. Emphasize to students that they should read the vocabulary list carefully before starting the Progress Self-Test. If students do not understand the meaning of a term, they should refer back to the indicated lesson.

SUMMARY

This chapter has three major themes: solving equations, the Distributive Property, and areas of common figures.

The many uses of multiplication—areas, arrays, and volumes; size changes; and rate factors—lead to situations in which one factor and a product are known, but the other factor is not. These situations translate into equations of the form $ax = b$. If you cannot solve such an equation in your head, you can use the Multiplication Property of Equality:

If $a \neq 0$, the solution to $ax = b$ is $x = \frac{b}{a}$. Other situations combine multiplication and addition and lead to equations of the form $ax + b = c$. These equations can be solved by first adding $-b$ to both sides.

The Distributive Property is the basic property connecting multiplication to addition. Its many forms are all consequences of the basic form

$$ax + bx = (a + b)x$$

that arises from adding like terms. Using the Commutative Property of Multiplication, a second form arises:

$$xa + xb = x(a + b).$$

Two other forms involve subtraction.

$$ax - bx = (a - b)x$$
$$xa - xb = x(a - b)$$

The surface area of a rectangular solid can be found by adding the areas of its six faces. Because it is an area, surface area is measured in square units. (The Distributive Property can make it easier to calculate this area.) The area of any triangle is $\frac{1}{2} bh$, where b is the base and h the height to that base. Adding the areas of two triangles and using the Distributive Property leads to the formula $A = \frac{1}{2}h(b_1 + b_2)$ for the area of a trapezoid.

VOCABULARY

You should be able to give a general description and specific example for each of the following ideas.

Lesson 10-1
Repeated Addition Property of Multiplication
like terms
unlike terms

Lesson 10-2
Multiplication Property of Equality

Lesson 10-4
equation of the form $ax + b = c$

Lesson 10-6
Distributive Property of Multiplication over
   Addition
Distributive Property of Multiplication over
   Subtraction

Lesson 10-7
net
surface area

Lesson 10-8
numerically equal
acre

Lesson 10-9
height, altitude, base of a triangle
Area Formula for Any Triangle

Lesson 10-10
trapezoid
Area Formula for a Trapezoid
trapezoid—height, altitude, base

584

Additional responses, p. 583

6. The following information is a sample of what students might include in their projects.
   Both the Chinese and Japanese abacuses are made up of vertical rods held in a wooden frame. Each abacus has a horizontal strip of wood that divides the abacus into two parts. The lower part has four beads on each rod and the upper part has one bead on each rod on the Japanese

abacus and two beads on the upper part on the Chinese abacus. The upper beads have a value of five units and the bottom beads each have a value of one unit. Numbers are recorded by bringing beads to the horizontal bar. To multiply 364 × 27, 364 would be multiplied by 7 with the product, 2548, represented on the abacus. Then 7280, the product of 364 × 20, would be added to 2548.

A knowledge of basic multiplication facts is necessary to multiply with an abacus. Multiplication of a large number by a one-digit number is often done using repeated addition. To multiply using Napier's bones, place the numbers 364 and 27 at the top and to the right of a lattice as shown at the right. Then multiply the digits of the

PROGRESS SELF-TEST

Take this test as you would take a test in class. Then check your work with the solutions in the Selected Answers section in the back of the book.

In 1–4, simplify.

1. $-y + y + y + 3 + y + y$ **3y + 3**
2. $m - 3m$ **-2m**
3. $7k - 2j - 4k + j$ **3k – j**
4. $x + 2x + 3x + 4x$ **10x**
5. Write the perimeter of the hexagon below in simplest form. **4b + 80**

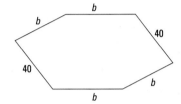

6. Explain how the Distributive Property can be used to calculate $49 \cdot 7$ mentally. **See below.**
7. The Distributive Property is used here in going from what line to what line? **line 5 to line 6**

Line 1	$5x + 2 - 2x - 2$
Line 2	$= 5x + 2 + -2x + -2$
Line 3	$= 5x + -2x + 2 + -2$
Line 4	$= 5x + -2x + 0$
Line 5	$= 5x + -2x$
Line 6	$= (5 + -2)x$
Line 7	$= 3x$

8. Suppose the shoreline of a lake is measured in kilometers. In what unit would you expect to measure the amount of room for fishing? **km²**
9. *Multiple choice.* Which is *not* necessarily a trapezoid? **(a)**
   (a) quadrilateral   (b) rectangle
   (c) square   (d) parallelogram
10. The area of a triangle is 400 square inches, and the height to one base is 25 inches. What must be that length of that base? **32 in.**

6) $49 \cdot 7 = (50 - 1) \cdot 7 = 50 \cdot 7 - 1 \cdot 7 = 350 - 7 = 343$

11. Explain how the Distributive Property can be used to find the total combined area of all these rectangles. **See below.**

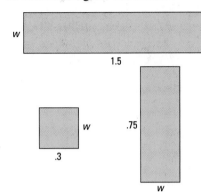

12. How much cardboard is needed to make the closed carton pictured below? **234 cm²**

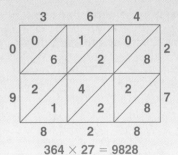

In 13–16, solve.

13. $35.1 = -9t$ **-3.9 = t**
14. $\frac{2}{5}m = -\frac{3}{4}$ **$m = -\frac{15}{8}$, or $-1\frac{7}{8}$**
15. $2 + 3a = 17$ **a = 5**
16. $12 - 4h = 10$ **$h = \frac{1}{2}$**
17. A person made $2000 more this year than last. This is 8% of last year's income. What was last year's income? **$25,000**

11) **Sample: Arrange the rectangles side by side with *w* as the common width. Then $A = w \cdot (1.5 + .3 + .75) = 2.55w$.**

---

two factors and put the products in the grid. Then, starting at the bottom right hand corner, add along the diagonals, carrying when necessary. The product is read from the left side to the bottom of the grid.

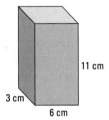

$364 \times 27 = 9828$

Responses continue on page 586.

For the development of mathematical competence, feedback and correction, along with the opportunity to practice, are necessary. The Progress Self-Test provides the opportunity for feedback and correction; the Chapter Review provides additional opportunities and practice. We cannot overemphasize the importance of these end-of-chapter materials. It is at this point that the material "gels" for many students, allowing them to solidify skills and understanding. In general, student performance should be markedly improved after these pages.

Assign the Progress Self-Test as a one-night assignment. Worked-out *solutions* for all questions are in the Selected Answers section of the student book. Encourage students to take the Progress Self-Test honestly, grade themselves, and then be prepared to discuss the test in class.

Advise students to pay special attention to those Chapter Review questions (pages 587–589) which correspond to questions missed on the Progress Self-Test.

PROGRESS SELF-TEST

In 18–20, find the area of each figure.

18.
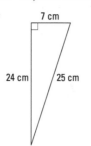
7 cm

24 cm   25 cm

84 cm²

20.
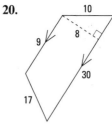
10

9   8

30

17

156 sq units

19.
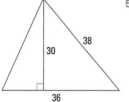
38

30

36

540 sq units

21. An ant is 4 meters up a tree and is crawling down at .02 meters per second. Assume this rate continues. **See below.**

a. How high will the ant be after 5 seconds?

b. When will the ant be 2.5 meters high?

22. The balance scale diagram below represents what equation? $3w + 1 = 10$

21a) 3.9 meters
b) after 75 seconds

Additional responses, page 583

To multiply 364×27 using the Russian Peasant algorithm, make a table with two columns. Write 364 at the top of the left column and 27 at the top of the right column. Divide 364 by two, ignoring any remainder, and record the quotient below 364 in the table. Double 27 and record that product below 27 in the table. Repeat this process until the number one is reached in the left column.

Cross out every row that has an even number in the left-hand column. Add the remaining numbers in the right-hand column, $108 + 216 + 864 + 1728 + 6912 = 9828$, to find the product.

364	27
182	54 (cross out)
91	108
45	216
22	432 (cross out)
11	864
5	1728
2	3456 (cross out)
1	6912

CHAPTER REVIEW

Questions on SPUR Objectives

SPUR stands for **S**kills, **P**roperties, **U**ses, and **R**epresentations. The Chapter Review questions are grouped according to the SPUR Objectives for this chapter.

SKILLS DEAL WITH THE PROCEDURES USED TO GET ANSWERS.

Objective A: *Solve and check equations of the form ax = b.* *(Lessons 10-2, 10-5)*

In 1–8, solve and check.

1. $40t = 3000$
   $t = 75$
2. $-22 = 4A$ $A = -5.5$
3. $0.02v = 0.8$
   $v = 40$
4. $\frac{2}{3}x = 18$ $x = 27$
5. $-49 = -7y$ $y = 7$
6. $2.4 + 3.6 = (5 - 0.2)n$
   $n = 1.25$
7. $\frac{4}{5}n = 12$
   $n = 15$
8. $700m = 14$ $m = .02$

Objective B: *Solve and check equations of the form ax + b = c.* *(Lessons 10-4, 10-5)*

In 9–16, solve and check.

9. $8m + 2 = 18$ $m = 2$
10. $-2.5 + .5y = 4.2$
    $y = 13.4$
11. $11 - 6u = -7$ $u = 3$
12. $23 + 4x - 10 = -39$
    $x = -13$
13. $2x + 3x + 5 = 17$
14. $44 = 10 - 2z$
    $z = -17$
15. $1.3 = 0.8 + 2x$
16. $160 = 9a - a + 16$
    $a = 18$

13) $x = 2.4$ 15) $x = 0.25$

Objective C: *Apply properties of multiplication to simplify expressions.* *(Lessons 10-1, 10-6)*

In 17–22, simplify.

17. $x + x + x + y + y + z + z$
18. $2v + 8v$ $10v$
19. $5x - x - 2x$ $2x$
20. $13a + 4b + 7a$
21. $-9 + 5m + 2 - 8m + m$
22. $m(1 + n) - m$
23. Multiply $6(a - b + 2c)$. $6a - 6b + 12c$
24. Multiply $2(3x + 5 - 2y)$. $6x + 10 - 4y$

17) $3x + 2y + 2z$
20) $20a + 4b$
21) $-7 - 2m$
22) mn

Objective D: *Find the area of a triangle.* *(Lesson 10-9)*

25. Find the area of $\triangle CAT$. 150 sq units

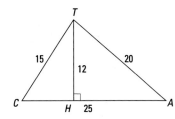

26. *SNOW* is a rectangle with dimensions in meters. Find the area of $\triangle SEW$. 750 m²

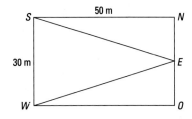

27. Use the triangles below.
    a. Find the area of $\triangle BUI$. 12 sq units

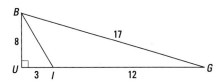

    b. Find the area of $\triangle BIG$. 48 sq units

Resources

From the **Teacher's Resource File**
■ Answer Master for
   Chapter 10 Review
■ Assessment Sourcebook:
   Chapter 10 Test, Forms A–D
   Chapter 10 Test, Cumulative
   Form

Additional Resources
■ TestWorks

The main objectives for the chapter are organized in the Chapter Review under the four types of understand-

...mend assigning the *evens* for homework the first night so that students get feedback in class the next day, then assigning the *odds* the night before the test, because answers are provided to the odd-numbered questions.

It is effective to ask students which questions they still do not understand and use the day or days as a total class discussion of the material which the class finds most difficult.

(handwritten: 10-1 to 10-4, 5-14, 17, 21, 22)

587

Assessment

Evaluation The *Assessment Sourcebook* provides five forms of the Chapter 10 Test. Forms A and B present parallel versions in a short-answer format. Forms C and D offer performance assessment. The fifth test is Chapter 10 Test, Cumulative Form. About 50% of this test covers Chapter 10, 25% of it covers Chapter 9, and 25% of it covers earlier chapters.

For information on grading, see *General Teaching Suggestions: Grading* in the *Professional Sourcebook* which begins on page T20 in Volume 1 of the Teacher's Edition.

28. Find the area of $\triangle ABC$. **126 sq units**

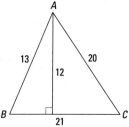

Objective E: *Find the area of a trapezoid.*
(Lesson 10-10)

In 29–32, *WEYZ* is a parallelogram.

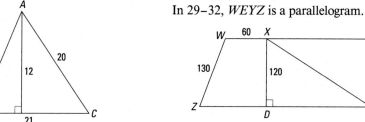

29) 24,600 sq units   **29.** If $ZY = 350$, find the area of *WXYZ*.

30) 42,000 sq units   **30.** If $ZY = 350$, find the area of *WEYZ*.

31) 28,800 sq units   **31.** If $XE = 180$, find the area of *WEYZ*.

32) 10,200 sq units   **32.** If $ZD = 110$, find the area of *WXDZ*.

PROPERTIES DEAL WITH THE PRINCIPLES BEHIND THE MATHEMATICS.

Objective F: *Recognize and use the Distributive Property, the Repeated Addition Property of Multiplication, and the Multiplication Property of Equality.*
(Lessons 10-1, 10-2, 10-6)

33. What property of multiplication can be used to solve $\frac{11}{3}y = \frac{2}{9}$? **Multiplication Prop. of Equality**

34. The Repeated Addition Property of Multiplication is a special case of what property of multiplication?
The Distributive Property

35. The Distributive Property is used here in going from what line to what other line?

Line 1	$3x - x$
Line 2	$= 3x - 1 \cdot x$
Line 3	$= (3 - 1)x$
Line 4	$= 2x$

from line 2 to line 3

36. Explain how the Distributive Property can be applied to calculate $\$19.95 \cdot 4$ in your head.
Think of 19.95 · 4 as (20.00 − .05) · 4; mentally calculate 20.00 · 4 − .05 · 4 = 80 − .20 = 79.80.

USES DEAL WITH APPLICATIONS OF MATHEMATICS IN REAL SITUATIONS.

Objective G: *Find unknowns in real situations involving multiplication.* *(Lessons 10-3, 10-4, 10-5)*

37. The floor of a store is in the shape of a rectangle. Find the length of the floor if its area is 3500 sq ft and the width is 40 ft.

38. A movie theater has 500 seats and 20 rows. There are the same number of seats in each row. How many seats are there per row?

37) 87.5 ft
38) 25 seats per row

39. Find the height of this box if its volume is 2400 cubic centimeters. **12 cm**

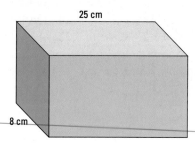

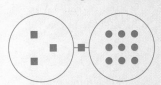

40. Elvis is currently 63 inches tall and is growing at the rate of $\frac{1}{4}$ inch every month.
  a. How tall will Elvis be in 6 months? $64\frac{1}{2}''$
  b. At this rate of growth, how long will it take Elvis to reach a height of 74 inches?

41. Melissa's car can hold 45 liters of gas. When she is driving on the highway, she uses 125 mL per minute.
  a. How much gas will Melissa have left after 1 hour? 37.5 L
  b. How long can she drive before she has less than 10 liters left? $4\frac{2}{3}$ hr or 4 hours, 40 minutes

Objective H: *Find the surface area of a rectangular solid in real contexts.* *(Lesson 10-7)*

42. A stick of margarine is approximately 11.5 cm long, 3 cm wide, and 3 cm high. To wrap the margarine in aluminum foil, what is the least area of foil needed? 156 cm²

40b) 44 mo

43. The mattress of a water bed is 7′ long, 6′ wide, and 3/4′ high. Explain why a quilt with an area of 48 square feet cannot cover the top and all sides of the mattress. 61.5 ft² is needed.

44. How much gift wrap is needed to cover a box that is 12″ by 8″ by 3″? 312 sq in.

Objective I: *Pick appropriate units in measurement situations.* *(Lesson 10-8)*

45. The perimeter of a vegetable garden is measured in feet. In what unit would you expect to measure the amount of space you have for planting? feet²

46. If the dimensions of a rectangular solid are measured in inches, in what unit would the surface area most probably be measured?

47. Name two units of volume.

48. *Multiple choice.* The acre is a unit of:
  (a) length.   (b) land area.
  (c) volume.   (d) weight. (b)

46) in²   47) Sample: in³, km³

REPRESENTATIONS DEAL WITH PICTURES, GRAPHS, OR OBJECTS THAT ILLUSTRATE CONCEPTS.

Objective J: *Represent equations of the form $ax = b$ and $ax + b = c$ with a balance scale diagram.* *(Lessons 10-2, 10-4)*

49. a. Draw a balance scale diagram representing the equation $3w = 9$.
  b. Solve the equation. a) See margin. b) $w = 3$

50. a. The balance scale diagram below represents what equation? $2w + 1 = 5$
  b. Solve the equation. $w = 2$

Objective K: *Represent the Distributive Property by areas of rectangles.* *(Lesson 10-6)*

51. What instance of the Distributive Property is pictured here? $x(20 + 5) = 20x + 5x$

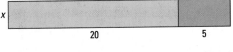
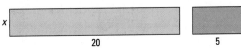

52. Use rectangles to show that $8.2 \cdot 13.6 + 9 \cdot 13.6 = (8.2 + 9)13.6$.

The sum of the areas of the first two rectangles is the same as the area of the rectangle on the right.

Setting Up Lesson 11-1
We recommend that you assign Lesson 11-1, both reading and some questions, for homework the evening of the test. It gives students work to do after they have completed the test and keeps the class moving.

Chapter **11** Planner

Adapting to Individual Needs

The student text is written for the vast majority of students. The chart at the right suggests two pacing plans to accommodate the needs of your students. Students in the Full Course should complete the entire text by the end of the year. Students in the Minimal Course will spend more time when there are quizzes and more time on the Chapter Review. Therefore, these students may not complete all of the chapters in the text.

Options are also presented to meet the needs of a variety of teaching and learning styles. For each lesson, the Teacher's Edition provides sections entitled: *Video* which describes video segments and related questions that can be used for motivation or extension; *Optional Activities* which suggests activities that employ materials, physical models, technology, and cooperative learning; and *Adapting to Individual Needs* which regularly includes **Challenge** problems, **English Language Development** suggestions, and suggestions for providing **Extra Help.** The Teacher's Edition also frequently includes an **Error Alert,** an **Extension,** and an **Assessment** alternative. The options available in Chapter 11 are summarized in the chart below.

Chapter 11 Pacing Chart

Day	Full Course	Minimal Course
1	11-1	11-1
2	11-2	11-2
3	11-3	11-3
4	11-4	11-4
5	Quiz*; 11-5	Quiz*; begin 11-5.
6	11-6	Finish 11-5.
7	11-7	11-6
8	11-8	11-7
9	Quiz*; 11-9	11-8
10	Self-Test	Quiz*; begin 11-9.
11	Review	Finish 11-9.
12	Test*	Self-Test
13		Review
14		Review
15		Test*

*in the Teacher's Resource File

In the Teacher's Edition...

Lesson	Optional Activities	Extra Help	Challenge	English Language Development	Error Alert	Extension	Cooperative Learning	Ongoing Assessment
11-1	●	●	●	●	●	●		Oral
11-2	●	●	●			●	●	Group
11-3	●	●	●	●		●	●	Oral
11-4	●	●	●			●		Written
11-5	●	●	●			●	●	Written
11-6	●	●	●			●	●	Group
11-7	●	●	●			●	●	Group
11-8	●	●	●	●		●		Oral
11-9	●	●	●			●	●	Written

In the Additional Resources...

| | In the Teacher's Resource File | | | | | | | | |
Lesson	Lesson Masters, A and B	Teaching Aids*	Activity Kit*	Answer Masters	Technology Sourcebook	Assessment Sourcebook	Visual Aids**	Technology Tools	Video Segments
11-1	11-1	105, 117		11-1			105, 117, AM	Spreadsheet	
11-2	11-2	117		11-2	Demo 11, Comp 25		117, AM	Spreadsheet	
11-3	11-3	117		11-3			117, AM		
11-4	11-4	87, 117	28	11-4		Quiz	87, 117, AM		
11-5	11-5	118		11-5			118, AM		
11-6	11-6	118		11-6			118, AM		Segment 11
11-7	11-7	118		11-7			118, AM		
In-class Activity		120					120, AM		
11-8	11-8	119, 121, 122		11-8	Comp 26	Quiz	119, 121, 122, AM	Geometry	
11-9	11-9	119		11-9			119, AM		

*Teaching Aids, except Warm-ups, are pictured on pages 590C and 590D. The activities in the Activity Kit are pictured on page 590C.

Teaching Aid 120 which accompanies the In-class Activity is pictured with the lesson notes on page 625.

**Visual Aids provide transparencies for all Teaching Aids and all Answer Masters.

Also available is the Study Skills Handbook which includes study-skill tips related to reading, note-taking, and comprehension.

Integrating Strands and Applications

	11-1	11-2	11-3	11-4	11-5	11-6	11-7	11-8	11-9
Mathematical Connections									
Algebra	●	●	●	●	●	●	●	●	●
Geometry	●	●		●	●	●	●	●	●
Measurement	●	●	●				●		●
Logic and Reasoning				●					●
Probability				●		●			
Statistics/Data Analysis		●			●		●	●	●
Patterns and Functions	●		●					●	
Interdisciplinary and Other Connections									
Literature							●		
Science	●			●	●		●		●
Social Studies	●	●		●	●	●	●	●	●
Multicultural					●		●	●	
Technology	●	●		●				●	●
Career	●	●	●						
Consumer		●	●	●	●	●	●	●	●
Sports			●		●	●	●		

Take it to the NET

On the Internet, visit **www.phschool.com** for UCSMP teacher support, student self-tests, activities, and more.

Teaching and Assessing the Chapter Objectives

In the Assessment Sourcebook

Chapter 11 Objectives (Organized into the SPUR categories—Skills, Properties, Uses, and Representations)	Lessons	Progress Self-Test Questions	Chapter Review Questions	Chapter Test, Forms A and B	Chapter Test, Forms C	D
Skills						
A: Divide fractions with numbers or variables.	11-3	3, 5	1–7	3, 12, 13	1	
B: Divide positive and negative numbers.	11-4	4, 6	8–12	14, 15	3	
C: Solve proportions.	11-6, 11-7, 11-9	9, 10	13–19	6, 16	4	
Properties						
D: Recognize the Means-Extremes Property and know why it works.	11-7	16, 17	20–22	7		
E: Know the general properties for dividing positive and negative numbers.	11-4	7	23, 24	4, 22	3	
Uses						
F: Use integer division in real situations.	11-1	21, 22	25–28	1, 17	3	✓
G: Use the Rate Model for Division.	11-2, 11-3, 11-4	1, 2, 8	29–35	2, 18	2	✓
H: Use the Ratio Comparison Model for Division.	11-5	11–13	36–39	5, 9–11, 19	2	✓
I: Recognize and solve problems involving proportions in real situations.	11-6, 11-7, 11-9	14, 15, 20	40–42	20	4	✓
Representations						
J: Find missing lengths in similar figures.	11-8	18, 19	43–45	8, 21	5	

Assessment Sourcebook
Quiz for Lessons 11-1 through 11-4   Chapter 11 Test, Forms A–D
Quiz for Lessons 11-4 through 11-8   Chapter 11 Test, Cumulative Form

TestWorks
Multiple forms of chapter tests and quizzes; Challenge items

Activity Kit

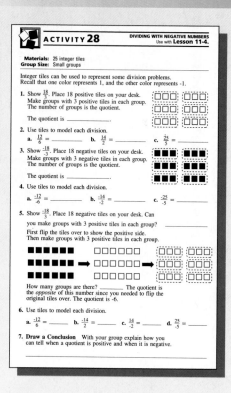

ACTIVITY 28

DIVIDING WITH NEGATIVE NUMBERS
Use with **Lesson 11-4.**

Materials: 25 integer tiles
Group Size: Small groups

Integer tiles can be used to represent some division problems.
Recall that one color represents 1, and the other color represents -1.

1. Show $\frac{18}{3}$. Place 18 positive tiles on your desk.
Make groups with 3 positive tiles in each group.
The number of groups is the quotient.

The quotient is _____.

2. Use tiles to model each division.
   a. $\frac{12}{6}$ = _____ b. $\frac{14}{2}$ = _____ c. $\frac{25}{5}$ = _____

3. Show $\frac{-18}{-3}$. Place 18 negative tiles on your desk.
Make groups with 3 negative tiles in each group.
The number of groups is the quotient.

The quotient is _____.

4. Use tiles to model each division.
   a. $\frac{-12}{-6}$ = _____ b. $\frac{-14}{-2}$ = _____ c. $\frac{-25}{-5}$ = _____

5. Show $\frac{-18}{3}$. Place 18 negative tiles on your desk. Can

you make groups with 3 positive tiles in each group? _____

First flip the tiles over to show the positive side.
Then make groups with 3 positive tiles in each group.

How many groups are there? _____ The quotient is
the *opposite* of this number since you needed to flip the
original tiles over. The quotient is -6.

6. Use tiles to model each division.
   a. $\frac{-12}{6}$ = _____ b. $\frac{-14}{2}$ = _____ c. $\frac{14}{-2}$ = _____ d. $\frac{25}{-5}$ = _____

7. **Draw a Conclusion** With your group explain how you
can tell when a quotient is positive and when it is negative.

Teaching Aids

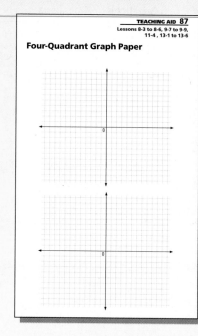

TEACHING AID 87

Lessons 8-3 to 8-6, 9-7 to 9-9,
11-4, 13-1 to 13-6

Four-Quadrant Graph Paper

TEACHING AID 105

Lessons 9-7 to 9-9

Size Changes

Magnitude _____

Preimage Point	Image Point

Magnitude _____

Preimage Point	Image Point

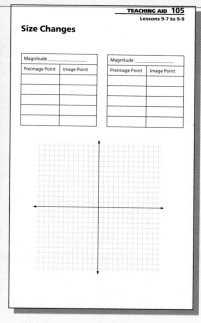

TEACHING AID 117

Warm-up Lesson 11-1

1. How many $7 baseball tickets can you buy
   with $25? How much money will you have left?
2. Box seats hold 7 people. How many box
   seats are needed for 25 people?
3. If the opening baseball game is 25 days from
   today, and today is a Wednesday, on what
   day of the week is the opening game?
4. Twenty-five days is how many weeks?

Warm-up Lesson 11-2

Think of as many rates as you can.
Then work with your classmates, and
write some of them on the chalkboard.

Warm-up Lesson 11-3

Calculator Write each fraction as a decimal.

1. $\frac{8}{5}$ 2. $\frac{9}{4}$ 3. $\frac{7}{16}$ 4. $\frac{29}{20}$ 5. $\frac{13}{13}$ 6. $\frac{9}{32}$

7. What is true about the numerator (n)
   and denominator (d) of a fraction
   when the number is

   a. less than 1?   b. greater than 1?

   c. equal to 1?

Warm-up Lesson 11-4

Multiply.

1. -7×-14 2. 23×-5 3. -4×11

4. $-9 \times -3 \times 0$ 5. -3^3 6. -2^4

7. $-4 \times 30 \times -5$ 8. $-5 \times 10 \times 5 \times -4$

590C

Warm-up
Lesson 11-5

1. If the sales-tax rate is 5%, what is the sales tax on a $15 CD?

2. If 60%, or 12, of the students in the chorus are girls, how many students are in the chorus?

3. In Question 2, what percent are boys?

Warm-up
Lesson 11-6

1. In your math class, what is the ratio of boys to students? What is the ratio of girls to students?

2. Assume the ratios for your class are the same for your grade and for your school.

   a. If there are 300 students in your grade, how many are girls? How many are boys?

   b. If there are 750 students in your school, how many are girls? How many are boys?

Warm-up
Lesson 11-7

The same brand of pen is sold by stores A, B, and C.

A: 3 for $0.50   B: 12 for $2.00   C: 8 for $1.50

1. Write a proportion using the prices at A and B.

   a. Identify the means.   b. Identify the extremes.

   c. Is the product of the means equal to the product of the extremes? Are the ratios equal?

2. Write a proportion using the prices at A and C. Are the ratios equal?

3. Is the price of the pens the same at

   a. A and B?   b. A and C?   c. B and C?

Warm-up
Lesson 11-8

On a road map, one inch represents 14 miles. The map distances between certain cities are listed below. Estimate the actual distances between the cities

1. Cincinnati, OH, and Lexington, KY: $5\frac{1}{2}$ inches

2. Eugene, OR, and Bend, OR: 9 inches

3. Bangor, ME, and Lewiston, ME: $7\frac{1}{2}$ inches

Warm-up
Lesson 11-9

For each exercise, select the proportion or proportions that could be used to solve the problem.

1. Zak drove 10 miles in 15 minutes. At this rate, how far can he drive in 40 minutes?

   a. $\dfrac{15 \text{ min}}{40 \text{ min}} = \dfrac{x}{10 \text{ mi}}$

   b. $\dfrac{15 \text{ min}}{10 \text{ mi}} = \dfrac{x}{40 \text{ min}}$

   c. $\dfrac{10 \text{ mi}}{15 \text{ min}} = \dfrac{x}{40 \text{ min}}$

2. If 3 boxes of pasta cost $1.59, how much will 5 boxes cost?

   a. $\dfrac{3 \text{ boxes}}{\$1.59} = \dfrac{5 \text{ boxes}}{x}$

   b. $\dfrac{3 \text{ boxes}}{5 \text{ boxes}} = \dfrac{x}{\$1.59}$

   c. $\dfrac{\$1.59}{3 \text{ boxes}} = \dfrac{x}{5 \text{ boxes}}$

Additional Examples

1. Given that △RUN is similar to △HOP, with corresponding sides parallel, list the pairs of corresponding sides.

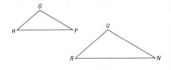

2. The two trapezoids are similar with corresponding sides parallel. Find the missing lengths.

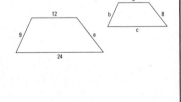

Tangram

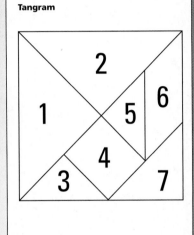

590D

Chapter Opener 11

Pacing

All lessons in this chapter are designed to be covered in one day. At the end of the chapter, you should plan to spend 1 day to review the Progress Self-Test, 1–2 days for the Chapter Review, and 1 day for a test. You may wish to spend a day on projects, and possibly a day is needed for quizzes. This chapter should therefore take 12–15 days. We strongly urge you not to spend more than 16 days on this chapter.

Using Pages 590–591

The seven applications of the division problem 20 ÷ 7 serve as an advance organizer for this chapter. Students know how to answer **Questions B and E** from their work in Chapter 10. However, in this chapter, they will see other equations they might use for these situations. **Question C** is usually answered with integer division, the subject of Lesson 11-1. **Questions A, D, and F** involve rates (area per person; children per child; miles at miles per hour), which are studied in Lesson 11-2. **Question G** involves ratio comparisons, which are covered in Lesson 11-5.

CHAPTER 11

11-1 Integer Division

11-2 The Rate Model for Division

11-3 Division of Fractions

11-4 Division with Negative Numbers

11-5 The Ratio Comparison Model for Division

11-6 Proportions

11-7 The Means-Extremes Property

11-8 Proportions in Similar Figures

11-9 Proportional Thinking

590

Chapter 11 Overview

Division, the last of the four traditional fundamental operations of arithmetic to be studied in this book, is by no means the least important. Rate and ratio comparison, the two principal uses of division, have applications throughout mathematics. Proportions, which arise from equal quotients, are also of fundamental significance.

Because hand calculation of answers to division problems is more difficult than the other fundamental arithmetic operations, most students in the past spent a great deal of time learning *how* to divide, but not *when* to divide. Your students' prior experiences may reflect that history. As a result, your students may have had very little work with applications of division. Thus, the applications of division tend to be unfamiliar, and intuition, particularly when the numbers are not small whole numbers, has never been developed.

The chapter begins by distinguishing the two types of division of whole numbers, integer division (quotient and remainder) and real-number division (single number). The next three lessons consider the Rate Model for Division and its applications. In Lesson 11-2, rates are calculated in which the divisor and dividend are either whole numbers or decimals. In Lessons 11-3 and 11-4, this model is used with fractions and with negative numbers.

PATTERNS LEADING TO DIVISION

There are many kinds of questions that can be answered by division. Here are seven questions that can be answered by dividing 20 by 7.

A. In Brazil, land is currently being offered to people for farming. Suppose a subdivision of 20 lots is split equally among 7 people. What will be the area of each person's share?

B. The distance from El Paso, Texas, to Boston is about 2000 miles, and from El Paso to Los Angeles is about 700 miles. How many times as far is it from El Paso to Boston as it is from El Paso to Los Angeles?

C. You expect 20 people at dinner. Seven people can be seated around each table you have. How many tables are needed?

D. Mr. and Mrs. Torrence have 3 daughters, 4 sons, and 20 grandchildren. On the average, how many children does each of their children have?

E. If $WX = 7$ cm, how long is $\overline{WZ}$?

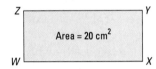

F. If you run at a constant rate of 7 mi/hr, how long will it take you to run 20 miles?

G. If you wished to expand the smaller figure below into the larger figure, what is the magnitude of the size change you would need?

This chapter is concerned with these and other situations that lead to division.

591

Teaching Lesson 11-1

Warm-up
1. How many $7 baseball tickets can you buy with $25? How much money will you have left?
   3 tickets, $4 left
2. Box seats hold 7 people. How many box seats are needed for 25 people? **4 boxes**
3. If the opening baseball game is 25 days from today, and today is a Wednesday, on what day of the week is the opening game?
   Sunday
4. Twenty-five days is how many weeks? $3\frac{4}{7}$ **weeks**

Division in a theme park. *Integer division can be used to determine the number of roller coaster cars needed to seat all members of a certain party. Shown here is the Scream Machine from Great America theme park in New Jersey.*

What Is Real-Number Division?

To answer the questions on page 591, you need to divide 20 by 7. But what are the answers? So far in this book, we have emphasized that

20 divided by 7 equals the quotient $\frac{20}{7}$, which equals $2\frac{6}{7}$, or 2.857142. . . .

This is the answer to questions **A, B, D, E, F,** and **G.** We call this *real-number division*. In **real-number division,** the result of dividing a by b is the single number $\frac{a}{b}$. The variable a can be any number; b can be any number except zero.

What Is Integer Division?

For some situations, however, a correct answer to 20 divided by 7 is

a quotient of 2 with remainder 6.

We call this *integer division*. Notice that the integer part of the quotient is the same regardless of the type of division. This is an appropriate division to use for situation **C** on page 591. If 20 people are to be seated at tables that seat 7 each, then 3 tables are needed. Of these, 2 tables will be filled, and there will be 6 people left over.

In **integer division** of a by b, the number a must be an integer and b must be a whole number. The result of dividing a by b is given by two numbers: an integer quotient and an integer remainder that is less than b. Although integer division may seem more complicated than real-number division, it is probably how you first learned to divide.

592

Lesson 11-1 Overview

Broad Goals This lesson introduces the familiar division of whole numbers leading to an integer quotient and integer remainder and the Quotient-Remainder Formula that relates the divisor, dividend, quotient, and remainder.

Perspective In this lesson, we try to clarify a confusing aspect of arithmetic. In the early grades, children are taught to find a quotient and a remainder as the answer to

a division problem such as 20 ÷ 7. In later study this is ignored—until one reaches a course in number theory or discrete mathematics, where the Quotient-Remainder Theorem (what is here called the Quotient-Remainder Property) is studied.

Is 25 ÷ 4 equal to 6.25 or is the quotient 6 with remainder 4? The answer depends on the situation. And even knowing the situation, such as the school-bus situation in

Example 1, either answer may be reasonable. The key here, as in so much of mathematics, is flexibility—the ability to give either answer.

In *UCSMP Precalculus and Discrete Mathematics* and many other advanced high school courses, students encounter an analogous situation with polynomials. When the polynomial $x^2 + 1$ is divided by $x - 1$, one could say that the quotient is the

Here are other examples of the two types of division.

Division problem	Real-number division answer	Integer division answer
184 divided by 5	quotient 36.8	quotient 36, remainder 4
12 divided by 4	quotient 3	quotient 3, remainder 0
7 divided by 12	quotient $\frac{7}{12} = 0.58\overline{3}$	quotient 0, remainder 7

Finding Answers in Integer Division

Most calculators give answers to real-number divisions, but not to integer divisions. Because some situations call for integer division, it is useful to be able to convert real-number division answers to integer division answers (sometimes called **quotient-remainder form**). The first example shows how to do this using arithmetic.

Example 1

Some school buses seat 44 people. If 600 people ride the buses to a game, how many buses could be filled? How many people would then be in an unfilled bus?

Solution

Divide 600 by 44. Our calculator shows [13.636364]. This indicates that 13 buses could be filled. Multiply 44 by 13 to determine how many students could be in those buses. 44 · 13 = 572. Now subtract 572 from 600 to indicate how many students will be left over. 600 − 572 = 28. Thus, the answer to the integer division is: quotient 13, remainder 28. 13 buses could be filled, and 28 people would then be in the 14th bus.

❶ The Quotient-Remainder Formula

Some people prefer using formulas. Notice in Example 1 how the divisor, dividend, quotient, and remainder are related.

$$d = \text{divisor} = 44$$
$$n = \text{dividend} = 600$$
$$q = \text{integer quotient} = 13$$
$$r = \text{remainder} = 28$$

In the solution, 600 was the sum of 572, the number of students on the full buses, and the remainder 28. Since 572 = 44 · 13, this tells us that

$$600 = 44 \cdot 13 + 28.$$

The more general formula is known as the **Quotient-Remainder Formula.** It relates the dividend n, divisor d, integer quotient q, and remainder r:

$$n = d \cdot q + r.$$

Lesson 11-1 *Integer Division* **593**

Notes on Reading

There is quite a bit of detailed reading in this lesson, so you might want to have students read it in class.

❶ The Quotient-Remainder Formula represents the way many students were taught to check a long division problem. Ask your students how they check a division answer. [Most students multiply the quotient and the divisor and then add the remainder. They know they are correct if the answer is the dividend.]

Optional Activities

rational expression $\frac{x^2+1}{x-1}$ or that it is $x + 1$ with remainder 2. The Quotient-Remainder Theorem for polynomials states that, if $p(x)$ is divided by $d(x)$ with quotient $q(x)$ and remainder $r(x)$, then $p(x) = d(x) \cdot q(x) + r(x)$. In the example given above, $x^2 + 1 = (x - 1)(x + 1) + 2$.

Technology Connection You may wish to have students do integer division using the *Spreadsheet Workshop*. Have them select "Operation forms" from the Forms menu and choose "division with remainders." Have them look up data about mountains, then use the form to change measurements in feet to miles and feet.
[Mt. Everest: 29,108 ft = 5 mi, 2,708 ft]

LESSON MASTER 11-1 A

Questions on SPUR Objectives
See pages 638-639 for objectives.

Uses Objective F

In 1-3, use the Quotient-Remainder Formula to write an equation relating the given numbers.

1. When 15 is divided by 2, the quotient is 7 and the remainder is 1. $15 = 2 \cdot 7 + 1$

2. $25\overline{)318}$ $\frac{12 \text{ R}18}{}$ $318 = 25 \cdot 12 + 18$

3. $w \div x$ gives y with a remainder of z. $w = x \cdot y + z$

4. The cloth for a banquet table is 160 inches long. Change this to feet and inches.   13 ft 4 in.

5. How many days, hours, minutes, and seconds are in 1,000,000 seconds?   11 d 13 hr 46 min 40 sec

6. One mile equals 160,934.4 cm. Change this to kilometers, meters, and centimeters.   1 km 609 m 34.4 cm

7. Which problem was easier to do, Question 5 or Question 6? Why?   Answers will vary.

8. a. In Cooperstown, 213 boys and girls are to be assigned to 15 Little League teams. How many players will each team have? How many teams will have an extra player?   14 players   3 teams

b. If an ideal number of players per team is 12, how many teams should there be? How many teams will have an extra player?   17 teams   9 teams

② The arithmetic in **Example 2** is the same in the metric system, but we do not notice it since it can all be done mentally. For instance, to determine how many meters are in 283 centimeters, we mentally divide 283 by 100 to find a quotient of 2 and a remainder of 83; there are 2 meters and 83 centimeters in 283 centimeters.

Additional Examples

1. A school counselor can see 4 students during a class period. How many periods will it take the counselor to schedule 225 students? **56.25 periods, or 56 full periods with 1 student left for the 57th period**

2. Mt. Aconcagua, the highest mountain in South America, is 22,834 feet high. How many miles and feet is this? **4 miles, 1714 feet**

3. One hundred days are how many weeks and days? **14 weeks and 2 days**

4. Identify *n*, *d*, *q*, and *r* in Question 3. **$100 = 7 \times 14 + 2$; $n = 100$, $d = 7$, $q = 14$, $r = 2$.**

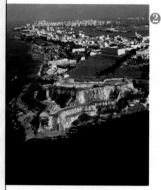

An oceanic trench, such as the Puerto Rico Trench, is a long, narrow, steep-sided depression in the ocean bottom. The Puerto Rico Trench lies about 75 mi north of Puerto Rico. Shown here is San Juan Bay on the northern coastline of Puerto Rico.

The power of the Quotient-Remainder Formula is that given any three of the divisor, dividend, quotient, and remainder, the fourth can be found by solving an equation.

② **Example 2**

The deepest spot in the Atlantic Ocean is the Puerto Rico Trench, 30,246 feet below sea level. How many miles and feet is this?

Solution

We need to find the integer quotient and remainder when 30,246 is divided by 5,280, the number of feet in a mile. Here $n = 30,246$ and $d = 5,280$.

A calculator displays the real-number quotient as $\boxed{5.7284091}$. This means that The integer quotient $q = 5$. That is, the trench is between 5 and 6 miles below sea level. (You could have done this part in your head.)

Now substitute into the Quotient-Remainder Formula.

$$n = d \cdot q + r$$
$$30,246 = 5,280 \cdot 5 + r$$

Solve the equation.

$$30,246 = 26,400 + r$$
$$3,846 = r$$

The Puerto Rico Trench is 5 miles, 3,846 feet below sea level.

QUESTIONS

Covering the Reading

1. Give the answer to 45 divided by 8:
   a. as a real-number division. **5.625**
   b. as integer division. **quotient 5, remainder 5**

In 2–4, *multiple choice.* Use these choices.
(a) integer division only
(b) real-number division only
(c) both integer and real-number division
(d) neither integer nor real-number division

2. has a quotient and a remainder **(a)**

3. has an answer that is a single number **(b)**

4. can be used with fractions **(b)**

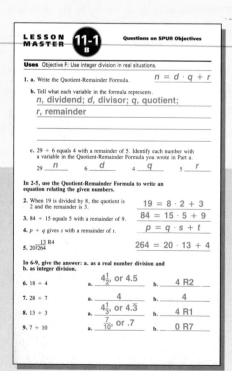
Adapting to Individual Needs

Extra Help
In problems involving integer division, some students fail to differentiate among (1) the integer quotient, (2) the remainder, and (3) one more than the quotient. Write $500 = 41 \cdot 12 + 8$ on the board, and have students use it to answer these questions.

1. If 12 people can sit at a table, how many tables are needed to seat 500 people? [42 tables]

2. A grocer has 500 oranges to put into bags of 12 oranges each. How many bags will be completely filled? [41 bags]

3. In Question 2, how many oranges will be left over? [8 oranges]

5. A class of 172 students is having a picnic. The school buses seat 44 people, including the 2 teachers who must ride on each bus.
   a. How many buses could be filled? **4 (42 students, 8 tchrs.)**
   b. How many people would then be on an unfilled bus?
      4 students plus 2 teachers
6. Write your answer for the Activity in this Lesson. **184 = 5 · 36 + 4**

7. A number w is divided by x, giving an integer quotient of y and a remainder of z. From the Quotient-Remainder Formula, how are these four numbers related? **$w = x \cdot y + z$**

8. The deepest spot in the Indian Ocean is the Java Trench, 23,376 feet below sea level. How many miles and feet is this? **4 miles, 2256 ft**

Applying the Mathematics

9. When 365 is divided by 7, the quotient is 52 and the remainder is 1.
   a. Show how these numbers are related using the Quotient-Remainder Formula. **365 = 7 · 52 + 1**
   b. What is the everyday significance of these numbers? **There are 52 full weeks in a year, with one day left over.**
10. a. How many years and days old is a person who is 10,000 days old?
    b. Is it possible for a person to live to be 50,000 days old? Why or why not? **a) 27 yr, 138 or 139 days (7 or 6 leap years); b) No. 50,000 days is almost 137 years, not a known length of human life.**
11. A teacher has 1000 sheets of paper and decides to distribute them equally to the 23 students in the class. How many sheets will each student get? How many sheets will be left over? **Each student gets 43 sheets; 11 sheets will be left over.**
12. What is the quotient and remainder when 31 is divided by 67? **quotient 0, remainder 31**
13. 450 is divided by an unknown number x, leaving a quotient of 32 and a remainder of 2. Is this possible? If so, what is x? If not, why not? **Yes, $x = 14$.**

14b) Sample: As the dividend increases by 1, the real-number quotient increases by $\frac{1}{9}$ and the integer remainder increases by 1.

14. a. Complete the following table.

dividend	divisor	real-number quotient	integer quotient	integer remainder
40	9	$4.\overline{4}$	4	4
41	9	$4.\overline{5}$	4	5
42	9	$4.\overline{6}$	4	6
43	9	$4.\overline{7}$	4	7
44	9	$4.\overline{8}$	4	8
45	9	5	5	0
46	9	$5.\overline{1}$	5	1
47	9	$5.\overline{2}$	5	2
48	9	$5.\overline{3}$	5	3
49	9	$5.\overline{4}$	5	4
50	9	$5.\overline{5}$	5	5

   b. Describe patterns you see in the table.

Lesson 11-1 *Integer Division* **595**

Notes on Questions

Question 9 Ask what the numbers in this question signify. [There are 52 weeks in a 365-day year with 1 day left over. Therefore, if a date falls on a particular day of the week (say Tuesday) this year, and this year is not a leap year, it will fall on the next day of the week (Wednesday) the next year.]

Question 12 Error Alert If students answer "quotient 2 with remainder 5," then they have divided 67 by 31. Suggest that they read the problem again and write the computation with a division symbol.

Question 14 Have students share the patterns they find.

▶ **LESSON MASTER 11-1 B** *page 2*

10. Mr. Dwyer brought a bag of 100 treats for his class. If there are 23 students in his class, how many treats should each child get? How many treats will be left over?
    4 treats   **8 treats left over**

11. A carpet runner is 54 inches long. Change this measure to feet and inches.
    4 feet 6 inches

12. Change 212,488 cm to kilometers, meters, and centimeters.
    2 km 124 m 88 cm

13. The school day is 5 hours 25 minutes long.
    a. How many minutes are in 5 hours 25 minutes? **325 minutes**
    b. The school day has 45-minutes periods, with the leftover time for homeroom. How many periods are there? How long is homeroom?
    7 periods   **10 minutes**
    c. If each period is changed to 43 minutes, how long would homeroom be?
    24 minutes

14. a. How many cups are in each unit?
    4 cups   **16 cups**
    a quart   a gallon
    b. How many gallons, quarts, and pints are in 74 cups?
    4 gallons 2 quarts 1 pint

15. a. How many seconds are in each unit?
    60 sec   **3,600 sec**   **86,400 sec**
    a minute   an hour   a day
    b. How many days, hours, minutes, and seconds are in 10,000,000 seconds?
    115 days 17 hours 46 minutes 40 seconds

Adapting to Individual Needs

English Language Development
You might want to review the division terms *dividend, divisor, quotient,* and *remainder* by putting the following diagram on the board.

$$
\begin{array}{r}
2 \\
7{\overline{)20}} \\
14 \\
\hline
6
\end{array}
$$

2 ← Quotient
Divisor → 7)20 ← Dividend
14
6 ← Remainder

Then relate each of the terms to the Quotient-Remainder Formula.

Dividend equals divisor times quotient plus remainder.

$$n = d \cdot q + r$$

$$20 = 7 \cdot 2 + 6$$

Notes on Questions

Question 15 Students might use **Teaching Aid 105** for this question.

Practice

For more questions on SPUR Objectives, use **Lesson Master 11-1A** (shown on page 593) or **Lesson Master 11-1B** (shown on pages 594–595).

Assessment

Oral Communication Have students describe situations for which a quotient of 8 with a remainder of 6 would be a solution. [Students need to realize that the divisor must be greater than 6 for any situation they describe.]

Extension

For 1–4, have students write a problem involving 50 divided by 12 for which the given number is the answer.

1. 4   **2.** 5
3. $4\frac{1}{6}$ **4.** 2

Sample problems: (1) How many 12-inch lengths can be cut from a 50-inch long board? (2) How many vans, each holding 12 students are needed to transport 50 students? (3) Fifty months is how many years? (4) How many apples are left over if 50 apples are put into bags of a dozen each?

Project Update Project 4, *Integer Arithmetic with Negative Divisors,* on page 635, relates to the content of this lesson.

16a) The perimeter of the image is $\frac{3}{2}$ the perimeter of the rectangle.

15. Perform a size change of magnitude $\frac{3}{2}$ on *ABCD*.   *(Lesson 9-7)*

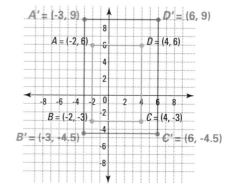

16. Suppose you have applied a size change of magnitude $\frac{3}{2}$ to a rectangle.   *(Lessons 9-1, 9-7)*
  a. How do the perimeter of the rectangle and its image compare?
  b. How do the area of the rectangle and its image compare? The area of the image is 9/4 times the area of the rectangle.

17. In the United States in 1991, about one in 4.5 births was by cesarean section. About one in 87 births was of twins.   *(Lessons 4-8, 9-4)*
  a. Which of these, a cesarean section or twins, was more likely?
  b. If these events are independent, about one in how many births would be a cesarean section birth of twins?
  a) cesarean section; b) 391.5

In 18 and 19, do the divisions in parts **a–d.**

18. Perform the divisions without a calculator if you can.   *(Lesson 2-4)*
  a. $\frac{20}{5}$ 4   **b.** $\frac{20}{0.5}$ 40   **c.** $\frac{20}{0.05}$ 400   **d.** $\frac{20}{0.00005}$ 400,000

19. Use a calculator only on part **a,** if needed.   *(Lesson 2-1)*
  a. $\frac{3}{16}$ 0.1875   **b.** $\frac{0.3}{16}$ 0.01875   **c.** $\frac{0.03}{16}$ 0.001875   **d.** $\frac{0.003}{16}$ 0.0001875

20. To divide a decimal *D* by 10^x, you should move the decimal point in *D* __?__ spaces to the __?__.   *(Lessons 6-5, 6-7)* x, left

21. Find the smallest positive integer *n* with *all* of the following properties.

The remainder is 1 when *n* is divided by 2.
The remainder is 2 when *n* is divided by 3.
The remainder is 3 when *n* is divided by 4.
The remainder is 4 when *n* is divided by 5.
The remainder is 5 when *n* is divided by 6.
The remainder is 6 when *n* is divided by 7.
n = 419

Adapting to Individual Needs

Challenge
Have students solve the following problem: In a physical-education class, the teacher sometimes separates all of the students into groups of equal size. If the class is split into 3, 5, or 6 groups, there is always 1 student left over. If the class is divided into 7 equal-sized groups, no students are left over. What is the smallest possible number of students in the class? [91 students]

Lower rates. *In 1960, the average family size was 3.67 people. Due to lower birth rates, the average family size had dropped to 3.17 by 1990.*

Here are some examples of **rates.**

55 miles per hour   1.9 children per family $1.95 for each 2-liter bottle

The **rate units** can be written as fractions.

$$\frac{miles}{hour} \qquad \frac{children}{family} \qquad \frac{dollars}{liter}$$

Example 1

A car is driven 250 miles in 5 hours. What is the average rate?

Solution

Since the unit of the answer will be $\frac{miles}{hour}$, divide miles by hours.

$$\frac{250 \text{ miles}}{5 \text{ hours}} = 50 \frac{miles}{hour}$$

People do Example 1 so easily that sometimes they do not realize they divided to get the answer. Example 2 is of the same type. But the numbers are not so simple.

Example 2

A car goes 283.4 miles on 15.2 gallons of gas. How many miles per gallon is the car getting?

Solution

The key to the division is "miles per gallon." This indicates to divide miles by gallons.

$$\frac{283.4 \text{ miles}}{15.2 \text{ gallons}} \approx 18.6 \frac{miles}{gallon}$$

The car is getting about 18.6 miles per gallon.

Do not let the numbers in rate problems scare you. If you get confused, try simpler numbers and examine how you got the answer.

Lesson 11-2 *The Rate Model for Division* **597**

Lesson 11-2 Overview

Broad Goals In this lesson, students calculate many kinds of rates and learn to associate these with division.

Perspective In chapter 9, students used rates in multiplication, but there those rates were given. Now students calculate the rates.

There is a difference between ratio comparison (the topic of Lesson 11-5) and rate.

If the quantities being compared have the same units, as in comparing 5 miles to 8 miles, the use is classified as *ratio comparison*. If the quantities being related have different units, as in 4 miles and 10 hours, the use is considered *rate*. The rates 4 miles in 10 hours (0.4 mi/hr) and 10 hours for 4 miles (2.5 hr/mi) are equal quantities. Notice that you must keep the rate units in mind for this to make sense.

Lesson 11-2

Objectives

G Use the Rate Model for Division.

Resources

From the **Teacher's Resource File**
- Lesson Masters 11-2A or 11-2B
- Answer Master 11-2
- Teaching Aid 117: Warm-up
- Technology Sourcebook
  Computer Demonstration 11
  Computer Master 25

Additional Resources
- Visual for Teaching Aid 117
- Spreadsheet Workshop

Teaching Lesson 11-2

Warm-up

Think of as many rates as you can. Then work with your classmates, and write some of them on the chalkboard. **Responses will vary.**

Notes on Reading

As you discuss the reading, have students do the following: (1) give examples of rates; (2) state the Rate Model for Division; (3) explain unit cost and why it is useful; and

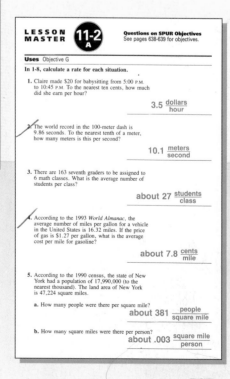

(4) note that whereas a count must be a whole number, a rate may be a fraction or negative number.

It is possible that all of the experience students have had with rates before this year involved only whole numbers. Use **Example 2** to emphasize that rates can involve other kinds of numbers.

Some students might think that rates only refer to speeds. Use **Examples 3 and 4** to point out that this is not the case.

The word *per* is a key word in rates, and it almost always signifies division. Many people think of the units in a rate as having been divided; for example, they think of mi/hr as miles divided by hours. Do not discourage students from thinking this way.

Now that each operation has been considered in this book, you might ask students to predict the topics in the remainder of this chapter. [Based on the treatment of other operations, they may predict, with some accuracy, just what is included—division of fractions, division of integers, another model, equations with division, and division applied to geometry.]

Good citizens. *Juliette Gordon Low formed the first girl scout troop in the U.S. in 1912. Then, as now, girls promised to follow a certain code of behavior, to participate in community service projects, and to develop skills by earning proficiency badges.*

Examples 1 and 2 are instances of the Rate Model for Division.

> **Rate Model for Division**
> If a and b are quantities with different units, then $\frac{a}{b}$ is the amount of quantity a per quantity b.

One of the most common examples of rate is *unit cost*.

Example 3

A 6-oz can of peaches sells for 89¢. An 8-oz can sells for $1.17. Which is the better buy?

Solution

Calculate the cost per ounce. That is, divide the total cost by the number of ounces.

Cost per ounce for 6-oz can: $\frac{89¢}{6 \text{ oz}}$ = 14.83 . . . cents per ounce.

Cost per ounce for 8-oz can: $\frac{117¢}{8 \text{ oz}}$ = 14.625 cents per ounce.

The cost per ounce is called the **unit cost**. The 8-oz can has a slightly lower unit cost. So the 8-oz can is the better buy.

Another common rate is items per person.

Example 4

Eleven people in a scout troop must deliver flyers to 325 households. If the job is split equally, how many flyers will each scout deliver? How many will be left over?

Solution

Think: flyers per scout. This means to divide the number of flyers by the number of scouts.

$$\frac{325 \text{ flyers}}{11 \text{ scouts}} = 29.54 \ldots \text{ flyers/scout}$$

Each scout will have to deliver 29 flyers. To find the remainder, use integer division.

$$n = dq + r$$

Here $n = 325$, $d = 11$, and $q = 29$.

$$325 = 11 \cdot 29 + r$$
$$325 = 319 + r$$

So $r = 6$, meaning that 6 flyers would be left over. The job could be finished if six of the scouts delivered 30 flyers.

Notice that the unit in Example 4 is *flyers per scout*. The number of flyers and the number of scouts are whole numbers. But the number of flyers per scout is a rate. Rates do not have to be whole numbers, they may also involve fractions or negative numbers.

598

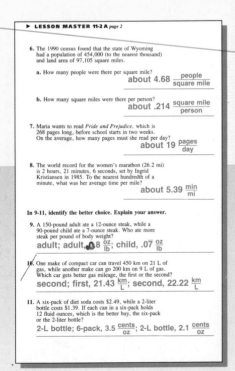

Optional Activities

Activity 1 Geography Connection As an extension of **Example 1**, have students find the average speed for the record-setting train runs listed below. You might also have the students find the locations on a world map.

1. TGV Train from Paris, France, to Macon, France: 225.7 miles in 100 minutes [≈ 135 mph]

2. Yamabiko Train from Morioka, Japan, to Sendai, Japan: 106.3 miles in 50 minutes [≈ 128 mph]

3. High Speed Train from Swindon, England, to Reading, England: 41.5 miles in 23 minutes. [≈ 108 mph]

Activity 2 Technology Connection You may wish to use *Technology Sourcebook, Computer Demonstration 11,* to show students how to use the *Spreadsheet Workshop* to make a table that computes rates automatically. Then, you could assign *Computer Master 25.*

Of course, rates can involve variables.

Example 5

Hal typed W words in M minutes. What is his typing speed?

Solution

The usual unit of typing speed is words per minute. So divide the total number of words by the total number of minutes.

His typing speed is $\frac{W}{M}$ words per minute.

QUESTIONS

Covering the Reading

In 1–7, calculate a rate suggested by each situation.

1. A family drove 400 miles in 8 hours. **50 $\frac{\text{miles}}{\text{hour}}$**

2. A family drove 400 miles in 8.5 hours. **≈ 47.1 $\frac{\text{miles}}{\text{hour}}$**

3. A family drove 600 kilometers in 9 hours. **≈ 66.7 km/hr**

4. An animal traveled d meters in m minutes. **$\frac{d}{m}$ meters per minute**

5. There were 28 boys and 14 girls at the party. **2 boys per girl**

6. 150 students signed up for 7 geometry classes. **about 21 students/class**

7. Six people live on 120 acres. **20 acres per person**

8. State the Rate Model for Division. **If a and b are quantities with different units, then a/b is the amount of quantity a per quantity b.**

9. The Smith family went to the grocery store. An 18-oz box of corn flakes costs $2.89, and a 24-oz box costs $3.99.
   a. Give the unit cost of the 18-oz box to the nearest tenth of a cent.
   b. Give the unit cost of the 24-oz box to the nearest tenth of a cent.
   c. Based on unit cost, which box is the better buy?
   a) 16.1¢ per ounce; b) 16.6¢ per ounce; c) the 18-oz box

10. a. Answer the questions of Example 4 if one of the troop members is sick and unable to deliver any flyers. **32 flyers; 5 flyers left over**
    b. How would you allocate the remaining flyers?
    Five scouts could deliver 33 flyers.

11. If in h hours you travel m miles, what is your rate in miles per hour?
    m/h miles per hour

Applying the Mathematics

12. Nine nannies need to nail nine hundred nineteen nails into a nook.
    a. If the job is split evenly, how many nails will each nanny nail?
    b. How many nails will be left over? **a) 102; b) 1 nail**

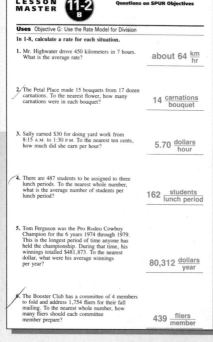

Lesson 11-2 *The Rate Model for Division* **599**

©Walt Disney Studios

Supercalifragilistic-expialidocious. *Mary Poppins is probably the most famous fictional nanny of all time. She is shown here with her friend Bert and her two charges in a scene from the movie* Mary Poppins.

Adapting to Individual Needs

Extra Help
If students are having trouble deciding what numbers to divide, stress the importance of labeling the rate. This will provide a clue as to how to divide and also how to label the answer.

In comparing rates it is important that the same units are used. For example, before comparing $1.59 for 12 ounces and $2.05 for $1\frac{1}{4}$ pounds, the ounces must be changed to pounds, or the pounds to ounces.

Practice

For more questions on SPUR Objectives, use **Lesson Master 11-2A** (shown on pages 597–598) or **Lesson Master 11-2B** (shown on pages 599–600).

Assessment

Group Assessment Have students **work in groups.** Tell each group to imagine that they have been hired to create an advertisement for a store. Explain that the items for sale can be either different sizes of the same thing for different prices, such as a quart of milk for $0.89 and a gallon for $2.59, or a number of items for a certain price, such as 5 pencils for 99¢. Then have groups exchange advertisements and find unit costs.

Extension

Consumer Connection Have students **work in groups** and discuss when they might *not* buy an item even though, based on its unit price, it is the best buy. Some things they might consider are size, brand, packaging, spoilage or shelf life, storage requirements, and availability.

Project Update Project 2, *Best Buys,* and Project 5, *World-record Rates,* on pages 634–635, relate to the content of this lesson.

600

Jute capital.
Bangladesh is a country about the size of Wisconsin, situated between Myanmar (formerly Burma) and India. It is the world's largest exporter of jute, a plant whose fiber is used to make carpets.

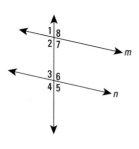

13. A person earns $222 for working 34 hours. How much is the person earning per hour? (Answer to the nearest penny.) **$6.53 per hour**

14. In Bangladesh, a laborer may earn $20 for working 80 hours. How much is this person earning per hour? **$0.25 per hour**

15. According to the *Statistical Abstract of the United States: 1992,* Hawaii had 2,491 active non-federal physicians and a population of 1,108,000 in 1990. California had 70,062 doctors for a population of 29,760,000. Which state had more doctors *per capita?* (The phrase per capita means "per person." It comes from the Latin words meaning "per head.") **California**

16. The school nurse used 140 bandages in 3 weeks. On the average, how many bandages were used per school day? **about 9 bandages per day**

17. Susannah calculated that she used an average of $8\frac{2}{5}$ sheets of paper per day. How many sheets of paper could she have used in how many days to get this rate? **Sample: 84 sheets in 10 days**

Review

18. Consider the division of 100 by 15. *(Lesson 11-1)*
    a. Give the real-number division answer. **6.6̄**
    b. Give the integer division answer. **quotient 6, remainder 10**

19. a. How many feet are in a yard? **3**
    b. How many square feet are in a square yard? **9**
    c. How many full square yards are in 250 square feet? How many square feet are left over? *(Lessons 3-2, 11-1)* **27 full square yards; 7 square feet are left over.**

20. Solve $-5 - 5m = 5$. *(Lesson 10-5)* $m = -2$

In 21–24, lines m and n are parallel. *(Lesson 7-7)*

21. Name all pairs of alternate interior angles. **angles 3 and 7, angles 2 and 6**

22. Name all pairs of corresponding angles. **angles 8 and 6, angles 1 and 3, angles 2 and 4, angles 7 and 5**

23. If m∠5 = 75°, what is m∠1? **75°**   24. If m∠4 = x, what is m∠7? **180 − x**

25. If $a = -2$, $b = 5$, and $c = 1$, what is $|a - b + c| - |a|$? *(Lessons 5-3, 7-2)* **4**

26. An octagon has __?__ sides, __?__ angles, and __?__ diagonals. **8, 8, 20**
    (Lessons 5-9, 6-3)

Exploration

27. Look in an almanac or other book to find at least one of these rates.
    a. the minimum number of grams of protein per day recommended for someone your age
    b. the number of people per square mile in the United States
    c. the number of miles per gallon you should expect to get from a certain car (you pick the car) **Answers may vary.**
    a) For ages 11−18, males should have **45−56 grams/day**; females, **46** $\frac{\text{g}}{\text{day}}$.
    b) about **69 people/square mile**

Adapting to Individual Needs

Challenge
Have students solve the following problem. Suppose a one-mile long train is traveling at 60 miles per hour. The train enters a tunnel that is one mile long. How much time does it take the train to pass through the tunnel? [2 minutes; it takes one minute for the engine to pass through the tunnel, but it takes another minute before the entire train is out of the tunnel.]

Setting Up Lesson 11-3

Materials If you are going to have your students do the activity for the *Extension* in Lesson 11-3, they will need the sports sections of newspapers.

Dividing the tab. *A knowledge of fractions is useful when dividing a restaurant bill among the people who ate.*

The Algebraic Definition of Division

May went with her friends June, Julius, and Augie to a restaurant. The bill totalled $27.30. Each person owed $\frac{1}{4}$ of the bill. Everyone knew that to find $\frac{1}{4}$ of $27.30 they could divide $27.30 by 4.

That is, $\frac{\$27.30}{4} = 27.30 \cdot \frac{1}{4}$.

In general, instead of dividing by b you can multiply by $\frac{1}{b}$, the reciprocal of b. We call this the *Algebraic Definition of Division*.

Algebraic Definition of Division
For any numbers a and b, $b \neq 0$,
    a divided by $b = a$ times the reciprocal of b, or
$$\frac{a}{b} = a \cdot \frac{1}{b}.$$

Why is this true? Just think of multiplying fractions. For any fraction $\frac{a}{b}$,

$$\frac{a}{b} = \frac{a}{1} \cdot \frac{1}{b}$$
$$= a \cdot \frac{1}{b}.$$

Using the Algebraic Definition of Division to Divide Fractions

Since the property holds for *any* numbers, it holds when a and b are themselves fractions. Then, it is critical to remember that the reciprocal of the fraction $\frac{x}{y}$ is the fraction $\frac{y}{x}$.

Lesson 11-3 *Division of Fractions* **601**

Lesson **11-3**

Objectives
A Divide fractions with numbers or variables.
G Use the Rate Model for Division.

Resources
From the *Teacher's Resource File*
■ Lesson Master 11-3A or 11-3B
■ Answer Master 11-3
■ Teaching Aid 117: Warm-up

Additional Resources
■ Visual for Teaching Aid 117
■ Sports sections of newspapers (Extension)

Teaching 11-3
Lesson

Warm-up
Calculator Write each fraction as a decimal.
1. $\frac{8}{5}$ 1.6   2. $\frac{9}{4}$ 2.25
3. $\frac{7}{16}$ .4375   4. $\frac{29}{20}$ 1.45
5. $\frac{13}{13}$ 1   6. $\frac{9}{32}$ .28125
7. What is true about the numerator (n) and denominator (d) of a fraction when the number is
   a. less than 1? $n < d$
   b. greater than 1? $n > d$
   c. equal to 1? $n = d$

Notes on Reading
Be sure to stress the Algebraic Definition of Division so students do not see division of fractions as involving a new property. You might use the following simple demonstrations to illustrate the definition.

Lesson 11-3 Overview

Broad Goals This lesson uses the Algebraic Definition of Division, $a \div b = a \cdot \frac{1}{b}$, to explain division of fractions, and the Rate Model for Division to supply a number of instances where division of fractions is needed.

Perspective Many people believe that division of fractions seldom occurs. This is not the case, since rates (and ratios) can

involve fractions. What actually happens is that people tend to avoid division of fractions when they can.

Consider the following problem. "A team won 64 games in 2 seasons. At this rate, how many games did the team win per season?" People know they should divide to obtain the answer; $\frac{64 \text{ games}}{2 \text{ seasons}}$ is equal to 32 games per season. Now replace the

number 2 with $\frac{2}{3}$ so the problem becomes, "A team won 64 games in $\frac{2}{3}$ season. At this rate, how many games did the team win per season?" Many people do not think of division, even though division of 64 by $\frac{2}{3}$ gives the correct answer, as seen in Example 4.

1. If 12 cookies are divided among 4 people, each person gets $\frac{12}{4}$. This is the same as $\frac{1}{4}$ of 12, or $\frac{1}{4} \cdot 12$. Thus $12 \div 4 = 12 \cdot \frac{1}{4}$.

2. Mary sold 7 sweaters in $\frac{1}{2}$ day. At this rate, how many sweaters will she sell in a full day? Students will immediately know that the answer is 14 sweaters. Point out that the rate being calculated could be found by the division $\frac{7 \text{ sweaters}}{\frac{1}{2} \text{ day}}$, but the answer of 14 shows that this rate equals $7 \cdot 2 \ \frac{\text{sweaters}}{\text{day}}$. This demonstrates that division by $\frac{1}{2}$ is the same as multiplication by the reciprocal of $\frac{1}{2}$.

You might also use Activity 1 of *Optional Activities* below to show instances of the Algebraic Definition of Division.

As you discuss **Examples 1–4,** ask students to explain how the Algebraic Definition of Division is used in each example. Have them notice that in the solution to **Example 1,** the division is written in two different ways—at the left as a fraction and at the right using the $\div$ sign.

Example 1

What is $\frac{6}{5}$ divided by $\frac{3}{4}$?

Solution

By the Algebraic Definition of Division, $\frac{6}{5}$ divided by $\frac{3}{4} = \frac{6}{5}$ times the reciprocal of $\frac{3}{4}$

You can think of the division in either of two ways.

$$\frac{\frac{6}{5}}{\frac{3}{4}} = \frac{6}{5} \cdot \frac{4}{3} \qquad\qquad \frac{6}{5} \div \frac{3}{4} = \frac{6}{5} \cdot \frac{4}{3}$$

$$= \frac{24}{15} \qquad\qquad\qquad = \frac{24}{15}$$

$$= \frac{8}{5} \qquad\qquad\qquad\quad = \frac{8}{5}$$

Check

To check that $\frac{8}{5}$ is the answer, you can change the original fractions to decimals. $\frac{6}{5} = 1.2$ and $\frac{3}{4} = 0.75$, so

$$\frac{\frac{6}{5}}{\frac{3}{4}} = \frac{1.2}{0.75} = 1.6.$$

Since $\frac{8}{5} = 1.6$, the answer checks.

Example 2

Simplify $\frac{\frac{2}{3}}{15}$.

Solution

Think: Instead of dividing by 15, multiply by $\frac{1}{15}$.

$$\frac{\frac{2}{3}}{15} = \frac{2}{3} \div 15 = \frac{2}{3} \cdot \frac{1}{15} = \frac{2}{45}$$

Rate situations can lead to division of fractions.

Example 3

Suppose you make $8 for babysitting 1 hour and 40 minutes. How much are you making per hour?

Solution

Earnings per hour is a rate, so divide the total earned by the number of hours. First change the hours and minutes to hours.

40 minutes $= \frac{40}{60}$ hour $= \frac{2}{3}$ hour, so 1 hour 40 minutes $= 1\frac{2}{3}$ hours $= \frac{5}{3}$ hours.

$$\text{Salary per hour} = \frac{8 \text{ dollars}}{1 \text{ hour } 40 \text{ min}} = \frac{8 \text{ dollars}}{\frac{5}{3} \text{ hours}}$$

602

Optional Activities

Activity 1 Before discussing the Algebraic Definition of Division on page 601, you might want to give students numerical examples to review the idea.

1. $24 \div 4 = ?$ $24 \times \frac{1}{4} = ?$ [6]
2. $5 \div 2 = ?$ $5 \times \frac{1}{2} = ?$ [$2\frac{1}{2}$]
3. $1 \div 3 = ?$ $1 \times \frac{1}{3} = ?$ [$\frac{1}{3}$]
4. $7 \div 9 = ?$ $7 \times \frac{1}{9} = ?$ [$\frac{7}{9}$]

Activity 2 The procedure shown at the right is an alternate way to divide fractions. To follow these steps, students must understand that: (1) the product of a number and its reciprocal is 1; (2) multiplying both the dividend and divisor by the same nonzero number does not change the quotient; (3) a number divided by 1 is the number itself.

$$\frac{\frac{6}{5}}{\frac{3}{4}} = \frac{\frac{6}{5} \cdot \frac{4}{3}}{\frac{3}{4} \cdot \frac{4}{3}}$$

$$= \frac{\frac{6}{5} \cdot \frac{4}{3}}{1}$$

$$= \frac{6}{5} \cdot \frac{4}{3}$$

$$= \frac{24}{15}$$

To divide 8 by $\frac{5}{3}$, use the Algebraic Definition of Division.

$$\frac{8 \text{ dollars}}{\frac{5}{3} \text{ hours}} = 8 \cdot \frac{3}{5} \frac{\text{dollars}}{\text{hour}}$$

$$= \frac{24}{5} \frac{\text{dollars}}{\text{hour}}$$

$$= 4.8 \frac{\text{dollars}}{\text{hour}}$$

You earn $4.80 per hour.

The next example shows how powerful division of fractions can be.

Example 4

Two-thirds of the way through the 1993 baseball season, the Atlanta Braves had won 64 games. At this rate, how many games would they win in the entire season?

Solution

$$\text{Games won per entire season} = \frac{64 \text{ games}}{\frac{2}{3} \text{ season}}$$

$$= 64 \cdot \frac{3}{2} \frac{\text{games}}{\text{season}}$$

$$= \frac{192}{2} \frac{\text{games}}{\text{season}}$$

$$= 96 \frac{\text{games}}{\text{season}}$$

At this rate, the Braves would win 96 games in the entire season.

Even better. *Actually, the Atlanta Braves won 104 games during the 1993 regular season and were the National League Western Division Champions for the third year in a row.*

QUESTIONS

Covering the Reading

1. Instead of multiplying a number by $\frac{1}{4}$, you can divide the number by __?__. 4

2. State the Algebraic Definition of Division. For any numbers a and b, $b \neq 0$, a divided by $b = a$ times the reciprocal of b, or $\frac{a}{b} = a \cdot \frac{1}{b}$.

3. Suppose a person earns $17 for working two and a half hours. How much did the person earn per hour? $6.80 per hour

In 4–7, simplify.

4. $\frac{\frac{8}{9}}{\frac{4}{3}}$ $\frac{2}{3}$

5. $\frac{\frac{2}{5}}{7}$ $\frac{2}{35}$

6. $\frac{\frac{17}{6}}{\frac{2}{3}}$ $\frac{17}{4}$

7. $\frac{\frac{10}{3}}{\frac{6}{5}}$ $\frac{25}{9}$

8. About three-fourths of the way into the basketball season, the Hornets have won 44 games. At this rate how many games will they win in the entire season? about 59 games

9. With one-fifth of the hockey season gone, the Red Wings have lost 7 games. At this rate, how many games will they lose in the season? 35 games

Lesson 11-3 *Division of Fractions* **603**

Additional Examples

1. Divide 10 by $\frac{2}{3}$. 15
2. Simplify.

   a. $\frac{\frac{1}{2}}{\frac{1}{8}}$ 4

   b. $\frac{8}{15} \div \frac{2}{5}$ $\frac{4}{3}$

3. Suppose you can read 35 pages of a novel in 90 minutes. At this rate, how many pages can you read per hour?
   $$\frac{35 \text{ pages}}{1.5 \text{ hours}} = 23\frac{1}{3} \frac{\text{pages}}{\text{hour}}$$

4. After riding $\frac{2}{3}$ of an hour, Lila had gone $7\frac{1}{2}$ miles. At this rate, how far will she ride in one hour?
   $$\frac{7\frac{1}{2}}{\frac{2}{3}} = 11\frac{1}{4} \text{ miles}$$

Adapting to Individual Needs

Extra Help

In problems involving division of fractions, students sometimes become confused about which number is the divisor and thus find the reciprocal of the wrong number. Show students the following three expressions, all of which mean 35 divided by 7.

$35 \div 7$ $\frac{35}{7}$ $7\overline{)35}$

Now have students identify the divisor in each of the following divisions.

1. $\frac{15}{4}$ [4]   2. $\frac{3}{9}$ [9]

3. $15\overline{)95}$ [15]   4. $-989 \div 131$ [131]

5. $\frac{18}{\frac{2}{3}}$ $[\frac{2}{3}]$ 6. $8\overline{).64}$ [8]

603

Notes on Questions

Questions 10–11 Students already know how to divide simple fractions. Suggest that they change each mixed number to a fraction. **Part d** in **Question 11** focuses on an important advantage of fractions over decimals in some situations.

Questions 13–14 Students should understand that they can simplify by using the Algebraic Definition of Division, or they can generalize the pattern from **Questions 4–7**.

Question 27 Laying 1.5 eggs in 1.5 days is simply 1 egg per day (for 1.5 hens); 3 hens could lay 2 eggs per day and two dozen hens could lay 8 times as many eggs, or 16 eggs per day. Thus in two dozen days, the hens would lay $24 \cdot 16$, or 384 eggs.

Follow-up
for Lesson **11-3**

Practice

For more questions on SPUR Objectives, use **Lesson Master 11-3A** (shown on page 603) or **Lesson Master 11-3B** (shown on pages 604–605).

604

Applying the Mathematics

10. **a.** Divide $4\frac{1}{4}$ by $3\frac{2}{5}$. $\frac{5}{4}$, or $1\frac{1}{4}$
    b. The answer you get to part **a** should be bigger than 1. How could you tell this before you did any division? $3\frac{2}{5}$ is less than $4\frac{1}{4}$.
    c. Check your answer to part **a** by changing each fraction to a decimal. $4.25/3.4 = 1.25 = 1\frac{1}{4}$

11. **a.** Divide $1\frac{2}{3}$ by $5\frac{4}{7}$. $\frac{35}{117}$
    b. The answer you get to part **a** should be less than 1. How could you tell this before you did any division? $5\frac{4}{7}$ is greater than $1\frac{2}{3}$.
    c. Check your answer to part **a** by changing each fraction to a decimal. $1.\overline{6} \div 5.\overline{571428} \approx .2991$ and $\frac{35}{117} \approx .2991$
    d. In this question, what advantage do the fractions have over the decimals? The decimals are repeating, so it is easier to work with the fractions.

12. Jay walked $\frac{1}{3}$ of a mile in $\frac{1}{6}$ of an hour.
    a. At this rate, how far would Jay walk in an hour? 2 miles
    b. Explain how you obtained your answer to part **a.** Sample: $\frac{\frac{1}{3} \text{ mile}}{\frac{1}{6} \text{ hr}} = \frac{1}{3} \cdot 6 \text{ mi/hr} = 2 \text{ mi/hr}$

In 13 and 14, simplify.

13. $\frac{\frac{2}{x}}{\frac{1}{y}}$ $\frac{2y}{x}$

14. $\frac{\frac{a}{b}}{\frac{c}{d}}$ $\frac{ad}{bc}$

15. Seven and one-half times a number is 375. What is the number? 50

Review

16. What is your hourly wage if you earn $21.12 in 3.3 hours? *(Lesson 11-2)* $6.40 per hour

In 17–18, use the cereal box pictured below.

30.8 cm

8.4 cm

20.4 cm

17. Find its total surface area. *(Lesson 10-7)* 2116.8 cm^2

18. **a.** Find its volume. *(Lesson 9-2)* 5277.888 cm^3
    b. Find its volume after rounding each dimension to the nearest cm. 4960 cm^3

Adapting to Individual Needs

English Language Development
Although *reciprocal* is not new to this book, you might want to review its meaning.

604

In 19–21, solve. *(Lessons 7-4, 7-5, 10-2)*

19. -4G = -3 $G = \frac{3}{4}$, or .75

20. -4 − G = -3 $G = -1$

21. -4 + G = -3 $G = 1$

22. The probability that an amateur golfer will make a hole-in-one on a par 3 golf hole is estimated to be 1 in 12,600. What then is the probability of making two holes-in-one in a row? *(Lesson 9-4)*
1 in 158,760,000

23. Nyasha planted 20 tomato plant seeds in her garden. Of these, 17 developed into tomato plants. Write the relative frequency that a seed developed into a plant:
  a. as a fraction. $\frac{17}{20}$
  b. as a decimal. .85
  c. as a percent. *(Lessons 1-6, 2-6, 4-8)* 85%

In 24–26, let $x = \frac{5}{4}$ and $y = \frac{1}{2}$. Write as a simple fraction.
(Lessons 5-5, 7-2, 9-3)

24. 8xy $\frac{5}{1}$ **25.** x − y $\frac{3}{4}$ **26.** x + y $\frac{7}{4}$

Exploration

27. Here is a famous puzzle. If a hen and a half can lay an egg and a half in a day and a half, at this rate how many eggs can be laid by two dozen hens in two dozen days? 384 eggs

Question 28? *Which came first—the chicken or the egg?*

Adapting to Individual Needs

Challenge
Two additional problems are given below. The second problem is made even more difficult because it is a tongue twister.

1. In 2 minutes, a carpenter sawed an 8-foot board into equal pieces with no wood left over. If each cut took $\frac{1}{2}$ minute, how many pieces were cut from the board? How long was each piece? [5 pieces; 1.6 feet long]

2. If six sextons can sift sixty thistles in sixteen seconds, how long would it take sixteen sextons to sift sixty-six thistles? [6.6 sec]

► **LESSON MASTER 11-3 B** *page 2*

Uses Objective G: Use the Rate Model for Division.

In 16-20, write a rate and answer the question.

16. A restaurant used two thirds of a sack of pancake mix to make 600 pancakes. At this rate, what is the total number of pancakes that can be made from a full sack?

600 pancakes/$\frac{2}{3}$ sack   900 pancakes
rate   answer

17. Iyo ran $2\frac{1}{2}$ miles in 18 minutes. At this rate, what is her rate in miles per hour?

$2\frac{1}{2}$ miles/$\frac{3}{10}$ hour $8\frac{1}{3}$ miles per hour
rate   answer

18. Ms. Lloyd earned $39 for $3\frac{1}{4}$ hours of work. How much did she earn per hour?

39 dollars/$3\frac{1}{4}$ hours $12 per hour
rate   answer

19. Halfway through the season the debate team had won 14 debates. At this rate, how many debates will they win in the entire season?

14 debates won/$\frac{1}{2}$ season   28 debates
rate   answer

20. Jack's car went 275 kilometers on 30 liters of gas. How many kilometers does the car get to the liter?

$\frac{275\ \text{kilometers}}{30\ \text{liters}}$ 9.1$\overline{6}$ km per liter
rate   answer

Review Objective A, Lesson 5-1; Objective A, Lesson 7-2; Objective D, Lesson 9-6

21. -6 + 19 13   **22.** 11 − 26 -15   **23.** -6 − 3 -9
24. -8 · -5 40   **25.** (3)(-12) -36   **26.** -9 + -14 -23
27. -20 − -7 -13   **28.** -5 · 5 -25   **29.** -22 + 10 -12

605

Assessment
Oral Communication Write the following problems on the board. For each problem, ask students to raise their right hand if the quotient is less than 1, their left hand if the quotient is greater than 1, and both hands if the quotient equals 1. [Students need to decide if the divisor is greater than, less than, or equal to the dividend.]

1. $\frac{5}{6} \div \frac{1}{6}$ [>1]   **2.** $\frac{3}{5} \div 6$ [<1]
3. $\frac{2}{3} \div \frac{3}{4}$ [<1]   **4.** $\frac{2}{4} \div \frac{3}{6}$ [=1]
5. $1\frac{3}{4} \div 2\frac{1}{2}$ [<1] **6.** $3\frac{1}{3} \div 2\frac{3}{4}$ [>1]

Extension
As an extension of **Example 4** on page 603, you might have students solve similar problems involving the records of sports teams that are playing now. Students might **work in groups,** and find statistics about current professional or school teams in the newspaper. They should research the teams' records to date and the number of games the team has left to play. Then, based on these data, they should predict the number of wins for the season.

Project Update Project 6, *A Different Way to Divide Fractions,* on page 635, relates to the content of this lesson.

Objectives

B Divide positive and negative numbers.

E Know the general properties for dividing positive and negative numbers.

G Use the Rate Model for Division.

Resources

From the Teacher's Resource File

■ Lesson Master 11-4A or 11-4B
■ Answer Master 11-4
■ Assessment Sourcebook: Quiz for Lessons 11-1 through 11-4
■ Teaching Aids
   87 Four-Quadrant Graph Paper (Question 24)
   117 Warm-up
■ Activity Kit, Activity 28

Additional Resources

■ Visuals for Teaching Aids 87, 117

Teaching Lesson **11-4**

Warm-up

Multiply.

1. -7×-14 98   **2.** 23×-5 -115
3. -4×11 -44 **4.** $-9 \times -3 \times 0$ 0
5. -3^3 -27 **6.** $(-2)^4$ 16
7. $-4 \times 30 \times -5$ 600
8. $-5 \times 10 \times 5 \times -4$ 1000

Division with Negative Numbers

A negative cash flow. *Although a person may spend only 50 cents to play a video game, Americans spend $5 billion a year playing arcade video games.*

Dividing a Negative Number by a Positive Number

❶ A person spends 10 dollars in a video arcade in 2 hours. What is the rate? The answer is given by division.

$$\frac{\text{spend 10 dollars}}{\text{2 hours}} = \text{spend 5 dollars per hour}$$

You can translate the dollars spent into a negative number.

$$\frac{-10 \text{ dollars}}{2 \text{ hours}} = -5 \frac{\text{dollars}}{\text{hour}}$$

This situation is an instance of the division $\frac{-10}{2} = -5$. Another way to do the division is to think as follows: Dividing by 2 is the same as multiplying by its reciprocal, $\frac{1}{2}$.

$$\frac{-10}{2} = -10 \cdot \frac{1}{2} = -5$$

In general, if a negative number is divided by a positive number, the quotient is negative.

Example 1

On five consecutive days, the low temperatures in a city were 3°C, -4°C, -6°C, -2°C, and 0°C. What was the mean low temperature for the five days?

Solution

Recall that the mean (or average) temperature is found by adding up the numbers and dividing by 5.

$$\frac{3 + -4 + -6 + -2 + 0}{5} = \frac{-9}{5} = -1.8$$

The mean low temperature was -1.8°C, or about -2°C. This temperature is a little below freezing.

Lesson 11-4 Overview

Broad Goals The rules for division of positive and negative numbers are developed in this lesson using the Algebraic Definition of Division and the Rate Factor Model for Multiplication.

Perspective If students have learned the rules for multiplication of integers, division of negative numbers is not difficult. Two ways to justify the division are given in **Example 2**. The first way is finding the

solution through properties, namely the Algebraic Definition of Division, and the second way is checking the answer by using the Rate Factor Model for Multiplication.

Some people consider the rate examples in this lesson as contrived. They are viewed that way because many people do everything they can to avoid using negative numbers—just as people tend to avoid fractions. For instance, though we automatically think

of weighing less some time ago as signifying an increase in weight, we often ignore the fact that the words *less* and *time ago* could relate to negative numbers.

Dividing a Positive Number by a Negative Number

In Example 2, a positive number is divided by a negative number. The quotient is again negative.

Example 2

What is 10 divided by -2?

Solution

Dividing by -2 is the same as multiplying by $-\frac{1}{2}$, the reciprocal of -2.

$$\frac{10}{-2} = 10 \cdot -\frac{1}{2} = -5$$

Check

Think of the video-arcade player at the beginning of this lesson, but go back in time for the 2 hours. The spender had $10 more 2 hours ago. What is the loss rate?

$$\frac{10 \text{ dollars more}}{2 \text{ hours ago}} = \frac{10 \text{ dollars}}{-2 \text{ hours}} = -5 \frac{\text{dollars}}{\text{hour}}$$

Heavy weights. *The typical weight of full grown African elephants is 3600 kg (8000 lb) for cows and 5400 kg (12,000 lb) for bulls. A baby elephant usually weights about 90 kg (200 lb).*

Dividing a Negative Number by a Negative Number

Here is a division question in which both numbers are negative. Is it obvious whether the answer will be positive or negative?

Example 3

What is -150 divided by -7?

Solution

$$\frac{-150}{-7} = -150 \cdot -\frac{1}{7} \quad (\text{Now we know the answer will be positive.})$$
$$= \frac{150}{7}$$
$$\approx 21.43$$

Division with two negative numbers can also be thought of using the rate model. Suppose an elephant gains 14 kg in weight in 3.5 months. It has gained weight at the rate of 4 kg per month. These are all positive quantities.

$$\frac{14 \text{ kg more}}{3.5 \text{ months later}} = \frac{4 \text{ kg}}{\text{month}} \text{ gain}$$

Another way of looking at the situation is that 3.5 months ago the elephant weighed 14 kg less. These are negative quantities.

$$\frac{14 \text{ kg less}}{3.5 \text{ months ago}} = \frac{4 \text{ kg}}{\text{month}} \text{ gain}$$

Notice the equal rates. $\frac{14 \text{ kg more}}{3.5 \text{ months later}} = \frac{14 \text{ kg less}}{3.5 \text{ months ago}}$

Ignoring the units but using negative numbers when appropriate:

$$\frac{14}{3.5} = \frac{-14}{-3.5}.$$

Lesson 11-4 *Division with Negative Numbers* **607**

Notes on Reading

If you wish to introduce this lesson using integer tiles, see Activity 1 in *Optional Activities* below.

❶ Notice that two rationales for the rules for dividing integers are given: the Algebraic Definition of Division and a rate situation. Make sure students recognize both reasons.

In **Example 1** students calculate a mean. Although most of them have done this before, they might not have used negative numbers. **Example 2** provides the same two types of solutions that are given in the opening paragraph on page 606, but this time a positive number is divided by a negative number. In **Example 3**, the division involves two negative numbers.

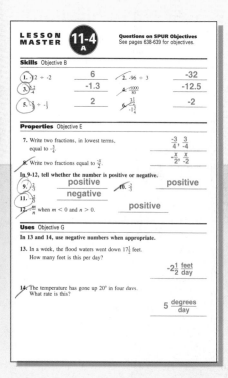

Optional Activities

Activity 1 You might want to use *Activity 28* in the *Activity Kit*, to introduce this lesson. In the activity, students use integer tiles to divide positive and negative integers.

Activity 2 After students have learned the generalization on page 608, you might have them complete the multiplication magic square shown on the right. [The magic product is -125.]

625	$[-\frac{1}{125}]$	25
$[-\frac{1}{5}]$	-5	$[-125]$
1	$[-3125]$	$\frac{1}{25}$

② The rules for division of positive and negative numbers are given here. Notice that if a and b are considered in all their generality, then the rules indicate the effects of opposites on division. If stated in words, the first part of the generalization states that if both the divisor and dividend are changed to their opposites, the quotient remains the same. The second part states that if either a divisor or a dividend is changed to its opposite, the quotient is changed to the opposite.

Additional Examples

1. Find the average weight gain or loss for the four weeks:
   Week 1: Lost 4 pounds
   Week 2: Lost 2 pounds
   Week 3: Lost 3 pounds
   Week 4: Gained 1 pound
   -2; Loss of 2 pounds
2. What is -150 divided by 5? **-30**
3. What is -150 divided by -5? **30**
4. Simplify.
   a. $10 \div 2.5$ **4**
   b. $10 \div -2.5$ **-4**
   c. $-10 \div 2.5$ **-4**
   d. $-10 \div -2.5$ **4**
5. *Multiple choice.* Which number is not equal to the other numbers?
   d
   (a) $-\frac{3}{5}$ (b) $\frac{-3}{5}$
   (c) $\frac{3}{-5}$ (d) $\frac{-3}{-5}$

That is, $\frac{-14}{-3.5} = 4.$

Because $\frac{-1}{-1} = 1$, we can multiply a fraction by $\frac{-1}{-1}$ and the value of the fraction is not changed. For instance, begin with $\frac{-10}{2}$. Multiplying both numerator and denominator by -1 yields the equal fraction $\frac{10}{-2}$.

Altogether, the rules for dividing with negative numbers are just like those for multiplying. If both divisor and dividend are negative, the quotient is positive. If one is positive and the other is negative, the quotient is negative. These properties can be stated with variables.

② For all numbers a and b, and $b \neq 0$,
$$\frac{a}{b} = \frac{-a}{-b}, \text{ and } \frac{-a}{b} = \frac{a}{-b} = -\frac{a}{b}.$$

If you forget how to do operations with negative numbers, there are two things you can do. (1) Change subtractions to additions; change divisions to multiplications. (2) Think of a real situation using the negative numbers. Use the situation to help you find the answer.

QUESTIONS

Covering the Reading

In 1–6, simplify.
1. $\frac{-14}{7}$ **-2**
2. $\frac{-100}{300}$ **$-\frac{1}{3}$**
3. $\frac{-56}{-8}$ **7**
4. $\frac{60}{-2}$ **-30**
5. $-\frac{144}{12}$ **-12**
6. $\frac{-80}{-100}$ **$\frac{4}{5}$**

In 7–9, find the mean of each set of numbers.
7. 40, 60, 80, 100 **70**
8. -40, -60, -80, -100 **-70**
9. -11, 14, -17, -20, 6, -30 **-9.6̄**

In 10–12, tell whether the number is positive or negative.
10. $\frac{-2.5}{6}$ **negative**
11. $\frac{-100}{300}$ **positive**
12. $\frac{-54}{-81}$ **negative**
13. $\frac{53}{-2} \cdot \frac{55}{-2}$ **positive**
14. Separate the numbers below into two collections of equal numbers.
$$-\frac{1}{2} \qquad \frac{-1}{2} \qquad \frac{-1}{-2} \qquad \frac{1}{-2} \qquad \frac{-1}{-2} \qquad \frac{1}{2} \qquad \frac{-1}{2}$$
$$-\frac{1}{2} = \frac{-1}{2} = \frac{1}{-2} = -\frac{-1}{-2}; \quad \frac{-1}{-2} = \frac{1}{2} = -\frac{-1}{2}$$

608

Adapting to Individual Needs

Extra Help

To help students realize that numbers such as $-\frac{3}{4}$, $\frac{-3}{4}$, and $\frac{3}{-4}$ are equal, have them use a calculator to find the quotients. Be sure they understand how to enter negative values into the calculator. Similarly, have them use a calculator to show that $\frac{3}{4} = \frac{-3}{-4}$.

LESSON MASTER 11-4 B — Questions on SPUR Objectives

Skills Objective B: Divide positive and negative numbers.
1. $18 \div -3$ **-6**
2. $-44 \div -11$ **4**
3. $\frac{-27}{-9}$ **3**
4. $\frac{-125}{25}$ **-5**
5. $\frac{-72}{-8}$ **9**
6. $\frac{950}{10}$ **95**
7. $\frac{-2000}{200}$ **-10**
8. $\frac{637}{-1}$ **-637**
9. $\frac{6.4}{-0.8}$ **-8**
10. $\frac{-14.4}{-6}$ **2.4**
11. $-\frac{1}{4} \div \frac{1}{8}$ **-6**
12. $-2\frac{1}{2} \div -7\frac{1}{2}$ **$\frac{1}{3}$**
13. $\frac{-\frac{1}{3}}{-\frac{4}{3}}$ **$\frac{1}{4}$**
14. $\frac{-6\frac{1}{4}}{3\frac{1}{3}}$ **$-\frac{15}{8}$, or $-1\frac{7}{8}$**

In 15–18, find $\frac{x}{y}$ for the given values of x and y.
15. $x = 63$ and $y = -7$ **-9**
16. $x = -.86$ and $y = -4.3$ **0.2**
17. $x = -42$ and $y = -42$ **1**
18. $x = -\frac{5}{8}$ and $y = \frac{9}{16}$ **$-\frac{10}{9}$, or $-1\frac{1}{9}$**

Properties Objective E: Know the general properties for dividing positive and negative numbers.
19. Write two fractions in lowest terms equal to $-\frac{3}{5}$. **$\frac{-3}{5}, \frac{3}{-5}$**
20. Write two fractions in lowest terms equal to $\frac{4}{7}$. **$\frac{4}{7}, \frac{-4}{-7}$**
21. Write two fractions in lowest terms equal to $\frac{5}{t}$. **$\frac{-5}{-t}, \frac{5}{t}$**

608

15b) $\frac{-4 \text{ inches}}{2 \text{ days}}$

d) $\frac{4 \text{ inches more}}{2 \text{ days ago}} = \frac{4 \text{ in.}}{-2 \text{ days}} = -2\frac{\text{in.}}{\text{day}}$

15. Four inches of snow on the mountain melted after two sunny days.
   a. Calculate a rate from this information. -2 inches per day
   b. What division problem with negative numbers gives this rate?
   c. Copy and complete: __?__ days ago, the mountain had __?__ inches of snow __?__ than it does now. 2, 4, more
   d. What division problem is suggested by part **c?**

16. What two things can you do if you forget how to calculate with negative numbers? Change subtractions to additions and divisions to multiplications; think of a real situation using the numbers to help find the answer.

Applying the Mathematics

17. In the twenty years from 1970 to 1990, Arizona's population rose by about 1,900,000.
   a. Calculate a rate from this information. 95,000 people per year
   b. Copy and complete: __?__ years before 1990, Arizona's population was 1.9 million __?__ than it was in 1990. 20, less
   c. What division problem is suggested by part **b?** What is the quotient? -1,900,000/-20; 95,000

In 18–21, calculate $x + y$, $x - y$, xy, and $\frac{x}{y}$ for the given values.

18. $x = -6$ and $y = -9$ See left.   **19.** $x = -12$ and $y = -12$ See left.

20. $x = -\frac{15}{8}$ and $y = -\frac{1}{8}$ See left.   **21.** $x = -\frac{1}{3}$ and $y = \frac{1}{2}$ See left.

22. Use $C = 5(F - 32)/9$ to convert -40° Fahrenheit to Celsius. -40°C

23. Round $\frac{350}{-6}$ to the nearest integer. -58

24. The *center of gravity* of a set of given points is the point whose first coordinate is the mean of the first coordinates of the given points, and whose second coordinate is the mean of the second coordinates of the given points.
   a. Find the coordinates of the center of gravity of the four points graphed below. $(5, \frac{1}{4})$
   b. Copy the drawing and plot the center of gravity on your copy.

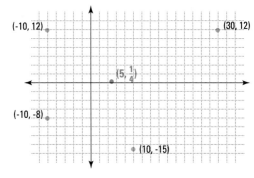

18) $-15, 3, 54, \frac{2}{3}$

19) $-24, 0, 144, 1$

20) $-2, -\frac{7}{4}, \frac{15}{64}, 15$

21) $\frac{1}{6}, -\frac{5}{6}, -\frac{1}{6}, \frac{2}{3}$

Lesson 11-4 *Division with Negative Numbers* **609**

Arizona attraction.
Located in northwest Arizona, the Grand Canyon extends for 277 miles and makes up most of Grand Canyon National Park. The natural beauty of the park attracts about 4 million visitors yearly.

Notes on Questions
Question 22 Point out that the formula works whether *F* is positive, negative, or zero. When *F* is less than 32, the quantity *F* – 32 is negative, so a negative number is divided by a positive number resulting in a negative answer. This agrees with what we expect—Fahrenheit temperatures below 32° correspond to negative Celsius temperatures.

Question 24 You can use **Teaching Aid 87** for this question.

▶ **LESSON MASTER 11-4 B** *page 2*

In 22-29, tell whether the number is positive or negative.
22. $\frac{-7}{-10}$ positive   23. $\frac{-7}{-10}$ positive
24. $\frac{-7}{-10}$ negative   25. $\frac{7}{10}$ positive
26. $\frac{-7}{-10}$ positive   27. $\frac{-7}{10}$ negative
28. $\frac{p}{q}$ when $p < 0$ and $q < 0$. negative
29. $\frac{p}{q}$ when $p < 0$ and $q > 0$. positive

Uses Objective G: Use the Rate Model for Division.
In 30-34, use negative numbers when appropriate.
30. The temperature has gone up 18° in six hours. What rate is this? $3 \frac{\text{degrees}}{\text{hour}}$
31. The temperature has gone down 25° in five hours. What rate is this? $-5 \frac{\text{degrees}}{\text{hour}}$
32. In a week, the flood waters went down $10\frac{1}{2}$ feet. How many feet was this per day? $-1\frac{1}{2} \frac{\text{feet}}{\text{day}}$
33. The price of a stock fell 9 dollars in six hours. How many dollars was this per hour? $-1.5 \frac{\text{dollars}}{\text{hour}}$
34. Gwen gained 4 kilograms in a year. How many kilograms was this per month? $.3 \frac{\text{kilograms}}{\text{month}}$

Review Objectives G and I, Lesson 2-4 and 2-6
In 35-46, write each decimal as a percent and each percent as a decimal.
35. .07 7%   36. 24% .24   37. 9% .09
38. 0.72 72%   39. 0.055 5.5%   40. 1.5 150%
41. 225% 2.25   42. $33\frac{1}{3}$% .3   43. .001 .1%
44. 12 1200%   45. 6.5% .065   46. $\frac{1}{4}$% .0025

Adapting to Individual Needs
English Language Development
Students with limited English might benefit from writing the generalization for dividing positive and negative numbers as follows.

$\frac{(+)}{(+)} = +$ $\frac{(-)}{(-)} = +$

$\frac{(-)}{(+)} = -$ $\frac{(+)}{(-)} = -$

Question 27 This question anticipates the next lesson where students are required to do the third
type of percent problem, which, for
these numbers is "40 is what percent
of 500?"

Question 31 Answers to **part d** may
suggest to some students that $\frac{5}{0}$ is
infinite. Remind students that they
cannot divide by 0. Thus, there is no
value of $\frac{5}{0}$. It is a colloquialism if
someone says that $\frac{5}{0}$ is infinity.

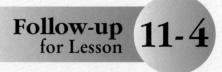

Follow-up 11-4
for Lesson

Practice

For more questions on SPUR Objectives, use **Lesson Master 11-4A**
(shown on page 607) or **Lesson
Master 11-4B** (shown on pages
608–609).

Assessment

Quiz A quiz covering Lessons 11-1
through 11-4 is provided in the
Assessment Sourcebook.

Written Communication Ask each
student to write three different sets
of numbers that each have a mean
of –4. Each set should contain at
least five numbers. [Some students
may include a set of numbers made
up of only –4s, some may list only
negative integers, and others may
include fractions and decimals in
their lists.]

Extension

Science Connection In **Question
22,** students found that –40°C =
–40°F. Ask them if they can find
another case in which the Fahrenheit
and Celsius temperatures are equal.
[There is no other number for which
the temperatures are equal. As
Fahrenheit temperatures increase
from –40°, Celsius temperatures
also increase, but at a slower rate.
Similarly, as Fahrenheit temperatures decrease from –40°, Celsius
temperatures also decrease, but at a
slower rate.]

Project Update Project 4, *Integer
Arithmetic with Negative Divisors*, on
page 635, relates to the content of
this lesson.

*These Jamaican
entertainers are
performing a traditional
dance for tourists.*

29) Sample:

25. In $3\frac{1}{2}$ days, a boat sailed the 500 miles from Kingston, Jamaica, to
Santo Domingo in the Dominican Republic. How many miles did
the boat average per day? *(Lessons 11-2, 11-3)* ≈ 142.9 mi/day

26. For the first 70 days of the year, the high temperature was above
normal on 21 days. If this rate continues, for how many days will the
temperature be above normal during the entire year? *(Lesson 11-2)*
≈ 110 days

27. **a.** 40% of a number is 500. What is the number? *(Lessons 2-6, 10-3)*
    b. What is 40% of 500? *(Lesson 2-6)*
    a) 1250; b) 200

28. Begin at the point (14, 6). Move 20 units to the left and 3 units
down. What are the coordinates of the image point? *(Lesson 8-5)*
(-6, 3)

29. Draw a hexagon *ABCDEF* in which $\overline{AB} \perp \overline{BC}$ and $\overline{AB} \parallel \overline{CD}$.
(Lessons 5-9, 7-7) **See left.**

30. **a.** Write 44% as a decimal. 0.44
    b. Write 44% as a simple fraction in lowest terms. *(Lesson 2-4)* $\frac{11}{25}$

31. **a.** Press 5 $\boxed{+/-}$ $\boxed{\div}$ 0 on your calculator. What does the display show?
    b. Press 5 $\boxed{+/-}$ $\boxed{\div}$ 0.001 on your calculator. What is displayed?
    c. Press 5 $\boxed{+/-}$ $\boxed{\div}$ 0.001 $\boxed{+/-}$ on your calculator. What is displayed?
    d. Divide -5 by other numbers near zero. Record your results.
    e. Explain what happens when the divisor gets nearer to zero and is
    positive.
    f. Explain what happens when the divisor gets nearer to zero and is
    negative.

    a) Sample: $\boxed{E \quad 0.}$, meaning error. b) -5000. c) 5000.
    d) Samples: $\frac{-5}{0.000001} = -5{,}000{,}000$; $\frac{-5}{-0.0000003} \approx 16{,}666{,}666$
    e) As the divisor gets closer to zero, the quotient is negative and its
    absolute value gets larger.
    f) The quotient becomes a larger positive number as the divisor gets
    closer to zero.

Adapting to Individual Needs
Challenge
Materials: Almanac

Geography Connection Have students
use an almanac to find at least three cities
or states where the population has declined
in recent years. Have them calculate the
negative rates of population growth.

11-5

The Ratio Comparison Model for Division

Open the gates! *Located at the junction of the Missouri and Mississippi Rivers, the St. Louis area was the site of record flood levels in 1993. Shown here is the Gateway Arch on the historic riverfront of St. Louis.*

In St. Louis, Missouri, it rained 11 of the 30 days of June, 1993. This rain saturated the ground and contributed to floods in July. Dividing 11 by 30 gives the relative frequency of rain.

$$\frac{11}{30} \approx .37$$

Relative frequency is often expressed as a percent. It rained about 37% of the days in June. You have calculated relative frequencies like this before.

What Are Ratios?

Notice what happens when the units are put into the numerator and denominator.

$$\frac{11 \text{ days}}{30 \text{ days}}$$

The units are the same. They cancel in the division, so the answer has no unit. Therefore, this is not an example of a rate. The answer is an example of a **ratio.** Ratios have no units. Because the 11 days is being compared to the 30 days, this use of division is called **ratio comparison.**

> **Ratio Comparison Model for Division**
>
> If a and b are quantities with the same units, then $\frac{a}{b}$ compares a to b.

All percents can be considered as ratio comparisons.

Objectives

H Use the Ratio Comparison Model for Division.

Resources

From the *Teacher's Resource File*
- Lesson Master 11-5A or 11-5B
- Answer Master 11-5
- Teaching Aid 118: Warm-up

Additional Resource
- Visual for Teaching Aid 118

Teaching **11-5**
Lesson

Warm-up
1. If the sales-tax rate is 5%, what is the sales tax on a $15 CD? **75¢**
2. If 60%, or 12, of the students in the chorus are girls, how many students are in the chorus? **20 students**
3. In Question 2, what percent are boys? **40%**

Notes on Reading
Emphasize that rates and ratios are similar, but that a rate has a unit, whereas in a ratio, there is no unit.

Lesson 11-5 Overview

Broad Goals In this lesson, quantities with the same units are compared using division.

Perspective Bill has $10, and Mary has $30. We can compare the quantities by saying that Bill has $\frac{1}{3}$ of Mary's amount or that Mary has 3 times what Bill has. These are two simple examples of ratio comparison division from the same situation.

We could also compare by subtraction. Since $10 - 30 = -20$, Bill has $20 less than Mary. Since $30 - 10 = 20$, Mary has $20 more than Bill. Just as numbers can be compared in either order using subtraction, numbers can be compared in either order with division.

In everyday usage, the words *rate* and *ratio* are often used synonymously. Sometimes the same quantity can be considered as

both a rate and a ratio. For instance, consider a batting average as a rate and as a ratio:

As a rate, it is $\frac{\text{number of hits}}{\text{number of at-bats}}$ and the unit is *hits per at bats*.

As a ratio it is $\frac{\text{number of at-bats with a hit}}{\text{total number of at-bats}}$.

More often we tend to think of a batting average as a ratio because it is never reported with a unit.

Example 3 illustrates the third type of percent problem. You may wish to use *Activity 1* in *Optional Activities* below to review all the types of percent problems.

If students have difficulty finding what percent 5 is of 40, ask the question in this way, "5 is what *part* of (or what *fraction* of) 40?" The answer, $\frac{5}{40}$ or $\frac{1}{8}$, equals 12.5%.

Another way to look at the three types of percent problems is to use the equation $ab = c$ where a is the *rate* or *ratio*, b is the *base*, and c is sometimes called the *percentage*. The three cases correspond to the three choices for the unknown. The reason we do not use this approach in this text is that in *Transition Mathematics* we are stressing the arithmetic of percent questions. In *UCSMP Algebra*, this algebraic approach is used.

Some people use the proportion $\frac{5}{40} = \frac{x}{100}$ to answer the question in **Example 3**. We feel that this complicates the issue, and we do not recommend its use.

Additional Examples

1. Jenny paid $2.60 tax on a $52 suit. What is the tax rate? **5%**
2. A house cost $120,000 in 1980 and $210,000 in 1993. Compare the prices. **The 1980 price is**

612

Example 1

Suppose the tax is $0.42 on a $7.00 purchase. What is the tax rate? (It's called a tax rate even though it is technically a ratio.)

Solution

Divide $0.42 by $7.00 to compare them. The units are the same, so they cancel.

$$\frac{\$0.42}{\$7.00} = \frac{0.42}{7.00} = .06$$

.06 = 6%, so the tax rate is 6%.

Check

A tax of 6% means you pay 6¢ tax for every dollar spent. So for $7, the tax should be $7 \cdot 6¢$, or 42¢.

Some comparisons can be done in either order.

Example 2

Compare the year 2000 estimated populations of the United States (270,000,000 people) and Canada (31,000,000 people).

Solution

The units (people) are the same. Divide one of the numbers by the other to compare them.

$\frac{270,000,000}{31,000,000} \approx 8.7$, so the population of the U.S. was about 8.7 times that of Canada.

Dividing in the other order gives the reciprocal.

$\frac{31,000,000}{270,000,000} \approx .11$, so Canada's population was about 11% of the population of the U.S.

Either answer is correct.

Percents as Ratios

Example 3

5 is what percent of 40?

Solution

This problem asks you to compare 5 to 40. So divide, and then convert the answer to a percent.

$$\frac{5}{40} = 0.125 = 12.5\%$$

Therefore, 5 is 12.5% of 40.

Check

Calculate 12.5% of 40.
12.5% of $40 = 0.125 \cdot 40 = 5$.

No horsing around. A mounted policeman is shown here on Parliament Hill in Ottawa, the capital of Canada.

612

Optional Activities

Activity 1 Before considering **Example 3**, you might review the three types of percent problems. In the examples below, the same numbers are used in each type of problem.

1. a. Find 5% of 40.   [2]
   b. 5% of what number is 2?   [40]
   c. 2 is what percent of 40?   [5%]
2. a. 60% of what number is 9?   [15]
   b. Find 60% of 15.   [9]
   c. 9 is what percent of 15?   [60%]

Activity 2
Materials: Newspapers

Give **groups of students** newspapers. Have them find 10 examples of percents and, for each percent, decide how it was obtained. For instance, if 63% of the voters in an election voted for Candidate A, ask how the 63% was calculated. [By dividing the number of people who voted for A by the total number of people who voted]

about 57% of the 1993 price; the 1993 price is 175%, of the 1980 price.

3. 85 is what percent of 200? 42.5%

QUESTIONS

Covering the Reading

1. In a city, it rained 70 of the 365 days in a year. What percent of the time is this? **about 19%**

2. A supermarket charges $0.64 tax on a grocery bill of $31.98. What is the tax rate? **2%**

3. Suppose there is a sales tax of 35¢ on a purchase of $5.83.
   a. What is the sales tax rate? **6%**
   b. 35 is what percent of 583? **≈ 6%**

4a) You can divide 6 by 25, or you can divide 25 by 6.

4. a. According to the Ratio Comparison Model for Division, what can you do to compare the numbers 6 and 25?
   b. 6 is what percent of 25? **24%**
   c. 6 is what part of 25? **$\frac{6}{25}$**

5. a. What percent is 6 of 12? **50%**
   b. What percent is 6 of 6? **100%**
   c. 6 is what percent of 3? **200%**

In 6 and 7, answer to the nearest whole-number percent.

6. 41 is what percent of 300? **14%**

7. 250 is what percent of 300? **83%**

8. The 1990 population of New York City was about 7.3 million. The population of York, England (from which New York got its name) was about 100,000.
   a. Then York, England had _?_ percent the number of people of New York City. **about 1.4**
   b. New York City had about _?_ times as many people as York, England. **73**

9. What is the difference between a rate and a ratio? **Rates have units of the form unit *a* per unit *b*. Ratios do not have units.**

Applying the Mathematics

10. 14 of the 25 students in the class are boys.
    a. What percent are boys? **56%**
    b. What percent are girls? **44%**

11. What number is 12 percent of 90? **10.8**

12. a. Banner High School won 36 of its last 40 games. What percent is this? **90%**
    b. What is 36 percent of 40? **14.4**
    c. 40 is 36 percent of what number? **111.$\overline{1}$**

13. If a $60 jacket is reduced $13.50, what is the percent of discount? **22.5%**

Lesson 11-5 *The Ratio Comparison Model for Division* **613**

Notes on Questions

Questions 3–7 Some people might answer these questions by solving proportions. We do not recommend the use of proportions with such simple division problems. For example, **Question 4b** asks, "6 is what percent of 25?" Dividing 6 by 25 yields 0.24, so if the question had been "6 is what *part* of 25?", 0.24 could be the answer. If the question had been "6 is what *fraction* of 25?", $\frac{6}{25}$ could be the answer. Only because the question calls for a percent is it necessary to translate 0.24 into percent and conclude that 6 is 24% of 25. To use proportions only when percent is involved misleads students into thinking that percents are totally separate from what they already know.

Question 8 Multicultural Connection Some students might enjoy investigating the origin of the name of their city or state.

Question 12a Stress the many equivalent ways that a situation might be described. Banner High has won 36 of 40 games, $\frac{36}{40}$ of their games, $\frac{9}{10}$ of their games, or 90% of their games. We also could say that if a game of Banner High were chosen at random, the probability is 0.9 that they won that game.

Adapting to Individual Needs

Extra Help
A percent can be represented by an unlimited number of equal fractions. Write the following on the board:

$16\% = \frac{16}{100} = \frac{8}{50} = \frac{4}{25} = \frac{32}{200}$.

Explain that, based on these equal fractions, the following percent statements can be made:

16 is 16% of 100.   8 is 16% of 50.
4 is 16% of 25.   32 is 16% of 200.

For each percent given below, have students write three equal fractions and then write percent statements they can make based on the equal fractions. [Answers will vary.]

1. 20%   2. 75%
3. 10%   4. 6%

Practice

For more questions on SPUR Objectives, use **Lesson Master 11-5A** (shown on page 612) or **Lesson Master 11-5B** (shown on pages 613–614).

Assessment

Written Communication Ask each student to write three instances of the ratio model for division. [Students should recognize that ratios have no units.]

Extension

Have students **work in groups**, and research pairs of numbers relating to the class, the school, or some other situation. Have them compare the numbers in as many different ways as they can. For example, if 20 out of 25 students ride the bus to school, the numbers can be compared by saying that four times as many students ride the bus as do not ride the bus. The numbers can be compared using fractions, decimals, or percents: $\frac{4}{5}$, or 0.8, or 80% of the students ride the bus. Students might also compare the numbers using subtraction. Since $5 - 20 = -15$, 15 fewer students walk than ride the bus. Similarly, 15 more students ride the bus than walk.

Walking is not only a popular form of exercise; it is a sport. Walking races have been a part of the Olympics since 1906.

14. If a population of 350,000 increases by 7000, what is the percent of increase? **2%**

Review

15. If $x = \frac{2}{3}$ and $y = \frac{3}{4}$, give the value of each expression.
    (Lessons 7-2, 9-3, 9-6, 11-3, 11-4)
    a. $3x + 4y$ **5** **b.** $3x - 4y$ **-1** **c.** $(-x)(-y)$ $\frac{1}{2}$
    d. $\frac{xy}{5}$ $\frac{1}{10}$ **e.** $\frac{x}{-y}$ $-\frac{8}{9}$ **f.** $\frac{-y}{-x}$ $\frac{9}{8}$, or $1\frac{1}{8}$

16. Let $a = 10$, $b = 20$, $c = 30$, and $d = 40$. What is the value of $\frac{a - c}{b - d}$?
    (Lessons 4-6, 7-2, 11-4) **1**

17. Suppose a person earns time and three quarters for overtime. If the overtime wage is $17.15 per hour, what is the person's normal hourly wage? *(Lessons 9-5, 10-3)* **$9.80**

18. Solve $10y = 43.8$. *(Lesson 10-2)* **y = 4.38**

19. A person walked for 2.5 hours at 2.5 miles per hour. How far did the person travel? *(Lesson 9-5)* **6.25 miles**

20. Determine the angle measures of $\triangle ABC$ below. *(Lessons 7-1, 10-2)*

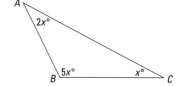

    m∠C = 22.5°
    m∠A = 45°
    m∠B = 112.5°

21. There are 12 members on the school math team. Sending them to the state tournament will cost C dollars per team member. If $200 has been collected, how much more needs to be collected?
    (Lessons 4-3, 7-1) **12C − 200 dollars**

22. Write 5 simple fractions equal to $\frac{6}{21}$. *(Lesson 1-10)*
    Samples: $\frac{2}{7}, \frac{4}{14}, \frac{8}{28}, \frac{10}{35}, \frac{12}{42}$

Exploration

23. What percent of English words have more consonants than vowels? Carry out an experiment using words from at least two different sources. **Answers will vary.**

► **LESSON MASTER 11-5B** *page 2*

17. At Southern Steelworks, 18% of the employees work the night shift. Explain how the 18% was calculated.
    The number of night-shift employees was divided by the total number of employees.

18. In 1983, the Romano family spent an average of $380 per month for food. In 1993, they spent an average of $535 per month.
    a. The Romanos' 1983 grocery bills were about __71__ % of their 1993 grocery bills.
    b. The Romano's 1993 grocery bills were about __141__ % of the 1983 grocery bills.
    c. The Romano's 1993 grocery bills were about __1.41__ times their 1983 grocery bills.

19. This year the Friel family planted 450 acres of corn. Last year they planted 600 acres of corn.
    a. This year's corn acreage was __75__ % of last year's.
    b. Last year's corn acreage was __133.3__ % of this year's.
    c. Last year's corn acreage was __1.3__ times this year's.

20. Last year, 3,041 babies were born at South Shore Hospital, and 1,218 babies were born at Hastings Hospital.
    a. Write a sentence comparing the number of births at South Shore Hospital to the number of births at Hastings Hospital.
    sample: There were nearly $2\frac{1}{2}$ times as many babies born at South Shore as at Hastings.
    b. Write a sentence comparing the number of births at Hastings Hospital to the number of births at South Shore Hospital.
    sample: Hastings had about 40% the number of births that South Shore had.

Adapting to Individual Needs

English Language Development
Students with limited English proficiency might have trouble distinguishing between *rates* and *ratios*. You might have these students work with classmates who understand the differences. The students can work together to make lists of rate situations and lists of ratio situations. Encourage them to talk about the differences.

Challenge
Give students the following problem to solve. A pet shop has 100 birds for sale–consisting of one myna and 99 parakeets. Assuming that the myna is not sold, how many parakeets must be sold so that the percent of parakeets drops from 99% to 98%? [50 parakeets; then 49 out of the remaining 50 birds are parakeets.]

LESSON

11-6

Proportions

Take a survey. *In this classroom, $\frac{8}{18}$ of the students are male, $\frac{1}{18}$ is wearing a green shirt, and $\frac{1}{12}$ of the girls are wearing glasses. Do these equal the ratios in your classroom?*

Equal Ratios and Equal Rates

Remember that the fraction $\frac{a}{b}$ is the result of dividing a by b. This means that every use of division gives rise to fractions. For instance, when 9 out of 12 students in a class ride a bus to school, then $\frac{9}{12}$ of the class ride the bus.

You know that $\frac{9}{12}$ is equal to $\frac{3}{4}$. In this case you could say that 3 of 4 students ride a bus to school. Equal fractions mean equal ratios.

Now consider a rate. A car goes 9 miles in 12 minutes. The fraction

$$\frac{9 \text{ miles}}{12 \text{ minutes}}$$

is the car's average rate. Simplify the fraction. Going 9 miles in 12 minutes is the same rate as going 3 miles in 4 minutes. Equal fractions mean equal rates.

$$\frac{9 \text{ miles}}{12 \text{ minutes}} = \frac{3 \text{ miles}}{4 \text{ minutes}}$$

What Is a Proportion?

A **proportion** is a statement that two fractions are equal. Here are three more examples.

$$\frac{730}{365} = \frac{2}{1} \qquad \frac{12ab}{3b} = \frac{4ab}{b} \qquad \frac{3 \text{ km}}{4 \text{ liters}} = \frac{d \text{ km}}{10 \text{ liters}}$$

Lesson 11-6 *Proportions* **615**

Lesson 11-6
Objectives
C Solve proportions.
I Recognize and solve problems involving proportions in real situations.

Resources
From the Teacher's Resource File
- Lesson Master 11-6A or 11-6B
- Answer Master 11-6
- Teaching Aid 118: Warm-up

Additional Resources
- Visual for Teaching Aid 118

Teaching Lesson 11-6

Warm-up
1. In your math class, what is the ratio of boys to students? What is the ratio of girls to students?
2. Assume the ratios for your class are the same for your grade and for your school.
   a. If there are 300 students in your grade, how many are girls? How many are boys?
   b. If there are 750 students in your school, how many are girls? How many are boys?

Responses will depend on the number of boys and girls in your class.

Notes on Reading
This lesson has three sections. The first introduces the terminology, the second shows students how to solve proportions using the Multiplication Property of Equality, and the third

---

Lesson 11-6 Overview

Broad Goals This lesson, the first of four on proportions, introduces the language of proportions and shows that the usual equation-solving rules can be applied to solve proportions.

Perspective Proportions are very important inside and outside mathematics. Some researchers feel that "proportional thinking," the ability to mentally find the unknown term in a proportion, is among the most

important mathematics concepts at this level. Such thinking is learned by doing a variety of problems in a variety of ways in both arithmetic and geometric situations. Thus, we devote a number of lessons to the solving of proportions.

It is not unusual for students to learn to solve a proportion like $\frac{a}{x} = \frac{b}{c}$ for x by "cross-multiplication." This is a valid procedure—its official name is the Means-

Extremes Property—and it will be studied in Lesson 11-7. However, we believe that if this procedure is learned first, two unfortunate outcomes are likely to result. First, students will not realize that a proportion is an equation and can be solved like all other equations, and second, the student will start looking for tricks to solve all equations. Consequently, in this lesson, we focus on the use of the Multiplication Property of Equality to solve proportions.

shows them how to set up a proportion using equal rates.

By saying "no new properties are needed" preceding **Example 1,** we mean students can solve proportions using properties they have already learned. Because a proportion is an equation, any property the students have learned might be used, but it is the Multiplication Property of Equality that is helpful. We use it to multiply both sides of the equation by a number large enough to eliminate the fractions. In general, we solve the proportion below by multiplying both sides by cx, which eliminates the denominators. Then we solve for x.

$$\frac{a}{x} = \frac{b}{c}$$

$$\frac{a}{x} \cdot cx = \frac{b}{c} \cdot cx$$

$$ac = bx$$

$$\frac{ac}{b} = x$$

Students may be overwhelmed by the length of **Example 1.** Make certain they realize that solving the equation took only a few steps. It is the two ways of checking that take most of the space.

Some equations with fractions are not proportions. Examine these two equations.

$$\frac{x+5}{8} = \frac{2}{1} \qquad\qquad \frac{x}{8} + \frac{5}{8} = \frac{x}{2}$$
$$\text{a proportion} \qquad\qquad \text{not a proportion}$$

The equation on the left is a proportion because on each side there is one fraction. The equation on the right is equivalent to the left equation. But it is not a proportion because its left-hand side is not a single fraction.

Solving Proportions

Like other equations, proportions can be true or false.

$$\frac{30}{100} = \frac{1}{3} \qquad\qquad \frac{320}{100} = \frac{16}{5}$$
$$\text{False} \qquad\qquad \text{True}$$

When a proportion has variables in it, the question is often to **solve the proportion.** That means to find the value or values that make the proportion true. For example:

$$\frac{320}{100} = \frac{16}{x} \text{ has the solution } x = 5, \text{ because } \frac{320}{100} = \frac{16}{5}.$$

Solving a proportion is just like solving any other equation. No new properties are needed. But it may take more steps. A nice feature is that there are many ways of checking proportions.

Example 1

Solve $\frac{32}{m} = \frac{24}{25}$.

Solution
Multiply both sides by $25m$, the product of the denominators.

$$25m \cdot \frac{32}{m} = \frac{24}{25} \cdot 25m$$

We put in a step here that you may not need to write. It shows the products before the fractions are simplified.

$$\frac{25m \cdot 32}{m} = \frac{24 \cdot 25m}{25}$$

Now simplify the fractions.

$$25 \cdot 32 = 24m$$
$$800 = 24m$$
$$\frac{800}{24} = m$$

Rewrite the fraction in lowest terms.

$$\frac{100}{3} = m$$

Video

Wide World of Mathematics The segment, *New York City Marathon,* brings out the excitement of that event and the large amount of mathematics that is naturally involved (such as pace, weight of the runner, etc.). This segment may be used to introduce or extend a lesson on proportions. Related questions and an investigation are provided in videodisc stills and in the Video Guide. A related CD-ROM activity is also available.

Videodisc Bar Codes

Search Chapter 54

Play

Check 1

To do a rough check, change $\frac{100}{3}$ to a decimal.

$$\frac{100}{3} = 33.3 \ldots$$

Then substitute this value for m in the original proportion.

Does it look right? Does $\frac{32}{33.3}$ seem equal to $\frac{24}{25}$? It seems about right, because in each fraction the numerator is just slightly less than the denominator.

Check 2

To do an exact check, substitute $\frac{100}{3}$ for m in the original proportion.

Does $\frac{32}{\frac{100}{3}} = \frac{24}{25}$?

Work out the division of fractions on the left-hand side.

$$\frac{32}{\frac{100}{3}} = 32 \cdot \frac{3}{100} = \frac{96}{100}$$

Since $\frac{96}{100}$ simplifies to $\frac{24}{25}$ (the right-hand side), the answer checks.

Many real situations lead to having to solve proportions.

Example 2

If you can stuff 100 envelopes in 8 minutes, how many could you stuff in 30 minutes? Assume that you can keep up the same rate.

Solution

Let N be the number of envelopes you can stuff in 30 minutes. Since the rates are equal,

100 envelopes in 8 minutes = N envelopes in 30 minutes.

$$\frac{100 \text{ envelopes}}{8 \text{ minutes}} = \frac{N \text{ envelopes}}{30 \text{ minutes}}$$

$$\frac{100}{8} = \frac{N}{30}$$

Multiply both sides by $30 \cdot 8$ to get rid of all fractions.

$$30 \cdot 8 \cdot \frac{100}{8} = \frac{N}{30} \cdot 30 \cdot 8$$
$$30 \cdot 100 = N \cdot 8$$
$$3000 = 8N$$
$$375 = N$$

At this rate, you can stuff 375 envelopes in 30 minutes.

Check

375 envelopes in 30 minutes is 12.5 envelopes per minute. 100 envelopes in 8 minutes is also 12.5 envelopes per minute.

In **Example 2**, and in **Questions 13–16,** there are many equivalent proportions that can be used. You can switch means, switch extremes, or do both. You can take reciprocals of both sides, and get an equivalent proportion. And of course, you can switch the sides of an equation. Different students will undoubtedly set up different equations for the same problem.

Additional Examples

1. Solve for p and check.

   a. $\frac{12}{p} = \frac{3}{4}$

   $p = 16$; $\frac{12}{16} = \frac{3}{4}$

   b. $\frac{p}{1.2} = \frac{1}{1.8}$

   $p = \frac{2}{3}$; $\frac{\frac{2}{3}}{1.2} = \frac{2}{3.6} = \frac{1}{1.8}$

2. On the school track, eight laps make a mile. Gloria ran 5 laps in $4\frac{1}{2}$ minutes. At this rate, how long would it take her to run a mile? 7.2 minutes, or 7 minutes and 12 seconds

3. *Multiple choice.* Which equation is not a proportion? c

   a. $\frac{x}{2} = \frac{5}{7}$

   b. $\frac{3+a}{5} = \frac{2}{9}$

   c. $\frac{3}{5} + \frac{a}{5} = \frac{2}{9}$

   d. $\frac{1}{2} = \frac{5}{6}$

Optional Activities

Sports Connection As an extension of **Question 16,** have students research how many regular season games Kareem Abdul-Jabbar played, [1560 regular season games] Then have them calculate the average number of points both Abdul-Jabbar and Jordan scored per game. [Abdul-Jabbar scored an average of 24.6 points per game; Jordan scored an average of 32.3 points per game.]

Notes on Questions

Question 2 Students should be able to answer this question without solving an equation. It is here so you can set up these equal rates: $\frac{300 \text{ words}}{10 \text{ minutes}} = \frac{x}{20 \text{ minutes}}$, and show students that they have solved many proportions in their heads before seeing this lesson. Explain that the purpose of this and the next lesson is to present techniques that can be used when the numbers are more complicated.

Question 16 The activity in *Optional Activities* on page 617 extends this question.

Question 17 Remind students that circle graphs are most effective when showing the ratios of parts to a whole.

Question 22 If we just compare the lengths of the diameters, $7.50 is a reasonable price for a 15-inch pizza. However, the area of the 15-inch pizza is more than $1\frac{1}{2}$ times the area of the 10-inch pizza ($\frac{3}{2}$ is the ratio of the diameters), so a pizza shop would tend to charge more than $7.50 for the larger pizza. In general, larger pizzas tend to cost more per inch of diameter but less per square inch of area.

QUESTIONS

Covering the Reading

1. Suppose 20 out of 60 students in a class are boys. In lowest terms, __?__ out of __?__ students are boys. 1, 3

2. Suppose you type 300 words in 10 minutes. At this rate, you would type __?__ words in 20 minutes. 600

3. Define *proportion*.
   A proportion is a statement that two fractions are equal.

4. *Multiple choice.* Which proportion is not true?
   (a) $\frac{100}{7} = \frac{50}{3.5}$
   (b) $\frac{1}{3} = \frac{33}{100}$
   (c) $\frac{24}{60} = \frac{14}{35}$ (b)

5. *Multiple choice.* Which equation is not a proportion?
   (a) $\frac{x}{5} = \frac{3}{4}$
   (b) $\frac{1}{9} = \frac{15}{23}$
   (c) $\frac{1}{2} + \frac{2}{2} = \frac{3}{2}$ (c)

6. Consider the equation $\frac{40}{t} = \frac{21}{15}$.
   a. By what can you multiply both sides to get rid of the fractions? 15t
   b. What equation results after that multiplication? 600 = 21t
   c. Solve this equation. $t = \frac{200}{7}$
   d. Check your answer. Sample: $\frac{40}{200} = 40 \cdot \frac{7}{200} = \frac{280}{200} = \frac{7}{5}$; $\frac{21}{15} = \frac{7}{5}$ also.
      $\frac{}{7}$

In 7–10, solve.

7. $\frac{8}{7} = \frac{112}{Q}$ Q = 98

8. $\frac{200}{8} = \frac{x}{22}$ x = 550

9. $\frac{L}{24} = \frac{0.5}{4}$ L = 3

10. $\frac{39}{a} = \frac{130}{7}$ $a = \frac{21}{10}$ or $2\frac{1}{10}$

11. Jennifer can assemble 3 cardboard boxes in 4 minutes. At this rate, how many boxes can she assemble in 24 minutes? 18 boxes

12. Victor can assemble 5 cardboard boxes in 6 minutes. At this rate, how many boxes can he assemble in 45 minutes? 37.5 boxes

Applying the Mathematics

13. In the book *Big Bucks for Kids,* the author says that a kid can earn $25 for singing 20 minutes at a wedding. At this rate, what should the fee be for singing 45 minutes? $56.25

14. If a car can travel 300 km on 40 liters of gas, can it travel 450 km on a tank of 50 liters? No, 60 liters are needed.

15. A recipe says to use 2/3 of a teaspoon of salt for 6 people. In using this recipe for 25 people, how many teaspoons of salt should be used? $2\frac{7}{9}$

16. At the end of the 1992–1993 season, basketball player Michael Jordan had scored 21,541 points in 667 regular season games. He then announced his retirement. If he had continued at this rate, in what game would he have broken Kareem Abdul-Jabbar's record of 38,387 points? in Jordan's 1,189th game

618

Adapting to Individual Needs

Extra Help
When students solve proportions, remind them that they can sometimes simplify a fraction on one side of the proportion. If this can be done, the computation involved will be easier. For example, $\frac{1.6}{3.2} = \frac{x}{6}$ can be simplified to $\frac{16}{32} = \frac{x}{6}$ and even further to $\frac{1}{2} = \frac{x}{6}$.

17. In 1990, female armed forces personnel were distributed among the four services as shown below. *Source: The Universal Almanac, 1993*

83,681	Army	37.5%
73,341	Air Force	32.8%
56,970	Navy	25.5%
9,305	Marine Corps	4.2%

a. What percent of all female armed forces personnel was in each service? **See percents above.**

b. Construct a circle graph showing this information. **See left.**
(Lessons 2-6, 2-7, 11-5)

17b)

Female Armed Forces Personnel

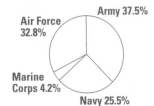

Army 37.5%
Air Force 32.8%
Marine Corps 4.2%
Navy 25.5%

18. a. What percent of 15 is 30? **200%**
b. What percent of 30 is 15? **50%**
c. What is the relationship between the answers to parts **a** and **b**?
(Lessons 10-3, 11-5) **They are reciprocals.**

19. Felice and Felipe folded fancy napkins for a Friday feast. In $\frac{2}{3}$ of an hour Felice folded 32 napkins. In 25 minutes Felipe folded 20 napkins. Who was folding faster? *(Lessons 11-2, 11-3)*
Neither, both fold 4/5 napkin per minute.

20. Pieces of paper numbered from 1 to 80 are put into a hat. A piece of paper is taken out. Assume each piece is equally likely. Mike's favorite number is 7. What is the probability that the number chosen has a 7 as one of its digits? *(Lesson 4-8)* **17/80**

21. The amount of material needed to make a cubical box with edge of length s is $6s^2$. How much material is needed to make a cubical box with an edge of length 30 cm? *(Lesson 4-4)* **5400 cm²**

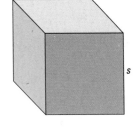

Exploration

22. Suppose a 10″ pizza costs $5.

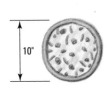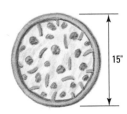

10″   15″

a. Using a proportion based on the diameters of the pizzas, what should a 15″ pizza cost? **$7.50**
b. Most pizza places charge more for a large pizza than the price calculated using proportions involving diameters. Why do they charge more?
c. Find a menu from a place that sells pizza. Do the larger pizzas cost more per inch of diameter? **Answers will vary.**

b) The price might be calculated using proportions involving areas instead of length of diameters. The area of the larger pizza is more than $1\frac{1}{2}$ times the area of the smaller pizza.

Lesson 11-6 *Proportions* **619**

Follow-up **11-6**
for Lesson

Practice
For more questions on SPUR Objectives, use **Lesson Master 11-6A** (shown on page 617) or **Lesson Master 11-6B** (shown on pages 618–619).

Assessment
Group Assessment Have students **work in groups,** and write about three situations in their everyday lives where using proportions is appropriate. [Students recognize that a proportion is a statement that two fractions are equal.]

Extension
Ask students to set up a proportion to answer the following question: If Bill reads p pages in m minutes, how many minutes will it take him to read g pages? [$\frac{p}{m} = \frac{g}{x}$; $x = \frac{gm}{p}$]

Project Update Project 2, *Best Buys*, on page 634, relates to the content of this lesson.

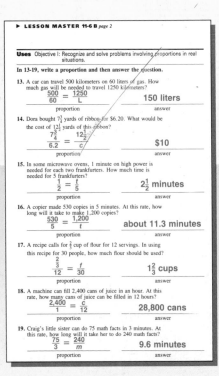

Objectives
C Solve proportions.
D Recognize the Means-Extremes Property and know why it works.
I Recognize and solve problems involving proportions in real situations.

Resources
From the Teacher's Resource File
■ Lesson Master 11-7A or 11-7B
■ Answer Master 11-7
■ Teaching Aid 118: Warm-up

Additional Resources
■ Visual for Teaching Aid 118

Warm-up
Diagnostic The same brand of pen is sold by stores A, B, and C.

A: 3 pens for $0.50
B: 12 pens for $2.00
C: 8 pens for $1.50

1. Write a proportion using the prices at A and B.
   Sample: $\frac{3}{\$0.50} = \frac{12}{\$2.00}$

   a. Identify the means.
      0.50 and 12
   b. Identify the extremes.
      3 and 2.00
   c. Is the product of the means equal to the product of the extremes? Are the ratios equal? **Yes, 6 = 6; yes**

Ageless calculations. *In Renaissance Europe, pictured here by a detail from a painting by Pieter Brueghel the Elder, 1559, merchants used a shortcut called the* Rule of Three *to solve proportions.*

The Means and the Extremes in a Proportion

In this lesson, you will learn a property that is very useful in solving proportions. First, however, you need to learn some new terms.

Here is a true proportion.

$$\frac{4}{10} = \frac{6}{15}$$

In some places in the world, this proportion is written

$$4:10 = 6:15.$$

In the United States, the colon sign indicates a ratio. We say "the ratio of 4 to 10 equals the ratio of 6 to 15." Or, we say "4 is to 10 as 6 is to 15."

Look again at 4:10 = 6:15. Since the numbers 4 and 15 are on the outside they are called the **extremes** of the proportion. The numbers 10 and 6 are in the middle and are called the **means**. Notice that 4 times 15 equals 10 times 6. The product of the means equals the product of the extremes.

> **Activity**
>
> Write down another true proportion. Verify that the product of the means of your proportion equals the product of the extremes. For instance, if you write down
>
> $$\frac{34.5}{23} \diagdown \diagup \frac{3}{2}$$
>
> means   extremes
>
> you would multiply to verify that
>
> $$23 \cdot 3 = 34.5 \cdot 2.$$

620

Lesson 11-7 Overview

Broad Goals One goal for studying this lesson is to learn to use the Means-Extremes Property (if $\frac{a}{b} = \frac{c}{d}$, then $ad = bc$) to solve proportions. A second broader goal is to show students that such properties are not isolated tricks, but are deducible from other properties.

Perspective In the previous lesson, students solved proportions by applying the Multiplication Property of Equality. In this lesson, the Multiplication Property of Equality is used to formulate the Means-Extremes Property. The Means-Extremes Property greatly simplifies the solving of proportions. Its drawback is that it is so easy that many students forget how the property was derived; they look for simple tricks for solving all equations, trying to avoid systematic procedures that take more than one step.

The general pattern can be shown to be true using the Multiplication Property of Equality. Suppose

$$\frac{a}{b} = \frac{c}{d}.$$

Now multiply both sides of the proportion by bd.

$$bd \cdot \frac{a}{b} = bd \cdot \frac{c}{d}$$
$$da = bc$$

❶ The right side of the equation $da = bc$ is the product of the means. The left side is the product of the extremes. This important property is stated below.

Means-Extremes Property

In any true proportion, the product of the means equals the product of the extremes. If $\frac{a}{b} = \frac{c}{d}$, then $b \cdot c = a \cdot d$.

Using the Means-Extremes Property to Solve Proportions

Example 1

Solve $\frac{2}{3} = \frac{12}{x}$.

Solution

You may be able to solve this equation in your head. But if you cannot, here is how to use the Means-Extremes Property.

The means are 3 and 12. The extremes are 2 and x. By the Means-Extremes Property,

$$3 \cdot 12 = 2 \cdot x.$$
$$36 = 2x$$

Solve this equation either mentally or by multiplying both sides by $\frac{1}{2}$.

$$18 = x$$

Check

Use substitution. Does $\frac{2}{3} = \frac{12}{18}$? Yes, because the fraction on the right simplifies to the fraction on the left.

Above is another detail of the Brueghel painting.

How Proportions Were Solved Before Algebra Was Invented

In the Middle Ages, there were no variables nor equations as we have them today. Here is a typical problem of that time. Can you solve it before turning the page?

Example 2

Suppose 6 bags of wheat cost 11 silver pieces. How much should 10 bags cost?

▶

Lesson 11-7 *The Means-Extremes Property* **621**

Optional Activities
You might use this activity after students have read the lesson. Have students **work in pairs**. (1) Have them write as many true proportions as they can using the numbers 6, 9, 40, and 60. If they need a hint, note that proportions can be found by starting with the equal products $6 \cdot 60 = 9 \cdot 40$, and thinking of one pair of factors as the means and the other pair as the extremes. (2) Now have students use this idea and write as many proportions as they can that are

equivalent to $\frac{a}{b} = \frac{c}{d}$, using only the four numbers a, b, c, and d.

[The following proportions can be written, along with the proportions obtained by interchanging the sides of the equation.

(1) $\frac{6}{40} = \frac{9}{60}, \frac{40}{6} = \frac{60}{9}, \frac{6}{9} = \frac{40}{60}, \frac{9}{6} = \frac{60}{40}$

(2) $\frac{b}{a} = \frac{d}{c}, \frac{a}{c} = \frac{b}{d}, \frac{c}{a} = \frac{d}{b}$]

Additional Examples

1. Solve and check.

   a. $\frac{4}{6} = \frac{n}{15}$

   $n = 10$; each side equals $\frac{2}{3}$.

   b. $\frac{\frac{1}{2}}{m} = \frac{5}{18}$

   $m = \frac{9}{5}$ or 1.8; each side equals $.2\overline{7}$.

2. Suppose it took you 34 minutes to read 20 pages of a novel. At this rate, how long would it take you to read the 175-page novel? **297.5 minutes, or almost 5 hours**

3. The scale on a map is 100 miles to 6 inches. If a lake is $1\frac{3}{4}$ inches long on the map, about how long is the real lake? **About 29 miles**

4. Consider the proportion $\frac{3}{4} = \frac{9}{12}$.

   a. Which numbers are the means? **4 and 9**

   b. Which numbers are the extremes? **3 and 12**

   c. Is the proportion true? **Yes**

   d. Does the product of the means equal the product of the extremes? **Yes**

622

Solution

Set up the two equal rates. $\dfrac{11 \text{ pieces}}{6 \text{ bags}} = \dfrac{p \text{ pieces}}{10 \text{ bags}}$

Now use the Means-Extremes Property. $6p = 110$

Multiply both sides by $\frac{1}{6}$.

$$p = \frac{110}{6}$$
$$= 18\frac{2}{6}$$
$$= 18\frac{1}{3}$$

The 10 bags should cost a little more than 18 silver pieces.

Students who wanted to solve proportions in the Middle Ages used a shortcut called the Rule of Three. They were taught to memorize: Multiply 10 by 11, and then divide by 6. But how could they remember which two numbers to multiply? Students were usually confused. A poem by an anonymous writer in the late Middle Ages indicates the confusion.

> Multiplication is vexation,
> Division is as bad,
> The Rule of Three
> Does puzzle me
> And practice drives me mad.

Good problem solvers try to find shortcuts like the Means-Extremes Property, or even the Rule of Three. But they also try to understand why the shortcuts work. A shortcut in which you have to guess what to do is no good at all.

With proportions, as with all other equations, it is essential to check answers. Here is a check for Example 2. Does $\frac{11}{6} = \frac{18.\overline{3}}{10}$? Yes, each equals $1.8\overline{3}$. Here is another check. Since 6 bags cost 11 pieces, 12 bags will cost twice as much, or 22 pieces. Ten bags should cost closer to 22 than 11 pieces, and they do.

QUESTIONS

Covering the Reading

1. Consider the proportion $\frac{15}{t} = \frac{250}{400}$.

   a. Identify the means. **t and 250**

   b. Identify the extremes. **15 and 400**

   c. According to the Means-Extremes Property, what equation will help you solve this proportion? **$250t = 400 \cdot 15$**

   d. Solve this proportion for t. **$t = 24$**

   e. Check your answer to part **d.**

   Does $\frac{15}{24} = \frac{250}{400}$? Yes, both are equal to 0.625.

Adapting to Individual Needs

Extra Help

The Means-Extremes Property is very useful for solving proportions. Unfortunately, some students try to apply the property to cases other than those involving proportions. The following equations involve some of the same fractions, but the Means-Extremes Property can only be used in the second equation. You might put each equation on the board, and demonstrate that only the numbers in the second equation form a proportion.

1. $\frac{1}{3} + \frac{7}{10} = x$ 2. $\frac{x}{3} = \frac{7}{10}$

3. $\frac{1}{3} \cdot \frac{7}{10} = x$ 4. $x + \frac{1}{3} = \frac{7}{10}$

2. Consider this situation. Eight small cans of grapefruit juice cost $1.79. You want to know how much ten small cans cost.
   a. Write a proportion that will help answer the question. $\frac{8}{1.79} = \frac{10}{c}$
   b. Solve the proportion using the Means-Extremes Property.
   c. Check your answer.   b) $c = \$2.2375 \approx \$2.24$;
   c) Does $8/1.79 = 10/2.24$? Yes, both are approximately 4.47.
3. Write down how the proportion $2:3 = 6:9$ is read.
   2 is to 3 as 6 is to 9
4. Why did the Rule of Three puzzle students in the Middle Ages?
   It was difficult to remember which two numbers to multiply.
5. Cyril went to market and found that 5 bags of salt cost 12 silver pieces. How much should he pay for 8 bags? $19\frac{1}{5}$ **silver pieces**

In 6–9, solve.

6. $\frac{n}{100} = \frac{72}{20}$ 7. $\frac{3}{10} = \frac{x}{25}$ 8. $\frac{200}{m} = \frac{21}{35}$ 9. $\frac{15}{8} = \frac{12}{v}$
   $n = 360$ $x = 7.5$ $m = 333.\overline{3}$ $v = 6.4$

Applying the Mathematics

10. Lannie tried to solve the proportion of Question 6 by multiplying both sides by 100. Will this work? Explain why or why not.
    Yes, because $100 \cdot n/100 = 100 \cdot 72/20$ results in $n = 7200/20 = 360$.

In 11–14, *true or false.* Consider the proportion $\frac{a}{b} = \frac{c}{d}$.

11. $ad = bc$ 12. $ab = cd$ 13. $ac = bd$ 14. $da = cb$
    True   **False**   **False**   **True**

15. If small cans of grapefruit juice are 5 for $1.69, how many cans can be bought for $10? **29 cans**

16. On the first two days of the week-long hunting season, 47 deer were taken.
    a. At this rate, how many deer will be taken during the week?
    b. Why might it be incorrect to assume the rate will stay the same all week? **a) 164 or 165 deer; b) There could be more hunters on the weekend.**

This 17th-century engraving shows laborers harvesting rice in China.

17. Why won't the Means-Extremes Property work on the equation $x + \frac{2}{3} = \frac{4}{5}$? **The equation is not a proportion.**

18. During approximately the first century A.D. the most important Chinese mathematics text of its time, the *Chiu Chang*, was written. Here is a problem from that text. (The *picul* was the average weight a man could carry on his back, about 65 kg.) If two and one-half piculs of rice were purchased for $\frac{3}{7}$ of a tael of silver, about how many piculs of rice could be bought for 9 taels? $52\frac{1}{2}$ **piculs of rice**

Lesson 11-7 *The Means-Extremes Property* **623**

Notes on Questions

Question 4 Use the story of the Rule of Three to point out that when properties are learned by rote (without connecting them to other properties), they are difficult to remember. Students learned how to solve proportions using the Multiplication Property of Equality so that if they forget, they can always go back to that property.

Questions 11–14 These questions combine the Commutative Property of Multiplication and the Means-Extremes Property. Since **Question 11** is true, **Question 14** must be true.

Questions 15–16 A proportion assumes the equality of rates, which is true only if the rate remains constant. Thus a solution to a proportion of this type will be accurate only for a constant rate.

▶ **LESSON MASTER 11-7 B** *page 2*

Properties Objective D: Recognize the Means-Extremes property, and know why it works.

In 13-16, use the proportion $\frac{p}{q} = \frac{r}{s}$.

13. __q__ and __r__ are the means.

14. __p__ and __s__ are the extremes.

15. Multiplying both sides of the equation by __qs__ will eliminate the fractions.

16. Use other properties to demonstrate that the Means-Extremes Property is true. (Start with $\frac{p}{q} = \frac{r}{s}$. Show $ps = qr$.)
    Given $\frac{p}{q} = \frac{r}{s}$, $qs \cdot \frac{p}{q} = qs \cdot \frac{r}{s}$ by the
    Mult. Prop. of Equality. Simplifying results in $sp = qr$, and the Commut. Prop. of Mult. gives $ps = qr$.

Uses Objective I: Recognize and solve problems involving proportions in real situations.

In 17-20, write a proportion and then answer the question.

17. During the first five days of summer, Scrumptious Scoops served 47 gallons of ice cream. At this rate, how many gallons will they serve in 75 days? $\frac{5}{47} = \frac{75}{g}$; **705 gal**

18. Five gallons of paint were used to paint two classrooms. If all the classrooms are the same, how many complete classrooms can be painted with 48 gallons of paint? $\frac{5}{2} = \frac{48}{r}$; **19 rooms**

19. A recipe serving eight people requires $2\frac{1}{2}$ pounds of ground beef. How much ground beef will be needed to serve 20 people? $\frac{2\frac{1}{2}}{8} = \frac{b}{20}$; $6\frac{1}{4}$ **lb**

20. If cans of pizza sauce are priced at 4 for $1.35, how many cans can be bought for $12? $\frac{4}{1.35} = \frac{c}{12}$; **35 cans**

Adapting to Individual Needs

English Language Development
Some of your students may have studied proportions in another country. Ask these students if they were taught to write proportions as, for example, 4:10 = 6:15, or 4:10 :: 6:15. Ask students if they feel there are advantages and disadvantages of writing 4:10 = 6:15 instead of $\frac{4}{10} = \frac{6}{15}$.

[Possible advantage: the means and extremes are easier to identify; possible

disadvantage: it is harder to see that the ratios are equal.]

Notes on Questions

Question 23 Students are calculating a *rate of change* in this question. This idea is exceedingly important in the study of algebra, functions, and calculus.

Follow-up 11-7
for Lesson

Practice

For more questions on SPUR Objectives, use **Lesson Master 11-7A** (shown on page 621) or **Lesson Master 11-7B** (shown on pages 622–623.)

Assessment

Group Assessment Have students **work in pairs**. Have one partner write a proportion involving 3 numbers and a variable. Then have the other partner write a problem that could be described by the proportion. Have students take turns writing proportions and problems. The student who writes the problem should solve the proportion. [Problems should be realistic and show an understanding of the Means-Extremes Property.]

Extension

✎ **Writing** Have each student pick at least one category below, and write and solve a proportion problem relating to it. Students should use real-world data and document their resources.

Art	Consumer topics
Geography	Health
History	Music
Science	Sports

Giant of a man. *Robert Wadlow is shown with part of his family on his 21st birthday, February 22, 1939.*

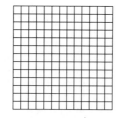

25b) The coordinates of the vertices of the image should be the result of multiplying the coordinates of the vertices of the first quadrilateral by -3.

Review

19. A telephone survey was conducted in a small city. Of 240 households called on the phone, 119 were watching television at the time.
    a. To the nearest hundredth, what percent of households were watching television? *(Lesson 11-5)* **49.58%**
    b. If 25,000 households are in this city, how many would you expect to have been watching TV? *(Lesson 11-6)* **about 12,400**
    c. What number might you choose as the probability that someone in a household was watching television? *(Lesson 4-8)* **1/2, or .5**

20. Simplify. *(Lessons 1-10, 11-4)*
    a. $\frac{12}{18}$ **$\frac{2}{3}$**   b. $\frac{12}{-18}$ **$-\frac{2}{3}$**   c. $\frac{-12}{-18}$ **$\frac{2}{3}$**   d. $\frac{-12}{18}$ **$-\frac{2}{3}$**

In 21 and 22, simplify. *(Lesson 11-3)*

21. $\frac{7}{10} \div \frac{2}{7}$ **$\frac{49}{20}$, or $2\frac{9}{20}$**   22. $1\frac{4}{5} \div \frac{1}{15}$ **27**

23. Robert Wadlow of Alton, Illinois, was $5\frac{1}{3}$ feet tall at the age of 5 and $8\frac{2}{3}$ feet tall at the age of 21. On the average, how fast did he grow during those years? *(Lesson 11-2)* **$\frac{5}{24}$ ft/yr, or 2.5 in./yr**

24. Ru-Niteroi, in Guanabara Bay, Brazil, is the world's largest continuous box-and-plate girder bridge, with a length of 45,603 ft.
    a. What is the bridge's length to the nearest tenth of a mile? *(Lesson 9-5)* **8.6 miles**
    b. Find the length in miles and feet. *(Lesson 11-1)* **8 miles, 3363 feet**

25. a. Graph four ordered pairs that are the vertices of a quadrilateral that is not a trapezoid. *(Lessons 8-3, 10-10)* **Answers will vary.**
    b. Apply a size change of magnitude -3 to your quadrilateral. *(Lesson 9-9)* **See left.**

26. Use the array of squares at the left. Assume each side of a little square has length $\frac{1}{8}$ inch.
    a. How many little squares are in the array? *(Lesson 9-1)* **169**
    b. What is the area of a little square? *(Lesson 9-3)* **1/64 square inch**
    c. What is the area of the entire figure? *(Lesson 10-1)* **≈2.64 sq in.**
    d. What is the perimeter of a little square? *(Lesson 10-8)* **1/2 inch**
    e. What is the total length of all the line segments in the figure? *(Lesson 10-1)* **$45\frac{1}{2}$ inches**

Exploration

For 27 and 28, look again at the poem in this lesson.

27. What is the meaning of the word *vexation?* **annoyance**

28. Approximately when were the Middle Ages? **between about 500 and 1500 A.D.**

Adapting to Individual Needs

Challenge
Have students solve the following problem: On a test, Mimi missed 6 items and received a score of 92%. The score was not rounded. If the same number of points was given to each item, how many items were on the test? [75 items]

Proportions in Similar Figures

IN-CLASS
ACTIVITY

Materials: Ruler
Work with a partner.

In Chapter 9 you learned that the image of a figure under a size change of magnitude k is similar to the original figure. In this activity you will learn how to determine the size change factor when given two similar figures. **See margin for answers.**

1 Polygons $ABCDE$ and $A'B'C'D'E'$ below are similar. Measure the lengths of corresponding sides. Then compute $\frac{A'B'}{AB}$, $\frac{B'C'}{BC}$, $\frac{C'D'}{CD}$, $\frac{D'E'}{DE}$, and $\frac{A'E'}{AE}$.

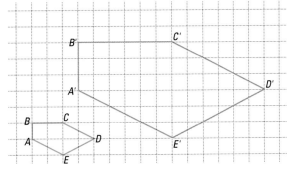

2 $A'B'C'D'E'$ is the size change image of $ABCDE$ under a size change of magnitude 3. How does this size change magnitude compare to the ratios of lengths of corresponding sides that you found?

3 Pick a size change magnitude to use to draw a picture of the house shown here that is similar to the original. Do not tell your partner the size change magnitude you chose. After you and your partner have both drawn the image of the house, trade pictures with your partner. Measure lengths of segments on your partner's drawing and compute appropriate ratios to try to find out what size change magnitude your partner used.

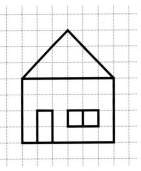

4 ***Draw conclusions.*** With your partner, determine what you can say about the ratios of lengths of corresponding sides of similar figures.

625

Additional Answers
1. $\frac{A'B'}{AB} = \frac{B'C'}{BC} = \frac{C'D'}{CD} = \frac{D'E'}{DE} = \frac{A'E'}{AE} = \frac{3}{1}$
2. The ratios are equal to the size change magnitude.
3. Answers will vary.
4. The ratios of the lengths of corresponding sides of similar figures are equal.

In-class Activity
Resources
From the **Teacher's Resource File**
- Answer Master 11-8
- Teaching Aid 120: Proportions in Similar Figures

Additional Resources
- Visual for Teaching Aid 120

To determine the ratios $\frac{A'B'}{AB}$ and $\frac{B'C'}{BC}$, students could simply count squares on the grid. In both cases it is clear that the ratio is $\frac{3}{1}$. However, in order to obtain the other requested ratios, students must measure with a ruler. Therefore, the ratios they obtain may not be exactly $\frac{3}{1}$ because all measurements are approximate.

For **Question 3,** some students may not remember how to draw an image under a size change with magnitude k. Remind them that they can draw an x-axis and a y-axis at any convenient point on the grid. Then every point on the drawing of the house can be designated by an ordered pair (x, y). To draw a size change with magnitude k, students simply multiply the coordinates of each point by k.

Have students record the results of the *Activity* for use in **Question 1** on page 628. Students can use **Teaching Aid 120** to help organize their work.

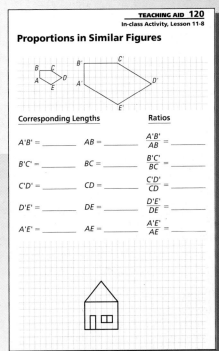

Warm-up

On a road map, one inch represents 14 miles. The map distances between certain cities are listed below. Estimate the actual distances.

1. Cincinnati, OH, and Lexington, KY: $5\frac{1}{2}$ inches **77 miles**

2. Eugene, OR, and Bend, OR: 9 inches **126 miles**

3. Bangor, ME, and Lewiston, ME: $7\frac{1}{2}$ inches **105 miles**

Notes on Reading

If students have not read this lesson for homework, the first two pages should be done in class.

LESSON

11-8

Proportions in Similar Figures

Scaled down. _A model airplane, such as the one being constructed in the photo, is called a scale model because its dimensions are scaled proportionally to those of the full-sized airplane it represents._

In the In-class activity on page 625, you examined the lengths of corresponding sides of similar figures. We call such lengths _corresponding lengths_. In the activity, you should have found that the following property is true.

> In similar figures, ratios of corresponding lengths are equal.

Finding Lengths in Similar Figures

If you know which sides of similar figures correspond, you can find unknown lengths.

Example 1

Triangles _CAT_ and _DOG_ are similar. Name the corresponding sides.

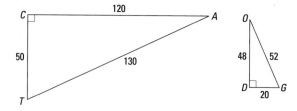

Solution

The sides will correspond in order of their lengths. The shortest sides, $\overline{CT}$ and $\overline{DG}$, correspond, as do the middle sides, $\overline{CA}$ and $\overline{DO}$, and the longest sides, $\overline{AT}$ and $\overline{OG}$. Notice that the ratios of these sides are equal: $\frac{50}{20} = \frac{120}{48} = \frac{130}{52}$.

Lesson 11-8 Overview

Broad Goals In this lesson, students examine lengths in similar figures, find that their ratios are equal, and use them to form proportions. Then they use the proportions to determine unknown lengths.

Perspective We have included a lesson on similar figures for three major reasons. First, the content and ideas are important in their own right. The understanding of similar figures is fundamental in geometry providing a basis for many applications as well as for trigonometry and other advanced topics. Second, this content pictures the ideas of the preceding lessons. For some students, this mental picture of proportions will help them to better understand the idea. Third, the topic of similar figures provides a different sort of application for the techniques of the previous lessons and is an interesting change of pace from the arithmetic and algebra that have dominated this chapter.

Many students can solve geometric problems only if the ratio of corresponding sides is an integer. This often occurs because students solve these problems by addition or multiplication rather than by proportions or ratios. If the sides of a figure are not integers, and if students are confused in setting up the proportion, suggest that they consider the problem with simpler numbers.

You can find lengths of sides in similar figures by solving proportions.

Example 2

The figures below are similar with corresponding sides parallel. Find *EF*.

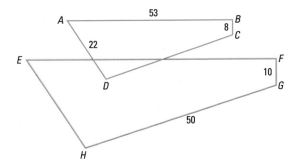

Solution

$\overline{EF}$ corresponds to $\overline{AB}$. The only corresponding sides with both lengths given are $\overline{FG}$ and $\overline{BC}$. Use them in the proportion.

$$\frac{EF}{AB} = \frac{FG}{BC}$$

Now substitute what is known. $FG = 10$, $BC = 8$, and $AB = 53$.

$$\frac{EF}{53} = \frac{10}{8}$$

Solve as you would any other proportion. Use the Means-Extremes Property.

$$53 \cdot 10 = 8 \cdot EF$$

Multiply both sides by $\frac{1}{8}$. $\frac{530}{8} = EF$

$$EF = 66.25$$

Check

For a rough check, look at the figure. Does a length of about 66 for $\overline{EF}$ seem correct? Yes, since *EF* should be longer than *AB*.

For an exact check, substitute the length of $\overline{EF}$ in the proportion.

$$\frac{66.25}{53} = \frac{10}{8}$$

Division shows each side to equal 1.25.

How Do Similar Figures Arise?

Begin with a real object. Take a photograph of it, or draw a picture of it. You may construct a scale model of a large object. You might magnify a small object. Any of these activities lead to similar figures in which you might want to find lengths of sides. In these ways, similar figures arise, and with them, situations involving proportions.

Lesson 11-8 *Proportions in Similar Figures* **627**

You might begin by noting that similar figures arise in many ways, such as magnification through a lens, taking pictures, and making models.

In **Example 1,** point out to students that they can check the lengths of corresponding sides by changing each ratio to a decimal.

In **Example 2,** make certain that students understand that to establish the ratio, they first need to look for a pair of corresponding sides with both lengths given. Then that ratio can be used in a proportion to find the missing sides.

Additional Examples

The following examples can be found on **Teaching Aid 121.**
1. Given that △*RUN* is similar to △*HOP*, with corresponding sides parallel, list the pairs of corresponding sides.

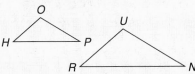

$\overline{RU}, \overline{HO}$; $\overline{UN}, \overline{OP}$; $\overline{RN}, \overline{HP}$
2. The two trapezoids are similar with corresponding sides parallel. Find the missing lengths.
$a = 12$; $b = 6$; $c = 16$

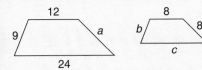

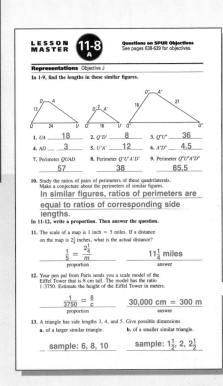

Optional Activities

Materials: Tangram pieces or **Teaching Aid 122,** centimeter ruler or **Geometry Template**

After teaching the lesson, you might give students these directions to use with tangram pieces.
1. Which tangram pieces are congruent? [See the diagram at the right: 1 and 2; 3 and 5]
2. Which pieces appear to be similar?

Measure each side, and set up proportions to verify your answers. [The triangles are similar, but since measurement is not precise, the proportions may not be exact.]
3. Make two similar figures by combining tangram pieces. [Sample: The triangle made with pieces 1 and 2 is similar to that made with 3, 4, and 5.]

627

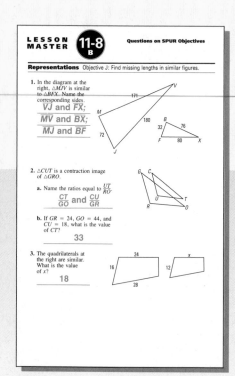

QUESTIONS

Covering the Reading

1. In the In-class activity on page 625, what value did you find for each ratio?
   a. $\frac{A'B'}{AB}$ $\frac{1.5 \text{ cm}}{.5 \text{ cm}} = 3$ b. $\frac{B'C'}{BC}$ $\frac{3 \text{ cm}}{1 \text{ cm}} = 3$ c. $\frac{C'D'}{CD}$ $\frac{3.3 \text{ cm}}{1.1 \text{ cm}} = 3$

2. In similar figures, what ratios are always equal? **ratios of lengths of corresponding sides**

3. a. Polygon *HUGE* at the left is an expansion image of polygon *TINY*. Name the ratios equal to $\frac{IN}{UG}$. $\frac{IN}{UG} = \frac{NY}{GE} = \frac{YT}{EH} = \frac{TI}{HU}$
   b. If $YN = 16$, $EG = 24$, and $TY = 26$, what is the value of *HE*? **39**

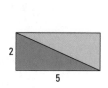

In 4 and 5, refer to Example 2.

4. Find *EH*. **27.5**   5. Find *CD*. **40**

6. Draw an example of similar figures whose corresponding sides are not parallel.

7. The figures below are similar. What is the value of *x*? **7.5**

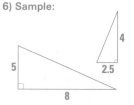

6) Sample:

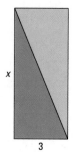

The pool shown here is in the Tuileries Gardens in Paris, France. Children often sail toy boats in this pool.

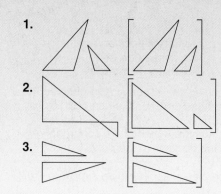

8. Name three places where similar figures can be found.
   Samples: photographs, scale models, magnifications

Applying the Mathematics

9. A right triangle has sides with lengths 3 cm, 4 cm, and 5 cm. The shortest side of a similar right triangle has length 9 cm.
   a. Draw an accurate picture of the original right triangle.
   b. Find the lengths of the other two sides of the similar right triangle.
   c. Draw an accurate picture of the similar right triangle.
   b) 12 cm, 15 cm;   a, c) Check student drawings.

10. A drawing is 20 cm long and 15 cm wide. It is put into a copy machine to be reduced to 60% of its original size.
   a. What will the dimensions of the copy be? **12 cm long; 9 cm wide**
   b. Are the ratios of corresponding sides of the drawing and its copy equal? **Yes**
   c. Are the drawing and its copy similar? **Yes**

11. A boat is 220 feet long. A scale model of the boat is 20 inches long. If the scale model is 8 inches wide, how wide was the original boat?
   88 ft

628

Adapting to Individual Needs

Extra Help
Students are sometimes confused by figures that are similar but have different orientations. Remind them that they can flip, slide, or turn any geometric figure. Draw pairs of similar figures with different orientations, similar to those at the right, on a piece of paper. Have students cut out one figure in each pair, and reposition it with the same orientation as the first figure. [Sample responses are given.]

COLORADO
285
SAN JUAN MTS.
84
64
84
285
NEW MEXICO
Espanola
Los Alamos
Santa Fe
JEMEZ MTS.
25
285
Albuquerque
40
40

0 10 20 30 miles

12. At the left is a map of the region around Santa Fe, New Mexico. The map is similar to the actual land. A distance of 14 mm on the map represents an actual distance of about 30 miles. The distance from Albuquerque to Santa Fe on the map is about 31 mm. How far is this in actual miles? **about 66 miles**

Review

In 13–15, solve. *(Lesson 11-6)*

13. $\frac{t}{40} = \frac{5}{16}$ *t = 12.5* **14.** $\frac{3.5}{11} = \frac{x}{132}$ *x = 42* **15.** $\frac{3}{4} = \frac{5}{A}$ *A = 6.\overline{6}*

16. A plane goes 300 miles in 36 minutes. At this rate, how far will it travel in an hour? *(Lesson 11-2)* **500 miles**

17. *Multiple choice.* If $x = 60$ and $y = -10$, which of the following are negative? *(Lessons 5-5, 7-2, 9-6, 11-4)*

(a) $x + y$ (b) $x - y$ (c) $y - x$ (d) xy (e) $\frac{x}{y}$ (f) $\frac{y}{x}$
(c), (d), (e), (f)

18. Solve $10A - 50 = 87$. *(Lesson 10-4)* *A = 13.7*

19. Consistent Constance constantly tips servers 15% of the bill for dinner. You see Constance leave a tip of $2.25. Estimate the dinner bill. *(Lesson 10-3)* **$15**

In 20–23, let $u = \frac{8}{5}$ and $v = -\frac{7}{5}$. Evaluate. *(Lessons 5-5, 7-2, 9-3, 11-3)*

20. $u + v$ $\frac{1}{5}$ **21.** $u - v$ 3 **22.** uv $-\frac{56}{25}$ **23.** $\frac{u}{v}$ $-\frac{8}{7}$

24. Merv knows that he can multiply both the numerator and denominator of a fraction by the same nonzero number without changing its value. He wonders what else he can do without changing its value.
a. Can he add the same number to the numerator and denominator? **No**
b. Can he subtract the same number from the numerator and denominator? **No**
c. Can he divide both the numerator and denominator by the same number? *(Lessons 6-4, 6-7)* **Yes**

25. Write 3,800,000,000 in scientific notation. *(Lesson 2-3)* $3.8 \cdot 10^9$

26. Write $17\frac{2}{11}$ as a simple fraction and as a decimal. *(Lessons 1-7, 1-10)* $\frac{189}{11}$; $17.\overline{18}$

27. Write $\frac{41}{8}$ as a decimal and as a mixed number. *(Lessons 1-6, 1-10)* 5.125; $5\frac{1}{8}$

28. Between which two whole numbers is $\frac{41}{8}$? *(Lesson 1-2)* **5 and 6**

29)
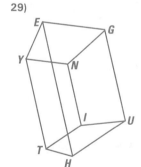
E
G
Y
N
I
U
T
H

Exploration

29. Look again at the drawing for Question 3. Some people think that the drawing might be a picture of a 3-dimensional object with missing lines. Trace the drawing, and add lines to picture an object.

Lesson 11-8 *Proportions in Similar Figures* **629**

Adapting to Individual Needs

English Language Development
Two words in this lesson that you might want to spend some extra time discussing are *similar* and *corresponding*. Emphasize the fact that the use of these words in the mathematical context of this lesson is more restrictive than their use in ordinary English.

Challenge
Suppose you have a picture that is 8 inches wide and 10 inches high. You want to reduce it on a copy machine to fit into a space that is 4.5 inches wide. The copy machine will reduce whole number percents of the original size from 99% to 64%. Explain how you can use this machine to reduce your picture. [Reduce to 75% and then reduce that reduction to 75%.]

Follow-up 11-8
for Lesson

Practice
For more questions on SPUR Objectives, use **Lesson Master 11-8A** (shown on page 627) or **Lesson Master 11-8B** (shown on pages 628–629).

Assessment
Quiz A quiz covering Lessons 11-5 through 11-8 is provided in the *Assessment Sourcebook.*

Oral Communication Draw a pair of similar figures on the board. Ask students to explain how to find corresponding sides. Then have them identify each pair of corresponding sides. [Explanations should include the fact that sides correspond in order of their lengths.]

Extension
Technology Connection You may wish to assign *Technology Sourcebook, Computer Master 26.* Students use the *Geometry Workshop* to explore lengths of corresponding sides.

Project Update Project 1, *Similar Objects,* on page 634, relates to the content of this lesson.

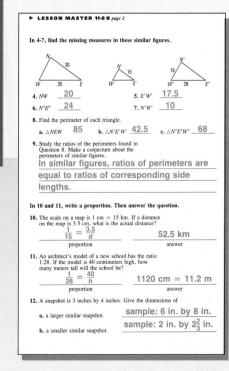

▶ **LESSON MASTER 11-8 B** *page 2*

In 4-7, find the missing measures in these similar figures.

4. NW ___20___ **5.** E'W' ___17.5___
6. N"E" ___24___ **7.** N'W' ___10___

8. Find the perimeter of each triangle.
  a. △NEW ___85___ **b.** △N'E'W' ___42.5___ **c.** △N"E"W" ___68___

9. Study the ratios of the perimeters found in Question 8. Make a conjecture about the perimeters of similar figures.
In similar figures, ratios of perimeters are equal to ratios of corresponding side lengths.

In 10 and 11, write a proportion. Then answer the question.

10. The scale on a map is 1 cm = 15 km. If a distance on the map is 3.5 cm, what is the actual distance?
$\frac{1}{15} = \frac{3.5}{d}$ proportion ___52.5 km___ answer

11. An architect's model of a new school has the ratio 1:28. If the model is 40 centimeters high, how many meters tall will the school be?
$\frac{1}{28} = \frac{40}{h}$ proportion ___1120 cm = 11.2 m___ answer

12. A snapshot is 3 inches by 4 inches. Give the dimensions of
  a. a larger similar snapshot. ___sample: 6 in. by 8 in.___
  b. a smaller similar snapshot. ___sample: 2 in. by $2\frac{2}{3}$ in.___

Objectives

C Solve proportions.
I Recognize and solve problems involving proportions in real situations.

Resources

From the *Teacher's Resource File*
■ Lesson Master 11-9A or 11-9B
■ Answer Master 11-9
■ Teaching Aid 119: Warm-up

Additional Resources
■ Visual for Teaching Aid 119

Teaching Lesson 11-9

Warm-up

For each exercise, select the proportion or proportions that could be used to solve the problem.

1. Zak drove 10 miles in 15 minutes. At this rate, how far can he drive in 40 minutes? **c**

   a. $\frac{15 \text{ min}}{40 \text{ min}} = \frac{x}{10 \text{ mi}}$

   b. $\frac{15 \text{ min}}{10 \text{ mi}} = \frac{x}{40 \text{ min}}$

   c. $\frac{10 \text{ mi}}{15 \text{ min}} = \frac{x}{40 \text{ min}}$

2. If 3 boxes of pasta cost $1.59, how much will 5 boxes cost?
   a and c

   a. $\frac{3 \text{ boxes}}{\$1.59} = \frac{5 \text{ boxes}}{x}$

   b. $\frac{3 \text{ boxes}}{5 \text{ boxes}} = \frac{x}{\$1.59}$

   c. $\frac{\$1.59}{3 \text{ boxes}} = \frac{x}{5 \text{ boxes}}$

How much forest is there? *Forests comprise a large portion of the land area of the United States. A forest near Corinth, Vermont, is shown above. See Example 2.*

Suppose 2 bags of peanuts cost 59¢. How much will 8 bags cost? You can answer this question by solving the following proportion.

$$\frac{2 \text{ bags}}{59¢} = \frac{8 \text{ bags}}{C}$$

Some people would notice that 8 is 4 times 2 and reason that the cost will be 4 times 59¢. These people have used *proportional thinking* to answer the question. **Proportional thinking** is the ability to get or estimate an answer to a proportion without solving an equation. Some people believe that proportional thinking is one of the most important kinds of thinking you can have in mathematics.

To improve your proportional thinking, try first to estimate answers to questions involving proportions. Then try to get the exact answer.

Example 1

If you travel at 45 mph, how much time will it take to go 80 miles?

Solution 1

Estimate. At 45 mph, you can go 45 miles in 1 hour. Therefore, you can go 90 miles in 2 hours. So it will take between 1 and 2 hours to go 80 miles. Since 80 is closer to 90 than to 45, it will take almost 2 hours.

Solution 2

Try simpler numbers. At 40 mph, it would take 2 hours. This answer is 80 divided by 40. This suggests that dividing 80 by 45 will get the answer.

$$\frac{80 \text{ miles}}{45 \frac{\text{miles}}{\text{hour}}} \approx 1.8 \text{ hours} = 1 \text{ hour } 48 \text{ minutes}$$

The answer seems right because it agrees with the estimate in Solution 1.

Lesson 11-9 Overview

Broad Goals In the past three lessons, students have studied algorithms for solving proportions. The goal of this lesson is to develop intuition for estimating the answers without using an algorithm.

Perspective This is a review lesson, both for proportions and for problem solving, but now the emphasis is on flexibility. Many students think that if they know one way to do a problem, there is no point in considering

alternatives. However, there are several advantages in knowing more than one way to approach a problem: (1) one method may be easier for one problem and more difficult for another; (2) a second method can be used to check the first; (3) preferences vary from person to person. For these reasons, we feel students should learn to think about a problem in a variety of ways.

Although the solution methods used in this lesson are important, the real point we want to emphasize is the flexibility to know how to solve problems in more than one way. As you discuss the lesson, you might ask students to identify advantages they see in knowing more than one way to solve a problem.

Solution 3

Set up a proportion.

$$\frac{45 \text{ miles}}{1 \text{ hour}} = \frac{80 \text{ miles}}{h \text{ hours}}$$

Use the Means-Extremes Property or multiply both sides by h.

$$45h = 80$$

Solve.

$$h = \frac{80}{45}$$
$$\approx 1.8 \text{ hours}$$

The important thing here is flexibility. You do not have to know every way there is of solving proportions. But you should have at least two ways to do these questions. Use one way to check the other.

Example 2 uses the hectare, a very common unit for measuring land area in the metric system.

Example 2

According to the *State of the World 1991*, about 296,000,000 hectares of the United States are forest. There are about 259 hectares in a square mile. About how many square miles of the U.S. are forest?

Solution 1

Estimate using proportional thinking. Since there are about 259 hectares in one square mile, there are 259 million hectares in 1 million square miles. 296,000,000 is more than 259 million, so more than 1 million square miles of the U.S. are forest.

Solution 2

The problem is to convert hectares to square miles. Use a method from Lesson 9-5. The abbreviation for hectare is ha.

$$296,000,000 \text{ ha} = 296,000,000 \text{ ha} \cdot \frac{1 \text{ square mile}}{259 \text{ ha}}$$
$$\approx 1,140,000 \text{ square miles}$$

Solution 3

Set up a proportion.

$$\frac{296,000,000 \text{ hectares}}{F \text{ square miles}} = \frac{259 \text{ hectares}}{1 \text{ square mile}}$$

Solve the proportion.

$$259F = 296,000,000$$
$$F = \frac{296,000,000}{259}$$
$$\approx 1,140,000 \text{ square miles}$$

The entire land area of the United States is about 3,536,000 square miles. Dividing 1,140,000 by 3,536,000, we get about 0.32. So about 32% (almost 1/3) of the land of the United States is forest.

Lesson 11-9 *Proportional Thinking* **631**

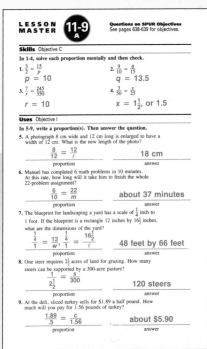

Optional Activities

Materials: Nutritional information from packages of food

Health Connection Use this activity after you have discussed the examples with students. Have students **work in groups,** and use nutritional information on packages of food to illustrate rates and write rate problems. For example, information on a peanut butter jar gives the number of Calories per 2-ounce serving as 185. Students might write a problem about the number of Calories in a 1-ounce portion, or they might write a problem about the number of Calories in the 28-ounce jar.

631

Notes on Questions

Questions 11–14 You might have students list the different ways to get answers.

Questions 19–20 Some students may still be confused by these problems. Tell them that they should obtain a rough estimate first. In **Question 19,** the answer will certainly be less than 200. In **Question 20,** the answer will be greater than 200.

Question 21b Consumer Connection You may need to explain the Consumer Price Index. The idea is simple. If something cost COST1 in a year in which the CPI was CPI1, then it should cost about COST2 in a year in which the CPI was CPI2.

The proportion is $\frac{COST1}{COST2} = \frac{CPI1}{CPI2}$.

For Question 21b, the proportion is $\frac{COST2}{11630} = \frac{136.2}{38.8}$. (The use of COST1, COST2, CPI1, and CPI2 as variables derives from names given to variables in computer programs.)

Follow-up for Lesson 11-9

Practice

For more questions on SPUR Objectives, use **Lesson Master 11-9A** (shown on page 631) or **Lesson Master 11-9B** (shown on pages 632–633).

LESSON MASTER 11-9 B   Questions on SPUR Objectives

Skills Objective C: Solve proportions.

In 1-8, solve each proportion mentally and check.   Student work is not shown.

1. $\frac{5}{3} = \frac{x}{21}$ 2. $\frac{42}{m} = \frac{14}{11}$
   $x = 35$ $m = 33$

3. $\frac{7}{10} = \frac{k}{25}$ 4. $\frac{u}{74} = \frac{56}{37}$
   $k = 17.5$ $u = 112$

5. $\frac{15}{8} = \frac{1}{r}$ 6. $\frac{5.1}{e} = \frac{1.7}{2.8}$
   $r = \frac{8}{15}$ $e = 8.4$

7. $\frac{6}{0.2} = \frac{30}{g}$ 8. $\frac{1\frac{1}{4}}{10} = \frac{3\frac{1}{4}}{y}$
   $g = 1$ $y = 30$

In 9-12, use proportional thinking to answer the question.

9. If cantaloupes are 2 for $1.19, 8 cantaloupes will cost ___$4.76___

10. At 55 mph (miles per hour),
   a. it takes __2__ hours to travel 110 miles.
   b. it takes __10__ hours to travel 550 miles.
   c. it takes between __3__ and __4__ hours to travel 200 miles. (Fill in the blanks with consecutive whole numbers.)
   d. the exact time needed to travel 200 miles can be found with this proportion: $\frac{55}{1} = \frac{200}{t}$

11. If a recipe for 6 servings uses 2 cups of flour, then __6__ cups of flour are needed for 18 servings.

12. If a recipe for 6 servings uses 2 cups of flour, then there is $\frac{1}{3}$ cup of flour in each serving.

---

3) $\frac{2 \text{ cans}}{\$2.50} = \frac{6 \text{ cans}}{\$c}$

8a) $2.\overline{18}$ hr
b) Sample:
$\frac{55 \text{ mi}}{1 \text{ hr}} = \frac{120 \text{ mi}}{x \text{ hr}}$
$55x = 120$
$x = 2.\overline{18}$ hr

9a) $8\frac{1}{3}$ dozen
b) Sample:
$\frac{12 \text{ eggs}}{1 \text{ doz}} = \frac{100 \text{ eggs}}{d \text{ doz}}$
$12d = 100$
$d = 8\frac{1}{3}$

12) 80 minutes, because they can mow 2 lawns in 40 minutes and twice as many lawns, or 4 lawns, in 80 minutes.

QUESTIONS

Covering the Reading

1. What is proportional thinking? the ability to get or estimate an answer to a proportion without solving an equation

2. Use proportional thinking to answer this question. If tuna is 2 cans for $2.50, how much will 6 cans cost? Multiply $2.50 by 3 to get $7.50.

3. What proportion will answer the question of Question 2?

4. About how many hectares equal one square mile? 259 ha

5. *True or false.* In a thousand square miles, there are more than 500,000 hectares. False

6. The area of the state of Illinois is about 56,000 square miles. About how many hectares is this? about 14,500,000 hectares

7. Suppose you travel 45 kph (kilometers per hour). Then
   a. it takes __?__ hours to travel 90 km. 2
   b. it takes __?__ hours to travel 450 km. 10
   c. it takes between __?__ and __?__ to go 200 km. 4 hr, 5 hr
   d. Exactly how long does it take to go 200 km? $4\frac{4}{9}$ hr, or $4.\overline{4}$ hr

In 8–10, **a.** answer the question using any method you wish.
b. Check your answer using a different method.

8. At 55 mph, how long will it take to drive 120 miles? See left.

9. There are 12 eggs in a dozen. 100 eggs is how many dozen? See left.

10. There are 640 acres in a square mile. Suppose a forest fire burned 12,000 acres of timberland. About how many square miles burned?
   a) 18.75 sq mi; b) Sample: Use estimation. Since 640 acres = 1 sq mi, 1200 acres is less than 2 sq mi, and 12,000 acres is less than 20 sq mi.

Applying the Mathematics

11. Speedy Spencer can type 30 words in 45 seconds. At this rate, how many words can he type in a minute? 40 words

12. Jack can mow his lawn in 40 minutes. Jill can mow the same lawn in 40 minutes. How long will it take Jack and Jill, working together to mow four lawns of the same size? Explain your reasoning.

13. Beatrice used 100 stamps in 2 weeks. At this rate, how many stamps will she use in 3 weeks? 150 stamps

14. If it costs $500/month to feed a family of 4, how much will it cost to feed a family of 5? $625/month

632

Adapting to Individual Needs

Extra Help
Some students might have trouble estimating. Point out that they should substitute numbers close to those given, but ones which they can compute mentally. You might give them problems like those at the right, and discuss what numbers could be used to estimate. You might also emphasize that often an answer *does not* have to be exact.

1. At a speed of 52 miles per hour, how far can you travel in $2\frac{3}{4}$ hours? [Sample: 52 is close to 50, and $2\frac{3}{4}$ is close to 3; $3 \times 50 = 150$; About 150 miles.]

2. If a 3-can package of orange juice costs $1.49 and a 6-can package costs $3.09, which is the better buy? [Sample: $1.49 is a little less than $1.50, so two 3-can packages cost a little less than $3.00 and are the better buy.]

Review

In 15 and 16, triangles *ABC* and *DEF* are similar with corresponding sides parallel. *(Lesson 11-8)*

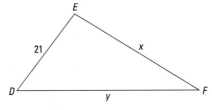

15. Find *x*. x = 30

16. Find *y*. y = 34.5

17. If $x = -4$ and $y = -2$, what is $-3x$ divided by $2y$?
(Lessons 4-4, 9-6, 11-4) -3

18. If 30% of a number is 51, what is 40% of that same number?
(Lessons 2-5, 10-3) 68

19. What is 14% of 200? *(Lesson 2-5)* 28

20. 200 is 14% of what number? *(Lesson 10-3)* about 1428.57

Exploration

21. You often hear that the cost of living is going up. The government calculates a number called the *consumer price index* (CPI) to measure the cost of living. When the CPI doubles, it means that, on the average, prices have doubled. The CPI scale used in 1991 considered average prices in the years 1982–84 to be 100.
  a. In 1991, the CPI was 136.2. In 1970, the CPI was 38.8. Between 1970 and 1991, did prices more than triple or less than triple?
  b. If a new car cost $11,630 in 1970, what would you expect a new car of the same type to cost in 1991?
  a) more than tripled; b) about $40,800

22. a. The following program prints the cost of peanuts if a bag costs $.59. See left.

```
10 FOR N = 2 TO 20 STEP 2
20 PRINT N; "BAGS OF PEANUTS COST $";.59 * N
30 NEXT N
40 END
```

Run the program and record its output.
  b. What could you do to print the costs for every whole number of bags from 1 to 20? Change line 10 to 10 FOR N = 1 TO 20
  c. Modify the program to print another similar table.
  Answers will vary.

The farm shown here grows peanut plants. The peanut plant is unusual in that its pods develop underground.

22a) Output is:
2 BAGS OF PEANUTS COST $1.18
4 BAGS OF PEANUTS COST $2.36
.
.
.
20 BAGS OF PEANUTS COST
$11.80

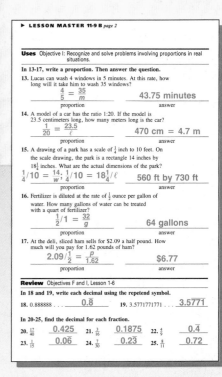

▶ **LESSON MASTER 11-9 B** *page 2*

Uses Objective I: Recognize and solve problems involving proportions in real situations.

In 13-17, write a proportion. Then answer the question.
13. Lucas can wash 4 windows in 5 minutes. At this rate, how long will it take him to wash 35 windows?
$\frac{4}{5} = \frac{35}{m}$ proportion
43.75 minutes answer

14. A model of a car has the ratio 1:20. If the model is 23.5 centimeters long, how many meters long is the car?
$\frac{1}{20} = \frac{23.5}{\ell}$ proportion
470 cm = 4.7 m answer

15. A drawing of a park has a scale of $\frac{1}{4}$ inch to 10 feet. On the scale drawing, the park is a rectangle 14 inches by $18\frac{1}{4}$ inches. What are the actual dimensions of the park?
$\frac{1}{4}/10 = \frac{14}{w}$; $\frac{1}{4}/10 = 18\frac{1}{4}/\ell$ proportion
560 ft by 730 ft answer

16. Fertilizer is diluted at the rate of $\frac{1}{2}$ ounce per gallon of water. How many gallons of water can be treated with a quart of fertilizer?
$\frac{1}{2}/1 = \frac{32}{g}$ proportion
64 gallons answer

17. At the deli, sliced ham sells for $2.09 a half pound. How much will you pay for 1.62 pounds of ham?
$2.09/\frac{1}{2} = \frac{p}{1.62}$ proportion
$6.77 answer

Review Objectives F and I, Lesson 1-6

In 18 and 19, write each decimal using the repetend symbol.
18. 0.888888 . . . . $0.\overline{8}$ **19.** 3.5771771771 . . . . $3.5\overline{771}$

In 20-25, find the decimal for each fraction.
20. $\frac{17}{40}$ 0.425 **21.** $\frac{3}{16}$ 0.1875 **22.** $\frac{4}{9}$ $0.\overline{4}$
23. $\frac{1}{15}$ $0.0\overline{6}$ **24.** $\frac{7}{30}$ $0.2\overline{3}$ **25.** $\frac{8}{11}$ $0.\overline{72}$

Chapter 11 Projects

Chapter 11 projects relate to the content of the lessons as follows.

Project	Lesson(s)
1	11-8
2	11-2, 11-6
3	11-9
4	11-1, 11-4
5	11-2
6	11-3

1 Similar Objects Different sizes of cereal boxes, books, windows, paper clips, tables, dog bones, and spoons are all examples of items students may choose to measure.

Students may find that items that are of different sizes are not necessarily similar. Explain that they may need to measure more than five pairs of items before they find five similar pairs. Some students may choose to use various sizes of balls as similar objects. They will have to find the circumference of each ball to determine the ratio of similitude. Also, the diameter of many balls used in sports can be found in sports encyclopedias or almanacs.

2 Best Buys Suggest that students inform the grocery store manager about this project before they begin. Some stores provide unit costs for each item as a service to the customer. Have students collect the data they need at the grocery store and then analyze the data at home or at school.

Make sure students understand that unit cost is found by dividing cost by number of units. Point out that they will need to change weights from pounds and ounces to ounces and fluid measurements to fluid ounces to facilitate finding unit costs. If necessary, have students review a table of equivalent measures.

3 Proportional Thinking Proportional thinking can be used to solve a wide variety of problems. Students may need help recognizing that many problems which can be solved using multiplication and division can also be solved using proportional thinking.

Remind students that both sides in a proportion must compare the same units.

634

A project presents an opportunity for you to extend your knowledge of a topic related to the material of this chapter. You should allow more time for a project than you do for typical homework questions.

PROJECTS 11 CHAPTER ELEVEN

1 Similar Objects
Find at least five pairs of similar objects around your house. (One pair might be different-sized photographs of the same scene.) Calculate the ratios of at least three corresponding lengths in each pair to verify that they are similar and to determine the ratio of similitude.

2 Best Buys
Go to a grocery store and find examples of at least five foods that are packaged in different sizes. Calculate the unit cost for each size to determine best buys. Write up what you find, and answer whether it is true that bigger packages are more economical.

3 Proportional Thinking
Invent ten real-world problems that can be solved with proportions and that are different from those given in this chapter. Include your solutions.

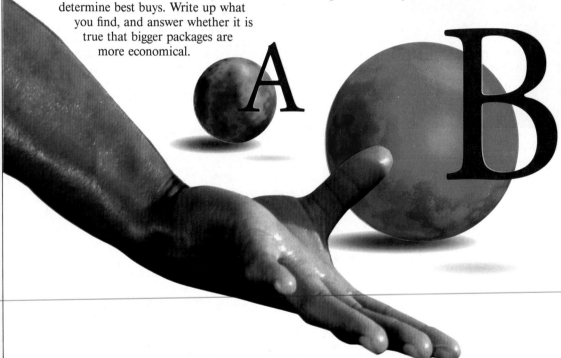

634

Possible responses
1. Responses will vary.
2. Responses will vary.
3. Sample responses:
   a. Michael reads 15 pages of his book each day. At this rate, how long will it take him to read a 300-page book? [20 days]
   b. Laura earned $4.00 an hour baby-sitting. How much will she earn if she baby-sits for five hours? [$20]
   c. One cup of uncooked rice makes three cups of cooked rice. How many cups of uncooked rice are needed to make 20 cups of cooked rice? [$6\frac{2}{3}$ cups]

Review

In 15 and 16, triangles *ABC* and *DEF* are similar with corresponding sides parallel.   *(Lesson 11-8)*

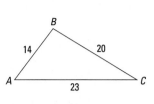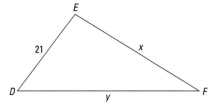

15. Find *x*. x = 30   **16.** Find *y*. y = 34.5

17. If *x* = -4 and *y* = -2, what is -3*x* divided by 2*y*?
(Lessons 4-4, 9-6, 11-4) -3

18. If 30% of a number is 51, what is 40% of that same number?
(Lessons 2-5, 10-3) 68

19. What is 14% of 200?   *(Lesson 2-5)* 28

20. 200 is 14% of what number?   *(Lesson 10-3)* about 1428.57

Exploration

21. You often hear that the cost of living is going up. The government calculates a number called the *consumer price index* (CPI) to measure the cost of living. When the CPI doubles, it means that, on the average, prices have doubled. The CPI scale used in 1991 considered average prices in the years 1982–84 to be 100.
  a. In 1991, the CPI was 136.2. In 1970, the CPI was 38.8. Between 1970 and 1991, did prices more than triple or less than triple?
  b. If a new car cost $11,630 in 1970, what would you expect a new car of the same type to cost in 1991?
  a) more than tripled; b) about $40,800

22. a. The following program prints the cost of peanuts if a bag costs $.59. See left.

```
10 FOR N = 2 TO 20 STEP 2
20 PRINT N; "BAGS OF PEANUTS COST $";.59 * N
30 NEXT N
40 END
```

Run the program and record its output.
  b. What could you do to print the costs for every whole number of bags from 1 to 20? Change line 10 to 10 FOR N = 1 TO 20
  c. Modify the program to print another similar table.
  Answers will vary.

The farm shown here grows peanut plants. The peanut plant is unusual in that its pods develop underground.

22a) Output is:
2 BAGS OF PEANUTS COST $1.18
4 BAGS OF PEANUTS COST $2.36
.
.
.
20 BAGS OF PEANUTS COST $11.80

Lesson 11-9   *Proportional Thinking*   **633**

Assessment
Written Communication
Example 2 on page 617 states that 100 envelopes can be stuffed in 8 minutes. Have students write a paragraph describing how they would use proportional thinking to estimate how long it would take to stuff 2,500 envelopes. [The paragraph should contain an example of a proportion.]

Extension
Project Update Project 3, *Proportional Thinking*, on page 634, relates to the content of this lesson.

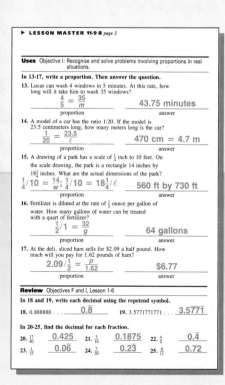

Adapting to Individual Needs
Challenge
Refer students to **Question 21**. Have them assume that the CPI rose from 100 in 1984 to 136.2 in 1991 at a constant rate, and find the rate of change. [An increase of 36.2 points in 7 years is a rate of 5.2 points per year.] Then have them assume that this rate continued to the present time and estimate the current CPI. Finally, have them research the current CPI and compare it to their estimates.

633

Chapter 11 Projects

Chapter 11 projects relate to the content of the lessons as follows.

Project	Lesson(s)
1	11-8
2	11-2, 11-6
3	11-9
4	11-1, 11-4
5	11-2
6	11-3

1 Similar Objects Different sizes of cereal boxes, books, windows, paper clips, tables, dog bones, and spoons are all examples of items students may choose to measure.

Students may find that items that are of different sizes are not necessarily similar. Explain that they may need to measure more than five pairs of items before they find five similar pairs. Some students may choose to use various sizes of balls as similar objects. They will have to find the circumference of each ball to determine the ratio of similitude. Also, the diameter of many balls used in sports can be found in sports encyclopedias or almanacs.

2 Best Buys Suggest that students inform the grocery store manager about this project before they begin. Some stores provide unit costs for each item as a service to the customer. Have students collect the data they need at the grocery store and then analyze the data at home or at school.

Make sure students understand that unit cost is found by dividing cost by number of units. Point out that they will need to change weights from pounds and ounces to ounces and fluid measurements to fluid ounces to facilitate finding unit costs. If necessary, have students review a table of equivalent measures.

3 Proportional Thinking Proportional thinking can be used to solve a wide variety of problems. Students may need help recognizing that many problems which can be solved using multiplication and division can also be solved using proportional thinking.

Remind students that both sides in a proportion must compare the same units.

634

A project presents an opportunity for you to extend your knowledge of a topic related to the material of this chapter. You should allow more time for a project than you do for typical homework questions.

PROJECTS 11 CHAPTER ELEVEN

1 Similar Objects
Find at least five pairs of similar objects around your house. (One pair might be different-sized photographs of the same scene.) Calculate the ratios of at least three corresponding lengths in each pair to verify that they are similar and to determine the ratio of similitude.

2 Best Buys
Go to a grocery store and find examples of at least five foods that are packaged in different sizes. Calculate the unit cost for each size to determine best buys. Write up what you find, and answer whether it is true that bigger packages are more economical.

3 Proportional Thinking
Invent ten real-world problems that can be solved with proportions and that are different from those given in this chapter. Include your solutions.

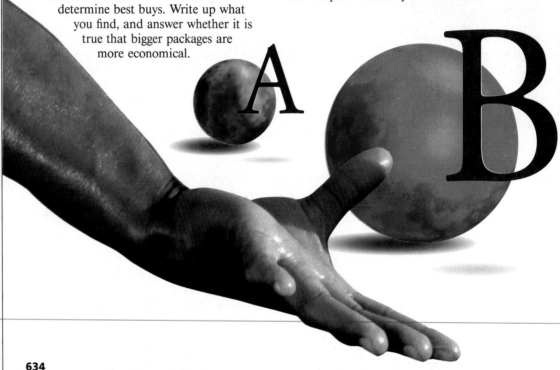

634

Possible responses
1. Responses will vary.
2. Responses will vary.
3. Sample responses:
   a. Michael reads 15 pages of his book each day. At this rate, how long will it take him to read a 300-page book? [20 days]
   b. Laura earned $4.00 an hour baby-sitting. How much will she earn if she baby-sits for five hours? [$20]
   c. One cup of uncooked rice makes three cups of cooked rice. How many cups of uncooked rice are needed to make 20 cups of cooked rice? [$6\frac{2}{3}$ cups]

4 Integer Arithmetic with Negative Divisors

Extend the idea of a quotient and remainder to cover division by -2, -3, and other negative integers. Assume that the remainder will always be positive, and calculate the quotient and remainder when 436 is divided by -7, and when -100 is divided by -6. Explain how you obtained your results and why you believe they are correct.

5 World-Record Rates

Look in an almanac or other reference book for all the world records in running or swimming, for men or for women. Calculate the average rate of speed of each of the record holders. Graph the ordered pairs (distance, average speed), and describe what you find.

6 A Different Way to Divide Fractions

One student had the following way of dividing fractions. First the student renamed the two fractions with a common denominator. Then the student ignored the denominators and just divided the numerators to obtain the answer. Does this method work? Try it on enough examples to form a conclusion about whether it *always, sometimes,* or *never* works.

4 Integer Arithmetic with Negative Divisors

If students use a calculator to divide 436 by -7, the quotient will be given as a negative decimal. Students will need to multiply the integer amount of the quotient by the divisor and subtract that amount from the number being divided to find the remainder. Checking each answer is an important part of understanding how to divide with negative divisors. Remind students that the remainder must be less than the absolute value of the divisor.

5 World-record Rates

Make sure students understand that they are to find the world records for a variety of swimming or running distances. If a student chooses to find swimming records, have him or her find the world records for a particular stroke, such as free-style, back-stroke, or butterfly.

6 A Different Way to Divide Fractions

Suggest that students test this method using fractions with different types of denominators. One pair of fractions could have relatively prime denominators, one pair could have one denominator that is a factor of another, and another pair could have denominators that have at least one factor in common. Once students have formed a conclusion about whether or not this division method works, you might want to point out that they are using the multiplicative identity property of one when they "ignore" the denominators. Therefore, they are not changing the value of the fractions they are dividing. Ask students if they think this method is easier than multiplying by the reciprocal of the divisor to divide fractions.

4. **Sample responses.**

(Responses continue on page 636.)

$$\begin{array}{r} -62 \ \text{R2} \\ -7\overline{)436} \\ \underline{42} \\ 16 \\ \underline{14} \\ 2 \end{array}$$

$$\begin{array}{r} 17 \ \text{R2} \\ -6\overline{)-100} \\ \underline{-6} \\ -40 \\ \underline{-42} \\ 2 \end{array}$$

Check: **Check:**
$-62 \times -7 + 2 = 436$ $17 \times -6 + 2 = -100$

The check shows that the results are correct.

Summary

The Summary gives an overview of the entire chapter and provides an opportunity for students to consider the material as a whole. Thus, the Summary can be used to help students relate and unify the concepts presented in the chapter.

Vocabulary

Terms, symbols, and properties are listed by lesson to provide a checklist of concepts a student must know. Emphasize to students that they should read the vocabulary list carefully before starting the Progress Self-Test. If students do not understand the meaning of a term, they should refer back to the indicated lesson.

SUMMARY

There are two types of division. For the integer division $x \div y$, x must be an integer, and y must be a positive integer. The answer is given as a quotient and remainder. For the real-number division $x \div y$, x and y can be any numbers with $y \neq 0$, and the answer is the single-number quotient $\frac{x}{y}$.

One basic use of division is to calculate rates. In a rate, the divisor and the dividend have different units. The unit of the rate is written as a fraction. For example, if x words are divided by y minutes, the quotient is $\frac{x}{y}$ words per minute, which can be written as $\frac{x}{y} \frac{\text{words}}{\text{minute}}$.

The numbers involved in rates can be fractions, or decimals, or negative numbers. So rates can help you learn how to divide these kinds of numbers. To divide fractions, you can use the Algebraic Definition of Division. Multiply by the reciprocal of the divisor. To divide with negative numbers, follow the same rules for signs that work for multiplication.

Another basic use of division is in calculating ratios. Ratios are numbers that compare two quantities with the same units. Since both divisor and dividend have the same units, the quotient has no unit. Ratios may be decimals, fractions, or integers. Percents are almost always ratios.

If two fractions, rates, or ratios are equal, a proportion results. The form of a proportion is $\frac{a}{b} = \frac{c}{d}$. Because it has many applications, proportional thinking is very important. You should be able to solve simple proportions mentally. If $\frac{a}{b} = \frac{c}{d}$, then $ad = bc$. This is known as the Means-Extremes Property. You could also solve the proportion by multiplying both sides of the equation by bd. Proportions occur in geometry and all other areas of mathematics. Proportions also occur in all sorts of daily experiences. So it helps to know more than one way to solve a proportion.

VOCABULARY

You should be able to give a general description and a specific example of each of the following ideas.

Lesson 11-1
real number division
integer division
Quotient-Remainder Form
Quotient-Remainder Formula

Lesson 11-2
rate, rate unit
Rate Model for Division
unit cost

Lesson 11-3
Algebraic Definition of Division

Lesson 11-5
ratio, ratio comparison
Ratio Comparison Model for Division

Lesson 11-6
proportion
solving a proportion

Lesson 11-7
extremes, means
Means-Extremes Property

Lesson 11-8
corresponding lengths

Lesson 11-9
proportional thinking

636

Additional responses, page 635

5. Sample responses: As of 1992, the men's world records in freestyle swimming are:

Distance in Meters	Record in Sec	Avg. Speed m/sec
50	21.81	≈2.29
100	48.42	≈2.07
200	1:46.69	≈1.87
400	3:45.00	≈1.78
800	7:47.85	≈1.71
1500	14:43.48	≈1.70

The average speed decreases as the distance increases, but it does not decrease as much for longer distances.

6. Sample response.

$$\frac{\frac{3}{7}}{\frac{2}{5}} = \frac{\frac{3}{7} \times \frac{5}{5}}{\frac{2}{5} \times \frac{7}{7}} = \frac{\frac{15}{35}}{\frac{14}{35}} = \frac{15}{14} = 1\frac{1}{14}$$

Check: $\frac{3}{7} \div \frac{2}{5} = \frac{3}{7} \times \frac{5}{2} = \frac{15}{14}$

This method will always work.

PROGRESS SELF-TEST

Take this test as you would take a test in class. Then check your work with the solutions in the back of the book.

1. What rate is suggested by this situation? A person types 300 words in 5 minutes. **60 wpm**

2. If you travel k kilometers in h hours, what is your average speed in kilometers per hour? **$\frac{k}{h}$ km/hr**

3. Divide $\frac{4}{9}$ by $\frac{1}{3}$. **$\frac{4}{3}$**

4. Simplify $\frac{-42}{-24}$. **$\frac{7}{4}$**

5. Simplify $\frac{\frac{3}{5}}{\frac{6}{5}}$. **$\frac{1}{2}$**

6. Give the value of $\frac{-2x}{8+y}$ when $x = -5$ and $y = -9$. **-10**

7. If a is negative and b is positive, which of the following are negative?
   $\frac{a}{b}$ $\quad$ $\frac{-a}{b}$ $\quad$ $\frac{-a}{-b}$ $\frac{a}{b'}$ $\frac{-a}{-b}$

8. Write a rate question about weight that results in division of -8 by 2. **See below.**

9. Solve $\frac{40}{x} = \frac{8}{5}$. **x = 25**

10. Solve $\frac{5}{12} = \frac{p}{3}$. **$p = \frac{5}{4}$**

11. To the nearest percent, 14 is what percent of 150? **9%**

12. If $0.30 is the tax on a $4 purchase, what percent tax rate is this? **7.5%**

13. If 60% of a number is 30, what is the number? **50**

14. At 45 mph, how long does it take to travel 189 miles? **4.2 hr**

15. There are 640 acres in a square mile. How many acres are in 10,000 square miles? **6,400,000 acres**

8) **Sample: Gunther lost 8 pounds in two months. What was the rate of change of his weight?**

16. State the Means-Extremes Property as it applies to the proportion $\frac{a}{b} = \frac{x}{y}$. **See below.**

17. Name the means in the proportion of Question 16. **b and x**

In 18 and 19, triangles ABC and DEF are similar with corresponding sides parallel.

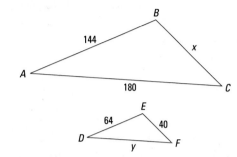

18. Find x. **90** $\qquad$ 19. Find y. **80**

20. A recipe for 4 people says to use $\frac{1}{4}$ teaspoon of pepper. How much should be used for 10 people? **$\frac{5}{8}$ teaspoon**

21. A book has 245 pages. Marissa feels she can read 15 pages a day. At this rate, how many days will it take her to read the book? How many pages will she need to read on the last day? **See below.**

22. Explain how Question 21 relates to the Quotient-Remainder Formula.
    $n = d \cdot q + r$ is translated as $245 = 15 \cdot 16 + 5$.

16) If $\frac{a}{b} = \frac{x}{y}$, then $b \cdot x = a \cdot y$.

21) Read 15 pages for 16 days, and 5 pages on the 17th day.

Progress Self-Test

For the development of mathematical competence, feedback and correction, along with the opportunity to practice, are necessary. The Progress Self-Test provides the opportunity for feedback and correction; the Chapter Review provides additional opportunities and practice. We cannot overemphasize the importance of these end-of-chapter materials. It is at this point that the material "gels" for many students, allowing them to solidify skills and understanding. In general, student performance should be markedly improved after these pages.

Assign the Progress Self-Test as a one-night assignment. Worked-out *solutions* for all questions are in the Selected Answers section of the student book. Encourage students to take the Progress Self-Test honestly, grade themselves, and then be prepared to discuss the test in class.

Advise students to pay special attention to those Chapter Review questions (pages 638–639) which correspond to questions missed on the Progress Self-Test.

Chapter 11 Review

CHAPTER REVIEW

Questions on SPUR Objectives

SPUR stands for **S**kills, **P**roperties, **U**ses, and **R**epresentations. The Chapter Review questions are grouped according to the SPUR Objectives for this chapter.

SKILLS DEAL WITH THE PROCEDURES USED TO GET ANSWERS.

Objective A: *Divide fractions with numbers or variables.* (Lesson 11-3)

1. What is 12 divided by $\frac{2}{3}$? 18
2. $\frac{3}{5} \div \frac{5}{3} = \frac{?}{?}$ $\frac{9}{25}$

In 3–5, simplify.

3. $\frac{\frac{2}{3}}{\frac{4}{3}}$ $\frac{1}{2}$
4. $\frac{1\frac{1}{6}}{3\frac{2}{3}}$ $\frac{7}{22}$
5. $\frac{\frac{x}{y}}{\frac{a}{b}}$ $\frac{bx}{ay}$

6. Divide $\frac{x}{3}$ by 2. $\frac{x}{6}$
7. Divide $3\frac{3}{4}$ by $2\frac{1}{7}$. $\frac{7}{4}$

Objective B: *Divide positive and negative numbers.* (Lesson 11-4)

8. Give the value of $\frac{2c}{d}$ when $c = 3$ and $d = -1$. -6

In 9–12, simplify.

9. $\frac{-10}{2}$ -5
10. $-\frac{-400}{-200}$ -2
11. $\frac{-40}{-30}$ $\frac{4}{3}$
12. $\frac{6}{-9}$ $\frac{-2}{3}$

Objective C: *Solve proportions.* (Lessons 11-6, 11-7, 11-9)

13. In solving $\frac{7}{t} = \frac{168}{192}$, Jenny got $t = 24$. Is she correct? No. $(t = 8)$

In 14–19, solve.

14. $\frac{40}{9} = \frac{12}{x}$
15. $\frac{y}{2} = \frac{9}{7}$
16. $\frac{700}{y} = \frac{20}{1}$
17. $\frac{7}{G} = \frac{1}{3}$
18. $\frac{6}{20} = \frac{AB}{50}$
19. $\frac{\frac{1}{2}}{CD} = \frac{5}{6}$

14) $x = \frac{27}{10}$; 15) $y = \frac{18}{7}$; 16) $y = 35$; 17) $G = 21$; 18) $AB = 15$; 19) $CD = \frac{3}{5}$

PROPERTIES DEAL WITH THE PRINCIPLES BEHIND THE MATHEMATICS.

Objective D: *Recognize the Means-Extremes Property and know why it works.* (Lessons 11-6, 11-7)

20. According to the Means-Extremes Property, if $\frac{a}{d} = \frac{b}{e}$, what else is true? $bd = ae$

21. To eliminate fractions in the equation $\frac{3}{x} = \frac{5}{6}$, by what can you multiply both sides? 6x

22. Why won't the Means-Extremes Property work on the equation $\frac{4}{5} + x = \frac{3}{.4}$? The equation is not a proportion.

Objective E: *Know the general properties for dividing positive and negative numbers.* (Lesson 11-4)

23. *Multiple choice.* Which does *not* equal $\frac{-x}{y}$?
(a) $\frac{-x}{y}$
(b) $-x \cdot \frac{1}{y}$
(c) $\frac{x}{-y}$
(d) $\frac{-x}{-y}$ (d)

24. If $\frac{a}{b} = c$ and a is negative, and c is positive, then is b positive or negative? negative

---

USES DEAL WITH APPLICATIONS OF MATHEMATICS IN REAL SITUATIONS.

Objective F: *Use integer division in real situations.* (Lesson 11-1)

25. a. How many gallons are in 25 quarts?
    b. Relate part **a** to the Quotient-Remainder Formula. a) $6\frac{1}{4}$ gallons; b) $25 = 4 \cdot 6 + 1$

26. a. How many feet and inches are in 218 inches? 18 ft, 2 in.
    b. How does this relate to the Quotient-Remainder Formula? $218 = 12 \cdot 18 + 2$

27. Twelve *Transition Mathematics* books can fit in a box.
    a. If a school orders 70 books, how many boxes could be filled and how many would then be in the unfilled box? **5; 10**
    b. Relate this situation to the Quotient-Remainder Formula. **70 = 12 · 5 + 10**

28. 700 students at a Model United Nations convention were split into groups of 16.
    a. How many full groups were formed? **43**
    b. How many students were left for a smaller group? **12**
    c. How does this relate to the Quotient-Remainder Formula? **700 = 16 · 43 + 12**

Objective G: *Use the Rate Model for Division.*
(Lessons 11-2, 11-3, 11-4)

29. A car travels 200 km in 4 hours. What is its average speed? **50 km/hr**

30. Sixteen hamburgers are made from 5 pounds of ground beef. How much beef is this per hamburger? $\frac{5}{16}$ **lb/hamburger**

31. On a diet, some people lose 10 pounds in 30 days. What rate is this? $-\frac{1}{3}$ **lb/day**

32. In 1990, Boston had a population of about 578,000 people and an area of about 47 square miles. About how many people per square mile is this? $\approx$ **12,300**

33. Two-thirds of the way through the summer, Jeremy had earned $120 mowing lawns. At this rate, how much will he earn mowing lawns during the entire summer? **$180**

34. Betty spent $200 on a 4-day vacation. Use this information to make up a question involving division and negative numbers. Answer your question. **Sample: How much did Betty spend per day?** $\frac{-\$200}{4 \text{ days}} = -\$50/\text{day}$

35) **Sample: How fast have they been repaving the road?** **-6 km/-3 days = 2 km/day**

35. Three days ago, the repaving crew was 6 km down the road. Use this information to make up a question involving division and negative numbers. Answer your question.
    See below.

Objective H: *Use the Ratio Comparison Model for Division.* *(Lesson 11-5)*

36. Bill bought 5 CDs last year. This year he bought 8. This year's amount is how many times last year's amount? **1.6**

37. If you get 32 right on a 40-question test, what percent have you missed? **20%**

38. In Seattle, Washington, it rains an average of 216 days a year. What percent of days in a year is this? (Answer to the nearest percent.) **about 59%**

39. In 1988, Ford Motor Company sold about 47,000 Lincoln Continentals. In 1989, the number of Continentals sold was about 9,000 more. In other words, in 1989 the company sold about __?__ times as many Continentals as in 1988. (Answer to the nearest tenth.) **1.2**

Objective I: *Recognize and solve problems involving proportions in real situations.* *(Lessons 11-6, 11-7, 11-9)*

40) ≈ **35.7 minutes**

40. You made 35 copies in 2.5 minutes using a duplicating machine. At this rate, how long will it take the machine to make 500 copies?

41. A recipe for 6 people calls for $1\frac{1}{3}$ cups of sugar. How much sugar is probably needed for a similar recipe for 10 people? $2\frac{2}{9}$ **cups**

42. You want to buy 5 cans of tuna. You see that 8 cans cost $5. At this rate, what will the 5 cans cost? **$3.12 or $3.13**

REPRESENTATIONS DEAL WITH PICTURES, GRAPHS, OR OBJECTS THAT ILLUSTRATE CONCEPTS.

Objective J: *Find missing lengths in similar figures.* *(Lesson 11-8)*

In 43 and 44, a right triangle has sides with lengths 5, 12, and 13. The shortest side of a similar right triangle has length 6.5.

43. Find the lengths of the other two sides of the similar right triangle. **15.6 and 16.9**

44. Draw accurate pictures of the two triangles using the same unit. **See margin.**

45. The figures below are similar. If $AB = 80$, $CD = 45$, and $EL = 56$, what is IK? **31.5**

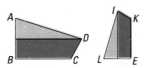

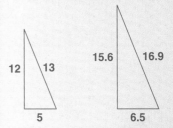
639

Adapting to Individual Needs

The student text is written for the vast majority of students. The chart at the right suggests two pacing plans to accommodate the needs of your students. Students in the Full Course should complete the entire text by the end of the year. Students in the Minimal Course will spend more time when there are quizzes and more time on the Chapter Review. Therefore, these students may not complete all of the chapters in the text.

Options are also presented to meet the needs of a variety of teaching and learning styles. For each lesson, the Teacher's Edition provides sections entitled: *Video* which describes video segments and related questions that can be used for motivation or extension; *Optional Activities* which suggests activities that employ materials, physical models, technology, and cooperative learning; and *Adapting to Individual Needs* which regularly includes **Challenge** problems, **English Language Development** suggestions, and suggestions for providing **Extra Help.** The Teacher's Edition also frequently includes an **Error Alert,** an **Extension,** and an **Assessment** alternative. The options available in Chapter 12 are summarized in the chart below.

Chapter 12 Pacing Chart

Day	Full Course	Minimal Course
1	12-1	12-1
2	12-2	12-2
3	12-3	12-3
4	Quiz*; 12-4	Quiz*; begin 12-4.
5	12-5	Finish 12-4.
6	12-6	12-5
7	12-7	12-6
8	Quiz*; 12-8	12-7
9	Self-Test	Quiz*; begin 12-8.
10	Review	Finish 12-8.
11	Test*	Self-Test
12		Review
13		Review
14		Test*

*in the Teacher's Resource File

In the Teacher's Edition...

Lesson	Optional Activities	Extra Help	Challenge	English Language Development	Error Alert	Extension	Cooperative Learning	Ongoing Assessment
12-1	●	●	●	●	●	●	●	Oral
12-2	●	●	●			●	●	Group
12-3	●	●	●			●	●	Written
12-4	●	●	●	●		●	●	Group
12-5	●	●	●			●	●	Written
12-6	●	●	●			●	●	Written
12-7	●	●	●	●		●	●	Written
12-8	●	●	●			●	●	Written

In the Additional Resources...

Lesson	Lesson Masters, A and B	Teaching Aids*	Activity Kit*	Answer Masters	Technology Sourcebook	Assessment Sourcebook	Visual Aids**	Technology Tools	Video Segments
					In the Teacher's Resource File				
12-1	12-1	123		12-1			123, AM		
12-2	12-2	123	29	12-2	Calc 11		123, AM		
In-class Activity		125			Demo 12		125, AM	Geometry	
12-3	12-3	86, 123	30	12-3		Quiz	86, 123, AM		Segment 12
In-class Activity		126, 127					126, 127, AM		
12-4	12-4	123, 127, 128		12-4	Comp 27		123, 127, 128, AM	Geometry	
12-5	12-5	124, 129, 130, 131		12-5	Comp 28		124, 129, 130, 131, AM	Spreadsheet	
12-6	12-6	124		12-6			124, AM		
12-7	12-7	124		12-7		Quiz	124, AM		
12-8	12-8	124, 132		12-8			124, 132, AM		
End of chapter				Review		Tests			

*Teaching Aids, except Warm-ups, are pictured on pages 640C and 640D. The activities in the Activity Kit are pictured on page 640C.

Teaching Aid 125 which accompanies the In-class Activity for Lesson 12-3 is pictured with the lesson notes on page 651.

Teaching Aid 126 which accompanies the In-class Activity for Lesson 12-4 is pictured with the lesson notes on page 657.

**Visual Aids provide transparencies for all Teaching Aids and all Answer Masters.

Also available is the Study Skills Handbook which includes study-skill tips related to reading, note-taking, and comprehension.

Integrating Strands and Applications

	12-1	12-2	12-3	12-4	12-5	12-6	12-7	12-8
Mathematical Connections								
Number Sense		●						
Algebra	●	●	●	●	●	●	●	●
Geometry	●	●	●	●	●	●	●	●
Measurement	●	●	●	●	●	●	●	●
Probability	●							
Statistics/Data Analysis		●						●
Patterns and Functions	●	●						
Interdisciplinary and Other Connections								
Music			●					
Literature								●
Science				●	●			●
Social Studies		●		●		●		●
Multicultural			●	●				●
Technology	●		●	●	●		●	
Consumer					●		●	
Sports			●					●

Take it to the NET

On the Internet, visit **www.phschool.com** for UCSMP teacher support, student self-tests, activities, and more.

Teaching and Assessing the Chapter Objectives

Chapter 12 Objectives (Organized into the SPUR categories—Skills, Properties, Uses, and Representations)	Lessons	Progress Self-Test Questions	Chapter Review Questions	Chapter Test, Forms A and B	Chapter Test, Forms C	Chapter Test, Forms D
Skills						
A: Find a simple fraction equal to any terminating or repeating decimal.	12-1	8, 9	1–4	8–10	3	
B: Estimate square roots of a number without a calculator.	12-2	4, 13	5–8	2, 3	1	
C: Use the Pythagorean Theorem to find unknown lengths of third sides in right triangles.	12-3	5, 6	9–12	7, 11–13	2	✓
D: Find the circumference and area of a circle or sector, given its radius or diameter.	12-4, 12-5	1, 15, 20	13–16	5, 6		
E: Find the surface area and volume of cylinders and prisms.	12-6, 12-7	11, 12	17–20	17, 18	4	
F: Find the surface area and volume of a sphere, given its radius or diameter.	12-8	18	21, 22	21, 22		
Properties						
G: Identify numbers as rational, irrational, or real.	12-4	7, 16	23–25	1		
Uses						
H: Apply formulas for the surface area and volume of cylinders and prisms in real situations.	12-6, 12-7	10	26–29	19, 20	6	✓
I: Apply formulas for the circumference of a circle and area of a circle or sector and surface area and volume of a sphere in real situations.	12-4, 12-5, 12-8	14, 17, 19	30–35	14–16, 21, 22	5, 6	✓
Representations						
J: Know how square roots and geometric squares are related.	12-2	2, 3	36–39	4		

In the Assessment Sourcebook

Assessment Sourcebook
Quiz for Lessons 12-1 through 12-3   Chapter 12 Test, Forms A–D
Quiz for Lessons 12-4 through 12-7   Chapter 12 Test, Cumulative Form

TestWorks
Multiple forms of chapter tests and quizzes; Challenge items

Activity Kit

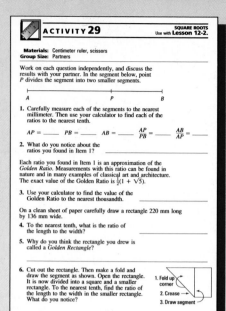

ACTIVITY 29
Use with **Lesson 12-2.**
SQUARE ROOTS

Materials: Centimeter ruler, scissors
Group Size: Partners

Work on each question independently, and discuss the results with your partner. In the segment below, point P divides the segment into two smaller segments.

A ———————— P ———————— B

1. Carefully measure each of the segments to the nearest millimeter. Then use your calculator to find each of the ratios to the nearest tenth.

$AP = $ _____ $PB = $ _____ $AB = $ _____ $\dfrac{AP}{PB} = $ _____ $\dfrac{AB}{AP} = $ _____

2. What do you notice about the ratios you found in Item 1? _____

Each ratio you found in Item 1 is an approximation of the *Golden Ratio*. Measurements with this ratio can be found in nature and in many examples of classical art and architecture. The exact value of the Golden Ratio is $\frac{1}{2}(1 + \sqrt{5})$.

3. Use your calculator to find the value of the Golden Ratio to the nearest thousandth.

On a clean sheet of paper carefully draw a rectangle 220 mm long by 136 mm wide.

4. To the nearest tenth, what is the ratio of the length to the width? _____

5. Why do you think the rectangle you drew is called a *Golden Rectangle*? _____

6. Cut out the rectangle. Then make a fold and draw the segment as shown. Open the rectangle. It is now divided into a square and a smaller rectangle. To the nearest tenth, find the ratio of the length to the width in the smaller rectangle. What do you notice?
 _____

1. Fold up corner
2. Crease
3. Draw segment

7. Now fold the smaller rectangle and divide it into a square and an even smaller rectangle. Find the ratio of the length to the width in the *smallest* rectangle. What do you notice?
 _____

4. Open rectangle

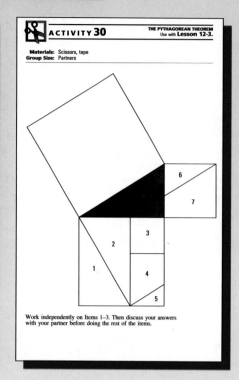

ACTIVITY 30
Use with **Lesson 12-3.**
THE PYTHAGOREAN THEOREM

Materials: Scissors, tape
Group Size: Partners

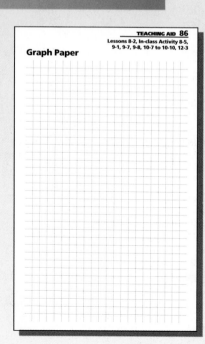

6

7

3

2

1

4

5

Work independently on Items 1–3. Then discuss your answers with your partner before doing the rest of the items.

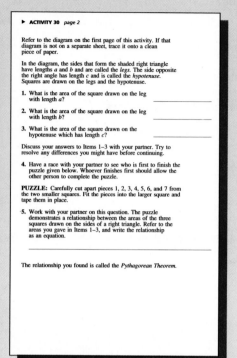

▶ **ACTIVITY 30** *page 2*

Refer to the diagram on the first page of this activity. If that diagram is not on a separate sheet, trace it onto a clean piece of paper.

In the diagram, the sides that form the shaded right triangle have lengths a and b and are called the *legs*. The side opposite the right angle has length c and is called the *hypotenuse*. Squares are drawn on the legs and the hypotenuse.

1. What is the area of the square drawn on the leg with length a? _____

2. What is the area of the square drawn on the leg with length b? _____

3. What is the area of the square drawn on the hypotenuse which has length c? _____

Discuss your answers to Items 1–3 with your partner. Try to resolve any differences you might have before continuing.

4. Have a race with your partner to see who is first to finish the puzzle given below. Whoever finishes first should allow the other person to complete the puzzle.

PUZZLE: Carefully cut apart pieces 1, 2, 3, 4, 5, 6, and 7 from the two smaller squares. Fit the pieces into the larger square and tape them in place.

5. Work with your partner on this question. The puzzle demonstrates a relationship between the areas of the three squares drawn on the sides of a right triangle. Refer to the areas you gave in Items 1–3, and write the relationship as an equation.

 _____

The relationship you found is called the *Pythagorean Theorem.*

Teaching Aids

TEACHING AID 86
Lessons 8-2, In-class Activity 8-5, 9-1, 9-7, 9-8, 10-7 to 10-10, 12-3

Graph Paper

TEACHING AID 123

Warm-up — Lesson 12-1

Write each decimal as a fraction in simplest form.

1. 0.8   2. 0.17   3. 0.842   4. 0.0804
5. 2.04   6. 5.07   7. 1.0006

Warm-up — Lesson 12-2

Without using a calculator or paper and pencil, write the squares of as many integers as you can. You should learn the squares of the integers 0–20.

Warm-up — Lesson 12-3

Tell if the statement is *true* or *false*.

1. A right triangle has a 90° angle.
2. The sum of the angle measures of a triangle is 360°.
3. A right triangle can have an obtuse angle.
4. A right triangle can have two equal angles.
5. A right triangle can have three equal sides.
6. All acute triangles are right triangles.

Warm-up — Lesson 12-4

1. Draw a circle and identify these parts.
 a. radius   b. diameter
 c. center   d. circumference
2. What do you know about the diameter and the radius of a circle?
3. What do you know about π?

TEACHING AID 124

Warm-up — Lesson 12-5

Mental Mathematics What fraction of a circle is represented by each of the following measures? Give the fraction in lowest terms.

1. 180°   2. 60°   3. 300°   4. 270°   5. 36°
6. 120°   7. 72°   8. 90°   9. 240°

Warm-up — Lesson 12-6

Select a cylindrical can with a label that can be removed.

1. Carefully remove the label from the can. What is the shape of the label?
2. Find the length and width of the rectangle. What is its area?
3. How can you find the area of the top and bottom of the can? What is the area?
4. Estimate the total surface area of the can.

Warm-up — Lesson 12-7

The interior of a trailer on a truck is 26 feet long, 8 feet wide, and 7.5 feet high. What is the greatest number of boxes, each 2 feet by 2 feet by 3 feet, that the trailer can hold?

Warm-up — Lesson 12-8

1. Make a list of objects in the real world that are shaped like spheres.
2. Select a spherical object. Find its diameter and explain how you did it.

First-Quadrant Graph Paper

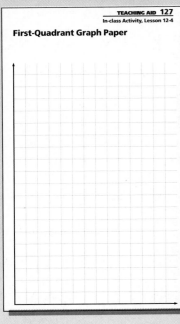

Real Numbers

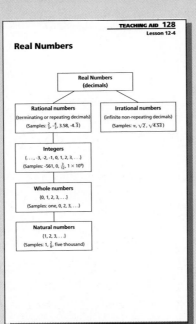

Real Numbers
(decimals)

Rational numbers
(terminating or repeating decimals)
(Samples: $\frac{2}{5}$, $-\frac{4}{3}$, 3.58, $-4.\overline{3}$)

Irrational numbers
(infinite non-repeating decimals)
(Samples: π, $\sqrt{2}$, $\sqrt{4.53}$)

Integers
{. . . , -3, -2, -1, 0, 1, 2, 3, . . .}
(Samples: -561, 0, $\frac{0}{1}$, 1×10^9)

Whole numbers
{0, 1, 2, 3, . . .}
(Samples: one, 0, 2, 3, . . .)

Natural numbers
{1, 2, 3, . . .}
(Samples: 1, $\frac{7}{8}$, five thousand)

Area of a Circle

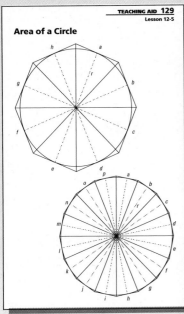

Additional Examples

1. A compact disc is 12 cm in diameter. Assume that the entire disc is for recording.
   a. Give the exact area of the recording surface.
   b. Give the area to the nearest square centimeter.

2. The radius of circle Q is 8 units, and in sector PQR, m$\angle PQR = 180°$.

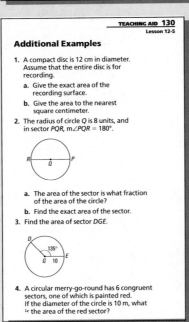

   a. The area of the sector is what fraction of the area of the circle?
   b. Find the exact area of the sector.

3. Find the area of sector DGE.

   a. The area of the sector is what fraction

4. A circular merry-go-round has 6 congruent sectors, one of which is painted red. If the diameter of the circle is 10 m, what is the area of the red sector?

Extension

Find each shaded area. The radius of each circle is 6 cm.

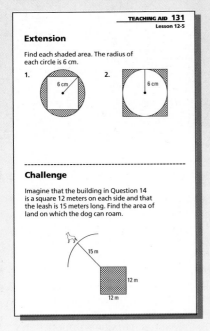

1. [6 cm]

2. [6 cm]

Challenge

Imagine that the building in Question 14 is a square 12 meters on each side and that the leash is 15 meters long. Find the area of land on which the dog can roam.

[15 m, 12 m, 12 m]

Formulas to Know

For each formula, make a sketch. Then label parts of the sketch with the appropriate variables from the formula.

Pythagorean Theorem $a^2 + b^2 = c^2$	Circumference of a circle $C = \pi d$	Area of a circle $A = \pi r^2$
Area of a sector of a circle $A = \frac{m}{360}\pi r^2$	Lateral area of a cylinder $L.A. = hC$	Surface area of a cylinder $S.A. = 2\pi rh + 2\pi r^2$
Volume of a cylindric solid $V = Bh$	Surface area of a sphere $S = 4\pi r^2$	Volume of a sphere $V = \frac{4}{3}\pi r^3$

Chapter Opener

Pacing

All lessons in this chapter are designed to be covered in one day. At the end of the chapter, you should plan to spend 1 day to review the Progress Self-Test, 1–2 days for the Chapter Review, and 1 day for a test. You may wish to spend a day on projects, and possibly a day is needed for quizzes. This chapter should therefore take 11–14 days. We strongly recommend that you not spend more than 16 days on this chapter.

Using Pages 640–641

We might have titled this chapter "Applications of Infinite Decimals" because each of its lessons involves some infinite decimals. If an infinite decimal repeats, then it is equal to a simple fraction. If an infinite decimal does not repeat, then it is not equal to a simple fraction. Most infinite non-repeating decimals have no special properties, but some of them are square roots and one is the special number π.

Photo Connections

The photo collage makes real-world connections to the content of the chapter: real numbers, area, and volume.

Cans: The formulas for volume, area, and circumference enable manufacturers to package, store, and shelve their products in the most cost effective ways. Manufacturers also want their products packaged so that they can be handled easily and shipped without damage, as well as used conveniently by consumers.

12-1 Converting Decimals to Fractions

12-2 Square Roots

12-3 The Pythagorean Theorem

12-4 The Circumference of a Circle

12-5 The Area of a Circle

12-6 Surface Areas of Cylinders and Prisms

12-7 Volumes of Cylinders and Prisms

12-8 Spheres

Lesson 12 Overview

The title of this chapter suggests the three major content areas with which the chapter deals. The first theme is that of real numbers and, in particular, two applications of infinite decimals. Repeating decimals are shown to be equal to simple fractions in Lesson 12-1. In Lesson 12-2, square roots are introduced. A square root of an integer is either an integer or an infinite non-repeating decimal. Square roots are necessary

with applications of the Pythagorean Theorem in Lesson 12-3.

The second theme is area. However, before area is introduced, π must be discussed. So, in Lesson 12-4 we return to the circumference of a circle which was first mentioned in Chapter 1. The formula for the area of a circle is the subject of Lesson 12-5. Then, Lesson 12-5 leads naturally into the discussion of surface areas in Lesson 12-6.

Cylinders and prisms are from the same family of three-dimensional figures, and they have the same general formulas for surface area ($S = 2B + ph$) and volume ($V = Bh$), where B and p are respectively the area and perimeter of the base, and h represents the height. Since the base of a cylinder is a circle, the calculations of its surface area and volume apply the formulas for the circumference and area of a circle. The corresponding measures for prisms apply

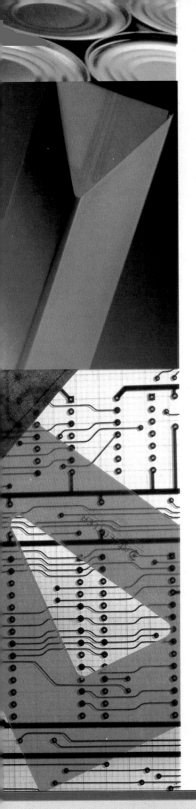

REAL NUMBERS, AREA, AND VOLUME

The numbers that can be represented by decimals are called real numbers. All of the numbers you have encountered in this book have been real numbers. Here are some examples.

Whole numbers, such as	6931
Simple fractions, such as	$\frac{24}{25} = 0.96$
Negative numbers, such as	$-7.3 \times 10^{-4} = -0.00073$
Infinite non-repeating decimals, such as	$\pi = 3.141592\ldots$
Mixed numbers, such as	$11\frac{4}{37} = 11.108108108108\ldots$

Some decimals are terminating; their decimals end. Others are infinite decimals. Some of the infinite decimals, such as the infinite decimal for $11\frac{4}{37}$ above, repeat. Others, like the decimal for π, have no repeating pattern. In this chapter, you will learn applications using some infinite non-repeating decimals. These numbers are important in finding the areas and volumes of common, everyday figures. For instance, the number π is involved in the volume formulas of both spheres and cylinders.

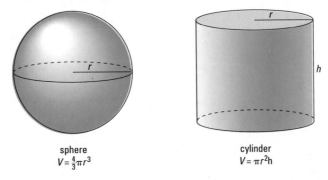

sphere
$V = \frac{4}{3}\pi r^3$

cylinder
$V = \pi r^2 h$

As a project, you can explore the *complex numbers*. These are numbers that are not real numbers. The complex numbers also have a variety of geometrical applications, but you will not usually study those uses until later mathematics courses.

641

Computer Chips: The arrangement of computer chips, each close to being square-shaped, presents a graphic representation relating the area of the circle to square units.

Prism: To determine the volume of a glass prism used to study color and light, use the formula, *V* = *Bh*, which is presented in Lesson 12-7.

Globes: The surface area of the earth is commonly represented on a sphere called a globe. Cartographers can map the earth more precisely on a sphere than on a flat map because parallels and meridians can be correctly drawn, and the scale is true everywhere over the curved surface.

Drafting Tool: A draftsman's triangle is pictured atop an enlargement of a computer chip. Tools of this type help produce accurate drawings which implement the use of the Pythagorean Theorem in the design of structures such as a gazebo.

Projects

At this time you might want to have students look over the projects on pages 684–685.

formulas for the perimeter and area of a polygon. These ideas are the subject of Lessons 12-6 and 12-7. The chapter ends with still another application of π—the volume and surface area formulas for a sphere.

Teaching
Lesson **12-1**

Warm-up

Diagnostic Write each decimal as a fraction in simplest form.

1. 0.8 $\frac{4}{5}$
2. 0.17 $\frac{17}{100}$
3. 0.842 $\frac{421}{500}$
4. 0.0804 $\frac{201}{2500}$
5. 2.04 $\frac{51}{25}$, or $2\frac{1}{25}$
6. 5.07 $\frac{507}{100}$, or $5\frac{7}{100}$
7. 1.0006 $\frac{5003}{5000}$, or $1\frac{3}{5000}$

Notes on Reading

It is important that students understand that a number can be represented in many ways; it can even be represented as a fraction in many ways. For instance, $0.\overline{5148} = \frac{0.\overline{5148}}{1}$. However, in this lesson, we not only want to represent a number as a fraction, but as a *simple fraction*, namely one with integers in the numerator and denominator.

LESSON

12-1

Converting Decimals to Fractions

Can you read these? *When you read a finite decimal aloud, you can write what you say as a fraction.*

Very early in this book, in Lesson 1-6, you studied how to convert a simple fraction $\frac{a}{b}$ into its decimal form. Just divide a by b. For instance, to find the decimal equal to $\frac{6}{11}$, divide 6 by 11. On a calculator, you will see something like $\boxed{0.5454545}$. Similarly, $\frac{873}{200} = 873 \div 200 = 4.365$. You should check these now on your calculator.

Fractions for Terminating Decimals

It is often useful to convert a decimal to its equivalent fraction. If the decimal is finite, you can do this by applying the Equal Fractions Property.

Example 1

Find a simple fraction equal to 4.365.

Solution

First write 4.365 as a fraction. $4.365 = \frac{4.365}{1}$

Multiply both numerator and denominator by a power of 10 large enough to obtain a whole-number numerator. In this case, the power is 10^3.

$$\frac{4.365}{1} = \frac{4.365 \cdot 10^3}{1 \cdot 10^3} = \frac{4365}{1000}$$

This simple fraction answers the question. If you want the fraction in lowest terms, look for common factors of the numerator and denominator. Here, 5 is obviously a common factor. Divide both the numerator and denominator by it.

So we find that $4.365 = \frac{4365}{1000} = \frac{4365 \div 5}{1000 \div 5} = \frac{873}{200}$.

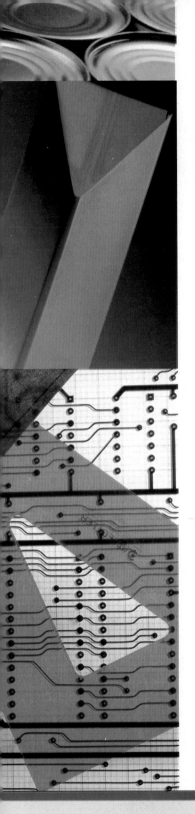

REAL NUMBERS, AREA, AND VOLUME

The numbers that can be represented by decimals are called real numbers. All of the numbers you have encountered in this book have been real numbers. Here are some examples.

Whole numbers, such as	6931
Simple fractions, such as	$\frac{24}{25} = 0.96$
Negative numbers, such as	$-7.3 \times 10^{-4} = -0.00073$
Infinite non-repeating decimals, such as	$\pi = 3.141592\ldots$
Mixed numbers, such as	$11\frac{4}{37} = 11.108108108108\ldots$

Some decimals are terminating; their decimals end. Others are infinite decimals. Some of the infinite decimals, such as the infinite decimal for $11\frac{4}{37}$ above, repeat. Others, like the decimal for π, have no repeating pattern. In this chapter, you will learn applications using some infinite non-repeating decimals. These numbers are important in finding the areas and volumes of common, everyday figures. For instance, the number π is involved in the volume formulas of both spheres and cylinders.

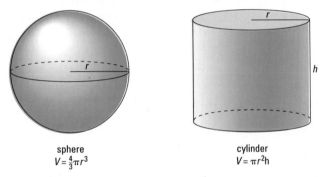

sphere
$V = \frac{4}{3}\pi r^3$

cylinder
$V = \pi r^2 h$

As a project, you can explore the *complex numbers*. These are numbers that are not real numbers. The complex numbers also have a variety of geometrical applications, but you will not usually study those uses until later mathematics courses.

Computer Chips: The arrangement of computer chips, each close to being square-shaped, presents a graphic representation relating the area of the circle to square units.

Prism: To determine the volume of a glass prism used to study color and light, use the formula, $V = Bh$, which is presented in Lesson 12-7.

Globes: The surface area of the earth is commonly represented on a sphere called a globe. Cartographers can map the earth more precisely on a sphere than on a flat map because parallels and meridians can be correctly drawn, and the scale is true everywhere over the curved surface.

Drafting Tool: A draftsman's triangle is pictured atop an enlargement of a computer chip. Tools of this type help produce accurate drawings which implement the use of the Pythagorean Theorem in the design of structures such as a gazebo.

Projects

At this time you might want to have students look over the projects on pages 684–685.

641

formulas for the perimeter and area of a polygon. These ideas are the subject of Lessons 12-6 and 12-7. The chapter ends with still another application of π—the volume and surface area formulas for a sphere.

Teaching Lesson 12-1

Warm-up
Diagnostic Write each decimal as a fraction in simplest form.

1. 0.8 $\frac{4}{5}$ 2. 0.17 $\frac{17}{100}$
3. 0.842 $\frac{421}{500}$ 4. 0.0804 $\frac{201}{2500}$
5. 2.04 $\frac{51}{25}$, or $2\frac{1}{25}$
6. 5.07 $\frac{507}{100}$, or $5\frac{7}{100}$
7. 1.0006 $\frac{5003}{5000}$, or $1\frac{3}{5000}$

Notes on Reading
It is important that students understand that a number can be represented in many ways; it can even be represented as a fraction in many ways. For instance, $0.\overline{5148} = \frac{0.\overline{5148}}{1}$.

However, in this lesson, we not only want to represent a number as a fraction, but as a *simple fraction*, namely one with integers in the numerator and denominator.

Can you read these? *When you read a finite decimal aloud, you can write what you say as a fraction.*

Very early in this book, in Lesson 1-6, you studied how to convert a simple fraction $\frac{a}{b}$ into its decimal form. Just divide a by b. For instance, to find the decimal equal to $\frac{6}{11}$, divide 6 by 11. On a calculator, you will see something like $\boxed{0.5454545}$. Similarly, $\frac{873}{200} = 873 \div 200 = 4.365$. You should check these now on your calculator.

Fractions for Terminating Decimals
It is often useful to convert a decimal to its equivalent fraction. If the decimal is finite, you can do this by applying the Equal Fractions Property.

Example 1

Find a simple fraction equal to 4.365.

Solution

First write 4.365 as a fraction. $4.365 = \frac{4.365}{1}$

Multiply both numerator and denominator by a power of 10 large enough to obtain a whole-number numerator. In this case, the power is 10^3.

$$\frac{4.365}{1} = \frac{4.365 \cdot 10^3}{1 \cdot 10^3} = \frac{4365}{1000}$$

This simple fraction answers the question. If you want the fraction in lowest terms, look for common factors of the numerator and denominator. Here, 5 is obviously a common factor. Divide both the numerator and denominator by it.

So we find that $4.365 = \frac{4365}{1000} = \frac{4365 \div 5}{1000 \div 5} = \frac{873}{200}$.

Lesson 12-1 Overview

Broad Goals This lesson discusses procedures that enable students to find a fraction for any repeating decimal.

Perspective In Chapter 2, students found fractions for terminating decimals. This material is reviewed in **Example 1.**

Determining fractions for repeating decimals provides a new and unusual use of the Distributive Property. Students generally find

the topic intriguing and are often surprised that the fractions can be found at all. This topic offers important background for understanding the difference between a rational number, which has a terminating or repeating decimal, and an irrational number, which has an infinite non-repeating decimal. Rational and irrational numbers are discussed in Lesson 12-4.

Converting repeating decimals to fractions also provides symmetry and closure to students' work with fractions. Since Chapter 1, they have had the tools to rewrite any simple fraction as a decimal. Now they have the tools to rewrite any repeating or terminating decimal as a fraction.

Fractions for Repeating Decimals

However, suppose you wanted to convert an infinite repeating decimal such as 0.5148148148148 . . . to a fraction. The method of Example 1 will not work because there is no power of 10 that can be multiplied by the numerator to make a whole number. One way to find a fraction equal to an infinite repeating decimal uses the Distributive Property in a surprising way.

Example 2

Find a simple fraction that equals $0.5\overline{148}$.

Solution

The idea is to solve an equation whose solution is known to be $0.5\overline{148}$.

Step 1: Let $x = 0.5\overline{148}$. Write x with a few repetitions of the repetend 148.

$$x = 0.5148148148\ldots$$

Step 2: The repetend has 3 digits, so multiply x by 1000. This moves the decimal point 3 places to the right.

$$1000x = 514.8148148148\ldots$$

Step 3: Subtract the first equation from the second equation.

$$1000x - x = 514.8\overline{148} - 0.5\overline{148}$$

Step 4: Use the Distributive Property on the left side of the equation. Subtract on the right side.

$$(1000 - 1)x = 514.8\overline{148} - 0.5\overline{148}$$
$$999x = 514.3$$

Step 5: Solve the resulting equation.

$$x = \frac{514.3}{999} = \frac{5143}{9990}$$

This is a simple fraction, but it is not in lowest terms. Dividing numerator and denominator by 37, this fraction equals $\frac{139}{270}$. Therefore,

$$0.5\overline{148} = \frac{139}{270}.$$

Check

Convert both $\frac{5143}{9990}$ and $\frac{139}{270}$ to decimals using a calculator.

Example 3

Find a simple fraction equal to $5.0\overline{3}$.

Solution

Step 1: Write $\quad x = 5.0333333333\ldots$

Step 2: Multiply both sides by 10. $\quad 10x = 50.33333333\ldots$

Step 3: Subtract. $\quad 10x - x = 50.3\overline{3} - 5.0\overline{3}$

Step 4: Simplify. $\quad 9x = 45.3$

Step 5: Solve. $\quad x = \frac{45.3}{9} = \frac{453}{90} = \frac{151}{30}$

$$\text{So, } 5.0\overline{3} = \frac{151}{30}$$

Cooperative Learning The process of writing fractions for repeating decimals is not easy for some students, so you might want them to do **Examples 2-4** together or in small groups. Note that each example involves a repetend with a different number of digits.

You may also wish to present the general algorithm.

1. Let x (or another variable) represent the repeating decimal. Write x with a few repetitions of the repetend.
2. Determine the number of digits in the repetend. Use that number as the power of 10 by which to multiply both sides of the equation. (Multiply by 10 for a one-digit repetend, by 100 for a two-digit repetend, and so on.)
3. Subtract the equation in Step 1 from the equation in Step 2.
4. Simplify using the Distributive Property.
5. Solve for x. If necessary, rewrite the solution as a simple fraction.
6. Finally, check by division.

Optional Activities

Give students the number patterns below. Have them find the pattern in the corresponding fractions.

1. $.\overline{1}, .\overline{2}, .\overline{3}, \ldots \quad \frac{1}{9}, \frac{2}{9}, \frac{3}{9}, \ldots$
2. $.\overline{01}, .\overline{02}, .\overline{03}, \ldots \quad \frac{1}{99}, \frac{2}{99}, \frac{3}{99}, \ldots$
3. $.\overline{001}, .\overline{002}, .\overline{003}, \ldots \quad \frac{1}{999}, \frac{2}{999}, \frac{3}{999}, \ldots$

LESSON MASTER 12-1 A — **Questions on SPUR Objectives** See pages 688-689 for objectives.

Skills Objective A

Find a simple fraction equal to each decimal.

1. .1875 $\quad \frac{3}{16}$
2. 6.475 $\quad \frac{259}{40}$
3. 8.25% $\quad \frac{33}{400}$
4. $0.\overline{4}$ $\quad \frac{4}{9}$
5. $.41\overline{6}$ $\quad \frac{5}{12}$
6. $.2\overline{4}$ $\quad \frac{11}{45}$
7. $2.7\overline{64}$ $\quad \frac{2737}{990}$
8. $808.\overline{568}$ $\quad \frac{807{,}760}{999}$
9. $.73\overline{09}$ $\quad \frac{7236}{990}$
10. 15.3% $\quad \frac{153}{1000}$

For 1–3, write each decimal as a simple fraction in lowest terms.

1. .312 $\frac{78}{250}$ 2. 4.2$\overline{81}$ $\frac{471}{110}$

3. 22.96$\overline{5}$ $\frac{20669}{900}$

4. A calculator display read 6.3636363. What numbers might have been divided?

Sample answer: $\frac{70}{11}$

Notes on Questions

Question 9c This answer can be found by adding 5 to the answer in **part b**.

Question 17 Some students do not want to believe that these two numbers are equal. You might show them the following explanation (which you may also have used in connection with **Question 36** in Lesson 1-6). Since $.\overline{3} = \frac{1}{3}$, students will agree that $3 \cdot .\overline{3} = \frac{1}{3} \cdot 3$. Simplification of both sides gives the result $.\overline{9} = 1$.

Question 18 Error Alert If students obtain $\frac{895}{9}$, remind them that 99.$\overline{4}$% means 99.$\overline{4} \cdot \frac{1}{100}$.

Question 25 Error Alert An answer of 0.$\overline{465}$ indicates that students added the repetends as if they did not repeat. Suggest that they write down the first 12 places of each decimal, and then add.

Fractions for Decimals that May Be Repeating

Example 4

Cleo had just done a division on her calculator when she was distracted. When she returned to her work she realized she had forgotten which numbers she had divided! The display on the calculator read [187.54545] What numbers might she have divided?

Solution

The display might be a rounding of the repeating decimal 187.$\overline{54}$.

Step 1: Let   x = 187.$\overline{54}$.
Step 2: Multiply both sides by 100.   100x = 18754.$\overline{54}$
Step 3: Subtract.   100x - x = 18754.$\overline{54}$ - 187.$\overline{54}$
Step 4: Simplify.   99x = 18567
Step 5: Solve.   x = $\frac{18567}{99}$ = $\frac{2063}{11}$

So Cleo may have divided 18,567 by 99. Or she may have divided 2063 by 11. Or, she divided any two other numbers whose quotient is $\frac{2063}{11}$.

Check

2063 [÷] 11 [=] [187.54545]

Remember that all simple fractions equal either repeating or terminating decimals. So if a decimal is infinite and does not repeat, it cannot be converted to a simple fraction. For instance, no simple fraction equals π.

QUESTIONS

Covering the Reading

In 1–4, classify the decimal as repeating, terminating, or cannot tell.

1. 3.04444   2. 3.0$\overline{4}$ 3. 3.040404 . . .   4. 3.$\overline{04}$
   terminating   repeating   cannot tell   repeating

5. Which of the decimals in Questions 1–4 are finite, which infinite?
   3.04444 is finite; the rest are infinite.

In 6–8, find the simple fraction in lowest terms equal to the decimal.

6. 11.6 $\frac{58}{5}$ 7. 0.061 $\frac{61}{1000}$ 8. 0.24 $\frac{6}{25}$

9. a. If $x = 0.\overline{24}$, then $100x = \underline{\ ?\ }$. 24.$\overline{24}$
   b. Find a simple fraction equal to 0.$\overline{24}$. $\frac{8}{33}$
   c. Find a simple fraction equal to 5.$\overline{24}$. $\frac{173}{33}$

10. Find a simple fraction equal to 0.$\overline{810}$. $\frac{30}{37}$

11. Convert 3.0$\overline{405}$ to a fraction. $\frac{30,101}{9900}$

12. Name two numbers other than 2063 and 11 which could have given Cleo's calculator display in Example 4. **Sample: 4126 and 22**

Adapting to Individual Needs

Extra Help
Refer to Step 2 in **Examples 2, 3, and 4** in which students must multiply by 1000, 10, and 100 respectively. Point out that the power of ten by which they must multiply depends on the number of digits in the repetend, *not* on the number of digits shown after the decimal point.

English Language Development
Have students write these terms on index cards: *terminating decimals, infinite repeating decimals, infinite non-repeating decimals*. Remind them that terminating means ending; repeating means occurring over and over; non-repeating means not occurring over and over; and infinite implies going on and on forever. Now have them **work in groups**, and give examples of each kind of number.

13. The digits of 0.12345678910111213 . . . are from the whole numbers. Explain why this decimal cannot be converted to a simple fraction. The decimal is not a repeating or terminating decimal, either of which is necessary for converting to a simple fraction.

Applying the Mathematics

14. A hat contains between 10 and 25 marbles. Some marbles are green, and the rest are yellow. Without looking you are to reach into the hat and pull out a marble. The probability of pulling out a green marble is 0.2.
  a. Rewrite the probability of pulling out a green marble as a simple fraction. $\frac{2}{9}$
  b. Use your answer to part **a** to determine how many marbles are in the hat. Describe how you arrived at this answer. See above left.
  c. How many of the marbles are green? 4

In 15 and 16, refer to this calculator display: [58.833333].

15. If the 3 repeats forever, name a division problem with this answer.
  Sample: 353 ÷ 6

16. Name a division problem with this exact answer.
  Sample: 58,833,333 ÷ 1,000,000

17. Use the method of this section to show that $1 = 0.\overline{9}$. See above left.

18. Write $99.\overline{4}\%$ as a simple fraction. $\frac{895}{900}$ or $\frac{179}{180}$

Review

In 19 and 20, use the drawing at the left.

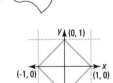

19. If the measure of angle 1 is $48\frac{2}{5}^\circ$, what is the measure of angle 2?
  (Lesson 7-6) $131\frac{3}{5}^\circ$

20. If angle 1 has measure x and angle 2 has measure $2x$, what is the value of x? *(Lessons 7-6, 10-2, 10-6)* 60°

In 21 and 22, use the figure at the left.

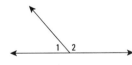

21. How many lines of symmetry does the figure have? *(Lesson 8-7)*
  none

22. Trace the figure and draw a tessellation using it as the fundamental region. *(Lesson 8-8)* See above left.

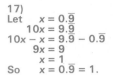

23. a. What is the area of a square with one side of length s? s^2
  b. What is the area of the square with vertices (1, 0), (0, 1), (-1, 0), and (0, -1)? *(Lessons 3-8, 8-3)* 2 square units

Exploration

24. What fraction with 1 in its numerator and a two-digit integer in its denominator equals $0.\overline{012345679}$? $\frac{1}{81}$

25. a. What decimal is the sum of $0.\overline{12}$ and $0.\overline{345}$? $0.\overline{466557}$
  b. What simple fraction is the sum? $\frac{5127}{10,989} = \frac{1709}{3663}$

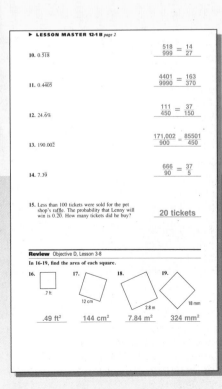

Objectives
B Estimate the square roots of a number without a calculator.
J Know how square roots and geometric squares are related.

Resources

From the *Teacher's Resource File*
- Lesson Master 12-2A or 12-2B
- Answer Master 12-2
- Teaching Aid 123: Warm-up
- Activity Kit, Activity 29
- Technology Sourcebook, Calculator Master 11

Additional Resources
- Visual for Teaching Aid 123

Teaching
Lesson **12-2**

Warm-up
Without using a calculator or paper and pencil, write the squares of as many integers as you can. You should learn the squares of the integers 0–20. **The squares of 0–20 are: 0, 1, 4, 9, 16, 25, 36, 49, 64, 81, 100, 121, 144, 169, 196, 225, 256, 289, 324, 361, 400**

Notes on Reading
1 History Connection Most students know the term *square root* but probably do not know its origin. When the ancient Greeks thought of a number as the area of a square—that is, the number 36 would be represented by a square with area 36—they also thought of the side upon which the square rests as the *square root*.

12-2

Square Roots

Mathmagic. *In this scene from the film* Donald in Mathmagic Land, *Donald chases a pencil and runs into many square roots.*

1 About 2500 years ago, Greek mathematicians began to organize the knowledge that today we call geometry. To the Greeks, numbers were lengths. They were probably the first to discover that some lengths could not be expressed as simple fractions. In this lesson you will learn about these lengths.

What Are Square Roots?
Here are two squares and their areas.

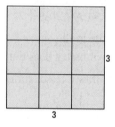
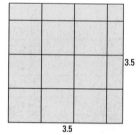

Area = $3 \cdot 3 = 3^2 = 9$ square units

Area = $3.5 \cdot 3.5 = 3.5^2 = 12.25$ square units

Recall that 9 is called the *square* of 3. We say that 3 is a *square root* of 9. Similarly, 12.25 is the square of 3.5, and we say that 3.5 is a square root of 12.25.

> If $A = s^2$, then s is called a **square root** of A.

646

Lesson 12-2 Overview

Broad Goals Square roots are introduced with their algebraic definition ($\sqrt{n}$ is a number whose square is n) and their geometric characterization ($\sqrt{n}$ is the side of a square whose area is n).

Perspective Until about 1980, most students learned a rather complicated paper-and-pencil algorithm to get a decimal approximation for a square root, and many of them did not understand it. Today,

calculators have made the square-root algorithm obsolete. In this lesson, students estimate square roots and then check their estimate by calculator multiplication and by using the square-root key. Because students can find square roots so quickly, the experimentation can help them understand the relationship between squaring and taking the square root of a number more readily than learning a lengthy procedure could.

In Europe, people generally write $\sqrt{(a + b)}$, while we write $\sqrt{a + b}$. This practice illustrates that the horizontal bar in our square root notation is actually the viniculum grouping symbol. Accordingly, work under that symbol must be done first.

② Since $-3 \cdot -3 = 9$, $(-3)^2 = 9$. So -3 and 3 are both square roots of 9. *Every positive number has two square roots.* The two square roots are opposites of each other. The symbol for the positive square root is $\sqrt{}$, called the **radical sign.** We write $\sqrt{9} = 3$. The negative square root of 9 is $-\sqrt{9}$, or -3. The symbol $\pm\sqrt{9}$, or ± 3, is sometimes used to refer to both square roots.

All scientific calculators have a square root key $\boxed{\sqrt{}}$. This key gives or estimates the positive square root of a number.

Activity 1

Find the positive square root of 12.25 using your calculator.

You should see 3.5 displayed. This tells you that the positive square root of 12.25 is 3.5. The two square roots of 12.25 are 3.5 and -3.5.

$$\sqrt{12.25} = 3.5 \text{ and } -\sqrt{12.25} = -3.5$$

area of square = 2
side of square = $\sqrt{2}$

Square Roots and Geometric Squares

The name square root comes from the geometry of squares. *If a square has area A, then its side has length $\sqrt{A}$.* In Question 23b of Lesson 12-1, you were asked to find the area of the square with vertices $(1, 0)$, $(0, 1)$, $(-1, 0)$, $(0, -1)$. One way to answer the question is to split the square into the four triangles shown at the left. Each triangle has area $\frac{1}{2}$ so the square has area 2. Therefore, each side of the square has length $\sqrt{2}$. The decimal for $\sqrt{2}$ is infinite and does not repeat. This means that although you can never write all the digits in the decimal for $\sqrt{2}$, you can draw a segment whose length is $\sqrt{2}$.

Estimating Square Roots

Activity 2

Determine what your calculator displays for $\sqrt{2}$.

Our calculator displays $\boxed{1.4142136}$, an estimate of $\sqrt{2}$. To check that 1.4142136 is a *good* estimate for $\sqrt{2}$, multiply this decimal by itself. Our calculator shows that

$$1.4142136 \cdot 1.4142136 \approx 2.0000001.$$

The negative square root of 2 is about -1.4142136.

Square roots of positive integers are either integers or infinite nonrepeating decimals. If a square root is an integer, you should be able to find it without a calculator. If a square root is not an integer, then you should be able to estimate it without a calculator.

Square roots?

The square-root key on the calculator makes finding an approximation to a square root (or an exact value if the radicand is a perfect square) automatic, but it does not provide much sense of what is going on. Encourage students to check their estimates on a calculator by multiplication. If, for example, they estimate that 25 is the square root of 500, they should multiply 25 by itself to see if their estimate was too large or too small. [Since $25 \cdot 25 = 625$, the estimate is too large.]

② Stress that $\sqrt{9}$ is not *the* square root of 9, but rather *the positive square root of 9.*

You might note that $\sqrt{x}$ may be read in at least four different ways: "radical x," "the positive square root of x," "the square root of x" (when it is clear that only positive square roots are being discussed), and "root x." We prefer the second and third phrases.

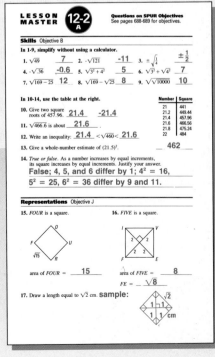

Optional Activities

Activity 1 After students complete **Questions 18–23**, you might show them that

$\sqrt{600} = \sqrt{100 \cdot 6} = \sqrt{100} \cdot \sqrt{6} = 10\sqrt{6}$. Then have them use this idea to find the square roots of the numbers below.

1. $\sqrt{500}$ $[\sqrt{100} \cdot \sqrt{5} = 10\sqrt{5}]$
2. $\sqrt{1600}$ $[\sqrt{100} \cdot \sqrt{16} = 40]$
3. $\sqrt{72}$ $[\sqrt{36} \cdot \sqrt{2} = 6\sqrt{2}]$
4. $\sqrt{450}$ $[\sqrt{25} \cdot \sqrt{9} \cdot \sqrt{2} = 15\sqrt{2}]$

Activity 2 You might want to use *Activity 29* in the *Activity Kit* as a follow-up for this lesson. This activity introduces students to the Golden Ratio and Golden Rectangles.

Activity 3 Technology Connection In *Technology Sourcebook, Calculator Master 11*, students investigate how accurate a square-root approximation is for a given number.

Additional Examples

1. **a.** Between which two whole numbers is $\sqrt{75}$? **8 and 9**

   b. What does your calculator show for $\sqrt{75}$? **Sample: 8.660254**

   c. Estimate $\sqrt{75}$ to the nearest tenth. **8.7**

   d. Estimate $\sqrt{75}$ to the nearest hundredth. **8.66**

2. Find each square root without using a calculator.

   a. $\sqrt{0}$ **0**   **b.** $\sqrt{484}$ **22**

   c. $\sqrt{2500}$ **50**   **d.** $\sqrt{1369}$ **37**

3. Simplify $\sqrt{16 + 20}$. **6**

Example

Between what two whole numbers is $\sqrt{40}$?

Solution

Write down the squares of the whole numbers beginning with 1. Stop when the square is greater than 40.

$$1 \cdot 1 = 1$$
$$2 \cdot 2 = 4$$
$$3 \cdot 3 = 9$$
$$4 \cdot 4 = 16$$
$$5 \cdot 5 = 25$$
$$6 \cdot 6 = 36$$
$$7 \cdot 7 = 49$$

This indicates that $\sqrt{36} = 6$ and $\sqrt{49} = 7$. Because larger positive numbers have larger square roots, $\sqrt{40}$ must be between $\sqrt{36}$ and $\sqrt{49}$. So $\sqrt{40}$ is between 6 and 7.

❸ The idea of square root was known to the ancient Egyptians thousands of years ago. The $\sqrt{\ }$ sign was invented in 1525 by the German mathematician Christoff Rudolff. The bar of the radical sign is a grouping symbol. Like parentheses you must work under the bar before doing anything else. For example, to simplify $\sqrt{36 + 49}$, you must add 36 and 49 first. Then find the square root.

$$\sqrt{36 + 49} = \sqrt{85} \approx 9.21954$$

QUESTIONS

Covering the Reading

1. Since $100 = 10 \cdot 10$, we call 10 a __?__ of 100. **square root**

2. When $A = s^2$, A is called the __?__ of s and s is called a __?__ of A. **square, square root**

3. $6.25 = 2.5 \cdot 2.5$. Which number is a square root of the other? **2.5 is the square root of 6.25.**

4. The two square roots of 9 are __?__ and __?__. **3, -3**

In 5-7, calculators are not allowed. Give the two square roots of each number.

5. 81 **9, -9**   6. 4 **2, -2**   7. 25 **5, -5**

8. The $\sqrt{\ }$ sign is called the __?__ sign. **radical**

In 9-11, calculators are not allowed. Simplify.

9. $\sqrt{64}$ **8**   10. $\pm\sqrt{1}$ **±1**   11. $-\sqrt{49}$ **-7**

12. Find the positive square root of 54.76 using your calculator. **7.4**

Adapting to Individual Needs

Extra Help

Students can develop a better sense of the meaning of square roots if they make and use a table of squares. For example, using their list, they can see that $12^2 = 144$ and $13^2 = 169$. Then they can estimate that $\sqrt{150}$ is between 12 and 13.

13. **a.** What does your calculator display for $\sqrt{2}$?
   b. Approximate $\sqrt{2}$ to the nearest thousandth.
   a) Sample: 1.4142136; b) 1.414
14. *Multiple choice.* The decimal for $\sqrt{2}$ is
   (a) finite.
   (b) infinite and repeating.
   (c) infinite and nonrepeating. (c)

15. **a.** Use your calculator to approximate $\sqrt{300}$. 17.320508
   b. How can you check that your approximation is correct?
   c. Round the approximation to the nearest hundredth.
   b) Multiply it by itself. c) 17.32

16. Suppose the area of a square is 400 square meters.
   a. Give the length of a side of the square. 20 m
   b. What is the positive square root of 400? 20
   c. Simplify: $-\sqrt{400}$. −20

Area 400 m²

17. A square has an area of 8 square units. To the nearest tenth, what is the length of a side of the square? 2.8

In 18–23, simplify.

18. $\sqrt{25} + \sqrt{16}$ 9   19. $\sqrt{25} - \sqrt{16}$ 1   20. $\sqrt{25 + 16}$ $\sqrt{41} \approx$ 6.4031

21. $\sqrt{25} \cdot \sqrt{25}$ 25   22. $\sqrt{25 - 16}$ 3   23. $\sqrt{5^2 + 4^2}$ $\sqrt{41} \approx$ 6.4031

24. $\sqrt{50}$ is between what two whole numbers? 7 and 8

Applying the Mathematics

25. A side of a square has length $\sqrt{10}$. What is the area of the square?
   10 square units
26. Which is larger, $\sqrt{2}$ or $\frac{239}{169}$? $\sqrt{2}$

27. The length of each side of a little square at the left is 1 unit.
   a. What is the area of the large tilted square? 8 square units
   b. What is the length of a side of this square? $\sqrt{8}$ units

In 28–31, use the table of numbers and squares at the left. Do not use a calculator. According to the table:

Number	Square
16.0	256.00
16.1	259.21
16.2	262.44
16.3	265.69
16.4	268.96
16.5	272.25
16.6	275.56
16.7	278.89
16.8	282.24
16.9	285.61
17.0	289.00

28. What is a square root of 268.96? 16.4
29. $\sqrt{285.6}$ is about __?__. 16.9
30. $\sqrt{270}$ is between __?__ and __?__. 16.4, 16.5
31. $\sqrt{250}$ is less than __?__. 16.0

Lesson 12-2 *Square Roots* **649**

Notes on Questions

Question 15 You might have students multiply to find how close 17.32² and 17.3205² are to 300. [17.32² = 299.9824; 17.3205² ≈ 299.99972]

Questions 18–23 These questions reinforce correct order of operations, and prepare students for generalizations with radicals. As an extension of this idea, see Activity 1 in *Optional Activities*, on page 647.

Question 26 This question provides an introduction to the notion of irrational numbers that will be discussed in Lesson 12-4. If you wish to provide some background now, see *Challenge* on page 650.

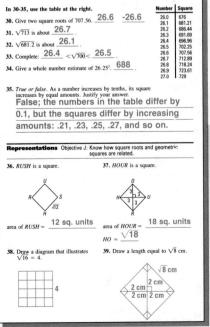

Notes on Questions

Question 37 This discussion introduces an important property of square roots. When *a* and *b* are nonnegative real numbers, $\sqrt{a} \cdot \sqrt{b} = \sqrt{ab}$. However there is no corresponding property connecting square roots to addition: $\sqrt{2} + \sqrt{3} \neq \sqrt{5}$. Only when *a* or *b* is zero is $\sqrt{a} + \sqrt{b}$ equal to $\sqrt{a+b}$.

Follow-up for Lesson 12-2

Practice

For more questions on SPUR Objectives, use **Lesson Master 12-2A** (shown on page 647) or **Lesson Master 12-2B** (shown on pages 648–649).

Assessment

Group Assessment Have students **work in pairs.** Have one partner give an area for a square and the other partner tell whether the length of the side of the square is or is not an integer. Then students should give an integer square root, or tell between which two integers a non-integer square root falls. [Students demonstrate an understanding of the geometric characterization of square roots.]

Extension

✎ **Writing** Interested students could research and prepare written reports on one of the following topics.
1. The meaning of cube root, fourth root, and other *n*th roots
2. The use of non-integer exponents for square roots, especially $x^{\frac{1}{2}} = \sqrt{x}$

Project Update Project 5, *The Number of Digits in a Repetend*, on page 685, relates to the content of this lesson.

650

In 32 and 33, find a simple fraction equal to the given decimal. *(Lesson 12-1)*

32. 4.26 $\frac{213}{50}$

33. $4.\overline{26}$ $\frac{422}{99}$

34. Find the area of triangle *ABC*. *(Lesson 10-9)* **140 square units**

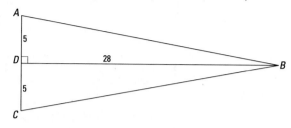

35. An article discussing some research in the learning of mathematics had references to other research articles published in the following years:
1982, 1987, 1987, 1989, 1982, 1990, 1992, 1989, 1974, 1987, 1988, 1981, 1990, 1969, 1989, 1992, 1988, 1987, 1989, 1991, 1989, 1989, 1981, 1989.

35a)
```
196 | 9
197 | 4
198 | 27792978198799919
199 | 02021
```

a. Plot the years in a stem-and-leaf display.
b. Give the median year for these references. **1988.5**
c. Give the mode year for these references. **1989**
d. In what year do you think the article was published?
(Lessons 6-1, 8-1) **Sample: 1992 (or 1993)**

36. *Multiple choice.* An item costs *C* dollars. The price is reduced by *R* dollars. You could buy the item at the reduced price and pay *T* dollars tax. How many dollars must you pay for the item? *(Lessons 5-1, 7-2)*
(a) $R - C + T$
(b) $C - R + T$
(c) $C - R - T$
(d) $R - C - T$ **(b)**

37a)
$\sqrt{1} = 1$, $\sqrt{2} \approx 1.414$,
$\sqrt{3} \approx 1.732$, $\sqrt{4} = 2$,
$\sqrt{5} \approx 2.236$, $\sqrt{6} \approx 2.449$,
$\sqrt{7} \approx 2.646$, $\sqrt{8} \approx 2.828$,
$\sqrt{9} = 3$, $\sqrt{10} \approx 3.162$,
$\sqrt{11} \approx 3.317$, $\sqrt{12} \approx 3.464$,
$\sqrt{13} \approx 3.606$, $\sqrt{14} \approx 3.742$,
$\sqrt{15} \approx 3.873$

b) $\sqrt{2} \cdot \sqrt{3} \approx$
$1.414 \cdot 1.732 \approx$
$2.449 \approx \sqrt{6}$

c) $\sqrt{3} \cdot \sqrt{5} \approx$
$1.732 \cdot 2.236 \approx$
$3.873 \approx \sqrt{15}$

37. a. Using your calculator, write down the square roots of the integers from 1 to 15 to the nearest thousandth.
b. Verify that the product of $\sqrt{2}$ and $\sqrt{3}$ seems equal to $\sqrt{6}$.
c. The product of $\sqrt{3}$ and $\sqrt{5}$ seems equal to what square root?
d. Find three other instances like those in parts **b** and **c**.
e. Write the general pattern using variables.
d) Samples: $\sqrt{2} \cdot \sqrt{4} \approx \sqrt{8}$; $\sqrt{2} \cdot \sqrt{5} \approx \sqrt{10}$; $\sqrt{3} \cdot \sqrt{4} \approx \sqrt{12}$.
e) $\sqrt{a} \cdot \sqrt{b} = \sqrt{ab}$

650

Challenge
Although there is no simple fraction equal to $\sqrt{2}$, it is possible to find fractions that are very close. Have students write decimal approximations for $\frac{7}{5}$, $\frac{17}{12}$, $\frac{41}{29}$, $\frac{99}{70}$, $\frac{239}{169}$, and compare them to an approximation of $\sqrt{2}$. [Sample answers using a calculator that rounds: 1.4, 1.4166667, 1.4137931, 1.4142857, and 1.4142012; $\sqrt{2} = 1.4142136$] Then have them look for a

pattern in the sequence, use it to write additional fractions, and compare the decimals for these fractions to the approximation for $\sqrt{2}$. [If one fraction is $\frac{a}{b}$, the next fraction is $\frac{a+2b}{a+b}$. Three more fractions in the sequence are $\frac{577}{408} \approx 1.4142157$, $\frac{1393}{985} \approx 1.4142132$, and $\frac{3363}{2378} \approx 1.4142136$. The approximations are approaching $\sqrt{2}$.]

The Pythagorean Theorem

IN-CLASS ACTIVITY

Materials: Ruler, scissors, paste or glue

Work with a partner.

This activity shows a way of finding the length of the hypotenuse of a right triangle without measuring it.

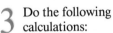

4 cm c

5 cm

1 Cut out a right triangle with legs of length 4 cm and 5 cm. We want to find c, the length of the hypotenuse.

2 Make 3 copies of the triangle and paste the four triangles on a piece of paper as shown here. This forms a large square and a tilted square in the middle with side c.

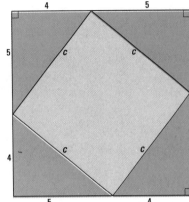

3 Do the following calculations:

a. What is the length of a side of the big square? **9 cm**
What is its area? **81 cm²**

b. What is the area of each corner right triangle? **10 cm²**
What is the total area of the four triangles? **40 cm²**

c. What is the remaining area, the area of the tilted square? **41 cm²**

d. What is the length of a side of the tilted square? **√41 or about 6.4 cm**

4 Measure a side of the tilted square (in centimeters). How close is your measure to what you calculated in Step 3?
Answers will vary. Measures should be close to 6.4 cm.

651

Optional Activities

Technology Connection You may wish to replace the activity on the student page by using *Technology Sourcebook, Computer Demonstration 12*, and the *Geometry Workshop* to show students how to draw geometric shapes by placing and connecting points. Then have students create the diagram on this page, and use options from the Measure menu to answer the questions.

In-class Activity

Resources

From the **Teacher's Resource File**
■ Answer Master 12-3
■ Teaching Aid 125: The Pythagorean Theorem
■ Technology Sourcebook, Computer Demonstration 12

Additional Resources
■ Visual for Teaching Aid 125
■ Geometry Workshop
■ Rulers or Geometry Templates

Students can use **Teaching Aid 125** to find the length of the hypotenuse of a right triangle with legs that measure 4 cm and 5 cm. The argument in this activity can be generalized to yield a proof of the Pythagorean Theorem. Using the diagram given on the pupil page, replace each 4 with a and each 5 with b. Then the area of the large square in the diagram can be found (1) by squaring the length of a side, or (2) by adding the areas of the triangles and the smaller square:
(1) $(a + b)^2 = a^2 + 2ab + b^2$.
(2) $4(\frac{1}{2}ab) + c^2 = 2ab + c^2$.
Thus, $a^2 + 2ab + b^2 = 2ab + c^2$. Now, subtracting $2ab$ from each side of the equation gives $a^2 + b^2 = c^2$, the Pythagorean Theorem.

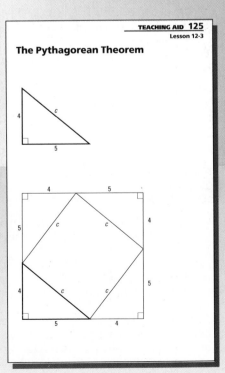

651

Objectives
C Use the Pythagorean Theorem to find lengths of third sides in right triangles.

Resources
From the Teacher's Resource File
- Lesson Master 12-3A or 12-3B
- Answer Master 12-3
- Assessment Sourcebook: Quiz for Lessons 12-1 through 12-3
- Teaching Aids
  86 Graph Paper
  123 Warm-up
- Activity Kit, Activity 30

Additional Resources
- Visuals for Teaching Aids 86, 123
- Rulers or Geometry Templates

Teaching Lesson 12-3

Warm-up
Tell if the statement is *true* or *false*.
1. A right triangle has a 90° angle. True
2. The sum of the angle measures of a triangle is 360°. False
3. A right triangle can have an obtuse angle. False
4. A right triangle can have two equal angles. True
5. A right triangle can have three equal sides. False
6. All acute triangles are right triangles. False

LESSON

12-3

The Pythagorean Theorem

Pythagorean action. *The carpenters are building triangular trusses, structural supports for a roof. They can use the Pythagorean Theorem to determine the lengths of the sides of the truss.*

In the In-class Activity, you began with a right triangle with legs 4 and 5. You should have found that the hypotenuse of the triangle has exact length $\sqrt{41}$. The numbers 4, 5, and $\sqrt{41}$ are related in a simple but not obvious way.

$$4^2 + 5^2 = (\sqrt{41})^2$$

That is, add the squares of the two legs. The sum is the square of the hypotenuse. *The Pythagorean Theorem* is the name commonly given to the general pattern. It is simple, surprising, and elegant.

Pythagorean Theorem
Let the legs of a right triangle have lengths *a* and *b*. Let the hypotenuse have length *c*. Then
$$a^2 + b^2 = c^2.$$

A **theorem** is a statement that follows logically from other statements known or assumed to be true. The Pythagorean Theorem is the most famous theorem in all geometry. With the theorem, you do not have to make copies of the triangle to find the length of a third side. This theorem was known to some Chinese, Egyptians, and Babylonians before the Greeks. But it gets its name from the Greek mathematician Pythagoras who was born about 572 B.C. He and his followers may have been the first people in the Western world to prove that this theorem is true for any right triangle.

652

Lesson 12-3 Overview

Broad Goals If the lengths of two legs of a right triangle are known, students should see how to obtain the length of the hypotenuse by using area. They should also see how the Pythagorean Theorem can be used to obtain the length of the third side.

Perspective The Pythagorean Theorem, one of the most important relationships in geometry, has many generalizations and more than 370 published proofs. It has been

independently discovered by people in many cultures; the ancient Chinese and Greeks deduced the theorem, and some ancient Egyptians and Babylonians knew of special cases and may have known the general property.

Students may wonder how people ever discovered the Pythagorean Theorem. It is likely that all discoverers generalized from a few specific cases, such as the 3-4-5 triangle.

The In-class activity, on page 651, shows students how to find the length of the hypotenuse of a right triangle without the Pythagorean Theorem. This idea can be generalized to give a proof of the theorem. Although the student text does not develop a proof, one is offered on page 651.

Example 1

What is the length of the hypotenuse of the right triangle drawn at the right?

Solution

Use the formula of the Pythagorean Theorem.

So

$$11^2 + 15^2 = h^2$$
$$121 + 225 = h^2$$
$$346 = h^2$$
$$h = \sqrt{346} \text{ or } -\sqrt{346}.$$

But h must be positive, so

$$h = \sqrt{346}.$$

A calculator shows that $\sqrt{346} \approx 18.6$.

The length of the hypotenuse is exactly $\sqrt{346}$, or about 18.6.

Activity

Draw a right triangle with legs 11 and 15 units. Then measure the hypotenuse. What is the difference between your measure and $\sqrt{346}$?

Applying the Pythagorean Theorem

Example 2 shows how to use the Pythagorean Theorem to find lengths that are difficult or impossible to measure directly.

Example 2

The bottom of a 12-foot ladder is 3 feet from a wall. How high up does the top of the ladder touch the wall?

Solution

First draw a picture. A possible picture is shown at the left. According to the Pythagorean Theorem,

$$3^2 + x^2 = 12^2.$$

Now solve the equation.
First simplify. $\qquad 9 + x^2 = 144$
Add -9 to both sides. $\qquad x^2 = 135$
Now, use the definition of square root.

$$x = \sqrt{135} \text{ or } -\sqrt{135}$$

Because x is a length, it cannot be negative. So

$$x = \sqrt{135}.$$

A calculator shows that $\sqrt{135} \approx 11.6$. This seems correct because the ladder must be less than 12 feet up on the wall.

The top of the ladder touches the wall about 11.6 feet up.

Caution: The Pythagorean Theorem works only for right triangles. It does not work for any other triangles.

Lesson 12-3 *The Pythagorean Theorem* **653**

Video

Wide World of Mathematics The segment, *Youthbuild,* highlights a program where urban youths are trained in the basics of construction and engineering, both in the classroom and on building renovation projects. The segment provides motivation to study the Pythagorean Theorem. Related questions and an investigation are provided in videodisc stills and in the Video Guide. A related CD-ROM activity is also available.

Videodisc Bar Codes

Search Chapter 59

Play

Notes on Reading

The In-class Activity on page 651 presents one of the many ingenious ways of finding the length of the hypotenuse of a right triangle when the lengths of the two legs are known. The process presented can always be used, but it is quite awkward. For that reason, it is nice to have a more general result. That general result, the Pythagorean Theorem, is discussed on page 652. **Examples 1 and 2** show the use of the theorem in finding the length of the hypotenuse and in finding the length of a leg of a right triangle.

Have students record the results of the *Activity* for use with **Question 7** on page 654.

Cooperative Learning As they work with the theorem, you might have students **work in small groups** and do additional measuring activities similar to the one in **Question 14** on page 656.

Emphasize that the Pythagorean Theorem is a generalization which applies to *all* right triangles and that it cannot be *proved* by using examples only. You might wish to note that many other statements in this book are theorems; the Triangle-Sum Property and the Means-Extremes Property are two examples. In each case, mathematicians use a logical argument to show that the property follows from other basic assumed properties.

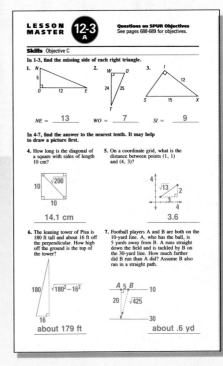

653

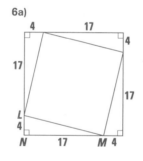

An arithmetic classic.
This Chinese block print shows a proof of the Pythagorean Theorem. The proof is from one of the oldest known sources of Chinese mathematics, the Chou Pei Suan Ching, *written about 500 B.C.*

6a)

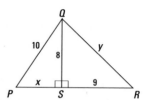

QUESTIONS

Covering the Reading

1. What is a theorem? a statement that follows logically from other statements known (or assumed) to be true
2. *Multiple choice.* Pythagoras was an ancient
   (a) Chinese.   (b) Greek.
   (c) Egyptian.   (d) Babylonian. (b)
3. State the Pythagorean Theorem. If the legs of a right triangle have lengths a and b, and the hypotenuse has length c, then $a^2 + b^2 = c^2$.

In 4 and 5, use the drawing below.

4. **a.** What relationship exists between 8, 9, and y? $8^2 + 9^2 = y^2$
   b. Find y. $y = \sqrt{145} \approx 12.04$
5. **a.** What relationship exists between x, 8, and 10? $x^2 + 8^2 = 10^2$
   b. Find x. $x = \sqrt{36} = 6$
6. Lee had to find LM in triangle LMN, but she forgot the Pythagorean Theorem. Take Lee through these steps to find LM.

   a. Trace $\triangle LMN$. Then draw three copies of the triangle to form a large square and a tilted square in the middle.
   b. Find the area of the large square. 441 sq units
   c. Find the area of $\triangle LMN$. 34 sq units
   d. Find the area of the tilted square in the middle. 305 sq units
   e. Find LM. $\sqrt{305}$
7. Answer the question of the Activity in this lesson. Answers will vary. The hypotenuse should be $\sqrt{346}$, or about 18.6 units
8. The bottom of a 3-meter ladder is 1 meter away from a wall. To the nearest cm, how high up on the wall will the ladder reach? $\sqrt{8}$, or about 2.83 meters
9. A right triangle has legs with lengths 6″ and 7″. Find the length of its hypotenuse, to the nearest tenth of an inch. 9.2 inches

Optional Activities

Activity 1 You can use *Activity 30* in the *Activity Kit* as a lead-in, an alternate approach, or a follow-up for this lesson. In the activity, students complete a dissection puzzle that verifies the Pythagorean Theorem.

Activity 2 You can use this activity after discussing **Example 2.** Have students **work in groups.** Give them a number that is the length of the hypotenuse of a right triangle. Have them find possible lengths of the legs. [Any two numbers for which the sum of their squares is the square of the number you gave are answers. For instance, consider a hypotenuse of 14. $14^2 = 196$. Since $100 + 96 = 196$, $\sqrt{100}$ and $\sqrt{96}$ are a possible solution.]

10. *Multiple choice.* For which of the following triangles can the Pythagorean Theorem be used? (b)

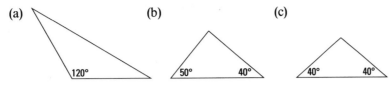

(a)   (b)   (c)

120°   50° 40°   40°   40°

11. A rectangular farm is pictured below. It is 9 km long and 2 km wide. Danny wants to go from point *A* to point *B*.

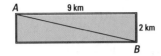

A   9 km

2 km

B

  a. What is the shortest distance Danny can travel going along the roads that surround the farm? 11 km
  b. What is the distance by tractor along the diagonal of the farm?
  c. Which path is shorter? How much shorter is it?
  b) √85 km, or about 9.2 km;   c) the diagonal path; about 1.8 km

12. The Chicago White Sox built a new stadium that opened in 1991. In the old ballpark, someone seated in the last row of the upper deck was about 150 feet away from home plate. Use the information about the new Comiskey Park in the diagram below. How much farther away from home plate is the last row of the new upper deck than it was in the old park? ≈ 100 feet

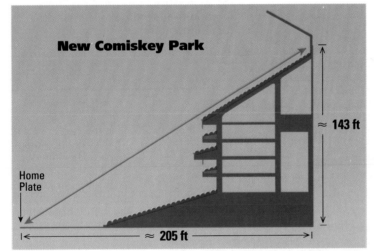

New Comiskey Park

≈ 143 ft

Home Plate

≈ 205 ft

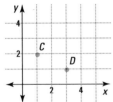

13. In the graph at the left, point *C* = (1, 2). *D* = (3, 1). What is the distance between these points? (Hint: Use a right triangle with hypotenuse *CD*.) *CD* = √5

Lesson 12-3   *The Pythagorean Theorem*   **655**

Notes on Questions

Question 10 This question reinforces the fact that the Pythagorean Theorem applies only to right triangles.

Question 13 This question relates the Pythagorean Theorem to coordinate graphs and anticipates the development of the distance formula in algebra.

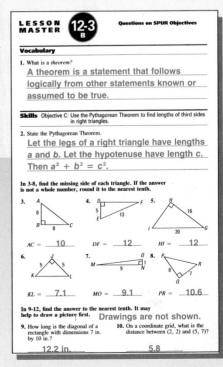

LESSON MASTER 12-3 B   Questions on SPUR Objectives

Vocabulary

1. What is a *theorem*?
   A theorem is a statement that follows logically from other statements known or assumed to be true.

Skills Objective C: Use the Pythagorean Theorem to find lengths of third sides in right triangles.

2. State the Pythagorean Theorem.
   Let the legs of a right triangle have lengths *a* and *b*. Let the hypotenuse have length *c*. Then $a^2 + b^2 = c^2$.

In 3-8, find the missing side of each triangle. If the answer is not a whole number, round it to the nearest tenth.

3.   4.   5.

  AC = __10__   *DF* = __12__   *HI* = __12__

6.   7.   8.

  KL = __7.1__   *MO* = __9.1__   *PR* = __10.6__

In 9-12, find the answer to the nearest tenth. It may help to draw a picture first. Drawings are not shown.

9. How long is the diagonal of a rectangle with dimensions 7 in. by 10 in.?
   __12.2 in.__

10. On a coordinate grid, what is the distance between (2, 2) and (5, 7)?
   __5.8__

Adapting to Individual Needs

Extra Help

Materials: Rulers or Geometry Templates, graph paper or **Teaching Aid 86**

Have students refer to the table at the right, where *a* and *b* represent the lengths of the legs of a right triangle, and *c* represents the length of the hypotenuse. For each row in the table, have students draw a right triangle with legs *a* and *b* on graph paper, and then measure *c*. Next have them calculate *c* using the Pythagorean Theorem.

	a	b	c	
1.	5	12	[13]	[25 + 144 = 169]
2.	6	8	[10]	[36 + 64 = 100]
3.	15	20	[25]	[225 + 400 = 625]
4.	9	12	[15]	[81 + 144 = 225]
5.	24	10	[26]	[576 + 100 = 676]

Notes on Questions

Question 25 Music Connection
The relationships the Pythagoreans found are used in all string instruments.

Follow-up for Lesson **12-3**

Practice

For more questions on SPUR Objectives, use **Lesson Master 12-3A** (shown on pages 653–654) or **Lesson Master 12-3B** (shown on pages 655–656).

Assessment

Quiz A quiz covering Lessons 12-1 through 12-3 is provided in the *Assessment Sourcebook.*

Written Communication Ask each student to write and solve two problems using the Pythagorean Theorem. [Students' problems require finding the length of the hypotenuse or a leg of a right triangle.]

Extension

Project Update Project 2, *A 3-Dimensional Pythagorean Pattern,* on page 684, relates to the content of this lesson.

▶ **LESSON MASTER 12-3 B** *page 2*

11. A rectangular park is 200 m by 260 m. To get from one corner of the park to the opposite corner, how much shorter is the route that cuts along the diagonal instead of following along the sides of the park?

132.0 m

12. Can an 8-foot ladder fit in a closet that is 3 feet wide, 4 feet deep, and 7 feet high?

yes

13. Draw a right triangle. Measure each leg to the nearest millimeter.
A sample is given.

20 mm, (36 mm), 30 mm

a. Use the Pythagorean Theorem to find the length of the hypotenuse to the nearest millimeter. **36 mm**

b. Now measure the hypotenuse. **36 mm**

c. How close are your answers to Parts a and b? How do you account for this?
Answers should be the same. If they are not, measurements might have been inaccurate.

14. Draw a triangle with three acute angles and sides of different lengths, *a*, *b*, and *c*.
A sample is given.

a. Measure *a*, *b*, and *c* to the nearest millimeter.
a = **40 mm**   *b* = **38 mm**   *c* = **30 mm**

b. Does $a^2 + b^2 = c^2$? Why do you think this is so?
$30^2 + 30^2 = 900 + 900 = 1800 \neq 784$ or 28^2;
no; the figure is not a right triangle.

656

---

14. Typing paper is often an 8.5″ by 11″ rectangle. Find the length of a diagonal of the rectangle using the given process.
 a. measuring with a ruler Sample: about $13\frac{7}{8}$″
 b. applying the Pythagorean Theorem about 13.9″

15. *Multiple choice.* There was no year 0. What year is 2500 years after the estimated year of Pythagoras's birth?
 (a) 1928 (b) 1929 (c) 1972 (d) 2072 (b)

Review

16. Simplify $\sqrt{225 - 144}$. *(Lesson 12-2)* 9

17. Simplify $\sqrt{2^2 + 3^2}$. *(Lesson 12-2)* $\sqrt{13} \approx 3.6056$

18. *True or false.* $\sqrt{9} + \sqrt{16} = \sqrt{25}$. *(Lesson 12-2)* False

19. a. The square of what number is 0? 0
 b. Simplify $\sqrt{0}$. *(Lesson 12-2)* 0

20. In the first 40 games of the baseball season, Homer had 31 hits. At this rate, how many hits will he have for the entire 125-game season? *(Lesson 11-6)* about 97

21. At 35 miles per hour, how long will it take to go 10 miles? *(Lessons 9-5, 10-2)* $\frac{10}{35}$ hour, or about 17 minutes

22. Solve $5000 = 50 + x - 25$. *(Lessons 5-8, 7-2)* 4975

23. *Multiple choice.* $0 + (x + 1) = 0 + (1 + x)$ is an instance of what property? *(Lessons 5-2, 5-7)*
 (a) Commutative Property of Addition
 (b) Associative Property of Addition
 (c) Additive Identity Property of Zero
 (d) Addition Property of Equality (a)

24. To the nearest integer, what is 2.5^7? *(Lesson 2-2)* 610

Donald Duck meets the Pythagoreans during one of their jam sessions, in a scene from Donald in Mathmagic Land.

© The Walt Disney Company

656

Exploration

25. The followers of Pythagoras, called the Pythagoreans, worshiped numbers and loved music. They discovered relationships between the lengths of strings and the musical tones they give. Look in an encyclopedia to find out one of the musical relationships discovered by the Pythagoreans. Sample: A string half as long as another sounds a note one octave higher than the other.

Adapting to Individual Needs

Challenge
A square is drawn on each side of a right triangle, with each side of the triangle forming one side of a square. If you know that areas of the three squares are 400 in.², 144 in.², and 256 in.², what is the area of the triangle? [96 in.²]

Setting up Lesson 12-4

Materials: Students will need circular objects to measure in the In-class Activity on page 657 and for Lesson 12-4. You might ask them to bring in empty food cans, paper-towel tubes, paper cups, paper plates, buttons, and other similar objects. Suggest that labels be left on the food cans so you can also use them for Lesson 12-6 which is on surface area. You will want to keep the cylindrical objects for use with Lessons 12-6 and 12-7.

The
Circumference
of a Circle

IN-CLASS
ACTIVITY

Materials: Circular objects, tape measure
Work with two or three other people, if possible,

Gather at least four objects in which you can see circles, such as cans, paper towel tubes, clocks, and bicycle wheels. You will also need a tape measure, (preferably cloth, so it bends).

1 Each person in the group should measure the distance across (the diameter) and the distance around (the circumference) each circle, as shown here. Answers will vary.

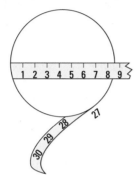

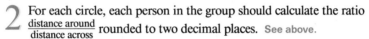

distance across ≈ 8.8 cm

distance around ≈ 27.6 cm

2,3) Answers will vary, but should be close to 3.14.

2 For each circle, each person in the group should calculate the ratio $\frac{\text{distance around}}{\text{distance across}}$ rounded to two decimal places. See above.

3 For each circle now find the average of the quotients found by the members of your group. This will give you a ratio for each of the circles. See above.

4 As a group, decide which of the following is the correct choice. As a circle gets larger, the ratio $\frac{\text{distance around}}{\text{distance across}}$ (b)
(a) becomes larger (b) stays about the same. (c) becomes smaller.

5 If the ratio becomes larger or smaller, how much larger or smaller does it become? If the ratio stays the same, about what number does it equal? The ratio should remain about 3.14.

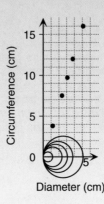

657

In-class Activity
Resources
From the *Teacher's Resource File*
- Answer Master 12-4
- Teaching Aids
  126 The Circumference of a Circle
  127 First-Quadrant Graph Paper

Additional Resources
- Visuals for Teaching Aids 126, 127
- A variety of circular objects from home and the classroom, such as empty food cans, paper towel-tubes, paper cups, paper plates, buttons, and other similar objects
- Tape measures

Have each group of students select four circular objects from those brought to class and from objects that are already in the classroom.

Students can use **Teaching Aid 126** to record their measures. In Step 3, have them compare quotients. Each quotient should be close to π. Point out that, in theory, with perfect circles and perfect measuring devices, the quotient would be π.

Students may be disappointed at how far their answers are from π. The reason is that very few quotients of small whole numbers are close to π. For numerators and denominators under 50, the closest fraction is $\frac{22}{7}$.

TEACHING AID 126
In-class Activity, Lesson 12-4

The Circumference of a Circle

Object	Diameter	Circumference	Circumference / Diameter

Optional Activities

Materials: Circular objects with diameters between 1 cm and 8 cm, centimeter grid or **Teaching Aid 127**

Have students draw the first quadrant on a centimeter grid, and label the x-axis "Diameter" and the y-axis "Circumference." Then, placing circular objects with diameters between 1 cm and 8 cm on the x-axis, tell them to (1) mark each diameter on the x-axis, (2) roll the object along the y-axis making one complete turn, and (3) mark off the circumference. After repeating the activity with several objects, students should see that the points (diameter, circumference) lie on a line.

Objectives

D Find the circumference of a circle, given its radius or diameter.
G Identify numbers as rational, irrational, or real.
I Apply the formula for circumference of a circle in real situations.

Resources

From the Teacher's Resource File
- Lesson Master 12-4A or 12-4B
- Answer Master 12-4
- Teaching Aids
  123 Warm-up
  127 First-Quadrant Graph Paper
  128 Real Numbers
- Technology Sourcebook, Computer Master 27

Additional Resources
- Visuals for Teaching Aids 123, 127, 128
- Compass (Extension)
- Geometry Workshop

Teaching
Lesson 12-4

Warm-up

1. Draw a circle and identify these parts. **Check students' work.**
   a. radius   **b.** diameter
   c. center   **d.** circumference
2. What do you know about the diameter and the radius of a circle? **Sample: The diameter is twice the length of the radius, or the radius is one half the diameter.**
3. What do you know about π? **Sample: π is approximately equal to 3.14.**

Swing time. *Hoops like this one were first introduced in the 1950s for exercising or playing. What is the circumference of a hoop with a 4-ft diameter?*
4π feet

The Idea Behind Circumference

Suppose you put a tape measure around your waist. Then you can measure the perimeter of your waist. You can do this even though your waist is curved.

The same idea works for circles. The perimeter of a circle can be measured. It is the distance around the circle, the distance you would travel if you walked around the circle.

The top of the aluminum can pictured below is a circle with diameter *d*. Think of the distance around this circle. (It is how far a can opener turns in opening the can.) This distance can be estimated by rolling the circle. We draw the circle with different shading so you can follow the circle as it rolls.

Lesson 12-4 Overview

Broad Goals The formula for the circumference of a circle is a vehicle not only for obtaining the circumference of a circle, but also for studying the number π and, more generally, irrational numbers.

Perspective The number π was introduced in Chapter 1 and should be familiar to students. One measure of its importance is the inclusion of a π key on scientific calculators.

Circumference in everyday language may refer to either a geometric object (the circle itself) or its length. Mathematicians tend to prefer only one meaning, that being circumference as a length. This meaning makes the use of *circumference* like the use of *perimeter*—the circumference *is* the perimeter of a circle.

Optional Activities

Activity 1 Technology Connection You may wish to assign *Technology Sourcebook, Computer Master 27*. Students use the *Geometry Workshop* to create a circle, mark points around the circle, and measure central angles.

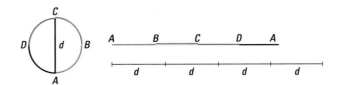

In the diagram above, the distance around the circle is compared to the diameter. The diagram shows that the distance around the circle is just a little more than 3 times the diameter. In fact, the unraveled length, called the **circumference** of the circle, is exactly 3.1415926535 . . . times the diameter. You have seen this number before. It is called **π** (pi), and its decimal never repeats or ends.

❶ **Formula for Circumference of a Circle**
In a circle with diameter d and circumference C,
$$C = \pi d.$$

The circumference of a circle is the circle's perimeter. Don't be fooled just because the word is long and different.

Example

To the nearest inch, what is the circumference of a can with a 4″ diameter?

4 in.

❷ **Solution**
Let C be the circumference. Using the formula $C = \pi d$,

$C = \pi \cdot 4 = 4\pi$ inches exactly.

To approximate C to the nearest inch, use 3.14 for π.

$C \approx 3.14 \cdot 4$, or 12.56, inches, so C is about 13″.

❸ **Some Facts About π**

When you divide both sides of the formula $C = \pi d$ by d, you get $\frac{C}{d} = \pi$. That is, the ratio of the circumference of a circle to its diameter is π. $\frac{C}{d}$ looks like a simple fraction. However, it was proved in 1767 that no whole numbers C and d can have a ratio equal to π. You should have found a number close to π for each ratio you calculated in the In-class Activity preceding this lesson.

Notes on Reading
Two important ideas are presented in this lesson—the circumference of a circle and the introduction of irrational numbers.

❶ Students give the circumference of a circle in terms of the radius in **Question 22**.

❷ Point out to students that π can be part of a meaningful answer. It is not always necessary to write a decimal or a fraction approximation. We give an exact answer in terms of π to questions that do not refer to an application as in **Question 5** or **Question 22**. We suggest decimal approximations when there is a real-world context as in **Question 24** or **Question 26**.

Ratios of whole numbers are either terminating or repeating decimals, and all terminating or repeating decimals are ratios of whole numbers. Therefore, when a number is an infinite non-repeating decimal, as π is, there is no ratio of whole numbers that is equal to it. This makes π irrational. Students may wonder how we know that the decimal for π never repeats. That is difficult to show and is well beyond high school mathematics. In 1767 Johann Lambert, a Swiss-German mathematician, first proved that π is irrational.

❸ The example $\pi = \frac{c}{d}$ shows that a number may look rational but be irrational, and conversely, may look irrational yet be rational. For instance, $\sqrt{6.25}$ may look irrational, but it is the rational number 2.5. The best way to tell the difference is to consider the number as a decimal. You may wish to write the following on the board:

Decimal	Number
finite	rational
infinite repeating	rational
infinite non-repeating	irrational

Activity 2
Materials: Circular objects, rulers or **Geometry Templates**

Have students **work in groups.** Give each group 3 or 4 circular objects. Have them estimate the circumference of each object and then measure the object to find the circumference.

As an extension of **Question 26,** students can measure the diameter of the wheel on a bicycle, and calculate the number of times the wheel turns in one mile. [Responses will depend on the diameter of the wheel. A 24-inch bicycle wheel will make about 840 revolutions; a 26-inch wheel will make about 776 revolutions.]

Activity 3 After completing the lesson, you might give students the following problem: Imagine that there are two circular train tracks around the earth at the equator— a ground-level one and an elevated one. The elevated track is one mile longer than the ground-level track. How far above the ground is the elevated track? Assume the diameter of the ground-level track is 7926.41 miles, the approximate diameter of the earth. [Answers may vary due to rounding. Using the π key gives about 0.16 miles, or about 840 feet.]

If you wish to give students experience finding the circumference of actual objects, see Activity 1 in *Optional Activities*, on page 658. Activity 2 in *Optional Activities* has them research the development of pi.

❹ This **Visual Organizer** is also found on **Teaching Aid 128.**

Cooperative Learning You might have students **work in groups.** Using the chart on page 660 or **Teaching Aid 128,** have one student in each group give a number to the other group members who must identify the number as rational, irrational, or real, and then explain their reasoning. Each student should have a turn naming a number.

It is within the scope of high school mathematics to show that the square roots of positive integers are either integers or irrational numbers, but that is outside the scope of this course. The proofs are given in two later UCSMP courses, *Geometry* and *Precalculus and Discrete Mathematics.*

The number π is so important that scientific calculators almost always have a key or keys you can press for π. Pressing that key will give you many decimal places of π. On one calculator, we press INV π and see 3.1415927. On another we press 2nd π ENTER and see 3.141592654. Without a calculator, people use various approximations. For rough estimates, you can use 3.14 or $\frac{22}{7}$. Use more decimal places if you want more accuracy.

Rational and Irrational Numbers

A number that *can* be written as a simple fraction is called a **rational number.** Finite decimals, repeating decimals, and mixed numbers all represent rational numbers. A number that *cannot* be written as a simple fraction is called an **irrational number.** Since π cannot be written as a simple fraction, it is irrational. Irrational numbers are those numbers whose decimals are infinite and do not repeat. When the square root of a positive integer is not an integer, then it is irrational. For instance, $\sqrt{2}$ and $\sqrt{3}$ are irrational. But $\sqrt{4}$ is rational, because $\sqrt{4} = 2$.

Irrational numbers are very important in many measurement formulas. Square roots often appear as lengths of sides of right triangles. As you will see in the next few lessons, many formulas involve π. As you study more mathematics, you will learn about other irrational numbers.

Every real number is either rational or irrational. The chart shows how some of the various kinds of numbers are related.

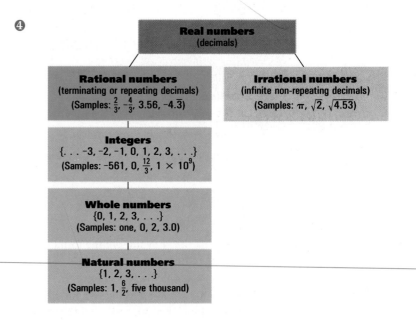

❹

Real numbers (decimals)

Rational numbers (terminating or repeating decimals) (Samples: $\frac{2}{3}$, $-\frac{4}{3}$, 3.56, $-4.\overline{3}$)

Irrational numbers (infinite non-repeating decimals) (Samples: π, $\sqrt{2}$, $\sqrt{4.53}$)

Integers $\{\ldots -3, -2, -1, 0, 1, 2, 3, \ldots\}$ (Samples: -561, 0, $\frac{12}{3}$, 1×10^9)

Whole numbers $\{0, 1, 2, 3, \ldots\}$ (Samples: one, 0, 2, 3.0)

Natural numbers $\{1, 2, 3, \ldots\}$ (Samples: 1, $\frac{6}{2}$, five thousand)

Adapting to Individual Needs

Extra Help

Materials: Strips of paper, such as adding machine tape, circular objects

Students can measure circles and their diameters in a comparative way by using a strip of paper. First, have them mark off the length of the diameter of any circle on the paper. Then have them turn the strip on its edge, and mark the circumference of the

circle by folding the paper as shown below. Students can see that the ratio of the circumference to the diameter is a little over 3 to 1.

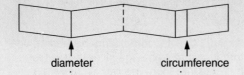

diameter   circumference

Covering the Reading

1. What is a *circle*? the set of points in a plane at a certain distance from a certain point

2. The distance across a circle through its center is called the __?__ of the circle. diameter

3. The perimeter of a circle is called the __?__ of the circle. circumference

4. A circle has diameter 10 cm. To the nearest cm, what is its circumference? 31 cm

5. The circumference of a circle with diameter s is __?__. πs

6. A simple fraction that is used as an approximation to π is __?__. $\frac{22}{7}$

7. A calculator shows π to be 3.141592654.
   a. Is this an exact value or an estimate? an estimate
   b. Round this number to the nearest hundredth. 3.14
   c. Round this number to the nearest hundred thousandth. 3.14159
   d. What does your calculator show for π? Sample: 3.1415927

8. The equator of the earth is approximately a circle whose diameter is about 7920 miles. What is the distance around the earth at its equator? about 24,900 miles

9. Solve the equation $C = \pi d$ for d. $d = \frac{C}{\pi}$

10. What is a rational number?
    a number that can be written as a simple fraction

11. What is an irrational number?
    a number that cannot be written as a simple fraction

In 12–17, a real number is given.
a. Tell whether the number is rational or irrational.
b. If it is rational, give a fraction in lowest terms equal to it.

12. $\frac{2}{3}$ b) $\frac{2}{3}$
a) rational

13. π b) none
a) irrational

14. $6.\overline{87}$ b) $\frac{227}{33}$
a) rational

15. $\sqrt{5}$ b) none
a) irrational

16. $5\frac{1}{2}$ b) $\frac{11}{2}$
a) rational

17. 0.0004 b) $\frac{1}{2500}$
a) rational

18. What is a real number?
    a number that can be written as a decimal

19. Which of the numbers of Questions 12–17 are real numbers?
    all of them

20. Are there any numbers that are not real numbers? (The answer is given on page 641.) Yes, complex numbers are not real numbers.

Additional Examples

1. The rim of a wheel is to be covered with rubber. If a spoke of the wheel (a radius) is 1 ft long, how long a strip of rubber will be needed to go around the rim?
   $\approx$ 6.28 ft

2. Find the circumference of a circle with:
   a. diameter 10 ft.
      10π ft $\approx$ 31.4 ft
   b. radius 3.5 cm.
      7π cm $\approx$ 21.98 cm

3. For each number, select all of the following categories that apply: whole number, integer, rational number, irrational number, real number
   a. 0 Whole number, integer, rational number, real number
   b. $-\sqrt{25}$ Integer, rational number, real number
   c. $\sqrt{5}$ Irrational number, real number
   d. π Irrational number, real number
   e. $\frac{25}{3}$ Rational number, real number
   f. 1×10^9 Whole number, integer, rational number, real number
   g. 1.2345678910111213 . . . Irrational number, real number

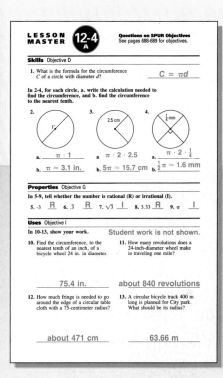

Adapting to Individual Needs

English Language Development
You might explain that the word *irregular* means "not regular" and *irresponsible* means "not responsible." Similarly, *irrational* means "not a ratio," and irrational numbers cannot be written as ratios of whole numbers.

Question 28 **History Connection**
Interested students might investigate some of the discoveries made by Archimedes.

Question 39 This question uses a famous infinite series approximation to π discovered by Leonhard Euler in the early 1700s:
$$\frac{\pi^2}{6} = 1 + \frac{1}{4} + \frac{1}{9} + \frac{1}{16} + \ldots..$$
The series converges slowly, however, and it is not until about the 600th term is added that the sum is greater than 3.14. The next 400 terms add only a little more than .00064 to the sum.

Follow-up for Lesson **12-4**

Practice
For more questions on SPUR Objectives, use **Lesson Master 12-4A** (shown on page 661) or **Lesson Master 12-4B** (shown on pages 662–663).

Assessment
Group Assessment Have students **work in pairs**. Have each partner make a list of ten rational and irrational numbers. Then have partners exchange their lists and identify each number as rational or irrational. [Students should be able to explain why each number is rational or irrational.]

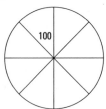

LESSON MASTER 12-4 B
Questions on SPUR Objectives

Vocabulary
1. Explain what the *circumference* of a circle is.
The circumference is the distance around a circle.

Skills Objective D: Find the circumference of a circle, given its radius or diameter.
2. Write the symbol for pi. Then give its approximate value to the nearest thousandth.
π   3.142
3. Write the formula for the circumference of a circle, and explain what each variable represents.
c = πd; c, circumference; d, diameter

In 4-9, a. write the calculation needed to find the circumference, and b. find the circumference to the nearest tenth.
4. (5 ft) a. π · 5 b. 15.7 ft
5. (1 cm) a. π · 2 b. 6.3 cm
6. (1 m) a. π · 1 b. 3.1 m
7. (8.2") a. π · 8.2 b. 25.8"
8. (1.5 mm) a. π · 3 b. 9.4 mm
9. (1"/8) a. π · 1/4 b. 0.8"

Applying the Mathematics

0.6"

In 21–22, use the fact that the diameter of a circle is twice its radius.
21. The circle at the left has radius 0.6″. What is its circumference? **1.2 π inches ≈ 3.77 inches**
22. A circle has radius *r*. What is its exact circumference? (You need to remember this formula.) **2πr**
23. The circle below is split into 8 congruent sectors. If the radius is 100, what is the length of the arc of one of the sectors, to the nearest tenth? **about 78.5 units**

(100)

24. In the seventeenth century, the Dutch built a circular fort at the southernmost point of New Amsterdam, what is now Manhattan Island in New York City. The fort was also used to protect the city during the War of 1812. Today it is a national monument known as Castle Garden. Castle Garden is about 236 feet across at its widest. What is the length of its outside wall? **about 741.4 feet**

The Castle Garden national monument is the circular building on the left in this detail of the 1855 painting, Immigrants Debarking at the Battery, *by Samuel B. Waugh.*

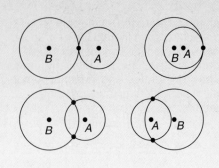

25. A plastic tube 50″ long is bent to make a circular hoop. To the nearest inch, what is the diameter of the hoop? **about 16 inches**
26. Some bicycle wheels are 24″ in diameter. How far will the bike go in 10 revolutions of the wheels? **≈ 754 in., or ≈ 63 ft**
27. The number $\frac{355}{113}$ was used by the Chinese as an estimate for π.
   a. Write $\frac{355}{113}$ as a mixed number. **$3\frac{16}{113}$**
   b. Which is a better approximation to π, $\frac{355}{113}$ or $\frac{22}{7}$? **$\frac{355}{113}$**

662

Adapting to Individual Needs
Challenge
Have students solve the following problem. A miser buried a can of money in a field. Later, someone found a note that said, "The money is 20 feet from point *A* and 30 feet from point *B*." How could you find the money without digging at random? [Draw a circle at *A* with a radius of 20 feet and a circle at *B* with a radius of 30 feet. The places where the circles intersect determine possible locations of the money.]

28. The Greek mathematician Archimedes knew that π was between $3\frac{1}{7}$ and $3\frac{10}{71}$. (Archimedes lived from about 287 B.C. to 212 B.C. and was one of the greatest mathematicians of all time.)
  a. Calculate the decimal equivalents of these mixed numbers.
  b. Why didn't Archimedes have a decimal approximation for π?
  a) See below left. b) Decimals had not been invented yet.

29. Which is larger, π or $\sqrt{10}$? $\sqrt{10}$

30. Approximate $\pi + 1$ to the nearest tenth. 4.1

Review

31. Simplify $\sqrt{841} - \sqrt{400}$. *(Lesson 12-2)* 9

32. Evaluate $5 \cdot \sqrt{3}$ to the nearest integer. *(Lesson 12-2)* 9

33. 6 is what percent of 30? *(Lesson 11-5)* 20%

34. 6% of what number is 30? *(Lesson 10-2)* 500

35. Olivia biked m miles at 20 miles per hour. How many hours did it take her to do this? *(Lessons 9-5, 10-2)* $\frac{m}{20}$ hours

36. Evaluate $|2 - n|$ when $n = 5$. *(Lessons 5-3, 7-2)* 3

37. Evaluate $9x^3 - 7x^2 + 12$ when $x = 6$. *(Lesson 4-4)* 1704

Exploration

38. a. What does your calculator show for π? Sample: $\pi \approx 3.1415927$
  b. Subtract the whole-number part of the decimal. (The first time this is 3.) Then multiply the difference by 10. Your calculator may show another digit of π. 1.4159265 ($\pi \approx 3.14159265$)
  c. Repeat part **b** several times if possible. Describe what happens.

39. a. Run this program, inputting a large number for the blank.

```
10 SUM = 0
20 FOR N = 1 TO ___
30 TERM = 1/(N*N)
40 SUM = SUM + TERM
50 NEARPI = SQR(6*SUM)
60 PRINT N, NEARPI
70 NEXT N
80 END
```

  a) **Sample:** If 100 is put in the blank, the last line is 100   3.13207653.

  b) It adds the reciprocals of the squares of integers from 1 to n, then takes the square root of 6 times this sum. As n gets larger and larger, the result gives a better approximation to π.

  c) **Sample:** If 1000 is put in the blank, the last line is 1000   3.14063806.

  Write down the last line the computer prints.
  b. What does the program do?
  c. Try a larger number in the blank. What happens?

Inventor, too! *Although a great mathematician and physicist, Archimedes was probably best known during his lifetime as an inventor. His inventions included systems of levers and pulleys for moving great weights. This portrait of Archimedes is by a 16th-century artist, André Thevet.*

28a) $3\frac{1}{7} \approx 3.1428571$;
$3\frac{10}{71} \approx 3.1408451$

38c) Sample: The calculator next shows 4.1592654, then 1.5926536, and then 5.926536. The calculator does not show places for π beyond 3.1415926536.

Extension

Materials: Compass, first quadrant grid or **Teaching Aid 127.**

In this activity, students graph numbers such as $\sqrt{2}$, $\sqrt{3}$, and $\sqrt{5}$. Begin by having students mark the axes so that 1 unit equals 3 centimeters, and then have them draw a right triangle with vertices $(0, 0)$, $(1, 0)$, and $(1, 1)$. Have them note that the length of the hypotenuse is $\sqrt{2}$ units. Have students open their compasses to this length, mark a segment $\sqrt{2}$ units long on the x-axis, and label it $(\sqrt{2}, 0)$. Have them use a triangle with vertices $(0, 0)$, $(\sqrt{2}, 0)$, and $(\sqrt{2}, 1)$ to find point $(\sqrt{3}, 0)$. Then have them continue this way to find the following points on the x-axis: $\sqrt{4}$, $\sqrt{5}$, $\sqrt{6}$, and so on.

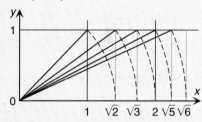

Project Update Project 1, *Complex Numbers,* and Project 4, *Approximations to π,* on pages 684–685, relate to the content of this lesson.

Objectives

D Find the area of a circle or sector, given its radius or diameter.
I Apply the formulas for the area of a circle or sector in real situations.

Resources

From the Teacher's Resource File
- Lesson Master 12-5A or 12-5B
- Answer Master 12-5
- Teaching Aids
  124 Warm-up
  129 Area of a Circle
  130 Additional Examples
  131 Extension/Challenge
- Technology Sourcebook, Computer Master 28

Additional Resources
- Visuals for Teaching Aids 124, 129–131
- Spreadsheet Workshop
- Rulers or Geometry Templates

Teaching Lesson **12-5**

Warm-up

Mental Mathematics What fraction of a circle is represented by each of the following measures? Give the fraction in lowest terms.

1. 180° $\frac{1}{2}$ **2.** 60° $\frac{1}{6}$ **3.** 300° $\frac{5}{6}$
4. 270° $\frac{3}{4}$ **5.** 36° $\frac{1}{10}$ **6.** 120° $\frac{1}{3}$
7. 72° $\frac{1}{5}$ **8.** 90° $\frac{1}{4}$ **9.** 240° $\frac{2}{3}$

Notes on Reading

❶ For this activity, students should find that the base of each triangle has a length of 1.9 cm and an

---

LESSON

12-5

The Area of a Circle

The circular advantage. *Each rotating arm of length r units in this irrigation system waters πr^2 square units of land. If the circles do not overlap, then some regions get no water from the system.*

Finding the Area of a Circle

Recall that the formula for the area of a triangle, $A = \frac{1}{2}bh$, was found by showing that two copies of a triangular region exactly fill up a rectangle.

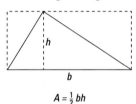

$$A = \frac{1}{2}bh$$

This idea does not work for finding the area of a circle. Sectors of a circle cannot be cut and pasted to fill up any rectangle exactly. However, the area of a circle can be estimated by splitting it up into small sectors, approximating each sector with a triangle, and adding up all the areas of the triangles.

❶ **Activity**

The circle at the top of page 665 has radius 5 cm. It has been split into 16 congruent sectors. Measure the height *h* and base *b* of the triangle drawn. Use these measurements to estimate the area of one of the sectors. Then multiply by 16 to estimate the area inside the circle.

Lesson 12-5 Overview

Broad Goals This lesson introduces the formulas for the area of a circle and the area of a sector of a circle.

Perspective The formula for the area of a circle is one of the most well known formulas in all of mathematics. This lesson offers one proof, and the teacher's notes on page 665 offer a second proof.

This is a good place to talk about the need

for *proof*. It took a long time for anyone to determine a formula for the area of a circle; the ancient Greeks seem to have been the first to develop it. The formula is not obvious because it involves π. Recall that π is irrational, and ancient people did not even have terminating decimals.

Most students find the area formula easy to apply. They need only be careful to use the radius not the diameter, and to follow the correct order of operations.

The formula for area of a sector looks much more imposing than it really is. The important thing for students to realize is that the area of a sector is just a fractional part of the area of a circle. That fraction depends on the size of the sector—so the fractional part is $\frac{m}{360}$, where *m* is the measure of the central angle of the sector. The formula could be stated as: Area of a sector = $\frac{m}{360}$ · Area of the circle.

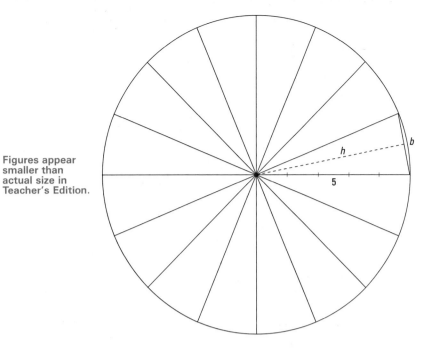

Figures appear smaller than actual size in Teacher's Edition.

The activity does not indicate how π gets involved with the formula for the area of a circle. This is harder to do, but try to follow the argument.

We take the 16 sectors from the Activity and rearrange them.

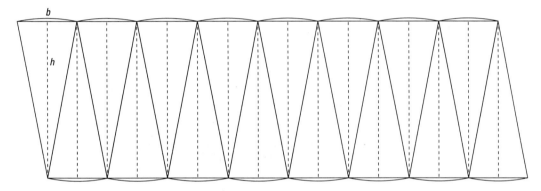

Now the figure resembles a parallelogram with height h. The top and bottom are not straight since they are made of arcs. The total length of the top and bottom arcs is the circumference of the circle, πd. So the top has length half that, or $\frac{1}{2}\pi d$, which equals πr.

altitude of about 4.9 cm, so the area of each sector is $\frac{1}{2} \cdot 1.9 \cdot 4.9$, or about 4.655 cm². Multiplying by 16 yields a total area of about 74.5 cm². The formula for the area of a circle gives 25π cm² as the area which is approximately 78.5 cm². The difference is the total area of the small regions between the triangles and the circle and in the thickness of the segments and arcs in the drawing. Have students record the results of this *Activity* for use with **Question 1** on page 668.

For another derivation of the formula for the area of a circle, have students circumscribe an octagon around a circle, or use **Teaching Aid 129**.

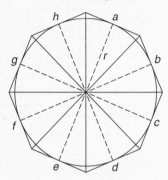

The area of the octagon is
$A = \frac{1}{2}ar + \frac{1}{2}br + \frac{1}{2}cr + \ldots + \frac{1}{2}hr$.
By the Distributive Property this is
$A = \frac{1}{2}(a + b + c + d + \ldots + h)r$.
The expression in parentheses is the perimeter of the polygon. Let this equal p, which gives $A = \frac{1}{2}pr$. The area of a polygon circumscribed about a circle will be $\frac{1}{2}pr$ regardless of the polygon used. Also, as the number of sides increases, its perimeter becomes closer and closer to the circumference of the circle, and its area becomes closer and closer to the area of the circle. Substituting $2\pi r$ for p gives
$A = \frac{1}{2}pr = \frac{1}{2}(2\pi r)r = \pi r^2$.

Optional Activities

Activity 1
Materials: Circular objects, rulers or **Geometry Templates**

You can use this activity after **Example 1.** Have students **work in groups.** Give each group 3 or 4 circular objects. Suggest that they estimate the area of each circle. Then have them measure the diameter or radius and use a formula to find the area.

Activity 2
Materials: Menus from pizza restaurants

You might use this activity after students complete the lesson. Have students find the areas of pizzas, and then, using the prices of various sizes of the same kinds of pizza, compare the prices per square inch. Have students compare, for example, two 12-inch pizzas and one 18-inch pizza. [Two 12-inch

pizzas have an area of 72π in², and one 18-inch pizza has an area of 81π in².]

Activity 3 Technology Connection
You may wish to assign *Technology Source-book, Computer Master 28*. Students use the *Spreadsheet Workshop* to compare areas of rings of various widths.

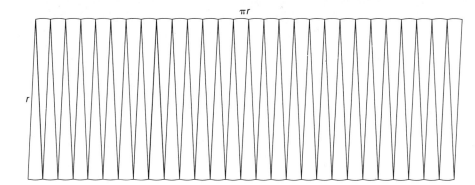

If the circle is split into more and more triangles, the height of each triangle becomes closer and closer to the circle's radius r. The "parallelogram" becomes more and more like a rectangle with width πr. And the area of that rectangle is $\pi r \cdot r$, or πr^2. This is why the area of the circle is πr^2.

> **Area Formula for a Circle**
> Let A be the area of a circle with radius r. Then
> $$A = \pi r^2.$$

Example 1

Find the exact area of a circle with a radius of 5 cm.

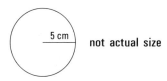

5 cm   not actual size

Solution

$$A = \pi \cdot (5 \text{ cm})^2 = 25\pi \text{ cm}^2$$

This is the exact answer. To estimate this to the nearest square centimeter, use an approximation to π.

$$\approx 25 \cdot 3.1416 \text{ cm}^2$$
$$\approx 78.54 \text{ cm}^2$$
$$\approx 79 \text{ cm}^2$$

Check

9 cm

10 cm

Notice that a square with side 9 cm has about the same area as the circle. The area of the square is 81 cm^2. So an area of about 79 cm^2 for the circle seems about right.

666

Adapting to Individual Needs

Extra Help
The formula for finding circumference, $C = \pi d$, is given in Lesson 12-4. However, since $d = 2r$, this formula sometimes appears as $C = 2\pi r$. Since the formula for the area of a circle is $A = \pi r^2$, students often confuse the two formulas. To help them avoid this mistake, write these expressions on the board:

3.14 · 5   3.14 · 5 · 5   3.14 · 5 · 2

Then, for **Questions 1–3,** have them pick the expression that answers the question.
1. Which expression shows the area of a circle with radius of 5? [3.14 · 5 · 5]
2. Which expression shows the circumference of a circle with a radius of 5? [3.14 · 5 · 2]
3. Which expression shows the circumference of a circle with a diameter of 5? [3.14 · 5]

666

Area of a Sector of a Circle

The area of a sector of a circle depends on the size of the central angle.

Example 2

In sector *VCS*, ∠*VCS* is a right angle, and *VC* = 8. Find the area of the sector.

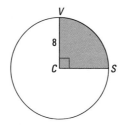

Solution

It may help you to draw the entire circle, as shown at the right.

A right angle has measure 90°. This is $\frac{90}{360}$ or $\frac{1}{4}$ of a revolution.

So the sector has $\frac{1}{4}$ the circle area. $A = \frac{1}{4} \cdot \pi \cdot 8^2 = \frac{1}{4} \cdot 64 \cdot \pi = 16\pi$.

Check

Notice that $16\pi \approx 16 \cdot 3.14 \approx 50$. A square with sides $\overline{VC}$ and $\overline{CS}$ has area 64. This is larger than the area of the sector, as it should be.

The area of any sector can be found if the radius and the measure of the central angle is known.

Example 3

Consider the figure at the left, with *AG* = 1 cm and m∠*BAG* = 145°. Find the area of sector *BAG*.

Solution

145 degrees is $\frac{145}{360}$ of a revolution. The area of circle A is $\pi \cdot 1^2 = \pi$ cm². So the area of sector BAG is $\frac{145}{360} \cdot \pi$ cm², or approximately 1.27 cm².

The process of finding the area of a sector of a circle is generalized in the next formula.

❷ **Area Formula for a Sector**

Let *A* be the area of a sector of a circle with radius *r*. Let *m* be the measure of the central angle of the sector in degrees. Then $A = \frac{m}{360} \cdot \pi r^2$.

Lesson 12-5   *The Area of a Circle*   **667**

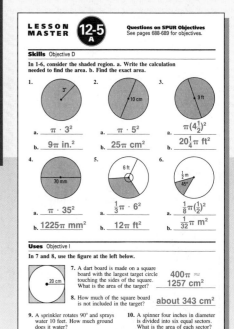

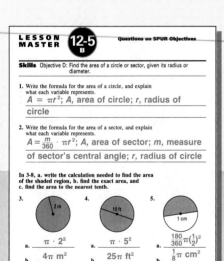
QUESTIONS

Covering the Reading

1. Refer to the Activity on page 664. What value did you get for each quantity?
   a. h about 4.9 cm
   b. b about 1.9 cm
   c. the area of one of the sectors about 4.655 cm²
   d. the area of the circle about 74.5 cm²

2. The area of a circle with radius r is equal to the area of a rectangle with dimensions r and __?__. πr

3. What is the area of a circle with radius r? πr^2

4. To the nearest integer, what is the area of a circle with radius 4?
   50 square units

5. What is the area of one half of a circle with radius 6? 18π sq units

In 6 and 7, use the figure at the left. G is the center of the circle.

6. What is the area of region GHI? about 78.5 square units

7. What is the area of region GIJ? about 52.4 square units

Applying the Mathematics

8. A quarter has radius 12.15 mm. What is the area of one of its faces?
   about 463.8 mm²

9. What calculator key sequence will give you an estimate to the area of a circle with radius 50? Sample: $\boxed{\pi}\boxed{\times}\boxed{50}\boxed{x^2}\boxed{=}$

10. A central angle of a sector has measure 50°. If the area of the circle is 180 square meters, what is the area of the sector? 25 m²

11. The smaller circle at the left has radius 0.5 inch, and the larger circle has radius 0.75 inch.
    a. What is the area of the ring? 0.3125π or about 0.98 in²
    b. Which has the greater area, the smaller circle or the shaded ring?
       the ring

12. Clyde decided to make a large spinner for a game. He wanted equal-sized sectors for each of three choices. Below is his plan.

    a. What should be the measure of the central angle of each sector?
    b. If the diameter of the circle is to be 11 in., what will be the area of each sector of the spinner?
       a) 120°; b) ≈ 31.7 in²

13. Lisa read that there were about 10 calories in each square inch of a 12-inch diameter cheese pizza. If she eats $\frac{1}{8}$ of a pizza, about how many calories would she consume? 141 calories

668

Adapting to Individual Needs

Challenge
The following problem is given on **Teaching Aid 131.** As an extension of **Question 14,** have students imagine that the building is a square 12 meters on each side and that the leash is 15 meters long. Have them find the area of land on which the dog can roam.
[About 544 m²]

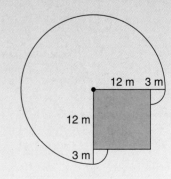

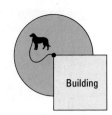

Building

14. A dog is on a leash tied to the corner of a building. This enables the dog to roam anywhere in a sector of the circle, as shown at the left. If the leash is 9 meters long, what is the area of land on which the dog may roam? **60.75π or about 191 m²**

15. Which gives you more for your money, one 14″ pizza, or three 7″ pizzas of the same kind? **one 14″ pizza**

25a) The circle; suppose the circumference of the circle equals the perimeter of the square $= 2\pi r$. Then the area of the circle $= \pi r^2 \approx 3.14 r^2$, and the area of the square $= \frac{\pi^2 r^2}{4} \approx 2.47 r^2$.

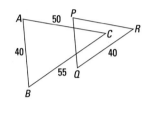

Review

16. To the nearest tenth of an inch, find the circumferences of the two circles in Question 11. *(Lesson 12-4)* **3.1 in., 4.7 in.**

17. When does a decimal represent an irrational number? *(Lesson 12-4)* **when it is infinite and does not repeat**

18. The hypotenuse of a right triangle has length 50. One leg has length 14. What is the length of the other leg? *(Lesson 12-3)* **48**

19. Order from smallest to largest: $\sqrt{5}, 3\sqrt{12}, 2\sqrt{3}, \sqrt{6}$. *(Lesson 12-2)* $\sqrt{5}, \sqrt{6}, 2\sqrt{3}, 3\sqrt{12}$

20. Find the simple fraction in lowest terms equal to $.0\overline{36}$. *(Lesson 12-1)* **2/55**

21. The triangles at the left are similar and tilted the same way. Find PR. *(Lesson 11-8)* **36.$\overline{36}$**

22. In $\triangle TON$ below, $NW = 80$, $TO = 60$, and $\overline{TO} \perp \overline{NT}$.
a. Is enough information given to find the area of $\triangle NOW$? **Yes**
b. If so, find its area. If not, explain why not. *(Lesson 10-9)*
A = 2400 sq units

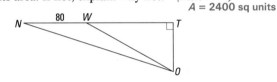

23. Multiply: $5(x - y + 12)$. *(Lesson 10-6)* **5x − 5y + 60**

24. A certain variety of lichen grows about 0.01 inch in a year. At this rate, how many inches would it grow in a century? *(Lesson 9-5)*
1 inch

Exploration

25. Take two pieces of string of equal length. Form the first string into a circle. Form the second string into a square.
a. Which figure has the greater area? Explain why you think as you do.
b. Does the answer to part **a** depend on the length of the string? **No**
a) **See above left.**

26. Copy the circle in the Activity on pages 664 and 665. Cut out the sectors and rearrange them to form a figure like that on page 665. Estimate the area of that figure in square centimeters. How close is your estimate to the area of the circle? **Answers will vary.**

Practice

For more questions on SPUR Objectives, use **Lesson Master 12-5A** (shown on page 667) or **Lesson Master 12-5B** (shown on pages 668–669).

Assessment

Written Communication Have students write an explanation of how the area of a sector can be found when the radius of the circle and the measure of the central angle are known. Tell students to include an example in their explanation. [Explanations demonstrate understanding of the area formula of a circle and of fractional parts of a circle.]

Extension

You might give students these diagrams which are given on **Teaching Aid 131**, and have them find each shaded area. The radius of each circle is 6 cm.

1. 6 cm   **2.** 6 cm

[Figure 1: If s is the side of the square, by the Pythagorean Theorem, $s^2 + s^2 = 12^2$, so $s^2 = 72$. Then $36\pi - 72 \approx 41$ cm².
Figure 2: $12^2 - 36\pi \approx 31$ cm²]

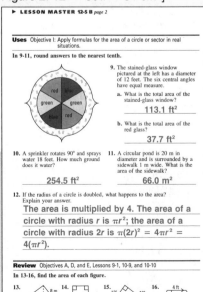

► **LESSON MASTER 12-5 B** *page 2*

Uses Objective I: Apply formulas for the area of a circle or sector in real situations.

In 9-11, round answers to the nearest tenth.

9. The stained-glass window pictured at the left has a diameter of 12 feet. The six central angles have equal measure.
a. What is the total area of the stained-glass window?
113.1 ft²
b. What is the total area of the red glass?
37.7 ft²

10. A sprinkler rotates 90° and sprays water 18 feet. How much ground does it water?
254.5 ft²

11. A circular pond is 20 m in diameter and is surrounded by a sidewalk 1 m wide. What is the area of the sidewalk?
66.0 m²

12. If the radius of a circle is doubled, what happens to the area? Explain your answer.
The area is multiplied by 4. The area of a circle with radius r is πr^2; the area of a circle with radius $2r$ is $\pi(2r)^2 = 4\pi r^2 = 4(\pi r^2)$.

Review Objectives A, D, and E, Lessons 9-1, 10-9, and 10-10

In 13-16, find the area of each figure.

13. 42 m² **14.** 24.57 cm² **15.** 96 in.² **16.** 23 ft²

Setting Up Lesson 12-6

Materials Students will need food cans with the labels attached for the *Warm-up*.

For Lesson 12-6 and Lesson 12-7, you may want to assemble cylinders and prisms with a variety of polygonal bases to show students as you discuss the lessons. Ask students to try to find boxes at home similar to those shown on the top of page 676, especially boxes with bases that are not rectangular.

Objectives

E Find the surface area of cylinders and prisms.
H Apply formulas for surface area of cylinders and prisms in real situations.

Resources

From the *Teacher's Resource File*
- Lesson Master 12-6A or 12-6B
- Answer Master 12-6
- Teaching Aid 124: Warm-up

Additional Resources
- Visual for Teaching Aid 124
- Food cans with labels that can be removed (Warm-up)

Teaching
Lesson **12-6**

Warm-up

Activity Select a cylindrical can with a label that can be removed.
1. Carefully remove the label from the can. What is the shape of the label? **A rectangle**
2. Find the length and width of the rectangle. What is its area? **Check students' answers. The length and width of the rectangle are the circumference and height of the cylinder; the area is their product.**
3. How can you find the area of the top and bottom of the can? What is the area? **Check students' answers.**
4. Estimate the total surface area of the can. **Students should add their answers to Questions 2 and 3.**

On a roll. *Large rotary printing presses use cylinders in the printing process. The greater the surface area of the cylinder, the larger each impression or printed sheet can be.*

Surface Areas of Cylinders

Many cans of food are shaped like *circular cylinders*. The top and bottom are the **bases** of the cylinder. Some cans have paper labels that can be peeled off. If you peel off the label, you will see that it is a rectangular piece of paper. The height of the rectangle is the height h of the can. If you ignore any overlap, the other dimension of the rectangle is the circumference of a base.

From this information, you can find the area of the side of the can, known as its **lateral area ($L.A.$).**

$$L.A. = hC,$$

where C is the circumference of a base. But since $C = \pi d$, another formula is

$$L.A. = \pi dh.$$

And since $d = 2r$, still another formula (and the most common) is

$$L.A. = 2\pi rh.$$

In these formulas d and r are the diameter and radius of a base, respectively.

670

Lesson 12-6 Overview

Broad Goals There are two goals in this lesson—to see cylinders and prisms as examples of the same type of figures, and to determine their surface areas by thinking of unrolling their lateral areas to form a rectangle.

Perspective One of the broad ideas that ranges through all of mathematics is the realization that things that look different may have common features that enable them to

be studied at the same time. For instance, polygons come in many different sizes and shapes, but when we group them all together, we find that their perimeters can all be found in the same way, that all of them can be separated into triangles, and (later in geometry) that there is a simple formula for the sum of the measures of their angles.

This lesson proceeds in analogous fashion. Prisms and cylinders are both types of

cylindric surfaces, and their surface areas (and volumes) can be found in analogous ways. We do not give the general formulas in the student text because we feel that students would then merely memorize them and lose track of their derivation. After students have done some activities, you might wish to generalize the results and mention the formulas as suggested in the *Extension* on page 674.

If you add the areas of the top and bottom of the can, you have calculated the **total surface area (S.A.)** of the cylinder.

Example 1

A typical soft-drink can is almost a circular cylinder with height of about $4\frac{3}{4}$ inches and a diameter of about $2\frac{1}{2}$ inches. Find the total surface area of such a can.

Solution

First draw a picture, as at the left. For convenience we have changed the dimensions to decimals. The lateral area is the area of a rectangle with height 4.75 inches and width $\pi \cdot 2.5$ inches.

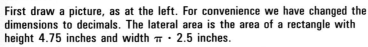

$$\begin{aligned} L.A. &= \pi dh \\ &\approx \pi(2.5)(4.75) \\ &\approx 37.3 \text{ square inches} \end{aligned}$$

The area of the circular top is $\pi(1.25)^2 \approx 4.9$ square inches. The bottom has the same area. So

$$\begin{aligned} S.A. &\approx 37.3 + 2 \cdot 4.9 \\ &= 47.1 \text{ square inches.} \end{aligned}$$

The total surface area of this typical soft-drink can is about 47.1 square inches.

To make a cylinder, you can reverse the process of unwrapping the paper off the side. If the bases are not included, then you will get something resembling the shape of a straw. Below we show a net for a circular cylinder including its bases. Notice that the length of the rectangle has to be the same as the circumference of the circular bases.

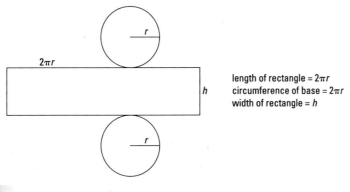

length of rectangle = $2\pi r$
circumference of base = $2\pi r$
width of rectangle = h

Activity

Make a circular cylinder, including at least one base.

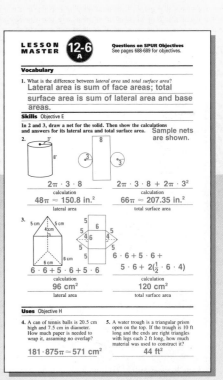

Surface Area of Prisms

Instead of a circular base, you can choose a polygon for a base. Then you can form a figure known as a prism. In a net for a prism, again the length of the rectangle must equal the perimeter of the base. Then the net can be folded into the prism.

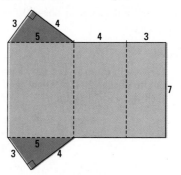

length of rectangle = 5 + 4 + 3 = 12
perimeter of one base = 12
width of rectangle = 7

Example 2

Find the total surface area of the triangular prism whose net is shown above.

Solution

The total surface area is the sum of the areas of the bases of the prism (the triangles) and the lateral area (the rectangle).

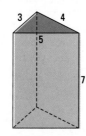

Because of perspective the bases do not look exactly like the net has them

Here is how the prism of Example 2 looks when folded.

Each 3-4-5 right triangle base has area $\frac{1}{2} \cdot 3 \cdot 4$, or 6. The rectangles have area $7 \cdot 3 + 7 \cdot 4 + 7 \cdot 5 = 7(3 + 4 + 5) = 7 \cdot 12 = 84$. So the total surface area is 6 + 84 + 6, or 96 square units.

QUESTIONS

Covering the Reading

9.5 cm

5.4 cm

1. Small juice cans often have a height of 9.5 cm and a base with diameter 5.4 cm.
   a. What is the lateral area of such a can? about 161 cm^2
   b. What is the area of one of its bases? about 23 cm^2
   c. What is its total surface area? about 207 cm^2

672

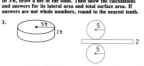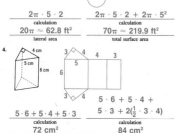
Adapting to Individual Needs

Extra Help

Students may be confused by the fact that some prisms have only rectangular faces, while others involve polygons such as triangles or hexagons. Point out that all prisms, as well as cylinders, have two congruent bases. For prisms, these bases can be any polygon. For circular cylinders, these bases are always circles. Show students diagrams like those below and have them shade both bases with a colored pencil.

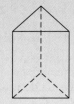

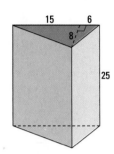

7)
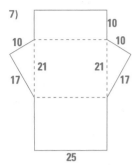
10
10   10
21   21
17   17
25

15   6
8
25

2. Consider the circular cylinder you made in the Activity of this lesson.
   a. What is the height of the cylinder you have made?
   b. What is the radius of its base?
   c. What is its lateral area?
      a, b, c) Answers will vary.

3. Draw a net for a circular cylinder with two bases that is twice as high as the cylinder you made in the Activity of this lesson.

4. Indicate why the net below will not form a circular cylinder with an open top. **The length of the rectangle is about 11.5 cm, and the diameter of the circle is about 2.5 cm. The circumference of the circle = 2.5 π ≈ 7.85 cm. The rectangle is too long for this circle.**

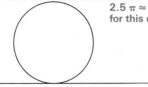

5. Trace the net used in Example 2. Make a triangular prism using the net. **See drawing on page 672. Check students' models.**

6. At the left a triangular prism is drawn.
   a. What is its lateral area? **1200 sq units**
   b. What is the area of one of its bases? **84 sq units**
   c. What is its total surface area? **1368 sq units**

7. Draw a net for the prism of Question 6.
   Placement of bases may vary. See sample net above left.

Applying the Mathematics

8. Convert the dimensions of the cylinder of Question 1 to the nearest $\frac{1}{8}$ inch. Use these dimensions to find the surface area in square inches.
   $d = 2.125''$, $h = 3.75''$, S. A. ≈ 32.125 in², (or ≈ 32.128 in²)

9. Many wood pencils are shaped like hexagonal prisms (prisms whose bases are hexagons). New pencils often have sides of length 4 mm and height (without eraser) of 170 mm. How much surface of the pencil is there to paint? **4080 mm²**

10. Draw a net for a pentagonal prism with a height of 4 cm. (Your pentagon may have any dimensions you wish.)
    Answers will vary. See margin for sample drawing.

11. *Multiple choice.* Suppose each dimension of the can of Example 1 were doubled. What would happen to the total surface area?
    (a) It would be doubled.
    (b) It would be multiplied by 4.
    (c) It would be multiplied by 8.
    (d) It would be multiplied by 16. **(b)**

Lesson 12-6 *Surface Areas of Cylinders and Prisms* **673**

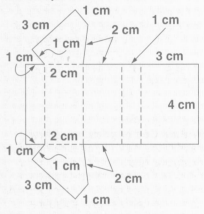

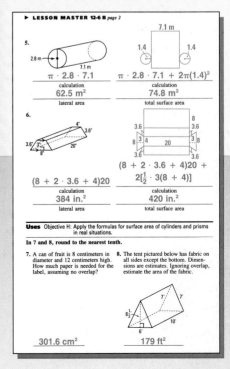

673

Notes on Questions

Question 12 History Connection
The first silver dollars issued in the United States in 1794 were composed of a little less than 90% silver. Most dollar coins minted in the 1970s were made of a copper-nickel combination. A few 1974D and 1977D dollars in silver clad composition were made in error. Interested students might interview coin collectors to learn more about the composition and value of dollar coins minted since 1794.

Follow-up for Lesson 12-6

Practice
For more questions on SPUR Objectives, use **Lesson Master 12-6A** (shown on page 671) or **Lesson Master 12-6B** (shown on pages 672–673).

Assessment
Written Communication Have each student find three different examples of cylinders or prisms in his or her home. Tell students to measure and find the surface area of each cylinder or prism. [Students might present the information in tables that show the dimensions of the figures.]

Students can use the same cylinders and prisms for the *Assessment* in Lesson 12-7. Have students save their data.

Extension
After students have done some activities, you might want to have them generalize and discuss formulas that apply to both right prisms and to right circular cylinders. If h is the height of a figure, and p and B are the perimeter and area respectively of its bases, then the lateral area (*L.A.*) and total surface area (*S.A.*) are:

$$L.A. = ph$$
$$S.A. = 2B + ph$$

Using the formulas for p and B when the base is a circle, we obtain the formula $2\pi r^2 + 2\pi rh$.

Project Update Project 3, *Cylindrical Packages*, and Project 7, *Cones and Pyramids*, on pages 684–685, relate to the content of this lesson.

12a) Area of a silver dollar ≈ 1140.1 mm²; area of a quarter ≈ 463.8 mm². Twice 464 = 928, and 1140 > 928.
b) Silver dollar: C = 38.1π ≈ 119.7 mm; quarter: C = 24.3π ≈ 76.3 mm. Twice 76.3 = 152.6, and 119.7 ≠ 152.6.

12. U.S. silver dollars minted from 1840 to 1978 have a diameter of 38.1 mm. U.S. quarters minted since 1831 have a diameter of 24.3 mm. **a, b)** See below left.
   a. Explain why a silver dollar covers more than twice the area of a quarter.
   b. Explain why a silver dollar does not have twice the circumference of a quarter. *(Lessons 12-4, 12-5)*

13. Suppose the top of a card table is a square 30″ on a side.
   a. What is the area of the tabletop?
   b. What is the perimeter of the tabletop?
   c. What is the length of a diagonal of the tabletop?
   (Lessons 3-8, 5-10, 10-8, 12-3)
   a) 900 in²; b) 120 in.; c) ≈ 42.4 in.

14. Round $\sqrt{500}$ to the nearest integer. *(Lessons 1-4, 12-2)* 22

15. Order from smallest to largest: $\sqrt{10}$ 10^0 10^{-1} 10^1. *(Lessons 2-8, 12-2)* $10^{-1}, 10^0, \sqrt{10}, 10^1$

In 16–19, write as a simple fraction. *(Lessons 2-6, 5-5, 9-3, 12-1)*

16. $\frac{1}{2} + \frac{1}{4} + \frac{1}{8}$ $\frac{7}{8}$

17. $\frac{1}{2} \cdot \frac{1}{4} \cdot \frac{1}{8}$ $\frac{1}{64}$

18. 2.48 $\frac{62}{25}$

19. $2.4\overline{8}$ $\frac{112}{45}$

20. Suppose the area of a triangle is 100 square inches, and its height is 10 inches. What is the length of the base for that height? *(Lessons 10-2, 10-9)* 20 inches

Exploration

21. a. Locate a cylinder or prism with dimensions different from any in this lesson. Describe what you find.
   b. Calculate its total surface area, including bases only if they are part of the object.
   Answers will vary.

Adapting to Individual Needs

Challenge
Have students solve the following problem: Twenty 1-inch cubes are used to make a rectangular prism. What is the greatest possible surface area of this 20-cube prism? What are the dimensions of this prism? [82 in.²; 1 in. by 1 in. by 20 in.]

Setting Up Lesson 12-7

Materials You may want to continue to use the materials suggested for Lesson 12-6. You may also want to have a deck of cards available to show students how a cylindric solid can be formed.

Volumes of Cylinders and Prisms

Silo trio. *Tower silos are often the preferred structure for storing grain crops. With a diameter of 30 ft and a height of 65 ft, one large silo can hold nearly 46,000 cubic feet, or 37,000 bushels, of grain.*

The surface area of a cylinder or prism-shaped container tells how much material is needed to cover the container, but it does not tell how much the container holds. For this the container's *volume* is needed.

In Lesson 9-2, two formulas were given for the volume of a box.

$V = abc$, where a, b, and c are the dimensions of the box.

$V = Bh$, where B is the area of a base and h the height to that base.

We included the second formula because a box is a type of prism, and the second formula applies to all prisms. Furthermore, all prisms and cylinders belong to the family of *cylindric surfaces,* and the formula $V = Bh$ applies to all members of that family.

❶ Cylindric Solids

Any **cylindric solid** can be formed in the following way. Begin with a two-dimensional region F. Now translate that figure out of its plane into 3-dimensional space. Call the image F'. Connect all points of F to the corresponding points on F'. The result is the cylindric solid. The surface of a cylindric solid is called a **cylindric surface.** F and F' are the **bases.**

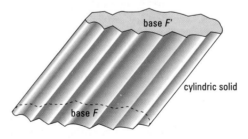

base F'

cylindric solid

base F

Objectives

E Find the volume of cylinders and prisms.

H Apply formulas for the volume of cylinders and prisms in real situations.

Resources

From the *Teacher's Resource File*
- Lesson Master 12-7A or 12-7B
- Answer Master 12-7
- Assessment Sourcebook: Quiz for Lessons 12-4 through 12-7
- Teaching Aid 124: Warm-up

Additional Resources
- Visual for Teaching Aid 124
- Deck of cards, models for cylinders and prisms with various polygonal bases

Teaching Lesson 12-7

Warm-up
The interior of a trailer on a truck is 26 feet long, 8 feet wide, and 7.5 feet high. What is the greatest number of boxes, each 2 feet by 2 feet by 3 feet, that the trailer can hold?
104 boxes

Notes on Reading
❶ You might use a deck of cards to illustrate this idea. Put one card on the table (the two-dimensional region). Then put additional cards on it to build a rectangular solid.

Emphasize that a cylindric solid is solid, like a cucumber. A cylindric surface is empty in the middle, like an empty tin can. The cylindric solids and surfaces include all prisms and all cylinders.

❷ You might want to show students examples of as many of these solids as you have available. Let them handle the figures and identify the bases.

❸ In $V = Bh$, B is an area and thus in square units, and h is the height and thus is a linear unit. When B and h are multiplied, the result is cubic units, as it should be for volume.

The suggestions in *Optional Activities* on page 677 give students hands-on experience finding the volumes of various cylinders and prisms.

❷ There are many kinds of cylindric solids, but in this lesson we are interested only in the simplest ones. For our solids, the translation will be perpendicular to the plane of the base F. Our base F or F' will either be a polygon or a circle. When F is a polygon, a **prism** is formed. Some bricks and some unsharpened pencils are prisms. When F is a circle, the solid is called a **circular cylinder,** or simply a **cylinder.** Aluminum juice cans are quite close to being cylinders.

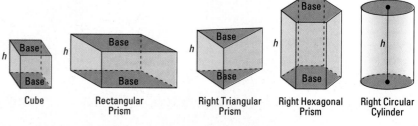

Cube   Rectangular Prism   Right Triangular Prism   Right Hexagonal Prism   Right Circular Cylinder

The distance between the bases is the **height** of the cylinder or prism. To see why the volume formula $V = Bh$ works, think of the prism or cylinder as made up of h layers of height 1 unit. If the base has area B, then each layer has volume B cubic units.

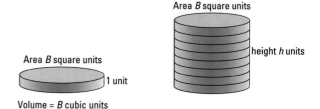

Area B square units

Area B square units

height h units

1 unit

Volume = B cubic units

❸ **Volume Formula for a Cylindric Solid**
The volume of a cylindric solid with height h and base with area B is given by $V = Bh$.

Example 1

A 12-ounce aluminum juice can is about 12 centimeters high. It has a radius of about 3 centimeters. What is its volume?

Solution

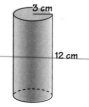

First it is always useful to draw a picture, as at the left. The base is a circle, so its area B is given by
$B = \pi r^2 = \pi \cdot 3^2 = 9\pi$ square centimeters
The volume V is given by
$V = Bh = 9\pi \cdot 12 = 108\pi$ cubic centimeters.
Now is the time to substitute for π.
$V = 108\pi \approx 339$ cubic centimeters.

Check

Information on 12-oz cans state that they contain 355 mL. Since 1 mL $= 1$ cm^3, the answer we found is quite close.

676

Example 2

Pictured here is the outline of a skyscraper that is a prism 356 ft high with a reflection-symmetric pentagon as a base. What is its volume?

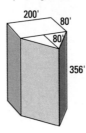

Solution

The pentagonal base, redrawn here, can be split into a triangle and a rectangle.

The area of the rectangle is 200 ft · 80 ft = 16,000 ft².

The area of the triangle is $\frac{1}{2}$ · 200 ft · 80 ft = 8,000 ft².

So the area of the base is 24,000 ft². This is B in the formula V = Bh.

$$V = Bh = 356 \text{ ft} \cdot 24{,}000 \text{ ft}^2 = 8{,}544{,}000 \text{ ft}^3$$

The volume of the skyscraper is about 8,544,000 cubic feet.

3) A cylindric surface is the 2-dimensional surface of a 3-dimensional cylindric solid.

6) Sample:

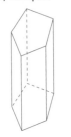

7)

QUESTIONS

Covering the Reading

In 1 and 2, *multiple choice.* Choose from these.
(a) volume   (b) surface area   (c) perimeter

1. how much a container holds (a)

2. how much material it takes to cover a container (b)

3. What is the difference between a cylindric surface and a cylindric solid?

4. A cylindric surface is a cylinder when its base is a __?__. circle

5. A cylindric surface is a prism when its base is a __?__. polygon

6. Draw a prism whose base is a pentagon.

7. Draw a cylinder whose height equals the radius of its base.

8. How is the height of a cylinder or prism measured?
It is the distance between the bases.

Lesson 12-7 *Volumes of Cylinders and Prisms* **677**

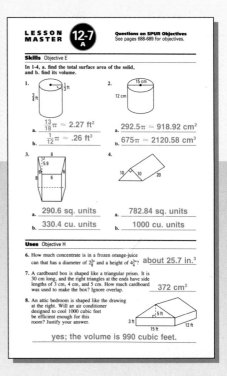
677

Notes on Questions

Question 14 The population would easily fit, which will surprise some students. A good part of the population of the United States could fit in the largest assembly building of Boeing Company in Seattle, Washington. The capacity of that building is about 200,000,000 cubic feet.

Question 25 Give special plaudits for ingenuity. Also, the base need not be a polygon or a circle.

Follow-up for Lesson 12-7

Practice

For more questions on SPUR Objectives, use **Lesson Master 12-7A** (shown on page 677) or **Lesson Master 12-7B** (shown on pages 678–679).

Assessment

Quiz A quiz covering Lessons 12-4 through 12-7 is provided in the *Assessment Sourcebook.*

Written Communication If students completed the assessment in Lesson 12-6, have them use their data to find the volume of the three shapes they found for that assessment. If not, have students find the volume of three cylinders or prisms they find in their homes. [Students demonstrate an ability to use the volume formula.]

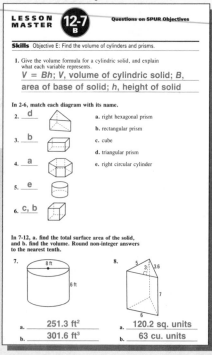

In 9 and 10, find the volume of the figure.

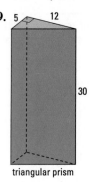

9. triangular prism
900 cubic units

10.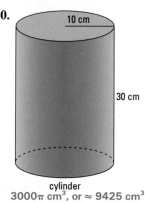
cylinder
3000π cm^3, or $\approx$ 9425 cm^3

11. Find the volume of a cylindrical potato-chip can whose height is 10″ and with a base with diameter 3″. about 71 in^3

12. Find the volume of a prism whose base is a hexagon with area 40 mm^2 and whose height is 30 mm. 1200 mm^3

Applying the Mathematics

13. Give an example of a figure with a large surface area for its volume.
Sample: a compact disc

14. Almost every adult human can easily fit in a space of 6 cubic feet. Could full-size replicas of the entire population of Jacksonville, Florida, about 673,000 people in 1990, fit inside the skyscraper of Example 2? Yes. The replicas would use about 4,000,000 cu ft of the 8,500,000 ft^3 space.

15. a. A book is a prism. Its base is a __?__. rectangle
b. What is the volume of a book whose base has dimensions 6″ and 9″ and whose height is $1\frac{1}{4}$″? 67.5 in^3

16. a. What is the capacity of a plastic straw that is 6 mm in diameter and 200 mm long? about 5655 mm^3
b. What is the surface area of this straw? about 3770 mm^2
c. If the plastic is 0.5 mm thick, how much plastic is needed to make the straw? about 1885 mm^3 of plastic
d. Would you say the straw has a lot of surface area for its volume, or not much surface area for its volume? Explain your choice.
The straw has a lot of surface area for its volume. Numerically, 3770 is about $\frac{2}{3}$ of 5655.

LESSON MASTER 12-7 B Questions on SPUR Objectives

Skills Objective E: Find the volume of cylinders and prisms.

1. Give the volume formula for a cylindric solid, and explain what each variable represents.
$V = Bh$; V, volume of cylindric solid; B, area of base of solid; h, height of solid

In 2-6, match each diagram with its name.
2. d — **a.** right hexagonal prism
3. b — **b.** rectangular prism
4. a — **c.** cube
5. e — **d.** triangular prism
6. c, b — **e.** right circular cylinder

In 7-12, a. find the total surface area of the solid, and b. find the volume. Round non-integer answers to the nearest tenth.
7. a. 251.3 ft^2 b. 301.6 ft^3
8. a. 120.2 sq. units b. 63 cu. units

Adapting to Individual Needs

Extra Help
Materials: A box and cubes or blocks that fit snugly and cover the bottom

Fill the bottom of the box with cubes. Relate the number of cubes used to the length, width, and area of the base. Measure the height of the box. Ask how many layers of cubes will be needed to fill the box. Then relate the total number of blocks needed to fill the box to the volume of the box.

English Language Development
To help students learn the vocabulary in this lesson, you might make a display using actual cylindric solids like those shown on the top of page 676. Label each by name—cube, rectangular prism, and so on. Then label the bases and height of each solid. Note how the name of the base is used in the name of the solid.

17. Here is a net for a cylinder with one base. Find its volume.

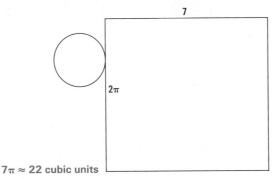

$7\pi \approx 22$ cubic units

Review

18. Give the length of the hypotenuse of the base of Question 9.
(Lesson 12-3) **13**

19. Triangle *ABC* below is equilateral. Find each indicated measure.
(Lessons 8-6, 12-3)

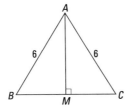

    a. *BC* **6**   **b.** *BM* **3**   **c.** *AM* $\sqrt{27}$, or ≈ 5.2

In 20–23, solve. *(Lessons 5-8, 7-3, 10-2, 10-5, 11-7)*

20. $-31 + x = 42$ **73**   **21.** $-31y = 42$ $-\frac{42}{31}$

22. $\frac{-31}{z} = 42$ $-\frac{31}{42}$ **23.** $-31w - 20 = 42$ **-2**

24. If $a + a + a + a + a + a = ba$, what is the value of *b*? *(Lesson 10-1)*
6

Exploration

25. Give dimensions for a cylindric solid whose volume is exactly 100 cubic meters and whose base is not a rectangle. **Answers will vary. The solid can be any prism in which the area of the base times the height of the prism equals 100 m³. Samples: $B = 2$ m², $h = 50$ m; $B = 10$ m², $h = 10$ m.**

Adapting to Individual Needs

Challenge
Have students solve the following problem. A cylindrical log will be cut into eight equal pieces by using only three straight cuts. How can this be done?

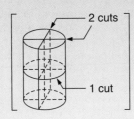
2 cuts
1 cut

Setting Up Lesson 12-8

Materials For Lesson 12-8 you may want to have several examples of spheres, such as balls, a globe, an orange, and so on.

If you use the *Warm-up*, each group of students will need an object shaped like a sphere.

Consumer Connection Have students **work in groups** to design a cereal box based on the following requirements.
1. The capacity is 60 cubic inches.
2. All dimensions are whole numbers less than 10 inches.
3 There is no need to overlap the cardboard.
4. The least possible amount of cardboard is used.
[The box is 3 in. by 4 in. by 5 in. high; it requires 94 in.² of cardboard.]

You might ask students why this might be an actual problem in industry. [Possible response: In real-world manufacturing, containers for products must meet certain requirements, one of which is the cost of materials.]

You might ask students why this might not be an actual problem. [Possible response: In real-world manufacturing, dimensions do not have to be integers and there will be overlap.]

Project Update Project 3, *Cylindrical Packages*, and Project 7, *Cones and Pyramids*, on pages 684–685, relate to the content of this lesson.

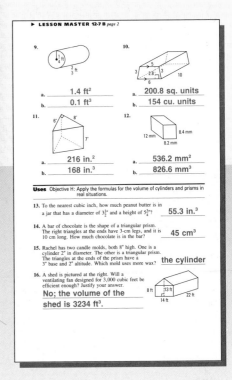

▶ **LESSON MASTER 12-7 B** *page 2*

9.   **10.**

a. 1.4 ft²   **a.** 200.8 sq. units
b. 0.1 ft³   **b.** 154 cu. units

11.   **12.**

a. 216 in.²   **a.** 536.2 mm²
b. 168 in.³   **b.** 826.6 mm³

Uses Objective H: Apply the formulas for the volume of cylinders and prisms in real situations.

13. To the nearest cubic inch, how much peanut butter is in a jar that has a diameter of $3\frac{1}{2}''$ and a height of $5\frac{1}{2}''$? **55.3 in.³**

14. A bar of chocolate is the shape of a triangular prism. The right triangles at the ends have 3-cm legs, and it is 10 cm long. How much chocolate is in the bar? **45 cm³**

15. Rachel has two candle molds, both 8″ high. One is a cylinder 2″ in diameter. The other is a triangular prism. The triangles at the ends of the prism have a 3″ base and 2″ altitude. Which mold uses more wax? **the cylinder**

16. A shed is pictured at the right. Will a ventilating fan designed for 3,000 cubic feet be efficient enough? Justify your answer. **No; the volume of the shed is 3234 ft³.**

Objectives

F Find the surface area and volume of a sphere, given its radius or diameter.

I Apply the formulas for the surface area and volume of a sphere in real situations.

Resources

From the Teacher's Resource File
- Lesson Master 12-8A or 12-8B
- Answer Master 12-8
- Teaching Aids
  124 Warm-up
  132 Formulas to Know

Additional Resources
- Visuals for Teaching Aids 124, 132
- A variety of objects shaped like spheres

Teaching
Lesson 12-8

Warm-up

Work in groups.

1. Make a list of objects in the real world that are shaped like spheres. **Samples: various balls, globes, marbles, oranges, bubbles, planets**

2. Select a spherical object. Find its diameter and explain how you did it. **Methods will vary. Some groups may put two cards parallel against the sphere and measure the distance between them; others may use a tape to find the circumference and then use the formula $C = \pi d$ to find the diameter.**

A sporting chance. *Can you name the sport for each of these balls?*

Formulas for Spheres

A **sphere** is the set of points *in space* at a given distance (its **radius**) from a given point (its **center**). Drawn below is a sphere with radius *r*.

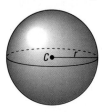

Planets and moons, baseballs, marbles, and many other objects are nearly the shape of spheres. A sphere is like a soap bubble. It doesn't include any points inside. Even the center *C* of a sphere is not a point on the sphere. A sphere together with all the points inside it is called a **ball**.

The formulas for the surface area and volume of a sphere were first discovered by the Greek mathematician Archimedes. You will learn how these formulas were found when you study geometry in more detail in a later course. Like formulas for the area and circumference of a circle, they involve the number π.

> **Surface Area and Volume Formulas for a Sphere**
> In a sphere with radius *r*, surface area *S*, and volume *V*,
> $$S = 4\pi r^2$$
> and $V = \frac{4}{3}\pi r^3$.

Lesson 12-8 Overview

Broad Goals Students should be able to apply the formulas for the surface area and volume of a sphere.

Perspective We study the formulas for the surface area and volume of a sphere here because spheres are so common, because these formulas also involve π, and because it is useful for students to see these formulas before they study geometry in more detail later.

The derivations of the formulas for the surface area and the volume of a sphere are more complicated than for other figures. The difficulty is reflected in the fact that a sphere does not have a two-dimensional net. As a result, all of the derivations utilize ideas of limits. You can find derivations in *UCSMP Geometry* and in many other geometry texts.

Students may look for some intuitive connection between the surface area formula $S = 4\pi r^2$ and the area formula $A = \pi r^2$ for a circle. It is natural to think that they are connected, but we know of no simple intuitive connection.

The exponents in these formulas signal the units in which surface area and volume are measured. The surface area of a sphere is measured in square units, just as any other area is, even though the surface of a sphere cannot be flattened. Volume is measured in cubic units.

Example 1

Find the volume of a sphere with radius 6.

Solution 1

Find the exact value. Let V be the volume.

$$V = \frac{4}{3}\pi r^3 = \frac{4}{3}\pi \cdot 6^3 = \frac{4}{3}\pi \cdot 216 = 288\pi \text{ cubic units.}$$

288π is the exact value. To get an approximate value, substitute an estimate for π, say 3.14. Then $V \approx 288 \cdot 3.14 \approx 904$ cubic units.

Solution 2

Use a calculator. Here is a key sequence that works on many calculators.

$$4 \boxed{\div} 3 \boxed{\times} \boxed{\pi} \boxed{\times} 6 \boxed{y^x} 3 \boxed{=}$$

To the nearest hundredth, a calculator will give 904.78. This differs from the answer of Solution 1 because a different estimate is used for π.

The Earth is not exactly a sphere because its rotation has flattened it slightly at the poles. The length of the equator is about 24,902 miles, while its circumference through the poles is about 24,860 miles. Dividing these circumferences by π, we find diameters of about 7927 and 7913 miles. These lengths are double the radii, so the Earth is nearly a sphere with radius 3960 miles.

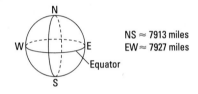

NS ≈ 7913 miles
EW ≈ 7927 miles

Example 2

Estimate the surface area of the Earth.

Solution

The formula for surface area is $S = 4\pi r^2$. Substitute 3960 for r. Here is a key sequence that will work on many calculators.

$$4 \boxed{\times} \boxed{\pi} \boxed{\times} 3960 \boxed{x^2} \boxed{=}$$

(By using the squaring key, 3960 does not have to be entered twice.) The calculator should display a result close to 197,000,000 square miles.

The surface area of the Earth is about 197 million square miles.

Lesson 12-8 *Spheres* **681**

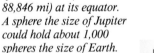

Shown is Jupiter, the largest planet in the solar system. It has a diameter of 142,984 km (about 88,846 mi) at its equator. A sphere the size of Jupiter could hold about 1,000 spheres the size of Earth.

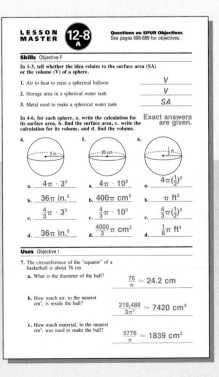

Optional Activities

Activity 1 Science Connection
As a follow-up activity for this lesson, you might ask students to draw a cross section of the earth, showing the liquid and solid cores, the mantle, and the crust. [The inner core extends from the center of the earth to about 800 miles; the liquid outer core extends another 1400 miles; the mantle extends from the outer core to within 5 to 25 miles of the earth's surface; the last 5 to 25 miles compose the earth's crust.]

Activity 2 Architecture Connection
After studying this lesson, some students might find examples of buildings or other structures that look similar to spheres or hemispheres (half spheres). You might suggest that they find information about the geosphere at Walt Disney World® Epcot Center, or the geodesic dome at Expo 67 in Montreal, or domed buildings such as the Capitol in Washington, D.C.

681

After discussing this lesson, you might want to review the formulas presented in the chapter. Use **Teaching Aid 132** or the list of formulas on page 686. For each formula, have students make a sketch, and identify the variables in the formula on the sketch.

Additional Examples

1. How much plastic is required to make a beach ball 20 inches in diameter? **400π in.² ≈ 1256 in.²**
2. How much air is needed to blow up the ball?
   $\frac{4000}{3}$ **π in.³ ≈ 4189 in.³**

Notes on Questions

Questions 10–13 These questions reinforce the difference between surface area and volume.

Question 16 Most people estimate an answer much greater than the actual percent. The smallest box that could be used is 12 cm by 12 cm by 12 cm.

Question 17 Multicultural Connection Students might research the game of *mancala*, and explain to the class the origin of the game and how it is played.

Question 25 Geography Connection Students might find the percent of the earth's total land area for each of the countries larger than the United States. [Russia ≈11.4%, Canada ≈ 6.6%, China ≈ 6.4%]

On the moon. *John Young is shown here walking on the moon in April of 1972 as part of the Apollo 16 mission. Young's crew brought back 98 kg of lunar rocks and soil for scientific research.*

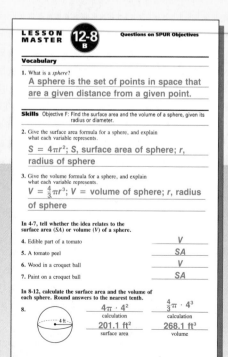
QUESTIONS

Covering the Reading

1. What is a *sphere*?
   the set of points in space at a certain distance from a certain point
2. Why is the Earth not exactly a sphere?
   The Earth is flatter at the poles due to the rotation on its axis.
3. Give a formula for the surface area of a sphere.
   In a sphere with radius *r* and surface area S, $S = 4\pi r^2$.
4. Calculate the surface area of a sphere with radius 12 cm.
   576π or about 1810 cm²
5. Give a formula for the volume of a sphere.
   In a sphere with radius *r* and volume V, $V = \frac{4}{3}\pi r^3$.
6. Calculate the volume of a sphere with radius 12 cm.
   2304π or about 7238 cm³
7. Who discovered the formulas for the surface area and volume of a sphere? Archimedes

8. **a.** What calculator sequence will yield the volume of a sphere with radius 7?   4 ÷ 3 × π × 7 y^x 3 =
   b. Find the volume of the sphere. about 1437 cubic units

9. The moon is approximately a sphere with radius 1080 miles.
   a. Estimate the surface area of the moon to the nearest million square miles. 15 million square miles
   b. The surface area of the Earth is how many times the surface area of the moon? about 13 times

Applying the Mathematics

In 10–13, tell whether the idea is more like surface area or volume.

10. how much land there is in the United States surface area

11. how much material is in a bowling ball volume

12. how much material it takes to make a basketball surface area

13. how much material is in a marble volume

In 14 and 15, use this information. A bowling ball is approximately 8.59 inches in diameter.

14. How much surface does a bowling ball have? (Ignore the finger holes.) about 232 square inches

15. How much material does it take to make a bowling ball? about 332 cubic inches

16. If a 12-cm diameter ball fits snugly into a box, what percent of the box is filled by the ball? about 52%

Adapting to Individual Needs

Extra Help
In the formula for surface area of a sphere, some students will incorrectly multiply the radius by 2 instead of taking the second power. Similarly, they may incorrectly multiply the radius by 3 when applying the formula for the volume of a sphere. Have students copy and complete the two sentences at the right for a sphere with a radius of 5.

Then have them complete the sentences for spheres with other numbers for the radii or diameter.

1. When the radius of a sphere is 5, the formula for surface area is $S = 4\pi r^2$.
   So $S \approx 4 \cdot 3.14 \cdot \_\_\_ \cdot \_\_\_$. [5 · 5]

2. When the radius of a sphere is 5, the formula for the volume is $V = \frac{4}{3}\pi r^3$.
   So $V \approx \frac{4}{3} \cdot 3.14 \cdot \_\_\_ \cdot \_\_\_ \cdot \_\_\_$.
   [5 · 5 · 5]

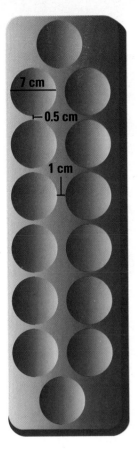

7 cm

0.5 cm

1 cm

17. At the left is a drawing of a board for the game *mancala,* played throughout the world. The version popular in Ghana begins by having players place stones in the "circles" (actually halves of spheres) on their side of the board. The end circles are used primarily to store the stones you "capture" from your opponent. Traditionally, the game board is carved out of a solid piece of wood.
   a. Determine the minimum dimensions of the piece of wood you would need for the game board shown at the left. **59.5 cm by 16 cm**
   b. If you had two pieces of wood, one 4 cm × 16 cm × 80 cm, and the other 4 cm × 32 cm × 60 cm, which would you use to make the game board? Explain your choice. **Answers may vary. Sample: Use the 4 cm × 32 cm × 60 cm piece and make two game boards with no waste. The other piece will have unusable waste.**

Review

In 18 and 19, consider a tube for carrying a fishing rod that is a cylinder 8′ long and 6″ in diameter.

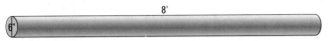

8′

6″

18. What is the volume of this tube?   *(Lesson 12-7)*   **about 2714 in³ or about 1.57 ft³**
19. What is the total surface area of this container?   *(Lesson 12-6)*   **about 1866 in² or about 13 ft²**
20. From the top of a tall building, a person can see 25 kilometers away in any direction. How many square kilometers are then visible?   *(Lesson 12-5)*   **625π km² or about 1963 km²**

21. The repeating decimal $1.\overline{41}$ is within .0002 of $\sqrt{2}$. What simple fraction equals $1.\overline{41}$?   *(Lesson 12-1)* $\frac{140}{99}$

22. The surface area of the Earth is given in this lesson. Only about 29.4% of the surface area is land.
   a. To the nearest million square miles, what is the total land area of the Earth?   *(Lesson 2-5)*   **58 million square miles**
   b. The area of the United States is approximately 3,540,000 square miles. What percent of the total land area of the Earth is in the United States?   *(Lesson 11-5)*   **about 6%**

23) Sample:
100 Most Influential Persons in History

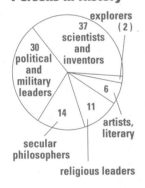

explorers (2)
37 scientists and inventors
30 political and military leaders
6
14
11
artists, literary
secular philosophers
religious leaders

23. According to Michael H. Hart in the book *The 100,* the 100 most influential persons in history include 37 scientists and inventors, 30 political and military leaders, 14 secular philosophers, 11 religious leaders, 6 artists and literary figures, and 2 explorers. Make a circle graph with this information.   *(Lesson 3-6)*

24. The mass of the Earth is about 6 sextillion, 588 quintillion short tons. Write this number as a decimal.   *(Lesson 2-2)*
   6,588,000,000,000,000,000,000

Exploration

25. Refer to Question 22b. What three countries of the world have more land area than the United States? (Look in an almanac for this information, or look at a globe.) **Russia, Canada, China**

Follow-up 12-8
for Lesson

Practice
For more questions of SPUR Objective, use **Lesson Master 12-8A** (shown on page 681) or **Lesson Master 12-8B** (shown on pages 682–683).

Assessment
Written Communication Tell students to write problems that involve using either the surface area or volume formula for a sphere. Then have them solve their problems. [Students recognize the difference between surface area and volume of a sphere, and demonstrate their ability to use a formula.]

Extension
You might have students find what happens to the volume of a sphere when the radius is doubled and when it is tripled. [Multiplied by 2³, or 8; multiplied by 3³, or 27]

Project Update Project 6, *Weights of Spheres,* on page 685, relates to the content of this lesson.

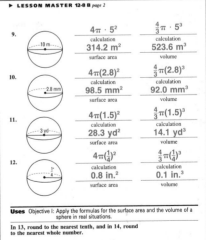

▶ **LESSON MASTER 12-8 B** *page 2*

	calculation	calculation
9. (10 m)	$4\pi \cdot 5^2$ **314.2 m²** surface area	$\frac{4}{3}\pi \cdot 5^3$ **523.6 m³** volume
10. (2.8 mm)	$4\pi(2.8)^2$ **98.5 mm²** surface area	$\frac{4}{3}\pi(2.8)^3$ **92.0 mm³** volume
11. (3 yd)	$4\pi(1.5)^2$ **28.3 yd²** surface area	$\frac{4}{3}\pi(1.5)^3$ **14.1 yd³** volume
12. ($\frac{1}{4}$)	$4\pi(\frac{1}{4})^2$ **0.8 in.²** surface area	$\frac{4}{3}\pi(\frac{1}{4})^3$ **0.1 in.³** volume

Uses Objective I: Apply the formulas for the surface area and the volume of a sphere in real situations.

In 13, round to the nearest tenth, and in 14, round to the nearest whole number.

13. The diameter of a ping-pong ball is 1.5″.
   a. How much air is inside the ball?   **1.8 in.³**
   b. How much plastic was used to make the ball?   **7.1 in.²**

14. The dome on a courthouse is shaped like a hemisphere (half of a sphere) with a diameter of 7.2 meters.
   a. How much copper covers the dome?   **81 m²**
   b. How much air is inside the dome?   **98 m³**

Adapting to Individual Needs

Challenge
Have students imagine that a sphere fits snugly into a cylinder—the diameter and the height of the cylinder being the same as the diameter of the sphere. Then suggest that they compare the formulas for the volume of each solid to determine what fraction of the volume of the cylinder gives the volume of the sphere.

First note the formula for the volume of a cylinder with the same diameter and height: $V = Bh = \pi r^2 \cdot 2r = 2\pi r^3$. Then compare the formulas.

$$\frac{\text{Volume of sphere}}{\text{Volume of cylinder}} = \frac{\frac{4}{3}\pi r^3}{2\pi r^3} = \frac{\frac{4}{3}}{2} = \frac{2}{3}$$

[The volume of the sphere is two thirds the volume of the cylinder.]

683

Chapter 12 Projects

Chapter 12 projects relate to the content of the lessons as follows.

Project	Lesson(s)
1	12-4
2	12-3
3	12-6, 12-7
4	12-4
5	12-1, 12-2
6	12-8
7	12-6, 12-7

1 Complex Numbers Students can find information about complex numbers in algebra textbooks, encyclopedias, and mathematics dictionaries. Carl Friedrich Gauss (1777–1855) is generally credited with being the first mathematician to use the term "complex number." He applied complex numbers to the study of electricity.

2 A 3-Dimensional Pythagorean Pattern Students may be surprised to discover that there is an infinite number of solutions to this problem. Encourage them to find solutions other than multiples of the dimensions given in the project.

3 Cylindrical Packages This can be presented as a group project. Have groups of students decide how many containers each person will measure. Then suggest that the groups combine and arrange the data in organized lists. Each group should decide if a particular ratio is the most common and if the diameter or height of a container is usually larger. Have each group discuss reasons for its findings.

4 Approximations to π A useful reference is *A History of π* by Petr Beckmann. Dorset Books Reprint Services offers a 1990 reprint of the 1971 edition, published by Golem Press, Boulder, Colorado.

Students may be interested in finding out about the Indian mathematician Srinivasa Ramanujan, who developed a method that allowed one to find millions of digits of π.

PROJECTS 12 CHAPTER TWELVE

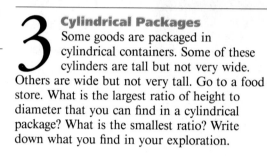

1 Complex Numbers
In the 16th century, Italian mathematicians began to realize that it was possible to work with square roots of negative numbers. These numbers, which are not real numbers—they cannot be represented by a single decimal—were later called *imaginary numbers* and are part of the set of numbers known as *complex numbers*. Write an essay about these numbers and where they are used.

2 A 3-dimensional Pythagorean Pattern
The longest diagonal of a box stretches inside the box from one corner to the far opposite corner. If the dimensions of the box are *a, b,* and *c* and the diagonal has length *d*, then $d^2 = a^2 + b^2 + c^2$. For instance, if the box has dimensions 3, 4, and 12, then the length *d* of the longest diagonal satisfies $d^2 = 3^2 + 4^2 + 12^2 = 9 + 16 + 144 = 169$, so $d = 13$. Find boxes of other shapes in which all the dimensions and the longest diagonal have *integer* lengths.

3 Cylindrical Packages
Some goods are packaged in cylindrical containers. Some of these cylinders are tall but not very wide. Others are wide but not very tall. Go to a food store. What is the largest ratio of height to diameter that you can find in a cylindrical package? What is the smallest ratio? Write down what you find in your exploration.

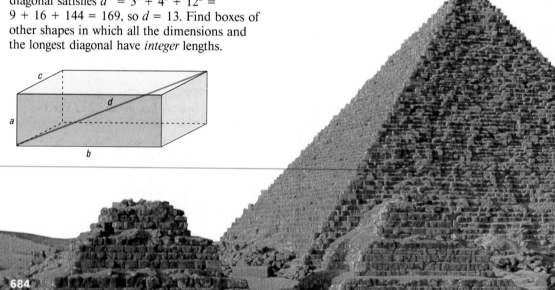

684

Possible responses
1. The following information is a sample of what students might include in their projects. A complex number is a number of the form *a* + *b*i where *a* and *b* are real numbers and i = $\sqrt{-1}$; *a* is called the real part and *b* is called the imaginary part. A complex number *a* + *b*i is a real number if *b* = 0 and an imaginary number if *b* ≠ 0. The Commutative, Associative, and Distributive Properties of Addition and Multiplication hold for complex numbers. Complex numbers are used in electrical engineering, in the study of geometry and acoustics, and to create computer-generated drawings.
2. Sample response: Any three numbers that are found by multiplying 1, 2, 2 or 2, 3, 6 or 3, 4, 12 by the same number will result in boxes for which all the dimensions and the longest diagonal will have integer lengths.

4 Approximations to π

The number π (pi) has a long history. People from many cultures, including the Chinese, Hindus, Egyptians, and Greeks, used approximations over 500 years ago. Find out what these approximations to π were. If possible, find out how at least one of the approximations was determined.

5 The Number of Digits in a Repetend

The number of digits in the repetend of a repeating decimal for a fraction is determined by the denominator of the fraction. If the denominator is not divisible by 2 or 5, then the length is determined by the first of the numbers 9, 99, 999, 9999, . . . into which it divides evenly. Use this information to find all the denominators of this type that have repetends with 1 digit, all with 2 digits, all with 3 digits, and all with 4 digits. Go further if you can.

6 Weights of Spheres

We come into contact with spheres of many different sizes. Tennis balls, basketballs, and ball bearings are just a few of the things with this shape. Find at least five different spheres and weigh them. Which has the greatest weight per unit volume? Which has the least weight per unit volume?

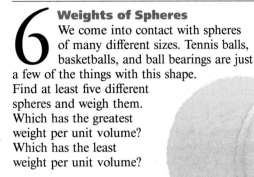

7 Cones and Pyramids

There are formulas for surface area and volume of cones and pyramids. Find out what these formulas are and how they are related to the formulas for cylinders and prisms. Make up some sample problems using these formulas.

cone   pyramid

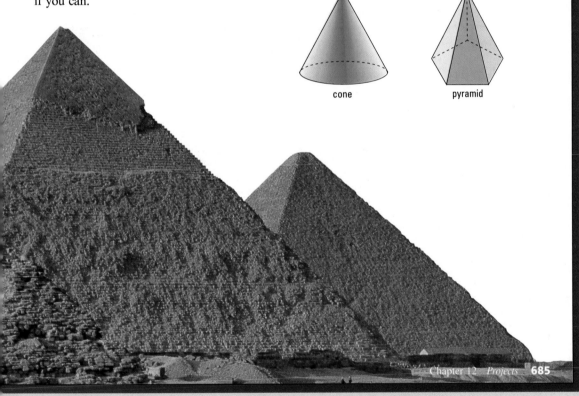

3. Responses will vary.
4. The following information is a sample of what students might include in their projects. Ancient Chinese mathematicians used 3 as a value of pi. Early sixth century Indian mathematicians confirmed a value of π that was equivalent to 3.1416. Egyptians used $\left(\frac{4}{3}\right)^4$ as a value of π. The Greek mathematician, Archimedes, used polygons of 96 sides inscribed in and circumscribed about a circle. His approximations of the area of a circle led to a value of π between $3\frac{1}{7}$ and $3\frac{10}{71}$.

(Responses continue on page 686.)

5 The Number of Digits in a Repetend
Students may require some assistance with this project. Make sure they understand that they will be using only denominators that do not have 2 or 5 as factors. Encourage them to look for patterns as they start finding denominators that have the required number of digits in the repetends. Lead them to see that denominators that have 1-digit repetends are factors of 9, and denominators that have 2-digit repetends are factors of 99. Suggest that students find the prime factorization of 999 [3 × 3 × 3 × 37] and 9999 [3 × 3 × 11 × 101], and use that information to find denominators with 3- and 4-digit repetends.

6 Weights of Spheres
Remind students that they can find the diameter of a sphere by finding the circumference and dividing by π. The circumference can be found by wrapping a string around the sphere and measuring the length of the string. Once the diameter is known, students should have little difficulty finding the volume of the sphere.

An almanac or sports dictionary will provide information about the standard size and weight of a variety of balls.

Remind students that the same units of volume and weight must be used for all spheres in order to compare weight per unit volume.

7 Cones and Pyramids
The relationship between the volumes of the cones and cylinders and between the volumes of the prisms and pyramids may be surprising to some students. You may wish to have students make pairs of paper cylinders and cones with the same height and radius. Then have students fill the cones with dry beans or popcorn kernels and pour them into the cylinders. Have students count the number of times they need to do this to fill the containers. They may repeat the activity with pairs of cones and cylinders of other sizes.

Summary

The Summary gives an overview of the entire chapter and provides an opportunity for students to consider the material as a whole. Thus, the Summary can be used to help students relate and unify the concepts presented in the chapter.

Vocabulary

Terms, symbols, and properties are listed by lesson to provide a checklist of concepts a student must know. Emphasize to students that they should read the vocabulary list carefully before starting the Progress Self-Test. If students do not understand the meaning of a term, they should refer back to the indicated lesson.

SUMMARY

Numbers that can be represented as decimals are called real numbers. The real numbers are of two types: rational and irrational. The rational numbers are those that can be written as simple fractions. All finite and all infinite repeating decimals are rational numbers. Using algebra, it is possible to find a fraction for any infinite repeating decimal.

Irrational numbers have infinite decimals that do not repeat. The number π is irrational. If a square root of a positive integer is not an integer, the square root is irrational. Lengths, areas, and volumes may be rational or irrational.

Formulas for the areas and volumes of many common figures show the importance of irrational numbers. The following formulas are in this chapter. You should look back at the lessons for the meanings of the variables in them.

Pythagorean Theorem: $a^2 + b^2 = c^2$

Circumference of a circle: $C = \pi d$

Area of a circle: $A = \pi r^2$

Lateral area of a cylinder: $L.A. = hC$

Total surface area of a cylinder: $S.A. = 2\pi r^2 + 2\pi rh$

Area of a sector: $A = \frac{m}{360}\pi r^2$

Volume of a cylindric solid: $V = Bh$

Surface area of a sphere: $S = 4\pi r^2$

Volume of a sphere: $V = \frac{4}{3}\pi r^3$

VOCABULARY

You should be able to give a general description and a specific example for each of the following ideas.

Lesson 12-1
infinite repeating decimal

Lesson 12-2
square root
radical sign, $\sqrt{}$, $\pm$

Lesson 12-3
Pythagorean Theorem
theorem
Pythagoras

Lesson 12-4
radii
circumference
π
Formula for Circumference of a Circle
rational number
irrational number
real number

Lesson 12-5
Area Formula for a Circle
Area formula for a Sector

Lesson 12-6
lateral area (*L.A.*)
total surface area (*S.A.*)

Lesson 12-7
cylindric surface
cylindric solid
base, height
prism
circular cylinder, cylinder
Volume Formula for a Cylindric Solid

Lesson 12-8
sphere, ball
center, radius, diameter of a sphere
Surface Area Formula for a Sphere
Volume Formula for a Sphere

686

Additional responses, page 685
5. Fractions with the following denominators have:
1-digit repetends: 3, 9
2-digit repetends: 11, 33, 99
3-digit repetends: 27, 37, 111, 333, 999
4-digit repetends: 101, 303, 909, 1111, 3333, 9999
5-digit repetends: 41, 123, 271, 369, 813, 2439, 11,111, 33,333, 99,999

6. Responses will vary.
7. Volume of a cone: $V = \frac{1}{3}\pi r^2 h$
Surface area of a cone: $S = \pi r^2 + \pi r\ell$
Volume of a pyramid: $V = \frac{1}{3}Bh$
Surface area of a pyramid:
$$S = \frac{1}{2}p\ell + B$$

The volume of a cone is one third the volume of a cylinder with the same height and radius, and the volume of a pyramid is one-third the volume of a prism with the same base and height. Sample problems will vary.

PROGRESS SELF-TEST

Take this test as you would take a test in class. Then check your work with the solutions in the Selected Answers section in the back of the book.

1. A circle has radius $\frac{3''}{8}$. Find its circumference and area to the nearest tenth. **1)** $C \approx 2.4''$; $A \approx 0.44\ in^2$

2. What is the area of a square if one side has length $\sqrt{3}$? **3 sq units**

3. If a square has area 10, what is the exact length of a side? $\sqrt{10}$ **units**

4. Estimate $\sqrt{33} + \sqrt{51}$ to the nearest integer. ≈ 13

5. Find x.

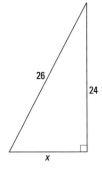

10

6. Find the length of $\overline{AC}$. $\sqrt{125}$

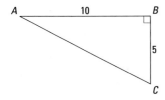

7. Which number is rational? $\sqrt{24}\ \ \sqrt{25}\ \ \sqrt{27}$. $\sqrt{25}$

In 8 and 9, Find a simple fraction in lowest terms equal to the given number.

8. -2.7 $-\frac{27}{10}$

9. $0.\overline{15}$ $\frac{5}{33}$

10. An empty 12-oz aluminum can has a diameter of approximately 57 mm and a height of approximately 123 mm. To the nearest 10 square millimeters, about how much aluminum was used to make this can? $\approx 27{,}130\ mm^2$

In 11 and 12, use the triangular prism shown below.

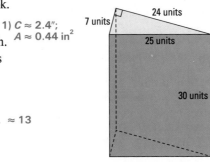

1680 sq units

11. What is the lateral area of this prism?

12. What is the volume of this prism? **2520 units³**

13. Name the two square roots of 16. **4 and -4**

14. To the nearest integer, what is the circumference of a 120-mm diameter compact disc? **377 mm**   **15)** 256π **units²**

15. A circle has radius 16. What is its exact area?

16. When does a decimal represent an irrational number? **See below.**

17. All basketballs are hollow. If one has a radius of about 12 cm, about how much material is needed to make it? **1810 cm²**

18. a. What is the exact volume of a sphere with radius 9? 972π **cubic units**

    b. Round your answer to the nearest cubic unit. **3054 cu units**

19. The diameter of Mars is approximately 7000 kilometers. Estimate the surface area of Mars. **about 154,000,000 km²**

20. A circle has a diameter of 12 cm. What is the exact area of a sector of this circle if the central angle of the sector is 60°? 6π **cm²**

16) **when the decimal does not terminate or infinitely repeat**

Progress Self-Test

For the development of mathematical competence, feedback and correction, along with the opportunity to practice, are necessary. The Progress Self-Test provides the opportunity for feedback and correction; the Chapter Review provides additional opportunities and practice. We cannot overemphasize the importance of these end-of-chapter materials. It is at this point that the material "gels" for many students, allowing them to solidify skills and understanding. In general, student performance should be markedly improved after these pages.

Assign the Progress Self-Test as a one-night assignment. Worked-out solutions for all questions are in the Selected Answers section of the student book. Encourage students to take the Progress Self-Test honestly to grade themselves, and then to be prepared to discuss the test in class.

Advise students to pay special attention to those Chapter Review questions (pages 688–689) which correspond to questions missed on the Progress Self-Test.

Chapter 12 Review

Resources

From the *Teacher's Resource File*
■ Answer Master for
  Chapter 12 Review
■ Assessment Sourcebook
  Chapter 12 Test, Forms A–D
  Chapter 12 Test, Cumulative
  Form

Additional Resources
■ TestWorks

The main objectives for the chapter are organized in the Chapter Review under the four types of understanding this book promotes—Skills, Properties, Uses, and Representations.

Whereas end-of chapter material may be considered optional in some texts, in *UCSMP Transition Mathematics*, we have selected these objectives and questions with the expectation that they will be covered. Students should be able to answer these questions with about 85% accuracy after studying the chapter.

You may assign these questions over a single night to help students prepare for a test the next day, or you may assign the questions over a two-day period. If you work the questions over two days, then we recommend assigning the *evens* for homework the first night so that students get feedback in class the next day and assigning the *odds* the night before the test because answers are provided to the odd-numbered questions.

It is effective to ask students which questions they still do not understand and to use the day or days as a total class discussion of the material which the class finds most difficult.

688

CHAPTER REVIEW

Questions on SPUR Objectives

SPUR stands for **S**kills, **P**roperties, **U**ses, and **R**epresentations. The Chapter Review questions are grouped according to the SPUR Objectives for this chapter.

SKILLS DEAL WITH THE PROCEDURES USED TO GET ANSWERS.

Objective A: *Find a simple fraction equal to any terminating or repeating decimal.* *(Lesson 12-1)*

In 1–4, find the simple fraction in lowest terms equal to the given number.

1. $-1.\overline{23}$ 2. $0.0\overline{46}$ 3. 81.55 4. 11.02
   $\frac{122}{99}$ $\frac{23}{495}$ $\frac{1631}{20}$ $\frac{551}{50}$

Objective B: *Estimate square roots of a number without a calculator.* *(Lesson 12-2)*

5. Between what two integers is $\sqrt{80}$? 8 and 9
6. Between what two integers is $-\sqrt{3}$? –2 and –1
7. Simplify $\sqrt{144 + 256}$. 20
8. Name the two square roots of 36. 6 and –6

Objective C: *Use the Pythagorean Theorem to find unknown lengths of third sides in right triangles.* *(Lesson 12-3)*

9. Find BI in the figure at the left below. $\sqrt{73}$
10. Find HA in the figure at the right below. 16

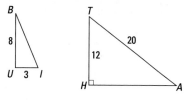

11. The legs of a right triangle have lengths 20 and 48. What is the length of the hypotenuse of this triangle? 52
12. Find y in the figure below. $\sqrt{3}$

Objective D: *Find the circumference and area of a circle or sector, given its radius or diameter.* *(Lessons 12-4, 12-5)*

13. Find the circumference and area of a circle with radius 10. $C = 20\pi$ units; $A = 100\pi$ sq units
14. To the nearest whole number, find the circumference and area of a circle with diameter 2 meters. $C \approx 6$ m; $A \approx 3$ m^2
15. Give the area of a 90° sector of a circle with radius 5 feet. $\frac{25}{4}\pi$ sq ft
16. To the nearest square unit, give the area of a 100° sector of a circle with radius 6. 31 sq units

Objective E: *Find the surface area and volume of cylinders and prisms.* *(Lessons 12-6, 12-7)*

In 17 and 18, a cylinder has a base of radius 5 units and height of 6 units.

17. Find its surface area. 110π units^2
18. Find its volume. 150π units^3

In 19 and 20, a prism has a base that is a right triangle with legs 20 and 21, and a height of 12.

19. Find its volume. 2520 units^3
20. Find its total surface area. 1260 units^2

Objective F: *Find the surface area and volume of a sphere, given its radius or diameter.* *(Lesson 12-8)*

21. A sphere has diameter 10. Give its exact surface area. 100 π units^2
22. To the nearest cubic inch, give the volume of a sphere with radius 4″. 268 in^3

PROPERTIES DEAL WITH THE PRINCIPLES BEHIND THE MATHEMATICS.

Objective G: *Identify numbers as rational, irrational, or real.* *(Lesson 12-4)*

23. Which of these numbers are rational?

π 3.14 $\frac{22}{7}$ $3\frac{1}{7}$

3.14, $\frac{22}{7}$, $3\frac{1}{7}$

24. Which of these numbers are irrational?

$\sqrt{2}$ $\sqrt{3}$ $\sqrt{4}$ $\sqrt{5}$ $\sqrt{2}$, $\sqrt{3}$, $\sqrt{5}$

25. When does a decimal represent a real number? **always**

USES DEAL WITH APPLICATIONS OF MATHEMATICS IN REAL SITUATIONS.

Objective H: *Apply formulas for the surface area and volume of cylinders and prisms in real situations.* *(Lessons 12-6, 12-7)*

26. How much wood is needed to make a cylindrical pencil 17 cm long and 1 cm in diameter? (Ignore the lead.) $\approx$ **13.4 cm³**

27. The side of a cylindrical oil storage tank is to be painted. If the tank is 60′ high and has a circumference of 400′, how much surface area needs to be painted? **24,000 ft²**

In 28 and 29, use the triangular prism ruler pictured here. The base of the prism is an equilateral triangle.

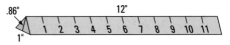

.86″   12″

1″

1 2 3 4 5 6 7 8 9 10 11

28. Give its lateral surface area. **36 in²**
29. Give its volume. **5.16 in³**

Objective I: *Apply formulas for the circumference of a circle and area of a circle or sector and surface area and volume of a sphere in real situations.* *(Lessons 12-4, 12-5, 12-8)*

30. A child is lost in the forest. Police decide to search every place within 2 miles of the place the child was last seen. To the nearest square mile, how much area must be searched? $\approx$ **13 mi²**

31. What is the surface area of a ball 20 cm in diameter? **400π or $\approx$ 1256.6 cm²**

32. Pearl is making a color wheel for school. She wants to put 12 equal-sized sectors on the wheel. What is the area of one of those sectors if the wheel is to be 18″ in diameter?

33. The Earth goes around the sun in an orbit that is almost a circle with radius 150,000,000 km. How far does the Earth travel in one year in its orbit?

34. How much clay is needed to make a ball with a 4″ diameter? $\frac{32}{3}\pi \approx$ **33.5 in³**

35. To the nearest cubic centimeter, what is the volume of a soap bubble with a radius of 1.5 centimeters? $\approx$ **14.1 cm³**

32) $\approx$ **21.2 in²**;   33) $\approx$ **942,000,000 km**

REPRESENTATIONS DEAL WITH PICTURES, GRAPHS, OR OBJECTS THAT ILLUSTRATE CONCEPTS.

Objective J: *Know how square roots and geometric squares are related.* *(Lesson 12-2)*

36. A square has area 50. What is the exact length of a side? $\sqrt{50}$

37. A side of a square has length $\sqrt{4.9}$. What is the area of the square? **4.9**

38. A farm of area 1 square mile is square.

   a. What is the length of each side? **1 mile**

   b. Relate your answer in part **a** to square roots. $\sqrt{1} = 1$

39. If the largest square to the right has area 4, what is the length of a side of the tilted square? $\sqrt{2}$

Assessment

Evaluation The *Assessment Sourcebook* provides five forms of the Chapter 12 Test. Forms A and B present parallel versions in a short-answer format. Forms C and D offer performance assessment. The fifth test is Chapter 12 Test, Cumulative Form. About 50% of this test covers Chapter 12, 25% of it covers Chapter 11, and 25% of it covers earlier chapters.

For information on grading, see *General Teaching Suggestions: Grading in the Professional Source-book* which begins on page T20 in Volume 1 of the Teacher's Edition.

Setting Up Lesson 13-1

Suggestions for Assignment We recommend that you assign Lesson 13-1, both reading and some questions, for homework the evening of the test. It gives students work to do after they have completed the test and keeps the class moving.

Materials Students will need graph paper (**Teaching Aid 86**) for Chapter 13. Or, you may want to give them Four-Quadrant Graph Paper (**Teaching Aid 87**).

Adapting to Individual Needs

The student text is written for the vast majority of students. The chart at the right suggests two pacing plans to accommodate the needs of your students. Students in the Full Course should complete the entire text by the end of the year. Students in the Minimal Course will spend more time when there are quizzes and more time on the Chapter Review. Therefore, these students may not complete all of the chapters in the text.

Options are also presented to meet the needs of a variety of teaching and learning styles. For each lesson, the Teacher's Edition provides sections entitled: *Video* which describes video segments and related questions that can be used for motivation or extension; *Optional Activities* which suggests activities that employ materials, physical models, technology, and cooperative learning; and *Adapting to Individual Needs* which regularly includes **Challenge** problems, **English Language Development** suggestions, and suggestions for providing **Extra Help.** The Teacher's Edition also frequently includes an **Error Alert,** an **Extension,** and an **Assessment** alternative. The options available in Chapter 13 are summarized in the chart below.

Chapter 13 Pacing Chart

Day	Full Course	Minimal Course
1	13-1	13-1
2	13-2	13-2
3	13-3	13-3
4	13-4	13-4
5	Quiz*; 13-5.	Quiz*; begin 13-5.
6	13-6	Finish 13-5.
7	Self-Test	13-6
8	Review	Self-Test
9	Test*	Review
10	Comprehensive Test*	Review
11		Test*
12		Comprehensive Test*

*in the Teacher's Resource File

In the Teacher's Edition...

Lesson	Optional Activities	Extra Help	Challenge	English Language Development	Error Alert	Extension	Cooperative Learning	Ongoing Assessment
13-1	●		●	●		●	●	Oral
13-2	●		●	●		●	●	Written
13-3	●	●	●	●	●	●	●	Group
13-4	●	●	●			●	●	Written
13-5	●	●	●	●		●	●	Written
13-6	●	●	●	●		●	●	Written

In the Additional Resources...

Lesson	Lesson Masters, A and B	Teaching Aids*	Activity Kit*	Answer Masters	Technology Sourcebook	Assessment Sourcebook	Visual Aids**	Technology Tools	Video Segments
Opener		135					135		
13-1	13-1	87, 127, 133		13-1	Demo 13, Comp 29, Calc12		87, 127, 133, AM	Graphing/ Probability	
In-class Activity		87					87		
13-2	13-2	87, 127, 133, 136		13-2	Comp 30		87, 127, 133, 136, AM	Graphing/ Probability	Segment 13
13-3	13-3	87, 133	31	13-3			87, 133, AM		
13-4	13-4	87, 134	32	13-4		Quiz	87, 134, AM		
13-5	13-5	87, 134		13-5	Calc 13		87, 134, AM		
13-6	13-6	87, 134		13-6	Calc 14		87, 134, AM		
End of chapter				Review		Tests			

*Teaching Aids, except Warm-ups, are pictured on pages 690C and 690D. The activities in the Activity Kit are pictured on page 690C.

Teaching Aid 135 which accompanies Chapter 13 Opener is pictured on page 690D.

**Visual Aids provide transparencies for all Teaching Aids and all Answer Masters.

Also available is the Study Skills Handbook which includes study-skill tips related to reading, note-taking, and comprehension.

Integrating Strands and Applications

	13-1	13-2	13-3	13-4	13-5	13-6
Mathematical Connections						
Number Sense						●
Algebra	●	●	●	●	●	●
Geometry	●	●	●	●	●	
Measurement			●	●	●	
Probability				●		
Statistics/Data Analysis			●			
Patterns and Functions	●	●	●	●	●	●
Discrete Mathematics	●					●
Interdisciplinary and Other Connections						
Science				●	●	●
Social Studies	●	●	●		●	
Multicultural					●	●
Technology	●	●		●	●	●
Career	●					
Consumer		●	●	●		●
Sports	●	●				

Teaching and Assessing the Chapter Objectives

Chapter 13 Objectives (Organized into the SPUR categories—Skills, Properties, Uses, and Representations)	Lessons	Progress Self-Test Questions	Chapter Review Questions	In the Assessment Sourcebook		
				Chapter Test, Forms A and B	Chapter Test, Forms	
					C	D
Skills						
A: Solve equations of the form $ax + b = cx + d$.	13-3	1, 2, 8, 14	1–8	1, 2, 9, 10	1	
B: Evaluate expressions using the symbols for rounding up or rounding down.	13-6	3, 4	9–14	6, 7	4	✓
Properties						
C: Find the line on which or near which the numerators and denominators of equal fractions or relative frequencies lie.	13-4	5, 6	15–18	14, 15	3	
Uses						
D: Translate situations of constant increase or decrease that lead to sentences of the form $ax + b = cx + d$.	13-2, 13-3	7	19–22	9	5	
E: Graph formulas for perimeter, area, and other quantities that involve two variables.	13-5	11, 12	23–26	11–13		
Representations						
F: Graph equations of the form $y = ax + b$.	13-1, 13-4	9, 10	27–30	3, 4	2	
G: Interpret the solution to $ax + b = cx + d$ graphically.	13-2	13	31–34	5	5	
H: Interpret graphs of equations using the symbols $\lceil\ \rceil$ or $\lfloor\ \rfloor$.	13-6	15	35–38	8	2	✓

Assessment Sourcebook
Quiz for Lessons 13-1 through 13-4 — Chapter 13 Test, Forms A–D — Comprehensive Test, Chapters 1–13
Chapter 13 Test, Cumulative Form

 TestWorks
Multiple forms of chapter tests and quizzes; Challenge items

Activity Kit

Materials: Envelopes, paper clips
Group Size: Partners

Place one sheet of paper toward the left side of your desk, and another sheet toward the right side.

1. Place 5 paper clips into each of 6 envelopes. Place 4 of the envelopes on the left sheet of paper and the other 2 envelopes on the right sheet. Then place another 9 clips on the left sheet of paper. How many clips are there altogether on the left sheet of paper?

On the right sheet of paper, place enough paper clips so that the right sheet has the number of clips equal to the *total* number of clips on the left sheet.

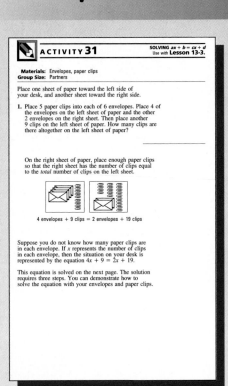

4 envelopes + 9 clips = 2 envelopes + 19 clips

Suppose you do not know how many paper clips are in each envelope. If x represents the number of clips in each envelope, then the situation on your desk is represented by the equation $4x + 9 = 2x + 19$.

This equation is solved on the next page. The solution requires three steps. You can demonstrate how to solve the equation with your envelopes and paper clips.

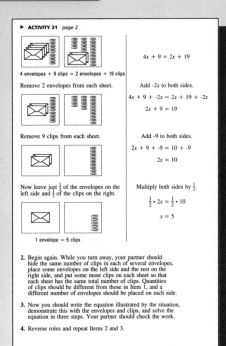

$4x + 9 = 2x + 19$

4 envelopes + 9 clips = 2 envelopes + 19 clips

Remove 2 envelopes from each sheet.

Add -2x to both sides.

$4x + 9 + -2x = 2x + 19 + -2x$

$2x + 9 = 19$

Remove 9 clips from each sheet.

Add -9 to both sides.

$2x + 9 + -9 = 10 + -9$

$2x = 10$

Now leave just $\frac{1}{2}$ of the envelopes on the left side and $\frac{1}{2}$ of the clips on the right.

Multiply both sides by $\frac{1}{2}$.

$\frac{1}{2} \cdot 2x = \frac{1}{2} \cdot 10$

$x = 5$

1 envelope = 5 clips

2. Begin again. While you turn away, your partner should hide the same number of clips in each of several envelopes, place some envelopes on the left side and the rest on the right side, and put some more clips on each sheet so that each sheet has the same total number of clips. Quantities of clips should be different from those in Item 1, and a different number of envelopes should be placed on each side.

3. Now you should write the equation illustrated by the situation, demonstrate this with the envelopes and clips, and solve the equation in three steps. Your partner should check the work.

4. Reverse roles and repeat Items 2 and 3.

Materials: 12″ × 18″ paper, toothpick, ruler
Group Size: Small groups

Prepare one sheet of lined paper for the group by drawing parallel lines on the paper. The distance between the lines should be the same as the length of the toothpick. Take turns holding the toothpick about one foot above the paper and dropping it. If the toothpick does not land entirely on the paper, drop it again.

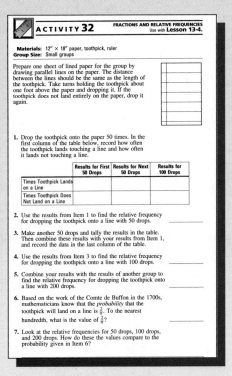

1. Drop the toothpick onto the paper 50 times. In the first column of the table below, record how often the toothpick lands touching a line and how often it lands not touching a line.

	Results for First 50 Drops	Results for Next 50 Drops	Results for 100 Drops
Times Toothpick Lands on a Line			
Times Toothpick Does Not Land on a Line			

2. Use the results from Item 1 to find the relative frequency for dropping the toothpick onto a line with 50 drops.

3. Make another 50 drops and tally the results in the table. Then combine these results with your results from Item 1, and record the data in the last column of the table.

4. Use the results from Item 3 to find the relative frequency for dropping the toothpick onto a line with 100 drops.

5. Combine your results with the results of another group to find the relative frequency for dropping the toothpick onto a line with 200 drops.

6. Based on the work of the Comte de Buffon in the 1700s, mathematicians know that the *probability* that the toothpick will land on a line is $\frac{2}{\pi}$. To the nearest hundredth, what is the value of $\frac{2}{\pi}$?

7. Look at the relative frequencies for 50 drops, 100 drops, and 200 drops. How do these the values compare to the probability given in Item 6?

Teaching Aids

Four-Quadrant Graph Paper

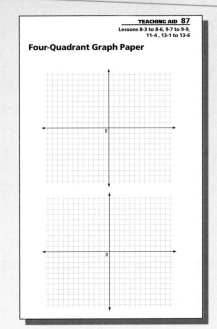

First-Quadrant Graph Paper

Warm-up — Lesson 13-1

For each equation, find the value of y when $x = -4, -2, 0, 2, 4,$ and 6.

1. $y = 3x + 1$ **2.** $y = -2x + 7$

Warm-up — Lesson 13-2

A student sports pass costing $20 allows students to attend 28 games at a cost of $2 per game. Individual tickets to these games are $4 each. Explain how you would decide whether or not to buy a student pass.

Warm-up — Lesson 13-3

Use the Distributive Property to simplify each expression.

1. $7t + 3t$ **2.** $6y - y$

3. $8x + 3 + 6x$ **4.** $r + r$

5. $11x + -5x$ **6.** $\frac{1}{2}s + \frac{1}{2}s + \frac{1}{2}$

7. $3.2z - 1.06z$ **8.** $-6m + 4m - 2m$

Warm-up

Find the probability that the spinner will land on

1. a two.
2. an even number.
3. a multiple of 3.
4. a number less than 4.
5. a number greater than 8.
6. a 3 or a 7.

Warm-up

The amount of gold in jewelry is measured in *karats*. The formula $p = \frac{25k}{6}$ tells the percent p of gold in a piece of jewelry when k is the number of karats.

Find the percent of gold in

1. an 18-karat gold ring.
2. a 14-karat gold pin.
3. a 24-karat gold necklace.

Warm-up

Work in groups. Give 3 real-world situations in which the numbers are rounded up.

Chapter Opener

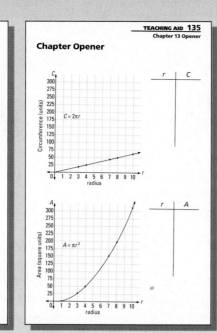

Examples 1 and 2

Example 1

Plan I
$C = 30 + .25m$

m	C
0	
100	
200	

Plan II
$C = 20 + .32$

m	C
0	
100	
200	

Example 2

Peggy
$A = 65 - 2w$

w	A
0	
2	
6	

Vanna
$A = 40 + 3w$

w	A
0	
2	
6	

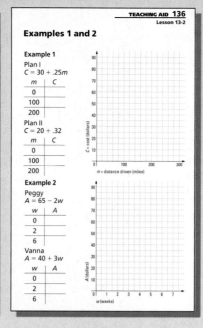

690D

Pacing

Every lesson in this chapter is designed to be covered in one day. At the end of the chapter, you should plan to spend 1 day to review the Progress Self-Test, 1–2 days for the Chapter Review, and 1 day for a test. You may wish to spend a day on projects, and possibly a day is needed for quizzes. This chapter should therefore take 9–12 days.

Using Pages 690–691

This page shows a different look at two formulas which students have previously seen. The graphs show that, as the radius of a circle increases, the circle's area increases faster than its circumference does. This represents the major theme of the chapter: the use of graphs to picture algebraic relationships.

Materials: **Teaching Aid 135**

When discussing the graphs on page 691, you might use **Teaching Aid 135.** Have students label the coordinates of the points on each graph and verify them in each formula. In both graphs, the second coordinates are given as multiples of π. Ask students to convert at least two values on each graph to decimals to check the placement of the points. For instance, the point $(8, 16\pi)$ on the graph of $C = 2\pi r$ is $(8, 50.265...)$. The decimal confirms its location near the intersection of the vertical line $r = 8$ and the horizontal line $c = 50$.

Then ask for the coordinates of two additional points on each graph. [Samples: for $C = 2\pi r$, $(1, 2\pi)$ and $(5, 10\pi)$; for $A = \pi r^2$, $(1, \pi)$ and $(5, 25\pi)$] Graph many of these points

13-1 Graphing $y = ax + b$

13-2 Situations Leading to $ax + b = cx + d$

13-3 Solving $ax + b = cx + d$

13-4 Fractions and Relative Frequencies Revisited

13-5 Graphs of Formulas

13-6 Graphs of Equations with Symbols for Rounding

690

Chapter 13 Overview

This chapter has two purposes, both appropriate for its position as the last chapter of the book. One purpose is to bring together many earlier ideas and to summarize some of the major ideas presented throughout the year. The other purpose is to introduce the student to a number of ideas that will be encountered in the next year of study. The vehicle that ties these purposes together is the connection between equations and coordinate graphs.

Lesson 13-1 begins by considering graphs of equations of the form $y = ax + b$. This lesson provides some opportunities to review the solving of linear equations with the unknown on one side. In Lessons 13-2 and 13-3, linear equations with the unknown on both sides are treated graphically and algebraically. Lesson 13-4 examines equations of the form $y = mx$ and relates these to equal fractions and relative frequencies. Lesson 13-5 examines some of the

formulas for perimeter and area, showing how they can be graphed. In Lesson 13-6, graphs of the equations for the rounding functions $y = \lceil x \rceil$ and $y = \lfloor x \rfloor$ are studied. Thus the chapter provides an opportunity to review and extend equation-solving, measurement formulas, probability and statistics, and the arithmetic of fractions and estimation.

COORDINATE GRAPHS AND EQUATIONS

It is possible to graph the formulas $C = 2\pi r$ and $A = \pi r^2$ for the circumference and area of a circle. Make r the first coordinate and C (or A) the second coordinate. The graphs are shown here.

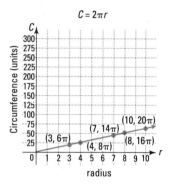

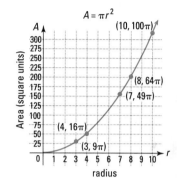

As you can see, the graphs are quite different. The graph on the left is a ray. The ray increases at a constant rate. This means the circumference of a pizza will increase the same amount when its radius is increased from 3″ to 4″ as when it is increased from 7″ to 8″. The graph on the right is part of a curve known as a *parabola*. The right graph goes up faster and faster as r increases more and more. This pictures the idea that the area of a circle increases more and more quickly as the radius gets larger and larger. So, for instance, changing the radius of a pizza from 7″ to 8″ will increase the area of the pizza quite a bit more than will changing the radius from 3″ to 4″.

In this chapter, you will study these and other graphs related to a variety of ideas you have seen in previous chapters.

691

to verify the shapes of the two graphs.

Have students move their fingers along the graphs from left to right. As they do this, explain that the points represent increases in the value of the radius. Because the area and circumference both increase as the radius increases, the graphs go up to the right. The area increases faster for larger values of r; its graph is not a line.

Photo Connections

The photo collage makes real-world connections to the content of the chapter: coordinate graphs and equations.

Computer Graphic: The line represented by this computer-generated graph increases at a constant rate.

Satellite Dish: Signals that are beamed down from satellites to Earth are received by ground stations with large parabolic-shaped dishes. The antenna in the dish transmitts the information to other relay stations.

Flashlight: In this picture, the light from the flashlight forms a parabolic shape on a surface.

Headlight: The reflecting surface of many automobile headlights has a parabolic shape.

Packages: The U.S. Postal Service charges according to the rounded weight of the item being mailed. For example, all packages weighing up to but not exceeding 2 pounds and being mailed to the same zone will be charged the same rate. This is an example of the ceiling function which is covered in Lesson 13-6.

Projects

At this time you might want to have students look over the projects on pages 725–726.

It will be helpful for students to have an ample supply of graph paper. It will also be helpful if they have access to calculators or computer software which enables them to automatically graph an equation of the form $y = \ldots$. We call this *automatic-grapher* technology.

Because this is the last chapter of the book, it can be skipped and students will still have all the ideas they need for success in their later work in mathematics. When this chapter is studied, the goal should not be for mastery of the ideas—many of them take a good deal of time to master—but for exposure, exploration, and fun.

Objectives

F Graph equations of the form
$y = ax + b$.

Resources

From the Teacher's Resource File
- Lesson Master 13-1A or 13-1B
- Answer Master 13-1
- Teaching Aids
   87 Four-Quadrant Graph Paper
   127 First-Quadrant Graph Paper
   133 Warm-up
- Technology Sourcebook,
   Computer Demonstration 13
   Computer Master 29
   Calculator Master 12

Additional Resources
- Visuals for Teaching Aids 87,
   127, 133
- Graphing and Probability
   Workshop

Teaching Lesson 13-1

Warm-up

For each equation, find the value of
y when $x = -4, -2, 0, 2, 4,$ and 6.
1. $y = 3x + 1$ –11, –5, 1, 7, 13, 19
2. $y = -2x + 7$ 15, 11, 7, 3, –1, –5

Notes on Reading

You might want to use **Teaching Aid 127** as you discuss this lesson. Notice that it allows students to reproduce the graphs on pages 692–693.

Carried out to the letter. *More than half of all letter mail in the United States is sorted and coded by machines that are programmed with algebraic functions.*

As of early 1994, costs of mailing a first-class letter were 29¢ for the first ounce and 23¢ for each additional ounce (up to ten ounces). The costs are in the table at the left below. At the right, the ordered pairs (weight, cost) are graphed.

weight in ounces	cost in cents
1	29
2	52
3	75
4	98
5	121
6	144
7	167
8	190
9	213
10	236

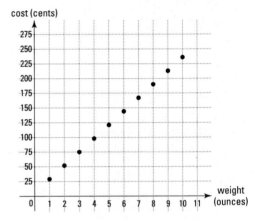

Call the weight w and the cost c. To find a formula relating w and c, you can rewrite the values of c without doing the arithmetic, a strategy used in Lesson 6-5.

w	c	
1	29	
2	29 + 23	
3	29 + 23 · 2	The number that changes in the
4	29 + 23 · 3	right column is always one less
5	29 + 23 · 4	than the value of w.
⋮	⋮	
w	29 + 23 · $(w - 1)$	

692

Lesson 13-1 Overview

Broad Goals The goal for students in this lesson is to see how a linear equation, the data that led to it, and its graph are related.

Perspective In Chapter 8, students graphed equations of the form $x + y = k$ and $x - y = k$. Solving these equations for y, they are respectively, $y = -x + k$ and $y = x - k$. This lesson generalizes the idea to cover equations where the coefficient of x is neither 1 nor –1. By now, students

should understand the relationship between ordered pairs and the graphs of points. They have also had experience in finding formulas that relate data. The new elements here are the recognition that the points lie on a line and the fact that the formula is an equation for that line.

The skill of graphing is covered in some detail in *UCSMP Algebra, Geometry,* and *Advanced Algebra*. At that time, students

will have ample time to learn about slope, intercepts, and equations in standard form.

There are only three questions that require graphs (**Questions 16, 18,** and **20**), but there are others in future lessons. We recommend that you supply graph paper with axes as shown on **Teaching Aid 87.** *Graphing is no fun if students have to recreate the graph paper themselves.*

So $c = 29 + 23(w - 1)$. Using the Distributive Property,

$$c = 29 + 23w - 23 = 23w + 6.$$

This formula shows that there is a simple pattern connecting w and c. If you multiply w by 23 and add 6, you get c.

$$c = 23w + 6$$

You might say that it costs 6¢ to mail anything, plus 23¢ for each ounce. For instance, suppose you want to mail some papers weighing 6.3 ounces. The post office always rounds weights up to the next ounce. So $w = 7$. Substitute 7 for w in the formula to find the cost.

$$c = 23 \cdot 7 + 6$$
$$c = 167$$

The cost is 167 cents. Dividing by 100 converts the cents to dollars. The cost to mail these papers is $1.67. The table at the beginning of the lesson gives the same cost.

You have just seen three ways to display postal rates: in a table, with a formula, and with a graph. Each way has some advantages. The table is easiest to understand. The formula is shortest and allows for values not in the table. Also, the formula can be used by a computer. The graph pictures the rates. It shows that they go up evenly.

Postal Rates in Three Different Years

The graph below shows the first-class postal rates for 1965, 1975, and 1990. The graph displays the changes over time in a way that is easy to understand.

Benjamin Franklin, pictured on the 13-cent stamp, was responsible for providing a more extensive, frequent, and speedy mail service. As deputy postmaster general for the American colonies in 1753, he built a solid foundation for a U. S. postal service. He became the first U.S. postmaster general in 1775.

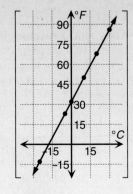

w = weight in ounces
c = cost in cents
1965: $c = 5w$
1975: $c = 11w + 2$
1990: $c = 20w + 5$

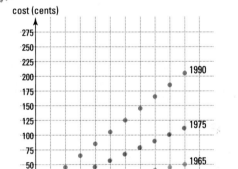

Lesson 13-1 *Graphing* $y = ax + b$ **693**

We have noted before that it takes a lot of time to draw graphs. Fortunately, computers enable us to graph more accurately and more easily than ever before, so the ability to draw graphs by hand is not as important as the ability to interpret them. However, students should be able to draw an accurate graph of a linear equation.

Additional Examples

Students can use **Teaching Aid 87** for their graphs.

1. Graph the line with the equation $y = -2x - 3$.

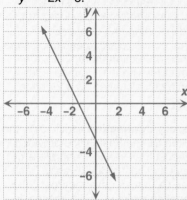

2. In the 1940s, it cost 3¢ to mail a letter and 1¢ for each additional ounce.
   a. Make a table of weight in ounces (w) and cost in cents (c) for integer values of w from 1 to 10.

w	1	2	3	4	5	6	7	8	9	10
c	3	4	5	6	7	8	9	10	11	12

   b. Graph the ordered pairs in the table. **Graph is shown on page 695.**

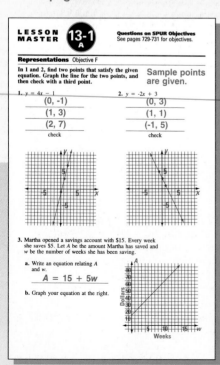

Each formula yields points on a line. The line $c = 5w$ is the lowest line. It shows that the 1965 costs were lowest. The line $c = 11w + 2$ is in the middle. The line $c = 20w + 5$ is the highest line, because costs were higher in 1990 than in 1975 or 1965.

In each of the three equations $c = 5w$, $c = 11w + 2$, and $c = 20w + 5$, w is multiplied by a number. This number indicates how fast the line goes up as you move one unit to the right. For instance, in $c = 11w + 2$, w is multiplied by 11. This causes the line to move up 11 units for every one unit increase in w. This is because, in 1975, each additional ounce of weight increased the cost of mailing a letter by 11¢.

Each of the postal rate equations is of the form $y = ax + b$, where a and b are fixed real numbers and the points (x, y) are graphed. For instance, in $c = 11w + 2$, $a = 11$, $b = 2$, and w and c take the place of x and y. Any equation of this form is a **linear equation.** The name *linear* is used because its graph is a line. When x is not restricted to be a whole number, then the graph of the equation consists of all points on the line.

Example

Graph the line with equation $y = -3x + 4$, and check that the graph is correct.

Solution

The graphs below show three steps. You should put all your work on one graph.

Step 1: Substitute numbers for x and find the corresponding values of y. For instance we choose $x = -1$. Then $y = -3 \cdot -1 + 4 = 3 + 4 = 7$. This means that $(-1, 7)$ is on the graph.

Now we choose $x = 2$. Then $y = -3 \cdot 2 + 4 = -6 + 4 = -2$. So $(2, -2)$ is on the graph.

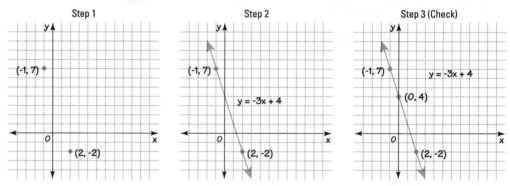

Step 2: Draw a line through the points. Label the line with the equation.

Step 3: Pick a third value for x. We pick $x = 0$. Then, according to the equation, $y = -3 \cdot 0 + 4 = 4$. This means that $(0, 4)$ should be on the graph. Is it? Yes, so the graph is correct.

Optional Activities

Activity 3 Technology Connection Students use a graphics calculator in *Technology Sourcebook, Calculator Master 12.* The master involves the graphing of equations of the form $y = ax + b$.

Adapting to Individual Needs

English Language Development
Help students understand that the word *linear* comes from *line*, even though it is pronounced differently. Tell them that a linear equation is any equation that can be graphed as a line. Mention other contexts for the word linear, such as linear measure or linear programming.

Caution: When graphing lines, it is easy to make errors in calculation. Then a point will be incorrect. You must check with a third point. If the three points do not lie on the same line, try a fourth point. Keep trying points until you see the pattern of the graph.

QUESTIONS

Covering the Reading

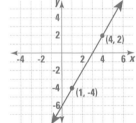

In 1–4, use the first-class postal rates for 1994.

1. What formula relates the weight of a letter and the cost to mail it?
cost = 23w + 6

2. What is the cost of mailing a letter that weighs 6 ounces? **$1.44**

3. What is the cost of mailing a letter that weighs 2.4 ounces? **$0.75**

4. For what weights does a letter cost 98¢? weights greater than 3 oz and less than or equal to 4 oz

5. Convert 213¢ to dollars.
$2.13

6. What is the general rule for converting cents to dollars?
Divide by 100.

7. What is an advantage of displaying postal rates in a table?
It is easy to understand.

8. What is an advantage of having a formula for postal rates? It is the shortest; it allows for values not in the table; it can be used by a

9. What is an advantage of graphing postal rates?   computer.
It pictures the rates.

In 10–14, use the first-class postal rates for 1965, 1975, and 1990.

10. What was the cost of mailing a 2-oz letter in 1965? 10¢

11. In 1965, what was the cost of mailing a letter weighing 9.2 oz? 50¢

12. You could mail a 3-oz letter in 1975 for what it cost to mail a __?__-oz letter in 1965. 7

13. What was the lowest cost for mailing a letter in the indicated year?
  a. 1965   **b.** 1975   **c.** 1990
     5¢   13¢   25¢

14. In 1975, by how much did the cost go up for each extra ounce of weight? 11¢

15. The line $y = -3x + 4$ is graphed in this lesson. Give the coordinates of two points on this line other than the points identified on the graph. Samples: (-2, 10), (1, 1)

16) Sample:

16. Graph the line with equation $y = 2x - 6$ and check your graph.
Sample: Graph (1, -4) and (4, 2), draw the line, and check if point (0, -6) lies on the line.

Lesson 13-1 *Graphing* $y = ax + b$ **695**

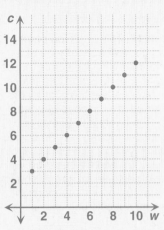

c. Write an equation relating w and c. $c = 3 + 1 \cdot (w - 1)$ or
$c = w + 2$

3. Graph the line $3x + 4y = 12$ on graph paper.

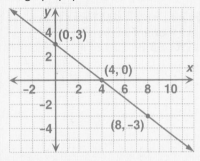

Notes on Questions

Question 5 One of the few times that decimals are preferred instead of whole numbers is in the treatment of money. We are so familiar with decimals in this context that we prefer $2.13 to 213¢.

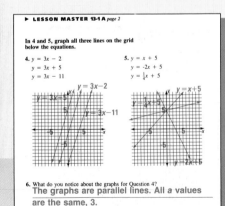
Adapting to Individual Needs

Extra Help
Some students may be confused by the general equation $y = ax + b$, when x and y are variables. Point out that x and y can be replaced by any real number. Yet a and b each stand for a particular number and remain fixed in a given equation. Then show students equations such as $y = 4x + 3$ or $y = 2x - 1$. Have students name the value of a and b in each case. Also, mention the special case where $a = 1$, for example,

$y = x + 3$. In this case, the 1 is usually not written, but it is still the value of a. Another special case occurs when $b = 0$, for example, $y = 5x$. Here again, the zero does not appear in the equation.

18a)

weeks from now	number of packages left
0	400
1	388
2	376
3	364
4	352
5	340
6	328
7	316
8	304
9	292
:	:

b)

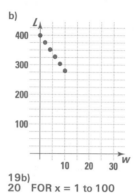

19b)
```
20   FOR x = 1 to 100
30     y = 2 * x − 6
```

20b)

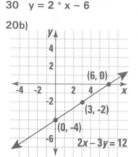

21a)

age	height
9 yr	56"
10 yr	59"
11 yr	62"
12 yr	65"

b) *inches*

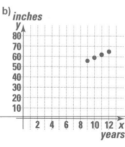

Applying the Mathematics

17. *Multiple choice.* Which line could be the graph of $y = 5x -- 2$? (a)

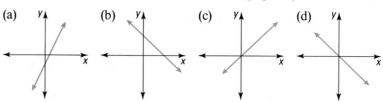

(a) (b) (c) (d)

18. Today there are 400 packages of duplicating paper at a school. Each week about 12 packages are used.
    a. Make a table with two columns, "weeks from now" and "number of packages left." Fill in at least 10 rows of your table.
    b. Graph six pairs of numbers in the table. Let *w*, the number of weeks, be graphed on the *x*-axis. Let *L,* the number of packages left, be graphed on the *y*-axis.
    c. What equation relates *w* and *L*? $L = 400 − 12w$
    d. Find the value of *w* when *L* = 0. What does this value mean?
       w = 33.3. All the paper will be used in about 33-1/3 weeks.

19. a. Coordinates of points on what line are found by this program?
       $y = 11x + 2$

```
10 PRINT "X", "Y"
20 FOR X = 1 TO 10
30 Y = 11*X + 2
40 PRINT X, Y
50 NEXT X
60 END
```

    b. Modify the program so that it will find 100 points on the line of Question 16.

20. Consider the equation $2x − 3y = 12$.
    a. Find the coordinates of three points that satisfy this equation.
    b. If you have answered part **a** correctly, the three points should lie on the same line. Graph this line.
    a) Samples: (0, -4), (3, -2), (6, 0)

21. Dan de Lion is 9 years old. His mother says he is growing "like a weed," 3 inches a year. He is now 56 inches tall.
    a. Suppose Dan continues to grow at this rate. Make a table with four pairs of numbers for his age *x* (in years) and his height *y* (in inches).
    b. Graph the four pairs.
    c. An equation that relates *x* and *y* is $y = 3x + b$. Find the value of *b*.
    d. Explain why $y = 3x + b$ will not relate Dan's age and height when he is an adult.
    c) *b = 29*; d) Sample: At age 25, his height from the equation would be 104" or 8'8", an unreasonable height.

696

Adapting to Individual Needs

Challenge

Materials: Graph paper or **Teaching Aid 87**

Give students the following equations:
$$y − 2x = 3$$
$$y − 3 = 2x$$
$$2y = 4x + 6$$
$$y = 2x + 3$$
For each equation, have them substitute three different numbers for *x* and then find the corresponding values for *y*. Next have

them graph each equation on a separate pair of axes. Ask them to try to discover what is similar about the graphs. [All the equations have the same graph.] Use this opportunity to point out that $y = ax + b$ is the commonly accepted way for writing the equation of a line, but any line has many different equations, all equivalent.

22) tee: $\frac{\pi}{4}$ ft^2;
blue ring: 20π ft^2;
white ring: 12π ft^2;
red ring: $\frac{15}{4}\pi$ ft^2

Smoothing the way.
*Curling players sweep
vigorously to smooth and
clean the ice as a
teammate's stone
approaches the house.*

22. Curling, a sport that probably originated in Scotland or the Netherlands around 400 years ago, involves sliding stones weighing over 40 pounds across ice at a target called the *house*. A point is scored by the team that gets closest to the middle of the target. Use the information below to find the area of the *tee*, or center. Then find the area of the red, white, and blue rings. *(Lesson 12-5)*

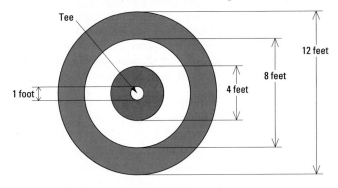

Tee

12 feet

8 feet

4 feet

1 foot

House

In 23 and 24, solve and check. *(Lessons 10-4, 11-6)*

23. $3(5n + 22) - 156 = 0$ 6;
$3(5 \cdot 6 + 22) - 156 = 0$

24. $\frac{x - 9}{2} = \frac{4}{5}$ 53; $\frac{\frac{53}{5} - 9}{2} = \frac{4}{5}$

25. Alvin ate about $\frac{1}{4}$ of the tossed salad. Betty ate half of what was left. How much salad now remains? *(Lesson 9-3)* $\frac{3}{8}$ of the salad

26. Diana gave P plants $\frac{1}{2}$ cup water each and Q plants $\frac{3}{4}$ cup water each. How much water did she use altogether? *(Lessons 5-7, 9-6)*   .5P + .75Q

27. A salesperson keeps a record of miles traveled for business. Last year, the salesperson drove 18,000 miles; 65% of this was for business. The company reimburses the salesperson 28¢ per mile traveled for business. How much money should the salesperson get back from the company? *(Lessons 10-1, 10-3)* $3276

28. Simplify. *(Lessons 5-3, 7-2, 9-1, 11-3)*
   a. $-5 + -3$ -8   **b.** $-5 - -3$ -2   **c.** $-5 \cdot -3$ 15   **d.** $\frac{-5}{-3}$ $\frac{5}{3}$ or $1\frac{2}{3}$

29. Use $\triangle BCD$ at the left to find m$\angle BCD$. *(Lesson 7-9)*   33°

D
83°
130°
B   C

30) Sample answers:
a) (1, 2), (5, −3), (9, −8)
b) If (*a, b*) is on the line, you can add 4 to the first coordinate and subtract 5 from the second coordinate to get another point, (*a* + 4, *b* − 5).

30. Consider the equation $5x + 4y = 13$.
   a. Find three points on this line in which both coordinates are integers.
   b. Describe how you could find many more points on the line in which both coordinates are integers.

Lesson 13-1   *Graphing y = ax + b*   **697**

Follow-up 13-1
for Lesson

Practice
For more questions on SPUR Objectives, use **Lesson Master 13-1A** (shown on pages 694–695) or **Lesson Master 13-1B** (shown on pages 696–697).

Assessment
Oral Communication Ask students to explain why graphing more than two points is a good idea when graphing a linear equation. [Explanations demonstrate an understanding of using a third point as a check.]

Extension
Have each student graph two lines, each on its own four-quadrant graph **(Teaching Aid 87),** and write the equations for the graphs on a separate sheet of paper. Each graph should have several points with integral coordinates. Then have students **work in pairs,** exchange graphs, and find the equation for each graph.

Project Update Project 1, *Graphs of Equations with Powers,* on page 725, relates to the content of this lesson.

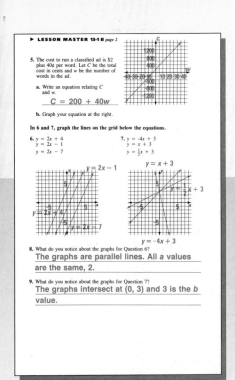

697

Resources

From the **Teacher's Resource File**
- Answer Master 13-2
- Teaching Aid 87: Four-Quadrant Graph Paper

Additional Resources
- Visual for Teaching Aid 87
- Automatic grapher

Technology Connection There is a variety of graphing software available for computers, as well as several different types of graphing calculators. So it is extremely important that you investigate the automatic grapher that will be used in this activity before students are asked to proceed. If possible, it would be better to have all students use the same type of grapher.

Step 3 is especially important. Unless an appropriate window is chosen, the screen will be blank. It might be helpful to have students choose several different ranges for *x* and *y* so that they see how the window displays different parts of the graph according to the chosen ranges.

In Step 5 students are asked to graph $y = 11x + 2$ and $y = 20x + 5$ on the same pair of axes. They can record their result on their own graph paper or on **Teaching Aid 87.**

For step 6, an appropiate window is given on page 700.

Introducing Lesson 13-2

Using an Automatic Grapher

IN-CLASS
ACTIVITY

The first computers were built in the 1940s. By the 1960s, software had been developed that enabled computers to print out graphs of equations. By 1985 this technology was available on relatively inexpensive hand-held calculators. Today most people graph equations with automatic graphers, either graphics calculators or computers equipped with software that can graph equations. For this activity you need to use an automatic grapher.

1 Turn on the machine you use and access the technology that enables equations to be graphed. What you need to do depends on the machine. Your teacher will help you.

2 Enter the equation that is to be graphed. You will begin by graphing the postal-rate equations from Lesson 13-1, so type in $y = 5x$. (Sometimes "$y = $ " is already typed in.)

3 Determine the window for the graph. The window is the part of the coordinate plane that appears on the screen. For the postal-rate graphs, *x* (the weight) ranges from 0 to 10. A window for *x* that shows these values and leaves some room at the side is $-1 \le x \le 11$. On some programs, you would type in XMIN = -1 and XMAX = 11. (These stand for the minimum and maximum values of *x*.) The costs range from 5¢ to 205¢, so type in values of *y* that include this range. One possibility is YMIN = -50 and YMAX = 250.

4 Display the graph of the equation. With some technology, you need only press a button or move a mouse to GRAPH. You should see a line that contains the blue points in the graph on page 693.

5 Follow steps 2 and 4 to graph $y = 11x + 2$ and $y = 20x + 5$ on the same axes. See margin for 4, 5.

6 Look at Example 1 of Lesson 13-2. Follow steps 2 through 4 above to graph the two equations in the example. See page 700.

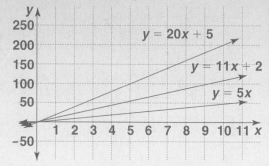

698

Optional Activities

After students have done the activity on this page, you might have them **work in pairs** using automatic graphers to graph the following equations. Ask them to generalize the pattern. [Sample: All lines of the form $y = 2x + b$ are parallel.]

$y = 2x + 5$,
$y = 2x - 3$
$y = 2x$
$y = 2x + 8$

Then have them graph the following equations, and again, ask for a generalization. [Sample: All lines of the form $y = ax + 5$ pass through the point (0, 5).]

$y = 2x + 5$
$y = 3x + 5$
$y = -x + 5$
$y = -4x + 5$

Additional Answers 4, 5

Car Return ↓ Stop Here

The algebra of renting a car. *Algebraic equations can be used to compare rates charged by different companies, such as car rental agencies, that provide the same services.*

In the last lesson, first-class postal rates for four different years were graphed and compared. In some situations there are choices of rates for the same time period. When this is the case, it is natural to want to know when a particular rate is cheaper. Example 1 shows how to compare the rates using graphs.

Example 1

A driver wants to rent a car for a day and is given a choice of two plans.

Plan I: $30 plus 25¢ a mile
Plan II: $20 plus 32¢ a mile

a. When is Plan I cheaper than Plan II?
b. When is Plan II cheaper than Plan I?
c. When do the two plans cost the same?

Solution

Begin by thinking about the situations. Plan I starts out with a higher cost but each mile driven costs less. This means that Plan I will be more expensive at first, but if enough miles are driven, it will cost less.

Find an equation for each plan. Let C be the cost (in dollars) for driving m miles. Here are equations relating m and C for each plan. (Do you see how these equations were found?)

Plan I: $C = 30 + .25m$
Plan II: $C = 20 + .32m$

▶

Lesson 13-2 *Situations Leading to ax + b = cx + d* **699**

Lesson 13-2

Objectives

D Translate situations of constant increase or decrease that lead to sentences of the form $ax + b = cx + d$.

G Interpret the solution to $ax + b = cx + d$ graphically.

Resources

From the *Teacher's Resource File*:
- Lesson Master 13-2A or 13-2B
- Answer Master 13-2
- Teaching Aids
   87 Four-Quadrant Graph Paper
   127 First-Quadrant Graph paper
   133 Warm-up
   136 Examples 1 and 2
- Technology Sourcebook, Computer Master 30

Additional Resources
- Visuals for Teaching Aids 87, 127, 133, 136
- Graphing and Probability

Teaching Lesson **13-2**

Warm-up

A student sports pass costing $20 allows students to attend 28 games at a cost of $2 per game. Individual tickets to these games are $4 each. Explain how you would decide whether or not to buy a student pass.
Sample response: If I plan to attend more than 10 games, it is less expensive to buy a student pass and pay $2 per game. If I plan to attend less than 10 games, it is cheaper to pay $4 per game.

Lesson 13-2 Overview

Broad Goals In this lesson, students see how situations that lead to an equation of the form $y = ax + b$ can lead to the solving of equations of the form $ax + b = cx + d$.

Perspective In many situations, a variable increases or decreases at a constant rate as in postal rates and many car-rental rates. We call such situations *constant increase* or *constant decrease* situations. Every constant increase or constant decrease

situation can be described by a linear equation of the form $y = ax + b$, where b is the starting amount and a is the amount of increase per unit time. (In graphing, b is the y-intercept and a is the slope, but that is not the concern here.) If there are two such situations involving the same variables x and y, then we have equations of the form $y = ax + b$ and $y = cx + d$. If we want to know when the values of y are equal, then

an equation of the form $ax + b = cx + d$ can be solved.

Note the reversal of the usual order of introducing these ideas. Often students are asked to solve large numbers of equations of the form $ax + b = cx + d$, and they have no idea why anyone would want to solve them. We give the rationale first. In Lesson 13-3, students will learn how these kinds of equations can be solved.

You can use **Teaching Aid 136** as you discuss **Examples 1 and 2**. In **Example 1**, if students have trouble seeing how the equations for Plan I and Plan II were found, you may wish to start a table. Then ask students to continue the table until they can see a pattern and fill in the row for *n* miles.

Miles	Cost Plan I	Cost Plan II
0	30	20
1	30 + .25	20 + .32
2	30 + .25 · 2	20 + .32 · 2
3	30 + .25 · 3	20 + .32 · 3
⋮	⋮	⋮
n	30 + .25n	20 + .32n

The next task is making a graph. It is important to pick scales on the two axes so that the point of intersection of the lines (if any) can be seen. Here marking the horizontal axis in hundreds of miles is reasonable.

The most important aspect of solving the problem is examining the graphs to learn how they show when one plan is less expensive or more expensive than the other. A useful way is to compare points on the same vertical line. Specifically, for 100 miles, Plan I is more expensive. But for 200 miles, Plan II is more expensive.

Pacing If you go over the reading for **Example 1** in as much detail as is suggested here, you should have students do **Questions 1–7** in class. Then have them do **Example 2** and **Questions 8–12** on their own.

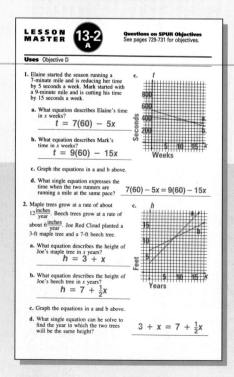

The graph of each equation is a line. We graph the lines on the same axes so that they can be compared easily.

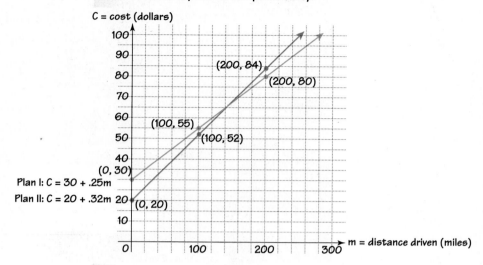

Plan I: $C = 30 + .25m$
Plan II: $C = 20 + .32m$

When the line for one of the plans is higher, then that plan is more expensive.
a. The lines intersect when m is about 150. This means: Plan I is more expensive when m is less than 150. If the car is to be driven more than 150 miles, Plan I should be chosen.
b. Plan II is cheaper if the car is driven less than 150 miles.
c. The two plans cost the same when the car is driven about 150 miles.

There are advantages and disadvantages to using a graph. A hand-drawn graph pictures the situation very nicely, but usually it is not very accurate. So it does not give an exact answer to any of the questions asked. However, some calculators and computer software automatically graph equations. With these, you can get enough accuracy to get an exact or nearly exact solution.

The key to an exact answer to part **c** of Example 1 is the location of the point of intersection of the lines. The first coordinate of that point is found by making the two values for *C* equal.

$$30 + .25m = 20 + .32m$$

This is called *equating* the values of *C*. This equation is of the form

$$ax + b = cx + d$$

because the unknown on each side of the equation is to the first power. In the next lesson, you will learn how to solve this kind of equation without a graph.

Optional Activities

Activity 1 After students have read **Example 2** and answered **Questions 8–12**, you might want to have them **work in pairs** to answer the following questions. Do not expect them to solve equations to find answers.
1. After how many weeks will Peggy have run out of money? [$32\frac{1}{2}$ weeks]
2. At the same time Peggy runs out of money, how much will Vanna have? [$137.50]

Activity 2 Technology Connection You may wish to assign *Technology Sourcebook, Computer Master 30*. Students graph sets of equations and determine points of intersection, if any.

Example 2

Peggy is spending money while her sister Vanna is saving it. At present, Peggy has $65 but she spends about $2 more than her allowance each week. Vanna has $40 but she is saving about $3 a week.

a. Use graphs to estimate when the two sisters will have the same amount of money.

b. Solving what equation will give the exact time when the sisters have the same amount?

Solution

a. First identify the variables you will use. Here we Let A be the amount of money that each sister will have after w weeks. Then

$$\text{for Peggy: } A = 65 - 2w$$
$$\text{for Vanna: } A = 40 + 3w.$$

Now graph these two equations.

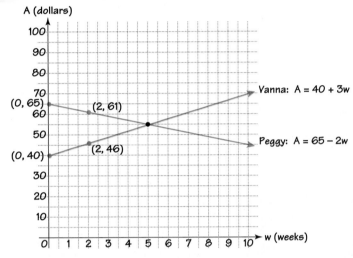

The graphs seem to intersect at (5, 55). This means that after 5 weeks, both girls will have $55. (Check that this is correct.) After that time, Vanna will have more money than Peggy will.

b. Equate the two values of A. Solving the equation

$$65 - 2w = 40 + 3w$$

will give the exact number of weeks.

Lesson 13-2 *Situations Leading to* $ax + b = cx + d$ **701**

Students will need graph paper for this lesson. They can use **Teaching Aid 87** or **Teaching Aid 127.**

Additional Examples

Spud owns 35 CDs and is trying to increase his collection by 3 CDs every 2 weeks. Mugsy owns 20 CDs and is trying to get 2 more CDs each week. Let w be the number of weeks from now, and y be the number of CDs owned.

a. For Spud, how are w and y related? $y = 35 + 1.5w$

b. For Mugsy, how are w and y related? $y = 20 + 2w$

c. Graph the equations of parts a and b to determine when Mugsy will own as many CDs as Spud owns. **Students' graphs should intersect at (30, 80); 30 weeks**

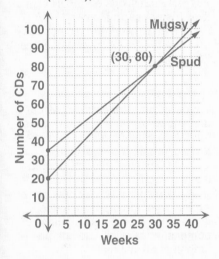

Video

Wide World of Mathematics The segment, *Balancing the Budget*, uses a variety of graphics to help explain what the deficit is and how it relates to the national debt. This, in turn, is related to balancing one's own budget. The segment may be used with Example 2 or as an extension of the lesson. Related questions and an investigation are provided in videodisc stills and in the Video Guide. A related CD-ROM activity is also available.

Videodisc Bar Codes

Search Chapter 64

Play

701

Question 6 This is a very important question. If students cannot answer it, they do not understand the title of the lesson.

Question 13 Project 6, *When Will One Person Overtake Another?*, on page 726, is related to this question.

Questions 16–18 These questions continue practice for the skills of Lesson 13-3.

Follow-up for Lesson 13-2

Practice

For more questions on SPUR Objectives, use **Lesson Master 13-2A** (shown on pages 700–701) or **Lesson Master 13-2B** (shown on pages 702–703).

Assessment

Written Communication Ask students to write two equations for the questions presented in the *Warm-up* for this lesson. [$C = 2g + 20$; $C = 4g$] Then tell students to graph the two equations and find where the lines intersect. Have students explain what the graphs and the intersection mean. [Explanations demonstrate an ability to interpret graphs of equations.]

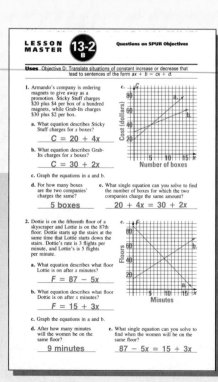

QUESTIONS

Covering the Reading

In 1–7, refer to Example 1.

1. **a.** What does it cost to drive 10 miles using Plan I? $32.50
   b. Name the point on the line for Plan I which determines the answer to part **a.** (10, 32.50)

2. **a.** What does it cost to drive 30 miles using Plan II? $29.60
   b. Name the point on the line for Plan II which determines the answer to part **a.** (30, 29.60)

3. How can you tell from the graph which plan is more expensive when you drive 200 miles? The line for Plan II is higher when $m = 200$.

4. How can you tell from the equations which plan is more expensive when you drive 200 miles? Substitute 200 for m in each equation. Plan II costs $84 while Plan I costs $80.

5. Solving what single equation tells when the plans cost the same? $30 + .25m = 20 + .32m$

6. $30 + .25m = 20 + .32m$ is an equation of the form $ax + b = cx + d$. Give the values of a, b, c, and d. $a = .25$, $b = 30$, $c = .32$, $d = 20$

7. With an automatic grapher, graph the lines of Example 1. Use a window that will show the answer to part **c** to the nearest mile. Graph should resemble that of Example 1 but be concentrated around (143, 66).

In 8–12, refer to Example 2.

8. After w weeks, how much money will Peggy have? $65 - 2w$

9. After w weeks, how much money will Vanna have? $40 + 3w$

10. Solving what equation tells when Peggy and Vanna have the same amount of money? $65 - 2w = 40 + 3w$

11. **a.** At what point do the lines in the graph intersect? (5, 55)
    b. What do the coordinates of this point mean? After 5 weeks, both girls have $55.00.

12. $65 - 2w = 40 + 3w$ is an equation of the form $ax + b = cx + d$. Give the values of a, b, c, and d. $a = -2$, $b = 65$, $c = 3$, $d = 40$

Applying the Mathematics

13. At the beginning of the 1994 baseball season, Barry Bonds had 222 home runs in his career and had averaged .190 home runs per game. Juan Gonzales had 120 home runs in his career and had averaged .260 home runs per game. Let P be the number of home runs in a career after g more games at these averages.
    a. For Barry, what equation relates P and g? $P = 222 + .190g$
    b. Graph the equation you found in part **a.** See graph on page 703.
    c. For Juan, what equation relates P and g? $P = 120 + .260g$

Valuable Bonds.
Barry Bonds of the San Francisco Giants was the unanimous choice for National League Most Valuable Player in 1993. In 1990 and 1992, he was NL MVP when he played for the Pittsburgh Pirates.

702

Adapting to Individual Needs

English Language Development

For students who are not proficient in English, special attention should be given to terms such as *equate, intersect,* and *coordinates.* For *equate,* remind students of the balance scale models used earlier. For *intersect,* use the example of roads crossing on a map. For *coordinates,* demonstrate pairs of *x*- and *y*-coordinates on a four-quadrant grid.

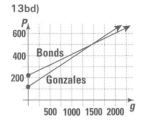

13bd)

15)

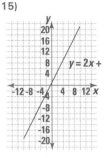

$y = 2x + 1$

18) $-\frac{1}{2}; (-\frac{1}{2} + 1) + (2 \cdot -\frac{1}{2} + 2) + (3 \cdot -\frac{1}{2} + 3) + (4 \cdot -\frac{1}{2} + 4) = \frac{1}{2} + 1 + \frac{3}{2} + 2 = 5$

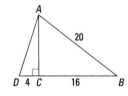

23) At $m = 142.86$, the second column is $30 + .25m = 65.7150$ and the third column is $20 + .32m = 65.7152$. The cost is the same when the mileage is 142.86 miles.

---

d. Graph the equation from part **c** on the same axes you used for part **b**.

e. From your graph, estimate the number of games it will take Juan to catch up with Barry in the number of home runs in his career.

f. Solving what equation will tell when the two players will have the same number of home runs?

e) Sample: about 1450 games; f) $222 + .19g = 120 + .26g$

14. Long-distance company I charges 20¢ for the first minute plus 15¢ for each additional minute of a long-distance call. Company II charges 26¢ for the first minute plus 13¢ for each additional minute. Let C be the cost (in cents) of an m-minute call.

a. Give an equation relating m and C for company I. $C = 5 + 15m$

b. Give an equation relating m and C for company II. $C = 13 + 13m$

c. Solving what equation will tell when the plans cost the same?
$5 + 15m = 13 + 13m$

Review

15. Graph $y = 2x + 1$ for values of x from -10 to 10. *(Lesson 13-1)*

In 16–18, solve and check. *(Lessons 10-1, 10-2, 10-4)*

16. $99 - 3x = 150$ -17;
$99 - 3(-17) = 150$

17. $\frac{2}{5}y = \frac{3}{4}$ 15. $\frac{2}{8} \cdot \frac{15}{5} \left(\frac{15}{8}\right) = \frac{3}{4}$

18. $(a + 1) + (2a + 2) + (3a + 3) + (4a + 4) = 5$

19. Suppose you have an 80% chance of getting an A on your next math test, and a 70% chance of getting an A on your next science test. If your scores on these tests are independent, what is the probability that you will get an A on both tests? *(Lesson 9-4)* **56%**

20. Use the figure at the left. *(Lessons 7-9, 12-3)*
a. What is the measure of $\angle ACB$? **90°**
b. $AC = \underline{\ ?\ }$ **12**
c. $AD = \underline{\ ?\ }$ **$\sqrt{160}$**

21. Along I-64 in Virginia, the distance from Staunton to Charlottesville is 34 miles. The distance from Waynesboro to Richmond is 91 miles. The distance from Staunton to Richmond is 103 miles. What is the distance from Waynesboro to Charlottesville? *(Lesson 7-5)* **22 miles**

22. Write 6×10^3 as a decimal. *(Lesson 2-3)* **6,000**

Exploration

23. Design a spreadsheet with the following columns.

m	$30 + .25m$	$20 + .32m$

By trying values of m between 100 and 200, make the values of $30 + .25m$ and $20 + .32m$ as close to each other as you can. Use this idea to determine m to two decimal places. This helps answer part **c** of Example 1.

Lesson 13-2 *Situations Leading to ax + b = cx + d* **703**

Extension

✎ **Writing** Have **groups of students** collect information from various sources on pricing situations that lead to equations of the form $ax + b = cx + d$. Examples include long distance telephone rates (one charge for the first minute and then a different constant rate for each additional minute), service charges at banks (one charge per month plus a different constant rate per check), and so on. Ask each group to find at least one example, write the equation, graph the equation, and interpret the graph in writing.

Project Update Project 6, When *Will One Person Overtake Another?*, on page 726, relates to the content of this lesson.

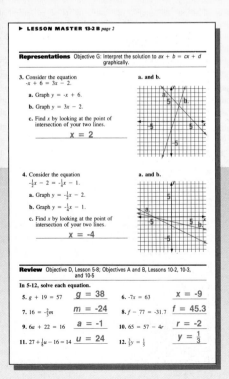

Adapting to Individual Needs

Challenge

Materials: Graph paper or **Teaching Aid 87**

Discuss with students the following plans that are available from a fitness center. Each plan involves an initial fee plus an additional charge for each visit.

Plan 1: $50 plus $4 per visit
Plan 2: $100 plus $2 per visit
Plan 3: $140 plus $1 per visit

Have students write an equation for each plan where C = cost and v = number of visits. [$C = 50 + 4v$, $C = 100 + 2v$, $C = 140 + v$] Then have them use graphing or trial and error to find the number of visits for which Plan 1 and Plan 2 will cost the same. [25 visits] Next have them find the number of visits for which Plan 1 and Plan 3 will cost the same. [30 visits] Finally, have them find the number of visits for which Plan 2 and Plan 3 will cost the same. [40 visits].

703

Objectives

A Solve equations of the form
$ax + b = cx + d$.
D Translate situations of constant
increase or decrease that lead
to sentences of the form
$ax + b = cx + d$.

Resources

From the Teacher's Resource File
■ Lesson Master 13-3A or 13-3B
■ Answer Master 13-3
■ Teaching Aids
87 Four-Quadrant Graph Paper
133 Warm-up
■ Activity Kit, Activity 31

Additional Resources
■ Visuals for Teaching Aids 87, 133

Teaching Lesson 13-3

Warm-up

Use the Distributive Property to simplify each expression.

1. $7t + 3t$ **10t**

2. $6y - y$ **5y**

3. $8x + 3 + 6x$ **14x + 3**

4. $r + r$ **2r**

5. $11x + -5x$ **6x**

6. $\frac{1}{2}s + \frac{1}{2}s + \frac{1}{2}$ **s + \frac{1}{2}**

7. $3.2z - 1.06z$ **2.14z**

8. $-6m + 4m - 2m$ **-4m**

Notes on Reading

Emphasize that the most common strategy for solving an equation that you cannot solve mentally is to transform it into one that you can solve.

Saving versus spending. *Example 1 provides two solutions to the equation of Example 2 from Lesson 13-2. It tells when Vanna will have as much money as her sister.*

In Lesson 13-2, you saw how an equation of the form $ax + b = cx + d$ can be solved with graphs. Using algebra, exact solutions can be found. Notice that

$$ax + b = cx + d$$

has the unknown x on both sides of the equal sign. By adding a carefully chosen expression to both sides of this equation, it can be converted to an equation with the unknown on only one side. The first example solves the equation from Example 2 of Lesson 13-2. Notice that you have a choice for the first step.

Example 1

Solve $65 - 2w = 40 + 3w$.

Solution 1

One way to start is to add $-3w$ to both sides. This results in an equation with w on only one side.

original equation	$65 - 2w = 40 + 3w$
Add $-3w$ to both sides.	$65 - 2w + -3w = 40 + 3w + -3w$
Add like terms.	$65 - 5w = 40$

Now proceed as you have previously with equations of this type.

Add -65 to both sides.	$-65 + 65 - 5w = -65 + 40$
Simplify.	$-5w = -25$
Multiply both sides by $-\frac{1}{5}$.	$-\frac{1}{5} \cdot -5w = -\frac{1}{5} \cdot -25$
Simplify.	$w = 5$

Lesson 13-3 Overview

Broad Goals After a lesson devoted to the uses and representations of linear equations with the unknown on both sides, this lesson is devoted to using properties learned earlier in the book to solve the equations.

Prospective The material in this lesson constitutes one of the most important goals of first-year algebra. It is covered in detail in first-year algebra texts and the introduction

here is meant to be just that—an introduction. Do not spend the time that might be necessary to gain proficiency at the expense of the material in the rest of the chapter.

Solving equations of the form $ax + b = cx + d$ can be difficult even if students can easily solve equations of the form $ax + b = c$. Stress that finding an equivalent equation with the variable on one side is a key to

solving the equations in this lesson. Once the equivalent equation is found, it is important that students focus on it and not get confused by going back to the original equation.

Lesson 13-4 is brief, allowing more time to be spent on the material in Lesson 13-3.

Solution 2

Another way is to add $2w$ to both sides. This avoids negative numbers.

original equation	$65 - 2w = 40 + 3w$
Add $2w$ to both sides.	$65 - 2w + 2w = 40 + 3w + 2w$
Add like terms.	$65 = 40 + 5w$

Solve this equation as you have done in earlier lessons.

Add -40 to both sides.	$-40 + 65 = -40 + 40 + 5w$
Simplify.	$25 = 5w$
Multiply both sides by $\frac{1}{5}$.	$5 = w$

Both solutions to Example 1 confirm that after 5 weeks Peggy and Vanna will have the same amount of money.

Example 2

Solve $3x + 5 = 10x + 26$.

Solution

We add $-10x$ to both sides. This gets rid of the variable on the right side.

original equation	$3x + 5 = 10x + 26$
Add $-10x$ to both sides.	$-10x + 3x + 5 = -10x + 10x + 26$
Simplify.	$-7x + 5 = 26$
Now add -5 to both sides.	$-7x + 5 + -5 = 26 + -5$
Simplify.	$-7x = 21$
Multiply both sides by $-\frac{1}{7}$.	$x = -3$

Check

Substitute -3 for x every place it occurs in the original equation. Does $3 \cdot -3 + 5 = 10 \cdot -3 + 26$? Yes, both sides equal -4.

The equation in Example 3 may look as if it is solved for L. But there is an L on the right side. The method of Examples 1 and 2 can be used to solve equations of this type.

Example 3

Solve $L = 15 - 4L$.

Solution

	$L = 15 - 4L$
Add $4L$ to both sides.	$L + 4L = 15 - 4L + 4L$
	$5L = 15$
	$L = 3$

Check

Does $3 = 15 - 4 \cdot 3$? Yes.

Lesson 13-3 *Solving $ax + b = cx + d$* **705**

An equation of the form $ax + b = cx + d$ has variables on both sides, so one strategy is to change it into an equivalent equation with all the variables on one side. The side chosen is not important. Some people prefer to keep the coefficient positive and choose the side that will accomplish that end; others prefer to keep the variable on the left side.

You may want to list solution steps:
(1) Simplify each side of the equation.
(2) Get all variables on one side of the equation; in other words, change the form to $ax + b = c$.
(3) Get all constants on the other side of the equation; in other words, change the form to $ax = b$.
(4) Solve the resulting equation.

Point out the purposes of the examples. **Example 1** provides an algebraic solution to **Example 2b** in Lesson 13-2. It also demonstrates that in solving equations of this type, one route will put the variable on the left side, while the other route puts the variable on the right side. Emphasize that either route will lead students to a correct answer. **Example 2** is a simpler example of the same type. **Example 3** looks different because there is no constant term on the left. Be certain that students read the paragraph before this example. **Example 4,** on page 706, is not in the form $ax + b = cx + d$, but it is easily transformed into an equation of that form.

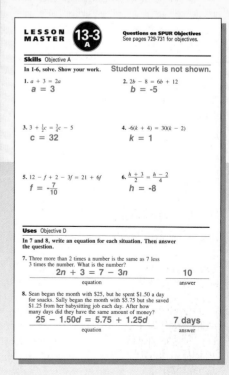

Optional Activities

Activity 1 You might want to use Activity 31 in the *Activity Kit* as a lead-in to this lesson. In this activity, students model equations of the form $ax + b = cx + d$, and use paper clips and envelopes to demonstrate how to solve these equations.

Activity 2 Have students **work in groups** of three or four. Ask each student to make up an equation of the form $ax + b = cx + d$ with a solution they know, and then give the equation to the other members of the group to be solved.

Additional Examples

In 1–4, solve and check:
1. $8w - 4 - 2w = 12 + 10w$
   $w = -4$; check: $-32 - 4 + 8 =$
   $12 - 40, -28 = -28$
2. $4x + 3 = 8x + 19$
   $x = -4$; check: $-16 + 3 =$
   $-32 + 19, -13 = -13$
3. $m = 28 - 3m$
   $m = 7$; check: $7 = 28 - 21$;
   $7 = 7$
4. $\frac{12 - u}{3} = \frac{u + 4}{5}$

   $u = 6$; check: $\frac{12 - 6}{3} = \frac{6 + 4}{5}, 2 = 2$

In 5–7 an equation is given. Have
students: (a) tell what can be added
to both sides of the equation to give
an equation with variables on the
right side only. (b) tell what can be
added to both sides of the equation
to give an equation with variables on
the left side only. (c) use one of
these methods to solve the equation.

5. $3p - 4 = 8 - 2p$
   a. $-3p$ b. $2p$ c. $p = 2.4$
6. $Q = 4 + \frac{1}{2}Q$
   a. $-Q$ b. $-\frac{1}{2}Q$ c. $Q = 8$
7. $8r - 4 + r = -3r - 5$
   a. $-9r$ b. $3r$ c. $r = \frac{-1}{12}$

8. Carol and Cathy are each saving
   money for a special vacation to
   Disney World. Carol started with
   $25 and saves $7.50 a week.
   Cathy started with $10 and saves
   $10 a week.
   a. How much money will Carol
      have saved after w weeks?
      $25 + 7.5w$
   b. How much money will Cathy

706

The next example combines a number of ideas from this and the
preceding chapters.

Example 4

Solve $\frac{x - 2}{2} = \frac{x + 3}{4}$.

Solution

First use the Means-Extremes Property.

$$4(x - 2) = 2(x + 3)$$

Now use the Distributive Property.

$$4x - 4 \cdot 2 = 2x + 2 \cdot 3$$
$$4x - 8 = 2x + 6$$

In this form, the equation is like those of Examples 1, 2, and 3. Add $-2x$
to both sides.

$$-2x + 4x - 8 = -2x + 2x + 6$$
$$2x - 8 = 6$$

Add 8 to both sides. $2x = 14$
Solve in your head. $x = 7$

Check

Substitute. Does $\frac{7 - 2}{2} = \frac{7 + 3}{4}$?

Does $\frac{5}{2} = \frac{10}{4}$? Yes.

QUESTIONS

Covering the Reading

1. In solving $65 - 2w = 40 + 3w$, name two things you could do to
   both sides to obtain an equation with the unknown on one side.
   Add $2w$ to both sides or add $-3w$ to both sides.
2. Solve $3x + 5 = 10x + 26$ by first adding $-3x$ to both sides.
   $5 = 7x + 26$; $-21 = 7x$; $x = -3$
3. a. To solve $s = 18 - 35s$, first add ___?___ to both sides. $35s$
   b. Solve this equation. $s = \frac{1}{2}$

In 4–9, solve and check.

4. $11A + 5 = 7A + 35$ 7.5;
   $11 \cdot 7.5 + 5 = 7 \cdot 7.5 + 35 = 87.5$
5. $12 - 3q = 2q - 2$ 2.8;
   $12 - 3 \cdot 2.8 = 2 \cdot 2.8 - 2 = 3.6$
6. $4 - y = 6y - 10$ $y = 2$;
   $4 - 2 = 6 \cdot 2 - 10 = 2$
7. $2(n - 4) = 3n$ $n = -8$;
   $2(-8 - 4) = 3 \cdot -8 = -24$
8. $\frac{t - 3}{4} = \frac{t + 6}{12}$ $t = 7.5$;
   $\frac{7.5 - 3}{4} = \frac{7.5 + 6}{12} = 1.125$
9. $0.6m + 5.4 = -1.3 + 2.6m$ $m = 3.35$;
   $.6 \cdot 3.35 + 5.4 = -1.3 + 2.6 \cdot 3.35 = 7.41$

706

Adapting to Individual Needs

Extra Help
The key to solving equations of the type
$ax + b = cx + d$ is to find an equivalent
equation in which the variable occurs on
one side only. Often students add an
expression to each side and still obtain
another equation that has variables on both
sides.

Refer students to the equation $28 - 5x =$
$42 + 2x$. Ask them to add each of the

following expressions to each side of the
original equation, and then tell what new
equation is obtained in each case.
1. $-28 [-5x = 14 + 2x]$
2. $-42 [-14 - 5x = 2x]$
3. $5x [28 = 42 + 7x]$
4. $-2x [28 - 7x = 42]$

Point out that only 3 and 4 yield an equation
with a variable on one side only.

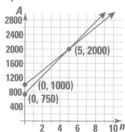

10. **a.** Solve $30 + .25m = 20 + .32m$. $m = 142\frac{6}{7} \approx 142.86$
    b. Use the answer to part **a** to answer the question of part **c** of Example 1 in Lesson 13-2. The two plans cost nearly the same at about 143 miles.

11. Under rate plan 1 a new car costs $1000 down plus $200 per month. Under rate plan 2 the car costs $750 down and $250 per month.
    a. Write an expression for the amount paid after n months under plan 1. $P = 1000 + 200n$
    b. Write an expression for the amount paid after n months under plan 2. $P = 750 + 250n$
    c. After how many months will the amount paid be the same for both plans? 5

12. Twice a number is 500 more than six times the number. What is the number? -125

In 13 and 14, solve and check.

13. $11p + 5(p - 1) = 9p - 12$ $p = -1$; $11(-1) + 5(-1 - 1) = -21$ and $9(-1) - 12 = -21$

14. $-n + 4 - 5n + 6 = 21 + 3n$ $n = -\frac{11}{9}$; $-(-\frac{11}{9}) + 4 - 5(-\frac{11}{9}) + 6 = \frac{52}{3}$ and $21 + 3(-11/9) = 52/3$

15. In $\triangle PIN$, the measure of angle N is $4x + 36$. The measure of angle P is $10x$. If the measure of $\angle N$ equals the measure of $\angle P$, find the measures of all three angles in the triangle. $m\angle P = 60$; $m\angle N = 60$; $m\angle I = 60$

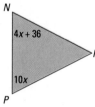

16. Hasty Harry wrote the following solution to $5x - 1 = 2x + 8$. When he checked the answer, it didn't work.
    a. In which step did Harry make a mistake? in Step 3
    b. What is the correct solution? $x = 3$

$$5x - 1 = 2x + 8$$
Step 1: $-2x + 5x - 1 = -2x + 2x + 8$
Step 2: $3x - 1 = 0 + 8$
Step 3: $3x = 8 - 1$
Step 4: $3x = 7$
Step 5: $x = \frac{7}{3}$

17) The lines intersect when $n = 5$, indicating when the amount paid is equal.

(graph with points $(5, 2000)$, $(0, 1000)$, $(0, 750)$; vertical axis A labeled 400, 800, 1200, 1600, 2000, 2400, 2800; horizontal axis n labeled 2, 4, 6, 8, 10)

---

have saved after w weeks?
$10 + 10w$
c. When will they have saved the same amount of money?
$25 + 7.5w = 10 + 10w$;
$w = 6$; after 6 weeks

Notes on Questions

Students will need graph paper or **Teaching Aid 87** for **Questions 17 and 22.**

Question 5 Error Alert Students will often anticipate that solutions are integers and make errors to ensure that their answers are integers. Here an answer $q = 2$ indicates that 2 was added to the right side of the equation and subtracted from the left side.

Question 11 You might extend the question and ask, "When will more money be paid in Plan 1 than is paid in Plan 2?" [During the first four months]

Question 16 If a check shows a mistake, then by going back through the solution, students can determine where the mistake was made. The number $\frac{7}{3}$ checks in Steps 5, 4, and 3, but not in Step 2. That shows that an error was made going from Step 2 to Step 3.

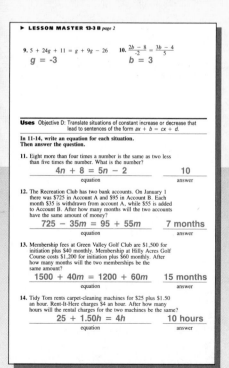

▶ **LESSON MASTER 13-3 B** *page 2*

9. $5 + 24g + 11 = g + 9g - 26$ $g = -3$
10. $\frac{2b - 8}{-2} = \frac{3b - 4}{5}$ $b = 3$

Uses Objective D: Translate situations of constant increase or decrease that lead to sentences of the form $ax + b = cx + d$.

In 11-14, write an equation for each situation. Then answer the question.

11. Eight more than four times a number is the same as two less than five times the number. What is the number?
$4n + 8 = 5n - 2$ 10
equation   answer

12. The Recreation Club has two bank accounts. On January 1 there was $725 in Account A and $95 in Account B. Each month $35 is withdrawn from account A, while $55 is added to Account B. After how many months will the two accounts have the same amount of money?
$725 - 35m = 95 + 55m$ 7 months
equation   answer

13. Membership fees at Green Valley Golf Club are $1,500 for initiation plus $40 monthly. Membership at Hilly Acres Golf Course costs $1,200 for initiation plus $60 monthly. After how many months will the two memberships be the same amount?
$1500 + 40m = 1200 + 60m$ 15 months
equation   answer

14. Tidy Tom rents carpet-cleaning machines for $25 plus $1.50 an hour. Rent-It-Here charges $4 an hour. After how many hours will the rental charges for the two machines be the same?
$25 + 1.50h = 4h$ 10 hours
equation   answer

Adapting to Individual Needs

English Language Development
Remind students that the *unknown* in an equation is the number represented by a variable. Also, be sure they understand that *converting* an equation simply means changing it to an equivalent form. Remind students of the properties of equality that allow such changes in an equation.

707

22)

23)

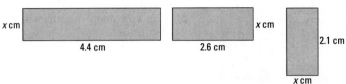

Future Farmers.
Shown here are two members of the Future Farmers of America. FFA helps prepare students for careers not only in farming, but in such related areas as agricultural marketing, agribusiness, forestry, communications, and horticulture.

26a) $x = -5$
b) Sample:

x	left side	right side	
10	43	39	left side bigger
12	53	45	left side bigger
5	18	24	right side bigger

So x is between 5 and 10.

8	33	33	

So x = 8.

708

Review

17. Let A be the amount paid after n months of the rate plans of Question 11. Graph the lines corresponding to each of these rate plans. Explain why these graphs check the answer to Question 11c. *(Lesson 13-2)* **See page 707.**

In 18 and 19, rewrite as a simple fraction in lowest terms. *(Lesson 12-1)*

18. 0.92 $\frac{23}{25}$

19. $6.\overline{36}$ $\frac{70}{11}$

20. What is the total area of these three rectangles? *(Lesson 10-5)* **9.1x cm²**

21. Trace the figure below. What word results when the figure is reflected over the given line? *(Lesson 8-6)* **Book**

◄BOOK►

22. Graph all pairs of solutions to $x - y = 4$. *(Lesson 8-4)*

23. Draw a cube. *(Lesson 3-9)*

24. In 1991 there were approximately two million, one hundred five thousand farms in the United States. *(Lessons 1-1, 2-3)*
   a. Write this number as a decimal. **2,105,000**
   b. Write this number in scientific notation. **2.105 × 10⁶**

25. Use the information in Question 24. In 1930 there were about 330% as many farms as in 1991. About how many farms were there in the U.S. in 1930? *(Lessons 2-6, 10-1)* **about 6,946,500**

Exploration

26. Paula wanted to solve $4x + 7 = 2x - 3$, but did not know the method of this lesson. She knew she wanted the value of the left side to equal the value of the right side. So she substituted a 2 for x to see what happened.

Left side	*Right side*
$4 \cdot 2 + 7 = 15$	$2 \cdot 2 - 3 = 1$

The left side was bigger than the right. Paula tried -10.

$$4 \cdot -10 + 7 = -33 \quad 2 \cdot -10 - 3 = -23$$

Now the right side was bigger than the left. She figured that the solution must be some number between -10 and 2.
a. Find the value that makes the two sides of the equation equal.
b. Use Paula's method to solve $5x - 7 = 3x + 9$.

Fractions and Relative Frequencies Revisited

Let's Make a Deal. *Game show host Bob Hilton is asking a contestant to consider trading a prize for a better prize concealed behind one of three doors. What is the probability of choosing a door that does not have the best prize?*

Objectives
C Find the line on which, or near which, the numerators and denominators of equal fractions or relative frequencies lie.
F Graph equations of the form $y = ax$.

Resources
From the *Teacher's Resource File*
- Lesson Master 13-4A or 13-4B
- Answer Master 13-4
- Assessment Sourcebook: Quiz on Lessons 13-1 through 13-4
- Teaching Aids
    87 Four-Quadrant Graph Paper
    134 Warm-up
- Activity Kit, Activity 32

Additional Resources
- Visuals for Teaching Aids 87, 134

Any ordered pair of real numbers can be graphed. Sometimes the graphs of sets of ordered pairs present a nice geometric picture. In this lesson, we look at fractions in a way that may surprise you.

Every rational number can be expressed using many different simple fractions. Here are some fractions that equal $\frac{2}{3}$.

$$\frac{2}{3} \;=\; \frac{4}{6} \;=\; \frac{-2}{-3} \;=\; \frac{6}{9} \;=\; \frac{12}{18}$$

Now think of these fractions as ordered pairs, with the denominator as the first coordinate and the numerator as the second coordinate.

$$(3, 2) \quad (6, 4) \quad (-3, -2) \quad (9, 6) \quad (18, 12)$$

When these pairs are graphed, they all lie on the same line.

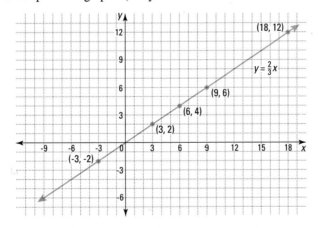

Lesson 13-4 Overview

Broad Goals This lesson relates numerators and denominators of equal and almost equal fractions to points on or near a line with equation $y = ax$.

Perspective This lesson is designed to be a brief excursion that allows more time to be spent on the material of Lesson 13-3. Still, it contains some key ideas. Because the ratio of the coordinates of points on any line through the origin is constant, these ratios

are all equal fractions. Since relative frequencies from the same experiment should be rather close to equal, when the numerators and denominators of the relative frequencies are graphed, they should lie close to the line.

This lesson provides a different look at equations of lines from those in the previous lessons. In previous lessons, the data have always been fixed, and it seems that lines

would only arise from particularly special data. But here there is quite a bit of latitude. *Any* repeated experiment can yield points nearly on a line. *Any* set of equal fractions will have pairs (denominator, numerator) lying on the same line.

Warm-up

Find the probability that the spinner will land on

1. a two. $\frac{1}{8}$
2. an even number. $\frac{1}{2}$
3. a multiple of 3. $\frac{1}{4}$
4. a number less than 4. $\frac{3}{8}$
5. a number greater than 8. 0
6. a 3 or a 7. $\frac{1}{4}$

Notes on Reading

You might want to use Activity 1, in *Optional Activities* below, to introduce this lesson. You can use Activity 2 in *Optional Activities* as a follow-up to the lesson.

To review the graphs at the top of page 711, you might ask students for other points on these lines.

Students will need graph paper for this lesson. You can use **Teaching Aid 87.**

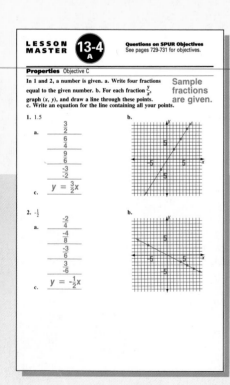

Here is the reason that all these points lie on the same line. Suppose y and x are numbers with

$$\frac{y}{x} = \frac{2}{3}.$$

Then after multiplying both sides of the equation by x,

$$y = \frac{2}{3}x.$$

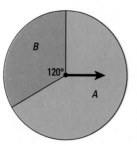

The equation $y = \frac{2}{3}x$ also appears in the following situation. Suppose that the probability that an event occurs is $\frac{2}{3}$. For instance, if the spinner pictured at the left is fair, then the probability that the spinner lands in region A is $\frac{2}{3}$. Thus, if you spin the spinner 60 times, you should expect that it will land in region A about $\frac{2}{3} \cdot 60$, or 40 times. More generally, if you spin the spinner x times, you should expect that it will land in region A about $\frac{2}{3}x$ times.

Below is a record of 150 spins of a spinner like the one pictured. After each 15 spins, we recorded the number of times that the spinner landed in region A. The data are given at the left and graphed at the right below.

Number of Spins	Spins in Region A
15	10
30	21
45	29
60	38
75	46
90	58
105	67
120	78
135	89
150	99

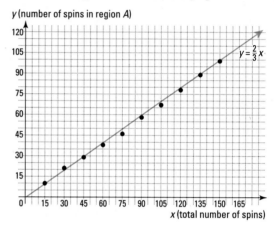

The points do not lie exactly on the line $y = \frac{2}{3}x$ because the relative frequencies are not exactly $\frac{2}{3}$, but they are close. In the long run, we would expect the relative frequencies to get closer and closer to $\frac{2}{3}$. The equation $y = \frac{2}{3}x$ is of the form $y = ax$. For any particular value of a, the graph of this equation is a line. Three such equations are graphed at the top of page 711.

Optional Activities

Activity 1
Materials: Graph paper or **Teaching Aid 87**, calendar

You might introduce this lesson by asking students to name fractions equal to $\frac{3}{7}$, to think of each fraction as an ordered pair, and then to graph the ordered pairs. [The points should all be on the line $y = \frac{3}{7}x$.] For a relative frequency near $\frac{3}{7}$, ask students to

find the day of the week on which their birthday falls this year. Let t be the total number of students and n be the number of students whose birthday is on a Monday, Wednesday, or Friday. The fraction $\frac{n}{t}$ should be close to $\frac{3}{7}$, and the point (t, n) should lie near the line $y = \frac{3}{7}x$.

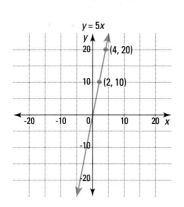

$y = 5x$

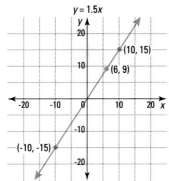

$y = 1.5x$

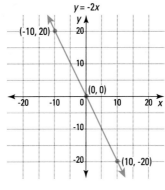

$y = -2x$

The number a in the equation $y = ax$ is called the **slope** of the line. It tells how much y changes for every increase of 1 unit by x. For instance, in $y = 5x$, $a = 5$, and as x increases from 2 to 3, y increases from 10 to 15, an increase of 5.

QUESTIONS

Covering the Reading

1b) Sample points:

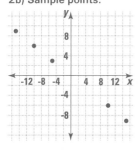

1. Consider the rational number $\frac{5}{4}$.
   a. Name five different fractions equal to it. Samples: $\frac{-5}{-4}, \frac{10}{8}, \frac{15}{12}, \frac{-15}{-12}, \frac{-10}{-8}$
   b. For each fraction $\frac{a}{b}$ that you named in part **a**, graph the ordered pair (b, a). See graph at left.
   c. The points in part **b** should lie on a line. What is an equation for that line? $y = \frac{5}{4}x$

2b) Sample points:

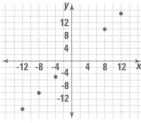

2. Repeat Question 1 for the number $\frac{-3}{5}$.
   a) Samples: 3/-5, 6/-10, -6/10, 9/-15, -9/15; c) $y = (-3/5)x$
3. Refer to the spinner experiment in the lesson.
   a. After 90 spins, how many times did the spinner land in region A?
   b. What point on the graph was determined by the information in part **a**?
   c. Why are the points on the graph close to the line?
   d. Why are the points on the graph not all on the line?

3a) 58 times;   b) (90, 58);
c) In the long run, the relative frequencies will get closer and closer to the probability.
d) Relative frequencies do not always equal probabilities.

Lesson 13-4   Fractions and Relative Frequencies Revisited   **711**

Activity 2 You might use *Activity 32* in the *Activity Kit* as a follow-up to this lesson. Students do a probability experiment based on the Buffon needle problem.

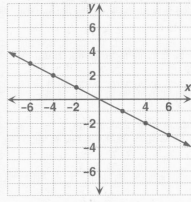
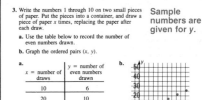
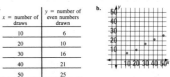
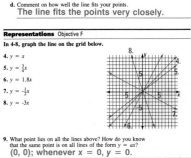
711

Question 8b The lines are parallel, but students may give other relationships. The points on $y = 2x$ are 1 unit above the points on $y = 2x - 1$. They are also a half unit to the left.

Question 9 As in **Question 8**, there are many possible answers to **parts b and c.** Probe to see how many different answers students gave.

Question 18 Science Connection In 1974, new cars averaged 13.2 miles per gallon. In 1975, a law was passed that forced automobile manufacturers to design more efficient cars. In 1991, the average car used 27.3 miles per gallon. Interested students might check the mileage on their family cars or on friends' cars.

✎ **Question 23 Writing** You might have students share the descriptions they wrote with the class.

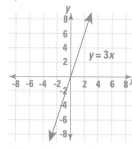

4a) Sample: (-1, -3), (0, 0), (1, 3)
b)

c) 3;   d) 3

Serve yourself! *In 1972, a few independent gas stations began offering savings of a few cents per gallon to customers willing to pump their own gas. Today, except in states where it is illegal to pump your own gas, almost all gas stations offer self-serve pumps.*

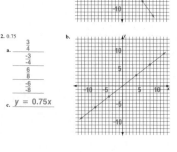

In 4–6, an equation of a line is given.
  a. Name three points on the line.
  b. Graph the line.
  c. As x increases from 10 to 11, by how much does y change?
  d. Give the slope of the line.

4. $y = 3x$
See left.

5. $y = -1.5x$
See page 713.

6. $y = \frac{1}{2}x$
See page 713.

Applying the Mathematics

7. a. Toss a coin 100 times, recording H or T after each toss.
  b. Make a table with the total number of heads after every ten tosses.
  c. Graph the pair of numbers in each row of the table.
  d. To what line should the ten points be near? Are your points near that line? $y = \frac{1}{2}x$;   Answers may vary.
  e. Do you think your coin was fair? Why or why not?
  a, b, c, e) Answers will vary.

8. a. Graph $y = 2x$ and $y = 2x - 1$ on the same pair of axes.   See p. 713.
  b. How are these graphs related?   The lines are parallel.
  c. Generalize the idea of parts **a** and **b.**   Sample: The graph of $y = 2x + k$ is parallel to the graph of $y = 2x.$

9. a. Graph $y = 2x$ and $y = -2x$ on the same pair of axes.   See page 713.
  b. How are the graphs of these equations related?
  c. Generalize the idea of parts **a** and **b.**
  b) They are reflection images of each other.   c) $y = ax$ and $y = -ax$ are reflection images of each other over the x-axis (or over the y-axis).

Review

10. Refer to Question 14c of Lesson 13-2. Solve the equation.
  (Lesson 13-3) $m = 4$

In 11–16, solve.   *(Lessons 10-5, 13-3)*

11. $12B + 5 = 10B + 17$
  $B = 6$

12. $3 - 4x = x + 23$
  $x = -4$

13. $18(x - 2) = 12(x + 3)$
  $x = 12$

14. $v - \frac{1}{2} = \frac{3}{4} - v$ $v = \frac{5}{8}$

15. $\frac{d}{4} = 11.22$
  $d = 44.88$

16. $\frac{30}{2x + 5} = \frac{20}{x - 1}$
  $x = -13$

17. About how long will it take to read a 312-page novel if the first 35 pages can be read in 45 minutes?   *(Lesson 11-6)*
  ≈ 401 minutes ≈ 6 hr, 41 min

18. When their odometer read 13,486 miles, the Villareal family filled the gas tank of their car with 12.4 gallons. At 13,869 miles they again filled the tank, now with 14.6 gallons. How many miles per gallon is their car getting?   *(Lesson 11-2)* about 26.2 mpg

19. A small store has two full-time employees. If each employee is absent about 3% of the days the store is open, what is the probability that both employees will be absent on the same day? Assume the absences are independent events.   *(Lesson 9-4)* .0009 or .09%

Adapting to Individual Needs

Extra Help

Materials: Graph paper or **Teaching Aid 87**

Remind students that each point (b, a) on a coordinate grid can represent the fraction $\frac{a}{b}$. Some students may not be convinced that all points on a given line through the origin represent equivalent fractions. Have students use a coordinate grid to draw any line through the origin and then find at least four points on the line. (The four points chosen should lie at grid intersections.) Then have students name the fractions for each point, and show that the four fractions are equivalent. In some cases, students may have to extend the line to find points at grid intersections.

5a) Sample: (-2, 3),
(0, 0), (2, -3)
b)

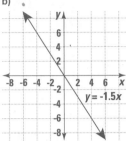

c) -1.5 d) -1.5

6a) Sample: (0, 0),
(-4, -2), (6, 3)
b)

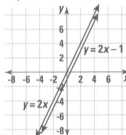

c) 1/2 d) 1/2

8a)

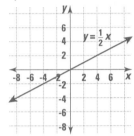

9a)

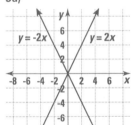

20. Figure *ABCD* is a parallelogram. m∠*BAD* = 65°. Find the measures of as many other sides and angles as can be found from this information. *(Lesson 7-8)* AD = 12, m∠C = 65°, m∠B = m∠D = 115°

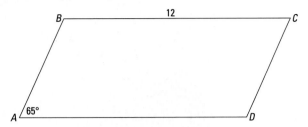

21. Name four metric units of length and tell how they are related to each other. *(Lesson 3-4)*
Sample: 1 km = 1,000 m = 100,000 cm = 1,000,000 mm

22. Round 4.921685 to the nearest thousandth. *(Lesson 1-4)* **4.922**

Exploration

23. a. Perform an experiment like the spinner experiment of this lesson.
  b. Record the results of your experiment in a table.
  c. Graph the pairs of numbers in the table.
  d. Graph the line that contains the points you would get if the relative frequencies of the event equalled the probability of the event.
  e. In a few sentences describe what you found.
    Answers will vary.

In 24 and 25, use an automatic grapher.

24. Graph $y = 2x$, $y = 3x$, $y = 4x$, and $y = 5x$ on the same window. Predict what the graphs of $y = 6x$, $y = 7x$, ... will look like.
  See below.

25. Graph $y = \frac{1}{2}x$, $y = \frac{1}{3}x$, $y = \frac{1}{4}x$, and $y = \frac{1}{5}x$ on the same window.
  Predict what the graphs of $y = \frac{1}{6}x$, $y = \frac{1}{7}x$, ... will look like.
  See below.

24)

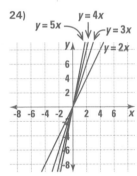

Sample:
The graphs of $y = 6x$, $y = 7x$, ... go through (0, 0) and are closer and closer to the y-axis.

25)

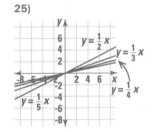

Sample:
The graphs of $y = \frac{1}{6}x$, $y = \frac{1}{7}x$, ... go through (0, 0) and are closer and closer to the x-axis.

Lesson 13-4 *Fractions and Relative Frequencies Revisited* **713**

Adapting to Individual Needs

Challenge
Materials: Graph paper or **Teaching Aid 87**

Have students **work in pairs** to do the following activity. One student draws a line through the origin on a coordinate grid. Then the other determines the equation of the line. Have students take turns drawing lines.

Practice

For more questions on SPUR Objectives, use **Lesson Master 13-4A** (shown on pages 710–711) or **Lesson Master 13-4B** (shown on pages 712–713).

Assessment

Quiz A quiz covering Lessons 13-1 through 13-4 is provided in the *Assessment Sourcebook*.

Written Communication Students can use **Teaching Aid 87**. Have students select a nonzero value for *a*, graph $y = ax$ and $y = -ax$ on the same pair of axes, and identify each graph. [Students' graphs should contain point (0,0), and $y = ax$ and $y = -ax$ should be reflection images of each other.]

Extension

Project Update Project 4, *An Experiment with Decimal Places*, on page 725, relates to the content of this lesson.

Objectives

E Graph formulas for perimeter, area, and other quantities that involve two variables.

Resources

From the Teacher's Resource File
- Lesson Master 13-5A or 13-5B
- Answer Master 13-5
- Teaching Aids
  87 Four-Quadrant Graph Paper
  134 Warm-up
- Technology Sourcebook, Calculator Master 13

Additional Resources
- Visuals for Teaching Aids 87, 134

Teaching
Lesson **13-5**

Warm-up

The amount of gold in jewelry is measured in *karats*. The formula $p = \frac{25k}{6}$ tells the percent p of gold in a piece of jewelry when k is the number of karats.

Find the percent of gold in

1. an 18-karat gold ring. **75%**
2. a 14-karat gold pin. **$58\frac{1}{3}$%**
3. a 24-karat gold necklace. **100%**

Notes on Reading

Multicultural Connection Satellites and satellite dishes like those shown on this page make it possible for pictures to be transmitted worldwide. You might have students discuss what this means. Ask them what live

---

13-5

Graphs of Formulas

Satellite dishes. *Large dishes, like these in Eagle River, Alaska, serve as stations for satellite communication systems. Each slice of this dish parallel to its face is a circle. As the diameter of the circle gets larger, so does its circumference.*

Some formulas, like the area formula $A = \ell w$ for a rectangle, involve three variables. To graph them requires graphs in three dimensions. But other formulas, like the formula $C = \pi d$ for the circumference of a circle, involve two variables. These formulas can be graphed just as you have done with other equations in previous lessons.

❶ Example 1

Graph $C = \pi d$, where C and d are the circumferences and diameters of circles.

Solution 1

We pick d as the first coordinate, and C as the second coordinate of each ordered pair. To plot points, use an approximation to π, such as 3.14.

When $d = 1$, $C = \pi \cdot 1 \approx 3.14 \cdot 1 = 3.14$.
When $d = 2$, $C = \pi \cdot 2 \approx 3.14 \cdot 2 = 6.28$.
When $d = 5$, $C = \pi \cdot 5 \approx 3.14 \cdot 5 = 15.7$

Plot as many points as you think you need to get a good graph. A graph is shown here.

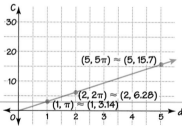

Because d and C stand for lengths, the graph contains only positive values of d and C. The graph is a ray without its endpoint.

Lesson 13-5 Overview

Broad Goals This lesson provides an opportunity to review measurement formulas and also to display graphs of lines and parabolas through the origin.

Perspective The formulas for the circumference of a circle ($C = \pi d$), and the perimeters of polygons, such as the perimeter of a square ($p = 4s$), and the perimeter of a hexagon ($p = 6s$), are of the form

$y = ax$. When graphed, these formulas give lines through the origin.

The formulas for the area of a square ($A = s^2$), area of a circle ($A = \pi r^2$), surface area of a sphere ($A = 4\pi r^2$), surface area of a cube ($A = 6s^2$), and braking distance ($d = \frac{s^2}{20}$) are of the form $y = ax^2$. When graphed, these formulas give half of a parabola with the vertex at the origin.

The purpose of this lesson is to show students that formulas have pictures, the pictures being graphs, and that the graphs can tell us things about the formulas. The equations of the form $y = ax^2$ are important for students to see so they realize that not every formula has a line as its graph.

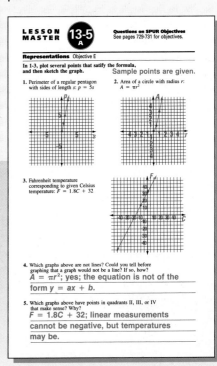

Solution 2

Use an automatic grapher. Think of d as x and C as y. On some calculators, you can enter

$\boxed{y}\ \boxed{=}\ \pi\ \boxed{x, t, \theta}\ \boxed{\text{GRAPH}}$.

You should see part of the line that contains the ray of Solution 1.

Another formula that involves only two variables is the formula $A = s^2$ for the area of a square. The graph of this formula is *not* part of a line, as Example 2 shows.

❷ Example 2

Let A be the area of a square with side s. Graph all possible pairs of values (s, A).

Solution

Since $A = s^2$, the values (s, A) are the same as the values (s, s^2). So the graph contains all ordered pairs in which the first coordinate is a positive number (it is a length), and the second coordinate is the square of that number. At the left is a table of some values. At the right is the graph.

s	A
2	4
1	1
3	9
4	16
$\frac{1}{2}$	$\frac{1}{4}$

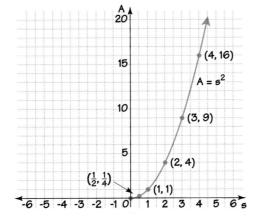

The arc in Example 2 is part of the curve known as a parabola. Another graph with this shape is found on page 691. The **parabola** is the shape of all graphs of equations of the form $y = ax^2$.

To graph all the possible pairs of numbers satisfying $y = x^2$, including possibly negative coordinates, remember that a number and its opposite have the same square. Thus $(-x)^2 = x^2$. For this reason, the graph is symmetric to the y-axis. The full graph cannot be shown because it extends forever. Its shape is the entire parabola.

▶

Lesson 13-5 *Graphs of Formulas* **715**

---

television programs they have seen recently that originated in another country.

❶ Be sure students recognize that π is a constant; therefore, C and d are the only variables in the circumference formula. You might also want to point out that the perimeter of any regular polygon will have a formula similar to the circumference formula ($P = 3s$, $P = 4s$, and so on). Some other formulas of this type are area formulas where one dimension is fixed. For instance, the area A of a rectangle with one side 70 is given by the formula $A = 70L$, where 70 and L are the dimensions of the rectangle.

❷ You may wish to introduce the term *quadratic equation* to describe equations of the form $y = ax^2$. The graphs of linear equations are always lines. The graphs of quadratic equations of this form are always parabolas.

Some other formulas of this type are volume formulas for figures where one dimension is fixed. For instance, the volume of a circular cylinder with height 10 is given by $V = 10\pi r^2$, where r is the radius of the base.

To understand the graph of $y = x^2$, there is no substitute for carefully plotting the points on the graph. Every student should do this with paper and pencil at least once. Do not expect students to be skilled at drawing in the curves between the points.

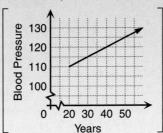

Optional Activities

Activity 1
Materials: Graph paper or **Teaching Aid 87**

After students have read **Example 1,** you might want to have them **work in pairs** to solve the following problem.
The formula $P = 100 + 0.5y$ gives the average systolic blood pressure P, in millimeters of mercury, for an adult who is y years old. Graph this equation and estimate the average blood pressure for adults who are 25,

35, and 45 years old. [112.5, 117.5, 122.5]

Additional Examples

1. A store charges $1.20 for each box of tissues. Let C be the cost of n boxes.
   a. How are C and n related?
      $C = 1.2n$
   b. Graph the relationship between n and C.

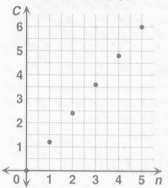

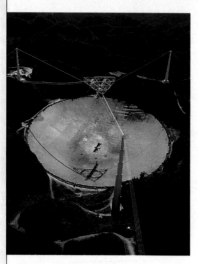

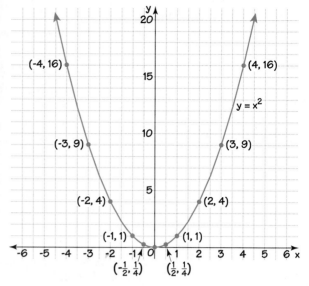

Any vertical cross section of a radio telescope receiving dish, like the one shown here in Arecibo, Puerto Rico, is part of a parabola. Compare this picture to the part of the graph from $x = -1$ to $x = 1$.

The parabola has important properties. Because of these properties, it is a shape used in the manufacture of automobile headlights, satellite dishes, and telescopes.

Graphs of equations may have shapes quite different from lines or parabolas. You are asked to explore these in the questions and in the next lesson.

QUESTIONS

Covering the Reading

In 1–4, consider the graph of $C = \pi d$ in this lesson.

1. Which variable is the first coordinate of points on the graph? *d*

2. Which variable is the second coordinate of points on the graph? *c*

3. *Multiple choice.* Which is the best description of the graph?
   (a) line   (b) ray without its endpoint   (c) line segment   (b)

4. Name a point on the graph other than those given in Example 1.
   Sample: $(3, 3\pi) \approx (3, 9.42)$

In 5–9, consider the graph of $A = s^2$.

5. Which variable is the first coordinate of points on the graph? *s*

6. Which variable is the second coordinate of points on the graph? *A*

7. The graph is part of the curve known as a __?__. parabola

8. Suppose the point $(5, t)$ is on this graph. What is t? 25

9. a. How does this graph differ from the graph of $y = x^2$?
    b. How is this graph the same as the graph of $y = x^2$?

9a) The graph of $A = s^2$ contains only positive values for s.
b) This graph is identical to the right half of the graph of $y = x^2$.

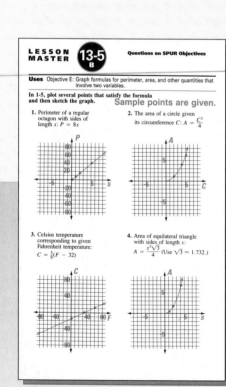

Optional Activities

Activity 2 Technology Connection In *Technology Sourcebook, Calculator Master 13,* students use a graphics calculator to graph various formulas.

Adapting to Individual Needs

English Language Development
Help students with the pronunciation of the term *parabola*. Point out that the accent is on the second syllable. You might also want to tell them that *parabola* is derived from the Greek word *parabole* which means comparison, as in the word parable.

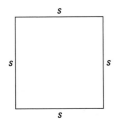

s

s   s

s

10a, b)

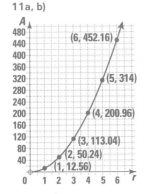

(5, 20)
(4, 16)
(3, 12)
(2, 8)
(1, 4)

10. A formula for the perimeter p of a square is $p = 4s$, where s is the length of a side of the square.
  a. Graph 5 pairs of values (s, p) that satisfy this formula.
  b. Sketch a graph of all pairs (s, p) that satisfy $p = 4s$.
  c. Describe the graph.
  The graph is a ray without its endpoint.

11. Recall that a formula for the surface area *S.A.* of a sphere with radius r is *S.A.* $= 4\pi r^2$. Let A stand for the surface area *S.A.*
  a. Graph 6 pairs of values (r, A) that satisfy this formula. (You may need to use an approximation to 4π.)
  b. Sketch a graph of all pairs (x, y) that satisfy $y = 4\pi x^2$.
  See below left.

12. a. Graph the equation $y = 3 - x^2$.
  b. Explain how this graph is related to the graph of $y = x^2$.
  a, b) Sample: The graph is like that of $y = x^2$, but reflected over the x-axis and then translated 3 units up.

13. Graph six points (x, y) such that $\dfrac{y}{x} = \dfrac{4}{3}$. *(Lesson 13-4)*
  Samples: (3, 4), (6, 8), (9, 12), (-3, -4), (-6, -8)

14. Solve $9x - 10 = 30 + x$. *(Lesson 13-3)* $x = 5$

15. Solve $36t = -\dfrac{2}{3} \cdot 12 - 28t$. *(Lesson 13-3)* $t = -\dfrac{1}{8}$

16. Triangle MIX is a size change image of $\triangle DEN$.

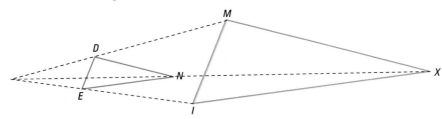

  a. *True or false.* The triangles are congruent. False
  b. If $DE = 10$, $MI = 22$, and $EN = 40$, what is the value of IX?
  (Lesson 11-8) $IX = 88$

11a, b)

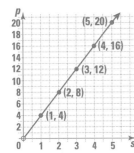

(6, 452.16)
(5, 314)
(4, 200.96)
(3, 113.04)
(2, 50.24)
(1, 12.56)

17. In 1990, the most populous Canadian province, Ontario, had 9,747,600 people living in 344,090 square miles. The least populous province, Prince Edward Island, had 130,400 people living in 2,185 square miles. Which of these provinces was more densely populated? Explain your answer. *(Lesson 11-2)*
Prince Edward Island, with about 60 people per square mile, was more densely populated than Ontario, with about 28 people per square mile.

Lesson 13-5 Graphs of Formulas **717**

2. The formula for the area of a semicircle with radius r is $A = \frac{1}{2}\pi r^2$. Graph this formula for values of r from 0 to 10.

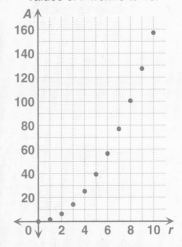

Notes on Questions

Question 12 Once you have established that the graph is a parabola, ask students what in the formula causes the parabola to open downward. [The subtraction of x^2] What does the 3 in the equation mean on the graph? [The highest point of the parabola is at the point (0, 3).] Looking at the numbers and operations in the equation can be used to predict how the graph will look. You might also wish to introduce the term *vertex* for the intersection of the parabola with its symmetry line.

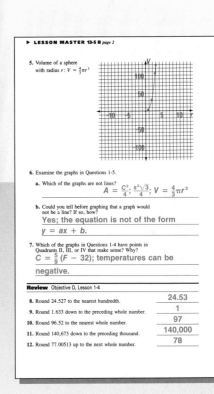

Adapting to Individual Needs

Extra Help
Students may be confused by the fact that the graph in **Example 1** is a straight line while the graph in **Example 2** is a curve. Point out that the variables in **Example 1** are c and d and that neither variable has an exponent. The variables in **Example 2** are A and s, but the variable s has an exponent of 2. Although students do not need to know the term *quadratic equation*, it is useful for them to know that the exponent of 2 for one or more variables leads to a graph that is curved.

Notes on Questions

Question 19 You might want to extend this question by asking students to generalize. If there are *r* rows of dried fruit with *p* pieces in each row, how many pieces are not next to a side of the box? $[(r-2)(p-2)]$

Question 20 This question reviews an important idea that is needed in Lesson 13-6.

Follow-up for Lesson 13-5

Practice

For more questions on SPUR Objectives, use **Lesson Master 13-5A** (shown on page 715) or **Lesson Master 13-5B** (shown on pages 716–717).

Assessment

Written Communication Have students graph $y = 2x$ and $y = 2x^2$. Then have them write a paragraph describing the differences between the graphs. [Paragraphs show understanding of the term *parabola* and the relationship between an equation and its graph.]

Extension

✎ **Writing** Have students do some research, and write a report on the use of the parabola in the manufacture of certain products. They might use the products mentioned on page 716 or others of their choice. The reports should include reasons for using the parabola shape.

Project Update Project 1, *Graphs of Equations with Powers*, on page 725, relates to the content of this lesson.

18. *TRAP* is a trapezoid with lengths given as shown.
    a. Is enough information given to find the area of *TRAP*? **Yes**
    b. If so, find the area. If not, tell what additional information is needed. *(Lessons 10-10, 12-3)* **210 square units**

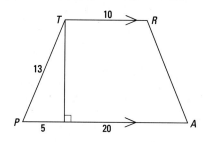

19. A box of dried fruit has 7 rows of fruit with 8 pieces in each row.
    a. How many pieces of fruit are in the box? **56**
    b. How many pieces of fruit are *not* next to a side of the box? **30**
    (Lessons 6-3, 9-1)

20a)
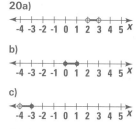

20. Graph on a number line.
    a. $2 < x < 3$
    b. $0 \leq x \leq 1$
    c. $-4 < x \leq -3$ *(Lesson 4-10)*

Exploration

21. An automatic grapher is recommended for this question. The graph of $y = x^2$ contains the points $(-1, 1)$, $(0, 0)$, and $(1, 1)$.
    a. Draw an accurate picture of the part of the curve from $(-1, 1)$ to $(1, 1)$ on the window $-1 \leq x \leq 1$, $-1 \leq y \leq 1$.
    b. Graph the equation $y = x^3$ on the same window as part **a**. Describe one similarity and one difference in the graphs of $y = x^2$ and $y = x^3$. **Answers may vary.**
    c. Explore these graphs with different windows. Describe what happens. **Answers will vary.**

21a)
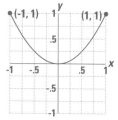

b)
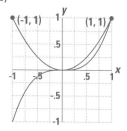

Sample: Both graphs are curves. The *y* values for $y = x^2$ are all positive but for $y = x^3$ they are both negative and positive.

Adapting to Individual Needs

Challenge
Have students find as many values of *x* and *y* as possible that satisfy the equation $xy = 36$. Remind them to use negative values for *x* and *y* as well as positive values. Then have them draw the graph of the equation.

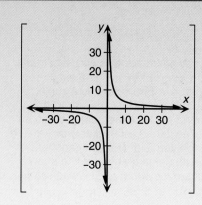

13-6

Graphs of Equations with Symbols for Rounding

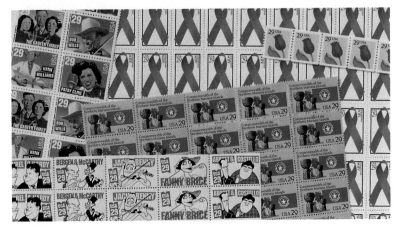

Stamp of approval. *The Postal Service offers a large variety of first-class stamps.*

There is a sense in which the postal-rate graphs from Lesson 13-1 are incomplete. They do not take into account weights that are not whole numbers. Below at the left is the graph of $c = 23w + 6$ from Lesson 13-1. At the right below is a more accurate graph for the situation.

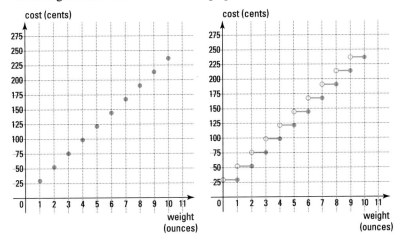

Notice how the graph at the right gets its shape. When a letter weighs less than 1 ounce, it costs 29¢ to mail. So for values of w between 0 and 1, the value of c is 29¢. This is represented by the bar that is farthest left and lowest. This bar has an open circle at its left because a weight of 0 is impossible. The closed circle at the right means that a weight of exactly 1 ounce costs 29¢.

The next bar goes from (1, 52) to (2, 52). This means that it costs 52¢ to mail a letter weighing between 1 and 2 ounces. The open circle means

Lesson 13-6 *Graphs of Equations with Symbols for Rounding* **719**

Lesson 13-6 Overview

Broad Goals This lesson introduces the symbols $\lceil x \rceil$ and $\lfloor x \rfloor$ for the results of rounding x up and down to the nearest integer, respectively, and graphs the simplest equations with these symbols.

Perspective Many situations in the real world involve rounding. Dealing with these situations mathematically requires a way of representing the rounded values. One symbol used for this purpose is the *greatest integer symbol* $\lfloor x \rfloor$, representing the greatest integer less than or equal to x. Or, put another way, it is the result of rounding x down to the nearest integer.

Another symbol commonly used as the greatest integer symbol is [ ]. This symbol has three weaknesses. First, it already has a meaning as a grouping symbol. Second, it favors rounding down when rounding up is just as common. Though rounding x up to

the nearest integer can be described by $-[-x]$, that is rather unwieldy. Third, it does not visually suggest what is happening. For these reasons, computer scientists and others who need precise ways of describing rounding use the symbols $\lceil \, \rceil$ and $\lfloor \, \rfloor$ described in this lesson.

---

before the cost of mailing them is determined; durations of phone calls are rounded up to the nearest minute or second to determine their cost; numbers of Calories in foods are rounded to the nearest integer in order to report them; percents of minimum daily requirements are rounded to the nearest integer percent. Also, calculators and computers cannot store infinite decimals, so they store approximations rounded to some decimal place.

Now consider the two graphs for postal rates on page 719. The graph at the right is more accurate and descriptive than the graph at the left. The question that will be answered in this lesson is, "How can the situation be described algebraically?"

❶ The symbols for rounding up and rounding down are introduced here, and examples of their use are found in **Example 1.**

❷ **Example 2** relates the idea of rounding to graphs. When the simplest equation using the rounding down symbol, $y = \lfloor x \rfloor$, is graphed in **Example 2**, the desired step-like graph appears.

that (1, 52) is not included in the graph. The closed circle means that (2, 52) is included. The other bars have similar meanings.

In this lesson, we introduce two new symbols. These symbols make it possible to write an equation for the graph at the right. They are the *rounding up* and *rounding down* symbols.

❶ $\lceil x \rceil$ is the result of rounding x up to the nearest integer.
$\lfloor x \rfloor$ is the result of rounding x down to the nearest integer.

Example 1

Evaluate each expression.

a. $\lceil 4.3 \rceil$ **b.** $\lfloor 4.3 \rfloor$ **c.** $\lceil 75 \rceil$
d. $\lfloor 75 \rfloor$ **e.** $\lceil -199.456 \rceil$ **f.** $\lfloor -199.456 \rfloor$

Solutions

a. 4.3 rounded up to the nearest integer is 5, so $\lceil 4.3 \rceil = 5$.
b. 4.3 rounded down to the nearest integer is 4, so $\lfloor 4.3 \rfloor = 4$.
c. and **d.** 75 is already rounded to the nearest integer. So $\lceil 75 \rceil = \lfloor 75 \rfloor = 75$.
e. -199.456 is between -199 and -200. The larger of these is -199. So, when rounded up, -199.456 goes to -199. Thus $\lceil -199.456 \rceil = -199$.
f. -199.456 rounded down to the nearest integer is -200. So $\lfloor -199.456 \rfloor = -200$.

Computers often have to deal with rounded values. So the symbols $\lfloor\ \rfloor$ and $\lceil\ \rceil$ are very commonly used in computer programming. Programmers sometimes call $\lfloor\ \rfloor$ the **floor function** symbol and call $\lceil\ \rceil$ the **ceiling function** symbol. Sometimes brackets [ ] are used for the floor function and it is called the **greatest integer function** symbol. In some programming languages and on some calculators, INT(x) has the same meaning as $\lfloor x \rfloor$.

It is possible to graph expressions using these symbols.

Optional Activities

Activity 1 You might want to have students **work in groups.** Use this activity after they have completed the lesson.

1. Evaluate the expressions $10\lceil \frac{x}{10} \rceil$ and $10\lfloor \frac{x}{10} \rfloor$ for many values of x.
   What do these expressions do? [They round x up and down to the nearest multiple of 10.]
2. What expression would round x up to the nearest 100? [$100\lceil \frac{x}{100} \rceil$]
3. What expression would round x down to the nearest 1,000,000? [$1{,}000{,}000\lfloor \frac{x}{1000000} \rfloor$]
4. What expression would round x up to the nearest .01? [$.01\lceil \frac{x}{.01} \rceil$ or $\frac{1}{100}\lceil 100x \rceil$]

Activity 2 Multicultural Connection As an extension of **Question 14**, you might have students investigate postal rates in other countries. Have them write a formula for the cost C of mailing a letter in terms of the weight w. Note that in most countries, the weight will be in grams. You might also ask students who have postage stamps from other countries to bring them to show to the class.

Graph the pairs (x, y) that satisfy $y = \lfloor x \rfloor$ for values of x from 0 to 3.

Solution

When $x = 0$, $y = \lfloor x \rfloor = \lfloor 0 \rfloor = 0$. This yields the point $(0, 0)$ at the lower left of the graph. When x has a value between 0 and 1, then $y = \lfloor x \rfloor = 0$. This yields the lowest segment of the graph. When x is between 1 and 2, $y = \lfloor x \rfloor = 1$. This yields the middle segment. The highest segment contains the points corresponding to values of x between 2 and 3. Then $y = \lfloor x \rfloor = 2$.

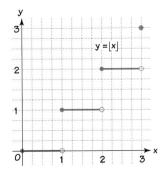

Today's graphing technology is very powerful. People now graph things that before would have been difficult, if not impossible, to graph, and newspapers and magazines now show many more graphs than they did a generation ago. As you study more mathematics, you will see graphs that a previous generation could not imagine. But the technology is not perfect. For instance, if you try to graph $y = \lfloor x \rfloor$ on today's automatic graphers, you may not get an accurate graph. Here is the output from one grapher.

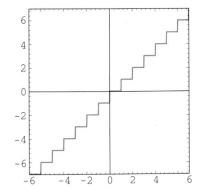

The segments of the graph are connected. This is not correct. It shows that when you use graphing technology, you should have some estimate of what an answer should be and be able to check whatever you get using a different approach. Of course, this is good advice even if you do not use technology!

Lesson 13-6 Graphs of Equations with Symbols for Rounding 721

Optional Activities

Activity 3 Technology Connection In *Technology Sourcebook, Calculator Master 14,* students use a graphics calculator to explore step functions.

Adapting to Individual Needs

Extra Help
The symbols $\lceil x \rceil$ and $\lfloor x \rfloor$ look almost the same, but they have different meanings. In case students have trouble distinguishing between the two, point out that the symbol with "upper bars" means that the number is rounded up, while the symbol with "lower bars" means that the number is rounded down.

LESSON MASTER 13-6 A

Questions on SPUR Objectives
See pages 729-731 for objectives.

Skills Objective B

In 1-10, evaluate each expression.
1. $\lfloor 3.42 \rfloor$ **3** 2. $\lfloor \frac{9}{8} \rfloor$ **2** 3. $\lceil -4 \rceil$ **-4**
4. $\lfloor -12.25 \rfloor$ **-13** 5. $\lceil 999 \rceil$ **999** 6. $\lceil -.3 \rceil$ **0**
7. $\lfloor -1000.001 \rfloor$ **-1001** 8. $\lceil \sqrt{30} \rceil + \lfloor \sqrt{30} \rfloor$ **11**
9. $\lfloor -8.3 \rfloor + \lfloor 8.3 \rfloor$ **-1** 10. $\lceil \frac{11.6}{5.8} \rceil$ **3**

Multiple choice. In 11 and 12, special cases could be helpful.

11. A school bus holds 44 students. If a class of c students taking a trip, how many buses are needed to transport all students by bus?
(a) $\lfloor \frac{c}{44} \rfloor$ (b) $\lfloor \frac{c}{44} \rfloor$ (c) $\lceil \frac{c}{44} \rceil$ (d) $\lceil \frac{c}{44} \rceil$ **b**

12. A recipe serving 4 people calls for 2 cans of chicken broth. If p people are attending a party, how many cans of broth are needed?
(a) $2 \lfloor \frac{p}{4} \rfloor$ (b) $\lfloor \frac{2p}{4} \rfloor$ (c) $2 \lceil \frac{p}{4} \rceil$ (d) $\lceil \frac{2p}{4} \rceil$ **d**

Representations Objective H

In 13 and 14, use this graph representing the cost of parking.

13. *Multiple choice.* Through 8 hours, this is the graph of
(a) $y = \lfloor x \rfloor + 3$.
(b) $y = \lceil x \rceil + 2$.
(c) $y = \frac{1}{2} \lfloor x \rfloor + 3$.
(d) $y = 2 \lceil x \rceil + 1$. **b**

14. What does the uppermost bar on the graph mean?
Cost is the same for 8 to 12 hours.

721

❸ The lesson ends by showing how the ⌈ ⌉ symbol solves the problem of representing the graph that was introduced at the beginnig of the lesson.

Be sure to have students examine at least one of the step function graphs to ensure that they understand why there are horizontal segments and why one side of the segment has an open circle while the other side has a filled-in circle.

Additional Examples

Students can use **Teaching Aid 87** to show their graphs for additional example 2.

1. Evaluate each expression.
   a. $\lceil 7.831 \rceil$ 8
   b. $\lfloor 7.831 \rfloor$ 7
   c. $\lceil -2.5 \rceil$ −2
   d. $\lfloor -2.5 \rfloor$ −3
   e. $\lceil 499 \rceil$ 499
   f. $\lfloor 499 \rfloor$ 499

2. Graph the pairs (x, y) that satisfy $y = \lceil x \rceil$ from −3 to 0.

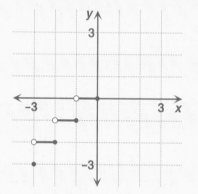

Look again at the graph in the Solution of Example 2. Notice that for integer values of x, the graph of $y = \lfloor x \rfloor$ contains the same points as the graph of $y = x$. For the non-integer values, the y-values are rounded down, as they should be. The graph resembles the steps of a staircase, so sometimes the symbols $\lfloor \; \rfloor$ and $\lceil \; \rceil$ are called **step function** symbols.

❸ Below is the graph of the full line $y = 23x + 6$ and the postage-rate graph that began this lesson. To find an equation describing the postage-rate graph, consider the steps in calculating the postage rate.

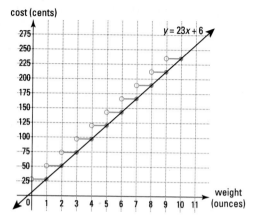

Step 1: Round the weight up to the nearest integer. If the weight was originally w, after rounding it is $\lceil w \rceil$.

Step 2: To find the postal cost, multiply the rounded weight by 23 and add 6. So the cost is $23\lceil w \rceil + 6$.

Consequently, an equation for the postage rate graph is $c = 23\lceil w \rceil + 6$. Notice how similar this is to the equation $y = 23w + 6$ that works for integer values of w.

Studying the rounding symbol is a fitting way to end this book. It returns us to an idea from arithmetic, rounding, that was discussed at the very beginning of the book. Graphs involving the rounding symbol have an interesting geometry. The equations with variables show how algebra is used by the programmer of the postal weighing machine to arrive at the postal rates when you weigh a letter. So, this one idea combines arithmetic, algebra, and geometry—using ideas you know and introducing you to ideas that you will encounter in your next mathematics courses.

An invention that lasts. *Jan Matzeliger was an inventor who industrialized shoe making in 1883. His invention, the shoe-lasting machine, shaped and fastened leather over a sole.*

722

Adapting to Individual Needs

English Language Development
You might ask students why they think ⌈ ⌉ is called the *ceiling* function and ⌊ ⌋ is called the *floor* function. It might help them to remember these functions if you relate the symbol ⌈ ⌉ to the ceiling and the symbol ⌊ ⌋ to the floor.

13)

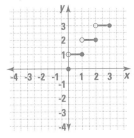

15)

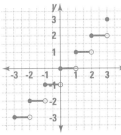

Math counts! *At the annual MATHCOUNTS National Competition in Washington, D.C., mathletes from each state meet and compete. The Countdown Round, shown here, decides the individual winner from among the 10 competitors with the highest scores.*

MATHCOUNTS

Covering the Reading

1. Examine the right-hand graph on page 719. Describe what the top segment represents. When a letter weighs between 9 and 10 ounces, the cost of mailing is 236 cents.

In 2–9, evaluate the expression.

2. $\lceil 11.3 \rceil$ 12

3. $\lfloor 11.3 \rfloor$ 11

4. $\lceil -8 \rceil$ -8

5. $\lceil 0.09\overline{1} \rceil$ 1

6. $\lfloor 600 \rfloor$ 600

7. $\lfloor -\pi \rfloor$ -4

8. $\lfloor \frac{3}{2} \rfloor$ 1

9. $\lceil \frac{47}{12} \rceil$ 4

10. Which two are equal? $\lceil \frac{1}{2} \rceil, \lfloor \frac{1}{2} \rfloor, \lfloor -\frac{1}{2} \rfloor, \lceil -\frac{1}{2} \rceil$ $\lfloor \frac{1}{2} \rfloor$ and $\lceil -\frac{1}{2} \rceil$ both equal zero.

11. Give three names for the symbol $\lfloor \ \rfloor$. rounding down function, floor function, greatest integer function.

12. Give two names for the symbol $\lceil \ \rceil$. rounding up function, ceiling function

13. Graph the pairs (x, y) that satisfy $y = \lceil x \rceil$ for values of x from 0 to 3.

14. In 1994, the cost of mailing a letter was calculated as follows.
    Step 1: Round the weight up to the nearest ounce.
    Step 2: Multiply the rounded weight by 23, then add 6.
    Give a formula for the cost C of mailing in terms of the weight w.
    $C = 23 \lceil w \rceil + 6$

Applying the Mathematics

15. Extend the graph of Example 2 to cover values of x from -3 to 0.

In 16 and 17, *multiple choice*. Use special cases to determine the answer.

16. A school is allowed one representative to a mathematics contest for every 250 students. (For instance, if the school has 251–500 students, it can send 2 representatives.) If the school has s students, how many representatives can it send?
    (a) $\lfloor \frac{s}{250} \rfloor$
    (b) $\lceil \frac{s}{250} \rceil$
    (c) $\frac{\lceil s \rceil}{250}$
    (d) $\frac{\lfloor s \rfloor}{250}$ (b)

17. Suppose a taxi ride costs $.75 plus $.25 for each $\frac{1}{4}$ mile. Assume the meter clicks on the quarter mile. What is the cost C of a ride of m miles?
    (a) $C = 0.75 + \lfloor m \rfloor$
    (b) $C = 0.75 + 4\lfloor 0.25m \rfloor$
    (c) $C = 0.75 + m$
    (d) $C = 0.75 + 0.25\lfloor 4m \rfloor$ (d)

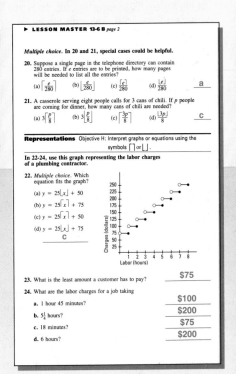

▶ **LESSON MASTER 13-6 B** *page 2*

Multiple choice. In 20 and 21, special cases could be helpful.

20. Suppose a single page in the telephone directory can contain 280 entries. If *e* entries are to be printed, how many pages will be needed to list all the entries?
    (a) $\frac{e}{280}$ (b) $\frac{\lceil e \rceil}{280}$ (c) $\lceil \frac{e}{280} \rceil$ (d) $\lfloor \frac{e}{280} \rfloor$ a

21. A casserole serving eight people calls for 3 cans of chili. If *p* people are coming for dinner, how many cans of chili are needed?
    (a) $3\lceil \frac{p}{8} \rceil$ (b) $3\lfloor \frac{p}{8} \rfloor$ (c) $\lceil \frac{3p}{8} \rceil$ (d) $\frac{\lfloor 3p \rfloor}{8}$ c

Representations Objective H: Interpret graphs or equations using the symbols $\lceil \ \rceil$ or $\lfloor \ \rfloor$.

In 22-24, use this graph representing the labor charges of a plumbing contractor.

22. *Multiple choice.* Which equation fits the graph?
    (a) $y = 25\lfloor x \rfloor + 50$
    (b) $y = 25\lceil x \rceil + 75$
    (c) $y = 25\lceil x \rceil + 50$
    (d) $y = 25\lfloor x \rfloor + 75$
    c

23. What is the least amount a customer has to pay? $75

24. What are the labor charges for a job taking
    a. 1 hour 45 minutes? $100
    b. $5\frac{1}{4}$ hours? $200
    c. 18 minutes? $75
    d. 6 hours? $200

Follow-up for Lesson 13-6

Practice
For more questions on SPUR Objectives, use **Lesson Master 13-6A** (shown on page 721) or **Lesson Master 13-6B** (shown on pages 722–723).

Assessment
Written Communication Have each student write a paragraph about what he or she has learned about symbols used for rounding. [Students distinguish between symbols used for rounding up and for rounding down and explain how equations with rounding symbols are graphed.]

Extension
✎ **Writing** Ask students to research various situations when prices and/or times are rounded up or down. They might include utility bills, equipment rental, or recreation facility fees. Students should compile their findings into a written class report.

Project Update Project 2, *Long-Distance Rates*, and Project 3, *Graphing Square Roots,* on page 725, relate to the content of this lesson.

19a) Samples:
At 10 mph, braking distance is 5 feet; at 20 mph, 20 feet; at 50 mph, 125 feet; at 60 mph, 180 feet.
b) Sample:(10,5),(20,20), (50, 125), (60, 180)

Making the grade.
To make new cars safe and marketable, automakers put cars through a variety of tests. The car pictured here is being tested for ease of steering, maneuverability, and braking distance.

22) Sample: Multiplying by a negative number reverses directions. Multiplying with two negative numbers brings the sign back to where it started.

---

18. Given that x is an integer, find x from these clues.

Clue 1: $\left\lceil \dfrac{x}{2} \right\rceil = 8$

Clue 2: $\left\lceil \dfrac{x-5}{2} \right\rceil = 5$
15

Review

19. If a car is traveling at s miles per hour, then once a driver steps on the brakes, it takes at least d feet to stop, where $d = \dfrac{s^2}{20}$. d is called the *braking distance*.
a. Give the braking distance for four different speeds.
b. Name four ordered pairs (s, d) that satisfy this formula.
c. What geometric figure is the graph of the formula? *(Lesson 13-5)*
part of a parabola

20. The graphs of $y = 3x$ and $y = 2x + 4$ intersect at what point? *(Lessons 13-1, 13-3, 13-4)* (4, 12)

21. Three more than half a number equals two more than a third of the same number. What is the number? *(Lesson 13-3)* -6

22. In a few sentences, explain why the product of two negative numbers is positive. *(Lesson 9-6)*

Exploration

23. Evaluate $\left\lfloor \dfrac{a}{b} \right\rfloor$ for many pairs of integers a and b, where a is quite a bit larger than b. From the results you get, tell how $\left\lfloor \dfrac{a}{b} \right\rfloor$ is related to the integer division of a by b. $\left\lfloor \dfrac{a}{b} \right\rfloor$ is the integer quotient when a is divided by b.

Adapting to Individual Needs

Challenge
The following method can be used for finding the day of the week for any date based on our current calendar.

Suppose y = year, d = day of the month, and m = the number of the month in the year. The exceptions are that January is considered the 13th month of the *previous* year, and February is considered the 14th month of the previous year. For example,

2/23/1993 = 14/23/1992 and 1/1/1994 = 13/1/1993. The months March through December are numbered 3 through 12 as usual. Then the number of the day of the week is the remainder when $\left(d + 2m + \lfloor \frac{3(m+1)}{5} \rfloor + y + \lfloor \frac{y}{4} \rfloor - \lfloor \frac{y}{100} \rfloor + \lfloor \frac{y}{400} \rfloor + 2 \right)$ is divided by 7.

Sunday is considered Day 1. Saturday is Day 7 and is indicated by a remainder of 0.

Have students use this method to find the day of the week on which they were born.

A project presents an opportunity for you to extend your knowledge of a topic related to the material of this chapter. You should allow more time for a project than you do for typical homework questions.

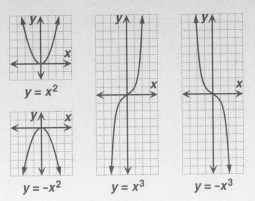

PROJECTS 13 CHAPTER THIRTEEN

1 Graphs of Equations with Powers

In this chapter, equations of the form $y = ax$ and $y = ax^2$ were graphed. Explore the graphs of the equations $y = ax^3$, $y = ax^4$, $y = ax^5$, $y = ax^6$, and so on, when x is any real number (positive, zero, or negative). Consider cases where a is positive and cases where a is negative.

2 Long-Distance Rates

Find out the precise long-distance rate from where you live to a place in another area you or someone in your family might call. Determine and graph at least six ordered pairs (,) based on your long-distance rate. Describe the graph with an equation using the rounding up or rounding down symbol.

3 Graphing Square Roots

a. Graph the equation $y = \sqrt{x}$. Explain how the shape of the graph compares with shapes that are mentioned in this chapter.
b. Graph $y = \sqrt{\lceil x \rceil}$ **c.** Graph $y = \lceil \sqrt{x} \rceil$.

4 An Experiment with Decimal Places

Locate a reference where a large number of digits (about 50) are given for an infinite decimal for an irrational number. (For instance, you might be able to find such a decimal for the number π or for some square roots.) Perform this experiment to see how often each of the even digits 0, 2, 4, 6, and 8 appears in the decimal. Make a table of the frequency of appearance of each digit in the first 10, 20, 30, 40, 50 places. Then graph the relative frequencies as was done in Lesson 13-4. If the digits appear at random, near what line should the points lie? Do they? Explain what has happened with the number you chose.

Chapter 13 *Projects* **725**

Chapter 13 Projects

Chapter 13 projects relate to the content of the lessons as follows.

Project	Lesson(s)
1	13-1, 13-5
2	13-6
3	13-6
4	13-4
5	13-3
6	13-2, 13-3

1 Graphs of Equations with Powers Students may wish to use automatic graphers for this project. Explain that equations of the form $y = ax^n$ are called powering functions. Lead students to understand that every powering function has symmetry. Have them name the type of symmetry that even- and odd-powering functions have. Even-powered functions have reflection symmetry with the y-axis as the line of symmetry. Odd-powered functions have rotation symmetry. The graph of the equation can be mapped onto itself under a 180° rotation around the origin.

2 Long-Distance Rates Point out that the time the call is placed, the day the call is placed, and the long-distance company that is used are factors that students will need to consider when finding long-distance rates. Some students may wish to make several graphs showing the cost of calling the same place at different times or using different long-distance companies.

3 Graphing Square Roots Some students may have difficulty understanding that the equations in **parts b and c** are not the same. In **part b**, the value of y is not necessarily an integer because y is equal to the square root of the integer to which x is rounded up. In **part c**, however, the value of y is always an integer because it is the square root of x that is being rounded up to the nearest integer. The graph of $y = \sqrt{x}$ is the upper half of the parabola with equation $x = y^2$.

4 An Experiment with Decimal Places The first fifty-one digits of π, $\sqrt{2}$ and $\sqrt{3}$ are:
π = 3.14159 26535 89793 23846 26433 83279 50288 41971 69399 37510

Project 4 continues on page 726.

Possible responses

1. The following information is a sample of what students might include in their projects. All graphs of the form $y = ax^n$ will pass through the origin. When n is even, the graph is a parabola. The parabola will be in quadrants I and II if a is positive and in quadrants III and IV if a is negative. When n is odd, the graph is in quadrants I and III when a is positive and in quadrants II and IV when a is negative.

$y = x^2$

$y = -x^2$

$y = x^3$

$y = -x^3$

$\sqrt{2}$ = 1.41421 35623 73095 04880
16887 24209 69807 85696
71875 37694

$\sqrt{3}$ = 1.73205 08075 68877 19352
74463 41505 87236 69428
05253 81038

5 How Often Is a Solution to
$ax + b = cx + d$ an Integer?
There are 1296 [$6 \times 6 \times 6 \times 6$] possible equations that can be formed by tossing four dice to find the values of a, b, c, and d.

There are several special groups of equations to consider in this project. When $a = c$ and $b = d$, the equation $ax + b = cx + d$ will be true for all values of x. When $a = c$ and $b \neq d$, the equation will not have a solution. Finally, any equation in which $a \neq c$, but $b = d$, will have zero as the solution.

As in Project 3 of Chapter 10, remind students that zero is an integer, and it is not positive.

6 When Will One Person Over-
take Another? This project would most appropriately be assigned to students who are avid sports fans. Football fans could find comparisons for yards rushed or passed, or for field goals kicked. Basketball fans could find comparisons for field goals, free throws, or rebounds. Baseball fans could find comparisons for number of triples, doubles, or singles hit.

Statistics for individual players can be found in newspapers, sport magazines, and sports almanacs.

5 How Often Is a Solution to
$ax + b = cx + d$ an Integer?
This project is similar to Project 2 of Chapter 10. Find four six-sided dice and call them a, b, c, and d. Toss the dice and record the numbers into the equation $ax + b = cx + d$. For instance, if the die a shows 3, b shows 1, c shows 4 and d shows 5, then the equation will be $3x + 1 = 4x + 5$. Write down 50 equations in this way. Determine the relative frequencies of the following events:
a. the solution is positive
b. the solution is an integer
c. the solution is a positive integer.
Write down what you think are the probabilities of these events, and explain how you have come to your conclusions.

6 When Will One
Person Overtake
Another?
In Lesson 13-2 there is a question asking when Juan Gonzales will overtake Barry Bonds in the number of home runs in his career. Find another actual example like this. You will need: two people, some count associated with each, and the count for the person who has less to be growing faster than the count for the person who has more. Determine when the person who has less will overtake the person who has more. Show this both with an equation and with a graph.

To get ideas for Project 6, think about people you know, sports and activities you like, and how people change at different rates.

Additional responses, pages 725–726
2. Responses will vary.
3. The graph of $y = \sqrt{x}$ is one half of a parabola.

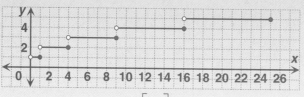

$$y = \lceil \sqrt{x} \rceil$$

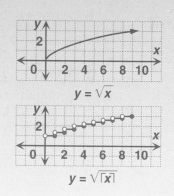

$y = \sqrt{x}$

$$y = \sqrt{\lceil x \rceil}$$

SUMMARY

Summary

The Summary gives an overview of the entire chapter and provides an opportunity for students to consider the material as a whole. Thus, the Summary can be used to help students relate and unify the concepts presented in the chapter.

The solutions to any equation can be graphed. If the equation has two variables, then the graph is a set of ordered pairs that can be plotted on a coordinate graph. In this chapter, four types of equations were discussed: $y = ax$; $y = ax + b$; $y = ax^2$; and $y = \lceil x \rceil$ or $y = \lfloor x \rfloor$.

In these descriptions, x is the first coordinate of the ordered pair, y is the second coordinate, and a and b are fixed real numbers.

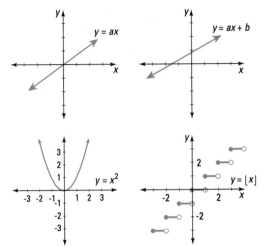

Equations of the type $y = ax$ occur in formulas for perimeter such as $p = 4s$ or $C = \pi d$. A graph of this type of an equation is a line containing the origin. This line contains all of the pairs (x, y) if $\frac{y}{x} = a$. Let an event occur y times out of x possibilities. If the event has probability a of occurring, then $\frac{y}{x}$ will be close to a, so the points (x, y) will lie close to the line $y = ax$.

Equations of the type $y = ax + b$ occur when an initial amount increases or decreases at a constant rate, such as the cost of a phone call. The graph of $y = ax + b$ is a line containing the point $(0, b)$. It is natural to compare two costs to see when one is lower. It is possible to determine which cost is lower if you know when the costs are equal. If the second equation is $y = cx + d$, then that value can be found by solving the equation $ax + b = cx + d$.

This equation, which has an unknown on both sides, can be solved by adding either $-ax$ or $-cx$ to both sides. The resulting equation has an unknown on only one side and can be solved using methods learned in earlier chapters.

Equations of the type $y = ax^2$ occur from formulas for area, like $A = s^2$ and $A = \pi r^2$. Their graphs are parabolas.

Equations involving the rounding up symbol $\lceil \ \rceil$ and the rounding down symbol $\lfloor \ \rfloor$ arise from situations in which rounding or estimating is necessary, such as when weights of letters are rounded before determining a postal rate. Their graphs resemble steps of a staircase.

VOCABULARY

Vocabulary

Terms, symbols, and properties are listed by lesson to provide a checklist of concepts a student must know. Emphasize that students should read the vocabulary list carefully before starting the Progress Self-Test. If students do not understand the meaning of a term, they should refer back to the indicated lesson.

You should be able to give a general description and a specific example of each of the following ideas.

Lesson 13-1
linear
linear equation

Lesson 13-2
automatic grapher, window

Lesson 13-4
slope

Lesson 13-5
parabola

Lesson 13-6
rounding up; rounding down
$\lceil x \rceil$, ceiling function
$\lfloor x \rfloor$, floor function, greatest
    integer function, INT(x)
step function

Chapter 13   *Summary and Vocabulary*   **727**

---

4. **Responses will vary. A sample response is given for π.**

No. of Digits	10	20	30	40	50
No. of Even Digits	3	8	13	19	21

If the digits appear at random, there should be about the same number of even numbers as odd numbers, so the points should lie near the graph of $y = \frac{1}{2}x$.

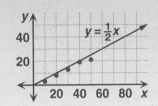

5. **Relative frequencies will vary but should be close to the following probabilities.**
   The probability of a unique positive solution is $\frac{5}{12}$ or 42%. The probability of a unique positive integer solution is $\frac{13}{81}$ or 16%.

6. **Responses will vary.**

PROGRESS SELF-TEST

Take this test as you would take a test in class. You will need a calculator and graph paper. Then check your work with the solutions in the Selected Answers section in the back of the book.

In 1 and 2, solve.

1. $60 + 14y = -20 + 30y$ $y = 5$
2. $3(2x - 8) = 4x + 9$ $x = \frac{33}{2}$
3. Evaluate $\lceil 987.654 \rceil$.   988
4. If $\lfloor x \rfloor = 8$, give two possible values of x.   See below.
5. The ordered pairs (10, 3), (20, 6), and (30, 9) all lie on the same line. What is an equation for that line? $y = \frac{3}{10}x$
6. Louise makes 30% of the 3-point shots she tries in basketball. If you were to graph ordered pairs (number of shots attempted, number of shots made), the points would tend to lie near what line? $y = \frac{3}{10}x$

In 7 and 8, use the following information. One car rental company charges $35 a day plus 48¢ a mile to rent a car. A second company charges $39 a day plus 41¢ a mile.

7. a. What will it cost to rent a car from the first company for 1 day, having driven m miles? $c = 35 + .48m$
   b. What equation can be solved to determine the number of miles m for which the car rental cost would be the same for these two companies? $35 + .48m = 39 + .41m$
8. Estimate, to the nearest mile, when the car rental cost would be the same for the two companies.   ≈ 57 miles
9. Graph $y = 4x$.   See margin.
10. Graph $y = -3x + 5$ See margin.

4) Any two numbers between 8 and 9, including 8, are acceptable.

13) Sample: The point where the lines meet is the solution to $y = 4x$ and $y = -3x + 5$, hence $4x = -3x + 5$ will determine the x-coordinate of the point where the lines meet.

In 11 and 12, use this information. A formula for the surface area of a cube is $A = 6s^2$, where s is the length of an edge of the cube.

11. a. What is the surface area of a cube whose edges have length 5?   150 sq units
    b. What point on the graph of $A = 6s^2$ is determined by the answer to part **a**? (Let s be the first coordinate.)   (5, 150)
12. Graph this formula.   See margin.
13. Explain how you can use the graphs from Questions 9 and 10 to solve the equation $4x = -3x + 5$.   See below left.
14. Solve the equation $4x = -3x + 5$ using any of the methods of this chapter.   See below.
15. *Multiple choice.* Which is the graph of $y = \lceil x \rceil$?   (c)

(a)   (b)

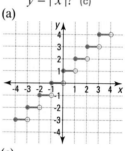   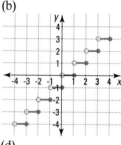

(c)   (d)

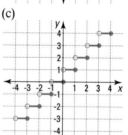   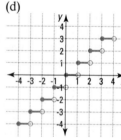

14) Sample:
$$4x = -3x + 5$$
$$4x + 3x = -3x + 3x + 5$$
$$7x = 5$$
$$x = \frac{5}{7}$$

Additional Answers

9.

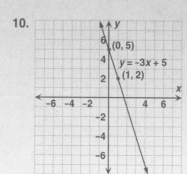

10.

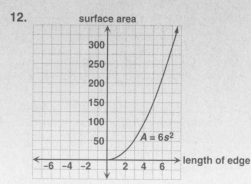

12.

surface area

$A = 6s^2$

length of edge

CHAPTER REVIEW

Questions on SPUR Objectives

SPUR stands for **S**kills, **P**roperties, **U**ses, and **R**epresentations. The Chapter Review questions are grouped according to the SPUR Objectives for this chapter.

SKILLS DEAL WITH THE PROCEDURES USED TO GET ANSWERS.

Objective A: *Solve equations of the form* $ax + b = cx + d$. *(Lesson 13-3)*

In 1–8, solve.

1. $12x + 7 = 2x + 11$ $x = \frac{2}{5}$
2. $8m - 2 = 17m - 20$ $m = 2$
3. $v = 3v - 1$ $v = \frac{1}{2}$
4. $5y = 100 - 3y$ $y = 12.5$
5. $6(2 + 3r) = 9 + r$ $r = -\frac{3}{17}$
6. $3s - (s - 15) = 4s + 5$ $s = 5$
7. $200 - 31t = 120 + 29t$ $t = \frac{4}{3}$
8. $\frac{1}{2}z + \frac{1}{2} = \frac{3}{2}z - \frac{1}{2}$ $z = 1$

Objective B: *Evaluate expressions using the symbols for rounding up or rounding down.* *(Lesson 13-6)*

In 9–12, evaluate.

9. $\lceil 2.5 \rceil - \lfloor 2.5 \rfloor$ 1
10. $\lceil \sqrt{10} \rceil + \lceil \sqrt{11} \rceil$ 8
11. $\lceil -40.8 \rceil$ -40
12. $\lfloor -\frac{2}{3} \rfloor$ -1
13. $\lceil 18.613 \rceil + 2\lfloor 4.2 \rfloor$ 27
14. If $\lfloor x \rfloor = 10$, give two possible values of x.
    Samples: 10, 10.3

PROPERTIES DEAL WITH THE PRINCIPLES BEHIND THE MATHEMATICS.

Objective C: *Find the line on which or near which the numerators and denominators of equal fractions or relative frequencies lie.* *(Lesson 13-4)*

15. **a.** Give three simple fractions equal to $\frac{7}{5}$.

    b. Think of each simple fraction $\left(\frac{y}{x}\right)$ you found in part **a** as a point (x, y) on a line. What is an equation for that line?

16. What is an equation for the line through $(3, 11)$ and $(9, 33)$? $y = \frac{11}{3}x$

15a) Samples: $\frac{-7}{-5}, \frac{14}{10}, \frac{49}{35}$; b) $y = \frac{7}{5}x$

17. Tornadoes occur with about equal relative frequency on each day of the week. Suppose you were to graph the ordered pair (number of tornadoes on Sunday last year, total number of tornadoes last year). Near what line would you expect this point to lie? $y = 7x$

18. Suppose you toss a coin you believe to be fair. Every so often you graph the points (number of heads, number of tosses). Near what line would you expect these points to be? $y = 2x$

Chapter 13 Review

Resources

From the **Teacher's Resource File**
■ Answer Master for Chapter 13 Review
■ Assessment Sourcebook Chapter 13 Test, Forms A–D Chapter 13 Test, Cumulative Form Comprehensive Test, Chapters 1–13

Additional Resources
■ TestWorks

The main objectives for the chapter are organized in the Chapter Review under the four types of understanding this book promotes—Skills, Properties, Uses, and Representations.

Whereas end-of-chapter material may be considered optional in some texts, in *UCSMP Transition Mathematics* we have selected these objectives and questions with the expectation that they will be covered. Students should be able to answer these questions with about 85% accuracy after studying the chapter.

You may assign these questions over a single night to help students prepare for a test the next day, or you may assign the questions over a two-day period. If you work the questions over two days, we recommend assigning the *evens* for homework the first night so that students get feedback in class the next day. Then assign the *odds* the night before the test since answers are provided to the odd-numbered questions.

It is effective to ask students which questions they still do not understand and to use the day or days as a total class discussion of the material which the class finds most difficult.

Assessment

Evaluation The *Assessment Sourcebook* provides five forms of the Chapter 13 Test. Forms A and B present parallel versions in a short-answer format. Forms C and D offer performance assessment. The fifth test is Chapter 13 Test, Cumulative Form. About 50% of this test covers Chapter 13, 25% covers Chapter 12, and 25% covers earlier chapters.

For information on grading, see *General Teaching Suggestions: Grading*, in the *Professional Sourcebook* which begins on page T20 of the Teacher's Edition.

Additional Answers

23.
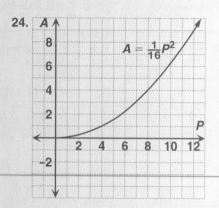

24.
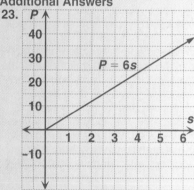

USES DEAL WITH APPLICATIONS OF MATHEMATICS IN REAL SITUATIONS.

Objective D: *Translate situations of constant increase or decrease that lead to sentences of the form $ax + b = cx + d$.* *(Lessons 13-2, 13-3)*

In 19–22, a situation is given.

a. Translate the given information into an equation of the form $ax + b = cx + d$ that will answer the question.

b. Solve the equation.

19. With one cellular car phone company, the monthly charge is $15, and calls cost 20¢ a minute. With another company, calls cost 34¢ a minute but the monthly charge is only $5. Determine the number of minutes for which the monthly bills from these companies would be the same. See below.

20. Kurt and Sara are saving money to buy their parents an anniversary present. Kurt now has $35 and is saving $6 a week. Sara has $60 and is saving $4 a week. When will they have the same amount?
a) $35 + 6w = 60 + 4w$;   b) after 13 weeks

19 a) $15 + .20m = 5 + .34m$; b) ≈ 71 min

21. Laura is now 57 inches tall and growing at a rate of about 1 inch each 100 days, or $\frac{1}{100} \frac{\text{in.}}{\text{day}}$. Robert is 59 inches tall and growing at about 1 inch each 150 days, or $\frac{1}{150} \frac{\text{in.}}{\text{day}}$. At these rates, in how many days will Laura and Robert be the same height? See below.

22. One football player currently has rushed for 3,000 yards in his career and gains an average of about 60 yards per game. A second player has rushed for 2,350 yards and gains an average of about 90 yards per game. If these rates continue, in how many games will the players have rushed for the same amount?
a) $3000 + 60g = 2350 + 90g$;
b) after 22 games

21 a) $57 + \frac{1}{100}d = 59 + \frac{1}{150}d$;
b) after 600 days

REPRESENTATIONS DEAL WITH PICTURES, GRAPHS, OR OBJECTS THAT ILLUSTRATE CONCEPTS.

Objective E: *Graph formulas for perimeter, area, and other quantities that involve two variables.* *(Lesson 13-5)*

23. In a regular hexagon, the perimeter P and the length s of a side are related by the formula $P = 6s$. Graph this formula. See margin.

24. The perimeter P and area A of a square are related by the formula $A = \frac{1}{16}P^2$. Graph this formula for values of P from 0 to 10. See margin.

25. The area A of a circle with diameter d is given by $A = \frac{\pi}{4}d^2$. Graph this formula for values of d from 0 to 10. See margin.

26. The circumference w of a person's wrist and the circumference n of that person's neck are said to be related by the formula $n = 2w$. Graph this formula. See margin.

25.
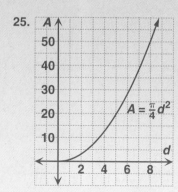

26.
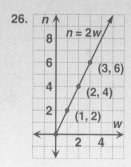

Objective F: *Graph equations of the form*
$y = ax + b.$ *(Lessons 13-1, 13-4)*

In 27–30, graph. **See margin for graphs.**

27. $y = -\frac{2}{3}x$

28. $y = 3x$

29. $y = 2x + 4$

30. $y = -\frac{1}{2}x - 1$

Objective G: *Interpret the solution to*
$ax + b = cx + d$ *graphically.* *(Lesson 13-2)*

31. Explain how Question 20 could be answered graphically. You do not have to draw the graphs. **See below.**

32. Graph $y = x + 5$ and $y = 3x - 1$. Use your graph to determine the solution to the equation $x + 5 = 3x - 1$. **See margin.**

33. Solve $4x - 7 = 2x + 1$ using graphs. **See margin.**

34. *Multiple choice.* Below is a graph of $y = ax + b$ and $y = cx + d$. Which of the coordinates (r), (s), (t), or (u), is the solution to $ax + b = cx + d$? **(t)**

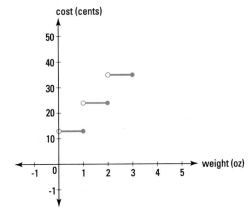

31) Graph $y = 35 + 6w$ for Kurt and $y = 60 + 4w$ for Sara. The w-coordinate of the point where the lines intersect is the solution.

35) $y = \lfloor x \rfloor$; In each bar the values of x are rounded down to the nearest integer.

36) When x is between 4 and 5 including 4, then $y = 4$.

Objective H: *Interpret graphs of equations using the symbols $\lceil\ \rceil$ or $\lfloor\ \rfloor$.* *(Lesson 13-6)*

In 35 and 36, refer to this graph.

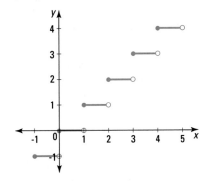

35. Is this the graph of $y = \lceil x \rceil$ or $y = \lfloor x \rfloor$? Explain how you know. **See below left.**

36. What does the uppermost bar on the graph describe? **See below left.**

In 37 and 38, refer to this graph below of postal rates in 1975.

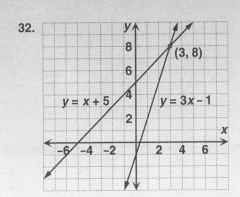

37. Is this the graph of $y = 11\lceil x \rceil + 2$ or $y = 11\lfloor x \rfloor + 2$? $y = 11\lceil x \rceil + 2$

38. In 1975, what did it cost to mail a letter that weighed 1.21 ounces? **24¢**

Chapter 13 *Chapter Review* **731**

27.
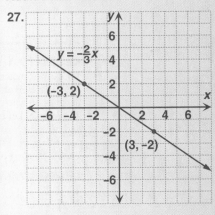

28.
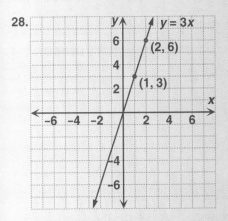

29.
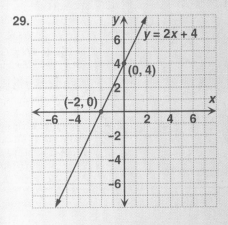

30.
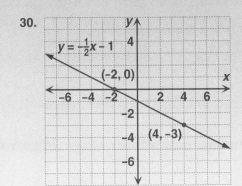

32.
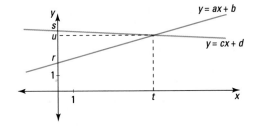

33.
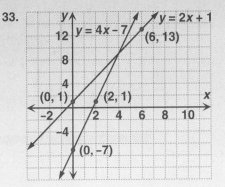

LESSON 7-1 (pp. 344–351)
13. $10 - x$ meters **15. a.** A and C **b.** BC **17. a.** $470.75
b. $510.75 - W$ dollars **19. a.** 17,558,165 **b.** 469,557 **c.** Answer depends on where you are. **21.** $b^2 - a^2$ **23.** 24.64 square units **25.** Sample: Let $a = 5$, $b = -2$. Then $-(a + b) = -(5 + -2) = -3$ and $-b + -a = -(-2) + -5 = -3$. Let $a = -9$ and $b = -4$. Then $-(a + b) = -(-13) = 13$ and $-b + -a = 4 + 9 = 13$. It seems true. **27.** 1 **29. a.** -5 **b.** 3.4 **c.** 0 **31.** 637

LESSON 7-2 (pp. 352–357)
25. 2 **27.** (c) **29. a.** $a - b = b - a$ **b.** No **31.** -7 **33.** $43 - m$ **35.** 7 **37.** 6°

LESSON 7-3 (pp. 358–361)
15. $327.61 **17.** $2\frac{1}{8}$ **19.** -17 **21.** 632,118 **23.** $88 **25.** 70 cm **27.** 10° **29.** 1.5 **31.** 5,000,000,000,000 **33.** .75

LESSON 7-4 (pp. 362–366)
19. $c = s - p$ **21. a.** $14 - d = -3$ **b.** $d = 17$ **c.** The temperature has decreased by 17°. **23.** $x = -120$ **25.** $K = 13$ **27.** (c) **29.** Algebraic Definition of Subtraction; Addition Property of Equality; Associative Property of Addition; Property of Opposites; Additive Identity Property of Zero; Addition Property of Equality; Associative Property of Addition; Property of Opposites; Additive Identity Property of Zero. **31.** $y = 48$ **33.** 58 or 59 **35.** $d = 90 - c$

37. a.   **b.** right angles

LESSON 7-5 (pp. 367–373)
11. a. Gabriella, Lakara, Jason, Kamal, Martha **b.** Lakara, Kamal, Martha, Jason **c.** Jason **d.** Contest 2 and Contest 3 **13.** 22
15. a. $\frac{1}{2}$ or 50% **b.** $\frac{33}{100}$ or 33% **c.** 67% **17. a.** $x - 39.725 = 0.12$
b. 39.845 **19. a.** Queen Victoria, 64 years **b.** 2016 **21.** (b)
23. ≈ 810 **25.** 2-liter watering can

LESSON 7-6 (pp. 374–380)
23. If the ramp is perpendicular to expressway, the driver has to accelerate into fast-moving traffic while making a 90° turn; if the ramp is nearly parallel, acceleration is much easier. **25.** $\angle NOM$ and $\angle POM$ **27. a.** False **b.** Vertical angles have the same measure. If one is acute, so is the other.
29. $x = y$ **31.** 140°
33. a. See right. **b.** 24 **35.** $y = 59$
37. $c = 300$

33. a.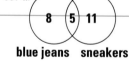

blue jeans   sneakers

LESSON 7-7 (pp. 381–386)
23. m∠1 = 90°, m∠2 = m∠4 = 40°, m∠3 = 140° **25.** 360°
27. See below. **29.** See below. **31.** $m = -\frac{1}{3}$ **33. a.** 16 square units
b. Samples: area surrounding a house; area of a path around a garden **35. a.** $C \approx 69.55$ dollars **b.** $C - W + D$ dollars

27. Sample:

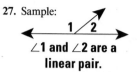

∠1 and ∠2 are a linear pair.

29. Sample:

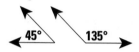

LESSON 7-8 (pp. 387–392)
17. rhombuses and squares **19.** parallelograms, rhombuses, rectangles, and squares **21.** 11 **23.** not enough information
25. a. 147° **b.** 57° **c.** 123° **d.** 33° **27.** ABG **29. a.** $\angle DBA$, $\angle CBD$, $\angle FBA$, $\angle GBC$, $\angle GBA$, $\angle GBD$, $\angle GBF$ **b.** m∠DBA = 30°;
m∠CBD = m∠FBA = 150°; m∠GBC = 60°; m∠ABG = 120°; m∠GBD = m∠GBF = 90° **31.** ⊥ **33. a.** from 1950 to 1960, 103,932; from 1960 to 1970, $-23,952$; from 1970 to 1980, $-81,160$; from 1980 to 1990, $-8,124$ **b.** $-9,304$ **c.** From 1950 to 1990, the population of Milwaukee decreased by 9,304 people.

LESSON 7-9 (pp. 392–398)
9. 74° **11.** m∠1 = 80°, m∠2 = 100°, m∠3 = 80°, m∠4 = 20°, m∠5 = m∠6 = 100°, m∠7 = 90°, m∠8 = 100° **13.** (a) **15.** If a triangle had two obtuse angles, the sum of their measures would be more than 180°. This contradicts the Triangle-Sum Property.
17. (d) **19. a.** True **b.** True **21.** $\overline{AB}$ and $\overline{AD}$ are perpendicular.
23. The angles have the same measure. **25.** See below. **27.** $x = 0$
29. 910

25. a. Line EF is perpendicular to line segment GH.

b.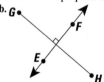

CHAPTER 7 PROGRESS SELF-TEST (p. 402)

1. $5 - (-5) = 5 + 5 = 10$ **2.** See p. 743 for drawing. $-6 - 22 = -28$
3. $\frac{9}{12} + \frac{-10}{12} = -\frac{1}{12}$ **4.** $5 - 13 + 2 - -11 = 5 + -13 + 2 + 11 = 5$
5. $x + -y + 5$ **6.** Use the comparison model. $V - N = L$, or $N + L = V$, or $V - L = N$. **7.** Use the comparison model or try simpler numbers. $Z - 67$ inches **8.** Use the Take-Away Model: Area of outer square = 8^2 square meters; area of inner square = 4^2 square meters; $8^2 - 4^2 = 64 - 16 = 48$ m². **9. a.** Use the slide model. $t° - 7° = -3°$ **b.** Add 7 to both sides. $t = 4°$

10. $y + -14 = -24$; add 14 to both sides; $y = -10$ **11.** Add x to both sides; $x + -50 = 37$; add 50 to both sides; $x = 87$
12. $g + -3.2 = -2$; add 3.2 to both sides; $g = 1.2$ **13.** $c + -a = b$; add a to both sides; $c = b + a$; add $-b$ to both sides; $c + -b = a$
14. (c); all others are equivalent to $x + y = 180$ **15.** $50 - 15 = 35$ people add something to their coffee. $25 + 20 - z = 35$ where z is the overlap, people drinking coffee with cream and sugar. $z = 10$, 10 people drink coffee with cream and sugar. **16.** m∠CBD = $90° - $m∠$ABD$ = $90° - 25° = 65°$ **17.** Angles ABE and ABD are a linear pair, so their measures add to 180. So m∠$ABE + 25° = 180°$,

742

from which m∠*ABE* = 155°. **18.** ∠5 and ∠6 are corresponding angles, so have the same measure, 74°. ∠2 forms a linear pair with ∠6, so 74° + m∠2 = 180°, from which m∠2 = 106°. **19.** ∠5, a corresponding angle; ∠3, a vertical angle; and ∠4, the vertical angle to ∠5 **20.** Angles 1 and 8 each form a linear pair with ∠5, so are supplementary. Angles 2 and 7, having the same measures as angles 1 and 8, are therefore also supplementary. **21.** 55° + 4° + *x* = 180°; 59° + *x* = 180°; *x* = 121° **22.** The sum of the angle

measures would be 270°. By the Triangle Sum Property, the sum must be 180°. **23.** ∠*CBE*, an alternate interior angle **24.** 130° **25.** rhombuses

2.

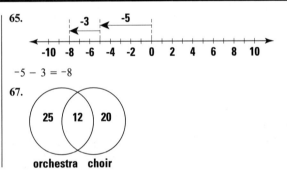

-6 − 22 = -28

The chart below keys the **Progress Self-Test** questions to the objectives in the **Chapter Review** on pages 403–405 or to the **Vocabulary** (Voc.) on page 401. This will enable you to locate those **Chapter Review** questions that correspond to questions students missed on the **Progress Self-Test**. The lesson where the material is covered is also indicated on the chart.

Question	1	2	3	4	5	6	7	8	9	10
Objective	A	O	A	A	G	M	M	K	L	B
Lesson	7-2	7-2	7-2	7-2	7-2	7-1	7-1	7-1	7-3	7-3
Question	11	12	13	14	15	16	17	18	19	20
Objective	B	B	B	G	N, P	C	C	D	H	H
Lesson	7-4	7-3	7-4	7-4	7-5	7-6	7-6	7-7	7-6, 7-7	7-6, 7-7
Question	21	22	23	24	25	26	27	28	29	30
Objective	E	J	D	F, I	I					
Lesson	7-9	7-9	7-7	7-8	7-8					

CHAPTER 7 REVIEW (pages 403–405)

1. -28 **3.** -0.7 **5.** $\frac{22}{15}$ or $1\frac{7}{15}$ **7.** 13.7 **9.** *x* = 72 **11.** *V* = -7.2 **13.** *b* = 197 **15.** *x* = 8 **17.** *c* = *e* + 45 **19.** 90 **21.** 180° − *x*° **23.** angles 7, 1, and 3 **25.** 180° − *y*° **27.** 50° **29.** 38° **31.** Yes, 10 cm **33.** 4 **35.** -3 **37.** *a* + *c* = *b* **39.** 140° **41.** 180° − *x*° **43.** angles 1, 8, 4, and 5 **45.** angles 1, 7, 5, and 3 **47.** rectangles and squares **49.** all **51.** Sample: Yes, angles could have measures 40°, 60°, and 80°, which add to 180°. **53.** 5500 square feet **55.** 21 **57.** (b) **59.** 2.5 million **61.** *F* − *R* = *L* **63.** 70%

65.

-3   -5

-5 − 3 = -8

67.

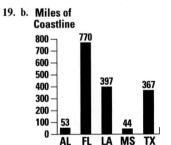

25   12   20

orchestra   choir

LESSON 8-1 (pp. 406–414)

15. a. Total hours of Democratic National Convention TV coverage by ABC, CBS, and NBC

year	hours
1960	85.6
1964	about 70
1968	about 80
1972	about 85
1976	about 65
1980	about 42
1984	about 40
1988	about 30
1992	24.0

b. Sample: The graph is easier to read and shows the decreasing trend more dramatically. **17.** about 6% **19.** 64° **21.** Samples: 10 + -7 + -1 = -(7 + -10 + 1); (-3) + -(-4) + -(-5) = -(-4 + -(-3) + (-5)); probably true. **23.** *G* < 24 or *G* >28 **25. a.** The segment should be approximately 1.7 cm long. **b.** The segment should be approximately 14 cm long. **c.** The segment should be approximately 3.1 cm long.

LESSON 8-2 (pp. 415–420)

11. a. Yes **b.** 2 **13. a.** No **b.** The first interval has length 1. The other intervals have length 0.05. **15.** 3.4 **17.** Samples: 1% or 0.5% **19. a.** Sample: 100 miles **b.** See below for graph. **21.** Samples: Graphs can be easier to read than tables or prose, and can take less space. **23. a.** *x* = 30 **b.** Sample: A triangle has two angles with measures 105° and 45°. What is the measure of the third angle? **25.** 3.99% **27.** $1.22 in 1990; $1.20 in 1991 **29.** 1,900,000; 1,400,000; 800,000; 600,000

19. b. Miles of Coastline

	AL	FL	LA	MS	TX
	53	770	397	44	367

743

29. III and IV **31.** II and III **33.** III **35.** II

37. North

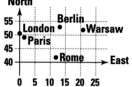
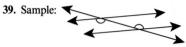
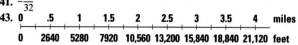

39. Sample:

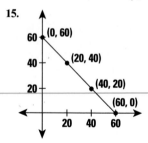

41. $-\frac{9}{32}$

43.

0	.5	1	1.5	2	2.5	3	3.5	4	miles
0	2640	5280	7920	10,560	13,200	15,840	18,840	21,120	feet

LESSON 8-4 (pp. 428–433)

13. (d) **15. a.** $x + y = 60$ **b.** See below.
17. a. The first two lines are

  X   Y
  10   80.

  Then the values of X increase by 1 and the values of Y decrease by 1. The last line is
  80   10.

b. The first two lines and last line are the same but now the values of X increase by 10 and the values of Y decrease by 10.

X	Y
10	80
20	70
30	60
40	50
50	40
60	30
70	20
80	10

c. Sample: Change line 20 to
  FOR X = 10 TO 100 STEP 5. Then the first two lines are the same but now the third line is 15   75; the values of X increase by 5 and the values of Y decrease by 5. The last line is
  100   −10. **19.** II **21.** (4, 2) **23.** (a) **25.** 2 liters ≈ 2.12 quarts

15.

LESSON 8-5 (pp. 434–439)
13. $B' = (320, 0)$, $C' = (320, 100)$, $D' = (280, 100)$, $E' = (260, 40)$, $F' = (60, 40)$, $G' = (40, 100)$, $H' = (0, 100)$ **15.** $A' = (-1, 9)$, $B' = (2, 9)$

17.

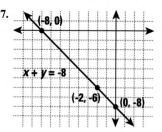

19. a. \$2.00 **b.** \$2.00 **c.** \$1.95 **d.** \$1.00

LESSON 8-6 (pp. 440–445)

11.

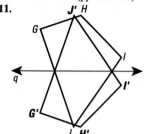

13. a and b.

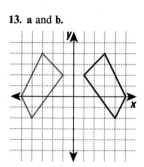

c. over the *y*-axis

15.

17.

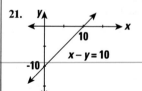

19. a and b.

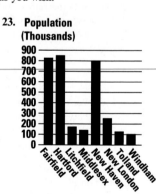

c. 16 **d.** Repeat steps **a** and **b** as many times as you wish.

21.

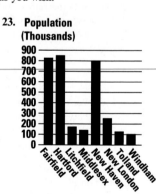

23.

Population (Thousands)

744

LESSON 8-7 (pp. 446–451)

9.

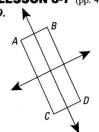

11.

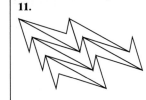

13. B, C, D, E, H, I, O, X **15.** perhaps O **17.** 5
19.

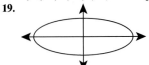

21. Sample:

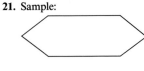

23. This line is a line of symmetry because all points on one side of the line are reflections of points on the other side. **25.** (−3, −8)

27.

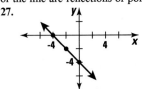

29. Circulation (millions)

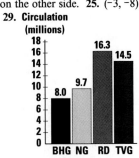

LESSON 8-8 (pp. 452–457)

9. Answers will vary.
11.

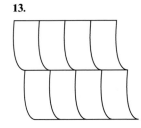

13.

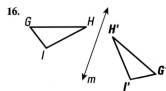

15. 60° **17.** square
19.

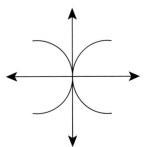

21. (c)
23.

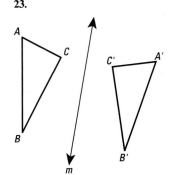

25. $c = 360 − a − b − d$

CHAPTER 8 PROGRESS SELF-TEST (pp. 461–462)

1. the week of November 9 **2.** about 3 million barrels
3. 0.4 million barrels **4.** The vertical axis does not begin at 0, so the bars look more different than they actually are. **5. See below.**
6. Add 10 to the second coordinate to get (2, 15). **7. See below.**
8. a. E **b.** A **9.** E **10.** B, since −4 + 2 = −2. **11.** M = (3, 6)
12. The hole is directly above (9, 3) so its first coordinate is 9. Its second coordinate is halfway between 9 and 12, so it is 10.5.
Hole = (9, 10.5) **13. See below.** **14. See below.** **15. See below.**

16. See below. 17. See below. 18. See below. 19. m∠V = m∠W;
m∠W = 72° **20.** Sample: Graphs can show a lot of information in a small place. Graphs can picture relationships. **21.** when they have the same size and shape
22. 4│9 8 6
5│7 7 7 7 8 7 4 1 0 2 6 4
6│1 1 8 4 5
23. a. 57 **b.** 68 − 46 = 22 **c.** 57

5.

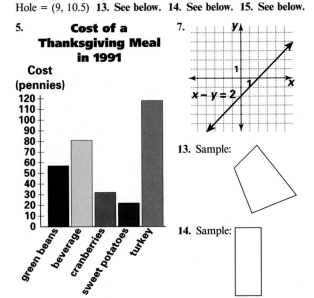

Cost of a Thanksgiving Meal in 1991
Cost (pennies)

7.

$x − y = 2$

13. Sample:

14. Sample:

15.

16.

17.

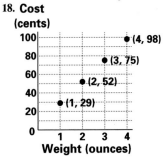

18. Cost (cents)

(4, 98)
(3, 75)
(2, 52)
(1, 29)

Weight (ounces)

745

The chart below keys the **Progress Self-Test** questions to the objectives in the **Chapter Review** on pages 463–465 or to the **Vocabulary** (Voc.) on page 460. This will enable you to locate those **Chapter Review** questions that correspond to questions students missed on the **Progress Self-Test.** The lesson where the material is covered is also indicated on the chart.

Question	1	2	3	4	5	6	7	8	9	10
Objective	F	F	F	F	F	J	J	J	J	K
Lesson	8-2	8-2	8-2	8-2	8-2	8-3	8-3, 8-4	8-4	8-5	8-4
Question	11	12	13	14	15	16	17	18	19	20
Objective	G	G	C	C	C	B	D	G	L	H
Lesson	8-4	8-4	8-7	8-7	8-7	8-6	8-8	8-3	8-6	8-1
Question	21	22	23							
Objective	E	I	A							
Lesson	8-6	8-1	8-1							

CHAPTER 8 REVIEW (pages 463–465)

1. median = 355, range = 222, mode = 350 **3.** median = 6, range = 4, mode = 6 **5.** and **7. See below.** **9. See below.** **11. See below.** **13. See below.** **15.** 90° **17.** Yes, a translation image is always the same size and shape as its preimage. **19.** 2″ **21.** 4′11″ **23.** The axis does not begin at 0, so the differences between the average heights of boys and girls are magnified. **25. a.** Sample: 1 million **b. See right.** **27.** 1983 **29.** 1988–1990 **31. See right.** **33.** Sample: The graph can show trends and sway the reader.

35.
```
0 | 8 7
1 | 1 0 4 9 9
2 | 4 4
3 | 1 6
4 | 4
5 | 0
```

37. $B = (-2, 4); C = (-2, 0)$ **39., 41. See below right.**
43. $x - y = 3$ **45.** $(-2, -3)$ **47.** $(9, 3); (7, 7); (10, 5)$

5.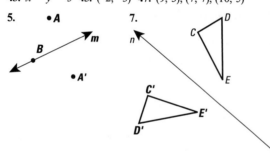

7.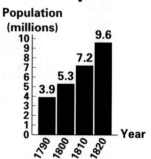

9.

11.

13. Sample: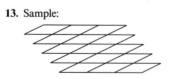

25. b. Sample:

U.S. Population
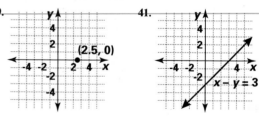

31.

U.S. Population

39.

41.

746

LESSON 9-1 (pp. 466–475)
13. 71 ft² **15.** Samples: 1 in. and 15 in., 2.5 in. and 6 in. **17.** (b)
19. 146.5 ft² **21.** 714 square units **23. a.** 24 miles
b. 36 square miles **25.** -25 **27.** 2.2 lb **29.** 1,440,000

LESSON 9-2 (pp. 476–481)
13. 864 ft³ **15. a. See drawing below. b.** cube **c. See below.**
17. (e) **19.** 262,080 dots **21. a.** fourth (or IV) **b.** Sample:
$y = x - 5$ **23.** $x = -27$ **25.** 595 **27.** < **29.** >

15. a.

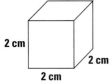

2 cm
2 cm
2 cm

c.

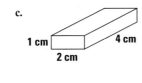

1 cm
2 cm
4 cm

LESSON 9-3 (pp. 482–487)
23. $0.625 \cdot 1.6 = 1$ **25.** Sample: The reciprocal would be $\frac{1}{0}$, but
you cannot divide by 0. **27. a.** $\frac{1}{24}$ **b.** Sample: $\frac{1}{2}$ of $\frac{1}{3}$ is less than $\frac{1}{3}$;
$\frac{1}{4}$ of that is even smaller. **29. a.** $9\frac{5}{8}$ **b.** Sample: Convert fractions to
decimals and multiply. **31.** 210 square units **33.** m∠SRT = 23°;
m∠S = 135°; m∠T = 22° **35.** 57%

LESSON 9-4 (pp. 488–492)
9. $\frac{8}{15}$ or about 53% **11.** No. Since $P(A) = \frac{9}{10}$ and $P(B) = \frac{17}{24}$, $P(A) \cdot$
$P(B) = \frac{51}{80}$. However, $\frac{3}{4}$ of the right-handed people are right-eyed, so
$P(A \text{ and } B) = \frac{3}{4} \cdot \frac{9}{10} = \frac{27}{40}$. This means $P(A \text{ and } B) \neq P(A) \cdot P(B)$.
13. ≈ 23.3% **15.** 3 **17.** $\frac{3}{5}$ **19.** 1 **21.** area is multiplied by 5^2 or 25
examples: $2 \cdot 3 = 6$ $5(2) \cdot 5(3) = 25(6) = 150$; $4 \cdot 1 = 4$
$5(4) \cdot 5(1) = 25(4) = 100$ Sample pattern: If dimensions of a
rectangle are multiplied by n, the area is multiplied by n^2.

LESSON 9-5 (pp. 493–498)
15. 100,800 beats **17.** 1299.6 pesetas **19.** $\frac{8}{35}$ **21.** $\frac{1}{12}$ **23.** $1\frac{1}{4}$ mi²
25. 21 games **27.** lb **29.** mL

LESSON 9-6 (pp. 499–504)
25. a. -10 **b.** -5 **c.** 0 **d.** 5 **e.** 10 **27.** Sample: Multiplication by
zero annihilates the number, making it 0. **29.** -64 **31.** 1
33. km/sec **35.** 600 minutes, or 10 hours **37.** $(90\%)^{10}$ ≈ 35%
39. It is multiplied by 27. **41.** Sample: -2 + 3 = 1

LESSON 9-7 (pp. 505–510)
13. a. 15 mm **b.** 150 **15.** 3 **17.** 96 **19.** -10 **21.** -10 **23.** .1
25. 101 **27.** 2% **29.** 45.3 **31.** Any number between -1 and 0 is
correct.

LESSON 9-8 (pp. 511–515)
11. Yes **13.** (b) **15. a.** 2 **b.** If figure A is the image of figure B
under a size change of magnitude k, then figure B is the image of
figure A under a size change of magnitude $\frac{1}{k}$. **17.** 62.5 cm
19. a. ≈10.8% **b.** Being poor and being white are not independent
events. A white person has a slightly smaller chance (about 17%
less) of being poor. **21.** The graph is translated five units down.
23. Sample: Graphs can contain a lot of information in a small
space, can show trends visually, and can be used to sway a reader.
25. ∠2 and ∠6, ∠3 and ∠7 **27. a.** $17 **b.** $5 + 2 \cdot w$ dollars
29. $3\frac{23}{24}$ miles

LESSON 9-9 (pp. 516–520)
11. True **13.** 2 **15.** $b - c + d$ **19.**
17. ≈ $.29 \cdot \frac{1}{7}$ ≈ $.04$ ≈ 4%
19. See right. 21. 16, 18, 20,
21, 22, 24 **23.** hexagon
25. pentagon **27.** -35
29. a. 945 **b.** equal to **31.** -0.6

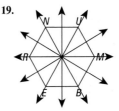

CHAPTER 9 PROGRESS SELF-TEST (p. 524)

1. $\frac{4}{3} \cdot \frac{5}{4} = \frac{5}{3}$, or $1\frac{2}{3}$ **2.** $\frac{7}{16x}$ **3.** -45 (positive · negative = negative)
4. -9 + 4 = -5 **5.** $a + a + b + 0 + -21c + c = 2a + b + -20c =$
$2a + b - 20c$ **6.** Associative Property of Multiplication
7. Property of Reciprocals **8.** $r \cdot s$ (or rs) is the total number of
seats. If 5 are broken, then the number of other seats is $rs - 5$.
9. Area equals $\frac{1}{2}$ base times height, so $\frac{1}{2} \cdot 17.3 \cdot 6.8 = 58.82$ m².
10. 4 hours $\cdot -3 \frac{\text{centimeters}}{\text{hours}} = -12$ centimeters **11.** $V = a \cdot b \cdot c =$
3 ft · 4 ft · 5 ft = 60 ft³ **12.** It would probably fit since the volume
of the drawer is 21,600 cm³, much larger than the volume of the
jewelry box. **13.** Two positive numbers whose product is 16.
Samples: 1 and 16, 1.6 and 10, 3.2 and 5. **14.** $\frac{1}{38}$ ≈ 0.0263158 ≈
0.026 **15.** (4 · 8, 4 · 2) = (32, 8) **16.** $5.80 \cdot 1\frac{1}{2}$ = $5.80 · 1.5 =
$8.70 per hour of overtime. **17. a.** $\frac{2}{3} \cdot \frac{1}{4}$ **b.** $\frac{2}{12}$ or $\frac{1}{6}$
18. a. 8.50 $\frac{\text{dollars}}{\text{hour}}$ · 37.5 $\frac{\text{hours}}{\text{week}}$ = 318.75 $\frac{\text{dollars}}{\text{week}}$ **b.** The person earns
$318.75 per week.

19.

(-5, 10)   (10, 10)

5

(-5, 0)   (2, 0)

-5   0   5   x

(-4, -4) -5 (2, -4)

20. Sample: The corresponding angles in the preimage and image
are equal. The corresponding sides in the preimage and image are
not equal. **21.** $\frac{3}{25}$ of the 850 students are in the band. $\frac{3}{25} \cdot 850 =$
102 students. **22.** $\frac{2}{3}$ of the $8400 is the value of the scholarship.
$\frac{2}{3} \cdot 8400 = 5600. **23.** $\frac{1}{10}$ chance for 3 independent digits =
$\frac{1}{10} \cdot \frac{1}{10} \cdot \frac{1}{10} = \frac{1}{1000} = 1$ in 1000. **24.** These are independent events.
$\frac{2}{3} \cdot \frac{2}{5} = \frac{4}{15}$. 4 in 15 of getting an A on both tests. **25.** (c) $\frac{1}{1.25} = \frac{4}{5} =$
$\frac{8}{10} = 0.8$ **26.** 1 mile = 5280 feet; $\frac{1 \text{ mi}}{5280 \text{ ft}} \cdot 19,340$ ft =
3.6629 . . . ≈ 3.66 mi

747

The chart below keys the **Progress Self-Test** questions to the objectives in the **Chapter Review** on pages 525–527 or to the **Vocabulary** (Voc.) on page 523. This will enable you to locate those **Chapter Review** questions that correspond to questions students missed on the **Progress Self-Test.** The lesson where the material is covered is also indicated on the chart.

Question	1	2	3	4	5	6	7	8	9	10
Objective	C	C	D	D	F	E	E	G	A	J
Lesson	9-3	9-3	9-6	9-6	9-6	9-2	9-3	9-1	9-1	9-5

Question	11	12	13	14	15	16	17	18	19	20
Objective	B	H	A, M	F	N	L	M	J	N	N
Lesson	9-2	9-2	9-1	9-3	9-7	9-7	9-3	9-5	9-9	9-9

Question	21	22	23	24	25	26
Objective	L	L	I	I	E	K
Lesson	9-8	9-8	9-4	9-4	9-3	9-5

CHAPTER 9 REVIEW (pp. 525–527)

1. 24.5 cm^2 **3.** 27 square units **5.** 1875 cubic units **7.** $\frac{1}{2}$ **9.** $\frac{75}{2}$, or $37\frac{1}{2}$ **11.** $\frac{405}{4}$, or $101\frac{1}{4}$ **13.** $\frac{2}{3}$ **15.** $\frac{8}{5}$, or $1\frac{3}{5}$ **17.** -87 **19.** -11 **21.** -320 **23.** For any x, $x \cdot 0 = 0$. **25.** Commutative Property of Multiplication **27.** False **29.** 0 **31.** 1 **33.** $\frac{x}{2}$ **35. a.** $\frac{1}{40}$ **b.** $0.125 \times 0.2 = 0.025$ **37.** 48 **39.** 42 in^2 **41.** 85,680 cm^3 **43.** $5\frac{1}{16} \approx 5$ cubic inches **45.** $\approx 98.34\%$ **47.** $\frac{1}{7}$ **49. a.** 125 miles **b.** Sample: How far can you drive in 5 hours if the average speed is 25 miles per hour? **51.** 360 people **53.** $\frac{1 \text{ ft}}{30.48 \text{ cm}}, \frac{30.48 \text{ cm}}{1 \text{ ft}}$ **55.** $6\frac{1}{4}$ days **57.** $18.75 **59.** $7.13 **61, 63.** See below. **65.** See right. **67.** contraction **69.** (−8, 16) **71.** See right.

61.

There are 20 dots in this 5×4 array.

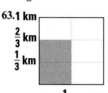

Area $= \frac{2}{6}$ or $\frac{1}{3}$ km^2.

65.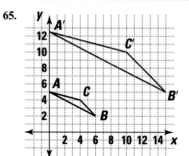

71.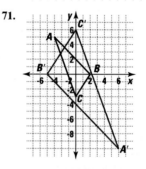

LESSON 10-1 (pp. 528–534)

11. $28s$ **13.** $3e$ **15. a.** $-\frac{1}{2} + -\frac{1}{2} + -\frac{1}{2} + -\frac{1}{2} + -\frac{1}{2} + -\frac{1}{2} + -\frac{1}{2} + -\frac{1}{2}$ **b.** -4 **17.** $u = -75$ **19.** (a), (b), (c), (d), (g) **21.** Associative Property of Multiplication **23.** Multiplication Property of Equality **25. a.** Yes **b.** $\ell w - ab$ **27. a.** $-1°F$ **b.** $w - z°F$

LESSON 10-2 (pp. 535–539)

15. $y = 2.3$; $16.56 = 7.2 \cdot 2.3$ **17.** $x = 1.912$; $1.912 + 1.912 + 1.912 = 5.736$ **19.** 675 **21.** $y + 3z$ **23.** $53.1\overline{6}$ **25. a.** 2 **b.** 6 **c.** 18 **d.** $2n - 2$ **27.** $152°$

LESSON 10-3 (pp. 540–543)

7. ≈ 13.27 hours **9.** 342 **11. a.** $T = 4w$ **b.** $T = 3600$ **c.** $T = 6w$ **d.** $T = 5400$ **13.** $a = 7.5$ **15.** -8 **17.** See right. **19.** 960 **21.** .02 m

17.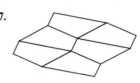

LESSON 10-4 (pp. 544–549)

21. a. $1500 + 90n$ dollars **b.** no longer than 11 days **23. a.** Addition Property of Equality **b.** Associative Property of Addition **c.** Property of Opposites **d.** Additive Identity Property of 0 **e.** Multiplication Property of Equality **f.** Associative Property of Multiplication **g.** Property of Reciprocals **h.** Multiplication Property of 1 **25. a.** $-n$ **b.** $x = \frac{p + -n}{m}$ **27.** $x = 121$ **29.** contraction **31.** $\frac{3}{130}$ **33.** Sample: $2500 - D + B - S = 2300$

LESSON 10-5 (pp. 550–554)

19. $n = -2.7$; $6 - 30(-2.7) - 18 = 6 + 81 - 18 = 87 - 18 = 69$ **21.** $b = 4$; $2(4) + 2 + 3(4) + 3 - 4(4) - 4 = 8 + 2 + 12 + 3 - 16 - 4 = 25 - 20 = 5$ **23.** $22\frac{1}{2}$ days **25.** y is positive **27.** $u = 29$ **29.** They will have the same shape, but the length of the sides of the image will be 4 times the lengths of the corresponding sides of the preimage, and the image will be rotated 180° from the position of the preimage. **31.** $13,468 **33.** $m\angle HEG = 98°$; $m\angle H = 50°$; $m\angle G = 32°$ **35.** $\frac{1}{18}$

748

LESSON 9-1 (pp. 466–475)

13. 71 ft^2 **15.** Samples: 1 in. and 15 in., 2.5 in. and 6 in. **17.** (b)
19. 146.5 ft^2 **21.** 714 square units **23. a.** 24 miles
b. 36 square miles **25.** −25 **27.** 2.2 lb **29.** 1,440,000

LESSON 9-2 (pp. 476–481)

13. 864 ft^3 **15. a. See drawing below. b.** cube **c. See below.**
17. (e) **19.** 262,080 dots **21. a.** fourth (or IV) **b.** Sample:
$y = x − 5$ **23.** $x = −27$ **25.** 595 **27.** < **29.** >

15. a.

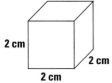

2 cm
2 cm
2 cm

c.

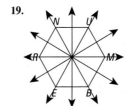

1 cm
2 cm
4 cm

LESSON 9-3 (pp. 482–487)

23. $0.625 · 1.6 = 1$ **25.** Sample: The reciprocal would be $\frac{1}{0}$, but
you cannot divide by 0. **27. a.** $\frac{1}{24}$ **b.** Sample: $\frac{1}{2}$ of $\frac{1}{3}$ is less than $\frac{1}{3}$;
$\frac{1}{4}$ of that is even smaller. **29. a.** $9\frac{5}{8}$ **b.** Sample: Convert fractions to
decimals and multiply. **31.** 210 square units **33.** m∠SRT = 23°;
m∠S = 135°; m∠T = 22° **35.** 57%

LESSON 9-4 (pp. 488–492)

9. $\frac{8}{15}$ or about 53% **11.** No. Since $P(A) = \frac{9}{10}$ and $P(B) = \frac{17}{24}$, $P(A) ·$
$P(B) = \frac{51}{80}$. However, $\frac{3}{4}$ of the right-handed people are right-eyed, so
$P(A$ and $B) = \frac{3}{4} · \frac{9}{10} = \frac{27}{40}$. This means $P(A$ and $B) ≠ P(A) · P(B)$.
13. ≈ 23.3% **15.** 3 **17.** $\frac{3}{5}$ **19.** 1 **21.** area is multiplied by 5^2 or 25
examples: 2 · 3 = 6   5(2) · 5(3) = 25(6) = 150; 4 · 1 = 4
5(4) · 5(1) = 25(4) = 100 Sample pattern: If dimensions of a
rectangle are multiplied by n, the area is multiplied by n^2.

LESSON 9-5 (pp. 493–498)

15. 100,800 beats **17.** 1299.6 pesetas **19.** $\frac{8}{35}$ **21.** $\frac{1}{12}$ **23.** $1\frac{1}{4}$ mi^2
25. 21 games **27.** lb **29.** mL

LESSON 9-6 (pp. 499–504)

25. a. −10 **b.** −5 **c.** 0 **d.** 5 **e.** 10 **27.** Sample: Multiplication by
zero annihilates the number, making it 0. **29.** −64 **31.** 1
33. km/sec **35.** 600 minutes, or 10 hours **37.** (90%)^{10} ≈ 35%
39. It is multiplied by 27. **41.** Sample: −2 + 3 = 1

LESSON 9-7 (pp. 505–510)

13. a. 15 mm **b.** 150 **15.** 3 **17.** 96 **19.** −10 **21.** −10 **23.** .1
25. 101 **27.** 2% **29.** 45.3 **31.** Any number between −1 and 0 is
correct.

LESSON 9-8 (pp. 511–515)

11. Yes **13.** (b) **15. a.** 2 **b.** If figure A is the image of figure B
under a size change of magnitude k, then figure B is the image of
figure A under a size change of magnitude $\frac{1}{k}$. **17.** 62.5 cm
19. a. ≈10.8% **b.** Being poor and being white are not independent
events. A white person has a slightly smaller chance (about 17%
less) of being poor. **21.** The graph is translated five units down.
23. Sample: Graphs can contain a lot of information in a small
space, can show trends visually, and can be used to sway a reader.
25. ∠2 and ∠6, ∠3 and ∠7 **27. a.** $17 **b.** 5 + 2 · w dollars
29. $3\frac{23}{24}$ miles

LESSON 9-9 (pp. 516–520)

11. True **13.** 2 **15.** $b − c + d$ **19.**
17. ≈ $.29 · \frac{1}{7}$ ≈ $.04$ ≈ 4%
19. See right. 21. 16, 18, 20,
21, 22, 24 **23.** hexagon
25. pentagon **27.** −35
29. a. 945 **b.** equal to **31.** −0.6

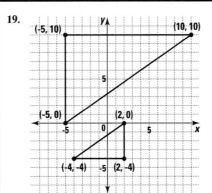

CHAPTER 9 PROGRESS SELF-TEST (p. 524)

1. $\frac{4}{3} · \frac{5}{4} = \frac{5}{3}$, or $1\frac{2}{3}$ **2.** $\frac{7}{16x}$ **3.** −45 (positive · negative = negative)
4. −9 + 4 = −5 **5.** $a + a + b + 0 + −21c + c = 2a + b + −20c =$
$2a + b − 20c$ **6.** Associative Property of Multiplication
7. Property of Reciprocals **8.** $r · s$ (or rs) is the total number of
seats. If 5 are broken, then the number of other seats is $rs − 5$.
9. Area equals $\frac{1}{2}$ base times height, so $\frac{1}{2} · 17.3 · 6.8 = 58.82$ m^2.
10. 4 hours $· −3 \frac{\text{centimeters}}{\text{hours}} = −12$ centimeters **11.** $V = a · b · c =$
3 ft · 4 ft · 5 ft = 60 ft^3 **12.** It would probably fit since the volume
of the drawer is 21,600 cm^3, much larger than the volume of the
jewelry box. **13.** Two positive numbers whose product is 16.
Samples: 1 and 16, 1.6 and 10, 3.2 and 5. **14.** $\frac{1}{38}$ ≈ 0.0263158 ≈

0.026 **15.** (4 · 8, 4 · 2) = (32, 8) **16.** $5.80 · $1\frac{1}{2}$ = $5.80 · 1.5 =
$8.70 per hour of overtime. **17. a.** $\frac{2}{3} · \frac{1}{4}$ **b.** $\frac{2}{12}$ or $\frac{1}{6}$

18. a. 8.50 $\frac{\text{dollars}}{\text{hour}}$ · 37.5 $\frac{\text{hours}}{\text{week}}$ = 318.75 $\frac{\text{dollars}}{\text{week}}$ **b.** The person earns
$318.75 per week.

19.

20. Sample: The corresponding angles in the preimage and image
are equal. The corresponding sides in the preimage and image are
not equal. **21.** $\frac{3}{25}$ of the 850 students are in the band. $\frac{3}{25} · 850 =$
102 students. **22.** $\frac{2}{3}$ of the $8400 is the value of the scholarship.
$\frac{2}{3}$ · $8400 = $5600. **23.** $\frac{1}{10}$ chance for 3 independent digits =
$\frac{1}{10} · \frac{1}{10} · \frac{1}{10} = \frac{1}{1000}$ = 1 in 1000. **24.** These are independent events.
$\frac{2}{3} · \frac{2}{5} = \frac{4}{15}$. 4 in 15 of getting an A on both tests. **25.** (c) $\frac{1}{1.25} = \frac{4}{5} =$
$\frac{8}{10}$ = 0.8 **26.** 1 mile = 5280 feet; $\frac{1 \text{ mi}}{5280 \text{ ft}}$ · 19,340 ft =
3.6629 . . . ≈ 3.66 mi

747

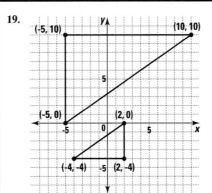 labels: N, U, R, M, E, B

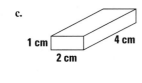 labels: (-5, 10), (10, 10), (-5, 0), (2, 0), (-4, -4), (2, -4)

Question	1	2	3	4	5	6	7	8	9	10
Objective	C	C	D	D	F	E	E	G	A	J
Lesson	9-3	9-3	9-6	9-6	9-6	9-2	9-3	9-1	9-1	9-5
Question	11	12	13	14	15	16	17	18	19	20
Objective	B	H	A, M	F	N	L	M	J	N	N
Lesson	9-2	9-2	9-1	9-3	9-7	9-7	9-3	9-5	9-9	9-9
Question	21	22	23	24	25	26				
Objective	L	L	I	I	E	K				
Lesson	9-8	9-8	9-4	9-4	9-3	9-5				

CHAPTER 9 REVIEW (pp. 525–527)

1. 24.5 cm^2 **3.** 27 square units **5.** 1875 cubic units **7.** $\frac{1}{2}$ **9.** $\frac{75}{2}$, or $37\frac{1}{2}$ **11.** $\frac{405}{4}$, or $101\frac{1}{4}$ **13.** $\frac{2}{3}$ **15.** $\frac{8}{5}$, or $1\frac{3}{5}$ **17.** -87 **19.** -11 **21.** -320 **23.** For any x, $x \cdot 0 = 0$. **25.** Commutative Property of Multiplication **27.** False **29.** 0 **31.** 1 **33.** $\frac{x}{2}$ **35. a.** $\frac{1}{40}$ **b.** $0.125 \times 0.2 = 0.025$ **37.** 48 **39.** 42 in^2 **41.** 85,680 cm^3 **43.** $5\frac{1}{16} \approx 5$ cubic inches **45.** $\approx 98.34\%$ **47.** $\frac{1}{7}$ **49. a.** 125 miles **b.** Sample: How far can you drive in 5 hours if the average speed is 25 miles per hour? **51.** 360 people **53.** $\frac{1 \text{ ft}}{30.48 \text{ cm}}$, $\frac{30.48 \text{ cm}}{1 \text{ ft}}$ **55.** $6\frac{1}{4}$ days **57.** $18.75 **59.** $7.13 **61, 63.** See below. **65.** See right. **67.** contraction **69.** (-8, 16) **71.** See right.

61.

There are 20 dots in this 5×4 array.

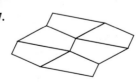

Area $= \frac{2}{6}$ or $\frac{1}{3}$ km^2.

65.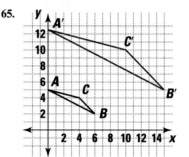

71.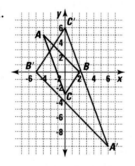

LESSON 10-1 (pp. 528–534)

11. $28s$ **13.** $3e$ **15. a.** $-\frac{1}{2} + -\frac{1}{2} + -\frac{1}{2} + -\frac{1}{2} + -\frac{1}{2} + -\frac{1}{2} + -\frac{1}{2} + -\frac{1}{2}$ **b.** -4 **17.** $u = -75$ **19.** (a), (b), (c), (d), (g) **21.** Associative Property of Multiplication **23.** Multiplication Property of Equality **25. a.** Yes **b.** $\ell w - ab$ **27. a.** -1°F **b.** $w - z$°F

LESSON 10-2 (pp. 535–539)

15. $y = 2.3$; $16.56 = 7.2 \cdot 2.3$ **17.** $x = 1.912$; $1.912 + 1.912 + 1.912 = 5.736$ **19.** 675 **21.** $y + 3z$ **23.** $53.1\overline{6}$ **25. a.** 2 **b.** 6 **c.** 18 **d.** $2n - 2$ **27.** 152°

LESSON 10-3 (pp. 540–543)

7. ≈ 13.27 hours **9.** 342 **11. a.** $T = 4w$ **b.** $T = 3600$ **c.** $T = 6w$ **d.** $T = 5400$ **13.** $a = 7.5$ **15.** -8 **17.** See right. **19.** 960 **21.** .02 m

17.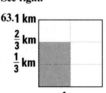

LESSON 10-4 (pp. 544–549)

21. a. $1500 + 90n$ dollars **b.** no longer than 11 days **23. a.** Addition Property of Equality **b.** Associative Property of Addition **c.** Property of Opposites **d.** Additive Identity Property of 0 **e.** Multiplication Property of Equality **f.** Associative Property of Multiplication **g.** Property of Reciprocals **h.** Multiplication Property of 1 **25. a.** $-n$ **b.** $x = \frac{p + -n}{m}$ **27.** $x = 121$ **29.** contraction **31.** $\frac{3}{130}$ **33.** Sample: $2500 - D + B - S = 2300$

LESSON 10-5 (pp. 550–554)

19. $n = -2.7$; $6 - 30(-2.7) - 18 = 6 + 81 - 18 = 87 - 18 = 69$ **21.** $b = 4$; $2(4) + 2 + 3(4) + 3 - 4(4) - 4 = 8 + 2 + 12 + 3 - 16 - 4 = 25 - 20 = 5$ **23.** $22\frac{1}{2}$ days **25.** y is positive **27.** $u = 29$ **29.** They will have the same shape, but the length of the sides of the image will be 4 times the lengths of the corresponding sides of the preimage, and the image will be rotated 180° from the position of the preimage. **31.** $13,468 **33.** m∠$HEG = 98°$; m∠$H = 50°$; m∠$G = 32°$ **35.** $\frac{1}{18}$

748

LESSON 10-6 (pp. 555–560)

23. $3x + 2x$, or $5x$ cents **25.** $a^2 + a^3$
27. $732(1,000,000,000,000,000 - 1) = 732 \cdot 10^{15} - 732 \cdot 1 =$
$732,000,000,000,000,000 - 732 = 731,999,999,999,999,268$
29. -6 **31.** $x = 3$ **33.** $y = -\frac{7}{2}$ or -3.5 **35. a.** $\frac{7}{6}$ **b.** $x = 98$

LESSON 10-7 (pp. 561–565)

9. a. ℓhw **b.** $2\ell w + 2\ell h + 2hw$ **11. a.** 16 in. by 14 in. **b.** 60 in^2
13. Move one of the top rectangles to the bottom. **15.** 1360 cm^2
17. $11x$ **19.** $-12m + n$ **21.** $x = \frac{1}{2}$ **23.** $-\frac{1}{9}$ **25.** Commutative
Property of Addition **27.** 125 cubic units

LESSON 10-8 (pp. 566–570)

15. $4\ell + 4w + 4h$ **17.** surface area **19.** volume **21.** (c) **23.** (c)
25. $c = 28.5$ **27., 29., 31. See below.**
33. a. $33.\overline{3}\%$ **b.** $66.\overline{6}\%$ **c.** 80%

27.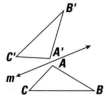

29.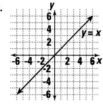

31.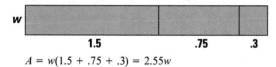

LESSON 10-9 (pp. 571–576)

9. 15 cm **11.** 132 square units **13.** $a^2 + 2a$ **15.** 113.42
17. 12 numbers **19.** A, B, C, D **21.** A, D **23.** $\frac{59}{60}$
25. three hundred forty-five and twenty-nine hundredths

LESSON 10-10 (pp. 577–581)

13. 1,100,000 square kilometers **15.** 7 meters
17. a. One example of an altitude is the dashed segment between
the parallel sides. **See below for sample figure. b.** $AB \approx 21$mm,
$DC \approx 39$mm, $AE \approx 25$mm; Area ≈ 750 mm^2. **19. a.** $x = 10$
b. $y = -10$ **c.** $z = -13$ **21.** 96 square ft **23.** 10

17.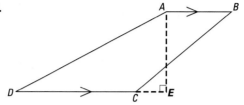

CHAPTER 10 PROGRESS SELF-TEST (pp. 585–586)

1. $(-y + y + y + y + y) + 3 = 3y + 3$ **2.** $-2m$ **3.** $(7k - 4k) +$
$(-2j + j) = 3k - j$ **4.** $10x$ **5.** $b + b + 40 + b + b + 40 =$
$(b + b + b + b) + 40 + 40 = 4b + 80$. **6.** Think of $49 \cdot 7$ as
$(50 - 1) \cdot 7$. Then using the Distributive Property, we can
mentally calculate: $50 \cdot 7 - 1 \cdot 7 = 350 - 7 = 343$. **7.** Between
lines 5 and 6. $5x + -2x = (5 + -2)x$. **8.** km^2 (area) **9.** (a)
10. $A = \frac{1}{2}hb$; $400 = \frac{1}{2} \cdot 25 \cdot b$; $\frac{2}{25} \cdot 400 = \frac{2}{25} \cdot \frac{25}{2} \cdot b$. The base
of the triangle is 32 inches.
11. Sample: The rectangles can be rearranged as shown.

w			
	1.5	.75	.3

$A = w(1.5 + .75 + .3) = 2.55w$

12. Front or back $= 6 \cdot 11$, sides $= 3 \cdot 11$, top or bottom $6 \cdot 3$
Surface area $= 6 \cdot 11 + 6 \cdot 11 + 3 \cdot 11 + 3 \cdot 11 + 6 \cdot 3 +$
$6 \cdot 3 = 66 + 66 + 33 + 33 + 18 + 18 = 234$ cm^2 **13.** $-\frac{1}{9} \cdot$
$35.1 = -\frac{1}{9} \cdot -9t$; $-3.9 = t$ **14.** $\frac{5}{2} \cdot \frac{2}{5}m = \frac{5}{2} \cdot -\frac{3}{4}$; $m = \frac{-15}{8}$, or $-1\frac{7}{8}$
15. $2 - 2 + 3a = 17 - 2$; $\frac{1}{3} \cdot 3a = \frac{1}{3} \cdot 15$; $a = 5$ **16.** $12 - 4h =$
10; $-12 + 12 - 4h = 10 + -12$; $-\frac{1}{4} \cdot -4h = -\frac{1}{4} \cdot -2$; $h = \frac{1}{2}$
17. $2000 = .08I$; $25000 = I$. Last year's income was \$25,000.
18. $A = \frac{1}{2}hb$; $A = \frac{1}{2} \cdot 24 \cdot 7$; $A = 84$ cm^2 **19.** $A = \frac{1}{2}hb$; $A = \frac{1}{2} \cdot$
$30 \cdot 36$; $A = 540$ square units **20.** $A = \frac{1}{2}h(b_1 + b_2)$; $A = \frac{1}{2} \cdot$
$8(9 + 30)$; $A = \frac{1}{2} \cdot 8 \cdot 39$; $A = 156$ square units **21. a.** $4 - 5 \cdot$
$.02 = 4 - .1 = 3.9$ meters **b.** $4 - .02x = 2.5$; $-.02x = 2.5 - 4$;
$x = \frac{-1.5}{-.02} = 75$; after 75 seconds **22.** $3w + 1 = 10$

The chart below keys the **Progress Self-Test** questions to the objectives in the **Chapter Review** on pages 587–589 or to the **Vocabulary**
(Voc.) on page 584. This will enable you to locate those **Chapter Review** questions that correspond to questions students missed on the
Progress Self-Test. The lesson where the material is covered is also indicated on the chart.

Question	1	2	3	4	5	6	7	8	9
Objective	C	C	C	C	C	F	F	I	Voc.
Lesson	10-1	10-1	10-1	10-1	10-1	10-6	10-6	10-8	10-10

Question	10	11	12	13	14	15	16	17	18
Objective	A, D	K	H	A	A	B	B	G	D
Lesson	10-2, 10-9	10-6	10-7	10-5	10-2	10-4	10-5	10-3	10-9

Question	19	20	21	22
Objective	D	E	G	J
Lesson	10-9	10-10	10-4	10-4

749

CHAPTER 10 CHAPTER REVIEW (pages 587–589)

1. $t = 75$; $40(175) = 3000$ **3.** $v = 40$; $.02(40) = .8$ **5.** $y = 7$; $49 = -7(-7)$ **7.** $n = 15$; $\frac{4}{5}(15) = 12$ **9.** $m = 2$; $8 \cdot 2 + 2 = 18$
11. $u = 3$; $11 - 6 \cdot 3 = -7$ **13.** $x = 2.4$; $2 \cdot 2.4 + 3 \cdot 2.4 + 5 = 17$ **15.** $x = 0.25$; $1.3 = 0.8 + 2 \cdot 0.25$ **17.** $3x + 2y + 2z$ **19.** $2x$
21. $-7 - 2m$ **23.** $6a - 6b + 12c$ **25.** 150 square units
27. a. 12 square units **b.** 48 square units **29.** 24,600 square units
31. 28,800 square units **33.** Multiplication Property of Equality
35. from line 2 to line 3 **37.** 87.5 ft deep **39.** 12 cm high

41. a. 37.5 liters **b.** $4\frac{2}{3}$ hr or 4 hours, 40 minutes **43.** The area needed to cover the mattress is $7 \cdot 6 + 2 \cdot 6 \cdot \frac{3}{4} + 2 \cdot 7 \cdot \frac{3}{4} = 61.5$ square feet, which is larger than 48 square feet. **45.** square feet **47.** Sample: in^3, km^3
49. a. See right. b. $w = 3$
51. $x(20 + 5) = 20x + 5x$

49. a. ■ = w
● = kilogram weights

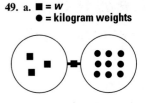

LESSON 11-1 (pp. 590–596)

9. a. $365 = 52 \cdot 7 + 1$ **b.** It shows that there are 52 full weeks in a 365-day year, with one day left over. **11.** Each student gets 43 sheets and 11 sheets are left over. **13.** Yes, $x = 14$.
15. See below. 17. a. Cesarean section **b.** 391.5 **19. a.** 0.1875
b. 0.01875 **c.** 0.001875 **d.** 0.0001875

15.

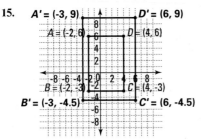

$A' = (-3, 9)$ $D' = (6, 9)$
$A = (-2, 6)$ $D = (4, 6)$
$B = (-2, -3)$ $C = (4, -3)$
$B' = (-3, -4.5)$ $C' = (6, -4.5)$

LESSON 11-2 (pp. 597–600)

13. \$6.53 per hour **15.** California **17.** Sample: 84 sheets in 10 days **19. a.** 3 **b.** 9 **c.** 27 full square yards; 7 square feet are left over **21.** angles 3 and 7; angles 2 and 6 **23.** 75° **25.** 4

LESSON 11-3 (pp. 601–605)

11. a. $\frac{35}{117}$ **b.** $5\frac{4}{7}$ is greater than $1\frac{2}{3}$. **c.** $1.\overline{6} \div 5.\overline{571428} \approx .2991$ and $\frac{35}{117} \approx .2991$ **d.** The decimals are repeating, so it is easier to work with the fractions. **13.** $\frac{2y}{x}$ **15.** 50 **17.** 2116.8 cm^2
19. $G = \frac{3}{4}$ or .75 **21.** $G = 1$ **23. a.** $\frac{17}{20}$ **b.** .85 **c.** 85% **25.** $\frac{3}{4}$

LESSON 11-4 (pp. 606–610)

17. a. 95,000 people per year
b. 20, less **c.** $\frac{-1,900,000}{-20}$; 95,000
19. -24, 0, 144, 1 **21.** $\frac{1}{6}, -\frac{5}{6}, -\frac{1}{6}, -\frac{2}{3}$
23. -58 **25.** ≈ 142.9 miles per day **27. a.** 1250 **b.** 200

29. Sample:

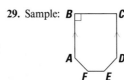

LESSON 11-5 (pp. 611–614)

11. 10.8 **13.** 22.5% **15. a.** 5 **b.** -1 **c.** $\frac{1}{2}$ **d.** $\frac{1}{10}$ **e.** $-\frac{8}{9}$ **f.** $\frac{9}{8}$
17. \$9.80 **19.** 6.25 miles **21.** $12C - 200$ dollars

LESSON 11-6 (pp. 615–619)

13. \$56.25 **15.** $2\frac{7}{9}$ (almost 3) teaspoons **17. a.** Army: 37.5%; Air Force: 32.8%; Navy: 25.5%; Marine Corps: 4.2%
b.

Female Armed Forces Personnel

Air Force 32.8%
Army 37.5%
Marine Corps 4.2%
Navy 25.5%

19. Neither. Both fold $\frac{4}{5}$ napkin per minute. **21.** 5400 cm^2

LESSON 11-7 (pp. 620–624)

11. True **13.** False **15.** 29 cans **17.** The equation is not a proportion. **19. a.** 49.58% **b.** about 12,400 households **c.** $\frac{1}{2}$ or .5 **21.** $\frac{49}{20}$ **23.** $\frac{5}{24}$ feet/year, or 2.5 inches/year **25. a.** Answers will vary. **b.** The coordinates of the vertices of the image should be the result of multiplying the coordinates of the vertices of the first quadrilateral by -3.

LESSON 11-8 (pp. 625–629)

9. a. See right. b. 12 cm, 15 cm
c. The triangle should show corresponding sides of 9 cm, 12 cm, and 15 cm. **11.** 88 feet
13. 12.5 **15.** $6\frac{2}{3}$ **17.** (c), (d), (e), (f) **19.** \$15 **21.** 3 **23.** $-\frac{8}{7}$
25. $3.8 \cdot 10^9$ **27.** 5.125, $5\frac{1}{8}$

9.

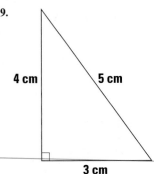

4 cm   5 cm
3 cm

LESSON 11-9 (pp. 630–633)

11. 40 words **13.** 150 stamps **15.** $x = 30$ **17.** -3 **19.** 28

CHAPTER 11 PROGRESS SELF-TEST (p. 637)

1. 60 words per minute ($300 \div 5$ words per minute)
2. $\frac{k}{h}$ kilometers per hour **3.** $\frac{4}{9} \cdot \frac{3}{1} = \frac{4}{3}$ **4.** $\frac{-42}{-24} = \frac{42}{24} = \frac{7}{4}$
5. $\frac{3}{5} \div \frac{6}{5} = \frac{3}{5} \cdot \frac{5}{6} = \frac{15}{30} = \frac{1}{2}$ **6.** $\frac{-2(-5)}{8 + -9} = \frac{10}{-1} = -10$ **7.** $\frac{a}{b}, \frac{-a}{-b}$
8. Sample: Gunther lost 8 pounds in two months. What was the rate of change of his weight? **9.** $40 \cdot 5 = 8x$; $200 = 8x$; $x = 25$
10. $5 \cdot 3 = 12 \cdot p$; $15 = 12p$; $p = \frac{15}{12} = \frac{5}{4} = 1\frac{1}{4}$ **11.** $\frac{14}{150} \approx 9.33 \approx$ 9% **12.** $\frac{.30}{4.00} = 7.5\%$ **13.** $.60x = 30$; $x = \frac{30}{.60}$; $x = \frac{300}{6}$; $x = 50$
14. $\frac{45 \text{ miles}}{1 \text{ hour}} = \frac{189 \text{ miles}}{x \text{ hours}}$; $45x = 189$; $x = 4.2$ hours

15. $\frac{640 \text{ acres}}{1 \text{ sq. mile}} = \frac{x}{10{,}000 \text{ sq. miles}}$; $640 \cdot 10{,}000 = x$; $x = 6{,}400{,}000$ acres **16.** In any true proportion $\frac{a}{b} = \frac{x}{y}$, $ay = bx$.
17. b and x are the means. **18.** $\frac{144}{64} = \frac{x}{40}$; $144 \cdot 40 = 64x$; $5760 \div 64 = x$; $x = 90$ **19.** $\frac{144}{64} = \frac{180}{y}$; $144y = 64 \cdot 180$; $y = 11520 \div 144 = 80$ **20.** $\frac{4}{1} = \frac{10}{x}$; $4x = 10 \cdot 1\frac{1}{4}$; $x = \frac{5}{8}$ teaspoon of pepper **21.** $245 \div 15 = 16$ with a remainder of 5; 15 pages for 16 days, 5 pages for the 17th day. **22.** $n = d \cdot q + r$ is translated as $245 = 15 \cdot 16 + 5$.

750

The chart below keys the **Progress Self-Test** questions to the objectives in the **Chapter Review** on pages 638–639 or to the **Vocabulary** (Voc.) on page 636. This will enable you to locate those **Chapter Review** questions that correspond to questions students missed on the **Progress Self-Test**. The lesson where the material is covered is also indicated on the chart.

Question	1	2	3	4	5	6	7	8	9	10
Objective	G	G	A	B	A	B	E	G	C	C
Lesson	11-2	11-2	11-3	11-4	11-3	11-4	11-4	11-4	11-9	11-6

Question	11	12	13	14	15	16	17	18	19	20
Objective	H	H	H	I	I	D	D	J	J	I
Lesson	11-5	11-5	11-5	11-9	11-9	11-7	11-7	11-8	11-8	11-6

Question	21	22
Objective	F	F
Lesson	11-1	11-1

CHAPTER 11 CHAPTER REVIEW (pp. 638–639)

1. 18 **3.** $\frac{1}{2}$ **5.** $\frac{bx}{ay}$ **7.** $\frac{7}{4}$ **9.** −5 **11.** $\frac{4}{3}$ **13.** No ($t = 8$) **15.** $y = \frac{18}{7}$
17. $G = 21$ **19.** $CD = \frac{3}{5}$ **21.** $6x$ **23.** (d) **25. a.** $6\frac{1}{4}$ gallons
b. $25 = 4 \cdot 6 + 1$ **27. a.** 5; 10 **b.** $70 = 12 \cdot 5 + 10$ **29.** $50 \frac{km}{hr}$ or

50 kilometers per hour **31.** $\frac{10 \text{ pounds}}{30 \text{ days}} = \frac{1 \text{ pound}}{3 \text{ day}}$ or $\frac{1}{3}$ pound each
day **33.** \$180 **35.** Sample: How fast have they been repaving
the road? $\frac{-6 \text{ km}}{-3 \text{ day}} = 2\frac{km}{day}$ **37.** 20% missed **39.** 1.2 times as many
Continentals **41.** $\frac{20}{9}$ cups **43.** 15.6 and 16.9 **45.** $IK = 31.5$

LESSON 12-1 (pp. 640–645)
15. Sample: $353 \div 6$ **17.** Let $x = 0.\overline{9}$; $10x = 9.\overline{9}$; $10x - x =$
$9.\overline{9} - 0.\overline{9}$; $9x = 9$; $x = 1$; So $x = 0.\overline{9} = 1$. **19.** $131\frac{3}{5}$ **21.** none
23. a. s^2 **b.** 2 square units

LESSON 12-2 (pp. 646–650)
25. 10 square units **27. a.** 8 square units **b.** $\sqrt{8}$ units **29.** 16.9
31. 16.0 **33.** $\frac{422}{99}$
35. a. 196 | 9
      197 | 4
      198 | 27792978198799919
      199 | 02021
b. 1988.5 **c.** 1989 **d.** 1992 or 1993
(It was published in 1992.)

LESSON 12-3 (pp. 651–656)
11. a. 11 km **b.** $\sqrt{85}$ km or about 9.2 km **c.** about 1.8 km
13. $\sqrt{5}$ **15.** (b) **17.** $\sqrt{13} \approx 3.6056$ **19. a.** 0 **b.** 0
21. 10/35 hours or about 17 minutes **23.** (a)

LESSON 12-4 (pp. 657–663)
21. 1.2π inches $\approx 3.77''$ **23.** $25\pi \approx 78.5$ units **25.** 16''
27. a. $3\frac{16}{113}$ **b.** $\frac{355}{113}$ **29.** $\sqrt{10}$ **31.** 9 **33.** 20% **35.** $\frac{m}{20}$ hours
37. 1704

LESSON 12-5 (pp. 664–669)
9. Sample: $\boxed{\pi}\boxed{\times}$ 50 $\boxed{x^2}\boxed{=}$ **11. a.** 0.3125π or about 0.98 in^2
b. the ring **13.** 141 calories **15.** one 14'' pizza **17.** when it is
infinite and does not repeat **19.** $\sqrt{5}$, $\sqrt{6}$, $2\sqrt{3}$, $3\sqrt{12}$ **21.** 36.36
23. $5x - 5y + 60$

LESSON 12-6 (pp. 670–674)
9. 4080 mm^2 **11.** (b) **13. a.** 900 in^2 **b.** 120 in. **c.** about 42.4 in.
15. 10^{-1}, 10^0, $\sqrt{10}$, 10^1 **17.** $\frac{1}{64}$ **19.** $\frac{112}{45}$

LESSON 12-7 (pp. 675–679)
13. Sample: a compact disc **15. a.** rectangle **b.** 67.5 in^3
17. $7\pi \approx 22$ cubic units **19. a.** 6 **b.** 3 **c.** $\sqrt{27}$ or ≈ 5.2
21. $y = -\frac{42}{31}$ **23.** $w = -2$

LESSON 12-8 (pp. 680–683)
11. volume **13.** volume **15.** about 332 cubic inches
17. a. 59.5 cm by 16 cm **b.** Answers may vary. Sample: Use the
4 cm × 32 cm × 60 cm piece to make two game boards with no
waste. The other piece of wood will make one game board with
unusable waste left over. **19.** about 1866 in^2 or about 13 ft^2
21. $\frac{140}{99}$

23. Sample: **100 Most Influential Persons in History**

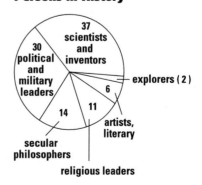

751

CHAPTER 12 PROGRESS SELF-TEST (p. 687)

1. $C = \pi d = \pi\left(\frac{3}{4}\right) \approx 2.4$ inches $A = \pi r^2 = \pi\left(\frac{3}{8}\right)^2 \approx$ 0.44 square inches **2.** $A = s^2$; $A = (\sqrt{3})^2$; $A = 3$ square units **3.** $A = s^2$; $10 = s^2$, $\sqrt{10}$ units **4.** $\sqrt{33} \approx 6$ and $\sqrt{51} \approx 7$; $\sqrt{33} + \sqrt{51} \approx 13$ **5.** $x^2 + 24^2 = 26^2$ (Pythagorean Theorem); $x^2 = 100$; $x = 10$ **6.** $5^2 + 10^2 = (AC)^2$; $125 = (AC)^2$; $\sqrt{125} = AC$ **7.** $\sqrt{25} = 5$; the other numbers are non-terminating, non-repeating decimals. **8.** $-2\frac{7}{10} = -\frac{27}{10}$ **9.** $n = 0.\overline{15}$; $100n = 15.\overline{15}$; $100n - n = 15.\overline{15} - .\overline{15}$; $99n = 15$; $n = \frac{15}{99} = \frac{5}{33}$ **10.** Determine surface area by adding the lateral area $(C \cdot h)$ and the area of the 2 bases. $S.A. = 57\pi \cdot 123 + 2 \cdot (28.5)^2 \cdot \pi \approx 27{,}130$ mm²

11. $L.A.$ = perimeter · height; $(7 + 24 + 25) \cdot 30 = 56 \cdot 30 = 1680$ square units **12.** V = area of base · h; $84 \cdot 30 = 2520$ cubic units **13.** 4 and -4 **14.** $C = \pi d \approx 120\pi \approx 377$ mm **15.** $A = \pi r^2 = \pi(16)^2 = 256\pi$ units² **16.** when the decimal does not terminate or infinitely repeat **17.** $S = 4\pi r^2 \approx 4\pi(12)^2 \approx 1809.6$ cm² ≈ 1810 cm² or $4\pi(.12)^2 \approx .18$ m² **18. a.** $V = \frac{4}{3}\pi r^3 = \frac{4}{3}\pi(9)^3 = 972\pi$ cubic units **b.** $972\pi \approx 3054$ cubic units **19.** $S.A. = 4\pi r^2 = 4\pi(3500)^2 = 49{,}000{,}000\pi \approx 1.5394 \cdot 10^8 \approx 153{,}950{,}000$ km² $\approx 154{,}000{,}000$ km² **20.** $A = \frac{60}{360}\pi \cdot 6^2 = 6\pi$ cm²

The chart below keys the **Progress Self-Test** questions to the objectives in the **Chapter Review** on pages 688–689 or to the **Vocabulary** (Voc.) on page 686. This will enable you to locate those **Chapter Review** questions that correspond to questions students missed on the **Progress Self-Test**. The lesson where the material is covered is also indicated on the chart.

Question	1	2	3	4	5	6	7	8	9	10
Objective	D	J	J	B	C	C	G	A	A	H
Lesson	12-4, 12-5	12-2	12-2	12-2	12-3	12-3	12-2	12-1	12-1	12-6
Question	11	12	13	14	15	16	17	18	19	20
Objective	E	E	B	I	D	G	I	F	I	D
Lesson	12-6	12-7	12-2	12-4	12-5	12-2	12-8	12-8	12-8	12-5

CHAPTER 12 CHAPTER REVIEW (pages 688–689)

1. $-\frac{122}{99}$ **3.** $\frac{1631}{20}$ **5.** 8 and 9 **7.** 20 **9.** $BI = \sqrt{73}$ **11.** $\sqrt{2704} = 52$ **13.** $C = 20\pi$ units; $A = 100\pi$ square units **15.** $A = \frac{25}{4}\pi$ square feet **17.** 110π square units **19.** 2520 units³

21. 100π units² **23.** 3.14, $\frac{22}{7}$, $3\frac{1}{7}$ **25.** always **27.** 24,000 ft² **29.** 5.16 in³ **31.** 400π or ≈ 1256.6 cm² **33.** $\approx 942{,}000{,}000$ km² **35.** $4.5\pi \approx 14.1$ cm³ **37.** 4.9 **39.** $\sqrt{2}$

LESSON 13-1 (pp. 690–697)

17. (a) **19. a.** $y = 11x + 2$
b. 20 FOR X = 1 TO 100
   30 Y = 2 * X − 6
21. a. Sample:

age	height
9 yr	56″
10 yr	59″
11 yr	62″
12 yr	65″

b. See below. **c.** $b = 29$ **d.** From the equation, at age 25, for example, height would be 104″ or 8′8″, an unacceptable human height. **23.** $n = 6$; $3(5(6) + 22) − 156 = 0$ **25.** $\frac{3}{8}$ of the salad **27.** \$3276 **29.** 33°

21. b.

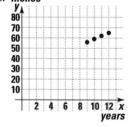

LESSON 13-2 (pp. 698–703)

13. a. $P = 222 + .190g$ **b.** See below. **c.** $P = 120 + .260g$ **d.** See below. **e.** Sample: about 1450 games **f.** $222 + .19g = 120 + .26g$ **15.** See below. **17.** $y = \frac{15}{8}$; $\frac{2}{5}\left(\frac{15}{8}\right) = \frac{3}{4}$ **19.** $0.56 = 56\%$ **21.** 22 miles

13. b., d.

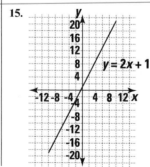

15.

LESSON 13-3 (pp. 704–708)

11. a. $P = 1000 + 200n$ **b.** $P = 750 + 250n$ **c.** 5 **13.** $p = -1$; $11(-1) + 5(-1 - 1) = -21$ and $9(-1) - 12 = -21$ **15.** $m\angle P = 60$; $m\angle N = 60$; $m\angle I = 60$ **17.** The lines intersect when $n = 5$, indicating when the amount paid is equal. **See below for graph.**
19. $\frac{70}{11}$ **21.** BOOK **23. See below. 25.** about 6,946,500

17.

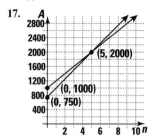

23.

LESSON 13-4 (pp. 709–713)

7. a., b., c. Answers will vary. **d.** $y = \frac{1}{2}x$; answers may vary.
e. Answers will vary. **9. a. See below. b.** They intersect at (0, 0).
c. $y = ax$ and $y = -ax$ are reflection images of each other over the x-axis (or over the y-axis). **11.** $B = 6$ **13.** $x = 12$
15. $d = 44.88$ **17.** ≈ 401 minutes ≈ 6 hours and 41 minutes
19. .0009 or .09% **21.** Sample: 1 km = 1000 m = 100,000 cm = 1,000,000 mm

9a.

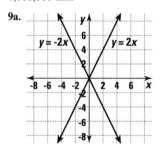

LESSON 13-5 (pp. 714–718)

11. a., b. See below. 13. Sample: (3, 4), (6, 8), (9, 12), (−3, −4), (−6, −8) **See below for graph. 15.** $t = -\frac{1}{8}$ **17.** Prince Edward Island, with about 60 people per square mile, was more densely populated than Ontario, with about 28 people per square mile.
19. a. 56 pieces **b.** 30 pieces

11.

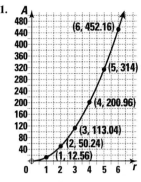

13.

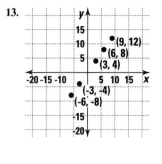

LESSON 13-6 (pp. 719–724)

15. See below. 17. (d) **19. a.** Samples: At 10 mph, braking distance is 5 feet; at 20 mph, 20 feet; at 50 mph, 125 feet; at 60 mph, 180 feet. **b.** Sample: (10, 5), (20, 20), (50, 125), (60, 180) **c.** part of a parabola **21.** −6

15.

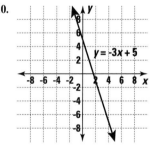

CHAPTER 13 PROGRESS SELF-TEST (page 728)

1. $60 + 14y - 14y = -20 + 30y - 14y$; $60 = -20 + 16y$;
$60 + 20 = -20 + 20 + 16y$; $80 = 16y$; $5 = y$ **2.** $6x - 24 = 4x + 9$; $6x - 4x - 24 = 4x - 4x + 9$; $2x - 24 = 9 + 24 + 24$;
$2x = 33$; $x = \frac{33}{2}$ **3.** 987.654 rounded up to the nearest integer is 988. **4.** Samples: 8, 8.3; any number between 8 and 9, including 8

5.

x	y
10	3
20	6
30	9
x	$\frac{3}{10}x$

$y = \frac{3}{10}x$ **6.** $y = \frac{3}{10}x$ **7. a.** $c = 35 + .48m$; **b.** $35 + .48m = 39 + .41m$ **8.** ≈ 57 miles **9. See right. 10. See right.**
11. a. $A = 6(5)^2$; $A = 150$ square units **b.** (5, 150) **12. See below.**
13. Sample: The point where the lines meet is the solution to $y = 4x$ and $y = -3x + 5$, hence $4x = -3x + 5$ will determine the x-coordinate of the point where the lines meet. **14.** Sample:
$4x = -3x + 5$; $4x + 3x = -3x + 3x + 5$; $7x = 5$; $x = \frac{5}{7}$ **15.** (c)

9.

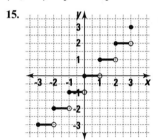

10.

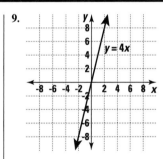

12.

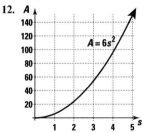

753

The chart below keys the **Progress Self-Test** questions to the objectives in the **Chapter Review** on pages 729–731 or to the **Vocabulary** (Voc.) on page 727. This will enable you to locate those **Chapter Review** questions that correspond to questions students missed on the **Progress Self-Test.** The lesson where the material is covered is also indicated on the chart.

Question	1	2	3	4	5	6	7	8	9	10
Objective	A	A	B	B	C	C	D	A	F	F
Lesson	13-3	13-3	13-6	13-6	13-4	13-4	13-2	13-3	13-1	13-1

Question	11	12	13	14	15
Objective	E	E	G	A	H
Lesson	13-5	13-5	13-2	13-3	13-6

CHAPTER 13 CHAPTER REVIEW (pp. 729–731)

1. $x = \frac{2}{5}$ **3.** $v = \frac{1}{2}$ **5.** $r = -\frac{3}{17}$ **7.** $t = \frac{4}{3}$ **9.** 1 **11.** -40 **13.** 27
15. a. Samples: $\frac{-7}{-5}, \frac{14}{10}, \frac{49}{35}$ **b.** $y = \frac{7}{5}x$ **17.** $y = 7x$ **19. a.** $15 +$
$.20m = 5 + .34m$ **b.** ≈ 71 minutes **21. a.** $57 + \frac{1}{100}d = 59 +$
$\frac{1}{150}d$ **b.** after 600 days **23. See below.** **25. See below.**

27. See below. 29. See below. 31. Graph $y = 35 + 6w$ for Kurt and $y = 60 + 4w$ for Sara. The w-coordinate of the point where the lines intersect is the solution. **33. See graph below.** Conclusion: $x = 4$ **35.** $y = \lfloor x \rfloor$; in each bar the values of x are rounded down to the nearest integer. **37.** $y = 11\lceil x \rceil + 2$

23.

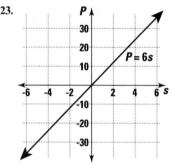

25.

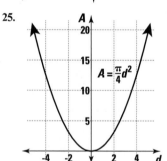

27.

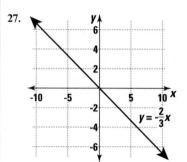

29.

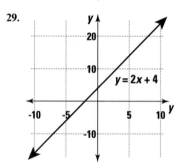

33.

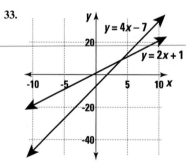

754

T106

absolute value   The distance that a number is from 0 on the number line. (248)

acre (a)   A unit of area equal to 43,560 square feet. (162)

acute angle   An angle with a measure less than 90°. (154)

addend   A number to be added. In $a + b$, a and b are addends. (239)

Adding Fractions Property   For all numbers a, b, and c, with $c \neq 0$, $\frac{a}{c} + \frac{b}{c} = \frac{a+b}{c}$. (260)

Addition Property of Equality   If $a = b$, then $a + c = b + c$. (277)

additive identity   The number zero. (244)

Additive Identity Property of Zero   For any number n, $n + 0 = n$. (244)

additive inverse   A number whose sum with a given number is 0. Also called *opposite*. (245)

adjacent angles   Angles that share a common side and have no common interior points. (256)

algebra   See *elementary algebra*.

Algebraic Definition of Division   For all numbers a and nonzero numbers b, $a \cdot \frac{1}{b} = \frac{a}{b} = a \div b$. (483)

Algebraic Definition of Subtraction   For any numbers x and y, $x - y = x + -y$. Also called the *Adding Opposites Property* or the *Add-Opp Property*. (353)

algebraic expression   An expression that contains either a variable alone or with number and operation symbols. (187)

algorithm   A finite sequence of steps that leads to a desired result. (302)

alternate exterior angles   Angles formed by two lines and a transversal that are on opposite sides of the transversal but not between the two given lines. (382)

alternate interior angles   Angles formed by two lines and a transversal that are between the two given lines and on opposite sides of the transversal. (382)

altitude   The perpendicular segment from a vertex of a triangle to the opposite side of the triangle. Also see *height*. (572)

ambiguous   Having more than one possible meaning. (189)

angle   The union of two rays with the same endpoint. (145)

Angle Addition Property   If $\overrightarrow{OB}$ is in the interior of $\angle AOC$, then $m\angle AOB + m\angle BOC = m\angle AOC$. (256)

Arabic numerals   See *Hindu-Arabic numerals*.

arc of a circle   A part of a circle connecting two points (called the **endpoints** of the arc) on the circle. (94)

area   A measure of the space inside a two-dimensional figure. (158)

Area Formula for a Circle   Let A be the area of a circle with radius r. Then $A = \pi r^2$. (666)

Area Formula for a Sector   Let A be the area of a sector of a circle with radius r. Let m be the measure of the central angle of the sector in degrees. Then $A = \frac{m}{360} \cdot \pi r^2$. (667)

Area Formula for a Trapezoid   Let A be the area of a trapezoid with bases b_1 and b_2 and height h. Then $A = \frac{1}{2} \cdot h(b_1 + b_2)$. (579)

Area Formula for Any Triangle   Let b be the length of a side of a triangle with area A. Let h be the length of the altitude drawn to that side. Then $A = \frac{1}{2}bh$. (572)

Area Formula for a Right Triangle   Let A be the area of a right triangle with legs of lengths a and b. Then $A = \frac{1}{2}ab$. (470)

Area Model for Multiplication   The area of a rectangle with length ℓ units and width w units is $\ell \cdot w$ (or ℓw) square units. (469)

array   See *rectangular array*.

Associative Property of Addition   For any numbers a, b, and c, $(a + b) + c = a + (b + c)$. (272)

Associative Property of Multiplication   For any numbers a, b, and c, $(ab)c = a(bc)$. (479)

automatic drawer   Technology that can be used to draw geometric figures. (400)

automatic grapher   A computer program or calculator that is used to make coordinate graphs. (458)

average   See *mean*.

ball   A sphere together with all the points inside it. (680)

bar graph   A display in which numbers are represented by bars whose lengths correspond to the magnitude of the numbers being represented. (415)

base   **1** In a power x^y, x. (68) **2** The side of a triangle perpendicular to an altitude. (572) **3** The bottom of a box, or rectangular solid. (476) **4** In a trapezoid, one of the parallel sides. (578) **5** In a cylindric solid, one of the plane regions translated to form the solid. (675)

base line of a protractor   A segment on a protractor connecting a 0° mark with a 180° mark opposite which is placed over one side of the angle being measured. (147)

billion   In the United States, a word name for the number 1,000,000,000 or 10^9. (65)

billionth   A word name for the number 0.00000 0001 or 10^{-9}. (101)

box   See *rectangular solid*.

brackets [ ]   **1** Grouping symbols that indicate that all arithmetic operations inside are to be done first. As grouping symbols, brackets mean exactly the same thing as parentheses. (203) **2** A notation sometimes used for the greatest integer function. (720)

capacity   See *volume*.

ceiling function symbol   See *rounding up symbol*.

cell   In a spreadsheet, the intersection of a column and a row. (325)

center of a circle   See *circle*.

755

center of a protractor The midpoint of the base line on a protractor. The center is placed over the vertex of the angle being measured. (147)

center of a sphere See *sphere.*

center of gravity The center of gravity of a set of points is the point whose first coordinate is the mean of the first coordinates of the given points, and whose second coordinate is the mean of the second coordinates of the given points. (609)

centi- A prefix meaning $\frac{1}{100}$. (137)

central angle of a circle An angle whose vertex is the center of the circle. (152)

certain event An event with probability one. (214)

circle The set of all points in a plane a given distance (its **radius**) from a fixed point in the plane (its **center**). (94)

circle graph A display in which parts of a whole are represented by sectors whose areas are proportional to the fraction of the whole taken up by each part. Also called *pie chart.* (93)

circular cylinder A cylindric solid whose bases are circles. Also called *cylinder.* (670)

circumference A circle's perimeter. (659)

clockwise The same direction as that in which the hands of a clock normally move. (253)

coincide To occupy the same position as. (442)

column One of the vertical arrangements of items in a table, rectangular array, or spreadsheet. (325)

common denominator A number that is a multiple of the denominator of every fraction in a collection of fractions. (262)

Commutative Property of Addition For any numbers *a* and *b*, $a + b = b + a$. (271)

Commutative Property of Multiplication For any numbers *a* and *b*, $ab = ba$. (470)

Comparison Model for Subtraction $x - y$ is how much more *x* is than *y*. (348)

complement of an event The event consisting of all outcomes not in the given event. (268)

complementary angles Two angles whose measures add to 90°. (376)

composite number Any positive integer exactly divisible by one or more positive integers other than itself or 1; opposed to *prime number.* (307)

congruent figures Figures having the same size and shape. Figures that are the image of each other under a reflection, rotation, or translation, or any combination of these. (436)

contraction A size change with a magnitude whose absolute value is between 0 and 1. (511)

conversion factor A rate factor that equals the number 1, used for converting quantities given in one unit to a quantity given in another unit. (495)

convex polygon A polygon in which every diagonal lies inside the polygon. (451)

coordinate graph A display in which an ordered pair of numbers is displayed as a dot located relative to a fixed point called the **origin.** (420)

corresponding angles Any pair of angles in similar locations in relation to a transversal intersecting two lines. (382)

corresponding sides Any pair of sides in the same relative positions in two figures. (626)

count A whole number tally of particular things. (7)

counterclockwise The direction opposite to that in which the hands of a clock normally move. (253)

counting unit The name of the particular things being tallied in a count. (7)

cube A three-dimensional figure with six square faces. (163)

cup (c) A unit of capacity in the U.S. system of measurement equal to 8 fluid ounces. (130)

customary system See *U.S. system of measurement.*

cylinder See *circular cylinder.*

cylindric solid The set of points between a plane region (its **base**) and its translation image in space, including the region and its image. (675)

cylindric surface The surface of a cylindric solid. (675)

data disk A disk used to store computer information. (328)

decagon A ten-sided polygon. (284)

deci- A prefix meaning $\frac{1}{10}$. (137)

decimal notation A notation in which numbers are written using ten digits and each place stands for a power of 10. (6)

decimal system A system in which numbers are written in decimal notation. (6)

degree A unit of angle measure equal to $\frac{1}{360}$ of a full revolution. (146)

deka- A prefix meaning 10. (137)

denominator In a fraction, the divisor. The number *b* in the fraction $\frac{a}{b}$. (31)

diagonal of a polygon A segment that connects two vertices of the polygon but is not a side of the polygon. (286)

diameter **1** Twice the radius of a circle or sphere. **2** A segment connecting two points on a circle that contains the center of the circle. (94) **3** A segment connecting two points on a sphere that contains the center of the sphere. (680)

diamond See *rhombus.*

difference The result of a subtraction. (347)

digit One of the ten symbols 0, 1, 2, 3, 4, 5, 6, 7, 8, 9 used in the decimal system to stand for the first ten whole numbers. (3)

dimension **1** The length or width of a rectangle. (469) **2** The number of rows or the number of columns in an array. (469) **3** The length, width, or height of a box. (476)

display **1** Numbers or other symbols that appear on the screen of a calculator or computer. (26) **2** A diagram, graph, table, or other visual arrangement used to organize, present, or represent information. (407)

756

Distributive Property of Multiplication over Addition For any numbers a, b, and x, $ax + bx = (a + b)x$ and $x(a + b) = xa + xb$. (556)

Distributive Property of Multiplication over Subtraction For any numbers a, b, and x, $ax - bx = (a - b)x$ and $x(a - b) = xa - xb$. (557)

dividend The number in a quotient that is being divided. In the division $a \div b$, a is the dividend. (31)

divisible An integer a is divisible by an integer b when $\frac{a}{b}$ is an integer. Also called *evenly divisible.* (34)

divisor **1** The number by which you divide in a quotient. In the division $a \div b$, b is the divisor. (31) **2** A number that divides into another number with zero remainder. Also called *factor.* (308)

dodecagon A 12-sided polygon (319)

double bar graph A display in which two bar graphs are combined into a single display. (416)

edges The sides of the faces of a rectangular solid. (476)

elementary algebra The study of variables and the operations of arithmetic with variables. (184)

ending decimal See *terminating decimal.*

endpoint of a ray See *ray.*

entering Pressing a key on a calculator to enter numbers, operations, or other symbols. (27)

Equal Fractions Property If the numerator and denominator of a fraction are both multiplied (or divided) by the same nonzero number, then the resulting fraction is equal to the original one. (51)

equally likely outcomes Outcomes in a situation where the likelihood of each outcome is assumed to be equal. (215)

equation A sentence with an equal sign. (219)

equilateral triangle A triangle whose sides all have the same length and whose angles all have the same measure. (452)

equivalent equations Equations that have the same solutions. (363)

equivalent formulas Formulas that have the same solutions. (364)

estimate **1** A number which is near another number. Also called *approximation.* **2** To obtain an estimate. (16)

evaluating an algebraic expression Replacing each variable with a particular number (the **value of the variable**) and then evaluating the resulting numerical expression. (193)

evaluating a numerical expression Carrying out the operations in a numerical expression to find the value of the expression. (176)

evenly divisible See *divisible.*

event Any collection of outcomes from the same experiment. (216)

exercise A question that you know how to answer. (302)

expansion A size change with a magnitude whose absolute value is greater than 1. (505)

exponent In a power x^y, y. (68)

exponential form A number written as a power. The form x^y. (99)

exterior angles Angles formed by two lines and a transversal that have no points between the two given lines. (382)

extremes In the proportion $\frac{a}{b} = \frac{c}{d}$, the numbers a and d. (620)

faces See *rectangular solid.*

factor **1** A number that divides evenly into another number. Also called *divisor.* (308) **2** To find the factors of a particular number. (51)

fair An object or experiment in which all outcomes are equally likely. Also called *unbiased.* (215)

finite decimal See *terminating decimal.*

first coordinate See *ordered pair.*

floor function symbol See *rounding down symbol.*

fluid ounce (fl oz) A unit of capacity in the U.S. system of measurement equal to $\frac{1}{128}$ of a gallon. Often called simply *ounce.* (130)

foot (ft) A unit of length in the U.S. system of measurement equal to twelve inches. (125)

formula A sentence in which one variable is written in terms of other variables. (208)

Formula for Circumference of a Circle In a circle with diameter d and circumference C, $C = \pi d$. (659)

fraction A symbol of the form $\frac{a}{b}$ which represents the quotient when a is divided by b. (31)

fraction bar The horizontal line in a fraction that indicates the operation of division. (31)

frequency of an outcome The number of times an outcome occurs. (213)

full turn A turn of 360°. Also called *revolution.* (253)

Fundamental Property of Turns If a turn of magnitude x is followed by a turn of magnitude y, the result is a turn of magnitude $x + y$. (255)

fundamental region A figure whose congruent copies make up a tessellation. Also called *fundamental shape.* (452)

fundamental shape See *fundamental region.*

furlong (fur) A unit of length in the U.S. system of measurement equal to 40 rods. (128)

gallon (gal) A unit of capacity in the U.S. system of measurement equal to 4 quarts. One gallon is equal to 231 cubic inches. (130)

generalization A statement that is true about many instances. (321)

giga- A prefix meaning one billion. (137)

gram (g) A unit of mass in the metric system equal to $\frac{1}{1000}$ of a kilogram. (136)

greatest common factor (GCF) The largest number that is a factor of every number in a given collection of numbers. (52)

greatest integer function symbol See *rounding down symbol.*

gross ton A unit of weight in the U.S. system of measurement equal to 2240 pounds. Also called *long ton.* (132)

grouping symbols Symbols such as parentheses, brackets, or fraction bars that indicate that certain arithmetic operations are to be done before others in an expression. (203)

half turn A turn of magnitude 180°. (253)

hectare (ha) A metric unit of area equal to 10,000 m². (159)

hecto- A prefix meaning 100. (137)

height **1** The perpendicular distance from any vertex of a triangle to the side opposite that vertex. (572) **2** The distance between the bases of the trapezoid. (578) **3** The distance between the bases of a cylinder or prism. (676) Also called *altitude.*

heptagon A seven-sided polygon. (284)

hexagon A six-sided polygon. (284)

Hindu-Arabic numerals The numerals 0, 1, 2, 3, 4, 5, 6, 7, 8, 9 used throughout the world today to represent numbers in the decimal system. (3)

hour (h) A unit of time equal to 60 minutes. (130)

hundred A word name for the number 100 or 10^2. (65)

hundred-thousandth A word name for 0.00001 or 10^{-5}. (12)

hundredth A word name for 0.01 or 10^{-2}. (11)

hypotenuse The longest side of a right triangle. (470)

image The result of applying a transformation to a figure. (435)

impossible event An event with probability zero. (214)

inch (in.) The basic unit of length in the U.S. system of measurement. One inch equals 2.54 centimeters exactly. (119)

independent events Two events *A* and *B* are independent events when and only when *Prob(A and B)* = *Prob(A) · Prob(B).* (489)

inequality A sentence with one or more of the symbols ≠, <, ≤, >, ≥. (224)

inequality symbols Any one of the symbols ≠ (not equal to), < (is less than), ≤ (is less than or equal to), > (is greater than), or ≥ (is greater than or equal to). (224)

infinite repeating decimal A decimal in which a digit or group of digits to the right of the decimal point repeat forever. (33)

instance A particular example of a pattern. (182)

integer A number which is a whole number or the opposite of a whole number. Any of the numbers 0, 1, -1, 2, -2, 3, -3, ... (43)

integer division Dividing an integer *a* by a positive integer *b* to yield an integer quotient and an integer remainder less than *b.* (592)

interior angles Angles formed by two lines and a transversal that have some points between the two given lines. (382)

international system of measurement See *metric system.*

irrational number A real number that cannot be written as a simple fraction. (660)

key in To press a key on a calculator to enter numbers or perform operations. (27)

key sequence A description of the calculator keys and the order in which they must be pressed to perform a particular computation. (27)

kilo- A prefix meaning 1000. (137)

kilogram (kg) The base unit of mass in the metric system. (136)

lateral area The area of the surface of a cylindric solid excluding the bases. (670)

least common denominator (LCD) The least common multiple of the denominators of every fraction in a given collection of fractions. (262)

least common multiple (LCM) The smallest number that is a multiple of every number in a given collection of integers. (262)

legs of a right triangle The sides of a right triangle that are on the sides of the right angle, or the lengths of these sides. (470)

light-year The distance that light travels in a year. (74)

like terms Terms that involve the same variables to the same powers. (532)

linear equation An equation of the form $y = ax + b$. An equation equivalent to $ax + b = cx + d.$ (694)

linear pair Two angles that share a common side and whose non-common sides are opposite rays. (374)

line of symmetry A line over which the reflection image of a figure coincides with its preimage. Also called *symmetry line.* (446)

line segment A pair of given points *A* and *B* (the **endpoints** of the line segment) along with all the points on $\overleftrightarrow{AB}$ between *A* and *B*. Also called *segment.* (283)

liter (L) A unit of volume in the metric system equal to 1000 cm³. (136)

long ton See *gross ton.*

lowest terms A fraction is in lowest terms when the numerator and denominator have no factors in common except 1. (51)

magic square A square array of numbers in which the sum along every row, column, or main diagonal is the same. (281)

magnitude **1** An amount measuring the size of a turn. (253) **2** The distance between a point and its translation image. (435) **3** A size change factor. (507)

make a table A problem-solving strategy in which information is organized in a table to make it easier to find patterns and generalizations. (320)

mean The sum of the numbers in a collection divided by the number of numbers in the collection. Also called *average.* (206)

means In the proportion $\frac{a}{b} = \frac{c}{d}$, the numbers *b* and *c.* (620)

Means-Extremes Property In any true proportion, the product of the means equals the product of the extremes. If $\frac{a}{b} = \frac{c}{d}$, then $b \cdot c = a \cdot d.$ (621)

758

measure A real number indicating an amount of some quantity. (10)

median In a collection consisting of an odd number of numbers arranged in numerical order, the middle number. In a collection of an even number of numbers arranged in numerical order, the average of the middle two numbers. (411)

mega- A prefix meaning one million. (137)

meter (m) The basic unit of length in the metric system, defined as the length that light in vacuum travels in $\frac{1}{299,792,458}$ of a second. (119)

metric system A decimal system of measurement with the meter as its base unit of length and the kilogram as its base unit of mass. Also called *international system of measurement.* (118)

micro- A prefix meaning one millionth. (137)

mile (mi) A unit of length in the U.S. system of measurement equal to 5280 feet. (125)

milli- A prefix meaning $\frac{1}{1000}$. (137)

million A word name for the number 1,000,000 or 10^6. (65)

millionth A word name for 0.000001 or 10^{-6}. (12)

minuend In a subtraction problem, the number from which another number is subtracted. In $a - b$, the minuend is a. (347)

minute A unit of time equal to 60 seconds. (130)

mirror See *reflection image.*

mixed number The sum of a whole number and a fraction. (37)

mode The mode of a collection of objects is the object that appears most often. (411)

Multiplication of Fractions Property For all numbers a and c, and nonzero numbers b and d, $\frac{a}{b} \cdot \frac{c}{d} = \frac{ac}{bd}$. (484)

Multiplication of Unit Fractions Property For all nonzero numbers a and b, $\frac{1}{a} \cdot \frac{1}{b}$. (483)

Multiplication Property of Equality When equal quantities are multiplied by the same number, the resulting quantities are equal. (125)

Multiplication Property of -1 For any number x, $-1 \cdot x = -x$. (501)

Multiplication Property of Zero For any number x, $0 \cdot x = 0$. (502)

Multiplicative Identity Property of One For any number x, $1 \cdot x = x$. (507)

multiplicative inverse A number whose product with a given number is 1. Also called *reciprocal.* (483)

mutually exclusive events Events that cannot occur at the same time. (267)

nano- A prefix meaning one billionth. (137)

natural number Any of the numbers 1, 2, 3, ... Also called *positive integer.* (43) (Some people like to include 0 as a natural number.)

negative integer Any of the numbers -1, -2, -3, ... (43)

negative numbers The opposites of the positive numbers. Numbers that are graphed to the left of zero on a horizontal number line. (41)

nested parentheses Parentheses inside parentheses. (199)

net A plane pattern for a three-dimensional figure. (561)

*n***-gon** A polygon with n sides. (284)

nonagon A nine-sided polygon. (284)

numerator In a fraction, the dividend. The number a in the fraction $\frac{a}{b}$. (31)

numerical expression A combination of symbols for numbers and operations that stands for a number. (176)

obtuse angle An angle whose measure is between 90° and 180°. (154)

octagon An eight-sided polygon. (284)

odds against an event The ratio of the number of ways an event cannot occur to the number of ways that event can occur. (218)

odds for an event The ratio of the number of ways an event can occur to the number of ways that event cannot occur. (218)

open sentence A sentence containing one or more variables that can be true or false, depending on what is substituted for the variables. (219)

Opposite of Opposites Property (Op-op Property) For any number n, $-(-n) = n$. (245)

opposite A number whose sum with a given number is 0. Also called *additive inverse.* (245)

opposite angles In a quadrilateral, two angles that do not share a side. (388)

opposite rays Two rays that have the same endpoint and whose union is a line. (374)

opposite sides In a quadrilateral, two sides that do not share a vertex. (388)

ordered pair A pair of numbers or objects (x, y) in which the first number x is designated the **first coordinate** and the second number y is designated the **second coordinate.** (422)

Order of Operations The rules for carrying out arithmetic operations: **1.** Work first inside parentheses or other grouping symbols. **2.** Inside grouping symbols or if there are no grouping symbols: **a.** First take all powers; **b.** Second, do all multiplications or divisions in order, from left to right; **c.** Finally, do all additions or subtractions in order, from left to right. (177)

origin The point (0, 0) in a coordinate graph. (424)

ounce (oz) A unit of weight in the U.S. system of measurement, equal to $\frac{1}{16}$ of a pound. (130)

outcome A possible result of an experiment. (213)

palindrome An integer which reads the same forward or backward. (433)

parabola The shape of all graphs of equations of the form $y = ax^2$. (691)

parallel Two lines in a plane are parallel if they have no points in common or are identical. (381)

parallelogram A quadrilateral with two pairs of parallel sides. (388)

parentheses ( ) Grouping symbols that indicate that all arithmetic operations inside are to be done first. (197)

759

pattern A general idea for which there are many examples. (182)

pentagon A five-sided polygon. (284)

percent A number written using the percent sign %. The percent sign indicates that the number preceding it should be multiplied by 0.01 or $\frac{1}{100}$. (79)

perfect number A positive integer n for which the sum of all its factors, except n, is equal to n. (310)

perimeter The sum of the lengths of the sides of a polygon. (289)

perpendicular Two rays, segments, or lines that form right angles. (153)

pi (π) The ratio of the circumference to the diameter of any circle. (12)

pico- A prefix meaning one trillionth. (137)

pie chart See *circle graph*.

pint (pt) A unit of capacity in the U.S. system of measurement equal to 2 cups. (130)

place value The number that each digit in a decimal stands for. For instance, in the decimal 123.45 the place value of the digit 2 is twenty. (7)

polygon A union of segments (its **sides**) in which each segment intersects two others, one at each of its endpoints. (283)

positive integer Any of the numbers 1, 2, 3, ... Also called *natural number*. (43)

positive numbers Numbers that are graphed to the right of zero on a horizontal number line. (43)

pound (lb) A unit of weight in the U.S. system of measurement equal to 16 ounces. One pound is approximately 455 grams. (130)

power The result of x^y. (68)

preimage A figure to which a transformation has been applied. (435)

prime number A positive integer other than 1 that is divisible only by itself and 1. (307)

prism A cylindric solid whose bases are polygons. (671)

Probabilities of Complements The sum of the probabilities of any event E and its complement *not E* is 1. (268)

probability A number from 0 to 1 that tells how likely an event is to happen. (214)

Probability Formula for Equally Likely Outcomes Suppose a situation has N equally likely possible outcomes and an event includes E of these. Let P be the probability that the event will occur. Then $P = \frac{E}{N}$. (216)

Probability of *A or B* If A and B are mutually exclusive events, the probability of A plus the probability of B. (267)

problem A question for which you do not have an algorithm to arrive at an answer. (302)

problem-solving strategies Strategies such as *read carefully, make a table, trial and error, draw a picture, try special cases,* and *check work* that good problem solvers use when solving problems. (303)

product The result of multiplication. (175)

Properties of Parallelograms In a parallelogram, opposite sides have the same length; opposite angles have the same measure. (388)

Property of Opposites For any number n, $n + -n = 0$. Sometimes called the *additive inverse property*. (245)

Property of Reciprocals For any nonzero number a, a and $\frac{1}{a}$ are reciprocals. That is, $a \cdot \frac{1}{a} = 1$. (484)

proportion A statement that two fractions are equal. (615)

proportional thinking The ability to get or estimate an answer to a proportion without solving an equation. (630)

protractor An instrument for measuring angles. (147)

Putting-Together Model for Addition Suppose a count or measure x is put together with a count or measure y with the same units. If there is no overlap, then the result has count or measure $x + y$. (238)

Putting-Together with Overlap Model If a quantity x is put together with a quantity y, and there is overlap z, the result is the quantity $x + y - z$. (368)

Pythagorean Theorem Let the legs of a right triangle have lengths a and b. Let the hypotenuse have length c. Then $a^2 + b^2 = c^2$. (652)

quadrant One of the four regions of the coordinate plane determined by the x- and y- axes. (424)

quadrilateral A four-sided polygon. (284)

quadrillion A word name for the number 1,000,000,000,000,000 or 10^{15}. (65)

quadrillionth A word name for the number 0.00000 00000 00001 or 10^{-15}. (101)

quart (qt) A unit of capacity in the U.S. system of measurement equal to 2 pints. (130)

quarter turn A turn of 90°. (253)

quintillion A word name for the number 1,000,000,000,000,000,000 or 10^{18}. (65)

quintillionth A word name for the number 0.00000 00000 00000 001 or 10^{-18}. (101)

quotient The result of dividing one number by another. (31)

Quotient-Remainder Formula Let n be an integer and d be a positive integer. Let q be the integer quotient and let r be the remainder after dividing n by d. Then $n = d \cdot q + r$. (593)

quotient-remainder form The result of an integer division expressed as an integer quotient and an integer remainder. (593)

radical sign The symbol $\sqrt{\ }$ used to denote a positive square root. (647)

radius **1** The distance that all points in a circle are from the center of the circle. **2** A segment connecting the center of a circle to any point on the circle. (94) **3** The distance that all points on a sphere are from the center of the sphere. **4** A segment connecting the center of a sphere to any point on the sphere. (680)

random experiment An experiment in which all outcomes are equally likely. (215)

range In a collection of numbers, the difference between the largest number and the smallest number. (411)

rate The quotient of two quantities with different units. A quantity whose unit contains the word ''per'' or ''for each'' or some synonym. (493)

760

rate factor A rate used in a multiplication. (494)

Rate Factor Model for Multiplication The product of (a $unit_1$) and (b $\frac{unit_2}{unit_1}$) is (ab $unit_2$), signifying the total amount of $unit_2$ in the situation. (494)

Rate Model for Division If a and b are quantities with different units, then $\frac{a}{b}$ is the amount of quantity a per quantity b. (598)

rate unit The unit in a rate. (493)

ratio The quotient of two quantities with the same units. (611)

Ratio Comparison Model for Division If a and b are quantities with the same units, then $\frac{a}{b}$ compares a to b. (611)

rational number A number that can be written as a simple fraction. (660)

ray A part of a line starting at one point (the **endpoint** of the ray) and continuing forever in a particular direction. (145)

real-number division Dividing one real number a by a nonzero real number b to yield the single real number $\frac{a}{b}$. (592)

real number A number that can be written as a decimal. (641)

reciprocal A number whose product with a given number is 1. Also called *multiplicative inverse*. (483)

rectangle A parallelogram with a right angle. (388)

rectangular array An arrangement of objects into rows and columns. Also called *array*. (469)

rectangular solid A three-dimensional figure with six **faces** that are all rectangles. Also called *box*. (476)

reflection A transformation in which the image of each point lies on a line perpendicular to a fixed line called the **reflection line,** or **mirror,** and is the same distance from the reflection line as the preimage point. (440)

reflection line See *reflection*.

reflection symmetry The property that a figure coincides with its image under a reflection over a line called a **line of symmetry.** Also called *symmetry with respect to a line*. (446)

regular polygon A convex polygon in which all sides have the same length and all angles have the same measure. (338)

relative frequency The frequency of a particular outcome divided by the total number of times an experiment is performed. (213)

Repeated Addition Property of Multiplication If n is a positive integer, then
$nx = x + x + \ldots + x$. (531)
$\qquad$ (n addends)

repeating decimal A decimal in which a digit or group of digits to the right of the decimal point repeat forever. (33)

repetend The digits in a repeating decimal that repeat forever. (33)

revolution A turn of 360°. Also called *full turn*. (253)

rhombus A quadrilateral with all sides the same length. Also called *diamond*. (388)

right angle An angle with a measure of 90°. (153)

right triangle A triangle with a right angle. (154)

rod (rd) A unit of length in the U.S. system of measurement equal to $5\frac{1}{2}$ yards. (128)

rotation symmetry The property that a figure coincides with its own image under a rotation of less than 360°. (451)

rounding down Making an estimate that is smaller than the actual value. (16)

rounding down symbol The symbol $\lfloor\ \rfloor$ used to indicate that the number inside is to be rounded down to the preceding integer. Also called the *floor function symbol* or the *greatest integer function symbol*. (720)

rounding to the nearest Making an estimate to a particular decimal place by either rounding up or rounding down, depending on which estimate is closer to the actual value. (21)

rounding up Making an estimate that is larger than the actual value. (16)

rounding up symbol The symbol $\lceil\ \rceil$ used to indicate that the number inside is to be rounded up to the next integer. Also called the *ceiling function symbol*. (720)

row One of the horizontal arrangements of items in a table, rectangular array, or spreadsheet. (325)

scale of a map The conversion factor used to convert real-world distances to distances on the map. (515)

scientific calculator A calculator which displays very large or very small numbers in scientific notation and which has powering, factorial, square root, negative, reciprocal, and other keys. (26)

scientific notation A notation in which a number is expressed as a number greater than or equal to 1 and less than 10 multiplied by an integer power of 10. A notation in which a number is written in the form *decimal* $\times 10^{exponent}$ with $1 \leq decimal < 10$. (74)

second coordinate See *ordered pair*.

second The fundamental unit of time in the metric and customary systems of measurement. (134)

sector A region bounded by an arc of a circle and the two radii to the endpoints of the arc. (94)

segment See *line segment*.

short ton A unit of weight in the U.S. system of measurement equal to 2000 pounds. Sometimes simply called *ton*. (130)

side **1** In an angle, one of the two rays that make up an angle. (145) **2** In a polygon, one of the line segments that make up the polygon, or the length of a side. (145) **3** In a rectangular solid, a face of the solid. (476)

similar figures Two figures that have the same shape, but not necessarily the same size. (507)

simple fraction A fraction with a whole number as its numerator and a nonzero whole number as its denominator. (31)

size change factor The number k by which the coordinates of the preimage are multiplied in a size change. (507)

Size Change Model for Multiplication (two-dimensional version) Under a size change of magnitude k, the image of (x, y) is (kx, ky). (507)

761

Size Change Model for Multiplication Let k be a nonzero number without a unit. Then ka is the result of applying a **size change of magnitude k** to the quantity a. (506)

slash The symbol / used to indicate division. (31)

slide image See *translation image*.

Slide Model for Addition If a slide x is followed by a slide y, the result is a slide $x + y$. (240)

Slide Model for Subtraction If a quantity x is decreased by an amount y, the resulting quantity is $x - y$. (352)

slope The amount of change in the height of a line as you move one unit to the right. For a line with equation $y = ax + b$, the slope is a. (711)

solution to an open sentence A value of the variable or variables in an open sentence that makes the sentence true. (219)

solve a proportion To find the values of all variables in a proportion that make the proportion true. (616)

solving a sentence Finding the values of the unknown or unknowns that make the sentence true. (220)

special case An instance of a pattern used for some definite purpose. (332)

sphere The set of points in space at a given distance (its **radius**) from a given point (its **center**). (680)

spreadsheet 1 A table. 2 A computer program in which data is presented in a table, and calculations upon entries in the table can be made. (325)

square A four-sided figure with four right angles and four sides of equal length. (158)

square root If $A = s^2$, then s is called a square root of A. (646)

statistic A number used to describe a set of numbers. (411)

stem-and-leaf display A display of a collection of numbers in which the digits in certain place values are designated as the **stems** and digits in lower place values are designated as the **leaves** and placed side-by-side next to the stems. (409)

step function symbols The symbols ⌊ ⌋ and ⌈ ⌉. (722)

Substitution Principle If two numbers are equal, then one can be substituted for the other in any computation without changing the results of the computation. (84)

subtrahend The number being subtracted in a subtraction. In $a - b$, the subtrahend is b. (347)

sum The result of an addition. (175)

supplementary angles Two angles whose measures add to 180°. (376)

Surface Area and Volume Formulas for a Sphere In a sphere with radius r, surface area S, and volume V, $S = 4\pi r^2$ and $V = \frac{4}{3}\pi r^3$. (680)

surface area The sum of the areas of the faces of a solid. (562)

symmetric figure A figure that coincides with its image under a reflection or rotation. (446)

symmetry line A reflection line over which the image of a reflection symmetric figure coincides with the preimage. Also called *line of symmetry*. (446)

symmetry with respect to a line See *reflection symmetry*.

table An arrangement of numbers or symbols into rows and columns. (320)

tablespoon (T) A unit of capacity in the U.S. system of measurement equal to $\frac{1}{2}$ of a fluid ounce. (264)

Take-Away Model for Subtraction If a quantity y is taken away from an original quantity x with the same units, the quantity left is $x - y$. (346)

teaspoon (tsp) A unit of capacity in the U.S. system of measurement equal to $\frac{1}{3}$ of a tablespoon. (264)

ten A word name for the number 10. (65)

ten-millionth A word name for 0.0000001 or 10^{-7}. (12)

ten-thousandth A word name for 0.0001 or 10^{-4}. (12)

tenth A word name for 0.1 or 10^{-1}. (11)

tenths place In a decimal, the first position to the right of the decimal point. (11)

tera- A prefix meaning one trillion. (137)

terminating decimal A decimal with only a finite number of nonzero decimal places. Also called *ending decimal* or *finite decimal*. (89)

tessellation A filling up of a two-dimensional space by congruent copies of a figure that do not overlap. (452)

test a special case A problem-solving strategy in which one or more special cases are examined to formulate a generalization or determine whether a property or generalization is true. (332)

theorem A statement that follows logically from other statements. (652)

thousand A word name for the number 1,000 or 10^3. (65)

thousandth A word name for 0.001 or 10^{-3}. (12)

ton (t) A unit of weight in the U.S. system equal to 2000 pounds. Also called *short ton*. (130)

transformation A one-to-one correspondence between a first set (the **preimage**) and a second set (the **image**). (440)

translation image The result of adding a number h to each first coordinate and a number k to each second coordinate of all the points of a figure. Also called *slide image*. (435)

transversal A line intersecting both of a pair of lines. (382)

trapezoid A quadrilateral with at least one pair of parallel sides. (577)

trial and error A problem-solving strategy in which potential solutions are tried and discarded repeatedly until a correct solution is found. (315)

triangle A three-sided polygon. (154)

Triangle-Sum Property In any triangle, the sum of the measures of the angles is 180°. (394)

trillion A word name for the number 1,000,000,000,000 or 10^{12}. (65)

trillionth A word name for the number 0.00000 00000 01 or 10^{-12}. (101)

truncate To discard all digits to the right of a particular place. To round down to a particular decimal place. (17)

try simpler numbers A problem-solving strategy in which numbers in a problem are replaced with numbers that are easier to work with so that a general method of solution can be found. (334)

twin primes Two consecutive odd numbers that are both prime numbers. (310)

unbiased See *fair*.

undecagon An eleven-sided polygon. (324)

uniform scale A scale in which the numbers are equally spaced so that each interval represents the same value. (416)

unit cube A cube whose edges are 1 unit long. (477)

unit fraction A fraction with a 1 in its numerator and a nonzero integer in its denominator. (483)

unit of measure A standardized amount with which measures can be compared. (10)

unit square A square whose sides are 1 unit long. (468)

U.S. system of measurement A system of measurement evolved from the British Imperial system in which length is measured in inches, feet, yards, miles and other units, weight is measured in ounces, pounds, tons, and other units, and capacity is measured in ounces, cups, pints, quarts, gallons, and other units. Also called *customary system*. (119)

unknown A variable in an open sentence for which the sentence is to be solved. (220)

unlike terms Terms that involve different variables or the same variable with different exponents. (532)

value of a numerical expression The result of carrying out the operations in a numerical expression. (176)

variable A symbol that can stand for any one of a set of numbers or other objects. (182)

Venn diagram A diagram using circles to represent sets and the relationships between them. (367)

vertex **1** The common endpoint of the two rays that make up the angle. (145) **2** A point common to two sides of a polygon. (283) **3** One of the points at which two or more edges meet. (476)

vertical angles Angles formed by two intersecting lines, but that are not a linear pair. (375)

Volume Formula for a Cylindric Solid The volume of a cylindric solid with height h and base with area B is given by $V = Bh$. (676)

volume The measure of the space inside a three-dimensional figure. Also called *capacity*. (163)

whole number Any of the numbers 0, 1, 2, 3, ... (6)

window The part of the coordinate plane that appears on the screen of an automatic grapher. (698)

x-axis The first (usually horizontal) number line in a coordinate graph. (424)

x-coordinate The first coordinate of an ordered pair. (424)

y-axis The second (usually vertical) number line in a coordinate graph. (424)

y-coordinate The second coordinate of an ordered pair. (424)

yard (yd) A unit of length in the U.S. system of measurement equal to 3 feet. (125)

763

$>$	is greater than		$\overleftrightarrow{AB}$	line through A and B
$<$	is less than		AB	length of segment from A to B
$=$	is equal to		$\overrightarrow{AB}$	ray starting at A and containing B
$\neq$	is not equal to		$\overline{AB}$	segment with endpoints A and B
$\leq$	is less than or equal to		$\angle ABC$	angle ABC
$\geq$	is greater than or equal to		$m\angle ABC$	measure of angle ABC
$\approx$	is approximately equal to		$\triangle ABC$	triangle ABC
$+$	plus sign		$\sqrt{n}$	positive square root of n
$-$	subtraction sign		$\lfloor x \rfloor$	floor of x; greatest integer less than or equal to x
$\times, \cdot$	multiplication signs		$\lceil x \rceil$	ceiling of x; least integer greater than or equal to x
$\div, \overline{)\,}, /$	division signs		$\pm$	positive or negative
%	percent		π	Greek letter pi; $= 3.141592...$ or $\approx \frac{22}{7}$.
ft	abbreviation for foot		?	computer input or PRINT command
yd	abbreviation for yard		INT( )	computer command rounding down to the nearest integer
mi	abbreviation for mile			
in.	abbreviation for inch		2*3	computer command for $2\cdot 3$
oz	abbreviation for ounce		4/3	computer command for $4 \div 3$
lb	abbreviation for pound		3^5	computer command for 3^5
qt	abbreviation for quart		SQR(N)	computer command for $\sqrt{n}$
gal	abbreviation for gallon			
$n°$	n degrees		y^x or x^y	calculator powering key
( )	parentheses		$x!$	calculator factorial key
[ ]	brackets		$\sqrt{n}$	calculator square root key
$\lvert x \rvert$	absolute value of x		$\pm$ or $+/-$	calculator negative key
$-x$	opposite of x			
$\perp$	is perpendicular to		π	calculator pi key
//	is parallel to		$1/x$	calculator reciprocal key
$\ulcorner$	right angle symbol		INV, 2nd, or F	calculator second function key
(x, y)	ordered pair x, y			
A'	image of point A		EE or EXP	calculator scientific notation key
$\overarc{AB}$	arc AB			
$\overarc{ABC}$	arc ABC		123456789.	calculator display

Acknowledgments

Unless otherwise acknowledged, all photographs are the property of Scott, Foresman and Company. Page abbreviations are as follows: (T) top, (C) center, (B) bottom, (L) left, (R) right.

COVER & TITLE PAGE Melvin L. Prueitt / Los Alamos National Laboratory **vi(L)** Ralph Mercer **vi(R)** Joe Vanos / The Image Bank **vii(L)** Roger Tully / Tony Stone Images **vii(R)** Scott Morgan / West Light **viii** Pictor / Uniphoto **ix** Charly Franklin / FPG **x** Michael Simpson / FPG **3T** Charlie Westerman / Gamma-Liaison **3B** Courtesy The Robinson Foundation **4T** Jon Davison / The Image Bank **4CL** Steven E. Sutton / Duomo Photography Inc. **4CC** Ralph Mercer **4CR** Index Stock International **4B** Paul Berger / Tony Stone Images **6** Brent Jones **8** P. Vandermark / Stock Boston **10** Focus On Sports **11** Photo: Mary Jane Koznick / Courtesy Special Olympics **15** Tadanori Saito / Photo Researchers **16** AP / Wide World **19** Bill Freeman / Photo Edit **21** Roger Tully / Tony Stone Images **24** Bob Daemmrich **29** Courtesy Texas Instruments **30** Dennis MacDonald / Photo Edit **35** Tony Freeman / Photo Edit **40** Carol Zacny **42** Carl Purcell / Photo Researchers **44** Focus On Sports **46** Michel Tcherevkoff / The Image Bank **48** Courtesy The Robinson Foundation **55C** Courtesy Evelyn Boyd Granville **55R** Courtesy The University of Michigan **61TL** Murray Alcosser / The Image Bank **61BL** Courtesy of the Trustees of the British Museum **61C** Robert Frerck / Odyssey Productions, Chicago **62T** John Turner / Tony Stone Images **62C** Royal Observatory, Edinburgh / AATB / Photo Researchers (SPL) **62BL** Tony Brain / SPL / Photo Researchers **62BR** Joe Vanos / The Image Bank **63L** Patrice Loiez,Cern / SPL / Photo Researchers **63R** ©1984 / Tribune Media Services **64** Focus On Sports **68** Melvin Prueitt / Los Alamos National Laboratory **72** Peter Arnold, Inc. **73** Tony Stone Images **75** Vic Cox / Peter Arnold, Inc. **78** AP / Wide World **80** Greg McRill **84** Bob Daemmrich **86** Milt & Joan Mann / Cameramann International, Ltd. **88** Takehide Kazami / Peter Arnold, Inc. **89** SCRABBLE®is a registered trademark of The Milton Bradley Company. © 1993 MBC, a division of Hasbro, Inc. Used with permission. **91** Everett Collection **92** Robert Frerck / Tony Stone Images **98** Bettmann **99** Steve Vidler / Leo de Wys **103** Beryl Goldberg **105** Courtesy, Sandia Laboratories **107** CNRI / SPL / Photo Researchers **108** Courtesy Penreal Estate Agency, Cornwall **110T** Focus On Sports **110TC** Everett Collection **110** Francolon / Gamma-Liaison **110BL** Everett Collection **110BR** Indy Car **114** Airphoto Jim Wark / Peter Arnold, Inc. **116T** Klaus Mitteldorf / The Image Bank **116C** Steve Satushey / The Image Bank **116BL** Roger Tully / Tony Stone Images **116BR** Chuck O'Rear / West Light **117T** Gerard Del Vecchio / Tony Stone Images **117BR** Alan Becker / The Image Bank **118** National Museum of American Art / Art Resource, NY **121** Everett Collection **125** Carol Zacny **128** Robert Frerck / Odyssey Productions, Chicago **130** Ed Pritchard / Tony Stone Images **134** U.S. Dept. of Commerce, National Institute of Standards and Technology **136** U. S. Dept. of Agriculture **138** David R. Frazier Photolibrary **140** Milt & Joan Mann / Cameramann International, Ltd. **141** Joseph Viesti **142** Bob Daemmrich **145** Jonathan Wright / Bruce Coleman Inc. **153** Wingstock / Comstock Inc. **155** Laura Dwight **156** Vince Streano / Tony Stone Images **158** Pugliano / Gamma-Liaison **162T** Mark Linfield / Green Umbrella Ltd. **163** NASA **165** U.S. Navy Photo / U.S. Department of Defense **167** N. Parfitt / Tony Stone Images **168T** Steve Vidler / Leo de Wys **168B** Orion SVC / TRDNG 1992 / FPG **171** National Portrait Gallery, London **174T** Richard Gorbun / Leo de Wys **174TC** Comstock Inc. **174BC** Hans R. Uthoff / Tony Stone Images **174B** Comstock Inc. **175B** Scott Morgan / West Light **182L** Smithsonian Institution / Courtesy of: National Museum of the American Indian **182R** Jake Rajs / The Image Bank **184** Library of Congress **185** Rooraid / Photo Edit **187** Will & Deni McIntyre / Photo Researchers **188** Bob Daemmrich / Stock Boston **189** Robert Fried / Stock Boston **191** The British Library **193** Courtesy The University of Chicago **196** Tony Stone Images **197** Joseph Viesti **201** Focus On Sports **207** Vandermark / Stock Boston **208** Ken Whitmore / Tony Stone Images **211** Ian Halperin **214** Bob Daemmrich / Stock Boston **218** Marka / Leo de Wys **219** Brent Jones **222** Mark Antman / The Image Works **224** Bill Gillette / Stock Boston **228** Everett Collection **229TL** K. Scholz / H. Armstrong Roberts **229TC** C. Ursillo / H. Armstrong Roberts **229TR** NASA **229BL** Addison Gallery of American Art Phillips Academy, Andover, MA **229BR** FPG **230TL** The Image Bank **230CL** Annie Griffiths Belt / West Light **230CR** Roy Gumpel / Mon-Tresor / Panoramic Stock Images **230B** Mark Segal / Panoramic Stock Images **230TR** Harald Sund / The Image Bank **235BL** Stokes Collection / New York Public Library, Astor, Lenox and Tilden Foundations **235TL** Bettmann Archive **235TC** Brown Brothers **235TR** NASA **235BR** Courtesy American Antiquarian Society **236TL** Comstock Inc. **236TR** Spencer Jones / FPG **236C** Hans N. Eleman / The Image Bank **236BL** H. Armstrong Roberts **236BR** Pictor / Uniphoto **238** Breck Kent / Earth Scenes **240** Les Stone / Sygma **242** Tony Freeman / Photo Edit **243** Michael Newman / Photo Edit **244** Carol Zacny **245** Joseph Viesti **247** D. MacDonald / Photo Edit **248** Vito Palmisano **252** Warren Jacobs / Tony Stone Images **254** G. Vandystadt / ALLSPORT USA **257** David Young-Wolff / Photo Edit **259** Chicago Historical Society **260** Bob Daemmrich **264** Bettmann **265** The Kobal Collection **266** Brent Jones **269** Tony Freeman / Photo Edit **271** Everett Collection **274** Milt & Joan Mann / Cameramann International, Ltd. **275** Milt & Joan Mann / Cameramann International, Ltd. **281** ©1959 / Cambridge University Press from SCIENCE AND CIVILISATION IN CHINA Vol. 3 by Joseph Needham **283** John Running **285** U.S. Government **288** Mike Powell / ALLSPORT USA **291** The Russian Museum, St. Petersburg "The Mowers" 1887 by Grigory Miasoyedov **293T** Mark Stephenson / West Light **293B** Picturesque **294TL** Pierre-Yves Goavec / The Image Bank **294C** Dave Burgering / Duomo Photography Inc. **294B** Sports Photo Masters, Inc. **300T** Pictor / Uniphoto **300C** Index Stock International **300BL** Comstock Inc. **300BR** Comstock Inc. **301CL** Gary Buss / FPG **302** Courtesy Lebanon Valley College Photo: Dwayne Arehart **304** Stanford University **307** William S. Favata **308** Tom McCarthy / Photo Edit **311** Courtesy Ford Motor Company **313** Bob Daemmrich / The Image Works **315** David Young-Wolff / Photo Edit **322** Hutchings / Photo Edit **323** Beryl Goldberg **325** Van Elton / Photo Edit **327** Tony Freeman / Photo Edit **334** A. Gyori / Sygma **336** Courtesy Ford Motor Company **338T** Peter Till / The Image Bank **338BL& BR(background)** Gary Commer / Index Stock International **338BC** C. Moore / West Light **338BR** W. Cody / West Light **339T** Illustration from OLD POSSUM'S BOOK OF PRACTICAL CATS by T. S. Eliot, illustration copyright © 1982 by Edward Gorey, reproduced by permission of Harcourt Brace & Company. **344TL** Natural Selection **344TR** Digital Art / West Light **344C** Index Stock International **344B** Rick Rusing / Leo de Wys **345B** Ralph Mercer **346** Courtesy Diamond B. Lumber Company / Photo: Milt & Joan Mann / Cameramann International, Ltd. **349** Courtesy United Airlines **350** Bettmann Archive **352** Barnwell / Stock Boston **355** Chip Peterson **357** Courtesy Chicago Youth Symphony Orchestra **358** Cornwell / Pacific Stock **359** Roessler / ANIMALS ANIMALS **360** Jerome Academia / Photo Edit **361** Nancy Rabener / Barker **362** Paul Conklin **366** Library of Congress **367** MacDonald / Photo Edit **369** Hutchings / Photo Edit **372L** Kennard / Stock Boston **372R** Hulton Picture Library **375** Holland / The Image Bank **380** ©1984 / UNIVERSAL PRESS SYNDICATE. Reprinted with permission. All rights reserved. **381** Joseph Viesti **385** Milt & Joan Mann / Cameramann International, Ltd. **387** J. L. Atlan / Sygma **393** Tribune Media Services **400T** Jim Richardson / West Light **406T** SuperStock, Inc. **406C** Ed Honowitz / Tony Stone Images **407T** Craig Aurness / West Light **407C** Kathleen Campbell / Gamma-Liaison **408** Yvonne Hemsey / Gamma-Liaison **410 411** Drawings by John Tenniel **415** Bob Daemmrich **421** Chip Peterson **427** Georgia Dept. of Tourism **428** Scott Berner / Visuals Unlimited **435** R. Saunders / Leo de Wys **439** David R. Frazier Photolibrary **440** David Boyle / Earth Scenes **442** David Wells / The Image Works **446** John Running / Stock Boston **449L** Doug Wechsler / Earth Scenes **452** D. Specker / ANIMALS ANIMALS **454** ©1941 / Escher Foundation-Haags Gemeentemuseum-The Hague **455** ©1994 / Escher Foundation-Haags Gemeentemuseum-The Hague **457** Adam Woolfit / Woodfin Camp & Associates **458TL** SuperStock, Inc. **458TC** Kathleen Campbell / Gamma-Liaison **458R** David Sutherland / Tony Stone Images **459T** Telegraph Colour Library / FPG **466TL** Andrew Sacks / Tony Stone Images **466TR** Comstock Inc. **466CL** Uniphoto **466B** Craig Aurness / West Light **467C** Paul Horsted / Direct Stock **471** Milt & Joan Mann / Cameramann International, Ltd. **473** Freeman / Photo Edit **476** D. Burnett / Contact / The Stock Market **482** David Spangler **484** Larry Lefever / Grant Heilman Photography **486** S. Grotta / The Stock Market **487** C. Mishler / AlaskaStock Images **488** T. Freeman / Photo Edit **491** MacDonald / Photo Edit **492** Focus On Sports **493** Courtesy British Airways **495T** Pollack / The Stock Market **495B** AP / Wide World **497** McCarthy / Photo Edit **498** Alex MacLean / Landslides **499** Walter Chandoha **503** T. Freeman / Photo Edit **505** J. Maher / The Stock Market **506** M. Newman / Photo Edit **508** V. Beller / The Stock Market **510** The Kobal Collection **511T** Janice Travia / Tony Stone Images **511C** Janice Travia / Tony Stone Images **511B** Janice Travia / Tony Stone Images **513** Charles Osgood / Copyrighted, Chicago Tribune Company, all rights reserved **515** P Beck / The Stock Market **519** NASA **521CL** S. Krasemann / Photo Researchers **521CL** S. Krasemann / Photo Researchers **521BL** S. Krasemann / Photo Researchers **521BR** S Krasemann / Photo Researchers **528T** Charly Franklin / FPG **528B** Freeman Patterson / Masterfile **529T** J Amos / H. Armstrong Roberts **529B** Steven E Sutton / Duomo Photography Inc. **530T** McCarthy / Photo Edit **535T** Jeff Speilman / The Image Bank **539** Markowitz / Sygma **541** M McVay / The Stock Market **542** D Young-Wolff / Photo Edit **544T** Walter Chandoha **546** Brenner / Photo Edit **548** The Image Bank **550** D Young-Wolff / The Image Bank **555** Stichting Beeldrecht Haags Gemeentemuseum, by Piet Mondrian **559** Simon Jauncey / Tony Stone Images **561** Courtesy California Raisin Advisory Board **562** Courtesy California Raisin Advisory Borad **564** Werner Bokelberg / The Image Bank **566** Thomas Tampy / The Image Bank **570** J R Eyerman 1973 Time, Inc. / TIME Magazine **571** The Walt Disney Company / Walt Disney Productions **575** Klaus Mitteldorf / The Image Bank **577** Carol Zacny **582T** Ric Ergenbright Photography (582 & 583) **582B** Brian Tolbert / brt Photo **583BL** Syguest **583BR** Bettmann Archive **590 TL** Robert Marien / RO-MA Stock **590TR** H. Abernathy / H. Armstrong Roberts **590BL** Steve Gottleib **590BL** David M. Philips / SS / Photo Researchers **591** David Madison **592** Savino / The Image Works **593** Bob Daemmrich **594** Frederick Grassle / Woods Hole Oceanographic Institution **596** Laura Dwight **597** Brent Jones **598** Bob Daemmrich / The Image Works **599** The Kobal Collection **600** Gillette / Stock Boston **602** Myrleen Ferguson / Photo Edit **605** Grant Heilman Photography **606** David Young-Wolff / Photo Edit **607** Anthony Bannister / ANIMALS ANIMALS **609** J. R. Williams / Earth Scenes **610** A. Tilley / Tony Stone Images **611** D. Jacobs / Tony Stone Images **612** Bill Brooks / Masterfile **614** Bob Daemmrich / The Image Works **615** Mary Kate Denny / Photo Edit **618** Bob Daemmrich / The Image Works **620** Kunsthistorisches Museum, / Art Resource, NY Gemaeldegalerie, Vienna / Photo: Erich Lessing, detail **621** Kunsthistorisches Museum, / Art Resource, NY Gemaeldegalerie, Vienna / Photo: Erich Lessing, detail **623** Courtesy of the Trustees of the British Museum **624** Bettmann **628** Brian Seed / Tony Stone Images **630** Grant Heilman Photography **633** Aresa Pryor-Adams / Earth Scenes **634T** C. Shotwell / Mon-Tresor **634 635** David Madison **635T** David Madison / Duomo Photography Inc. **640T** Jaime Villaseca / The Image Bank **640C** Karageorge / H. Armstrong Roberts **640B** Jim Barber Studios **641T** Pete Saloutos / The Stock Market **641B** J. McDermott / Tony Stone Images **642** David Madison **646** Walt Disney Productions **647** Rita Boserup **652** Milt & Joan Mann / Cameramann International, Ltd. **656** Walt Disney Productions **658** Bob Daemmrich / Stock Boston **662** by Samuel B. Waugh / The Museum of the City of New York **663** by Andre Thevet, Keruert et / The Burndy Library Chaudiere, Paris, 1584 **664** Grant Heilman Photography **670** Courtesy R. R. Donnelley **675** W. Johnson / Stock Boston **681** NASA **682** NASA **684T** Jaime Villaseca / The Image Bank **684B** D. Sutherland / Tony Stone Images **685** Neveux / H. Armstrong Roberts **690T** Eugen Gebhardt / FPG **690BL** Baron Wolman **690BR** Comstock Inc. **691T** Michael Simpson / FPG **692** Milt & Joan Mann / Cameramann International, Ltd. **695** Milt & Joan Mann / Cameramann International, Ltd. **697** David Madison / David Madison **699** Milt & Joan Mann / Cameramann International, Ltd. **702** David Madison **707** Bachmann / The Image Works **708** Courtesy Future Farmers of America **709** Everett Collection **714** Milt & Joan Mann / Cameramann International, Ltd. **716** Stephanie Maze / Woodfin Camp, Inc. **723** Courtesy Illinois Society of Professional Engineers **724** Courtesy Road & Track Magazine **725** Scott Morgan / West Light **726T** M. Angelo / West Light **726TC** The Stock Shop **726BC** Richard Price / West Light **726BL** Tony Freeman / Photo Edit **726BR** D. Degnan / H. Armstrong Roberts

abacus, 99, 583
Abdul-Jabbar, Kareem, 618
absolute value, 248
abundant number, 339
acre, 569, 583
active cell, 326
Activities, in the student's edition, 26, 27,
    32, 70, 73, 74, 75, 79, 100, 106, 120,
    122, 127, 148, 177, 178, 179, 199, 209,
    250, 311, 312, 326, 327, 328, 387, 393,
    424, 430, 447, 448, 454, 505, 507, 518,
    550, 555, 556, 562, 571, 573, 594, 620,
    647, 653, 664, 671
  In-class, 104, 152, 213, 253, 282, 374, 434,
    625, 657, 698
  in the teacher's edition, 7, 12, 18, 22, 27,
    32, 38, 42, 47, 51, 65, 69, 74, 79, 86, 90,
    91, 94, 95, 106, 119, 126, 131, 136, 141,
    146, 147, 152, 154, 160, 164, 177, 178,
    183, 188, 198, 204, 209, 214, 216, 220,
    225, 239, 245, 250, 253, 255, 261, 267,
    272, 277, 282, 284, 289, 303, 308, 309,
    312, 316, 326, 334, 347, 353, 359, 363,
    368, 374, 376, 382, 388, 394, 410, 416,
    422, 429, 434, 436, 441, 447, 453, 469,
    470, 477, 483, 490, 494, 500, 506, 512,
    517, 531, 536, 541, 545, 551, 556, 557,
    562, 569, 573, 574, 576, 578, 593, 598,
    602, 607, 612, 617, 621, 627, 631, 643,
    647, 651, 653, 657, 658, 665, 670, 671,
    677, 681, 693, 698, 700, 705, 710, 715,
    716, 720, 721
acute angle, 154
Adapting to Individual Needs
  Challenge, 14, 30, 45, 49, 54, 67, 71, 77,
    83, 88, 97, 102, 108, 120, 129, 133, 143,
    148, 156, 162, 166, 181, 186, 191, 201,
    207, 210, 218, 223, 228, 242, 247, 252,
    264, 270, 275, 280, 287, 292, 306, 310,
    313, 319, 320, 321, 323, 329, 337, 350,
    356, 361, 366, 372, 379, 386, 391, 397,
    414, 419, 425, 432, 439, 444, 450, 456,
    472, 480, 486, 492, 498, 503, 509, 515,
    520, 534, 539, 543, 548, 553, 559, 565,
    575, 581, 596, 600, 605, 610, 614, 619,
    624, 629, 633, 645, 650, 656, 662, 668,
    674, 679, 683, 696, 703, 708, 713, 718,
    724
  English Language Development, 9, 14, 19,
    24, 29, 33, 39, 43, 53, 66, 71, 77, 82, 88,
    97, 101, 122, 127, 132, 139, 144, 147,
    155, 165, 180, 185, 190, 196, 200, 206,
    210, 222, 227, 241, 246, 257, 263, 269,
    274, 279, 286, 291, 305, 309, 313, 318,
    322, 328, 336, 349, 355, 365, 370, 378,
    385, 390, 396, 413, 418, 424, 431, 438,
    443, 449, 455, 471, 479, 485, 491, 496,
    502, 508, 514, 519, 538, 543, 547, 552,
    559, 564, 580, 595, 604, 609, 614, 619,
    623, 629, 644, 649, 655, 661, 673, 678,
    694, 702, 707, 716, 722
  Extra Help, 8, 13, 20, 24, 28, 34, 35, 40,
    44, 48, 52, 66, 70, 76, 82, 87, 92, 96,
    100, 107, 122, 128, 132, 138, 147, 155,
    161, 166, 179, 184, 189, 195, 199, 205,
    210, 217, 221, 226, 240, 246, 251, 256,
    262, 268, 273, 285, 290, 304, 313, 317,
    322, 327, 335, 348, 354, 360, 364, 369,
    377, 384, 389, 395, 412, 417, 423, 430,

    437, 442, 448, 454, 470, 478, 484, 495,
    501, 507, 513, 518, 532, 537, 542, 546,
    551, 558, 563, 570, 572, 579, 594, 599,
    603, 608, 613, 618, 622, 628, 632, 644,
    648, 654, 660, 666, 672, 678, 682, 695,
    701, 706, 712, 717, 721
addends, 239
Adding Fractions Property, 260
addition
  addends, 239
  models
    putting-together, 238–239
    slide, 240–241
  of fractions, 260–263
  properties
    associative, 271
    commutative, 271
    equality, 277
    opposites, 245
  symbol, 175
Addition Property of Equality, 277
additive identity, 244
Additive Identity Property of Zero,
    244
additive inverse, 245
adjacent angles, 256
Africa Counts, 167
Agassi, Andre, 124
Ahmes Mathematical Papyrus, 191
algebra, (Variables are used throughout
    the text.)
  elementary, 184
  equation(s), 219
    addition, 276–279
    equivalent, 363
    graphing, 429, 694, 714–716, 725
    linear, 694
    multiplication, 535–537, 540–542,
      544–546, 550–552
    subtraction, 358–359, 362–363
    two-step, 545–546, 551–552
    using multiplication property of equality,
      536
    with fractions, 536–537
    with percents, 542
    with proportions, 616–617, 621–622
    with variables on both sides, 704–706
  evaluating expressions, 193–194
  formulas, 208–210
  graphing
    coordinate, 421–424, 428, 692–694
    equation with powers, 725
    formulas, 714–716
    inequalities, 224–226
    linear equation, 429–430, 694
    square roots, 725
    using rounding symbols, 719–722
  inequalities, 224–226
  open sentences, 219–220
  patterns, 183–184
  problems, See *problem-solving strategies.*
  solving equations, See *solving equations.*
  translating expressions, 187–189
  using formulas, See *formulas.*
  variables, 182
Algebraic Definition of Division, 483,
    601
**Algebraic Definition of Subtraction
    (Add-Opp Property),** 353

algebraic expressions, 187–189
  evaluating, 193
algorithm, 302
al-Hassar, 175
Alice's Adventures in Wonderland, 407,
    410
al-khowarizmi, 230
alternate exterior angles, 382
alternate interior angles, 382
altitude
  of a trapezoid, 578
  of a triangle, 572
amicable numbers, 339
angle(s)
  acute, 154
  adjacent, 256
  alternate exterior, 382
  alternate interior, 382
  central, 152
  complementary, 380
  corresponding, 382
  exterior, 382
  interior, 382
  interior of, 256
  linear pair, 374
  measuring, 146–149
  obtuse, 154
  opposite, 388
  right, 153
  sides of, 145
  straight, 374
  supplementary, 376
  symbol, 382
  vertex of, 145
  vertical, 375
Angle Addition Property, 256
Aouita, Said, 543
applications, (Applications are found
    throughout the text. The following are
    selected applications.)
  activities in a day, 237
  allowance, 157
  architecture, 293
  area of your residence, 521
  area of rectangles, 540
  babysitting, 602
  balance of trade, 252
  bank account, 19, 80
  baseball gate receipts, 64
  batting "averages," 77
  braking distance, 724
  bricklayer's formula, 229
  checking account, 273, 274
  consumer price index, 633
  curling, 697
  driving distance, 288
  earth's surface area, 681
  elections, 79
  employment, 65
  Ferris wheel, 258, 259
  graphing, 426
  height comparison, 126
  hurricane damage, 16
  inflation, 86
  large edifices, 168
  lengths, 653
  library fine, 193, 195
  long distance rates, 725
  magazine circulation, 451

monetary system, 138, 139, 142
parabola, 716
playing cards, 399
population, 8, 75, 103, 306, 345
postal rates, 692–693
probability of grand prize, 489
protein in cereal, 144
recipe, 348
salary, 188, 190
sale price, 85
school supply store, 326–327
seating capacity of American League
   baseball stadiums, 492
shopping, 56
size change, 541
solar distance, 75
space shuttle, 42
special numbers, 338
speed of light, 21, 73–74
Sports Illustrated cover appearance, 124
stock prices, 39, 43, 44
street map, 376–377, 378
student grades, 337
systems of measurement, 167
temperature change, 278, 421–422
temperature conversion, 197–198
tessellations, 458
thickness of pennies, 109
units on food, 168
virus, 102, 107
"What America Eats," 66
weight, 167
women's track record, 10–11, 15
world records, 635
Arabic numerals, 5
arc, 94
Archimedes, 663, 680
area, 158–160
lateral, 670
model for multiplication, 469
of a circle, 666
of a rectangle, 208
of a right triangle, 470
of a sector of a circle, 667
of a square, 159
of a trapezoid, 579
of a triangle, 572
surface, 163, 670–672
Area Formula for a Circle, 666
Area Formula for a Right Triangle, 470
Area Formula for a Sector, 667
Area Formula for a Trapezoid, 579
Area Formula for any Triangle, 572
Area Model for Multiplication, 469
Assessment
ongoing, 9, 15, 20, 25, 30, 35, 40, 45, 49,
   54, 60, 67, 71, 76, 82, 88, 92, 97, 103,
   108, 114, 124, 129, 134, 139, 144, 151,
   157, 162, 166, 172, 181, 186, 192, 196,
   202, 207, 212, 218, 223, 228, 234, 243,
   247, 252, 259, 265, 270, 275, 281, 287,
   292, 297, 306, 310, 314, 319, 324, 331,
   337, 343, 351, 357, 360, 366, 373, 380,
   385, 392, 397, 405, 414, 420, 427, 433,
   439, 445, 451, 457, 464, 475, 481, 487,
   492, 498, 504, 510, 515, 520, 526, 533,
   539, 543, 549, 554, 560, 565, 570, 575,
   581, 588, 596, 600, 605, 610, 614, 619,
   624, 629, 633, 639, 645, 650, 656, 662,
   669, 674, 678, 683, 697, 702, 708, 713,
   718, 724, 730

progress self-test, 58, 112, 170, 232, 296,
   341, 402, 461, 524, 585, 637, 687, 728
Associative Property of
Addition, 271
Multiplication, 479
automatic grapher, 458, 698, 700, 715,
   718, 721
average, 206, 606

ball, 680
Ball, Lucille, 110
bar graph, 415–417
Barkley, Charles, 420
base(s), 68
of a rectangular solid, 477
of a trapezoid, 578
of a triangle, 572
Bell, John, 419
Bibliography, T56–T57
billion, 65
billionth, 101
Bill James Baseball Abstract, 212
bisect, 397
Bonds, Barry, 702
box, 476
volume, 477
brackets, 203
Bradley, Shawn, 48
Breckenridge, John C., 419
Bricklin, Dan, 325
Browne, Marjorie Lee, 55
Brueghel, Pieter, the Elder, 620
Bruhn, Wilhelm, 546

calculator instruction (Scientific
   calculators are assumed throughout this
   book. See also *graphics calculator*.)
constant key, 534
converting fraction to decimal, 31–34
display, 26
dividing by zero, 30
entering, 27
key sequence, 27, 28
keying in, 27
memory key, 28
negative numbers, 43
opposite key, 245, 250
order of operations, 176
parenthesis keys, 199
percent key, 79
pi (π), 660
powering key, 70
reciprocal key, 484
scientific calculator, 26
scientific notation, 73–76, 77, 106
square root key, 647
capacity, 163
customary, 130–131
metric, 137
career
accountant, 325
architect, 438
artist, 171, 439, 454
bricklayer, 229
builder, 438
carpenter, 35
photographer, 336
salesperson, 514, 530, 697
Carroll, Lewis, 407, 410, 580

ceiling function, 720
cell, 325
center
of circle, 94
of gravity, 609
of sphere, 680
centimeter, 119, 135, 137
central angle, 152
Challenge, 14, 30, 45, 49, 54, 67, 71, 77,
   83, 88, 97, 102, 108, 120, 129, 133, 143,
   148, 156, 162, 166, 181, 186, 191, 201,
   207, 210, 218, 223, 228, 242, 247, 252,
   264, 270, 275, 280, 287, 292, 306, 310,
   313, 319, 320, 321, 323, 329, 337, 350,
   356, 361, 366, 372, 379, 386, 391, 397,
   414, 419, 425, 432, 439, 444, 450, 456,
   472, 480, 486, 492, 498, 503, 509, 515,
   520, 534, 539, 543, 548, 553, 559, 565,
   575, 581, 596, 600, 605, 610, 614, 619,
   624, 629, 633, 645, 650, 656, 662, 668,
   674, 679, 683, 696, 703, 708, 713, 718,
   724
Chapter Review, These sections include
   questions on Skills, Properties, Uses,
   and Representations (SPUR). 59–61,
   113–115, 171–173, 233–235, 297–299,
   342–343, 403–405, 463–465, 525–527,
   587–589, 638–639, 688–689, 729–731
Charlemagne, 117
Chern, Shiing-Shen, 110
circle(s)
arc, 94
area, 666
center, 94
circumference, 657–659
diameter, 94
graph, 152
radius, 94
sector, 94
turns, 253
circle graph, 93–96, 152, 168
circular cylinder, 676
circumference, 657–659
Clinton, Bill, 78
clockwise turn, 253
coincide, 442
Columbus, Christopher, 229
common denominator, 262
Communications, See *Reading
   Mathematics* and *Writing.*
Commutative Property
of Addition, 271
of Multiplication, 470
comparing
decimals, 12
integers, 46–47
mixed numbers, 47
positive and negative numbers, 47
Comparison Model for Subtraction,
   348
complementary
angles, 380
events, 268
complex numbers, 641, 684
computer instruction
automatic drawing programs, 400, 458
ceiling function, 720
converting fraction to decimal, 25
digital, 68
floor function, 720
greatest integer function, 720

INT( ) command, 20
powering symbol, 72
PRINT (?) command, 20
step function, 722
computer program
approximation for pi, 663
calculating volume and surface area of a
box, 569
circle graphs, 98
converting inches to centimeters, 144
converting miles to feet, 129
coordinates of points, 696
drawing software, 168, 398, 400
evaluating expressions, 196, 317, 318, 202,
432
congruent figures, 436
Connections
Architecture, 681
Art, 379, 445, 451
Biology, 80
Consumer, 600, 632, 679, 719
Ecology, 225
Environmental, 152
Geography, 42, 72, 361, 365, 486, 510,
548, 598, 610, 682
Geometry, 51, 54
Health, 73, 138, 206, 329, 631
History, 22, 24, 30, 108, 124, 130, 138, 154,
178, 191, 204, 285, 289, 303, 308, 351,
432, 454, 456, 474, 514, 538, 574, 646,
648, 662, 674, 693
Literature, 126, 292, 410
Multicultural, 7, 12, 25, 49, 64, 65, 66, 71, 83,
86, 90, 94, 99, 124, 144, 155, 166, 200,
238, 252, 259, 324, 334, 377, 392, 416,
436, 447, 454, 480, 495, 497, 519, 553,
564, 567, 613, 628, 654, 682, 714, 720
Music, 656
Photo, 5, 63, 116, 175, 198, 237, 301, 345,
405, 467, 529, 591, 640, 691
Reading, 18, 197, 308
Safety, 724
Science, 74, 150, 162, 245, 247, 264, 350,
441, 478, 532, 559, 610, 681, 712
Social Studies, 119, 178, 217, 380, 386,
542, 580
Sports, 368, 603, 617
Technology, 12, 32, 47, 74, 83, 88, 91, 95,
106, 129, 136, 147, 157, 178, 183, 204,
212, 220, 255, 270, 284, 309, 316, 321,
326, 376, 386, 388, 398, 416, 422, 429,
432, 434, 441, 447, 470, 506, 512, 517,
551, 574, 578, 593, 598, 629, 647, 651,
658, 665, 693, 694, 698, 713, 716, 721
contractions, 511, 522
conversion
equations, 125
factor, 495
relations, 140
convex polygon, 451, 452
Cooperative Learning, 10, 14, 26, 27, 28,
32, 35, 40, 42, 45, 74, 76, 79, 84, 88, 94,
100, 119, 121, 124, 126, 135, 136, 141,
152, 153, 154, 155, 164, 166, 177, 183,
186, 188, 189, 190, 192, 196, 198, 202,
204, 207, 212, 223, 228, 244, 245, 247,
256, 265, 275, 281, 282, 289, 292, 302,
305, 309, 310, 312, 314, 319, 321, 324,
326, 337, 357, 366, 368, 374, 380, 381,
385, 386, 397, 410, 411, 414, 416, 420,
422, 433, 438, 439, 447, 483, 490, 492,
494, 539, 541, 549, 554, 556, 557, 562,

564, 565, 570, 600, 605, 612, 614, 619,
621, 624, 631, 643, 644, 650, 653, 659,
660, 665, 671, 677, 679, 680, 697, 698,
700, 703, 705, 708, 713, 715, 719, 720
coordinate graph, 421–424
corresponding
angles, 382
lengths, 626
sides, 516
count, 7
counterclockwise turn, 253
counting unit, 7
cryptarithms, 339
cube, 163
surface area, 163
volume, 163–164
cubic centimeter, 163
cubic units, 163
cup, 130
Curie, Marie, 350
customary system of measurement
capacity, 130–131
length, 119, 120–122
volume, 130–131
cylinder, 676
cylindric solid, 675

data disk, 328
decagon, 284
decimal notation, 6
decimal system, 5, 6
decimals, 6, 68–69
comparing and ordering, 12–13
converted from fractions, 32–34, 91
converted from mixed numbers, 38
converted to fractions, 89–90
converted to percents, 90
infinite repeating, 33
on a number line, 11
repeating, 643
terminating, 642
deficient number, 339
degrees, 146
denominator, 31
depth, 476
Descartes, René, 175, 178–179, 406
diagonal of a polygon, 286, 338
diameter, 94
diamond, 388
difference, 347
digital computer, 68
digits, 5–7
dimensions, 469
Diophantus, 230
discrete mathematics
develop and analyze algorithms, 238–243,
346–357, 468–475, 493–498, 583,
592–614
games and puzzles, 71, 162, 259, 281,
319, 351, 497, 543, 605
linear equations and inequalities, 224–228,
276–281, 358–366, 535–554, 692–708
probability, 213–218, 230, 266–270, 294,
367–373, 399, 488–492, 522, 582, 710,
726
sequences, 186
set theory, 367–373
systems of linear equations and
inequalities, 698–708
display, 407
bar graph, 415
calculator, 26

stem-and-leaf, 409
Distributive Property
of Multiplication over Addition, 556
of Multiplication over Subtraction, 557
used to multiply mentally, 556–557
dividend, 31
divisibility, tests for, 54
divisible, 34
division, 31, 32, 33
algebraic definition, 483, 601
by zero, 31
integer, 592
rate model, 598
ratio comparison model, 611
real-number, 592
symbols for, 31, 175
with fractions, 601–603, 635
with negative numbers, 606–608, 635
divisor, 31, 308
Dmitriev, Artur, 254
double bar graph, 416–417
Douglas, Stephen A., 419
draw a picture, See *problem-solving
strategies.*

edge, 476
Elizabeth I, Queen of England, 372
Elizabeth II, Queen of England, 372
endpoints of segment, 283
English Language Development, 9,
14, 19, 24, 29, 33, 39, 43, 53, 66, 71, 77,
82, 88, 97, 101, 122, 127, 132, 139, 144,
147, 155, 165, 180, 185, 190, 196, 200,
206, 210, 222, 227, 241, 246, 257, 263,
269, 274, 279, 286, 291, 305, 309, 313,
318, 322, 328, 336, 349, 355, 365, 370,
378, 385, 390, 396, 413, 418, 424, 431,
438, 443, 449, 455, 471, 479, 485, 491,
496, 502, 508, 514, 519, 538, 543, 547,
552, 559, 564, 580, 595, 604, 609, 614,
619, 623, 629, 644, 649, 655, 661, 673,
678, 694, 702, 707, 716, 722
Enrichment, See *Extensions* and
Challenge.
equal fractions, 50–52
Equal Fractions Property, 51
equation(s), 219. See also *solving
equations.*
addition, 276–279
equivalent, 363
graphing, 429, 694, 714–716, 725
linear, 694
multiplication, 535–537, 540–542,
544–546, 550–552
subtraction, 358–359, 362–363
two-step, 545–546, 551–552
using multiplication property of equality, 536
with fractions, 536–537
with percents, 542
with proportions, 616–617, 621–622
with variables on both sides, 704–706
equilateral triangle, 452
equivalent equations, 363
equivalent formulas, 364
Error Alert, 7, 8, 14, 19, 24, 29, 34, 39, 42, 44,
69, 81, 92, 107, 123, 128, 143, 150, 156,
179, 184, 188, 189, 206, 227, 249, 261,
291, 313, 330, 349, 350, 355, 356, 371,
390, 391, 397, 432, 438, 447, 470, 484,
532, 548, 553, 569, 574, 595, 644, 707
Escher, Maurits, 439, 454, 455

Espinosa, Andres, 495
estimation, 16, 55
  rounding down, 16–17, 21
  rounding to the nearest, 21–22
  rounding up, 16–17, 21
Euclid, 308
evaluating expressions, 176, 193–194, 197–199, 203–206
event, 216
expansion, 507
Exploration question(s), 9, 15, 20, 25, 30, 36, 40, 45, 49, 54, 67, 72, 77, 83, 88, 92, 98, 103, 108, 124, 129, 134, 139, 144, 151, 157, 162, 166, 181, 186, 192, 196, 202, 207, 212, 218, 223, 228, 243, 247, 252, 259, 265, 270, 275, 281, 287, 292, 306, 310, 314, 319, 324, 331, 337, 351, 357, 361, 366, 373, 380, 386, 392, 398, 414, 420, 427, 433, 439, 445, 451, 457, 475, 481, 487, 492, 498, 504, 510, 515, 520, 534, 539, 543, 549, 554, 560, 565, 570, 576, 581, 596, 600, 605, 610, 614, 619, 624, 629, 633, 645, 650, 656, 663, 669, 674, 679, 683, 697, 703, 708, 713, 718, 724
exponent, 68, 99–101
exponential form, 68, 99
expression(s)
  algebraic, 187–189
  evaluating, 176, 193–194, 197–199, 203–206
  English, 187–189
  numerical, 187
  simplifying, 197–198, 203–204
Extensions, 9, 15, 20, 25, 30, 35, 45, 49, 54, 67, 71, 77, 83, 88, 98, 103, 108, 124, 129, 134, 139, 144, 151, 157, 162, 166, 181, 186, 192, 196, 202, 207, 212, 218, 223, 228, 243, 247, 252, 259, 265, 270, 275, 281, 287, 292, 306, 310, 314, 319, 324, 331, 337, 351, 357, 361, 366, 373, 386, 392, 398, 414, 420, 427, 433, 445, 451, 457, 475, 481, 487, 498, 504, 510, 515, 520, 533, 539, 543, 549, 554, 560, 565, 570, 576, 581, 596, 600, 605, 614, 619, 624, 629, 633, 645, 650, 656, 663, 669, 674, 679, 683, 697, 703, 708, 713, 718, 724
exterior angles, 382
Extra Help, 8, 13, 20, 24, 28, 34, 35, 40, 44, 48, 52, 66, 70, 76, 82, 87, 92, 96, 100, 107, 122, 128, 132, 138, 147, 155, 161, 166, 179, 184, 189, 195, 199, 205, 210, 217, 221, 226, 240, 246, 251, 256, 262, 268, 273, 285, 290, 304, 313, 317, 322, 327, 335, 348, 354, 360, 364, 369, 377, 384, 389, 395, 412, 417, 423, 430, 437, 442, 448, 454, 470, 478, 484, 495, 501, 507, 513, 518, 532, 537, 542, 546, 551, 558, 563, 570, 572, 579, 594, 599, 603, 608, 613, 618, 622, 628, 632, 644, 648, 654, 660, 666, 672, 678, 682, 695, 701, 706, 712, 717, 721
extremes of a proportion, 620

faces, 476
factor, 51, 308
Farmer, Fannie Merritt, 264
Fermat, Pierre, 406
Ferris, George Washington Gale, 259
Fibonacci, 5, 7, 31
first coordinate, 422

floor function, 720
fluid ounce, 130
foot, 125
formula(s), 208–210
  area
    circle, 666
    rectangle, 208
    sector of a circle, 667
    square, 159
    trapezoid, 579
    triangle, 572
  circumference of a circle, 659
  equivalent, 364
  graphing, 714–715
  perimeter
    rectangle, 532
    square, 531
  probability for equally likely outcomes, 216
  surface area of sphere, 680
  volume
    box or rectangular solid, 477
    cylindric solid, 676
    sphere, 680
fraction bar, 203
fraction(s),
  adding, 260–263, 266–268
  calculator, 263
  converted from decimals, 642–644
  converted to decimals, 31–34
  converted to percents, 90
  denominator, 31
  dividing, 601–603
  equal, 50–52
  for repeating decimals, 643
  for terminating decimals, 642
  lowest terms, 51–52
  multiplying, 482–485, 522
  numerator, 31
  simple, 31, 34, 263
  subtracting, 348–349, 369–370
  unit, 293
Frankston, Bob, 325
frequency, 213
Fuller, Buckminster, 571
functions
  absolute-value functions, 433
  exponential functions, 691, 714–718, 725
  graphing, 428–433, 691–697, 714–725
  linear functions, 428–433, 691–713
  modeling, 42, 213, 230, 238–243, 273, 274, 287, 315–319, 346–351, 367–373, 376–378, 385, 386, 393, 399, 459, 468–474, 493–498, 506–507, 521–522, 562, 597–600, 611–614, 625, 651, 657, 665, 670, 699–703, 719–724
  probability functions, 214–218
  quadratic functions, 223, 316–317, 716
  step functions, 719–725
  use of tables, 8, 61, 139, 155, 192, 237, 306, 320–324, 345, 356, 362, 392, 417, 420, 421, 426, 439, 445, 451, 492, 510, 539, 642, 649, 710, 715
Fundamental Property of Turns, 255
fundamental
  region or shape, 452
furlong, 128

gallon, 130
Galois, Evariste, 407
generalization, 321
geometry, 646
  acute angle, 154

  adjacent angles, 256
  alternate exterior angles, 382
  alternate interior angles, 382
  altitude of a trapezoid, 578
  altitude of a triangle, 572
  area, See *area.*
  base of rectangular solid, 477
  base of a trapezoid, 578
  base of a triangle, 572
  bisect, 397
  box, 476
  center of a circle, 94
  center of a sphere, 680
  central angle, 152
  circle, 94
  circumference, 659
  complementary angles, 380
  congruent figures, 436
  corresponding angles, 382
  corresponding lengths, 626
  corresponding sides, 516
  degrees of an angle, 146
  diameter, 94
  exterior angle, 382
  face, 476
  height, 572, 578
  hypotenuse, 470
  image, 435, 440–441, 506, 512
  interior angles, 382
  legs of right triangle, 470
  linear pair, 374
  obtuse angle, 154
  parallel lines, 381
  perpendicular, 153
  polygons, 154, 158, 282, 284, 319, 324, 338, 388–389, 451, 452, 577
  preimage, 435, 442, 506, 512
  protractor, 147
  Pythagorean theorem, 651–653
  radius of a circle, 94
  ray, 145
  rectangular solid, 476
  reflection, 440–442
  rhombus, 388
  right angle, 153
  right triangle, 154
  segment, 283
  similar figures, 507
  straight angle, 374
  transformation, 440
  translation, 434–435
  vertex of a triangle, 145
  vertical angles, 375
Geyer, Georgie Anne, 108
Gonzales, Juan, 702
googol, 72
grad, 151
gram, 136–137
Granville, Evelyn Boyd, 55
graph(s), 408–411. See also *number line.*
  bar, 415–417
  circle, 93–96
  coordinate, 421–424, 428, 692–694
  equation with powers, 725
  formulas, 714–716
  inequalities, 224–226
  linear equation, 429–430, 694
  square roots, 725
  stem-and-leaf display, 409–411
  using rounding symbols, 719–722
graphics calculator, 458, 698, 700, 715, 718, 721

greatest common factor, 52
greatest integer function, 720
Griffith-Joyner, Florence, 10–11, 15
gross ton, 132
grouping symbols, 203–205
Gutsu, Tatiana, 372

Hamilton, Sir William Rowan, 272
Harriot, Thomas, 46
Hart, Michael H., 683
hectare, 159, 582
height, 476
  of a cylinder, 676
  of a prism, 676
  of a trapezoid, 578
  of a triangle, 572
Henry I, King of England, 117
Henry II, King of England, 372
Henry VIII, King of England, 372
heptagon, 284
hexagon, 282, 284
  regular, 452
Hillary, Edmund, 88
Hindu-Arabic numerals, 5
history of mathematics, 5, 12, 31, 46,
  54, 80, 96, 99, 110, 145, 146, 175, 184,
  191, 229, 271, 272, 411, 483, 621, 646,
  648, 652, 680, 684, 685
How to Solve It, 303
How Much Land Does a Man Need, 292
Hui, Liu, 54
hypotenuse, 470

identity
  additive, 244
  multiplicative, 507
image
  reflection, 440–441
  size change, 506, 512
  slide, 435
  translation, 435
imaginary numbers, 684
In-class Activities, 104, 152, 213, 253,
  282, 374, 434, 625, 651, 657, 698. See
  also *Activities.*
inch, 119, 125
independent events, 489
inequality(ies), 224–226
  graphing, 224–226
  double, 225–226
  symbols, 46–48, 224
infinite repeating decimal, 33, 643
instance of a pattern, 182
integer(s), 43
  adding, 240–241, 244–245
  comparing, 46
  division, 592
  function, 720
  multiplying, 499–502
  on a number line, 41
  subtracting, 352–355
Interdisciplinary, See *Connections.*
interior angles, 382
**international system of
  measurement,** 135
interval, 10–11
inverse
  additive, 245
  multiplicative, 483
irrational number, 660

Jahre Viking, 132
Jefferson, Thomas, 118, 122
Jemison, Mae, 229
Johnson, Alex, 77
Jordan, Michael, 110, 124, 420, 134, 618

kilogram, 136–137, 140
kilometer, 135–137, 140
King, Martin Luther, Jr., 98
Kristiansen, Ingrid, 543

Lambert, Johann, 659
Landon, Michael, 405
lateral area, 670
leaf, 409
least common multiple, 262
legs of a right triangle, 470
Leibniz, Gottfried, 175
length, 476
  customary units, 125
  metric, 137
  segment, 289
Leonardo of Pisa, 5
light-year, 74
like terms, 532
Lincoln, Abraham, 419
line(s)
  parallel, 381
  perpendicular, 153
  reflecting, 440–441
  slope, 711
  transversal, 382
line segment, 283
linear equation, 694
linear pair, 374
liter, 136–137, 140, 164
Livy, 350
long ton, 132
Low, Juliette Gordon, 598
lowest terms of a fraction, 51–52

magic square, 281
magnitude, 253
make a table, See *problem-solving
  strategies.*
Malone, Karl, 420
Manipulatives, See *Activities.*
Marx Brothers, 110
mass, 137
mathematicians, See *history of
  mathematics* and individual
  mathematicians.*
mathematics in other disciplines
  (Applications and uses of mathematics
  in other disciplines are found throughout
  the text.)
  agriculture, 337, 467, 474
  art, 171, 439, 454
  business, 64, 82, 181, 298, 325–327, 427
  consumer education, 17–19, 22, 41, 43,
    60, 79, 85, 87, 95, 273, 321–322, 360,
    417, 533, 598, 612
  economics, 86, 207, 252
  everyday life, 193, 198, 237, 264, 288, 308,
    313, 336
  government, 65, 66, 118–119, 323
  health, 499–500
  language arts, 498
  music, 170, 232, 264

science, 73–74, 87, 102, 105, 107, 243, 509
social sciences, 7, 8, 305, 409, 415–416, 513
sports, 10, 11, 77, 211, 212, 275, 299, 492,
  543, 702
Mayas, 5, 293
mean, 206
means of a proportion, 620
Means-Extremes Property, 621
measurement, 117
  angles, 145–149
  area, 158–160
  converting between systems, 140–142
  customary system
    capacity, 130–131
    length, 119, 120–122, 125
    weight, 130–131
  international system, See *metric system.*
  metric system
    capacity, 136–137
    length, 118–119, 122, 135, 137
    mass, 136–137
    volume, 136
  numbers in, 10
  U.S. system, See *customary system.*
  volume, 163–164
median, 411
meter, 119, 135, 137
metric system
  capacity, 136–137
  length, 118–119, 122, 135, 137
  mass, 136–137
  volume, 136
mile, 125, 140
Miller, Shannon, 372
milligram, 136–137
milliliter, 136–137
millimeter, 119, 135, 137
million, 65
millionth, 101
minuend, 347
Mishkutienok, Natalia, 254
mixed numbers, 37–38
  converting to decimals, 38
  on a number line, 37
mode, 411
model
  addition
    putting together, 238–239
    slide, 240–241
  division,
    rate, 598
    ratio comparison, 611
  multiplication
    area, 469
    rate factor model, 494
    size change, 506–507
  Putting-Together with Overlap, 368
  subtraction
    comparison, 348
    slide, 352
    take-away, 346
Mondrian, Piet, 555
monetary systems, 142
Moscow Mathematical Papyrus, 191
Mother Teresa, 110
multiplication
  by powers of ten, 64–65, 69
  models
    area, 469
    rate factor, 494
    size change, 506–507

of fractions, 484
of negative numbers, 499–502
of percents, 84–85
of unit fractions, 482–483
property(ies)
  associative, 479
  commutative, 470
  of equality, 125, 536
  of fractions, 483
  of negative one, 501
  of zero, 502
symbols, 175, 182
using Distributive Property, 556–557
Multiplication of Fractions Property, 484
Multiplication of Unit Fractions Property, 483
Multiplication Property of Equality, 125, 536
Multiplication Property of -1, 501
Multiplication Property of Zero, 502
multiplicative identity, 507
Multiplicative Identity Property of One, 507
multiplicative inverses, 483
mutually exclusive events, 267

nanosecond, 103
Napier's bones, 583
negative numbers, 41–43
  rules for adding with, 248–250
  rules for dividing with, 606–608
  rules for multiplying with, 499–502
  rules for subtracting, 353
nested parentheses, 199
net, 561
n-gon, 284
nonagon, 284
Norgay, Tenzing, 88
not, 268
number(s)
  as count, 7
  complex, 641, 684
  integers, 43
  irrational, 660
  mixed, 37
  negative, 41–43, 245
  perfect, 310
  positive, 43
  prime, 307, 339
  rational, 660
  real, 641, 660
  whole, 6
  zero, 245
number line, 10–11
  graphing
    decimals, 11
    inequalities, 224–226
    integers, 41
    mixed numbers, 37
    percents, 80
    rational numbers, 43
  interval, 10–11
  tick marks, 10–11
numerator, 31
numerical expression, 176
numerically equal, 567

obtuse angle, 154
octagon, 284

odds, 218
Olajuwon, Hakeem, 420
Open-ended questions, 6, 8–10, 15–20, 24, 25, 28–30, 36, 40, 42, 44, 45, 53–56, 58–61, 64, 66, 67, 71, 72, 76, 77, 83, 84, 87, 88, 93, 97, 98, 102, 103, 106–110, 115, 121, 123, 125, 127, 129, 131, 134, 139, 142, 144, 149, 157, 160, 165–168, 173, 180, 181, 185–187, 190, 191, 195, 197, 200, 202, 206, 207, 210, 212, 214, 216–218, 221–224, 227–230, 241–243, 252, 253, 258, 259, 264, 265, 269, 270, 273, 275, 281, 285, 286, 291, 293, 294, 296, 304, 308–311, 314, 317–319, 323, 325, 329, 331, 335, 338, 339, 341–343, 351, 356, 361, 366, 370, 372, 373, 379–381, 383, 385, 386, 391, 392, 396, 398–400, 404, 411–420, 427, 430–433, 438–440, 444, 445, 448, 450, 452, 455–459, 462, 464, 465, 473, 475, 480, 481, 486, 487, 491–493, 496, 498, 503, 504, 510, 514, 515, 518, 520–522, 533, 534, 542, 543, 558, 563, 564, 568–570, 576, 580–583, 585, 595, 597, 599, 600, 604, 610, 614, 615, 619, 624, 628, 632–635, 639, 644, 645, 649, 650, 654, 656, 658, 661, 663, 668–670, 673, 674, 677–679, 683–685, 695–699, 703, 708, 711–713, 716–718, 724–726, 728, 729
open sentence, 219–221
operations
  order of, 176–179
  symbols for, 175
opposite(s)
  in addition, 244
  of opposites (Op-op) property, 245
  property of, 245
  rays, 374
Opposite of opposites (Op-op) Property, 245
order of operations, 176–179
  grouping symbols, 203–205
  parentheses, 197–199
  summary of rules, 205
Order of Operations Parentheses Rule, 197
ordered pair, 422
  first coordinate, 422
  second coordinate, 422
origin, 424
Oughtred, William, 12, 145, 175
ounce, 130
outcomes, 213
  random, 215

palindrome, 433
parabola, 691, 715
parallel lines, 381
  symbol, 382
parallelogram, 388–389
  opposite angles, 388
  opposite sides, 388
  properties of, 388
parentheses, 197
pattern(s), 182–184
  addition, 238, 240, 249–250, 260, 271, 272
  algebraic, 182–186, 320–323, 332–337, 596
  division, 598, 611
  geometric, 162, 166, 311–314, 320–324, 338, 439, 452–458

multiplication, 469, 494, 500, 501, 506
number, 33–36, 64–72, 78–83, 135–139, 182–186, 320–324, 475, 487
probability, 267
subtraction, 346, 348, 352
pentagon, 284
percent(s)
  as ratios, 612
  converting to decimals, 79–80
  converting to fractions, 79
  graphing on number line, 80
  of a quantity, 84–86
  on a number line, 80
perfect number, 310
perimeter, 289
  rectangle, 532
  square, 531
Perot, Ross, 408
perpendicular, 153
  symbol, 383
pi π, 12, 27, 685
pie chart, 93–96, 152, 168
pint, 130
Pippen, Scottie, 124
Pippig, Uta, 495
place value, 7, 11, 12, 13, 21, 64–65
Playfair, William, 96, 406
Polya, George, 300–301, 303, 304
polygon, 283–284
  angle of, 284
  architecture, 293
  convex, 451, 452
  decagon, 284
  diagonal, 286
  dodecagon, 319
  heptagon, 284
  hexagon, 282, 283–284
  naming, 284
  n-gon, 284
  nonagon, 284
  octagon, 284
  pentagon, 284
  perimeter, 289
  quadrilateral, 284
  regular, 338, 452
  sides, 283
  triangle, 284
  type of, 284
  undecagon, 324
  vertex, 283
Portrait of a Man in a Red Turban, 171
positive numbers, 43
pound, 130, 140
power, 68–70
  negative integer, 100
  positive integer, 69–70
  zero, 99
powering
  symbol for, 175
Powers of Ten, 110
preimage, 435, 442, 506, 512
Price, Mark, 526
prime number, 307
prism, 676
probability, 214–216, 710
  addition of, 266–268
  event, 216
  formula for equally likely outcomes, 216

independent events, 489
mutually exclusive events, 267
odds, 218
of *A* and *B,* 488
of *A* or *B,* 267
of complements, 268
outcome, 215
relative frequency, 213, 230, 294, 522, 710, 726
with overlap, 367–370, 399

problem, 302

problem solving (Problem solving is found throughout the book. Below are selected appearances.)
addition, 238, 240, 273, 278, 288, 321–322, 368
area and surface area, 160, 220, 468–471, 484, 521, 540, 555, 557, 562, 568, 577, 583, 631, 671, 681
circumference, 657, 658–659
cost and value, 321–322
distance/rate/time, 597, 630–631
division, 334–335, 592–594, 597–599, 601–603, 606–607, 611–612
factorization, 342
fractions and mixed numbers, 260, 348, 482–483, 522, 601, 602–603, 622
geometry, 311–312, 316, 320, 334
integers, 593
involving turns, 257–258
mean, 606
multiplication, 321–322, 326–327, 493–496, 500–502, 516–518, 531–532, 535–536
percent, 85, 86, 91, 95, 542
perimeter, 288–289, 313, 566
probability, 268, 488–490
proportions, 615, 617, 620–622, 627
rate, 334, 493–496, 499, 521, 559, 597–599, 602, 606–607
ratio, 611–612, 620
subtraction, 346–348, 352–354, 358–359, 362–363, 551–552
too little information, 308
too much information, 308
size change, 505–507, 509, 511–513, 541, 627
volume, 476–479, 677

problem-solving strategies (Problem-solving strategies are found throughout this book. Below are selected appearances.)
advice, 303
draw a picture, 95, 220, 261, 311–312, 343, 367–369, 393, 506, 515, 676
find a pattern, 182–184, 186, 333–334, 531–532, 546–547
make a generalization, 321
make a graph, 152, 415–416, 422, 521, 692–693, 700, 701, 710, 715–716
make a table, 152, 320–322, 342, 399, 428, 710
read carefully, 307–308
testing a special case, 332–334, 343
trial and error, 315–317, 342
try simpler numbers, 334–335
use a diagram/picture, 288, 371, 372, 376, 477, 478, 480, 482, 509
use a formula, 208–209, 220, 572–573, 579, 653, 668, 671, 677, 681
use a graph, 82, 93, 353, 408–409, 722
use a spreadsheet, 325–328, 337, 338, 343, 417

use a table, 317, 320, 421
use alternate approach, 320
use estimation, 16–17, 21–22
use physical models, 627
use proportional thinking, 630–631, 634
use proportions, 615, 617, 620–622, 627
use ratios, 611–612, 620
use technology, 28, 316
write an equation, 220, 258, 278, 280, 537, 540–542, 546, 547, 551, 556–557, 692–693, 699, 701

Professional Sourcebook, T20–T57
Progress Self-Test, 58, 112, 170, 232, 296, 341, 402, 461, 524, 585, 637, 687, 728

Projects
A 3-dimensional Pythagorean Pattern, 684
A Different Way to Divide Fractions, 635
A Large Triangle, 400
A Parentheses Problem, 229
A Probability Experiment, 294
An Experiment with Decimal Places, 725
An Experiment with Dice, 229
Angles of Chairs, 399
Approximations to π, 685
Area of Your Residence, 521
Areas of Special Types of Trapezoids, 582
Arithmetic Time Line, 229
Automatic Drawing Programs, 400
Automatic Graphers, 458
Best Buys, 634
Circle Graph Summary, 168
Comparing Estimates, 55
Complex Numbers, 684
Computer Drawing Programs, 168
Cones and Pyramids, 685
Copies of All Sizes, 521
Cryptarithms, 339
Cylindrical Packages, 684
Diagonals of Regular Polygons, 338
Different Methods of Multiplication, 583
Display of Temperature, 459
Displays in Newspapers, 459
Displays of the Tchokwe, 459
Effects of Different Rates, 521
Financial Log, 294
Fractions That Add to 1, 293
Graphing Square Roots, 725
Graphs of Equations with Powers, 725
Half-size You, 522
How Often Is a Solution to an Equation an Integer?, 582
How Often Is a Solution to $ax + b = cx + d$ an Integer?, 726
Integer Arithmetic with Negative Divisors, 635
Large Edifices, 168
Long Distance Rates, 725
Metric Units, 167
Multiplication of Numbers in Scientific Notation, 583
Multiplying Fractions Versus Multiplying Decimals or Percents, 522
Numbers in the Newspaper, 55
One Million Pennies, 109
Other Numeration Systems, 56
Other Traditional Units, 167
Percents in Print, 109
Polygons in Architecture, 293
Population Changes, 399
Powers of 10, 110

Probabilities with Playing Cards, 399
Problem Solving, 338
Proportional Thinking, 634
Scientific Notation, 110
Similar Objects, 634
Special Cases That Work, but Generalizations That Do Not, 339
Special Numbers, 339
Spreadsheets, 338
Streaks, 522
Surface Areas and Volumes of Boxes, 583
Symmetry, 458
Tessellations, 458
The Advantage of Rounding, 56
The Beginning of Algebra, 230
The Bricklayer's Formula, 229
The Maya, 293
The Number of Digits in a Repetend, 684
Turns in Sport, 294
Units for Land Area, 583
Units on Food, 168
Using Inequality Symbols, 230
Using the Symbols 1, 2, 3, and a Decimal Point, 109
Weighing a Collection, 167
Weights of Spheres, 685
When Will One Person Overtake Another?, 726
When $x - y$ Is Small, 400
Which Fractions Equal Repeating Decimals?, 56
World-Record Rates, 635
Your Own Data, 459

Property(ies)
adding fractions, 260
addition, of equality, 277
additive identity, of zero, 244
Algebraic Definition of Subtraction (Add-Opp), 353
angle addition, 256
associative, of addition, 272
associative, of multiplication, 479
commutative, of addition, 271
commutative, of multiplication, 470
distributive, of multiplication over addition, 556
distributive, of multiplication over subtraction, 557
equal fractions, 51
fundamental, of turns, 255
means-extremes, 621
multiplication, of equality, 125
multiplication of fractions, 484
multiplication, of negative one, 501
multiplication of unit fractions, 483
multiplication, of zero, 502
multiplicative identity, of one, 507
of opposites, 245
of parallelograms, 388
of reciprocals, 484
opposite of opposites (op-op), 245
repeated addition, of multiplication, 531
triangle-sum, 394

proportion, 615
extremes, 620
in similar figures, 625–627
means, 620

proportional thinking, 630
prose, 415

protractor
base line, 147
center, 147
Putting-Together Model for Addition, 238–239
Putting-Together with Overlap Model, 368
Pythagoras, 652
Pythagorean Theorem, 651–653

quadrant, 424
quadrilateral, 284
quadrillion, 65
quadrillionth, 101
quart, 130, 140
quintillion, 65
quintillionth, 101
quotient, 31
quotient-remainder form, 593
Quotient-Remainder Formula, 593

radian, 151
radical sign, 647
radius
of a circle, 94
of a sphere, 680
Rahn, Johann, 174–175
random outcome, 215
range, 411
rate, 493, 521, 597
conversion factor, 495
unit, 493
Rate Factor Model for Multiplication, 494
Rate Model for Division, 598
ratio comparison, 611
Ratio Comparison Model for Division, 61
rational number, 660
ray, 145
Reading Mathematics, 7, 11, 17, 18, 22, 26, 32, 36, 38, 42, 47, 51, 64, 68, 73, 79, 85, 90, 94, 99, 106, 119, 125, 130, 136, 140, 145, 153, 158, 164, 176, 183, 187, 194, 197, 203, 208, 215, 219, 225, 239, 244, 249, 255, 261, 267, 272, 277, 283, 289, 303, 308, 312, 315, 321, 326, 328, 333, 347, 353, 358, 363, 367, 376, 382, 388, 394, 409, 416, 423, 429, 436, 441, 447, 453, 469, 477, 482, 488, 494, 500, 506, 512, 517, 530, 536, 540, 545, 551, 555, 562, 567, 571, 577, 593, 597, 601, 607, 611, 615, 621, 626, 631, 642, 646, 653, 659, 664, 671, 675, 681, 692, 700, 704, 714, 719
real number, 641, 660
real-number division, 592
reciprocals, 483
property of, 484
rectangle, 388, 469
area of, 208
perimeter, 532
rectangular array, 469
rectangular solid, 476, 562
surface area, 562
volume, 477
reflection, 440–442
reflection image over the line *m*, 440
reflection symmetry, 446–447

regular hexagon, 452
regular polygon, 338, 452
relative frequency, 213, 230, 294, 522, 710, 726
relatively prime numbers, 339
Repeated Addition Property of Multiplication, 531
repeating decimals, 643
repetend, 33, 685
Review questions, 9, 15, 19, 24, 30, 36, 39, 45, 49, 54, 67, 72, 77, 83, 88, 92, 98, 103, 107–108, 124, 128, 134, 139, 143–144, 151, 157, 162, 166, 181, 186, 191–192, 196, 201–202, 207, 212, 218, 223, 228, 243, 247, 252, 258–259, 265, 270, 274–275, 281, 286–287, 291–292, 305–306, 310, 314, 319, 324, 331, 337, 351, 357, 360–361, 366, 372–373, 380, 385–386, 391–392, 397–398, 413–414, 419–420, 427, 432–433, 439, 445, 450–451, 456–457, 475, 481, 486–487, 492, 497–498, 504, 509–510, 514–515, 519–520, 533–534, 539, 543, 548–549, 553–554, 559–560, 564–565, 569–570, 576, 581, 596, 600, 604–605, 610, 614, 619, 624, 629, 633, 645, 650, 656, 663, 669, 674, 679, 683, 697, 703, 708, 712–713, 717–718, 724
revolution, 253
rhombus, 388
right angle, 153
right triangle, 154
area formula, 470
hypotenuse, 470
legs, 470
Robinson, David, 3, 48
rod, 128
Roentgen, Wilhelm, 40
Roman numerals, 5
rotation symmetry, 451
rounding, 56
down, 16–17, 21, 720
to the nearest, 21–22
up, 16–17, 21, 720
Rubik, Erno, 71
Rubik's Cube, 71
Rudolff, Christoff, 648
Rules
for adding a positive and negative number, 250
for adding two negative numbers, 249
for multiplying a number by a negative number, 500
for multiplying a number by a positive number, 500
for multiplying by a negative integer power of 10, 100
for multiplying by a positive integer power of 10, 69
for multiplying two numbers with the same sign, 501
for order of operations, 177, 197, 205
Russian Peasant algorithm, 583

Sanders, Barry, 72
scientific notation
for large numbers, 73–76, 110
for small numbers, 104–106, 110
multiplication, 583
second coordinate, 422

sector, 94
area, 667
segment, 283
length, 289
sentence, 219
equation, 219
inequality, 224
open, 219
solution, 219
Servois, François, 271
short ton, 130
sides
of an angle, 145
of a polygon, 283
similar figures, 507, 625
Sinclair, Debra, 526
size change factor, 505
contraction, 511
expansion, 507
Size Change Model for Multiplication, 506
(two-dimensional version), 507
slide, 435
image, 435
Slide Model for Addition, 240–241
Slide Model for Subtraction, 352
slope, 711
Smith, Margaret Chase, 539
solution, 219
solving equations
changing subtraction to addition, 358–359
mentally, 276
proportions, 616–617, 621–622
the sentence, 220
using addition property of equality, 277–279
using equivalent equations, 362–364
using properties of equality, 550–552
using two steps, 544–547
with variables on both sides, 704–706
solving proportions, 616
using means-extremes property, 621
sphere, 680
center, 680
radius, 680
surface area, 680
volume, 680
weight, 685
spreadsheets
active cell, 326
bar graph, 417
cell, 325
columns, 325
COPY, 327
data disk, 328
design, 703
FILL, 327
REPLICATE, 327
row, 325
square, 158, 388
area of, 159
perimeter, 532
square kilometer, 159
square root, 646, 725
square units, 158, 209
State of the World 1991, 631
statistic(s), 411 (Statistical data are used throughout the text. See *applications* for selected uses of such data.)
bar graphs, 415–417
circle graphs, 93–96, 152, 168

coordinate graphs, 421–424
mean, 206
median, 411
mode, 411
range, 411
stem-and-leaf display, 409–411
survey, 55, 152, 168, 459
table, 421
stem-and-leaf display, 409–411
step function, 722
Stevin, Simon, 12, 20
Stifel, Michael, 175
Substitution Principle, 84
subtraction
  Algebraic Definition of Subtraction (Add-Opp Property), 353
  difference, 347
  minuend, 347
  model
    comparison, 348
    slide, 352
    take-away, 346
  subtrahend, 347
  symbol for, 175
subtrahend, 347
supplementary angles, 376
surface area, 163
  cylinders, 670–671
  prisms, 672
  rectangular solid, 562, 583
  sphere, 680
surface area and volume formulas for a sphere, 680
symmetric with respect to a line, 446, 458

table, 320, 421
Take-Away Model for Subtraction, 346
Tchokwe, 459
terminating decimal, 89
tessellation, 452–454, 458
test a special case, See *problem-solving strategies.*
The Book of Chapters on Indian Arithmetic, 12
The 100, 683
theorem, 652
Thoreau, Henry David, 347
Three Stooges, 271
Through the Looking Glass, 580
tick marks, 10–11
Tolstoy, Leo, 291
ton
  gross, 132
  long, 132
  short, 130
total surface area, 670
transformation, 440
  reflection, 440–442
  translation, 435–436
translation, 434
transversal, 382
trapezoid, 577
  altitude, 578

area formula, 579
bases, 578
height, 578
trial and error, See *problem-solving strategies.*
triangle, 154
  altitude, 572
  area formula, 572
  equilateral, 452
  exterior angle, 395
  height, 572
  right, 154
  symbol for, 154
Triangle-Sum Property, 394, 400
trillion, 63, 65
trillionth, 101
truncate, 17, 20
try simpler numbers, See *problem-solving strategies.*
Tukey, John, 406, 411
turn(s)
  clockwise, 253
  combining, 255
  counterclockwise, 253
  full, 253
  fundamental property of, 255
  magnitude, 253
  quarter, 253
  revolution, 253
twin primes, 310

undecagon, 324
uniform scale, 416
unit cost, 598
unit fractions, 293
  multiplication of, 482–483
unit of measure, 10, 119
  area, 158, 209
  customary
    capacity, 130
    length, 125
    weight, 130
  metric
    capacity, 137
    length, 137
    mass, 137
    volume, 163
unit square, 468
unknown, 220
unlike terms, 532
Unser, Al Jr., 110
use a spreadsheet, See *problem-solving strategies.*

Valdes, Manuel Antonio, 31, 175
value
  of an expression, 176, 193
  of a variable, 193
van Eyck, Jan, 171
variable, 182
Venn diagram, 367
vertex
  of an angle, 145
  of a box, 476

of a polygon, 283
vertical angles, 375
Victoria, Queen of England, 372
Viète, François, 184
VisiCalc, 325
volume, 163
  box, 477, 583
  cube, 164
  cylindric solid, 676
  rectangular solid, 477
  sphere, 680
Volume Formula for Cylindric Solid, 676

Wadlow, Robert, 624
Washington, Booker Taliaferro, 366
Waugh, Samuel B., 662
weight
  customary units, 130–131
whole numbers, 6, 13, 34
Widman, Jaohann, 175
width, 476
Wilkins, Dominique, 420
window, 698
Writing, 8, 14, 18, 20, 36, 40, 49, 54, 70, 71, 76, 82, 98, 103, 108, 129, 133, 144, 151, 157, 162, 181, 186, 188, 192, 196, 197, 202, 207, 212, 223, 228, 243, 244, 247, 252, 265, 270, 281, 286, 287, 303, 306, 314, 319, 331, 351, 368, 373, 378, 392, 414, 416, 433, 451, 481, 487, 498, 504, 510, 517, 520, 533, 534, 543, 570, 575, 581, 610, 614, 624, 633, 650, 656, 669, 674, 678, 683, 702, 703, 712, 713, 718, 724

x-axis, 424
x-coordinate, 424

y-axis, 424
y-coordinate, 424
Yamaguchi, Kristi, 124
yard, 125
Yastrzemski, Carl, 77
Young, John, 682

Zaslavsky, Claudia, 167
zero
  absolute value, 249
  additive identity, 244
  division by, 30, 31
  as an integer, 42–43
  multiplying by, 502
  opposite of, 245
  place value, 13
  power, 100
  symbol, 100
zero power, 99

NOTES